2017

CRISI

MW00582526

Bob
Bonnorumno

CRISIS IN GREECE

PETER SIANI-DAVIES

With the assistance of
Mary Siani-Davies

OXFORD
UNIVERSITY PRESS

OXFORD
UNIVERSITY PRESS

Oxford University Press is a department of the
University of Oxford. It furthers the University's objective
of excellence in research, scholarship, and education
by publishing worldwide.

Oxford   New York
Auckland   Cape Town   Dar es Salaam   Hong Kong   Karachi
Kuala Lumpur   Madrid   Melbourne   Mexico City   Nairobi
New Delhi   Shanghai   Taipei   Toronto

With offices in
Argentina   Austria   Brazil   Chile   Czech Republic   France   Greece
Guatemala   Hungary   Italy   Japan   Poland   Portugal   Singapore
South Korea   Switzerland   Thailand   Turkey   Ukraine   Vietnam

Oxford is a registered trade mark of Oxford University Press
in the UK and certain other countries.

Published in the United States of America by
Oxford University Press
198 Madison Avenue, New York, NY 10016

Library of Congress Cataloging-in-Publication Data is available
Peter Siani-Davies.
Crisis in Greece.
ISBN: 9780190456726

Printed in the United Kingdom by Bell and Bain Ltd, Glasgow

For Michael

CONTENTS

ACKNOWLEDGEMENTS

Research for this book has taken place in a number of libraries. In London these were principally the library of the London School of Economics and Political Science and the British Library, and in Athens the library of the Bank of Greece and the National Library of Greece. We would like to thank in particular the staff of the last two institutions for their frequent help and kindness in assisting us to track down various sources. Countless people from all walks of life across Greece have also been instrumental in shaping our ideas. Some knew that we were working on this book but others did not. All gave generously of their time as they talked to us, usually informally, about their lives during these long years of crisis. There are too many for us to list by name although in a few instances specific assistance is acknowledged in the notes, but we would like to extend to them all our grateful and heartfelt thanks. In particular, we would like to thank our closer friends and family who invariably provided the lens through which we saw much of the crisis. These years have affected them all in many ways, providing endless challenges both great and small, but they have weathered them with a spirit of fortitude which commands respect and serves as a microcosm for the inhabitants of Greece themselves. In particular, we would like to thank Paraskevi and Michael, who put up with much, and to whom this book is dedicated.

INTRODUCTION

For the best part of a decade the international media has been reporting a crisis in Greece. Often the story has been confined to specialist financial reports but at other times it has dominated global headlines, becoming the major news item of the day. Over the years the crisis has been presented in many guises, ranging from the economic and political to the social and humanitarian, but the underlying narrative, especially for the outside world, has centred on the soundness of Greek public finances and whether the country was about to default on its loans or even exit the euro and return to the drachma. The consequences of either of these courses of action were totally unknown but at an early stage in the crisis a general consensus emerged among the vast majority of policy makers, media commentators and financial analysts that they would be calamitous not only for Greece but also for the global economy, which risked being plunged into another crippling recession. Faced with this prospect and the possibility that the single currency itself might not survive the crisis, in the spring of 2010 Greece's euro area partners, along with the International Monetary Fund (IMF), overcame their many reservations and agreed to provide the country with billions of euros of financial assistance but only under strict conditions. Under the watchful eye of a team of officials from the IMF, the European Commission and the European Central Bank (ECB), which came to be known as the 'troika', the Greek government was expected to enact a series of austerity measures designed to stabilise public finances while at the same time implementing a programme of structural reforms intended to improve the competitiveness of the economy. The measures provoked intense popular opposition inside Greece, with countless strikes and demonstrations, some of which led to serious outbreaks of civil unrest, and, as several other euro area countries were forced to seek similar financial

1

assistance, a sense of crisis came to engulf the currency zone as a whole. With many of the key players regularly differing in public, in a series of high profile meetings stretching over many months, foreign and domestic politicians struggled to agree on how to further assist Greece and strengthen the euro area in general. Every twist and turn of this convoluted process was played out under intense media scrutiny, leading Greece to be regularly held responsible for the volatility of global financial markets. With central bankers declaring the euro zone crisis to be the worst economic upheaval since the 1930s, a more substantial assistance package was eventually put in place for Greece and the national debt was reduced in the largest restructuring of sovereign borrowing the world has so far seen. However, this was not before the Greek prime minister had resigned (in late autumn 2011) in favour of a non-elected leader amid a general fracturing of the established political arena that facilitated the rise of parties on both the left and the right. All this time, the economy, which had begun to contract at the onset of the global financial crisis, continued to experience the deepest and most prolonged downturn seen in a member state of the Organisation for Economic Co-operation and Development (OECD) in recent times, leaving tens of thousands of businesses closed, over a quarter of the working population jobless and average household disposable income cut by a third.

Following the agreement of the second assistance package and the restructuring of the debt, a general election was called for May 2012. This proved inconclusive but, after a second ballot the next month, a multi-party government was sworn in which mostly drew its members from the ranks of the existing political establishment. This government never enjoyed an entirely comfortable relationship with the troika but, as the violent mass demonstrations came to an end and some key economic indicators started to turn to the better, Greece faded from the international news headlines. However, with the majority of the population seeing little sign of economic recovery in their own lives a sense of crisis persisted and this helped ensure that a general election that was called in January 2015 was won by an overtly left-wing party, the Coalition of the Radical Left (SYRIZA), that had never before held power. Stressing their willingness to challenge prevailing economic norms, SYRIZA pledged to bring the era of austerity to a close by leaving the troika-inspired adjustment programme. However, it was not long before the continuing weakness of both the banking sector and the country's finances as a whole became apparent. Last minute negotiations led to the external funding arrangement being extended until early summer, but weeks of further talks failed to make much headway towards securing a new assistance package. As the end of the extension loomed, the government called a referendum on its negotiating partners' latest proposals. Speculation about the country defaulting on its loans or leaving the euro reached an apogee in the media and in an increasingly tense atmosphere capital controls were imposed and Greece failed to make a payment to the IMF. With the government urging rejection of the terms, the referendum was easily won by those opposed to the proposals but in another series of late night talks an agreement was eventually reached paving the way for a third adjustment programme, which was duly signed in August 2015. This only led to a splintering of the main ruling party, prompting another general election to be called. Despite the upheavals of the previous months, this returned to power the same coalition that had ruled the country since January, in a victory that could also be seen as giving some legitimacy to the new economic adjustment programme, especially since a dissident group that had split from the main ruling party over the issue did not gain enough votes to enter parliament. Over the next months some progress was made in implementing the new programme, leading to further funding being released. But points of contention remained not just between the Greek authorities and the institutions, as the troika expanded to include officials from the European Stability Mechanism (ESM) now came to be known, but also among the institutions themselves. With the financial problems of Greece increasingly overshadowed by a wider international migration crisis, which saw hundreds of thousands of displaced people from the Middle East crossing into Europe through the Greek islands, a determination seems to have arisen to avoid returning to the sense of crisis of previous years. Yet, at the start of 2017, the story still seemed to be little changed. The Greek economy struggled to show any signs of significant recovery and a new bout of tension over the implementation of the adjustment programme led once more to talk of Greece's position in the euro area being at risk.

And yet this brief chronicle of events tells only part of the story, because the crisis cannot be reduced merely to dramatic headlines and aggregate numbers. It was and always will be about individual lives, and amid all the drama everyday existence in Greece has continued in its own mundane way. Primary school children still wheeled bags stuffed with textbooks to class in the morning, the bars and restaurants of fashionable Athenian areas, like Gazi, thronged with life throughout much of the night, summer beaches were covered with bathers, families gathered together to celebrate the feast day of a namesake saint, and outside the cities, in the countryside, life ran to its old seasonal rhythms. However, even within this everyday life, subtle signs of changes in fortune were often visible. The cakes brought to the celebrations were more likely to come from new, cheaper, chain delicatessens; the advertising flyer alluring customers to the bar in Gazi promised special weekday discounts to 'unfortunates born and living in Greece beset by the economic crisis'; the setting of the sun over the sea was marked by the pitching of tents across the beach as people avoided the cost of accommodation; the restaurant meal was paid not in full but with a cut-price coupon purchased on the internet; and the old lady in the village sat and talked not of her own life but about her concerns for her unemployed grandchildren in a faraway city. For these people and countless others, the crisis has not been defined by the clashes in Syntagma Square nor the endless meetings of grey-suited politicians and officials. It has been a crisis of households scrabbling for money to pay bills, the unemployed despairing of ever finding work, the shop owners fending off demands from the bank for the repayment of loans, the workers retiring with a smaller pension than they had expected, facing a life with little purpose and only poverty as company, and the parents ceaselessly worrying about the future of their sons and daughters. In relating the story of the crisis this book inevitably concentrates on the wider politico-economic scene, but it should never be forgotten that this tells only one part of what is a complex and often highly personal tale.

Crisis is not unknown to Greece. From the struggle for independence in the nineteenth century through defeat in the war in Anatolia in the early 1920s, which led to the arrival of over one million refugees in the country, to the German occupation of the Second World War and the subsequent bitter Civil War, the history of Greece as an independent state has often been turbulent.[1] The post-dictatorship era dawned in the midst of the Cyprus crisis and since 1974 the word has frequently appeared in local political discourse, often in relation to the economy, especially in the 1990s.[2] Some would argue that a sense of crisis even lingered after Greece adopted the euro, and in the north of the country, particularly central and western Macedonia, many associate the onset of the current difficulties with the unemployment left in the wake of the departure of local industries to Bulgaria.[3] However, it was in 2007 that the term 'crisis' started to reappear regularly in the local media both in the context of the domestic political arena, especially after the poor performance of the Panhellenic Socialist Movement (PASOK) in the general election of that year, and, increasingly, also in relation to events in the outside world after the onset of the financial crisis in the United States. The stories at first mostly concentrated on developments abroad, but by early 2008 speculation was growing that local banks might also be affected and by the spring a rise in inflation was leading to talk of Greek households in general facing a crisis.[4] These concerns initially intensified after the collapse of Lehman Brothers Holdings in September 2008 but, after the government had reassured the public that local banks were well financed, the word 'crisis' disappeared a little from the main headlines. Stories continued to appear suggesting that Greeks were responding to the shock waves of the wider global financial turmoil by cutting down on their spending and eating cheap fast food, but at this stage the crisis was still seen as something largely external to the country even if it was 'knocking on the door'.[5] This changed in December 2008, when a rash of stories started to appear, highlighting the growing problems of the local economy as companies reporting declining profits began to cut jobs. Some journalists talked about 'recession' but most, utilising the language of the previous months, began to refer to a domestic 'economic crisis' or more succinctly 'The Crisis'.[6] Soon the word was infiltrating reports on every aspect of life, with talk of a crisis in healthcare, in pharmaceuticals, even in the arts. The civil unrest of December 2008, while rarely described in terms of crisis itself, only added to the feeling of dislocation, and by January 2009 the idea that Greece was in crisis was firmly entrenched in the local media, even if stories could still appear questioning its depth.[7] By this time the political leadership was also regularly employing the word as was the general public, with nearly three-quarters of respondents in an opinion poll in March 2009 deciding, when given a range of options, that 'crisis' best described the situation in the country, and, as the year proceeded, this figure only continued to rise.[8]

The word 'crisis' was first employed in Greece largely to describe a local economic downturn that coincided with a period of international financial turmoil and domestic social unrest. The word 'recession' was occasionally used in news reports but the widespread discussion of the global financial crisis and a strong domestic tradition of describing troubles in the local economy in such terms meant that the majority of people felt that 'crisis' was the most appropriate word to use, especially at a time when their personal finances were coming under pressure. This decision to see the economic downturn as a crisis had certain implications because the word itself holds particular powers. As in the English word 'crisis', which is derived from the Greek κρίση, it firstly carries with it a suggestion of malfunction in which the smooth operation of a process is disrupted and longstanding structures and values are questioned. With most Greeks already downbeat about their own economic prospects, this recognition that the country was in crisis was sufficient for them to further rein in their spending. This sent the economy into a deeper downturn than expected and the crisis became to a certain extent self-fulfilling. However, the word 'crisis' also signifies a critical turning point, and in Greek as well it can imply thinking deeply and logically about an issue and drawing conclusions.[9] In a 2011 television interview, the philosopher Christos Yiannaras drew these meanings together, when he questioned whether a nation schooled by an education system that prepared its members to accept rather than actively participate had the κρίση to tackle the κρίση.[10] So, immediately the term was adopted, an expectation arose that the government would react and take the necessary decisions to reverse the economic downturn, because a crisis by its very nature begs attention and once conjured cannot be easily dismissed. Christine Lagarde, the managing director of the IMF, discovered this to her cost in May 2012 when she forgot to draw a distinction between absolute and relative deprivation and implied that Greece in comparison with a country such as Niger could not really be considered to be in crisis.[11] Within hours her Facebook page was reportedly bombarded with 10,000 irate messages.

By the beginning of 2009 many Greeks considered their country to be in crisis, but its transmission to the outside world was not immediate. Across Europe in the second half of 2008 there was a tendency to translate the global financial crisis into a domestic context but, as yet, there was no appearance of a generalised narrative of crisis, as had encompassed Latin America in the 1980s or Asia in 1997. In the first months of 2009, the economic imbalances of Greece attracted some attention in the international press but there was no suggestion that the country was in crisis. However, financial analysts, casting an eye at current account figures and also debt and budgetary deficit levels within the euro area, had since early 2008 begun to (re-)employ the pejorative acronym PIGS (Portugal, Italy, Greece and Spain), first apparently used by EU bureaucrats in the 1990s, to suggest that the economic weaknesses of these southern European states might be exposed by the global financial crisis.[12] Still, international media interest in Greece remained limited until November 2009, when the widening of the spread between the yields on Greek government bonds and their German equivalents coincided with the need for Dubai World, the state-run investment vehicle of Dubai, to reschedule its borrowing, sparking speculation about a sovereign debt crisis.[13] Within weeks, the possibility that Greece and other southern European countries might be about to default on their debts, worries about the stability of the euro area and continuing concerns about the banking institutions of northern European countries had all prompted talk about a more general 'euro zone crisis'.[14] Almost a year after

Greeks had first come to see their country as being in crisis, the outside world had also started to use the term. However, in contrast to the domestic narrative that had arisen in large part as a response to the local economic downturn, external commentators, at least in the Anglo-Saxon world, saw the situation developing in Greece, even if they chose to ascribe it to financial profligacy, mostly as an offshoot of global financial woes, a symptom of deeper rooted problems within the euro area and increasingly as a sovereign debt crisis. Consequently, two of the first English language books on the subject had the word 'debt' in their titles.[15] Indeed there are some, particularly on the political left, who even contest the very notion of a specifically Greek crisis, seeing the application of such a label as yet another example of negative ethnic stereotyping; for them the crisis which has afflicted the country is merely part of a wider international phenomenon.

This idea that the crisis was a sovereign debt crisis now came to dominate but there was still little agreement as to whether it was caused by the Greek state being fundamentally insolvent or whether it was due to a temporary shortage of liquidity—a situation which usually arises when investors are unwilling to advance funds to roll over debt coming to maturity, most typically, due to the size and structure of existing borrowing.[16] If this was the case, once assistance was given to meet immediate funding needs, Greece could be expected to return relatively quickly to the international financial markets to meet its borrowing requirements, as was initially foreseen. Others, however, from an early stage, judged that the country was insolvent—a situation brought about not so much by the state not having sufficient assets to meet its liabilities but by the inability or unwillingness of the government to bear the considerable political and economic costs associated with raising the revenue needed to meet its obligations.[17] At the time of the signing of the memorandums of understanding with the institutions of the troika in 2010, the prevailing view still seems to have been that Greece was suffering from a liquidity crisis. However, there were already some who were arguing that the rising debt level, combined with a weakening economy and the constraints imposed by the single currency, meant that the country was effectively insolvent.[18] This issue of the nature of the sovereign debt crisis reaches into a wider theme that perhaps not surprisingly, given its centrality in the Greek political discourse over the years, has frequently reappeared during the crisis, and this is the relationship between external and internal factors in the country's life. Often visualised in terms of the simple imposition of alien demands on Greece, this relationship, as this book will show, is complicated and multifaceted. In terms of the issue of solvency, it might be asked whether the crisis resulted from internal structural weaknesses which brought the country to the verge of bankruptcy, or from an unexpected disruption of capital flows from outside.[19] In a wider politico-economic context it might be rephrased to question whether the origins of the crisis lay in systemic imbalances within the global financial system and the shortcomings of what is cast as a neo-liberal capitalist model as well as the euro itself as a single currency, or in domestic failings, principally the excessive politicisation of the two party-system, patronage, corruption, tax evasion and endemic administrative mismanagement.[20] Finally, in relation to the adjustment programme itself, the same issue reappears in the discussion as to whether the depth and length of the depression has been due to flaws within the memorandum, including its steep fiscal adjustment targets, or the inability of Greek governments to correctly implement the measures required.

Whatever the causes, from the second quarter of 2008 until the beginning of 2014 Greece recorded six years of negative growth, during which real GDP fell from its pre-crisis peak by a cumulative total of around 26 per cent.[21] In terms of length and severity, this economic contraction bears some analogy with the Great Depression in the USA, which saw a similar fall in economic output but by most counts lasted for a shorter period of time.[22] Yet, surprisingly, perhaps in part because in Greek the distinction between economic depression and recession is lost in the word ύφεση, the term 'depression' has seldom been used in relation to Greece in English language reports.[23] This partly reflects a general tendency since the 1930s to avoid using a word which has become synonymous with a particular image of hardship caught in the novels of John Steinbeck and the photographs of the Farm Security Administration.[24] The relative moderation of the business cycle in Western economies since 1945, which has limited the size of economic downturns, may also have played a role, as has the tendency to cast extraordinary economic events as crises. Still, in recent times, downturns in Finland between 1991 and 1993 and Argentina between 1998 and 2002 have been called 'depressions' and periodically the term has also been used in press coverage of Greece and in books.[25] Significantly, the OECD also openly used the word in both the 2013 and 2016 editions of its *Economic Survey of Greece* and, following this lead, it will be employed in this book alongside the term 'recession'.[26] The two terms will not be ascribed distinct meanings. Instead they will be used to show how the crisis was perceived at different times, with recession gradually giving way to depression as the downturn deepened. Likewise the word 'crisis' will be used in general terms without further definition. The decline in the global economy brought about by the international financial crisis has been termed the 'Great Recession' and, perhaps partly in reflection of this, the events in Greece have been cast as the 'Great Crisis', with the Bank of Greece calling its history of this period by that name.[27] In doing so, however, the Bank was also merely reflecting the fact that in Greece the troubled times since 2008, with or without capitalisation, are invariably described as 'the crisis' and any attempt to impose a more academic definition on the word would ignore its considerable significance.[28] Therefore, the word, with the addition of modifiers such as 'financial', 'economic', 'sovereign debt', and even 'great' when applicable, will be used throughout this book within a general understanding that in the case of Greece a term which usually describes a transient phenomenon has evolved to encompass a much greater period of time. In general, perhaps because of their nebulous nature, crises seem to peter out rather than come to a declared end—their passing determined as much by the fact that the term ceases to be used to describe the current situation as anything else. Indeed, by the end of 2016 the word 'crisis' was being heard less in relation to Greece, but such are the problems the crisis has created that few inside the country seemed willing to accept that it had come to an end. Therefore, in part due to the general reluctance to use the word 'depression' in relation to Greece, it may be better to view the crisis as having taken yet another guise. In the light of the failure of the Greek economy to stage any meaningful recovery after its precipitate decline between 2008–2014, it has come to represent a sustained period of stagnation and hardship. Therefore, although this book is predominately concerned with the height of the crisis during the period 2009–2012, with the Epilogue bringing the story up to date, the economic and social problems that continue to beset the country and the periodic tensions that arise over the implementation of the third economic adjustment programme make it not yet possible to place the crisis in Greece in the past tense.

Indeed, the lack of precision inherent in the usage of the word 'crisis' is significant. It may in part derive from the fact that the nature of the crisis has changed over the years as it has evolved and taken different forms. That it has often been viewed as part of a series of wider intersecting economic and financial crises also plays a role, as does the fact that inside Greece the crisis has often been interpreted as being not just limited to these fields but as encompassing many other facets of life. In the rhetoric of politicians and social commentators it has frequently acquired political, social, cultural, moral and ethical dimensions, even becoming a crisis of values and, most poignantly, a crisis of humanity. The reasons for this diversification were many: it was partly due to the fact that the memorandums of understanding signed by Greece with the institution of the troika demanded wider socio-economic reforms; it was partly because an argument was increasingly advanced that the crisis was rooted in the matrix of institutions and values that had arisen from the post-dictatorship democratic transition or *metapolitefsi* to give it its Greek name; it was partly to give relevance to different voices because only by widening the crisis beyond the field of economic data could cultural commentators and others claim to have a legitimate opinion; it was partly because the notion of crisis fitted within an existing discourse which held that the future prosperity of Greece could only be secured through the completion of a radical pro-gramme of modernisation; and it was partly because the crisis became so all-encompassing. However, this broadening of the idea of crisis also reflects and accentuates the difficulties the Greeks themselves have had in establishing who should be held responsible for placing the country in such a plight. This was nowhere more clearly shown than when the Deputy Prime Minister, Theodoros Pangalos, expounding on the reasons for the size of the national debt, raised the issue of patronage appointments in the public sector and suggested that the answer to the question, 'How did we eat the money?' was 'We appointed you. We all ate it together, within the framework of relationships based on political clientelism, corruption, bribery and the debasement of the meaning of politics.'[29] Pangalos' remarks about 'eating the money', which intentionally or not mirrored the dialogue of a Greek film of 1960, were widely lampooned, often being accompanied with crude jokes about his girth, but the vehemence of the reaction was an indication of not only how important but also problem-atic the issue of apportioning responsibility for the crisis continues to be for Greeks, with many perceiving, unfairly or not, that Pangalos by his remark was trying to shift the blame from the political elite to society as a whole.[30]

This opening out of the concept to encompass not just the sovereign debt crisis and the economic depression but virtually every aspect of Greek life understandably makes it very difficult not only to pinpoint the nature of the crisis in Greece but even to describe what it means. Aside from a general acceptance that the country faces serious economic problems and that it has been in crisis, little else seems to be widely agreed about its origins, nature or, more seriously, the remedies to be applied. Furthermore, even if a generally accepted interpretation were to emerge, it would still only be an approximation of crisis for most people, because there can be no universal experience. The term obviously means different things to different people—the perceptions of the businessman from the northern Athenian neighbourhood of Maroussi, the shop assistant from the western suburb of Aegaleo and the international financier in his office in London are bound to differ. However, as best as can be divined from a series of opinion polls taken in the first years of the crisis asking respondents to rate a series of fixed concerns, the defining issue for most was a lack of money, with about 40 per cent consistently stating this was their biggest worry. Yet, even at the start of the recession in 2008, a third of those asked expressed the same concern, so this changed less than might be expected, although, of course, within this sizeable proportion of the population, individual hardship may have worsened considerably. In contrast, the number concerned about the next most pressing issue, unemployment, doubled, rising from 13.1 per cent in June 2007 to 27 per cent in December 2012, a figure which quite closely matched the rise in unemployment itself and, given the difficulties faced by many of the jobless, may stand as a proxy for concerns about money.[31] Other concerns have also tended to vary with the progress of the crisis, with worries about high prices declining in the face of deflation at the same time as anxieties about the future prospects of children have risen.

The crisis means different things to different people but the ambition of this book is to give as clear an account as possible of its causes and consequences. It does so mostly through a chronological framework in the belief that this is the most accessible and coherent way in which to examine the issue. As such, the book is primarily a work of contemporary history, although it also draws heavily on the insights of other disciplines in the belief that only such an interdisciplinary approach allows the crisis to be placed in sufficient context to permit a proper understanding of its origins and scale to emerge. The first chapters consider developments between 1972 and 2008 but, in initially looking to the past, the book is neither trying to establish a line of causation between the institutions and values of the *metapolitefsi* and the crisis nor suggesting a direct lineage can be traced with the long sequence of similar crisis-like situations that have beset Greece over the years, although similarities, of course, do abound. Instead, a critical reading of this past can elucidate the causes of the crisis and help us to understand why many of the prescriptions have been less successful than expected. The crisis has also constantly being interpreted in relation to this past.[32] This is not only in terms of personal understandings of the unfolding events but also in relation to a key narrative that holds that the crisis results from an incomplete process of modernisation, with the inference being that only when this has been achieved will imbalances in the economy be corrected and the paradoxes that have held back the country's development be resolved.

1

THE TEMPEST OF PROGRESS

THE SEARCH FOR ECONOMIC STABILITY
AFTER THE DICTATORSHIP

On 13 December 1972 the police were called to the heart of the commercial district of Athens to attend to a crowd. On arrival they found a group of excited small investors looking to buy and sell shares on the stock exchange in Sophocleous Street.[1] At first sight this scene might have been taken as another indicator of the success of an economy that overseas observers were still rating one of the best performing in the world, but in fact it was marking the end of an era. The same forces which had led the stock market to boom, with many shares quintupling in price over previous months, were also bringing to an end two decades that some have called the 'Greek economic miracle'.[2] Usually dated from a steep devaluation of the drachma in 1953, this had been marked by sustained economic growth, rising exports, increasing productivity, low inflation, minimal unemployment and monetary stability. The reasons for the change in fortunes lay both inside Greece, with the expansionary economic and monetary policies followed by the ruling military regime, and beyond its borders, with the breakdown of the Bretton Woods system of fixed exchange rates producing a rise in global commodity prices that was aggravated in Europe by distortions created by the Common Agricultural Policy of the European Economic Community (EEC).[3] In combination these created a surge in the rate of inflation which rose from being one of the lowest in the countries of the Organisation for Economic Co-operation and Development (OECD) at the beginning of 1972 to one of the highest by the close of 1973.

The turbulence of the early 1970s, and especially the oil price rises of 1973 following the Arab-Israeli Yom Kippur War, created problems for many West European economies, but in Greece the recovery of economic stability was to prove a particularly difficult and protracted affair, partly because the 'miracle' itself had rested on underlying structural deficiencies, including serious regional and social inequalities.

To cool the overheating of the economy, at the end of 1972, the military regime announced a series of austerity measures that threw its expansionist policies into reverse.[4] The public investment budget was slashed, interest rates were raised and restrictions were placed on loans, especially for housing. Amid warnings that investors should ignore the irresponsible rumours of profiteers, limits were placed on daily trading on the stock exchange and promises given that more shares would be made available through the part flotation of state companies such as the Public Power Corporation and the Hellenic Telecommunications Organisation (OTE). To curb inflation, price controls were also intensified, with market inspections stepped up and consumers urged to report shopkeepers overcharging. Soon the newspapers were full of stories of arrests. The manager of a poultry breeding association faced prosecution for deliberately holding back chickens from the market, a trader for selling beef as higher price veal, and a group of fruit merchants for offering oranges above the official price. At the same time the administration also embarked on a process of price liberalisation. This was partly due to the fact the controls had already effectively broken down, with shopkeepers asking purchasers of merchandise for an additional unofficial surcharge or 'hat', which could be up to three-quarters of the official price. Importers were also said to be unhappy because their goods, which the government hoped would help bring down high local prices, could be stuck in warehouses for weeks while they waited for new prices to be approved. Now, the prices of many goods, from household appliances to ladies underwear were freed, with the process intensifying after the installation of a new government under Spyros Markezinis in October 1973, when the 'hat' was effectively legalised. The government argued that it was only removing market distortions to end food shortages and justified the increases as being necessary to converge with European norms but with some prices doubling overnight even the officially appointed union leadership voiced their disapproval of measures that, they claimed, were 'sentencing the workers to starvation.'[5]

Markezinis accepted that the government was following a policy of 'austerity' but promised that it would not 'ignore and underestimate the needs of the

Greek people'.[6] However, the government was swept away by another coup d'état after just a month, following the brutal suppression of a student uprising at the Athens Polytechnic on 17 November 1973.[7] The new military regime and its civilian government followed a policy of austerity in all fields. It ruthlessly persecuted its opponents, sending many to reopened island prison camps, 'purified' society by arresting people deemed to be guilty of such deviant behaviour as smashing plates in tavernas, and tabled what it openly called an 'austerity budget'. This brought further cuts in public investment, new taxes on construction and extra levies on the likes of foreign-flagged yachts, which led to reports of boats sailing surreptitiously to Italy by night to avoid the imposition. There were also clampdowns on corruption, with a former minister being jailed for his part in a scandal involving imported meat, and tax evasion, although the military authorities were not averse to using this as an excuse to persecute their opponents.[8] To curb oil usage, the price of petrol was raised so it became almost twice as expensive as in leading West European countries, limits were placed on the use of cars at weekends, and television channels ordered to close early. The squeeze cooled the economy, leading to a sharp fall in industrial production, but at the expense of growing social tensions, with reports speaking of groups of unemployed building workers loitering on street corners in Athens and consumers hoarding foodstuffs, especially sugar. However, by May 1974, the Prime Minister, Adamantios Androutsopoulos, felt confident enough to claim that inflation had been brought under control 'by means of economic measures only, without having recourse to the police measures used in the past, which never succeeded in preventing prices from rising'.[9] By then, though, the military regime was already in its last days, although its eventual demise was due neither to the troubled economy nor the student protests but its decision to back a coup d'état in Cyprus in July 1974. A few days later a Turkish army landed in the north of the island. The Greek armed forces mobilised to meet any challenge but with chaotic scenes in Athens, in the midst of panic buying by civilians and open dissent among military reservists, the military regime effectively collapsed.[10] In the early hours of 24 July 1974, the former Prime Minister, Konstantine Karamanlis, returned from exile in France and amid tumultuous scenes of celebration quickly formed a civilian government drawn from the political centre and the anti-dictatorship right.

In order to contest elections in the restored democratic environment Karamanlis founded a party, appropriately called New Democracy, which he positioned 'between the extreme right and the left, both Marxist and non-

Marxist'.[11] Ideologically the party reflected a breadth of thinking which could lead the essentially conservative Karamanlis at times to speak approvingly of social democracy.[12] In terms of social and economic policy its approach was to be 'radical liberal', which was defined in terms of a commitment to social justice and a willingness to use the state to 'limit inequalities and replace private initiative wherever economic and social reasons so dictate'.[13] The philosophical base of these ideas was drawn from an eclectic blend of schools of thought ranging from socialist state planning to post-1945 American developmentalism, Keynesianism and the German *ordoliberal* social-market tradition.[14] To these might also be added a strong streak of pragmatism embodied in Karamanlis' constant quest for efficiency and his meticulous eye for detail, which once saw him raise a minister from bed early on a Sunday morning to check whether the price of chicory really was as stated in that day's newspaper.[15] Facing challenges from both inside the country and outside, with war with Turkey seen as a distinct possibility throughout much of this period, the chief imperative for the new government was the consolidation of democracy. In line with the other post-authoritarian states of southern Europe, this was to be pursued through a relatively lax monetary policy, as controlling inflation gave way to maintaining economic growth, creating jobs, raising standards of living and delivering social justice. To further the latter, the wealthy and bigger businesses were taxed more heavily, wage differentials compressed within the civil service and strict rent controls imposed, which kept rises to about half the rate of inflation, effectively transferring resources from landlords to tenants. However, within this 'progressive' programme the tenor often remained distinctly paternalistic, with one report suggesting that a relaxation of the six day working week might not only harm the economy but also lead to 'psychological and social problems' among those not accustomed to such leisure.[16]

The new regime presided over a successful democratisation process and this helped create a general narrative of achievement that even stretched into the economic field, precluding any talk of crisis for much of this period, although words such as 'recession' and 'austerity' remained within the political lexicon.[17] The episode of military rule in Greece, which had lasted just over seven years, had been relatively short in comparison with Spain and Portugal. This allowed it to be seen as little more than a brief aberration and helped give the *metapolitefsi* its own particular character. There was to be no radical caesura with the past. Familiar political faces were able to re-emerge alongside old practices, such as the system of securing votes through the granting of favours. The intricate network of professional and trade bodies also survived. Even the dictators had failed in their attempt to change this. When they had announced plans to alter the organisational structure of the Athens bus service in 1973, the drivers had responded by threatening to set their vehicles alight in front of the Tomb of the Unknown Soldier. Whether from fear of reaction or a need to win over a natural constituency, changes in the civil administration were also more limited than desired by many, especially the young. Some judges, members of local authorities and university professors were dismissed, but otherwise there were relatively few changes either in personnel or practices, with individual ministers retaining considerable powers of patronage.[18] When new competences, such as dealing with the Common Agricultural Policy, were added, the response was invariably to take on more staff, and, as a consequence, the numbers employed within the public sector continued to grow, so that a 1979 efficiency study by American consultants, perhaps not unexpectedly, is reported to have found that 4,000 of 72,000 civil service jobs examined were superfluous.

Under the leadership of Karamanlis, New Democracy won two consecutive elections. In 1974 it achieved a landslide victory over the old pre-dictatorship Centre Union and in 1977 defeated a new alignment that had in part supplanted the centrist party, the Panhellenic Socialist Movement (PASOK) of Andreas Papandreou, the son of the prominent Centre Union politician and previous Prime Minister, Georgios Papandreou.[19] For the first time since the Civil War of the 1940s, the elections were also contested by communists, after the government had legalised both the Communist Party of Greece (KKE) and a splinter group, the Communist Party of Greece-Interior. This was part of a general policy of removing the trappings of the past designed to curb the political left, such as the requirement for citizens to produce certificates of social responsibility attesting to a patriotic, non-communist character when applying for many jobs or in transactions with the civil administration.[20] However, some vestiges of the old ways were not so easily swept away, with the military continuing to keep records of the political views of conscripts and officers being refused permission to marry girls from families that were perceived to be left-wing.[21] Memories of the Civil War in which royalist forces had defeated their communist opponents also continued to be evoked to shape the political identities of both right and left, leading one contemporary observer to suggest that, with the possible exception of Northern Ireland, Greece remained the most divided polity in Europe.[22] This gave a special twist to Greek political life, which continued to be marked by a particularly bitter right-left polarisation, as all too often preventing the opposition gaining power became the *sine qua non* of political life.[23] Virtually all policy could be subverted to achieve this end, whether it be the buying off of influential interest groups or the customary tearing up of the economic balance sheet at the time of elections in order to allure voters.[24]

Yet, aside from continuity, the *metapolitefsi* also brought considerable change as, free from the constraints of dictatorship, the country embraced the concept of democracy. For much of the population this seems to have meant little more than welcoming the new political system and its ideals of moderation, maturity and national pride.[25] However for many others, especially the young, it entailed a more radical rejection of the past. Democracy for them stood as the antithesis of dictatorship, with its attendant values of anti-communism, pro-Americanism, social conservatism and, as they saw it, anti-modernism. It meant instead an openness to the political views of the left, implacable opposition to authoritarianism and American imperialism and a growing acceptance of social liberalism, in part inspired by changes in attitudes elsewhere in the world. Such values were not new to Greece since many were grounded in the traditions of the pre-dictatorship United Democratic Left as well as sections of the Centre Union. However, for the first time they could now be openly and clearly articulated in a cultural outpouring which completely subverted the old right-wing order which in various guises had held sway since the Civil War. Instead of being lauded as the restorers of democracy, in this new discourse the familiar political faces of the past were cast as representatives of a failed conservative system and, when people were asked in an opinion poll who should be held responsible for the Civil War, more now chose to blame the right than the previously demonised left, although significantly only a third thought it would have been better for the country if the outcome of the conflict had been different.[26]

Politically this new leftism took many forms, from support for the communist parties and increasingly, as time progressed, for PASOK, to participation in protest marches on the streets of Athens which periodically ended in violent clashes between police deploying tear gas and missile throwing demonstrators, whom the media were quick to dub 'anarchists'. There were also a growing number of strikes, some of which, such as the one at the white-goods manufacturer, Izola, were held explicitly to 'end the dictatorship of the boss'.[27] Others enrolled in one of the multitude of organisations that appeared, many of which were affiliated to the political parties, with each of the main groupings having its own student, youth and women's associations. In a country already encouraged after the Civil War to see virtually everything in political terms, this not only led to an even deeper politicisation of society but also in the eyes of some curbed their effectiveness. The women's groups, for instance, although they did provide an opportunity for a few, often well-connected, women to enter party life, in general blunted the impact of the wider feminist movement by tending to focus on challenging formal constraints rather than changing more ingrained behaviour patterns.[28] The same was also true of the trade union movement, which had long been heavily politicised, but now became increasingly dominated by public sector workers. This allowed it to pressurise the government into raising pay and enacting a host of regulations protecting jobs but only, it was later claimed, at the expense of introducing rigidities into the labour market. Many found their way into the youth groups of the parties of the left where they mingled with members of anti-dictatorship resistance groups to form complex networks of relationships. Dubbed the 'Polytechnic generation' after the 1973 student uprising, under the influence of the radicalism of their international contemporaries they formed an influential avant-garde.[29] Employing a radical new political language, through their positions in the expanding state sector, including the banks, they were effectively able to infuse society with their values, shaping its relationship to democracy, left-wing ideological thought, modernisation and, ultimately, Europe as a whole.

The rejection of the values of the dictatorship also extended to the field of economics, but in contrast to the political and social arenas there was no general shift towards liberalisation. This was perhaps because the culture of regulation and control was not particularly associated with the dictatorship, having been in part shaped by Karamanlis and other members of the incoming political leadership during his earlier tenure in power. As a result the Greek economy remained far more bound by controls than most of its free-market trading partners within the EEC. An enormous multitude of petty regulations covered every aspect of economic life from the opening hours of different categories of shops to the amount of gold sovereigns that could be purchased in any one day.[30] Typically, in the banking sector there were at least fifty types of interest rate at any one time, determined not so much by the amount of money being lent but by usage, as the government tried to steer credit towards what it called 'productive investments'.[31] Infringements of the many rules brought sanctions, with businessmen who sold goods at higher than designated prices risking jail, while those who tried to carry too much currency overseas could have their money seized. Indeed, faced with an economic challenge, the first response of the government was usually to create new regulations. An untoward rise in the rate of inflation would see the imposition of further price controls and complex attempts to limit profit margins while a similar increase in imports would find traders required to place large deposits in blocked bank accounts and special taxes applied to what were deemed luxury goods, which could range from fur coats to light bulbs.[32]

Instead of this system of regulation and control it was the dictatorship's mishandling of the economy that was highlighted by the incoming government. On entering office, Karamanlis quickly established a commission to review state finances. This revealed that the budgetary deficit was far greater than previously thought, largely, it was said, because state subsidised goods had been released at a price below which they had been purchased. This discrepancy allowed Karamanlis to look little further for the cause of the country's economic ills than the 'incoherent and irresponsible' policies of the dictators.[33] Foremost amongst these were the granting of 'uncontrolled benefits' to private firms, which included the direct, and by inference underhand, negotiating of public works contracts, and the favouring of monopolies and oligarchies.[34] Again, much of this chimed with pre-dictatorship narratives which had stressed the rapacious behaviour of middlemen in their dealings with peasant producers, exploitative practices in industries such as tobacco processing and the alien nature of large industrial plants established by American companies in the 1960s.[35] In the post-dictatorship environment these views were reflected in opinion polls which showed that the vast majority wanted to see a redistribution of wealth on a more equitable basis. With the owners of larger businesses seen as being part of a privileged elite and as inherently dishonest, more than anywhere else in Western Europe respondents declared themselves in favour of greater protection against what were perceived to be the ravages of capital, with overwhelming numbers pronouncing themselves in favour of prohibiting redundancy if no alternative jobs were available, and of greater government involvement in the economy, including nationalisation.[36]

Indeed, one of the most striking features of the economy under the Karamanlis government was the expansion of state ownership. In 1974 the incoming government had pledged to 'free the economy from unnecessary state interference...' but by 1979 the state either directly or through assets it controlled dominated the banking, energy, communications, utility and public transport sectors, as well as sizeable proportions of the insurance, oil refining, shipyard and fertiliser production industries.[37] When pressed on the reason for this massive expansion of state control, the minister most involved,

Panayiotis Papaligouras, regularly denied it was due to any ideological leanings towards socialism.[38] Instead, he insisted that every takeover was
approached pragmatically on its own merit, although it seems likely that the
French tradition of *dirigisme* experienced by Karamanlis in exile exerted some
influence on policy.[39] Nonetheless at times allegations of personal animosities
surfaced. In particular, a dispute over an apartment between Karamanlis and
the shipowner-banker, Stratis Andreadis, was said to have motivated the
takeover of the latter's empire.[40] However, in reality the nationalisations were
just part of a wider reappraisal of the business practices of the junta era which
saw over three hundred contracts with foreign firms reviewed at this time.
Only a handful of these were deemed worthy of revision, but Renault-Peugeot
did abandon plans to build a car plant, and this foreshadowed a general tendency for foreign companies to henceforth look for investment opportunities
outside Greece. During this period the government took control of companies
such as Olympic Airways, after Aristotle Onassis renounced his concession to
run the airline, the extensive holdings of Andreadis, including the Ionian and
Commercial banks, and the Aspropyrgos oil refinery, after it had reacquired
Stavros Niarchos' stake. In doing so, it not only neutralised the domestic influence of a group of powerful shipowners, who to a greater or lesser extent had
been associated with the previous regime, but it also ensured that the levers of
economic development, especially the banking sector, lay almost entirely
within its control.[41] Indeed, by 1977 Karamanlis had come to see state investment as virtually the sole instrument for promoting economic growth. Yet,
already the limits of such an approach were also becoming apparent. A petro-
chemical plant bought from the UK using investment credits remained moth-
balled in store and Olympic Airways was soon posting losses. Ministers started
to voice their frustration about the inability of the bureaucracy to enact their
plans. An undersecretary at the Ministry of Industry in 1978, noting that the
staff of his department had authority but no responsibility and worked in a
mechanical way, was reported to have bitterly complained, 'Nobody knows
what he is doing, why he is doing it, what he writes, what he signs and why he
signs it'.[42] In the face of growing competition from state enterprises, private
businessmen also began to object to the administration's 'social mania' and
claim it was anti-business. However, in reality the relationship between the
two sides was always complex and often highly personal, as owners instinc-
tively turned to ministers to solve their problems, whether in the form of new
regulations to protect against foreign competition or an intervention to help
secure a loan. As a result differing opinions increasingly came to be heard

within New Democracy so that a key minister within a government still ostensibly pursuing a policy of state-led industrial development could declare, 'We have learnt from bitter experience that the State is not a successful businessman and that the State should not be allowed to undertake ventures which can be implemented much better by the private sector'.[43]

The stress on the primacy of the state in the economy was part of a general policy of building national self-sufficiency and strengthening international links to meet the challenge from Turkey. This led to massive arms purchases, which put a strain on the budget, and considerable investment in a defence industry; it also underpinned the decision to actively pursue EEC membership. In 1961 Greece had signed an Association Agreement with the EEC in anticipation of eventual membership but, when this possibility was first raised after the dictatorship, the response was initially guarded. After Karamanlis' first tour of Europe, one jaundiced French diplomat remarked that everybody had said 'yes' to his request in the expectation that somebody else would say 'no'.[44] Even after negotiations began, attempts by the European Commission to prescribe a lengthy period of harmonisation and delay Greece's application, so that it had to be considered with those of Portugal and Spain, were only thwarted by personal interventions from the Greek premier. Those in favour of the Greek application argued that rejecting its membership bid after it had so recently re-established democracy would undermine the basic values on which the EEC rested, although the growing importance of bilateral trade links between Community states and Greece no doubt also weighed heavily in the calculations. Greece, stressing its role as a bridge between Europe and the Middle East, for its part sought geopolitical security, new markets for its goods and cash inflows. As always, the balance to be struck was between political imperative and economic cost and, according to at least one observer, the Greek government was slow to appreciate the latter, but in the end the main points of difficulty in the negotiations were settled with transition periods of various lengths.[45] However, equally important were the wider moves towards convergence associated with membership. These ranged from steep rises in food prices, which probably added more than the oil price shock of 1979 to the consumer price index, to a requirement to open an interbank foreign currency market in Athens. Beyond these, there were also measures that were not required but became expected, either because they moved Greece closer to West European norms, such as the introduction of a five-day week in 1981, or because they were necessary to make the economy competitive in a wider Community environment. Indeed, it has been suggested that the wave of strikes which hit Greece from 1977 onwards was in large part driven by opposition to Karamanlis' desire to 'rationalise' and 'modernise' the economy prior to EEC entry. Thus, while the owner of the newspaper, *Kathimerini*, Eleni Vlachos, might have complained at the time that 'too many Greeks think of the EEC as a kind of Santa Claus from whose bag we can take countless treasures without having to contribute much', in reality by no means all the population were convinced of the benefits of joining the Community, with a clear majority being either hostile or indifferent immediately prior to accession.[46] Among the most trenchant critics was Andreas Papandreou who saw membership as consolidating Greece's position as a peripheral state within Europe, ensuring its 'transformation into a satellite economy under the control of the Brussels decision-making centre'.[47] Shorn of its ability to apply measures such as import and capital controls, he saw the country being placed at a permanent disadvantage, unable to achieve true national sovereignty and full economic development, with Greek industry only remaining competitive if wages were kept lower than European norms.

Those who argued for a longer harmonisation period did so because they were aware of the differences between the Greek and other EEC economies. The number of people living in villages might be continuing to decline, but in 1980 about a third of the economically active population, defined as those over fourteen years old, were still working on the land. Most of the people who had left the countryside headed for the growing metropolises where the need for housing helped fuel economic growth throughout this period. Once in their new homes, many of the male arrivals found jobs in industry, artisanal workshops or the retail trade, while the women, in contrast to the countryside, tended to be occupied in domestic duties. This led to less than half of the population aged over fourteen declaring they were economically active, which helped keep the official unemployment rate virtually non-existent, although one contemporary study estimated that in reality it was running at about 10 per cent and that without emigration, especially to West Germany, that figure might have been almost double.[48] Much of the manufacturing industry in which the new arrivals found jobs was still in the hands of its original founding families. Most were orientated towards the domestic market with little of their production exported. Indeed, half of all non-agricultural exports were handled by less than 200 companies. This lack of merchandise exports left the country with a perpetual trade deficit in goods which was only countered by earnings from services, primarily tourism and shipping, as well as remittances sent home by Greeks living abroad. However, while helping balance the books, these also kept the exchange rate high, making Greece increasingly uncompetitive against international rivals and the country unattractive to foreign direct investment.[49] Partly as a result, by the late 1970s, many businesses, heavily dependent on bank borrowing, were already beginning to falter. In 1979 about a third of the leading 2,680 firms reported losses and with non-performing loans mounting alarmingly, state controlled banks were already urging the government to establish an industrial holding body on the lines of the Italian *Istituto per la Ricostruzione Industriale* (IRI) for what were starting to be known as 'problematic companies'.[50]

By the close of its period in office, New Democracy could point to achievements in the field of economic governance. After the immediate post-dictatorship downturn, the economy had grown relatively strongly and in general the *metapolitefsi* is recollected as a time of plenty when new goods entered the market. However, the problems were also familiar. The government blamed the troubles of industry on poor management but equally or more important were a persistent lack of investment, increasing labour costs, which almost doubled in companies with more than ten workers during the period 1974–1980, and falling productivity.[51] Inflation also remained far higher than in many European competitors. It reached 18.9 per cent again in 1979, driven by a continuing monetary expansion that Xenophon Zolotas, the governor of the Bank of Greece, chose to blame on the persistently high budget deficit but which Papandreou, dropping into the familiar language of Greek politics, said was due to the 'immense and irrational increase of public expenditures and bank credits in order to facilitate party and personal interests'.[52] The considerable difference in inflation rates between Greece and its main trading rivals further exacerbated the competitiveness problems of industry. In response the government adopted a crawling-peg exchange rate policy, allowing the drachma to decline broadly in line with the inflation differential. However, critics increasingly argued this was self-defeating since it only stymied the fight against inflation and removed an incentive to introduce structural reforms.[53]

In the euphoria surrounding the return of democracy not only had discussion of crisis been impossible but 'the very concept itself was unthinkable'.[54] Instead, crisis had remained a phenomenon encountered outside Greece. However, by the early 1980s the vicissitudes of the economy in conjunction with conservative unease at changing social norms had led the term to reappear, with Karamanlis speaking of the existence of a general political, economic and moral crisis.[55] Along with selfishness, he rooted this in the materialism increasingly visible in Greek society, seeing prodigality and excessive consumption as having not only economic repercussions but as 'distorting… our whole social structure, and even… the Greek character'.[56] Such a view was in tune with a society in which ostentatious behaviour was seen by many as running counter to a moral code that was rooted in essentially rural but also deeply Christian values. These excoriated laziness and exhibition and instead held hard work to be the best 'remedy to misfortune' in a life which was viewed as being an almost continual struggle with the adversities of nature and human temptation.[57] It was perhaps partly as a result of ideas such as these that discussions about economic issues commonly came to carry a moral tinge, as with the administration's attempt to root the causes of inflation in the profligate behaviour of certain sections of society, especially the self-employed and professional classes. They were regularly decried for 'wasting' vast sums of money in *bouzoukia*, tavernas and the like, and Zolotas argued that the only way inflation could be brought under control was if the spending capacity of this group was checked through a campaign against tax evasion. When justifying the imposing of import controls, a minister in a similar vein also insisted that spending on imported alcohol, jewellery and musical instruments was a mark of 'excessive consumption and waste' that undermined economic progress.[58] Indeed, critics argued that with external remittances from emigrants, tourism and shipping, accounting for up to 20 per cent of GDP, Greece was 'in thrall to the easy and quick inflow of currency', allowing it to display to the world 'the image of a country living beyond its means'.[59] However, despite the persistence of this narrative blaming profligacy for the nation's woes, the country gave no appearance of being ready for austerity. In an opinion poll in May 1981 only 33 per cent agreed that the standard of living should be lowered to fight inflation and a mere 29 per cent thought it was necessary to raise taxes to pay for free health care and other social benefits.[60]

As in 1973, the rise in inflation also coincided with an increase in global oil prices, this time caused by the overthrow of the Shah of Iran early in 1979. This placed the balance of payments under further pressure in part because importers, anticipating the imposition of new regulations, built up stocks beforehand, leading to more goods entering Greece than normal. The government's response was, as usual, to impose additional controls, but by the late 1970s the effectiveness of these was waning. They had been undermined by both the growing complexity of the marketplace, which made it impossible to calculate comparative costs and profit margins, and a global drift towards free-market solutions, with international organisations such as the EEC and International Monetary Fund (IMF) as well as the General Agreement on Tariffs and Trade (GATT) all pressing Greece to lift restrictions. With rumours circulating that the country's foreign exchange reserves were running low, the IMF was said to be standing ready to intervene, but the central bank still possessed sufficient international credibility to secure a series of 'emergency' overseas loans—with one excused by a minister as being due to 'a slight miscalculation'.[61] By 1980 the position had stabilised. The government claimed that the import restrictions had worked, although a decline in demand following a loss of consumer confidence and later a fall in oil prices were probably more important. Inflation, though, remained high, the budget deficit was expanding, with a leaked government report prior to the 1981 general election saying it was running at twice the level officially admitted, and public debt was rising sharply. During the 1981 election campaign the two parties clashed over economic policy, with PASOK claiming that New Democracy was following a scorched earth policy. However, a rating of European credit risk produced by international banks in September 1979, which placed Greece in position fifteen out of eighteen, just above Iceland, Yugoslavia and Portugal and just below Spain, Ireland and Italy, so closely mirrors similar exercises thirty years later that it raises interesting questions as to the extent that macroeconomic fundamentals change, regardless of policy.[62]

The Panhellenic Socialist Movement came to power in the general election of 18 October 1981 and aside from a brief interregnum between 1989 and 1993 the party was to remain in office until 2004. At the time PASOK's victory was cast as the fulfilment of historic destiny.[63] However, when it was suggested to Papandreou by the British ambassador that it was only the dictatorship that had made socialism popular, he did not demur.[64] During the election campaign, the party had instead preferred to dwell on its slogan of 'change', which remained vaguely defined, but seems in part to have been viewed as a pragmatic policy designed to unleash the full potential of the economy and society. Some still chose to interpret this as carrying the possibility of radical transformation, but many Greeks reassured by the presence of Karamanlis in the presidency saw it more as a chance to move beyond the limits of New Democracy's rule without embarking on a totally different path to the future.

PASOK had been founded by Papandreou in 1974 following his return to Greece after the dictatorship. During its turbulent early years, the movement had been marked by a series of mass expulsions, mostly due to disagreements over organisation, but subsequently it had become a disciplined, hierarchical and frequently highly bureaucratic organisation. However, this did not mean that various tendencies did not continue to exist. The radicalism of some members, such as the youth group, which tended in the early days to see Yugoslavia or developing world national liberation movements as providing a better model than traditional European socialist parties, was not necessarily shared by more pragmatic parliamentary deputies or indeed voters. At the helm was Papandreou, lauded by party propagandists as the 'single and stable point of reference in the unsettled consciousness' of both the people and PASOK.[65] Papandreou gained his prestige not only from being the founder of the movement and his undoubted charisma but also from his ability to act as arbitrator between its various factions.

Indeed, in its early years the party was described as an intellectual 'babel', providing a home for an eclectic mesh of ideas including socialist, Marxist, Trotskyite and Maoist currents.[66] Its economic policy was also heavily influenced by dependency theory as espoused by the Argentine economist Raúl Prebisch, with its notion of 'peripheral' and 'core' states. Over the years the party's position gradually evolved towards a social democratic stance, so that by the early 2000s one prominent minister could even envision it following a similar path to the British Labour Party of Tony Blair.[67] However, as originally conceived, PASOK's ideology held that Greece, as a peripheral country lying on the margins of the world system, was little more than an economic, political, social and cultural dependency of what were termed the 'metropoles of capitalism'. Chief of these was the USA and its main European satellite, West Germany. A visiting British Labour Party politician in private conversation with Papandreou was shocked by the depth of the Greek premier's dislike of the social democratic government of Chancellor Helmut Schmidt.[68] According to PASOK, dependency had been created by the metropoles both formally through institutional arrangements, such as membership of NATO and the EEC and the stationing of American bases on Greek soil, but also through the activities of foreign multinationals which, it argued, continued to dominate the local economy.[69] In this formulation true popular sovereignty, and not the titular sovereignty that Greece enjoyed, could only come from the rejection and expulsion of all these forms of dependency—although party ideologues recognised this would probably provoke a reaction from the metropoles which might try and prevent it by backing another seizure of power by the military or taking some form of economic action, such as encouraging the flight of capital from the country or even withholding loans.

Moreover, in PASOK's worldview, dependency had not just been imposed on the country by outside forces, it had also arisen because some Greeks had chosen to associate themselves with foreign interests to benefit from their presence. These 'unpatriotic forces', as they were known, formed the backbone of a privileged elite and true freedom from dependency would only come when the people were mobilised to destroy their influence.[70] In this process politics would cease to be a formal procedure limited to national and local government. Instead, it would expand to embrace the population as a whole, producing in the process the conditions for the creation of a new socialist society that would solve once and for all the problems of development and social justice that continued to blight Greece. Such a transformation was seen as feasible because the privileged elite were facing in PASOK not just a narrow class based party but a popular mass movement representing both the working people of Greece as well as the 'unprivileged', which featured among its ranks another oppressed group, the lower-middle strata (*micromesaioi*). This term was developed primarily to encompass the vast numbers of self-employed within Greek society, especially the merchants and shopkeepers, but ultimately it became so broadly defined that it was able to encompass almost all who wanted to be included.[71] The term 'lower-middle strata' has long since disappeared from the rhetoric of everyday political life and the extent to which the first PASOK governments succeeded in transforming Greek society still remains a matter of dispute. However, the key dichotomies of privileged/ unprivileged and Greek/foreign, the latter usually identified with the United States and international capital, continued to be deeply embedded at all levels within the political discourse. Thus, PASOK's gradual drift towards a less radical political posture was not matched by any lessening in its rhetorical attacks on the privileged, as they were held to account for tax evasion, holding more than one position or salary or just driving a particular model of car beyond the means of average Greeks. In this way, society and the world at large was neatly divided into opposing categories of the dominant and domi- nated, allowing the party to cultivate a sense of collective identity with the population in general based on the notion that together they formed a broadly based 'us' opposed to a narrow 'them'. Within such a discourse blame and responsibility could be shifted and a sense of victimisation easily built, and it is in this way that the tropes of populism, according to many interpretations, came to pervade the political landscape of Greece.[72] Perhaps in part this was a response to fear, insecurity and marginalisation within Europe, but listening to any conversation about politics in Greece, whether it be around the kitchen table or in the local cafe, soon raises questions as to the extent to which such constructions reflect the prevailing party political discourse or whether the parties are merely responding to longstanding popular rhythms.[73]

As with the *metapolitefsi* in general, PASOK's ascent to office brought a mixture of continuity and change. Despite frequent pledges in the past to the contrary, Greece remained a member of the EEC and NATO and American bases stayed on Greek soil. However, this was only after negotiations had extracted armaments from the USA and better terms from the EEC, following the submission by PASOK of a petition, which, with some irony given later developments, is known in Greece as the 'memorandum'. Change came in areas like the civil service, which PASOK saw as being potentially hostile to its plans of socialist transformation. Senior posts were abolished and several thousand party workers, colloquially known as 'Green Guards', due to PASOK's official colour, introduced. With responsibility for other appointments also passing to councils representing broad swathes of the workforce, including trade unions, critics have long argued that the changes weakened coordination, undermined the authority of senior personnel and made the administration more open to political pressure.[74] At a lower level, PASOK offices were besieged by thousands of people, many previously excluded by personal and political criteria from the patronage networks of New Democracy, seeking party assistance in finding jobs in the public sector. Recruitment into the state-controlled enterprises and banks was particularly heavy, and, since the new employees were easily recognisable as PASOK supporters, a more polarised workplace became the norm. Indeed, security of tenure, relatively good pay, rising annually on a preordained scale, generally lax employment conditions, and a series of perks from cheap housing loans to discounts in major shops in Athens helped consolidate the idea that the best jobs were to be found in the public sector. In an opinion poll of the time, 64 per cent of young Greeks said it would be their favoured place of work, with only 10 per cent preferring the private sector.[75] This process, though, was mutually supporting, because, while large numbers of PASOK supporters were entering the state sector, at the same time, many public employees were joining PASOK.[76] Indeed, the overwhelming majority of recruits to the party after 1981 were linked to this part of the economy, but this raised its own difficulties; and Papandreou was aware of the danger that PASOK might be almost entirely absorbed by the state machinery, losing its identity and becoming little more than an electoral mechanism to further the interests of a technocratic elite and, it might be added, the public sector in general.[77]

Many of the members of the first PASOK cabinet taking up economic portfolios had been trained in British and American universities. Papandreou himself had been a professor of economics at the University of California,

Berkeley and co-authored, among other books, *Competition and its Regulation*.[78] They had to shape policy within the context of an external economic downturn, which allowed Papandreou to talk of a 'blizzard from abroad', and a rapidly weakening local economy.[79] In keeping with the party's general philosophical principles, policy initially focused on strengthening autarkic economic development and mobilising the domestic market to promote growth.[80] In practice this meant that within a broader budgetary framework designed to ensure macroeconomic stability the party kept its election promises and increased wages, especially to poorly paid manufacturing workers, and pensions, which were also granted to a wider range of recipients, including the wives of farmers.[81] The policy had an irrefutable moral, as well as an ideological and economic base. Many workers were poorly paid and international comparisons of standards of living continued to show Greeks having to work far longer than their equivalents in other West European countries to earn the money to purchase the same amount of goods. Low wages were also seen as arising from the domination of the metropoles and by increasing them the government was hoping to boost demand within domestic industry which had considerable unused capacity. This, it was thought, would stimulate growth, increase employment and spur investment, especially in technology, which would allow any loss in economic competitiveness caused by the pay rises to be compensated by a rise in productivity. However, measures intended to boost productivity failed to have the expected impact and with domestic industry choosing to offset the wage rises by either increasing prices or trying to reduce costs in other ways, the overall result was a growing number of strikes and a general loss of competitiveness.[82] Amid a growing perception that the government was anti-business, industrial investment, already weak, diminished even further. The number of companies posting losses continued to grow and, with unemployment rising and the state-controlled banks nursing more and more non-performing loans, the government established an Organisation for Rehabilitation of Business Firms (OAE). The organisation was not given *carte blanche* to rescue every firm in trouble, but by 1986 it had over twenty-one enterprises employing 50,518 people under its wing, the largest being the textile producer, Piraiki-Patraiki, the munitions manufacturer, Pyrkal, and Athens Paper Mills. Taken together with the nationalisations of the Karamanlis governments and some others by PASOK, including the ESSO Pappas refinery and the cement maker AGET Heracles, about 70 per cent of domestic industry was now under the direct or indirect control of the state. The OAE could be compared with the Italian IRI and the National

Enterprise Board in the UK, but by the time it was founded some of Greece's European partners were already moving towards privatising their state-controlled holdings. As a result, Greece not only increasingly found itself out of step with wider European currents, but it was also saddled with a seemingly bottomless pit of expenditure, as the OAE companies continued to accumulate enormous debts, many of them owed to state-controlled banks.

The failure of the economy to respond to the initial policies as hoped, coupled with a change in personnel in key ministries, led to a shift in rhetoric, as increasingly words like 'restructuring' and 'reshaping' were heard alongside 'change'. With neither the technological base to compete with advanced economies nor the low wages of the developing world, Greece was seen as operating outside normal economic cycles. The need was for the economy to be rebalanced and this would be through a combination of demand management to reduce inflation, which would include a socially just incomes policy, and a supply-side fiscal policy designed to curb consumption in favour of investment in technology and innovation. However, a tough budget, which initially saw wages falling quite sharply in the first half of 1983, only led to a surge in industrial action. Much of the loss in earnings seems to have been quickly made up, but by the beginning of 1984, amid stories of thousands of households being cut off by the utility companies due to non-payment of bills, the leader of the KKE was openly talking about the country being in a state of 'economic crisis'.[83] The government's supply-side measures had been predicated on any increase in spending funding investments that would promote growth. It tried to ensure this in part through regulation but much of the lending seems to have leached towards consumption, with sixty senior bankers at one point being referred to the prosecutor for granting loans to small manufacturing companies that were actually used to import whiskey. As a result, and also perhaps because of a certain amount of complacency due to the low level of public debt it inherited when it assumed office, it has been suggested that many in PASOK underestimated the problems posed by a budget deficit that had reached 18 per cent of GDP by 1985.[84] The same may also have been true of the current account deficit which was still calibrated in American dollars and subject to exchange rate fluctuations.[85] Despite an increasingly strident 'insist on buying Greek' campaign, this again expanded rapidly at this time to over 10 per cent of GDP per annum. Both the current account and budget deficits were running at high levels and not for the last time in the face of such imbalances a Greek government was on the verge of having to seek assistance from its European partners.

During 1985 rising wages and further recruitment to the public sector produced a sense of economic wellbeing that helped PASOK win the general election of that year, but, in reality, the country was increasingly becoming dependent on foreign borrowing. Much of this had come from Japanese banks which had originally seen Greece as a more secure home for their money during the Latin American debt crisis. However, from the middle of 1984, rumours began to circulate that the Greek government and its public utilities were experiencing difficulties in securing foreign loans and, with the country facing a distinct hump in repayments later in the decade, a visiting IMF mission at the beginning of 1985 was reported to have come to the conclusion that Greece was heading for an 'obvious crisis'.[86] Still, it was, by all accounts, a complete surprise when the new Minister of National Economy, Kostas Simitis, in October 1985 appeared on television to announce a package of austerity measures after the foreign reserves of the Bank of Greece had fallen to levels which were deemed dangerously low. Hailed by New Democracy for its 'irreproachable neo-liberal orthodoxy', the adjustment programme, according to its proponents, was intended to impact equally across Greek society.[87] It aimed to not only slash the current account and budget deficits and reduce inflation but also implicitly to restore business confidence and encourage investment.[88] Most importantly, it also paved the way for Greece to formally apply for external assistance from the EEC through a facility established to provide emergency funding to states facing balance of payments problems, Papandreou having apparently ruled out approaching the IMF.

Under the EEC facility, funding could come from either bilateral loans provided by other member states or finance raised on international markets by commercial banks, with the European Commission acting as a guarantor, which happened in the case of Greece. The Economic and Financial Affairs Council of the Council of the EEC, frequently known as the Ecofin Council, approved an application for a 1.75 billion European Currency Unit (ECU) loan in November 1985 and the first tranche was distributed in January 1986. As a condition of the stabilisation loan, the Greek authorities were expected to draw up an adjustment programme in consultation with the Commission. Many of the measures were familiar. To boost exports and improve the competitiveness of the tourist industry the drachma was devalued by 15 per cent and exchange rate policy once more adjusted to fully accommodate the differential between the inflation rate of Greece and its main EEC trading partners.[89] Imports, as before, were to be curbed through requiring the importers of many goods to place six-month interest-free deposits with the Bank of

Greece, and in the case of some cars these could amount to 80 per cent of their value.[90] The budget deficit as measured by the Public Sector Borrowing Requirement (PSBR) would be reduced by 4.0 per cent of GDP in 1986 and by a similar amount in the following year, largely through increasing revenues. Thus, tax brackets were not raised in line with inflation, a reduction in oil prices not passed on to consumers and a one-off surtax applied to company profits, amid a further clamp down on tax evasion.[91] Some cuts were planned in expenditure, including agricultural subsidies, although the EEC was expected to partially compensate for these. The indexation of wages designed to maintain purchasing power in the face of inflation, which had been introduced in 1982, was also first frozen and then a new formula introduced based on projected price rises, which stripped out import costs and led wages to fall by between 7.0 and 12 per cent.[92]

Following long discussion, Ecofin authorised the release of the second tranche of the stabilisation loan in December 1986 after it was judged progress had been made in meeting the required targets. Under the programme the current account deficit fell sharply from 9.8 per cent of Gross National Product (GNP) in 1985 to 2.7 per cent in 1987. This was partially due to an increase in exports, following the devaluation and cuts in wages, which were held to have boosted competitiveness, but equally important seems to have been increased payments from the EEC, higher remittances from abroad, due to renewed confidence in the drachma, and, from 1987, sizeable capital inflows as foreign companies started to invest in Greece in anticipation of the creation of a single European market.[93] Lower world oil prices helped cut the import bill as well by about $900 million per annum. Inflation also fell from 22 per cent to 15.7 per cent in 1987, and, if the effect of the newly imposed Value Added Tax (VAT) was removed, it would have declined to 12 per cent.[94] Less successful was the attempt to curb the budget deficit, with the PSBR, after initially falling, remaining at 13 per cent of GNP in 1987, far higher than the EEC average of 5.4 per cent in that year.[95] Indeed, the tendency during this period was for public expenditure to rise due to the increasing cost of servicing the rapidly expanding debt, which had grown from approximately 34 per cent of GDP in 1981 to around 87 per cent in 1987 if the deficits of social security funds are also taken into account. By that year debt servicing was already accounting for about a quarter of all government expenditure and, with large amounts of borrowing denominated in foreign currencies, fluctuations in exchange rates could have a huge impact on public finances, with about half the increase in the budget deficit in 1987 attributable to a depreciation in the value of the American dollar. Still, by June 1987, enough confidence had been restored to enable the Bank of Greece to return to the international financial markets to raise a $300 million loan, with both the lead banks in the syndicate being Japanese.[96] Most importantly, domestic buyers had also entered the market and were purchasing government debt in large quantities, encouraged by interest rates up to 5 per cent above those on ordinary deposits, ushering in an era Papandreou was to disparagingly call the 'golden age of the rentiers'.[97]

The economy contracted by approximately 2.3 per cent of GDP in 1987 but, in marked contrast to the adjustment programmes of the early twenty-first century, by the following year it was growing strongly, led by both high domestic demand and buoyant exports to important markets such as Italy and Germany, which were expanding again after the downturn at the beginning of the decade. The rise in unemployment was also relatively mild and less marked than in Ireland, which had embarked on a similar stabilisation programme at this time, perhaps partly because the Greek programme appears to have included some stimulus measures. Aside from additional tax exemptions and credits, there was a temporary relaxation of rent controls, which is said to have produced a minor building boom.[98] The adjustment in exchange rate policy may also have helped, as did the continuing strength of consumer spending. This may partly have been because people tended to view the programme as being short-term and raided their savings to compensate for any loss in earnings, but there was also speculation that the informal economy was taking up much of the slack, in part due to the findings of an influential general study of this issue which appeared at the time.[99] However, equally important was probably the fact that the programme appears to have produced a general increase in business confidence. Profits outside the 'problematic companies' rose by about a half in 1986, helped by the wage cuts, devaluation of the currency and some liberalisation. Relations with the private sector had reached their nadir in May 1984, when a protest against the government's perceived anti-business bias was dubbed by its critics the 'meeting of the saucepans' after an event held in Chile by analogous interests reacting against a programme enacted by Salvador Allende when cooking utensils had been banged together. Now, the apparent change of emphasis was driven by both a reappraisal of policy within PASOK and the requirements of the EEC. This was clearest in the financial services sector where willing internal actors pushed through an agenda of change, including in 1987 a partial liberalisation of interest rates. In addition a law guaranteeing the repatriation of profits from business transactions in Greece and the approaching single European market also led to a wave of foreign multinationals, such as Nestlé and Suchard, buying controlling stakes in a number of Greek firms. It was a far cry from the beginning of the decade but was justified by Papandreou on the grounds that it 'is not the nationality of the capital that matters but the nationality of the management'.[100]

The stabilisation programme sparked strikes and protests, and the fall in wages was to leave a bitter memory. The opposition parties, including New Democracy, were highly critical, calling on workers to resist the austerity measures, which the KKE claimed had been imposed by Brussels.[101] Perhaps though, because Papandreou continued to stress that the EEC loan had saved Greece from having to turn to the IMF, which it was widely believed would have imposed far harsher terms, the period of the stabilisation programme saw a marked change in public sentiment in favour of the EEC—although this might also have been due to the growing flow of funds from Brussels as well as a general loss of faith in the domestic political establishment.[102] The communists also charged that in implementing the programme PASOK was abandoning the political left for the right and within the ranks of the ruling party itself, as well as its trade union affiliates, there was open dissent amid much heart searching. PASOK fared badly in the October 1986 local elections, losing all three of the major conurbations, and, with tens of thousands of members deserting its ranks, critics began to highlight what they saw as a growing gap between the party and the people. Faced with the growing discontent, Papandreou failed to back Simitis in a dispute over wage indexation. Simitis resigned and in reaction to this and the imposition of an extraordinary tax the main stock exchange index lost 40 per cent of its value in five days. Afterwards, with Papandreou increasingly ill and at one stage hospitalised in London, political life became more and more chaotic and obsessed with a welter of corruption scandals, the most notorious involving the banker and media owner, Giorgos Koskotas, who made a series of allegations that implicated the leaders of PASOK in financial malpractice while facing accusations of embezzlement himself.[103] Economic policy also became more contradictory but, with a general election pending, the pendulum swung away from fiscal austerity, with the atmosphere of the times supposedly caught in a well-known aside made by Papandreou at a meeting in the Athenian suburb of Peristeri in which he is said to have told the Minister of Finance, Dimitris Tsovolas, 'to give it all [to them]', although it seems that Tsovolas was not present at the time and Papandreou was merely responding to the chants of the crowd for a popular minister whose surname rhymes with the expression 'give it all' in Greek.[104]

The first part of the PASOK era, which had opened with so much expectation, closed in scandal and recrimination, but there are still many who see the period 1981–1985 as something of a golden age in which the country asserted its national independence, righted some of the wrongs of the Civil War, made progress in tackling income inequalities and erected the framework of a modern welfare state. The 1985–1989 government with its stabilisation programme, austerity and corruption scandals is not remembered with such fondness, but, as PASOK left office, the economy was still growing and some had even begun to venture the thought that the EEC with its directives and regulations might provide a framework for development free from political interference. This was not to be the case but the stabilisation programme in conjunction with EEC mandated liberalisation measures had provided a roadmap for the future. It could be read both as a success, in the sense that it was believed that it had achieved results when applied, and as a failure in the way that it had unravelled afterwards, partly due to the opposition it had provoked both inside PASOK and within society as a whole. From these understandings a broader movement arose that was not exclusively drawn from PASOK but which at its core had an important group of party members favouring what was termed 'modernisation'. This creed rested on a belief that a paradox existed between the external reality of Greek life and the inner potential of the country's citizens.[105] By releasing the latent capacities of the people themselves, modernisation would free Greece from obstructive bureaucratic practices, patron-client relations and self-centred antisocial behaviour, such as tax evasion. Education and new forms of social dialogue would empower society, fostering responsibility, ending alienation from the collective and removing the divide between the public and the private. As a result a strong and self-confident Greece would emerge, with a welfare state not distributing benefits by favours but genuinely aiding the weakest in society, because at the heart of the project lay a belief that resources had to be used in an efficient and rational manner. Simitis saw modernisation as being compatible with socialism but, nonetheless, it seems to have been accepted that it would encounter opposition from both the political left as well as the right. Indeed, in the work of the social scientist Nikiforos Diamandouros the process was conceptualised as a struggle between a relatively narrow modernising elite and a society dominated by a populist underdog culture which stood as its antithesis. In this model, while the modernisers were open minded reformers seeking to integrate Greece into world systems, the underdogs sought sanctuary in a defensive culture, built on a xenophobic view which tended to divide the world into pro- and anti-Greek forces. Powerfully statist, ambivalent to capitalism and market mechanisms and diffident to innovation, such beliefs according to Diamandouros were 'particularly entrenched among the very extensive, traditional, more introverted and least competitive strata and sectors of society'. Areas which were marked by 'low productivity, low competitiveness... [and an] aversion to reform'.[106] Conceptualisations such as these effectively subverted the old dichotomy of privileged and unprivileged, as, instead of a mass movement struggling against an elite, a narrow elite was now to lead the way against a resistant and backward society. Indeed, in this sense it was not difficult to see the creed of modernisation in spite of its focus on the citizen as following in the footsteps of the top-down policymaking of the developmental state.[107]

The roots of the underdog/moderniser dichotomy can be located in concepts of identity long detected in Greek society which ultimately rest on experiences perceived to have arisen from encounters with, on the one hand, Ottoman rule and, on the other hand, a European Enlightenment heavily influenced by its own reading of the Ancient Greek past.[108] Subsequently, the model was to be both refined and contested by other scholars, but mapped out onto the political world it provided a ready base for dividing the ranks of PASOK and society in general into Europeanising reformers and populist defenders of Greek exceptionalism.[109] The timelessness of these constructions also makes it not unexpected that they have found strong echo in the crisis. Diamandouros in a 2013 work argued that this 'noxious legacy of cultural dualism continues to bedevil the country', but, while some have not been slow to pin the blame on the underdog culture for the country's ills, others have recast the divide, suggesting it could better be seen as being between those with a symbiotic relationship with the public sector and those without special access.[110] However, at the same time as it was providing an opportunity to reconceptualise divisions within Greek society, modernisation was also helping foster a new consensus, because its adherents also subscribed to the view that shifting balances of power caused by globalisation and the ending of the Cold War were creating a unique opportunity for Greece to enhance its influence in the Balkans and eastern Mediterranean. For this to occur, though, it was considered necessary for the country to be at the core of the European project and this could only be ensured if it fully participated in the process of Economic and Monetary Union (EMU) upon which the EEC was embarked.[111] This had been given new impetus by both the creation of the single European market and the accession of Greece and the Iberian states, with its proponents arguing that economic divergence otherwise threatened to make the Community little more than a customs union.[112] Under the guidance of Karamanlis, New Democracy had long favoured closer European integration but through a mixture of geo-political necessity and economic pragmatism PASOK had also gradually come to adopt a similar stance. This new consensus meant that the idea of EMU was embraced not only by the vast majority of the political elite but also by much of the heavily politicised economics profession. However, the country's poor fiscal position left it little credibility in the subsequent intergovernmental negotiations and so externally Greece had virtually no influence on shaping the forms of the currency union, while internally little space was provided for any meaningful discussion about the overall merits of membership, the effects of meeting the necessary convergence criteria on the Greek economy or even the long-term impact of the policies of liberalisation prescribed by the Commission.[113] Nonetheless, the story of the search for economic stability from this point converges with that of the quest for participation in monetary union, although the coincidence was always based on a presumption rather than certainty.

The February 1992 Treaty on European Union, more familiarly known as the Maastricht Treaty, aside from creating the institutions of monetary union, including the European Central Bank (ECB), laid down convergence criteria revolving around: the stability of each currency; levels of inflation, public debt and budget deficit; and a requirement that interest rates should be converging. Many of these criteria were essentially arbitrary, with the stipulation that the general government deficit should not exceed 3.0 per cent of GDP apparently being based on a ceiling set by the French government in its 1983 restructuring.[114] Nonetheless, at the time Greece was far from meeting this and the other reference values. The drachma had been devalued twice during the 1980s, the inflation rate was 20.4 per cent against an EEC average of 6.7 per cent and public debt levels at 105 per cent of GDP were far above the treaty reference value of 60 per cent as was the budgetary deficit of 14.6 per cent of GDP. Indeed in 1989, fuelled by pre-election spending, this had reached 21.5 per cent, prompting the European Commission to remind Greece of its commitments under the 1985 stabilisation agreement. However, a short-lived coalition government formed, following the June 1989 election, by New Democracy and the KKE dominated Coalition of the Left and Progress, concerned mostly with 'cleansing' the body politic of the transgressions judged to have been committed by PASOK, regularly denounced the fiscal profligacy of the socialists but proved unable to take decisive action. A new election in November 1989 again proved inconclusive but, after two weeks of hard bargaining, an ecumenical government drawing its members from across the political spectrum was formed under the leadership of the eighty-five-year old Zolotas. After the uncertainty the new government was greeted with enthusiasm, leading one member to quip that it was the only time in history that the entry of communists into power had produced a rise in the stock market. Yet in reality government finances were again in a parlous state, with reports circulating that funds were hardly sufficient to pay salaries and pensions.[115] Faced with the pending repayment of the stabilisation loan, Zolotas seems to have sounded out the European Commission about the possibility of Greece being extended a new line of credit. However, he received a sharp letter from the President of the Commission, Jacques Delors, and Henning Christophersen, the European commissioner for macroeconomic affairs, in which they urged the country to keep to the existing stabilisation programme, pointing out that otherwise the European Commission would 'find itself in an awkward position for having participated in and having linked its own creditworthiness in any decision concerning a loan whose terms were not honoured by the debtor'.[116] Furthermore, they contended that Greek debt levels were growing so rapidly that they posed a threat not only to the realisation of the single European market but to the project of monetary union as a whole. Rebuffed by its partners, Greece was rumoured to be about to ask the IMF for help, but Delors is reported to have warned against this, asking the government to keep the matter 'within the family'; and no crisis arose, largely because domestic sources could still be tapped for funding and there was an excess of liquidity within the international banking system as a whole at this time.[117] Indeed, even though rumours circulated that the country was poised to reschedule its foreign debt, the only immediate response within the financial markets to the Delors letter being made public seems to have been that a group of banks negotiating a $500 million loan with the Bank of Greece decided to enlarge their syndicate to thirty-five members in order to spread the risk a little further.[118]

Another general election in April 1990 brought New Democracy to power again, under the leadership of Konstantine Mitsotakis. The party remained an ideologically imprecise grouping but partly through the influence of the think-tank, the Centre for Political Research and Training, a view had been gaining ground that it needed to adopt a more distinct identity. It was argued that a sense of guilt acquired from victory in the Civil War had hobbled the right, leading it to effectively abandon the field of ideology to the left whose values had permeated society. If this was to continue, the right risked being placed at a permanent disadvantage, so it needed to challenge this situation by developing its own ideas. In search of these, though, the younger members of the party turned not to the social-market models of Germany but the free-market liberalism of America and the United Kingdom.[119] However, despite the growing influence of these younger voices, many members of the party still felt more comfortable with the paternalistic *dirigisme* of the Karamanlis era. These differences imparted tensions throughout the government's term of office and together with its extremely narrow parliamentary majority they not only constrained its room to manoeuvre but also made it susceptible to the pleadings of various interest groups.

When it tabled its draft budget in November 1990, the government also announced that it was negotiating with the European Commission for a further loan. Initially, Mitsotakis had been confident that Greece would receive the backing of its European partners, but unexpectedly at its December 1990 meeting the Ecofin Council declined to give its authorisation on the grounds that the proposed adjustment programme presented alongside the request was short on detail. Two months later, however, in January 1991 it changed its mind and endorsed a loan of 2.2 billion ECU but only after the government had made a number of promises, including a pledge to tax many farmers as well as the interest on savings. The loan was made conditional on the fulfilment of a twenty point medium-term adjustment programme which in the toughness of its targets bore some resemblance with the 'shock therapy' measures then in vogue in parts of Eastern Europe.[120] Government borrowing was expected to be sharply reduced until Greece posted a primary surplus (when revenues exceed expenditure, if the interest paid on government liabilities is excluded), allowing the public debt to GDP ratio to stabilise. The civil service was to be reduced in size, although, after what was rumoured to be hard bargaining, the number of dismissals was limited to 10 per cent of a stated complement of 525,000. To facilitate the fight against inflation, which was running at an annual rate of 23 per cent in 1990, but was expected to fall to 9.5 per cent in 1993, an anti-inflation exchange rate policy that had been followed since 1988 was to continue. Under this 'hard drachma' regime the currency was to decline in value at less than the rate of inflation. The tax base was also to be widened, subsidies to public enterprises cut, privatisation speeded up and legislation introduced to free markets in goods, labour and services. Moreover, to help ensure compliance, the money was to be released in three tranches, following thrice yearly inspections by a team of monitors from the European Commission's Directorate General II (Economic and Social Affairs).

The first tranche of one billion ECU was duly released in March 1991. However, amid rumours that a substantial part had been diverted from its intended usage to fund the budget deficit and pay the Easter bonuses of civil servants, the first monitoring mission in May ended with the inspectors declaring that there were 'no margins for deviations from the programme' and later in the year the European Commission was to be more damning when it spoke of inadequate implementation and results 'seriously out of line'.[121] Accepting that the failure to control the budgetary deficit was partly due to unavoidable reasons, such as an increase in debt servicing costs and shortfalls in revenues because of a recession, the Commission nonetheless stressed that there had been less progress than it had expected in structural reforms such as market deregulation and privatisation, as well as the inadequacy of the crackdown on tax evasion. As a result it advised the government that the second tranche was unlikely to be released until it had tabled a credible EMU convergence programme designed to both fulfil the Maastricht criteria and create the conditions for sustainable economic growth. The government duly produced a programme but the second tranche of the loan seems never to have been requested, largely it appears because alternative funds could still be raised from both domestic and international sources. By the beginning of 1992 some stability had been restored to public finances, with revenues increasing from 25.8 per cent of GDP in 1988 to 30.4 per cent in 1992, and the PSBR in the same year standing at just 7.9 per cent of GDP as compared with 21.5 per cent in 1989, a level of readjustment which was occasionally cited as a precedent during the crisis. However, in the context of a global downturn, which saw lengthy recessions in other parts of Europe, the squeeze on demand led the economy to contract. Amid general talk of imminent collapse it was reported that every single day thirteen businesses were going bankrupt and, with tens of thousands of enterprises failing, an effective PASOK poster during the 1993 general election campaign simply showed a shop with its shutters permanently padlocked. Measures to curb tax evasion had also merely served to dampen the construction sector and with revenues continuing to decline it was even rumoured that the government was thinking of selling some small uninhabited islands to raise cash.

In the face of the economic downturn and growing unease within EEC bodies about the pace of reform, Mitsotakis reshuffled his cabinet in an effort to invigorate the process of change.[122] Stefanos Manos was appointed minister of finance and later national economy. Legislation was promulgated deregulating the oil market and liberalising prices, although proposals to open the closed professions seem to have been shelved in the face of protests. Sweeping changes were also made to the tax system which was simplified in an effort to build trust and curb the informal economy. A potential revenue shortfall was made up by a special property tax levied in two instalments through electricity bills. Other taxes were also increased, with a rise in petrol duty causing particular outcry, and there was a campaign against tax evasion. Inspectors were reported to have been promised 3.0 per cent of any tax arrears gathered as an incentive and rumours circulated that empty hotels were being requisitioned to serve as prisons to hold offenders.[123] Progress was even made in privatisation which was seen not so much as a cash generating process but as a way to stem some of the enormous losses the state continued to incur. However market conditions remained difficult, many companies needed restructuring before they could be considered for sale and in some sectors regulatory frameworks still had to be created. There was also a freeze on public sector wages both to lower expenditure and to set a precedent for the private sector, which was perceived as losing international competitiveness, partly due to the hard drachma policy. The policies produced a sharper contraction, with growth turning negative in 1993, but even amidst the downturn, foreign companies kept investing in the Greek market, with the German home improvement retailer Praktiker and the French supermarket chain Carrefour opening stores and the Belgian Delhaize Frères 'Le Lion' buying a majority stake in the AB Vassilopoulos supermarkets. However, by then the strains of imposing the austerity programme were showing both outside and inside New Democracy. A group of senior former-ministers proposing an alternative manifesto pushing for growth rather than austerity argued that 'The Greek people are in danger of losing hope that the economic crisis can be overcome. They have repeatedly been called upon to make sacrifices without seeing any improvement... The medium and small income citizen sees his living standard constantly decreasing and he can no longer endure it... The government must take the initiative for a dialogue with social groups'.[124] Mitsotakis dismissively called them pedlars of 'antiquated economic models which use as levers overheating of the economy through deficits and étatism' but, when the 1993 budget was presented to parliament, many New Democracy MPs were conspicuous by their absence.[125] Attempts to push through the part-privatisation of OTE by sale to a strategic partner, which would have placed under question lucrative supply contracts, proved exceptionally divisive and, when this was coupled with policy differences over an attempt by the southernmost republic of the disintegrating Yugoslav federation to gain international recognition under the name Macedonia—a dispute which led to the Foreign Minister, Antonis Samaras, resigning and establishing his own party, Political Spring—the party began to fracture and, deprived of its slim majority, the government fell.

Despite the enthusiasm of key ministers the Mitsotakis government had been unable to meet its ambitious macroeconomic targets and had achieved only limited success in implementing its structural adjustment programme in areas such as the downsizing of the public sector and privatisation. Throughout it had encountered concerted opposition from the unions and, in the eyes of Mitsotakis, the 'entangled interests' which bound together certain businesses and political groups.[126] Critics at the time accused the government of extreme monetarism and, partly due to its ideological inclinations, the brusque manner of some ministers and newspaper reporting of its austerity measures, it has come to be associated with Greece enduring its own period of hard-line Thatcherism.[127] However, in reality, although the government did undoubtedly preside over a period of readjustment which brought hardship, policy at this time, was not consistently austere, with the OECD even considering the 1992 tax reforms to be effectively a covert stimulus programme.[128] Likewise, the reduction in the budget deficit was only achieved in part by lowering debt servicing costs through extraordinary measures that were termed by contemporaries 'rescheduling'. Foreign bond holders were still paid in full to preserve the country's credit rating but domestic banks received new bonds with extended maturities.[129] At the same time the government was also taking on more liabilities, partly to meet the requirements of EEC accounting standards, with these amounting to 836 billion drachmas in 1993 alone. The overall effect was that, in spite of the fact that the first budgetary primary surplus for two decades was posted in 1992, public debt actually grew in this period. Despite reports of soup kitchens opening in unemployment black spots such as the town of Lavrio, the government also seems to have been mindful of the problem of unemployment, offering those made redundant by OAE enterprises in 1991 a choice of retraining, special payments to allow them to open their own businesses or twelve months of full pay.

The upheavals surrounding the liquidation of the OAE companies and privatisation gave political capital to PASOK, allowing it to stress a narrative that it alone was able to protect society from the depredations of the untrammelled market, a stance which was increasingly shared by New Democracy after its defeat in the 1993 election as it shifted to try to occupy the same centre ground and began to speak of finding a middle way between socialism and neo-liberalism. This may have been a rhetorical device designed to strengthen internal positions and rehabilitate the party with the electorate, but in its public rejection of the Mitsotakis era the party was also consolidating a wider narrative that not only ruled out neo-liberalism as a policy option but also cast it as the antithesis of domestic values and traditions. Yet, during its relatively brief life, the government had changed the terms of political debate. Building on PASOK's 1985 stabilisation programme, it laid the foundations for monetary convergence and furthered public acceptance of this goal, with both main parties now adopting a common language stressing 'macroeconomic stability', 'sustainability', 'efficiency', and 'restructuring'. It also reversed the pattern of ever increasing state control. Henceforth, privatisation rather than nationalisation was to be the point at issue. However, this was to remain highly controversial and a clumsy privatisation of the Athenian bus service, which had not been part of the main programme and caused considerable disruption, together with the allegations of corruption that surrounded the sale of AGET Heracles to an Italian firm in partnership with a Greek state-controlled bank, did little to win public support and instead merely fuelled a growing belief that it was just another way for politicians to enrich themselves and distribute favours.

This change in the terms of debate meant that when PASOK and Andreas Papandreou did return to office after the general election of October 1993, despite much talk of 'undoing the wrongs committed by the right', the new government did little to alter the policies of its predecessor. A few of the OAE holdings that had been closed were reopened but only to be sold on to private buyers. Otherwise, the differences were more in the pace of change, with a new EMU convergence plan setting milder targets, and an aspiration that it should be achieved through greater social consensus. The narrative of the transfer of power followed what was becoming a familiar pattern. There was a dispute over the size of the PSBR, which New Democracy had said was 10.8 per cent of GDP but PASOK revised upwards to 13.9 per cent. This made the central government debt 116 per cent of GDP, although, if the borrowings of all the public enterprises, OAE and the military were added, by some calculations by the end of 1994 the public debt overall totalled an enormous 162.1 per cent of GDP.[130] This was followed by talk of a crisis, with rumours circulating that the government would soon be unable to make salary and pension payments and that foreign bondholders were hedging their holdings amid fears that the country might default. There were even expressions of concern from international rating agencies. Public debt, as Papandreou observed, had brought the state budget to its knees.[131] Then, after a period of post-electoral stasis in which PASOK ministers accustomed themselves to their new jobs, a series of revenue gathering measures were announced, the moral base of these being established through the use of statistics, and a campaign mounted against tax evasion. Promises were also made to the Ecofin Council to restrict hirings in the public sector, although other pledges to re-employ previously ousted PASOK supporters together with court rulings that temporary posts should be made permanent, meant that, in reality, recruitment seems to have continued much as before. The talk of crisis then eased, but despite a recalibration of the national accounts to bring them in line with European practices, which raised national output by nearly a quarter, allowing the budget deficit to fall to 12 per cent of GDP, Greece in September 1994 was still placed under the excessive deficit procedure outlined in Article 104c of the Treaty on European Union for states failing to keep within the 3.0 per cent reference value.

In the middle of November 1995 Papandreou fell ill for the last time and entered intensive care but it was only in the middle of January 1996 that he was eventually persuaded to relinquish the premiership. In two rounds of close voting PASOK deputies then chose Simitis as his replacement and, after the death of Papandreou in June 1996, he was also elected leader of the party. Simitis then called an early general election for September 1996 in which, due to a change in the law, he was able to translate a relatively narrow electoral victory into a substantial parliamentary majority. The accession to power of Simitis ensured the ascendency of the modernising faction within PASOK and the standard narrative of the period that follows is one of triumph in the face of adversity, as Greece, against the odds, gained admittance to the EMU. In handling his cabinet Simitis saw himself as conducting an orchestra rather than imposing his will and the macroeconomic adjustments of this period were impressive, but they were not achieved without the government once more resorting to a rhetoric of austerity and economic as well as social costs that were not to be easily forgotten.[132] By 1996 government finances had already been placed on a more stable footing. The budget deficit was under control and Greece was posting a primary surplus. The economy was growing at a good rate, inflation was declining and with interest rates falling debt levels were beginning to ease. In this new atmosphere of stability many companies began to flourish as profitability increased. The government signalled its commitment to meet the EMU convergence targets by signing the Stability and Growth Pact at the December 1996 European Council and by tabling a tough 1997 budget in which revenue was projected to rise twice as fast as expenditure, partly due to the cutting of a host of special exemptions. This produced the first of the waves of mass protests that were to characterise the search to meet the convergence criteria, but they eventually subsided, literally, in the case of the farmers who had the tyres deflated on their tractors after they had blocked major roads.

Before applying for membership of the third stage of EMU, which would see the introduction of the euro, Greece had to spend two years within the Exchange Rate Mechanism (ERM) and in 1997 it was the only aspiring member not to have joined. As part of the ERM the drachma would be allowed to deviate only a small amount from a fixed parity with the ECU and it was widely assumed that it would have to be devalued prior to entry to make its position sustainable. In the autumn of 1997 turbulence from a financial crisis then gripping Asia spread first into the Greek secondary sovereign bond market and from there into the currency markets. The Bank of Greece responded by spending reserves to defend the national currency and raising interest rates to soak up excess liquidity. This, though, put the convergence targets under strain as it led the spread between Greek and comparable German government bonds that stood as an effective proxy for determining the interest rate criterion to widen considerably. As a result an estimated 40 billion drachmas were added to debt servicing costs in the first quarter of 1998 alone, putting the budget deficit and debt targets under threat as well.[133] After lengthy negotiations, in March 1998 the drachma was finally admitted to the ERM at a central parity of 357 drachmas to 1 ECU, which meant that the Greek currency depreciated by 12.1 per cent. The drachma had entered the ERM at a time of crisis in part to ward off a potentially deeper crisis but, contrary to some views at the time, it proved not only able to sustain its parity but actually rose in value to offset much of the devaluation. Entering the ERM helped curb inflation but at the cost of potentially eroding long-term economic competitiveness, with some economists suggesting that the currency might have been overvalued by as much as a quarter when its value was fixed.[134] As part of the ERM, the drachma would now be defended by the central banks of fellow members of the mechanism if it came under pressure and the new confidence this engendered led to large amounts of currency flowing into Greece attracted by interest rates which were relatively high compared to the other states. To keep this process orderly, the Bank of Greece in just three weeks was forced to mop up 2.5 trillion drachmas of excess liquidity through the placement of a succession of bonds with increasingly long maturities and lower yields. By the beginning of the summer the spread between Greek and comparable German sovereign bonds had fallen to the required 200 basis points (bps) and in the autumn the international rating agencies began a cautious series of upgrades. Despite some further turbulence during the subsequent Russian financial crisis, Greece was well on the way to meeting the convergence criteria as regards both the stability of the currency and interest rates and had also put an important element of its anti-inflation strategy in place.

Some of the increased liquidity flowing into the country found its way into the stock exchange. The main Athens Stock Exchange (ASE) index rose precipitously, passing 2000 in March 1999 until it peaked in September of that year at an astonishing 6,355, by which time hundreds of thousands of small investors were actively 'playing the market'. In the subsequent decline, which by the end of 2000 saw the index fall to 3,377, businesses were left bankrupt and thousands of households teetering on the edge of ruin, as dreams of wealth were swept away in an anguish of anxiety and stress.[135] Trust was eroded, not just in the stock exchange but also in market economics in general as well as the government, which in public perceptions had become associated with the fortunes of the stock market, especially after PASOK produced a poster for the 1999 European Parliament elections openly connecting itself with the boom. Amid tales of insider dealing, sham companies, profiteering and a general search for scapegoats, the explanatory narrative took a strong moral twist. The boom was considered democratic, because anybody, even a vegetable market porter could hope to acquire a fortune, but the collapse selective. The winners were seen as being a group of wealthy, well-connected Athenian investors, who had flourished at the expense of the rest of society, which was perceived as having been effectively abandoned by Simitis and PASOK. Within this critical worldview it was easy for some to once again argue that the country had fallen thrall to a culture of easy money which eroded collective values and fed the vacuous consumer orientated individualism flaunted in glossy magazines and morning television chat shows. The stock market bubble had given a sense of spurious prosperity at a time of austerity, taking the edge off the government's measures and allowing it to maximise its privatisation gains. However, in the process, it became intimately bound in the public perception with the convergence programme and the whole project of modernisation, and in its traumatic collapse, as one observer acutely remarked, 'Somehow, somewhere along the way... popular expectations of a vibrant, prosperous Greece fizzled out.'[136]

In March 1998 a European Commission convergence report surveying the progress of various states towards EMU ruled that only Greece was not eligible to participate in the third stage, due to start on 1 January 1999, on the basis of its 1997 performance. The country was given eighteen months to meet the criteria and introduce measures designed to increase competitiveness, including a schedule for privatisation through either sale to strategic investors or the public flotation of stakes on the stock exchange. Jolted into action the government began to divest itself of assets. The final vestiges of OAE were closed down, with one of the last companies to be sold, Athens Paper Mills, passing to a consortium that included Goldman Sachs and Bain & Co.[137] However, the privatisation campaign was vigorously opposed by the unions and by the middle of 1998 the country was facing almost daily strikes, the longest and bitterest being a six-week confrontation with staff at the Ionian Bank. This brought dissent in the ruling party into the open, with the PASOK nominated European commissioner at one point publicly warning his former colleagues that reforms cannot be enforced by riot police.[138] Simitis was expected to come under more pressure at a PASOK party congress held in March 1999. However, his only open rival failed to gather the signatures required to contest the leadership and the prime minister was re-elected but with only a handful more votes than in 1996. The challenges of meeting the convergence criteria had revealed fault lines within the ruling party and Simitis' standing in opinion polls fell below 30 per cent. However, other surveys still showed the public to be broadly in favour of the single currency and Simitis was also helped by the fact that despite the demands of convergence the economy continued to grow at rates that, after 1996, surpassed EU averages, although this was in large part due to the high levels of transfers from Brussels. This continued growth also meant that, as before, fiscal adjustment occurred largely on the basis of increasing revenues rather than cutting expenditure, much of which was increasingly cast as non-elastic.[139] Thus, while elsewhere in Europe the ideological climate was often leading to a reappraisal of the role of the state, this was not apparent in Greece, where ministers in affirming the left-wing credentials of modernisation declared they were not concerned with replacing the state with the market but consolidating the role of the former. With the government also choosing to follow a strategy of making concessions when policies were challenged providing core convergence targets were not threatened, key issues were left unaddressed. The deeper reform process, which many saw as being necessary to furnish sustainable growth, remained incomplete and from the beginning of the decade some had been arguing that in the process public debt was being stabilised at levels that in the long-term could prove to be unsustainable.[140]

When President Bill Clinton visited Athens in November 1999, he declared that, if there was an Olympic medal for economic recovery, Greece would get gold. Indeed, in many ways, driven by large public sector investment projects, the country was performing strongly, not only in terms of growth but also company profitability which rose sharply in 1998 and 1999. With the government declaring it was running a primary surplus of 6.7 per cent of GDP, there was even space in the autumn of 2000 to promise a package of tax cuts and benefit increases, especially pensions. Most importantly, the debt, budgetary deficit and inflation convergence criteria all seemed to be within grasp. The greatest gains in the reduction of the deficit had come from lower debt servicing costs, but in the last push for convergence the government began to adopt a series of exceptional measures, such as withholding payments to suppliers, especially within the healthcare sector, to lower the figure further. It also engaged in what might be seen as some 'creative accounting' that the statistical office of the European Union, Eurostat, was later to question. However, in an era in which the rules of accountancy in both the private and public realms were often being pushed to the limits to enhance balance sheets, Greece was by no means alone among the aspirant EMU states in adopting such tactics. France used pension fund transfers to lower its budget deficit. When the reported figure fell below the convergence criteria reference value in December 1999, Ecofin was finally able to lift the 1994 excessive deficit decision, clearing the way for entry. Somewhat similar tactics were also used with inflation, with a 'gentlemen's agreement' being reached with manufacturers through which they assented to temporarily refrain from raising prices. A wage restraint package was concluded with the unions, limiting pay increases to 4.5 per cent over two years and a series of strategic cuts made in indirect taxes on items such as petrol, heating oil and cars, with the latter estimated to have lowered the price of vehicles by 10 per cent on average. With world commodity prices also remaining low, the result was that by the end of 1999 inflation had been reduced to 2.4 per cent and a helpful recalibration of the Harmonised Index of Consumer Prices by Eurostat then pushed it down to 1.6 per cent in January 2000. This made its average rate over the year between April 1999 and March 2000 less than 1.5 per cent above that recorded in the three countries posting the lowest rates of inflation within the ERM, enabling Greece to meet the convergence criteria.

On 9 March 2000 Greece made a formal application to join the EMU and almost two months later two convergence reports issued by the European Commission and the ECB confirmed that the country had fulfilled the requirements. Shortly afterwards, on the basis that the government needed a clear mandate to take such a historic step, Simitis requested the dissolution of parliament and an early election. The two main parties entered the campaign neck-and-neck in the opinion polls. PASOK was facing a strong challenge from parties to its left but New Democracy for once had a clear field on the right. The programmes of the two main parties were broadly similar, with both being committed to convergence and joining the EMU. Competition rested mostly on which party could offer the most blandishments to the electorate and on competence to rule. Simitis still polled better than the leader of New Democracy, Kostas Karamanlis, the nephew of the elder statesman, on this score and partly as a result of this on 9 April 2000 PASOK gained a narrow victory. Since the vast majority of voters had continued to support the two main parties, the result could also be interpreted as indicating that the people of Greece had given their backing to the country joining the EMU and it was fitting that it was Simitis who attended the European Council meeting in Santa Maria da Feira in Portugal at which its application was approved.[141] Shortly after midday on 20 June 2000 the assembled heads of state and government broke into applause as it was announced that Greece would become the twelfth member from 1 January 2001, a success which was appropriately toasted with a bottle of port wine produced in 1981, the year Greece had first joined the EEC.[142] When he spoke, Simitis stressed that a strong and modern Greece had deservedly entered the EMU as an equal partner.[143] In the past the evils of Civil War, dictatorship and political patronage may have left the country reliant on loans and prone to deficits and inflation but now, he said, there was a chance for a true transformation, because entry into the EMU had not been an aim in itself but only the beginning of a real economic convergence.[144] The main union groups also supported joining the EMU, although the General Confederation of Workers of Greece (GSEE) was careful to stress that the new era should not mean further compression of wages and pensions but rather a raising of levels of social protection. Hostility mostly came from the left, with the KKE warning that it would only mean the Greek people facing a new period of austerity.

Confounding the doubts of some of its partners Greece had successfully met the criteria to join the EMU but both the main party leaders continued to stress it was the start rather than the end of a process.[145] In their convergence reports the European Commission and the ECB had raised caveats about inflation and debt levels as well as stressing the necessity of future wage rises being matched by productivity gains.[146] On the broader stage, there were also some voices suggesting that the whole EMU project might be fundamentally flawed because the economic cycles of the states remained unsynchronised and it lacked the true labour mobility, financial integration and monetary transfer mechanisms of an optimum currency area.[147] In the first flush of success, though, these risks were downplayed, as policymakers purposefully looked at the euro area as a whole and stressed the benefits that were to be gained from lower borrowing costs and the removal of exchange rate fluctuations.[148] This was partly because the asymmetries between the nations of northern Europe were generally perceived as being little more than those between US states. However, the differences with countries such as Greece were greater and in the event of any financial or economic shock the corrective mechanisms available were considerably less effective than in America.[149] Indeed, the political choices made when designing the architecture of the single currency meant that a country had few ways to respond other than, as one Greek academic noted prior to the crisis, 'a suppression of real labour costs and prices to bolster competitiveness... and labour mobility towards other EU economies'.[150] The limits on macroeconomic policy imposed at a euro area level also meant that the pursuit of 'responsible' structural reform policies now came to be seen as being even more crucial. To this end, the more rigid requirements of the Stability and Growth Pact, which included within a broader surveillance mechanism the possibility that sanctions might be taken against a state breaching its 3.0 per cent budget deficit reference value, were complemented by softer policy coordination within a series of processes and strategies, which were given geographic monikers on the basis of where they were signed, with Cologne being followed by Cardiff and Lisbon.[151] Through a system of timetables and benchmarks these ostensibly provided more space for national interpretations of policy but, in reality, little room was left for manoeuvre. Reform along the prescribed lines was effectively becoming non-negotiable but in contrast to the convergence process, when policy had been shaped by a small elite working in a limited technocratic area, this broader process would require the involvement of a greater range of domestic actors; and in a society in which, the IMF noted, mistrust of market mechanisms and between social partners remained high this was always going to be difficult.[152] Nonetheless, with entry into the EMU the search for economic stability had apparently reached a conclusion. Just as in the pre-dictatorship period, it was to be based on a stable currency, monetary and fiscal prudence, low inflation and sustained economic growth. However, unlike that time, Greece now carried high levels of government borrowing and, as the ECB presciently noted in its final Greek convergence report, this could produce problems in the future if 'slippages in the country's fiscal performance were to raise the perceived credit risk of public debt'.[153]

2

THESE GAMES WITH NUMBERS HAVE TO STOP[1]

GREECE IN THE EURO AREA

The formal fixing of the exchange rate at 340.75 drachmas to the euro was followed on 1 January 2001 with entry into the Economic and Monetary Union (EMU) and then, exactly one year later, by the appearance of the new currency itself which in the Greek case appropriately included a two euro coin bearing an image of Europa. Under the new euro regime, monetary policy was no longer to be decided in the stately building of the Bank of Greece in the centre of Athens but in an anonymous tower block in distant Frankfurt am Main. Here the European Central Bank's (ECB) governing council, first under the presidency of Wim Duisenberg and afterwards Jean-Claude Trichet, with Loukas Papademos, the former governor of the Bank of Greece, as his deputy, would henceforth be fixing interest rates for a euro area of which Greece was only one small part. As one observer noted, the member states in their 'unprecedented, self-willed abrogation of state prerogative' had enacted something little short of a 'bloodless, noiseless, bureaucratic revolution'.[2] Yet, it was not only membership of the EMU that was giving Greece a new international standing. The Olympic Games, for the first time since the inception of the modern cycle in 1896, were about to return to Athens and aided by EU funding the face of the city was being transformed, with an expanded motorway network, state-of-the-art airport and new metro system boasting stations imaginatively adorned with ancient artefacts or contemporary Greek artwork. The construction boom was not confined to the public sector. In the outer suburbs, rows of new apartment blocks lined the streets. Some furnished in a contemporary minimalist fashion, with fittings chosen from a host of kitchen and bathroom showrooms that had appeared alongside a rash of shops selling smart designer clothes and other consumer goods. Greece was changing, and books and articles written at this time could be more than excused for ending on an optimistic note, with one even daring to suggest the country might be a giant in the making.[3]

The new era also seemed to stretch to the macroeconomic field where Greece, along with several other smaller euro area states, appeared to be exhibiting a creditable fiscal discipline as it continued to post budgetary deficits well below the Stability and Growth Pact's reference value of 3.0 per cent.[4] Greek sovereign bonds became increasingly attractive to a wider range of buyers, with 90 per cent of the first ten-year issue in the new currency being sold overseas, although this was no doubt helped by the fact that the spread over comparable German bonds at 54 bps was still the highest within the euro area. Beginning with Moody's in November 2002, the credit rating agencies also began a series of upgrades, so that by the autumn of 2003 the country's long-term sovereign debt rating stood at the equivalent of Standard & Poor's A+, the highest it had ever reached.[5] There were some suggestions that this had been driven in part by a need to maintain a differential between euro area members and Eastern European states, many of which had also been upgraded at this time, but in January 2004 an editorial in the *Financial Times* could still confidently state, 'Greece has passed from economic laggard to disciplined member of the euro zone'.[6] This initial narrative of prudence was short lived. It was to be swept away in an audit of state accounts following a change of government in March 2004. This revealed that fiscal policy had been far more expansive than previously reported and that throughout this period Greece had consistently breached the Stability and Growth Pact's reference value. Indeed, according to the European Commission among the root causes of the sovereign debt crisis of the end of the decade, alongside an inadequate reaction to mounting economic imbalances, structural weaknesses and statistical mis-reporting, were 'inappropriate' fiscal policies.[7] However, at this point Greece was by no means alone in apparently paying only cursory heed to the strictures of the Pact. Portugal had breached the budget deficit reference value in 2001 and shortly afterwards Germany and a host of other member states followed suit. Indeed, it was the larger states that were regarded as finding it harder to keep to the new constraints. Germany, in particular, wrestling with the challenges of unification, was faced with sluggish growth. As a result, and with leading economists warning that 'implementing rigid rules for public sector

borrowing would risk turning downturn into depression', the country abandoned any attempt to stick to the budgetary deficit reference value, causing
the Stability and Growth Pact's coercive mechanisms to be effectively suspended in November 2003.[8] The Pact might have helped confer fiscal stability
to the euro area in its first years of existence but it had yet to bring fiscal discipline. Indeed, in many ways the weakening of the Pact was merely a symptom
of a general waning of appetite for further integration once the euro had been
successfully launched, which meant, among other things, that the political
leadership gave little thought to creating a common crisis resolution mechanism able to deal with future financial and economic shocks.[9]

On paper, and rhetorically, the Panhellenic Socialist Movement (PASOK)
government remained committed to securing 'real convergence' with its euro
area partners, with its first stabilisation and growth programme, which
replaced the old convergence document now Greece was inside the EMU,
setting ambitious macroeconomic and structural reform targets. To achieve
these, in September 2001, Simitis, during his annual premier's address at the
Thessaloniki International Fair, unveiled a three-year action plan which within
a pledge to improve the country's competitiveness promised extensive privatisation, tax, health and social security reform and the removal of restrictions
surrounding the so-called 'closed professions'.[10] The government had clearly
stated its intention to press ahead with reforms, but during the first years of its
new term of office its attention often seemed to lie elsewhere. Negotiations
over proposals put forward by the UN Secretary General, Kofi Annan, to
resolve the Cyprus dispute and the admittance of the island to the EU dominated the foreign agenda, while a prolonged dispute with the leadership of the
Orthodox Church over whether religious affiliation should be declared on
identity cards stirred controversy at home. There was also the need to prepare
for the forthcoming XXVIII Olympiad, which continued to lag behind
schedule, amid persistent rumours of problems with tenders and escalating
costs. Most of all, though, despite being returned to power for the third consecutive time at the 2000 election and holding a comfortable parliamentary
majority, PASOK's political position was far from secure. New Democracy
had only narrowly lost the election and, by the middle of 2001, it was already
ahead in the opinion polls. When voters were asked their preferences, Simitis
might still usually be preferred to Kostas Karamanlis as prime minister, but
PASOK was to spend most of the next three years trying to make up lost
political ground. Therefore, although it remained under constant pressure
from outside institutions, such as the International Monetary Fund (IMF)

and the Organisation for Economic Co-operation and Development (OECD), as well as the European Commission and the Economic and Financial Affairs (Ecofin) Council, to speed up structural reforms, the government continued to be, understandably, wary of pursuing any policies that might alienate voters or rekindle divisions within the ranks of the ruling party.[11]

Nevertheless, in April 2001, under prodding from European partners and well aware that the existing system was untenable, the government presented a programme of pension reform. However, even before the proposals had been officially tabled, they sparked mass unrest, with the unions once again accusing the government of waging war against society. Dissent already simmering within PASOK also broke to the surface and in the face of this tumult the legislation was withdrawn.[12] At a subsequent party congress in October 2001 Simitis secured re-election as leader but, as in 1999, he failed to gain the endorsement of nearly a third of the delegates, and in response an influential segment of the pro-PASOK press started to speculate that a better choice might have been Giorgos, the son of Andreas Papandreou. Eventually, after a cabinet reshuffle, a new pension reform bill was tabled but this was generally considered as being less radical and failed to deal with the issue of long-term sustainability.[13] Subsequently, the government promulgated a number of market liberalisation decrees and continued to press ahead with its privatisation plans, but following the withdrawal of the first pension bill it was generally perceived as lacking the will to implement major changes, leaving the chairman of the Hellenic Federation of Industrialists not alone in bewailing its failure to 'exploit creatively the historic opportunity presented by membership of the euro'.[14]

Prior to entry into the EMU, the government had used the stock exchange to bring privatisation offers to the market, but the sharp fall in the Athens Stock Exchange (ASE) index after the ending of the stock market boom forced it to employ other strategies. These included issuing bonds which would be convertible into shares at preferential rates once market conditions had improved sufficiently to allow state companies to be privatised. In a series of deals named after figures from Greek mythology, money was also raised in advance against upcoming revenue streams, with future air traffic control fees appropriately being pledged under the guise of Aeolus, the god of the winds.[15] At the same time, the government also engaged in a series of currency swaps, partly to remove exchange rate vulnerabilities identified in the 2000 European Central Bank (ECB) convergence report. By 2002, nearly all the 15 per cent or so of public debt denominated in foreign currencies, principally US dollars and Japanese yen, had been successfully converted into euros. However, in the process Greece's balance sheet had been bolstered by around €2.8 billion in a complex cross-currency swap arranged by the London-based Fixed-Income Currency and Commodities Division of the American investment bank, Goldman Sachs.[16] This was achieved through the expedient of using a lower exchange rate than the one prevailing at the time when re-denominating the foreign currency into euros and, since the deal was technically a currency swap, it seems not to have been treated as borrowing, although Greece, following a grace period of two years, was due to repay the equivalent of the difference to Goldman Sachs in annual payments stretching to 2019, which would give an estimated profit of $100 million to the bank.[17]

Details of the original 2001 deal, which was one of a dozen or so swaps arranged for Greece by Goldman Sachs, were published in *The New York Times* in February 2010 at the height of the sovereign debt crisis.[18] It was then widely taken as evidence that Greece and the American bank had conspired together to deliberately mask the country's debts—an act the German Chancellor, Angela Merkel, reportedly suggested would be a 'scandal'.[19] However, despite what was suggested in the American newspaper report the deal never seems to have been particularly hidden. It may not have been publicly announced at the time, which was apparently quite customary, but details appeared in the specialist press and Goldman Sachs even seems to have contacted Eurostat to check its legitimacy, although the agency maintains that it was never specifically asked about a deal involving Greece.[20] Nor was Greece unique within the euro area in using such financial instruments. Italy in particular also made wide use of them, although, taken as a percentage of GDP, no country seems to have been as active in this field as Greece. Indeed, deals of this kind were even initially permitted by Eurostat, but they and other similar arrangements used by Greece and its euro area partners always remained controversial.[21] In July 2002, the agency ruled that bonds securitised against future revenue rather than a pre-existing asset should be considered borrowing, and in a subsequent audit that autumn various transfers the Greek government had made to public entities were also judged to be subsidies and considered as part of the public debt.[22] This had already reached 107 per cent of GDP in 2001, which meant that it was not only well above the 60 per cent reference value of the Stability and Growth Pact but also that rather than diminishing, as was envisaged at the time Greece was admitted into the EMU, it had actually increased.[23] Indeed, it continued to grow throughout the decade, so that by 2009 it had reached €299.7 billion, which was almost double the 2001 figure of €151.9 billion, and as a proportion of the total public and private debt far higher than in countries like Portugal.[24] At the same time, increasing amounts of this debt were also passing into foreign hands, with the result that by the end of the decade 78.7 per cent was held outside Greece. This freed space for the domestic banks to lend more money at home, fuelling the rise in private consumption, but also, as it was to prove later, increased the country's vulnerability at times of international financial crisis.[25]

However, at this stage it was not just debt levels that were under scrutiny, because questions were also being asked about budgetary practices, with doubts in particular surfacing over defence spending which the State Audit Council towards the end of 2002 suggested was not being properly recorded.[26] The government dismissed the reports as being politically inspired but New Democracy built on this and other revelations to create a narrative that charged that PASOK was not only failing to control public spending but that it was deliberately manipulating the figures through creative accounting. The accusations may have been largely motivated by electoral gain but New Democracy also had a practical concern, since the securitisation deals, by effectively mortgaging future revenues, were depriving any forthcoming conservative government of funds. By playing on stories of malpractice during the stock market collapse, corruption in the granting of contracts for the Olympics and shady links between the ruling party and certain business interests, personified in Kostas Karamanlis' alleged comment about five pimps manipulating the political life of Greece, New Democracy was able to gain support, even from those on the political left.[27] PASOK tried to counter New Democracy's narrative by taking steps against corruption. It proposed a law forbidding the principals of companies with more than a 5.0 per cent stake in the media from tendering for public works' contracts and extended a requirement to declare sources of wealth to judges, senior policemen and football referees among others, but the party could not throw off the allegations.[28] The economy might be continuing to grow strongly—by 6.6 per cent of GDP in 2003—but with the inflation rate over double the euro area average, unemployment rising and opinion polls showing that half of households expected their income to decline during 2003, a pessimism was taking root, which even led to comparisons being made between Greece and the contemporary collapse of the Argentine economy. Eventually, with PASOK continuing to struggle in the polls, just weeks before the election, Simitis stepped down as party president to be replaced by Giorgos Papandreou. The new leader promised 'revolution everywhere' but his attempt to create a broad-based coalition similar to the centre-left Olive Tree grouping in Italy sowed confusion about the party's intentions, especially after the former New Democracy minister and architect of the Mitsotakis government's free-market reforms, Stefanos Manos appeared on the state list of PASOK parliamentary candidates. When this was coupled with a lacklustre performance in a television debate by the new party leader, early optimism about his appointment dissipated. New Democracy won the election and after a decade out of power returned to office with a clear majority of thirty seats in parliament.[29]

During the election campaign, Kostas Karamanlis had spoken of reinventing the state, rolling back bureaucracy and promoting meritocracy and now, with a strong popular mandate behind him, it was widely expected that the forty-eight-year-old with his mixture of easygoing bonhomie and natural self-confidence would make good his promises. The sense of the dawning of a new era was further reinforced by the totally unexpected triumph of the national football team at the 2004 UEFA European Football Championships and, then, by the success of the Olympics, which were described by Jacques Rogge, president of the International Olympic Committee, as 'unforgettable, dream games'.[30] Greece basked in the accolades and none at the time could have foreseen that the success of the Olympics within a handful of years would come to stand in stark antithesis to the humiliations of the crisis, although the opening ceremony cast a tenuous link to this future when the appearance of the Icelandic singer Björk inadvertently connected two states that were to be caught in the financial maelstrom at the close of the decade. It has regularly been suggested that the serious cost overruns of the Olympics, resulting in part from lavish payments made to ensure facilities were completed on time, caused lasting harm to the finances of the state. A decade after the games, the exact cost remained far from clear but most estimates suggested it was around €8.5 billion. This contributed to the large budget deficit in 2004, but, given the scale of Greek borrowing in general, it is difficult to see it as being instrumental in pushing the country to crisis.[31] However, the rumours of excessive profits and corruption that surrounded the granting of Olympic Games contracts not only tarnished PASOK but also further reinforced a narrative that cast important segments of the Greek business world as exploitative and, at best, only semi-legal. Moreover, public spending on the Olympic Games and the various infrastructure projects associated with them had been an important factor driving economic growth in the early years of the new millennium and, now that they had taken place, the government was faced with the dilemma of devising a fresh model to maintain momentum. The new Minister of Economy and Finance, Giorgos Alogoskoufis, spoke of the country adopting a more export oriented, business friendly growth strategy, with less bureaucracy, lower corporate and small business taxes as well as further privatisation. The government was eventually to fulfil some of this programme, especially as regards reducing tax rates and privatisation.[32] However, merchandise exports were to remain weak and so, in reality, growth came to rest more on a mixture of increased public sector consumption, private investment in housing and credit driven consumer spending, all of which were to be disrupted in the forthcoming crisis.[33]

Ideologically Karamanlis positioned New Democracy within the 'social centre' which he defined in terms of showing sensitivity to the needs of the general population and rejecting extremes. Consensus was to be the watchword and the legacy of the Mitsotakis government firmly banished to the past as mild adjustment and moderation replaced shock therapy.[34] This was not just in economic policy but the approach of the government in general as Karamanlis adopted a rhetoric of moral piety which bore more than a passing resemblance to that employed earlier by his uncle, Konstantine Karamanlis. In his first address to his cabinet the new premier declared his detestation of 'every display of pride, arrogance, opulence and ostentation'.[35] Adhering to the 'social centre' meant New Democracy continued to maintain a statist view, heavily flagged its social protection programmes, which among other things gave higher pensions and offered farmers new low cost loans to help them restructure debts, and downplayed more contentious privatisations, amid talk of 'natural monopolies' existing in areas such as electricity and water supply. Changes were pushed through in some domains, leading to claims that Karamanlis was showing more conviction and tactical guile than his predecessors when dealing with issues like shop opening hours, but in other areas, such as pension reform, a desire to avoid confrontation and build consensus through social dialogue led to endless delays.[36] Overall, the impression was of a change more in form than content although the shifts in personnel were considerable not only within governing structures but also public enterprises, where some attempts at restructuring initiated by the previous government appear to have been disrupted.[37] Indeed, a combination of these personnel changes, the Olympic Games and an audit of state accounts were sufficient to occupy the government's attention for much of its first year in office, producing even by Greek standards a particularly protracted period of initial stasis.

Immediately the government entered office Karamanlis had highlighted a clutch of worrying economic trends, and one economist writing at the time went so far as to suggest that the combination of a high growth rate driven by construction and private borrowing, inflation, widening deficits and lack of competitiveness could be seen as the 'classic symptoms of a dangerously overheating economy'.[38] Most attention, though, was paid to the 2003 budgetary deficit. In its 2002 stability and growth programme PASOK had projected that this would be 0.9 per cent of GDP but by the time of the election it had risen in a series of steps to 1.7 per cent. However, in his first speech to parliament, Alogoskoufis, after affirming that these 'games with numbers have to stop', suggested that the figure could actually be higher, and it was little more than six weeks later when Eurostat revealed that it was in fact 3.2 per cent of GDP.[39] This was an exceptionally large amount of revision in percentage terms, being nearly double the previous government's figure, which Karamanlis blamed on the cost of the Olympic Games, the absorption of less EU funds than expected and what he termed PASOK's 'systematic and organized' attempt to distort the economic picture in which critical figures had been 'persistently concealed'.[40]

With confirmation that the deficit was over 3.0 per cent, the European Commission on 19 May 2004 published a strongly worded budget surveillance report that was the first step towards placing the country again under its excessive deficit procedure (EDP). Greece was only one of eleven EU countries facing this prospect at the time, but in its statement the Commission particularly stressed the pro-cyclical nature of a deficit that had arisen at a time when the country was enjoying robust economic growth. On 5 July 2004 the Commission supplemented this initial report with a series of recommendations and, after these were endorsed by the Ecofin Council, Greece was given four months under Article 104c(7) of the Treaty on European Union to take actions to reduce the deficit by 2005 to less than 3.0 per cent and to improve the collection and processing of statistical data.[41] Alogoskoufis' response came in November when in an open letter to the Commission he outlined a series of measures which were to form the base of the 2005 budget. Frequently citing an ECB study that suggested that the Greek state was inefficient, he proposed a fiscal readjustment which was largely led by reductions in expenditure, although there was also to be a crackdown on tax evasion and, from 1 April 2005, a series of tax increases, with higher duties on spirits and tobacco as well as a 1.0 per cent rise in VAT.[42] However, by this stage, it had also become clear that the 2004 budget deficit, partly due to the Olympic Games, would be around 7.5 per cent of GDP. This would make it the largest recorded in the euro area since its formation, and within a general atmosphere of unhappiness arising from statistical discrepancies, on 22 December 2004, the Commission decided that Greece had not complied with the earlier Council recommendation.[43] In consequence, at its February 2005 meeting the Ecofin Council, for the very first time, activated the second stage of the EDP process, which under Article 104c(9) of the Treaty permitted the Council to give notice to a government to take, within a specified time limit, whatever measures for deficit reduction it judged necessary to remedy the situation.[44] In response PASOK and other members of the opposition spoke of the country being put 'under supervision', but Alogoskoufis denied this was the case, arguing that its only real consequence was that Greece had to submit bi-annual fiscal progress reports to the Commission to allow it to judge if the country's efforts at adjustment were sufficient.[45]

The statistical discrepancies that had upset the Ecofin Council related to the budget deficit figures. New Democracy had long alleged that PASOK had been misreporting these and, with Eurostat pronouncing itself unwilling to certify the 2003 figure, the new government on entering office had ordered an audit of state finances.[46] New Democracy was not the first incoming government to engage in such an exercise in 2004. The new Spanish government did the same and in 2002 the incoming administration in Portugal had also taken a similar step.[47] Indeed, beginning with the Plural Left government of Lionel Jospin in France in 1997, the fiscal demands of the Stability and Growth Pact had led a number of governments to order audits in an attempt to clean up their balance sheets so as not to be encumbered by the spending of parties now in opposition. The 2004 Greek audit, which was termed 'informal', was carried out with the co-operation of Eurostat by the National Statistical Service (NSS) under the leadership of a head newly installed by the incoming government. Its remit was limited to the last years of PASOK's rule and it was only after this initial enquiry had turned up sizeable discrepancies that the Ecofin Council considered extending the investigation. The issue seems to have been discussed at an informal Ecofin Council held in Scheveningen in the Netherlands on 10–11 September 2004, but it was only at the end of that month that it was publicly announced that Eurostat was to 'examine all possible consequences of these updated figures for the years before 2000', with it being confirmed that this meant as far back as 1997 at an October Ecofin Council gathering in Luxembourg.[48] However, prior to this, on 8 September 2004, it had already been disclosed in Athens that the 2003 budget deficit had not been 3.2 per cent of GDP, as previously announced, but in fact 4.6 per cent. This was even higher than expected and afterwards, under pressure from the media, a rather defensive Alogoskoufis was forced to dismiss suggestions that the country's credit rating might be at risk and that Greece's membership of the euro area could even be questioned, emphatically stating 'history cannot be reversed'.[49] Alogoskoufis' comments were made in Greece and elicited little international reaction, but when Eurostat shortly afterwards published revised figures for the whole 2000–2003 period and it emerged that ever since the establishment of the euro the Greek deficit had breached the 3.0 per cent reference value, a storm of criticism was unleashed. Trichet called the new figures an 'enormous problem', while less circumspect German and Austrian politicians openly talked about Greek 'trickery' and called for sanctions to be imposed on the country.[50] At the October Ecofin Council Greece came under pressure but no immediate action was taken, with the finance ministers preferring instead to wait for the publication of the official Eurostat report before taking any decisions.[51] It seems that at this stage the immediate concern was not so much that Greece had broken the rules, but how its behaviour might be interpreted by the ten new members of the EU, many of which were struggling to keep up with the fiscal demands of the EMU convergence process.

The *Report by Eurostat on the Revision of the Greek Government Deficit and Debt Figures* was eventually released on 22 November 2004.[52] It showed that Greece had breached the deficit reference value not only since joining the euro but, crucially, also in the years immediately prior to its entry into the single currency when it was one of the convergence criteria. Within the report, eleven areas of concern were highlighted. Three of these related to military expenditure, social security funds and taxation revenue had been important in the period 2000–2003, while the others concerned with areas such as the capitalisation of interest and capital injections together with the aforementioned military expenditure had been most significant in the period 1997–1999. Defence spending accounted for the majority of the overrun between 2000 and 2002. The problem was not expenditure on salaries and maintenance, which Eurostat acknowledged had always been correctly recorded, but money spent on military durables, such as tanks and submarines. Greece was not alone in facing problems in the recording of this type of expenditure. The process lacked transparency in many EU countries and recognising this Eurostat in 2003 had created a special task force to clarify how the rules should be applied in complex cases. Under the prevailing ESA95 accountancy rules, best practice was that expenditure on military equipment should be recorded at the time of final delivery, with any payments made between ordering and that time being considered financial advances. However, Eurostat also accepted that it was frequently impossible to record military expenditure in this way, because domestic statistical authorities often did not have access to delivery information which was deemed sensitive for reasons of national security. Therefore, it was also accepted that expenditure could be recorded in the year that it occurred. Following lengthy discussions, the Greek authorities had informed Eurostat in 2002 that they would conform with ESA95's best practice and this choice was validated by the agency not only because it was preferable but also because it had been told that the NSS had access to the necessary information. However, the result of this change, according to Eurostat, was that virtually no expenditure on military equipment had been recorded from 1997 onwards. In talks with a Eurostat mission after the 2004 elections it was agreed that the NSS would try and obtain the necessary delivery date information but, when this was still not forthcoming, it was agreed by all sides that Greece would, like the majority of EU states, switch to recording payments when they had been made and this was the chief reason for the upward adjustment of the deficit figures for the years preceding the audit. The extent to which delivery data was actually available remains unclear, but it seems fair to say that the retrospective shifting of expenditure backward was as advantageous to New Democracy as its shifting forward had earlier been to PASOK.

The other important area highlighted by Eurostat in the post-2000 period related to the assets of social security funds. ESA95 methodology allowed the capital surpluses of public entities, such as local authorities, pension funds, hospitals and universities, to be set against central government borrowing to produce a figure for the general government deficit. In Greece local government usually ran a deficit but some pension funds ran surpluses and, once these were factored into the calculations, they regularly allowed the general deficit to come in some two or three percentage points below that of the central government. In 1998 Eurostat had noticed that Greece was reporting much larger social security surpluses than other member states. The Greek authorities said this was because many of the schemes, which had only been recently established, had received large transfers from central government. They also held assets that had risen in value during the stock market boom, while at the same time having relatively low costs since they were as yet paying few pensions. Prior to the election, PASOK had retained the same figures as before but, after it assumed power, New Democracy sharply revised the surplus downwards by a cumulative total of €2.8 billion. On the basis of this and further investigations, Eurostat revised the deficit figures for 2000 and the years following upwards but, since most of the funds had not filed audited accounts since that year, even these new figures were little more than estimates. Of the other categories in the period before 2000, the most important were capitalisation of interest and capital injections. The other categories all raised the deficit by less than 0.25 per cent of GDP per year. The capitalisation of interest problem arose from an agreement made by the PASOK administration in 1995 with domestic banks, most of which were state controlled, to allow interest payments on certain government bonds to accumulate as capital. These should have been recorded as payments and notified to Eurostat but for unknown reasons this had not occurred. Likewise, capital injections were a notably complicated part of ESA95 methodology but, following the Eurostat ruling of October 2002 relating to subsidies, the government should have corrected the figures not just for the years after 2000, which it did, but also for those before. However, this, again, had not happened.

In welcoming the report, Alogoskoufis said it signalled a 'new era of transparency' but, even after despatching a series of missions to Greece, Eurostat in 2008 was still expressing concerns about the accuracy of the figures it received.[53] In that year, when it released its preliminary 2007 government debt and deficit data for the EU as a whole, it openly voiced its doubts about the Greek figures, emphasising that there was 'insufficient coverage of source data for extra-budgetary funds, local government and social security funds'.[54] However, in his statements in 2004 Alogoskoufis firmly pinned the blame for the faulty figures on the previous government which he charged had denigrated the Greek people 'in front of our partners'.[55] In response the leaders of PASOK mounted a robust defence, with Simitis penning an article in the *Financial Times*. In this he stressed that Eurostat was constantly revising its regulations to take into account changes in the economic environment as well as advances in methodology, before suggesting that in this case it could be seen as changing the rules after the fact.[56] This was denied by the head of Eurostat in a letter published in the same newspaper a few days later but the agency itself was hardly an uninterested party.[57] It had come under criticism from the Ecofin Council in December 2003 for its failure to monitor Greece more closely, and a European Commission spokeswoman later accepted that in confining itself to technocratic detail and not giving the problem sufficient 'political dimension' Eurostat bore some of the blame, continuing that, furthermore, other member states that had been aware of the problem did as well.[58]

Within Greece, disputes over budgetary deficit figures had become commonplace over the years, often being employed as a political weapon to cast doubts on the competence of opponents, but the 2004 audit was to remain a particularly deep wound, continuing to sour relations between the main parties and leaving them more polarised than ever. By throwing a spotlight on the opaque defence budget it also fuelled discussion of corruption. Initially attention focused on some relatively minor cases but, following revelations that a German company had paid bribes in Portugal to secure a submarine contract, interest switched to a similar deal concluded with Greece.[59] Although it was to be many years before charges were laid, the revelations that followed strengthened the perception that the political system was riddled with corruption, and subsequently the government seemed to be endlessly beset by scandal. One, involving the purchase of a €280 million structured bond by state controlled funds at allegedly disadvantageous prices, was much discussed at the time of the 2007 election, but it was two others that came to dominate political life.[60] The first of these involved allegations that the German electronics company Siemens and its local subsidiary over many years had paid millions of euros in bribes to both individuals and, it seems, to the two leading political parties in order to gain lucrative contracts.[61] The second concerned a complicated swap of agricultural land around a lake in Northern Greece for prime real estate near Athens, which it was alleged benefitted the Athonite monastery of Vatopedi at the expense of the Greek state. The heady mixture of monks, ministers and high finance made this scandal particularly newsworthy, leading to every twist and turn of what was an extremely convoluted tale being reported in enormous detail in the media, although repeated parliamentary attempts to uncover the truth behind the deal invariably broke down in partisan infighting.[62] The New Democracy leadership continued to allege that the issue had been largely manufactured by the pro-PASOK press, but the Vatopedi scandal came to haunt the government, with some suggesting that it was Karamanlis' decision to publicly back a number of ministers linked with the affair during his appearance at the Thessaloniki International Fair in September 2008 that effectively sealed the fate of his second administration in the public eye.[63]

In contrast to the political fury inside Greece the response of the financial markets to the results of the audit was mild. This lack of reaction was attributed to both the relative insignificance of the Greek economy within the euro area as a whole and the fact that it had been a comparatively minor deception by a country long perceived as having weak public finances.[64] Not everybody, though, was persuaded and, contrary to Alogoskoufis' earlier dismissal of the possibility, Standard & Poor's did downgrade the country's sovereign rating on 17 November 2004 from A+ to A, with Fitch following suit on

16 December 2004.[65] The downgrades led to some speculation that demand for Greek debt would weaken, but the authorities found little difficulty in placing €5 billion of ten-year bonds in mid-February 2005 and even their first thirty-year bond at the end of that month. In an era of low interest rates, in which investors were said to be 'desperately looking for yield', the weaknesses of the Greek economy seem to have been easily overlooked, especially since new rules relating to pension funds on both sides of the Atlantic had generated demand for longer dated bonds.[66] However, the downgrade by Standard & Poor's was only the second time such a ratings action had been taken against a euro area state since the creation of the single currency, and it meant that Greek sovereign bonds now only just met the requirement to be accepted as collateral by the ECB. The existence of this condition seems only to have been publicly admitted in November 2005 but, according to Trichet, a prerequisite that collateral be rated above A− had applied since the creation of the bank, with reports suggesting that the issue was only brought to public attention at this time to put additional pressure on states such as Greece running deficits above the Stability and Growth Pact's reference value.[67] Yet, in contrast to 2009, when worries that the ECB might again raise its collateral requirement to A− were a significant factor in destabilising the Greek bond market, at this time there was little reaction, presumably because investors could see no immediate danger. Later, studies trying to explain the rise in spreads during the crisis at the end of the decade suggested it was partly a natural correction after the markets had effectively ignored macroeconomic fundamentals throughout this period, keeping the difference between Greek and German yields unreasonably small.[68] However, this was not just specific to Greek bonds because there was a global tendency to underplay risk in the quest for higher yields during these years. In the euro area pricing was also influenced by a generalised belief that if one of its member states encountered difficulties the others would come to its aid.[69] Indeed, the financial markets were not alone in their apparent complacency. After their initial downgrades, the rating agencies also took no further actions, with both Moody's and Fitch confirming their ratings in 2006 and 2007, although Greece was still the lowest rated of all the euro area countries. Fitch, at the beginning of 2006, held its sovereign rating for the country at A, when Portugal, as well as Italy, was at AA, and Ireland, together with Spain, was at the top-ranking AAA.

The external political response to the final Eurostat report was equally muted. The European Commission viewed the New Democracy government as being cooperative and doing the best it could to reduce the budgetary deficit so, although infringement proceedings were started and there were a few calls for the withholding of cohesion funds, no tangible sanctions seem to have been applied.[70] This was partly because, following their effective undermining in November 2003, when the Ecofin Council had decided to put on hold proceedings against France and Germany after they had both breached the deficit reference value, the rules had been rewritten so that in special circumstances or when it was warranted by the economic cycle countries were permitted more leeway.[71] It was difficult to see Greece fitting these criteria, but the fact that its problems arose while these changes were under discussion seems to have played to its advantage.[72] However, with the weakening of the Stability and Growth Pact, the euro more than ever came to rest on mutual trust between the partner states, with respecting the rules seen as an act of self-interest in the name of the collective good. Greece was perceived to have breached the expected code of conduct. This brought much criticism, but amid firm affirmations from the Ecofin Council that such a situation would never be allowed to occur again, the matter was allowed to drop. Even a request by Eurostat to increase its powers so that instead of relying on notifications it could mount on-site inspections was blocked.[73] However, seeds of doubt had been sowed. One leading outside observer afterwards cautiously wrote, 'In hindsight, Greece's euro entry appeared misjudged, even fraudulent', and such sentiments were to be easily resurrected during the crisis when the assertion by a German former ECB chief economist in a 2011 interview that Greece had cheated in order to join the single currency probably only gave voice to the thoughts of many.[74]

Most of all the figures that continued to be reported throughout this period gave the impression that state finances were under control and, with the economy growing strongly, there seemed little reason for concern. From its peak of 7.9 per cent of GDP in 2004 the budget deficit by 2006 was reported to have fallen to a mere 2.6 per cent, suggesting that Greece had achieved a considerable fiscal readjustment in just two years.[75] Early on Alogoskoufis had ruled out following a policy of austerity, which he defined as applying a shock to the economy, on the basis that it was 'something that has failed whenever it's been attempted'.[76] So, apart from an extension of VAT to new housing and a few other minor changes, he chose not to impose any major tax rises which he saw as only stunting economic growth. Instead, a series of one-off special measures were used to increase revenue. These included gathering extra dividends from state-controlled banks and selling the rights to electronic games operated by the state lottery, although an attempt in 2006 to securitise up to €1.5 billion of uncollected tax revenue was opposed by the European

Commission and eventually dropped.[77] Alogoskoufis justified his strategy on the basis that many of the costs the state was facing were also one-off, ranging from the Olympic Games themselves and the repayment of EU structural funds to a series of large fines for illegal subsidies to Olympic Airways.[78] Most importantly, though, revenues were rising due to continuing economic growth and, after GDP was recalibrated upwards on a new base year of 2000 by 9.6 per cent, the change in figures was sufficient to push the budget deficit below the 3.0 per cent reference value.[79] With the 2007 figure, with no one-off budgetary measures, also projected to be just 2.4 per cent, on 16 May 2007 the European Commission ruled that Greece was in compliance with the terms of the Stability and Growth Pact; and, following its recommendation, the Ecofin Council lifted the EDP the following month. For his performance in handling the economy Alogoskoufis won plaudits, with the *Financial Times* in November 2007 ranking him fifth out of twelve euro area finance ministers, giving him high marks for technical abilities but low ones for political skills.[80] Indeed, in all regards the praise appeared well deserved. The Greek economy had grown by 5.8 per cent of GDP in 2006, the number of registered unemployed had fallen from 10.5 per cent of the workforce in 2004 to 8.4 per cent in 2007 and household incomes were said to be approaching 90 per cent of the EU-15 average. Indeed, so impressive was its handling of the economy thought to be that it was the main focus of New Democracy's advertising during the 2007 election campaign. Stories in the international press at this time also dwelt on the 'feel-good factor' that the party was said to be enjoying, although it was also accepted this was to be found more in major cities and tourist areas than in lesser population centres.[81]

In reality any sense of economic well-being was relatively superficial and in large part founded on borrowing. From a low base consumer credit had expanded rapidly after Greece had joined the EMU, until it was growing by nearly 33 per cent per annum in the middle of the decade. As late as 2007, only around half of all households carried any debt, but this figure was distorted by the low number of mortgages, and proportionately levels of consumer borrowing were among the highest in the euro area. Consumer groups and the media highlighted the risks, with one TV channel even introducing a game show where the prize was the paying off of credit card bills and the public shredding of statements.[82] Borrowing was so attractive partly because it was much cheaper than before due to the low interest rates set by the ECB under its one-size-fits-all policy. Indeed, once Greece's higher inflation was taken into account, these actually became negative for much of this period, which not only encouraged borrowing but also gave little incentive to save. Aside from Poland, Greece had the lowest gross saving rate in the OECD throughout this period and, according to one set of calculations, interest rates should have been up to three times higher than they actually were at this time to regulate the expansion of the money supply.[83] The ECB's interest rate policy, high aggregate domestic demand and supply-side constraints all combined to keep the inflation rate in Greece consistently about 1.0 per cent above the euro area average. However, the popular perception was that prices, especially those of everyday items, were rising far faster, and this, to a certain extent, was borne out by official figures covering essential items such as foodstuffs. The initial rise in prices at this time seems to have resulted from the ending of the unofficial control through 'gentleman's agreement' that had facilitated entry into the EMU. Once this had been achieved, manufacturers and retailers quickly sought to make up any lost ground and restore, if not increase, profits, with many immediately rounding up the new prices to the nearest fifty cents, if not euro.[84] Even more insidiously, the new currency also brought a change in basic perceptions of value, as consumers, used to dealing exclusively with banknotes and hundreds, thousands and even millions of drachmas, had to adjust to coins and thinking in terms of prices denoted in hundreds, tens and single euros. Faced with the new euro-denominated prices, many consumers, especially the elderly, handed over their notes without any real notion of value. The rising prices brought some protests, with a one day boycott called by a consumer group in September 2002 reportedly seeing supermarket takings drop by one third, but the new scale of values soon became entrenched. It was visible in everything from coffees in a cafe to a simple children's party at the local play centre, which could easily cost over €1,000, and more than anything else it was the escalating cost of living that fuelled the mood of unhappiness caught in opinion polls throughout this period. So much so that by the middle of the decade almost twice as many saw the new currency in a negative light as positive, and there were the first signs of consumer resistance.[85] Retail sales peaked in 2006 and then began to flatten, presenting the first signs of a weakening of the economy which was to gather steam in 2008.

The increasing prices were only one aspect of an ongoing commercial revolution which saw many traditional stores with un-enticing window displays of often locally made goods, especially in the field of clothing, swept away in favour of shiny boutiques selling expensive imported wares often produced in low-wage developing economies. This trend was epitomised by the appearance of a number of glossy shopping malls in the Athenian suburbs, similar to those encountered elsewhere in the world. At first sight, Greece seemed to be embracing this new material culture with enthusiasm, with executives of companies selling luxury brands quoted as saying that the country was a hidden market for their products and importers of designer goods reputed to be making enormous profits.[86] The culture was blatantly promoted in hordes of glossy magazines bearing names like *Status*, which lay stacked in piles around the news kiosks, and the stylish interiors of the sets of the ubiquitous soap operas on television. It was also reflected in everyday comment about the number of big new cars on the roads and the extravagance of orders in the tavernas, which left tables groaning under the weight of food. Yet, many of the journalists received a pittance for their writings and, while the pages of the magazines were adorned with pictures of slender young models, the reality was that Greece was posting one of the highest childhood obesity rates in the world.[87] Perhaps in part due to the growth of the local fast-food industry, which was driven among other things by household members having to devote increasing amounts of their time to earning the money necessary to maintain their lifestyles. OECD statistics showed Greeks to work long if not always particularly productive hours although such figures were skewed by the lengthy days worked by the self-employed. In a society always highly conscious about appearance, people could save for weeks to buy a precious branded item, and when import figures were studied the much commented upon big new cars turned out not to be as numerous as popularly supposed. Even those that were on the road often seem to have been bought on credit. Ostentatious display may have become more noticeable but, in truth, it was still more a society of aspiration than reality. This, however, did not stop many, including the Church of Greece, from later rooting the causes of the crisis in the moral decline of a society which had too readily succumbed to the vices of hedonism, hubris and greed.[88] Excess and a self-centred quest for material gains could again be blamed for the nation's ills and this theme was readily taken up by some politicians, with Papandreou speaking of the 'deification of wealth' as PASOK preached a narrative of decline that highlighted the 'prevalence of the law of the powerful'.[89]

A feeling among employees that they needed to make up ground lost during the period of austerity prior to admittance to the single currency, along with the rising prices fed demands for higher pay, and in 2002 nominal wages rose almost twice as fast as the euro area average. In the years that followed this trend continued, with two rounds of national pay negotiations in 2004 and, acrimoniously, in 2006, ensuring that Greece remained at the top of the table when it came to average wage gains within the euro area.[90] So much so that by the beginning of 2007 the lowest monthly minimum wage had increased to €730, slightly more than in Spain, and far above the €470 of Portugal and neighbouring Bulgaria where it stood at just €92.[91] Nonetheless, this was still widely perceived as being insufficient as a living wage and there was much anguished comment about the fate of young people consigned to what became known as the €700 generation. An influential union movement, a desire to match West European norms and higher inflation all combined to keep pay rises in Greece relatively high during this period and this was nowhere more noticeable than in the public sector. In keeping with a longstanding trend, salaries here on average tended to be about a third higher than in the private sector and in certain entities, such as Hellenic Petroleum, Olympic Airways and the urban transport companies, they stood even further above the norm.[92] In Greece the 'golden boys' were usually not the bankers of other countries but the executives and administrators of public sector entities.[93] These pay discrepancies and the failings of the bureaucracy in general helped consolidate a narrative that cast many civil servants as being overpaid, aloof and work-shy and the state administration as overmanned, inefficient and often corrupt. This fuelled the mood of unhappiness and disillusion caught in opinion polls prior to the crisis and gave rise to endless stories of corruption, waste and malpractice.[94] Prior to 2009 this discourse remained largely confined to Greece, but after that date, as external interest in the country quickened following the onset of the crisis, it diffused outwards to intersect with national stereotypes long held within northern Europe and elsewhere. From this there arose a powerful new narrative of Greece being a profligate, easy-living country, squandering borrowed money and EU grants on favoured constituencies, such as farmers, an excessively remunerated civil service and lavish pensions to those who in many other countries would be considered to have at least fifteen more years of working life. Greece was again cast as a country living beyond its means and afterwards this was to make it in the words of one author the 'perfect culprit' for the ire of its euro area partners.[95]

The steady increase in wages helped bring the issue of the lack of international competitiveness of the economy again to the fore. However, the differential between the domestic inflation rate and those in other euro area states may have been sufficient to account for much of any loss.[96] Furthermore, since wholesale export prices rose by less than half the increase in wages during this time, it could be argued that it was often as much a case of other states gaining competitiveness as Greece losing ground.[97] This was especially true as regards euro area partners such as Germany which under Chancellor Gerhard Schröder's Agenda 2010 reform programme was reinvigorating its manufacturing base. Moreover, as the German economy prospered, some of its fiscal surplus was recycled across southern Europe, lured by the higher returns available and reassured by the security granted by common membership of the single currency and the creditworthiness of local banks. Theoretically this process should have been beneficial, since within a currency union funds are expected to move to where they can be most productively invested, but in reality the money, aside from driving the local credit boom that sucked in more imports from countries such as Germany, was utilised to fund the borrowing of the Greek state.[98]

The government responded to the loss of competitiveness by taking a series of initiatives to boost investment and increase labour flexibility. However, much of the money seems to have flowed into already problematic sectors like textiles, and a law mandating high rates of overtime pay was not replaced by one freeing the market but by another involving a complex sliding scale. Productivity nevertheless increased during this period above the euro area average. And while levels remained below Western European norms, in certain key areas of the economy, such as tourism and agriculture, an influx of migrant workers often prepared to work for less than the minimum wage and without social security contributions, meant that any rise in costs was muted, allowing these sectors in general to retain international competitiveness.[99]

Those who wished to highlight the economy's loss of competitiveness frequently pointed to the accelerating current account deficit, which they suggested resulted from Greek producers, unable to compete against cheaper imports and trading rivals, effectively pricing themselves out of both domestic and foreign markets. In fact other factors might have been responsible for the rise in the deficit, with the OECD suggesting that it may have been primarily due to a large reduction in net private and official inflows, including EU transfers, and a rise in outflows, especially remittances from migrants.[100] Nonetheless, it is undeniable that the current account deficit did rise sharply from an average of 3.0 per cent of GDP in the period 1990–1998 to 14 per cent in 2007–2008. Some economists were not alarmed by the rise, arguing that it was sustainable.[101] In this view, as long as investment financed by the inflows produced sufficient rate of return to allow external liabilities to be met, and the increase in consumption was only a temporary phenomenon in order to secure economic convergence, it was not likely to be especially problematic.[102] Certainly, when pressed on the matter in 2008, Alogoskoufis spoke confidently, suggesting that capital inflows from shipping and Balkan investments would help cover the country's needs. However, many others differed and saw it as a significant problem. Papademos was by no means alone when, also speaking in 2008, he warned that 'the adverse effect of the external imbalances may be very important' and another Governor of the Bank of Greece, Giorgos Provopoulos, in hindsight was to call it an 'accident waiting to happen'.[103] Yet, although the trade imbalances posted by Greece and other southern European euro area members occasioned discussion in the media and academic circles prior to the crisis and the European Commission even suggested there was a need to 'broaden surveillance to address macroeconomic imbalances', little action was taken.[104] The ECB had few policy options, the political leaders tended to focus on their own domestic economies, the European Commission seemed content to put its faith in the Stability and Growth Pact and the voice of the Eurogroup, which was 'never much more than the ghost of an absent government', was rarely heard.[105]

The ballooning current account deficit did not become an immediate problem, as it had in the past, because it was counteracted by balances elsewhere within the euro area which as a whole was posting a trade surplus.[106] Prior to 2008, Greece had been able to fund its current account deficit largely through commercial interbank transactions but with the full onset of the wider financial crisis, banks and insurance companies in northern euro area member states began to balk at increasing their exposure. Interbank lending froze and it was this 'sudden stop' of funds that led some to suggest that the crisis in Greece was at root a balance of payments issue.[107] A full breakdown was only avoided due to the Eurosystem's facility for offsetting balance of payments differences between member states known as Target-2 (Trans-European Automated Real-Time Gross Settlement Express Transfer), which allowed central banks in countries where payment deficits were causing an outflow of commercial bank reserves to extend extra credits, although in the process the Bank of Greece's external liabilities within the system rose in direct relation to the claims of its euro area counterparts, especially the Bundesbank.[108] The significance of the large imbalances that were created has been much debated, with some economists choosing to portray them as an effective rescue programme predating the official mechanism established in the spring of 2010.[109] However, more generally they can be seen as either helping the country cope with the outflow of funds during the first years of the crisis and moderating the contraction in domestic credit or as prolonging the subsequent readjustment period by further distorting the market.

When Karamanlis called a general election for 16 September 2007, he cited economic and constitutional reasons for an early vote.[110] During the campaign both leading parties offered the usual blandishments to the electors, with those proffered by New Democracy calculated by one source likely to cost €1.5 billion in 2008 alone.[111] New Democracy also made much of the leadership qualities of Karamanlis and the need for solidarity at a time of difficulty, and one reading of the election is that it was effectively won when Alogoskoufis offered generous compensation to households affected by some particularly serious wildfires, which in the Peloponnese claimed many lives.[112] The result was that New Democracy gained a second consecutive victory over PASOK, although the combined votes of the two parties fell below 80 per cent, allowing the Communist Party of Greece (KKE) and the other main left-wing grouping, the Coalition of the Radical Left (SYRIZA), to increase their representation and the Popular Orthodox Rally (LAOS), a right-wing party formed by Giorgos Karatzaferis following his expulsion from New Democracy, to enter parliament for the first time.[113] Afterwards, rent by recriminations, PASOK embarked on a leadership contest in which Papandreou defeated his main rival Evangelos Venizelos, in part due to a new procedure giving the 'friends' of the party a chance to participate in choosing the leader, which boosted the number of voters to over three-quarters of a million. While PASOK was preoccupied, New Democracy was also facing its own problems. Beside continuing protests against its plans to reorganise higher education, from March 2008 it also faced concerted opposition from the unions over its proposals for pension reform, with industrial action breaking out even before the bill was presented to parliament, leading to power cuts, the closure of the stock exchange and piles of rubbish in the streets. PASOK vigorously opposed the law. It tabled a parliamentary no-confidence motion to delay the final vote and even suggested the issue should be put to a referendum, an unusual idea for Greece, where previous referenda had been almost entirely concerned with the monarchy, but one which was fully in keeping with Papandreou's ideal of creating a more participational democracy.

Prior to the election, the government had moved to fulfil long-delayed promises from the 2004 campaign to increase the pensions of farmers and those on lower incomes as well as benefits to families with three children or more. This, together with a rise in the public sector wage bill well above the rate of inflation and a series of one-off payments, including the costs of compensation for the forest fires, pushed up general government expenditure, which rose from 45.3 per cent of GDP in 2006 to 47.5 per cent in 2007. In

2008 the public sector wage bill was again forecast to rise sharply and, with Standard & Poor's as well as Fitch already publicly warning of the need to limit expenditure, the government seems to have initially pondered making up any budgetary shortfall by increasing VAT. However, this was seen as being potentially inimical to growth and so, instead, in September 2008 Alogoskoufis introduced legislation increasing tax on motor vehicles, corporate dividends and capital gains as well as imposing a blanket levy on all the self-employed earning a taxable income of more than €10,500, justifying this as the only way to deal with tax evasion.[114] This may have had a more neutral effect on the economy as a whole, but it was greeted with dismay by many within his own party, who saw it as targeting a natural constituency of voters. As ever, the balancing act depended on the government maintaining economic growth. After hitting 5.8 per cent of GDP in 2006, this was initially thought to have reached similar levels in 2007, although it was later revised downwards to 3.5 per cent. The first projections for 2008 were also optimistic, but global conditions were already weakening, following the onset of the wider financial crisis. Inside Greece the slowdown was led by a decline in consumer spending. Retail sales had fallen from their peak and remained flat, despite continued wage growth. Some areas, such as car sales, stayed strong until the autumn of 2007, perhaps because of a continuing growth in long-term hire-purchase credit agreements. However, with the Bank of Greece urging the commercial banks to show greater circumspection in their lending in the deteriorating financial environment, by the beginning of 2008 vehicle purchases were also starting to tail off. Nonetheless, Alogoskoufis remained optimistic.[115] As late as June 2008, he was still talking about 'plenty of ammunition' being available to help meet growth targets and, instead, it was inflation that was seen as presenting the greatest challenge, with ministers talking of a 'crisis' within household budgets and hinting at the need for a 'self-regulation of the market' similar to the gentlemen's agreements of the past to curb the rise in prices.[116] Initially business confidence also remained resilient, aided by a reduction in corporation tax and the government continuing to offer grants and subsidies, especially to the service sector. Public investment remained high as well, as the authorities sought to maximise the drawdown of the EU's Common Strategic Framework (CSF) funds. However, by early 2008 business sentiment was also starting to weaken as companies readjusted to lower consumer demand. Only exports were still growing. However, the slowdown in the global economy, which saw euro area partners, such as Germany, edging into recession, and a collapse in south-eastern European markets, following the onset of the crisis in that region, meant that by the late summer of 2008 even these were falling as well, by which time Greece, although it was not apparent from the figures released at the time, had also slipped into recession.[117]

3

AN UNPRECEDENTED CRISIS[1]

THE SECOND KOSTAS KARAMANLIS GOVERNMENT, GLOBAL FINANCIAL TURMOIL AND A LOCAL ECONOMIC DOWNTURN

The underlying causes of the international financial crisis that was eventually to envelop Greece are complex and involve global economic imbalances, but most narratives start with the collapse of the American housing market after a sustained boom. This translated into a wider financial crisis because many of the properties had been bought with mortgages that had been sold on by the initial sellers to the larger banks which had packaged them together into complex and opaque bonds. This meant that, when property values fell and homeowners started to default on their loans, not only the value of these bonds was put into question but also, ultimately, the solvency of virtually every financial institution operating in the American market. In an atmosphere of doubt and uncertainty, in which few could be certain loans would be repaid, banks became increasingly wary of taking on counterparty risk. Interbank lending, vital to the short-term borrowing model many had adopted, began to breakdown and, with liquidity flows dwindling, the financial world tumbled into crisis. Indeed, in the eyes of the European Central Bank (ECB), it was a spike in short-term money market rates and spreads on 9 August 2007 caused by a sudden evaporation of confidence that signalled the onset of the global financial turmoil in Europe.[2] In response, the ECB had taken what Trichet called the 'bold' step of offering €95 billion of overnight credit against collateral to euro area banks to increase liquidity, but at this stage it still seems to have been believed by its board members in general that the euro area economy would be spared the full impact of the crisis. Therefore, when the Federal Reserve and the Bank of England began to cut interest rates to try and stave off recession, the ECB did the opposite and on 9 July 2008 actually raised its refinancing rate to 4.25 per cent, judging that inflation still posed the greatest immediate risk.

The ECB's assessment seems to have been broadly shared by the Greek government. Karamanlis in his speeches repeatedly stressed that the origins of the crisis lay outside the country and that its effect had been mostly to drive up inflation due largely to speculative 'games' that were forcing up international food, oil and commodity prices.[3] He acknowledged that shockwaves from the crisis might be affecting the revenues and expenditures of the state, but, as he invariably noted, the Greek economy was still growing at double the pace of the euro area average, the unemployment rate was at its lowest level in years and the local banking system was well capitalised. Karamanlis was not alone in seeing the situation in relatively benign terms. A similar view was held by the Organisation for Economic Co-operation and Development (OECD) which suggested that Greece, tied into the developing markets of south-eastern Europe and cushioned by EU inflows, was potentially in a good position to weather the crisis.[4] The opposition parties, however, including the Panhellenic Socialist Movement (PASOK), were less sanguine, but they nonetheless couched their arguments more in terms of the failings of the New Democracy government than the threat posed by the outside world. Therefore, according to Papandreou, the 'explosive' rise in the cost of living was not so much due to imported inflation, which had been partly offset by changes in the euro-dollar exchange rate, but by the failure of the government to tame the 'rackets' which manipulated the domestic markets for foodstuffs, oil and medicines.[5] The real problem facing the country for him was the scandal-ridden governance of New Democracy, with inflation and the acute over-borrowing of households only being the symptoms of a deeper malaise, which Papandreou termed a 'crisis of values'.[6] Yet, in the first half of 2008 the idea that Greece was in crisis was still not fully formed. There was as yet no generalised perception that the country was in any particular difficulty either in Greece or abroad, although international investors were beginning to show the first signs of being aware of potential weaknesses. The main Athens Stock Exchange (ASE) index, after posting a healthy net gain for most of 2007, had started to fall, partly due to the exit of foreign investors from the market.[7] In this, though, it was only mirroring other stock markets. Likewise, a rise in the spread between German and Greek government securities also only reflected a wider trend within the bond markets, as investors, after years of apparently paying little heed to macroeconomic fundamentals, with the onset of the financial crisis, started to be more wary of differentials in risk and looked afresh at debt and deficit levels.[8] The pejorative acronym PIGS (Portugal, Italy, Greece and Spain) reappeared to bind together the euro area states under scrutiny and, with questions also being asked about the economic soundness of Iceland and a bevy of East European states, financial analysts began to talk about a 'psychology of contagion'.[9] The overall result was that by early summer 2008, the yield on Greek ten-year bonds was approaching 5.0 per cent and the spread with their German equivalents from 40 bps at the beginning of the year had widened to around 70 bps. This was slightly greater than the other southern euro area states—even Italy which bore the highest level of national debt as a proportion of GDP—but it was not sufficient to cause much comment at the time and was probably as much due to the marginality of the Greek market, with its low trading volumes, as to the country's weak macroeconomic fundamentals and lower credit rating.[10]

The defining moment of the global financial crisis came on Monday 15 September 2008 when the American investment bank, Lehman Brothers Holdings, filed for bankruptcy. The liabilities of the bank were far greater than the national debt of a country like Greece and, as the largest company failure in American history, it sent reverberations around the globe. However, initially, aside from the ASE index falling in line with other stock exchanges, there was little suggestion that it would have much impact on Greece. The total exposure of Greek commercial banks to Lehman Brothers was said to be a relatively modest €270 million, and, as might be expected, much of this was through the local subsidiary of the American Citibank. Indeed, part of the Greek press still considered PASOK taking a lead in the opinion polls to be the main news story and, when Karamanlis spoke to New Democracy party members in a televised address on 26 September, the state of the economy seems to have warranted no special attention.[11] It was the near-collapse of financial institutions at the other end of Europe that was to bring the first sense of alarm in Greece. A series of emergency takeovers and nationalisations in the United Kingdom was followed by the neighbouring Irish government guaranteeing all deposits in six major banks and building societies. With financial institutions in Belgium, the Netherlands and Germany also seeking assistance, this turbulence in northern Europe caught the attention of the Greek media. Taking its cue from events across the Atlantic, they had been running increasingly dramatic stories about the financial crisis, and, when pressed on the matter, Alogoskoufis made a statement about deposits at all banks operating in the country being 'absolutely guaranteed'.[12] However, by law only the first €20,000 was protected and the issue was soon seized upon by the media and parliamentary opposition. Confusion reigned and, with 'senior ministerial sources' continuing to indicate that the government would follow the example of Ireland, the overseas media began to report events in Greece as part of their broader coverage of the developing European financial crisis.[13] In this way Greece, which until this point had just occasionally featured in stories about rising bond spreads, almost inadvertently, became part of the emerging international narrative of crisis—even though there were no real indications of anything being particularly untoward with local financial institutions, which senior officials continued to reassure the public were fundamentally sound.

The deepening sense of crisis in Europe as a whole together with the local worries about bank deposits seems to have changed the political atmosphere inside Greece as the politicians afterwards vied with each other to describe the developing situation in increasingly dramatic terms. Papandreou talked of 'an unprecedented crisis', albeit one 'not due to the repercussions of the international crisis' but to New Democracy's rule in recent years, while Karamanlis spoke of the greatest crisis since the period of the Second World War, although he was also careful to state that he was sure Greece would weather the storm.[14] Responding in part to an agenda set by PASOK, which was maintaining a slight lead in the opinion polls, and stung by allegations that New Democracy favoured the rich over the poor, the government repeatedly stressed its priority in tackling the crisis would be to protect the socially vulnerable from unemployment and the high prices arising from the actions of 'speculators'. In keeping with this pledge, legislation was introduced to strengthen consumer protection and a draft law tabled making it more difficult for lenders to repossess homes, but in general the government continued to argue that the crisis was best met by it sticking to its existing reform programme. In particular this meant trying to curb the losses at Olympic Airways and the Hellenic Railways Organisation (OSE), which were said to be running at €3 million a day. In taking this approach the charitable might say that the government was merely not overreacting but others more pointedly suggested it was in a state of virtual denial, although Greece was by no means alone in adopting such a tactic, since the response of its European partners in general to the burgeoning crisis at this time has been said to lack 'conviction and coordination'.[15]

In early October 2008 Karamanlis made an official visit to Malta. In statements after the meeting the prime ministers of the two countries took differing approaches to the financial crisis. While his Maltese counterpart, Lawrence Gonzi, used the opportunity to stress that it would mean taking tough domestic decisions, the Greek premier in his comments chose instead to focus on the need for Europe as a whole to address the crisis.[16] Seeing the crisis as an external phenomenon the government sought a European response and this was to emerge during the second half of 2008 and involve the ECB, the European Commission, the EU finance ministers within the Economic and Financial Affairs (Ecofin) Council and, increasingly, as the scale of the crisis became apparent, the political leadership of the union as a whole. By the time Karamanlis spoke, the ECB had already taken a series of significant measures, which were termed 'non-standard', in order to introduce extra liquidity into the Eurosystem. Aside from a series of cuts in interest rates taken in 'coordination' with other central banks, this also included an announcement that from 15 October it would conduct its weekly refinancing operation through a fixed rate tender procedure with full allotment.[17] Intended to revive confidence and encourage lending, this effectively allowed the euro area's commercial banks to borrow as much as they wanted from the central bank provided they posted adequate collateral. One week later, in a move which was to prove highly significant, the ECB eased this process even further by issuing another press release saying that until the end of 2009 it was lowering its minimum credit rating threshold for collateral from A− to the equivalent of Standard & Poor's BBB-.[18] At the time the ECB's strategy was seen as providing vital support to the banks, but by shifting demand towards shorter-term securities it may also have made it more difficult for states to place longer-term bonds, thereby inadvertently contributing to the development of what was to become a sovereign debt crisis.[19] At the same time as the ECB was introducing its non-standard measures, the European political leadership was also attempting to shape its response to the crisis in a series of meetings. At a 7 October Ecofin Council the finance ministers committed themselves 'to take all necessary measures' to enhance the soundness and stability of a banking system which was coming under increasing pressure after the collapse of Lehman Brothers.[20] The European Commission's favoured option was to create an integrated pan-European fund to support illiquid but basically solvent banks, but the political leaders decided against this and instead agreed to provide assistance through coordinated national plans. Rather than the US approach of buying toxic debts through a Troubled Asset Relief Program (TARP), these would follow the line of the scheme devised to support the British financial sector and provide loan guarantees while also allowing banks to be taken into partial public ownership. The decision to adopt this national approach was largely based on the need for speed and flexibility in addressing what was seen as a highly fluid and dangerous situation, but it also reflected a reluctance among many of the northern European states to divulge further details about the balance sheets of their own banks for fear this would trigger more instability. As was noted at the time, in life the banks might be global but in death they remained steadfastly national.[21]

As they were grappling with the financial crisis, the policymakers also acknowledged that the economic downturn it had caused was proving deeper and more serious than they had expected. As arguments raged on both sides of the Atlantic about the desirability of economic stimulus programmes, in some quarters an expectation arose that the same flexibility that had seen EU competition and state subsidy rules pushed to the limits and beyond to safeguard the banking sector might in the 'current exceptional circumstances' also apply to budget deficits.[22] However, when the issue was broached at an Ecofin Council, while it was accepted that countries facing a severe slowdown might take temporary and targeted measures, particularly to help citizens most affected, it was also stressed that this could only be 'where room for manoeuvre exists'.[23] No *carte blanche* was given for the increase of deficits beyond the Stability and Growth Pact's reference value and, in particular, any measures were expected to take into account specific challenges, such as the need to recover economic competitiveness. To this end, in a message familiar to the Greek government, much stress was laid on the need for continued structural reforms, including the need to introduce flexibility into labour markets. However, the immediate priority of the New Democracy government remained economic growth and, although ostensibly poor public finances gave little space for pump-priming, nonetheless, the decision by member states to endorse a €200 billion European Economic Recovery Plan, even if it was largely to be financed at the national level, could be interpreted as indicating a shift in climate towards stimulus and flexibility regarding the strictures of the Stability and Growth Pact.[24] Indeed, as will be seen, the Greek government was to present its own bank recapitalisation scheme as something of a covert stimulus programme for the economy as a whole, but elsewhere in the EU such plans were being put in place to secure an increasingly fragile financial sector. This was especially the case in Ireland, Germany, and the Benelux countries, where banks such as the Dutch-based ING Group were so large that they exceeded or equalled their country's GDP.[25] France at this stage was not seen as being equally affected, partly because, while French banks were often just as large and had been active in the American market, when they had expanded overseas, as in Greece, they had mostly concentrated on buying retail banks.[26] They had, though, like their German and Dutch counterparts, in the search for yield invested heavily in Greek and other southern European sovereign bonds.[27] In contrast, in Germany heavy exposure to American mortgage backed securities led to a string of banks seeking assistance and the government creating the state-backed Financial Market Stabilisation Fund (*Sonderfonds Finanzmarktstabilisierung*, or SoFFin) to offer guarantees, including €23 billion to Commerzbank and about €100 billion to Hypo Real Estate Holdings A.G. The German authorities had not taken these steps lightly. They had only reluctantly agreed to provide support to the country's banks and, when they did, they repeatedly insisted that other financial institutions share the costs and that those who had behaved irresponsibly be held to account because, as Merkel stated, 'we owe this to the taxpayers of Germany'—a position which, in hindsight, was to be remarkably close to the approach the country was to take to assistance packages in the euro area as a whole.[28]

Alogoskoufis unveiled Greece's own bank recapitalisation plan on 15 October 2008. It had three main components. Firstly, it would provide €15 billion to guarantee bonds issued by banks operating in Greece to increase liquidity in the local system. Secondly, €8 billion in special government bonds would be issued, which could be used by local banks as collateral to borrow from the ECB. Thirdly, €5 billion was set aside to recapitalise the banking sector through the purchase of preference shares from local banks.[29] As a percentage of GDP, the €28 billion Greek plan was less than the schemes put forwards by Germany, Austria and Spain but considerably more than that of Italy whose banking sector, like Greece's, was considered to be basically solvent. It was opposed by the opposition parties which argued that any extra funding should be provided by shareholders, and found only limited favour among a suspicious public, which largely held the banks responsible for the crisis.[30] It was widely believed that the plan would just boost profits and even the head of Marfin Egnatia Bank was quoted as questioning whether it would achieve its goals.[31] Indeed, the bankers themselves were just as uneasy about the package, fearing that the preference share scheme might presage greater government control. Sensing their reluctance, but also probably pandering to public sentiment, Karamanlis intervened to warn them that he would not permit them to heedlessly defy common efforts.[32] Under pressure from all sides, the Hellenic Banking Association eventually gave its muted support,

with the largely state-controlled ATEBank becoming the first financial institution to announce its participation in the scheme, although it was careful to
state that it did not actually need the capital. The other major banks gradually
followed suit, especially after the government made some concessions, and
parliament eventually backed the scheme. However, this was only after a torrid
debate, reports of demonstrations outside banks accusing them of being loan
sharks and the resurgence of a fiercely anti-capitalist rhetoric which was aptly
caught in a slogan that appeared during the disturbances later in the year:
'Billions for the banks, bullets for the young'.[33]

The wider European bank recapitalisation scheme had been designed to
shore up troubled financial institutions, and there were commentators who,
casting an eye at the weakening profitability of some of the state-controlled
banks, wondered if the Greek proposal might not also in reality be a covert
rescue plan. However, when it was presented to the public, the government
spoke of the plan in broader terms as being designed to help reduce interest
rates, make liquidity available to small and medium-sized enterprises and
generally support the economy.[34] Indeed, to maintain economic growth at the
projected level and ultimately to balance its books, the government did need
the supply of credit to continue to expand at rates similar to previous years.
However, perhaps heeding warnings about overexposure, the first response of
the banks to the crisis had been to curb lending and increase interest rates,
partly because the amount they needed to offer to attract deposits had risen.
This might have been commercially justifiable, but it attracted the ire of ministers and the Governor of the Bank of Greece, Giorgos Provopoulos, who
complained of unreasonable rate rises made without transparency.[35] To try
and maintain growth the government could try and cajole the local banks into
maintaining the supply of credit at previous levels, but a greater problem was
that the fortunes of Greece could not be so easily separated from its euro area
partners, and the economies of many of these were already faltering. As in
Greece, weaknesses apparent earlier in the year accelerated after the collapse
of Lehman Brothers. World trade shrank as dramatically as the supply of
credit, with German exports alone down by 18 per cent in the last quarter of
2008.[36] The myth that continental Europe could somehow be decoupled from
the Anglo-Saxon crisis was well and truly buried as the economies of the euro
area contracted, led by Ireland which in the last quarter of 2008 registered a
fall in GDP of 8.8 per cent compared to the previous year. In 2009 the process
continued with the Finnish economy shrinking by 8.3 per cent of GDP, the
Irish by 6.4 per cent and the German by 5.6 per cent. Indeed, with the euro

area shedding 4.5 per cent of GDP in that year, the 3.2 per cent decline in Greece was below average and later was to provide the basis for some unfavourable comparisons with countries that were perceived to have taken more resolute steps to counteract the crisis.[37]

Outside the euro area the situation was sometimes even worse, especially in Eastern Europe, where the Latvian economy declined by 18 per cent of GDP in 2009 and its Estonian and Lithuanian neighbours by almost as much. As their situation grew more parlous, a growing number of countries looked for outside help. Many, including Hungary, Romania, Latvia and Serbia, sought assistance from the International Monetary Fund (IMF), which after spending nearly a decade in the doldrums was given a new lease of life by the crisis.[38] However, Hungary also secured a €5 billion line of credit from the ECB and then, along with Latvia and Romania, turned to the European Commission, seeking help from a long-standing medium-term financial facility designed to assist non-euro member states with balance of payments problems.[39] These events in Eastern Europe and, especially the Balkans, directly impacted on Greece, because the region had become both a major trading partner and an important hub for Greek investment. They removed an important export market, weakened bank profitability and provided another reason for investors to steer clear of the ASE and Greek government bonds. Together with events in Iceland, where the banking sector effectively collapsed in the autumn of 2008, they also revived the spectre of sovereign default that many thought had been banished from Europe. In the end this was thwarted through the intervention of international organisations, with all the institutions that were eventually to constitute what came to be called the 'troika' in Greece playing a role in one country or another. However, no clear structure for giving assistance arose, although, as a precursor to what was to follow in Greece, Latvia under the influence of the European Commission had refused to follow the urgings of the IMF and devalue its currency and had instead instituted a policy of internal devaluation, with mixed opinions as to its success. Not only were models appearing that would eventually be used in Greece but also expectations were rising that a country requiring assistance would respond by taking actions that the outside world considered to be resolute.

Eastern Europe had provided some pointers as to how similar assistance packages might subsequently evolve within the euro area, but, as yet, there was no sign that any of its countries would require such help. Economic growth as a whole might be turning negative but, in late 2008, the area still seemed to be weathering the crisis more successfully than countries outside its bounds, like the United Kingdom. Indeed, the early indications were that the Greek economy in particular was performing well. When Alogoskoufis tabled the 2009 budget in October 2008, he forecast that the economy would continue to grow by 3.6 per cent of GDP in the coming year, although he lowered the 2008 figure a little to 3.4 per cent. He also amended the 2008 budget deficit target, raising it slightly from 1.6 per cent of GDP to 2.3 per cent and set a 2009 goal of 1.8 per cent.[40] However, increasing signs of strain were also starting to appear, with the October Purchasing Managers' Index (PMI) falling to 48.1, which pointed to a contraction of the economy rather than expansion. In November it dropped even further to 42.3. The Foundation for Economic and Industrial Research's (IOBE) economic sentiment index also hit a record low, crashing to 66.7, which was far below the 100.6 recorded at the beginning of the year.[41] These surveys, though, were only reflecting wider public opinion which was also turning increasingly pessimistic, partly due to media reporting of the global financial crisis, which left more people in Greece than any other EU country believing the world economy to be in a bad state. Indeed, at a time when economic conditions were deteriorating across the EU, people in Greece still tended to believe the domestic economy to be in a worse condition than that of any other member state, with many also expecting things to deteriorate further over the next twelve months.[42] Partly as a consequence, consumers continued to cut back on their purchases and later when the figures were revised it was revealed that growth had turned negative in the second quarter of the year.[43] Indeed, as early as June 2008 three-quarters of respondents in a survey had declared they were worried about their jobs but now, as a number of major companies began to lay off workers, unemployment became a major public concern.[44] In response the government at the beginning of December 2008 announced a €370 million package of benefit increases as well as a number of schemes designed to create tens of thousands of new jobs. Other steps also seem to have been taken to minimise the growth in unemployment, with it being reported that under recent regulations the whole staff of a food processing factory in Xanthi threatened with closure would be offered jobs in the local authorities of the area.[45] As a result of the growing economic gloom as the autumn turned to winter, the pressures and tensions of the crisis were increasingly reflected in the speeches of the leadership. Thus, while Alogoskoufis continued to say that debt was the 'Achilles' heel' and to stress that it needed to be reduced further, Karamanlis suggested that unemployment was now the greatest problem facing the country.[46] However, although it might now be generally accepted that the country was in crisis, the term was still being used very broadly and the idea was largely confined to Greece. Admittedly the spread with German bonds was continuing to widen, reaching 160 bps by the beginning of December 2008, but this was still broadly in line with the performance of the securities of other southern euro area states. Indeed, the increase was almost as much a consequence of German bond yields falling in reaction to the wider financial crisis, as investors turned to perceived low risk assets, as it was of their Greek equivalents rising. The deviation occasioned some comment in the local press, but the international media, even in relation to the evolving financial crisis in general, continued to look elsewhere for its stories.[47]

This situation was to change in the evening of Saturday 6 December 2008 when in the central Athenian district of Exarcheia, during an altercation with a group of youngsters, a uniformed police officer drew a gun and fired several shots, one of which killed fifteen-year-old Alexis Grigoropoulos.[48] The shabby streets of Exarcheia have long been the haunt of anarchists and other alternative voices and, as news of the shooting spread, crowds began to gather at both the scene of the death and in nearby university and polytechnic buildings. Soon improvised barricades were being thrown across streets and, when the police tried to intervene to remove them, they were pelted with petrol bombs and other missiles. Other young people, many of whom had left nearby bars and tavernas, joined the fray as the violence spread across the heart of the commercial centre of Athens. Amid clouds of tear gas and smoke as the police battled with the protesters the sound of sledgehammers breaking glass could also be heard. Hundreds of shop windows were smashed, many in a nihilistic expression of rage, but others with more obvious intent as store contents were looted. One of the most evocative photographs taken at this time shows two beheaded shop dummies stripped bare of their clothes lying amid burnt-out wreckage in the street. That night the authorities effectively lost control of the centre of Athens and the pattern was to be repeated sporadically through the coming nights in the capital and other larger urban centres. The media graphically caught the intensity of the disturbances but also exaggerated their extent.[49] At times the reports made it seem as if much of Athens was being torched but in the cold light of day the damage was less widespread. A few buildings were gutted by fire, including a library of the university, and perhaps a hundred cars were burnt, some lingering on the streets for several days cordoned behind red and white police tape. In daytime, Athens lay in a strange half-life, with people going about their daily lives passing by rows of shops whose windows were either smashed or lined with black bin bags, not to mourn lost business but to catch shards of glass if attacked afresh. Meanwhile, in Syntagma Square and elsewhere, crowds of youngsters continued to gather under protest banners, watched by curious onlookers, as detachments of riot police trotted by. Karamanlis had pledged that the state would protect its citizens but there was a tangible feeling of loss of control, and, at times, it seemed that only routines and norms stopped society breaking down. The day of the funeral of Alexis Grigoropoulos there were further skirmishes but by then the heat was dying out of the violence. Without leadership and focus the destruction had run its course, and the burning of a large Christmas tree erected in Syntagma Square, which some protesters saw as a symbol of material consumption, seemed to breach a symbolic line of public acceptance. On 10 December a rally organised by the two main union federations, the General Confederation of Workers of Greece (GSEE) and The Confederation of Civil Servants (ADEDY), attracted only a few thousand but brought some regularity to the protests and, with the beginning of the Christmas holidays, the violence eventually fizzled out. Until the end of December, though, hundreds of schools remained occupied, as pupils continued to protest largely outside the media gaze, offering apparent confirmation of the widely held belief that only violence could confer political visibility.[50]

The disturbances took the scale they did because of the large numbers who took to the streets, which made the response of the police uncertain. Under the hooded sweatshirts of those who were known in Greek as the *koukouloforoi* because of their attire there were many identities. Not just anarchists and other antiauthoritarian groups, but a supporting cast that included scores of teenagers radicalised during protests against New Democracy's education reforms as well as some immigrants. The protesters were helped by new technologies, including mobile phones and social media, which gave fresh abilities to coordinate actions—at one point secondary school pupils simultaneously demonstrated outside police stations across Athens and other parts of Greece—and this seems to have contributed to the police being caught off-guard and ill-prepared. They ran short of tear gas and at one point there even seems to have been a discussion about calling in the army to help quell the disturbances, with troops in bases close to Athens put on standby. Such a move would have been politically disastrous for a conservative government that was already trailing PASOK in the opinion polls, and so, instead, it seems to have mandated a defensive policy designed to protect state institutions and avoid inflaming the situation through further bloodshed.[51] This tactic probably prolonged the disturbances since it effectively gave the protesters control of the streets, which fuelled public discontent with the police response, but it was successful in avoiding further deaths. The disturbances were interpreted in various, sometimes contradictory ways. In one opinion poll taken shortly after the events about 60 per cent of respondents thought they had been something akin to a social revolt, while just under half saw them as spontaneous and not politically motivated.[52] Indeed, for many they were another link in a long chain of riots that stretched from the post-dictatorship marches on the American Embassy through demonstrations against visiting leaders such as Bill Clinton to protests against proposed reforms, especially those involving pensions or education.[53] Cast as the work of the usual malcontents, they could be seen as being little more than a formalised ritual of rebellion—a 'unique rite of passage of real battle'.[54] Such views did not necessarily discount the problems faced by young people but primarily they saw the events as an opportunistic outbreak of meaningless violence, which had been facilitated by a political culture that accepted or even encouraged such behaviour and was deeply suspicious of the police.[55] Others, however, traced more direct political intent, linking the disturbances with past events—even calling them a new *Dekemvriana* after the period in December 1944 when forces of the left-wing wartime resistance had battled with British and Greek government troops for control of Athens—while at the same time projecting them as 'an image from the future', which at least one commentator read as being apocalyptical.[56] In interpretations such as these, if not a full-scale social revolt or insurrection, the disturbances could be seen as an act of active resistance against prevailing political, social and economic orthodoxies.[57] This allowed them to be presented as both part of a wider anti-globalisation narrative foretelling the collapse of capitalism as well as a local howl of wrath or rage from a marginalised generation trapped by a failing education system in interminable degrees from which they would eventually graduate to find at best a job for which they were overqualified on an inadequate minimum wage.[58] Some though, while still seeing the disturbances as a rupture in traditional Greek political life, chose not to dwell on the violence but instead focused on the wider social mobilisation they saw as arising from the disturbances, highlighting the appearance of local community groups, including neighbourhood and student assemblies, although these were not particularly apparent to those not connected to the events at the time. They saw this 'diffuse, inarticulate, emergent political expression' as giving a voice to the previously invisible.[59] The most obvious was perhaps the solidarity movement which arose in support of Konstantina Kuneva, a Bulgarian union activist working for a company subcontracted to clean the electric railway in Athens, who was subject to a horrific sulphuric acid attack at this time, although it was not directly connected with the disturbances.[60] Her case helped bring the treatment of migrants and others termed 'precarious workers' into the mainstream debate and Kuneva later was elected a member of the European Parliament for the Coalition of the Radical Left (SYRIZA). Indeed, the links this party forged with these social movements was to be a factor in its subsequent rise, but at this time the increased visibility of migrant and other groups in an environment of crumbling state authority also brought forth other forces, with the first reports appearing of patrols of right-wing groups, like Golden Dawn, in inner city areas.[61]

There was much talk at the time of the disturbances being a historical moment and the possible harbinger of further discontent in Greece and elsewhere in Europe. The French President, Nicolas Sarkozy, was reported to have postponed education reforms in France because he feared they would provoke Greek-style unrest, and the former French Minister of Economy and Finance and Managing Director of the IMF, Dominique Strauss-Kahn, to have warned that similar social unrest could erupt elsewhere if economic inequalities were not addressed.[62] In fact, there were to be no further confrontations on the same scale in Greece until 2010 and the era of the memorandum, but at least one commentator afterwards, drawing parallels with Italy in the 1970s, wondered nonetheless whether the country had not entered 'a low intensity civil war'.[63] In the first months of 2009 there were a number of terrorist incidents, with one police officer shot outside the Ministry of Culture and another in front of Korydallos prison, as well as almost daily reports of blasts at the premises of banks, ministries and commercial ventures, usually by small gas-canister bombs.[64] On the 2 January 2009 it was reported that six banks and three car dealerships had been attacked in Athens alone and a further five banks in Thessaloniki along with a number of shops. Gangs of youths could also still go on the rampage. One group attacked the offices of the conservative newspaper *Apoyevmatini*, setting fire to cars parked outside, while another, disguised as carnival revellers, torched six Electric Railway Athens-Piraeus (ISAP) carriages late at night, allegedly causing about €16 million of damage. Such incidents combined to continue the narrative of the December disturbances that society was on the verge of collapse and that the government was barely in control. This sense was augmented by news reports of robberies, murders and kidnappings. In particular the authorities were made to look especially incompetent when two convicted criminals absconded from the roof of Korydallos jail by helicopter in an almost carbon copy re-enactment of an earlier escape they had made in 2006.[65] However, it was not just the crime reported on the television news each night that bred the feeling of hopelessness. Endless stories also circulated. Everybody seemed to have either been the victim of a robbery or a mugging themselves or to know somebody who had been. Conversation regularly returned to the migrants openly trading their wares on the pavements of the city centre, the drug addicts brazenly accosting passersby for money, and the gangs of people of different coloured skins roaming downtown Athens. People began to declare they were not only afraid to leave their homes at night but also to venture into certain areas of the city during the day. The December disturbances may have ended but unease and uncertainty were entering everyday life, a state of affairs caught in opinion polls which showed Greeks to be more pessimistic about their prospects than any other nation in the EU other than the Hungarians, who were already the recipients of an international assistance package.

This growing sense of pessimism coupled with anger was reflected in popular commentary. The furore over the bank recapitalisation plan had already sharpened these sentiments and now, in the wake of the disturbances and the deteriorating economic climate, a popular discourse started to emerge which also found expression on the world wide web where bloggers began to rail against the technocrats and politician-criminals who, they claimed, had ransacked the country. In bitter prose these usually anonymous voices condemned this group for their mafia-like business dealings and cuts on deals that had left Greece bleeding from debt. The money had been squandered on 'villas, [Porsche] Cayenne[s], boats, apartments, membership of tennis clubs, sea cruises...', leaving the ordinary citizen to pay for the excesses of 'Vatopedi... the greed of the bankers... [and] the criminals of the stock exchange'.[66] At the heart of much of the commentary was the sleek but invariably black top-of-the-range sports utility vehicle the Porsche Cayenne. Previously almost a subject of mockery, owned just to impress girls, they now became 'filthy Cayenne' driven by the 'the wrecks of the capitalist class... the editors, ministers and MPs [that] operate in the media, private television stations and the banks'. The same list of culprits appeared regularly—a leaflet circulating in Athens at the time declared 'We are in civil war with the fascists, the bankers, the state, the media wishing to see an obedient society'—but it was not new and neither was the theme of dominant and dominated.[67] At a party political level it was echoed in PASOK's claims that New Democracy served only the interests of the establishment and that it was treating the state as its own private fiefdom. Familiarity made the discourse politically effective, but it undercut any attempt to build social consensus for fiscal consolidation and reform, since responsibility for the crisis could be entirely pinned on a narrow privileged elite. It also offered a solution which was potentially painless to the vast majority of citizens, since it was almost universally believed that, if only the ill-gotten gains of this elite could somehow be retrieved by the state, sufficient money would be produced to rescue Greece from its fiscal predicament.[68] It was a simple argument but highly persuasive and totally credible not only to the vast majority of Greeks but also increasingly to the outside world, since it chimed so well with the emerging narrative that held that the misfortunes of Greece were due to profligacy and the inability of the state to gather sufficient revenues from its citizens.

The discourse further eroded the legitimacy of a New Democracy government which was already under pressure due to the Vatopedi scandal and public unease with its handling of both the disturbances and the economy. To try and regain the initiative on 7 January 2009 Karamanlis reshuffled his cabinet. Strikingly, none of those involved in dealing with the disturbances were replaced although some had offered to resign, but Alogoskoufis was dispatched in favour of his deputy, Yiannis Papathanassiou. Antonis Samaras also re-entered the government as minister of culture. The long-serving Alogoskoufis had won few friends within his party when he had changed the tax rates of the self-employed in 2008, and his brief departing statement that seemed to imply that in economic policy those that spend are not the ones who pay the price also suggests he may have had his differences with his colleagues over expenditure.[69] In contrast, his successor, Papathanassiou contented himself with some remarks about improving coordination and pushing ahead with reforms. The new finance minister was said to be liked by many in the business community because of his background as a former head of the Athens Chamber of Commerce and certainly his arrival produced a succession of policies giving support to small and medium sized enterprises. He revoked some of Alogoskoufis' controversial September 2008 measures, reduced taxes for companies working in tourism and offered state guarantees and grants to small businesses. The reshuffle was popular, particularly among New Democracy voters, and in an effort to further strengthen his position Karamanlis also took some steps to try and build a wider political consensus. A series of meetings were held with other political leaders but they showed little enthusiasm, with Papandreou in a speech in Ioannina declaring that seeking consensus without a plan was like giving a blank cheque to New Democracy to 'continue the looting of state coffers'.[70] In return Karamanlis could only bemoan the obstructionist tactics of the opposition. PASOK was now persistently ahead in the opinion polls, but it did not gain the type of lead that other opposition parties were enjoying elsewhere in the EU due to the wider financial crisis. Voters still seemed doubtful of its prescriptions. Nonetheless, the ruling party's continued low ratings in the polls led to tensions emerging, with a small group of rebellious parliamentary deputies ensuring its majority was never secure. Karamanlis imposed iron discipline and his government was never defeated in a parliamentary vote but these uncertainties made it difficult for him to achieve a consensus in favour of introducing tougher measures within his own party, let alone with the opposition.

After the disturbances, it was blithely said that it would take years to repair the damage, but most signs of the violence disappeared within weeks. Various claims were made about the overall cost, and the unrest may have contributed to a subsequent fall in tourism as well as a further decline in retail sales, but its longer-term effect seems to have been to reinforce existing tendencies. Dramatic images of confrontation, which had been splashed across television screens around the world, not only fed the myth that Greece was a society particularly prone to urban unrest but also prompted some outside reassessment, with a column in the *Financial Times* finishing, 'Not only has Greece gone on general strike; investors, increasingly, have too'.[71] The spread between Greek and ten-year German bonds, which until then had been widening at about the same rate across all the southern euro area states, started to diverge more sharply, although trading was thin, with the value of transactions in December 2008 only a quarter of a year before. On 18 December it reached 230 bps while in contrast the difference between Italian and German bonds was just 132 bps. At the beginning of 2009, the New Democracy government was therefore facing an increasingly difficult balancing act. Firstly, it needed to make sure that it could raise the considerable amount of funding it required for the year from the financial markets. Secondly, it had to persuade the European Commission and the members of the Ecofin Council that it was making a concerted effort to keep the budget deficit in check. Thirdly, it had to prevent the economy from plunging into a deeper recession which would merely aggravate the fiscal situation and could lead to it losing office. Trying to balance these three imperatives within the exigencies of the crisis was not to prove an easy task and the result was a succession of what often appeared to be contradictory policies, with some designed to raise revenue and curb spending while others sought to stimulate growth.

In 2009 Greece was confronted with the prospect of raising around €42 billion to cover its funding needs. This target, daunting enough in itself, was made more difficult by the fact that it faced considerable competition in attracting funds, since the eleven largest euro area economies alone were said to be seeking to raise an unprecedented €1.05 trillion at a time when banks and other institutions were still facing massive write-downs due to the wider financial crisis.[72] Indeed, this increased demand for funding and the surfeit of government securities that it produced was probably sufficient in itself to put upward pressure on yields at this time.[73] By December 2008, local analysts were already suggesting that international investors would probably buy no more than €10 to €15 billion of the Greek government bonds on offer in 2009 and the chances of them purchasing more diminished even further when, on 14 January 2009, in a move which took at least one commentator by surprise, Standard & Poor's downgraded Greece's sovereign rating from A to A-, citing structural weaknesses in fiscal management, including a longstanding overreliance on raising revenue rather than cutting expenditure. Papathanassiou's response to the downgrade was measured. He acknowledged that the main reason was Greece's continuing high debt and deficit levels but stressed that both were lower than they had been in 2004. Furthermore, they only remained elevated because of the 'government's decision to put the real economy and supporting weaker classes as a top priority' and that in such circumstances 'minimising deficits by ignoring social consequences cannot be a target'.[74] Nonetheless, the downgrade meant that Greek sovereign bonds were now perilously close to becoming ineligible as collateral at the ECB and in response the spread with German ten-year bonds on 24 January reached 300 bps.

Greece was not alone in coming under the scrutiny of the rating agencies as within days Standard & Poor's had also downgraded Spain and Portugal.[75] At the same time, the spread between German and Irish bonds was also rising as the authorities nationalised Anglo Irish Bank amid rumours that Ireland might be on the verge of approaching the IMF for assistance. Almost surreptitiously, the northern European banking crisis had started to evolve into a southern and western euro area sovereign debt crisis and this, in turn, sparked speculation about the future of the single currency itself.[76] These concerns were fully expressed in a 23 January 2009 article in *The New York Times* which bore the title, 'Once a boon, euro now burdens some nations'.[77] This openly raised the possibility that a euro area state might be forced into bankruptcy or even to leave the single currency before singling out Greece for having the worst problems, arguing that the country had run into trouble because of fiscal profligacy and a loss of economic competitiveness. This was to become the standard narrative line throughout the crisis but, nonetheless, the Greek interviewees espoused complete faith in both the country and the single currency, with the economist, Yiannis Stournaras, explicitly ruling out the possibility of bankruptcy and Greece leaving the euro. In the following weeks European policymakers were also equally adamant in their pronouncements. Trichet speaking at the Davos World Economic Forum insisted that there was no danger of the euro zone falling apart and the European Commissioner for Economic and Monetary Affairs, Joaquín Almunia, was equally clear, saying that there was zero possibility of this happening, before rhetorically asking, 'Who is crazy enough to leave the euro area?'[78] The message was that both Greece and the euro area as a whole were fully able to deal with the crisis but some seemed less certain. After a presentation by Provopoulos, in which he had urged the government to embark on a more rapid fiscal consolidation, the domestic newspapers the next day carried headlines about austerity amid warnings that otherwise the country might be facing bankruptcy.[79] This possibility was quickly ruled out by the government, but interviewed for *The New York Times* article the former New Democracy minister, Stefanos Manos, also said he could not be certain the situation would not 'spiral out of control', while the leader of the Popular Orthodox Rally (LAOS), Karatzaferis, was already pressing for the creation of a broad all-party government led by Papademos to 'exit the crisis'.[80]

Despite the public assurances of confidence, behind the scenes European Commission officials seem to have become increasingly concerned about the rising bond yields of a number of euro area states. The Italian Finance Minister, Giulio Tremonti, and Jean-Claude Juncker, the prime minister of Luxembourg, had already proposed some sort of debt union, possibly based on Eurobonds, but a number of states had objected to the idea, including Germany. Nonetheless, in an event in Düsseldorf in mid-February, presciently—but perhaps not in the way intended at the time—entitled 'The New Decade', the German Finance Minister, Peer Steinbrück, after openly admitting that a number of euro area states were facing problems, pragmatically continued, 'The euro-region treaties don't foresee any help for insolvent countries, but in reality the other states would have to rescue those running into difficulty'.[81] The statement was clear and forthright and, according to press comment at the time, the German Finance Ministry had been examining various options for helping troubled states. These it was said could involve Germany either issuing bonds itself on behalf of other euro area members or doing so as part of a group of countries, the creation of an emergency fund or some sort of action from the IMF. Commentators were already suggesting that the most likely option would be a combination of the last two, although much was to happen before this came to pass. The proposals were controversial, particularly the idea of an emergency fund, because this could be interpreted as running counter to various articles of the Treaty on the Functioning of the European Union. Article 122 allowed for the possibility of providing financial assistance but only when a member state was in difficulties 'caused by national disasters or exceptional occurrences beyond its control'. And Article 125, which stipulated that the Community should 'not be liable for or assume the commitments of central governments, regional, local or other public authorities' of another member state, had been widely interpreted, especially in Germany, as a 'no bail-out' clause making individual states responsible not only for their own debts but also for ensuring that their fiscal policies were sustainable.[82] Loans between member states were not explicitly proscribed but with Article 124 also prohibiting privileged access to financial institutions, it was easy enough for critics like Jürgen Stark, the chief economist of the ECB, to argue that any assistance was forbidden. Signs of future trouble were also apparent in *Der Spiegel's* reporting of Steinbrück's speech, which was subtitled, 'Will Germany have to bail out other EU states the way it is rescuing its banks and industry?' Nonetheless, Steinbrück's intervention, backed by similar assurances from the German Foreign Minister, Frank-Walter Steinmeier, has generally been seen as crucial in stabilising the financial markets and preventing the crisis from escalating at this time. Indeed, not only were the euro area states apparently willing to act in solidarity but the impression was also given that they had the means to do so, with Almunia on the 3 March explicitly stating that 'if a crisis emerges in one euro area country, there is a solution... before visiting the IMF... Don't fear for this moment—we are equipped intellectually, politically and economically to face this crisis scenario, but by definition these kinds of things should not be explained in public'.[83]

On the eve of the February 2009 Ecofin Council, the Greek government presented its annual updated stability and growth programme. Amid its stress on reducing state expenditure and supporting lower income groups, this raised the projected budget deficit for 2009 to 3.7 per cent of GDP. Presenting the programme, Papathanassiou emphasised it was not designed to impose austerity but to ensure growth which remained 'our strongest weapon against the crisis'.[84] Greece was by no means alone in projecting a budget deficit above 3.0 per cent of GDP. In response to the deepening recession a clutch of other euro area members had also increased expenditure above the reference value and, during the next few months, Papathanassiou regularly defended his policies by pointing out that the projected Greek figure was less than the area average, an argument that later made it difficult for him to revise the figure upwards. Nonetheless, with the 2007 budget deficit verified by Eurostat at over 3.0 per cent of GDP and the 2008 deficit forecast to be 3.4 per cent the European Commission concluded the problem was structural rather than cyclical and that Greece along with France, Spain, Ireland, Latvia and Malta should be placed under the first stage of its excessive deficit procedure (EDP).[85] In its report on the Greek stability programme the Commission, on the basis of the figures it was given, which projected continuing economic growth and a relatively small 2009 budget deficit, urged the government to act quickly to both consolidate state finances and implement structural reforms in areas such as pensions and labour laws. The government had already raised tobacco and alcohol duties, but on 25 February 2009 a further package was announced aimed at curbing pay and freezing recruitment in the public sector, reducing duplication in state agencies and rationalising health service procurements. However, the pay caps only applied to high earning managers and the recruitment freeze excluded many categories. In reality, public sector remuneration levels continued to rise and market sentiment was not influenced.[86] The spread continued to hover around 300 bps, with a ten-year bond issued on 11 March 2009 carrying a yield 1.27 per cent above a comparable October 2008 issue. Yet, only six weeks later, the spread had fallen to near 200 bps and, when a three year bond was reopened at the end of April to raise €7.5 billion, it was oversubscribed and placed at just 189.6 bps above a German four-year bond.

The decline in the spreads is often attributed to investors regaining confidence after Steinbrück and other politicians had been so emphatic in their assurances that they were prepared to act decisively to head off the emerging crisis and that assistance would be provided to any country running into difficulties. The tabling of an emergency budget in Ireland on 7 April 2009, which contained sharp tax increases and deep cuts in public spending, was also presented as being indicative of the resolve that euro area members as a whole were prepared to show in addressing the issue. A change in the global economic climate also probably helped, as the fall in the spreads took place at a time when the sense of crisis was ebbing, partly due to a belief that after the introduction of quantitative easing in the USA and the UK the ECB might be about to take similar steps to stimulate economic activity. Inside Greece the Public Debt Management Agency (PDMA) also played a role, as it offered easier to sell short-term T-bills and switched to placing bonds through syndicated sales to eliminate the risk of failure. Most importantly, though, the Greek commercial banks stepped in and began to buy large amounts of bonds. On 17 February 2009 the National Bank of Greece (NBG) announced that since the beginning of the year it alone had increased its holdings by just over a quarter, taking them to €10.7 billion.[87] The bank justified the purchases on the basis that it had previously been 'light' on government bonds, and, indeed, Greek sovereign debt had been in such demand from buyers outside the country since it had joined the euro that its holdings were far lower than they had been previously. It can also be argued that the NBG and the other Greek banks were following a general tendency for commercial banks to retain extensive holdings of the bonds of the state in whose jurisdiction they are headquartered, in part because it acts as the ultimate guarantor of the means of payment within this area.[88] However, the trade also made commercial sense, because the relatively high yielding bonds, which were still presumed to be effectively without risk, could be bought with money borrowed from the ECB at a far lower rate due to its non-standard measures. From the deal the banks not only stood to make a tidy profit from the differential in rates, enhancing their own bottom line, but they could also use the newly purchased bonds as collateral with the ECB to borrow more money. This would then allow them to buy more bonds in what came to be termed the 'sovereign-bank loop'.[89] This trade was not confined to Greece but seems to have been followed as unofficial policy throughout the euro area, with one estimate being that the commercial banks of member states increased their holdings of their respective governments' debt by €280 billion between October 2008 and August 2009. Later, a variant was openly endorsed by the European political leadership and popularly given the moniker the 'Sarko trade' in sections of the British media after the name of the French president. The understanding at this time seems to have been that in return for the ECB effectively supplying a closet fiscal stimulus through its longer-term refinancing operations (LTROs), which gave the banks access to unlimited finance providing adequate collateral was posted, member states would make sure that they controlled their budgetary deficits in a deal that one author terms the 'grand bargain'.[90] If this interpretation is correct, it might in part explain the anger displayed later in the year by the members of the ECB's governing council when it was revealed that Greece had so brazenly breached the deficit limit. Longer-term, the sovereign-bank loop was also to have catastrophic consequences for the Greek banks once the possibility of debt restructuring was raised, but in the late spring of 2009 the strategy seemed to be working. Eurostat announced that the 2008 budget deficit had in fact been

5.0 per cent of GDP instead of 3.6 per cent, but it hardly caused a ripple in the financial markets; and with a few minor hiccups along the way, yields continued to drop until on 24 July the PDMA was able to raise €1.9 billion through thirteen week T-bills bearing just 0.52 per cent. The issue, which was six times oversubscribed, took total borrowing for the year to €56 billion, well in excess of the €42 billion projected in January, yet rather than being perturbed by this the ten-year bond spread fell to 138 bps and, on average, coverage rates in 2009 were actually better than they had been in 2006.[91]

The immediate sovereign debt crisis might have ebbed but the recession was continuing to deepen led by a precipitate fall in demand. In January 2009 alone new car sales fell by 40 per cent and in the same month the economic sentiment index of IOBE declined to 55.4. This was its lowest level since the dark days of January 1990. Only Hungary had a worse reading in the EU and in February the index fell even further to 47.2. In the same month the PMI also hit a new record low of 38.9. Only the unemployment rate seemed to be rising. It reached 9.4 per cent in April 2009, with a survey by the Athens Chamber of Small and Medium Industries revealing that a quarter of its members had already shed labour.[92] The government had pledged €600 million to farmers after protests in January and, in the face of the continuing deterioration of the economy, somewhat to the suspicion of the IMF, at the beginning of April 2009 Papathanassiou announced a further package of spending. Apparently in part influenced by policies adopted elsewhere, this included a programme designed to boost car sales by cutting vehicle registration duty and other taxes.[93] Greece has no real indigenous car industry but the scheme was justified by the government on the basis that large numbers of people were employed in the import and sale of vehicles, which was also an important source of tax revenue. In a similar vein there were also programmes designed to refurbish older houses to make them more energy efficient and to replace out-of-date air conditioning systems. This attracted 110,402 applicants, double the initial target, boosting the cost to the state to €40 million, but with suppliers reportedly taking advantage of the situation to raise prices many consumers felt they gained little. These and other measures were not enough to turn growth positive but, together with increased spending prior to the June 2009 European Parliament elections, they seem to have led to an easing of the decline. Although still suggesting contraction, the PMI began to move upwards, as did the IOBE index quite sharply in June, recovering ten points. After March, in keeping with other stock markets, the ASE index also rebounded, continuing to climb until late autumn. Signs were detected that consumer confidence was returning, and some companies, including a property group, announced expansion plans. Moreover, the government's credit expansion targets were more or less being fulfilled, with both household and commercial borrowing still growing quite strongly until April, although by June it was starting to dwindle—a decline which was not unexpected, since in a recession healthy businesses and households tend to retrench and cut back on borrowing. With signs that the outlook might be brightening, the government clung to its optimistic predictions, despite the National Statistical Service (NSS) reporting that growth had turned negative in the second quarter, and more guarded projections from international organisations, such as the OECD and the IMF, although they continued to foresee any downturn as being relatively brief and shallow.[94]

The problem was that any success in lessening the decline in economic activity in the private sector had only been achieved through increasing public expenditure and deepening a budgetary deficit which the government was under pressure to diminish. An informal Ecofin Council held in Prague at the beginning of April had instructed that this should be brought below 3.0 per cent in 2010, and set a deadline of 24 October 2009 for the government to present measures to achieve this target.[95] In response Papathanassiou declared that the rising debt level was now the government's greatest concern, and with Juncker speaking of not fighting debt with new debt and deficits with new deficits, Almunia was asked to draw up a memo.[96] Presented to finance ministers during a July Eurogroup meeting, this explicitly warned that the Greek 2009 central government deficit, which is generally higher than the more regularly quoted general government deficit, might be double what had been budgeted and exceed 10 per cent of GDP.[97] Soon afterwards the IMF also gave its opinion on the state of the country's economy. It welcomed another batch of revenue raising measures announced in June, which included further tax increases on petrol, gambling and mobile telephony charges, but in noting that 'large and growing data discrepancies... between cash accounts and those of the SGP [stability and growth programme] could harbor a worse underlying deficit than currently reported' it suggested that this could amount to 5.9 per cent of GDP before concluding that 'fiscal consolidation can no longer be postponed'.[98] The official projection remained that the 2009 deficit would be 3.7 per cent of GDP but, with PASOK repeatedly suggesting that the increased public borrowing was derailing budgetary targets and IOBE ruling the target 'unfeasible', there were plenty of signs that it would be higher.[99]

By the summer of 2009 the sense of crisis in Greece was all pervasive. It did not just stem from the December disturbances or the collapsing economy but from every aspect of life. In this atmosphere it was all too easy to see the New Democracy government as weak and ineffective. However, it was struggling to cope not only with an embryonic sovereign debt crisis but also a sharp economic downturn from a very weak fiscal position. By the late summer the government was still able to secure a majority in parliament, there had been no recurrence of the December disturbances and, although the economy had slowed, there were signs that the decline was beginning to flatten out. The IMF was projecting that the country would fall into recession, but the government was still insisting that the economy would continue to grow, even if it was only by a small amount, which led one observer to opine, 'In a land where mythology has a special magic, a new myth has been born that the flourishing black market... will somehow protect the economy from the full force of the crisis'.[100] To most Greeks, though, it was the weakness of the economy rather than the budget deficit that was the main challenge facing the country. Indeed, writing in November 2008, one well-informed local commentator had suggested that the greatest mistake Alogoskoufis had made was to overestimate the threat of a return to European Commission supervision and underestimate the economic crisis.[101] Well into the summer of 2009, New Democracy continued to receive relatively high ratings in the opinion polls and its performance in the June European Parliament elections, which Papandreou had urged should be treated as a 'referendum of condemnation', was no disgrace.[102] Indeed, a Eurobarometer poll taken in the summer of 2009 recorded figures of trust in government which were not that far off the EU average and strikingly not greatly different than before the December disturbances.[103] The government had weathered the onset of the crisis and, despite the urging of the opposition, the prospect of a general election was not immediate. However, PASOK had made it clear that it would force an election in the spring of 2010—when parliament was due to choose a new president—by blocking whoever New Democracy proposed, even if it was the veteran PASOK incumbent Karolos Papoulias. Karamanlis was thus forced to choose between waiting until the spring, when he could have cast PASOK as being opportunistic, or going to the polls in the autumn. In the end he decided to choose the latter, giving PASOK the chance to grasp the poisoned chalice of dealing with the country's growing problems.

4

EVEN IN OUR WORST NIGHTMARES[1]

THE PAPANDREOU GOVERNMENT, THE SOVEREIGN DEBT CRISIS AND THE SIGNING OF THE MEMORANDUM

The old man wandering along the school corridor through the slanting rays of sun carried a wooden pole that was almost as tall as him. Festooned with colourful slips of paper it invited passers-by to try their luck. Someone asked 'who let him in here' but on a sunny October afternoon in 2009 it did not seem altogether inappropriate for a lottery ticket seller to be roaming the corridors of an Athenian school-cum-polling station. In the face of the problems confronting the country the voters could be excused for thinking that casting their ballot was little more than a game of chance. At the time there was much speculation about why Karamanlis had called an early poll but he insisted it was the state of the economy that had determined his choice, and on the very day the general election was announced Papathanassiou at an informal Economic and Financial Affairs (Ecofin) Council meeting in Brussels had handed to Almunia revised data that was described as 'less than optimistic'.[2] The widespread perception was that the New Democracy government had run out of steam. Its reputation had been tarnished by its poor handling of the December 2008 disturbances, the endless talk of scandal, the faltering economy and a clumsy response to another outbreak of forest fires around Athens in the summer of 2009. Yet, although the Panhellenic Socialist Movement (PASOK) was ahead in the opinion polls, there was no certainty it would gain sufficient seats to rule. Many voters professed themselves to be undecided and others continued to say they found the premier the more plausible leader. However, at the end of the day, even Karamanlis could not save New Democracy from its worst ever defeat and, with the help of the reinforced electoral system, PASOK was able to obtain 160 seats in the 300 seat parliament.[3] Yet rather than being won by PASOK, which gained an extra quarter of a million votes, the election in many ways was lost by New Democracy whose vote fell by nearly three quarters of a million. Relatively few of these electors seem to have transferred their vote directly to PASOK. Most either switched to the Popular Orthodox Rally (LAOS), which was the only party to see a significant improvement in its vote, augmenting its representation in parliament by five seats, or were lost in the higher than usual number of abstentions. The other two major parties, the Communist Party of Greece (KKE), still led, as it had been since 1991, by Aleka Papariga, lost a few votes, as did the Coalition of the Radical Left (SYRIZA), headed by the young, newly appointed Alexis Tsipras, who had first gained prominence when he had stood for the mayoralty of Athens in the 2006 local elections. The overwhelming majority of electors had still chosen to vote for the twin behemoths of Greek politics and yet, when asked in an opinion poll, who they thought would form the best government, nearly half said neither PASOK nor New Democracy.

When the new premier, Giorgos Papandreou, announced his cabinet it contained a record nine female members and this, together with the inclusion of some new faces in their forties, who were seen as being close to the prime minister, such as the Minister of Finance, Giorgos Papaconstantinou, gave the impression that it was a break from the past. Its public approval rating was also high, with 83 per cent in an opinion poll expressing a positive view, even more than after the installation of the New Democracy government in 2004.[4] Nevertheless, it was the experienced Andreas Loverdos and Michalis Chrysochoidis who were voted the most trusted ministers in an opinion poll, and their inclusion, alongside such PASOK veterans as Theodoros Pangalos, who became deputy prime minister, and Papandreou's erstwhile rival for the leadership, Venizelos, meant that the new cabinet was not without familiar faces. In a brief victory statement Papandreou spoke of bringing back hope and smiles to the faces of Greeks and, after the troubled last months of the previous administration, a new spirit of optimism did seem to be in the air.[5] The Foundation for Economic and Industrial Research's (IOBE) economic sentiment index climbed to its highest level for a year, although it was still some way below the European average.[6] Outside Greece, PASOK's electoral triumph brought relatively little comment apart from some asides about the dynastic traits of Greek politics.[7] Foreign funds continued to invest in the Athens Stock Exchange (ASE), whose main index had risen 45 per cent since the beginning of the year, far outstripping increases in other European indexes such as the London FTSE and Frankfurt DAX. The euro remained stable and the spread between German and Greek ten-year bonds even decreased a little to 126 bps, a far cry from the 300 bps it had reached earlier in the year. The only potential blot on the landscape was a comment from a senior director of Fitch Ratings when asked about Greece's sovereign debt rating, who said he thought it should be secure providing there was no surprise revision of fiscal data.[8]

Inside Greece the crisis was still largely seen in terms of the downturn in the economy and to tackle this Papandreou during the electoral campaign had outlined an ambitious package of measures designed to rekindle growth. He had promised above inflation pension and public sector wage rises, debt relief for companies and individuals, and increased public investment in areas such as education, research and development, and green technology.[9] The government would also follow an 'aggressive policy' protecting employees from employers, make solidarity payments to poorer members of society, freeze utility bills, give subsidies to promote employment and gradually raise unemployment benefit to 70 per cent of the basic wage.[10] The package was priced at €3 billion but, when questioned, the PASOK leader, repeating a statement he had been making since at least 2007, reiterated that the money was available.[11] After the election, Papandreou continued to espouse many of the same policies but, when he faced parliament on 16 October, along with talk of a new campaign against tax evasion and moves to increase the transparency of government and deal with the 'unprecedented lack of competitiveness', there was also a fresh sense of urgency and alarm as he spoke of the economy being in a 'state of emergency' due to 'large hidden debts and spending'.[12] The root cause of this new tone was the public acknowledgement, just a few days before, that the 2009 budget deficit was going to be far greater than previously projected. Despite a stream of negative economic indicators and suggestions that it would be higher from the European Commission and the International Monetary Fund (IMF), New Democracy in public had maintained its revised deficit projection of 3.7 per cent of GDP until the beginning of the election campaign, when Papathanassiou, almost in passing, had mentioned in an emailed response to questions from Bloomberg that he now expected it to be in the region of 6.0 per cent.[13] Subsequently a slightly higher figure appeared in the press and prior to the ballot both Karamanlis and Papandreou also seem to have been warned by Provopoulos that it could be greater.[14] However, when it emerged immediately after the election that the deficit would be at least 12 per cent, this, according to Papaconstantinou, was beyond what PASOK had envisaged 'even in our worse nightmares....'[15] Indeed, even a projection of 12.5 per cent made by the minister of finance at a press conference following the October 2009 Ecofin Council was not to be the end of the matter because, after Eurostat had used new powers it had been granted to exhaustively work through the Greek books, in November 2010 it signed off on a figure of 15.4 per cent, almost eight times greater than the original target.[16]

In his first statement to Eurogroup colleagues, Papaconstantinou blamed the raising of the deficit forecast on the negative economic environment, which had brought increased public spending and lower revenues, the effects of the electoral cycle and the 'omission of certain expenditure items'; but, later, in a letter sent to Almunia on 30 October 2009, he pinned more of the blame on a collapse in revenues.[17] This in part may have arisen as an unintended consequence of a change in the law by the previous government designed to help small and medium sized businesses weather the recession by staggering VAT payments. This apparently not only produced an immediate shortfall but also disrupted the pattern of payments as some companies almost ceased paying a tax that contributed about a fifth of all government revenues.[18] The raising of the projected deficit proved highly controversial. At home allegations were made that PASOK had added losses from public enterprises that had previously not been entered into the government accounts so as to be able to take the political credit for a subsequent reduction in the figure in 2010, and afterwards it became a matter of parliamentary inquiries and possible criminal proceedings.[19] Abroad, when he attended the October 2009 Ecofin Council in Luxembourg, Papaconstantinou, by his own admission, found his European colleagues 'frustrated and angry'.[20] Aside from any rancour caused by the wayward 2009 figures, their ire was also provoked by the fact that two completely different sets of data for the 2008 budget deficit were being submitted before and after the election, with the second being 2.1 per cent of GDP higher than the first. Afterwards, Juncker could scarcely conceal his unhappiness when he openly declared 'The game is over—we need serious statistics'.[21] As in 2004, when Greek data had last been seriously called into question, Eurostat was asked to draw up a report and, when this was released, it suggested that the discrepancy between the two sets of figures for 2008 was due to various factors. These included the addition of previously unrecorded hospital liabilities and an overlooked transfer to the Public Power Corporation (DEH) pension fund, as well as an over-recording of surpluses from social security funds and methodological weaknesses which led to an overestimation of tax revenue.[22] In a damning assessment the report found not only technical flaws within the procedures of the National Statistical Service (NSS) and in several other authorities that provided it with data but also other failings, including an 'absence of written instruction and documentation, which leave the quality of fiscal statistics subject to political pressures and electoral cycles'.[23] The government responded to the criticism by embarking on a major overhaul of the statistics service, upgrading its status, giving it a new name, the Hellenic Statistical Authority (EL.STAT), and greater independence under a president and a nine-person board of directors. And, after Eurostat lifted a reservation on Greek data on 15 November 2010, subsequent relations between the two statistical agencies appear to have been amicable. In particular, there have been no caveats about the Greek figures recorded in the European agency's biannual press release on deficit and debt data, which is in marked contrast to previous years.[24] However, the revision of the statistical data had sowed seeds of distrust which continued to influence policymaking, with the depth of feeling vividly caught by a comment Trichet is reported to have made in a television interview many months later in March 2010 when he declared, 'The Greeks provided wrong figures, something that is absolutely unforgivable and must never be repeated'.[25]

The new 2009 deficit projection meant that Greece was clearly going to breach the 3.0 per cent Stability and Growth Pact reference value, but it was not alone, with Ireland, Spain and Portugal all heading towards double digit deficits and France also forecasting a substantial overshoot. These higher figures were partly due to the adoption of programmes to offset the impact of the financial crisis but, as the first signs of economic recovery began to appear, the mood within the euro area under the influence of a newly elected and more conservative German government was beginning to shift, with the press release of the October Ecofin Council speaking of the need for 'a coordinated strategy for exiting from the broad-based policies of stimulus' and 'substantial fiscal consolidation'.[26] The switch in policy remained controversial. It contrasted with the quantitative easing introduced by both the USA and UK as part of a broader policy of providing greater assistance for the private sector to allow it to recover and was questioned by the authorities of a number of states, including France. They argued that it was too early to think of retrenchment, and this gave some commentators hope that the Greek government's plan to reduce its deficit through additional revenues generated by its own ambitious stimulus package might find favour. However, in talks with EU officials the atmosphere according to the PASOK spokesman had been 'exceptionally negative'.[27] The other ministers, though, did recognise that the new deficit projection for

2009, together with the increase in the 2008 figure, made it impossible for Greece to meet the goal of lowering its deficit below 3.0 per cent of GDP by 2010, which they had established at the beginning of the year. A new target would have to be set. The revision of the fiscal data also led Fitch to make good its earlier warning and on 22 October it downgraded Greece's sovereign debt rating from A to A− with a negative outlook. The response of the financial markets was low key, as it had been when the deficit projection had been raised in the first place, perhaps because it was more or less expected. There were no dramatic movements in the ASE index and the spread between Greek and German ten-year bonds remained steady, fluctuating between 130 and 139 bps. With global interest rates low, there was still demand for higher yielding government securities and the prevailing consensus remained that 'despite the high macro risk' Greek bonds were still effectively a risk-free investment since its European partners would not allow the country to fail.[28] Commission officials were not alone in believing that the establishment of the euro had effectively ended the possibility of any of the participating countries defaulting on their debts and, as a result, at the beginning of November, Greece was still able to syndicate €7 billion of fifteen-year bonds with only a slightly higher yield.[29]

Perhaps partly due to the calmness of the market reaction and the differing opinions within the Ecofin Council about when fiscal consolidation should begin, the government's response to the higher than projected deficit appeared equally low key. At one level, it gave every indication of being aware of the problem. After all, Papandreou had spoken of an 'emergency situation' and the government spokesman, in a speech at the beginning of November 2009, starkly warned that the country was 'on the verge of bankruptcy'.[30] There were also reports that the premier had met a team from Goldman Sachs to discuss the possibility of using financial instruments to extend the maturities of debts within the healthcare system and, although nothing seems to have come of this, within days of returning from the October Ecofin Council Papaconstantinou had written to Almunia promising to reform public finances.[31] Yet, at the same time, the government still only spoke about the deficit falling to single digits in 2010 as part of a 'medium-term reduction to 3 per cent of GDP' and, in general, the focus of policy seemed to be more on fulfilling election commitments than dealing with a fiscal situation which sometimes appeared to be treated more as rhetorical device to offload responsibility and lambast the opposition than a problem to solve.[32] Thus, an early bill designed to raise €1.6 billion through special taxes on the largest companies and wealthiest individuals was tabled not to reduce the deficit but to fulfil an election pledge to support those on lower incomes. The cautious response may have been driven by the fact that opinion polls were already turning against the new government, with a majority of respondents in one already expressing dissatisfaction with its performance and less than a third happy with the direction the country was heading.[33] The government also had to transcend the customary settling in period, with the process being more prolonged than usual due to a decision to open up ninety senior administrative appointments to online applications, which produced thousands of responses and led to some posts remaining unfilled at Christmas. Thus, although the government entered office with a flurry of announcements and proposals, the overall impression during its first months was as much of dysfunction as dynamism.[34]

During this time, the new government also faced little challenge from the main opposition party, as New Democracy retreated into a protracted leadership contest in order to choose a successor to Karamanlis, who had resigned following the party's poor showing during the election. It was only in late November that Antonis Samaras was pronounced the victor after defeating Dora Bakoyanni. The new leader benefited from the ambiguous feelings many within the party continued to harbour about the period in office of Bakoyanni's father, Konstantine Mitsotakis, as well as a more general backlash against what was perceived as dynastic politics. Most of all, though, the lack of a more decisive response was attributed to splits within PASOK, with Papandreou facing repeated questioning about divisions at a press conference. The stories inevitably boiled down to suggestions that a populist faction within the party was opposing attempts by certain ministers to take more decisive actions to curb the deficit and, indeed, an attempt at this time to freeze public sector salaries and pensions above €2,000 a month was opposed by a group of PASOK deputies. Arguing that the government should adhere to its election pledges, they suggested that any savings would be modest and that it would be wrong to ask people on such relatively low salaries to bear the cost of the crisis.[35] Unsure as to the seriousness of the situation, many ministers displayed similar doubts particularly because any switch to fiscal retrenchment would have meant not only the party abandoning its whole strategy for combating the crisis but also a fundamental revision of the model on which the Greek economy had come to rest, and this was a challenge which New Democracy had also been either unable or unwilling to face.

In keeping with the promise made to Almunia in his October letter, on the eve of the November Ecofin Council, Papaconstantinou tabled a draft 2010 budget that proposed to shave 3.3 per cent of GDP off the projected general government deficit, reducing it from 12.7 per cent in 2009 to 9.4 per cent. However, since a number of items of expenditure from 2009, such as election expenses, were non-recurring, the extent of any proposed adjustment could be questioned, especially, since the budget also continued to project higher than inflation rises in salaries and pensions, a one-off subsidy to low income families and the recruitment of an extra 3,000 staff within the health service.[36] There was little immediate reaction in the financial markets to the proposed budget. Stocks on the ASE index registered a small rise the next day and the spread remained at 139 bps. In the press release issued after the 10 November Ecofin Council the ministers also confined themselves to expressing 'regrets' about the renewed problems with Greek statistics and inviting the European Commission to produce a report on the issue which would propose 'appropriate measures'.[37] However, the next day the European Commission with the consent of the relevant member states issued its judgement on whether 'effective action' had been taken to reduce budgetary deficits following the recommendations it had given in April 2009. The Commission found that Spain, France, Ireland and the United Kingdom had broadly met its expectations but that Greece had not, noting that more than half of its expenditure overrun could be attributed to 'higher-than-budgeted outlays for compensation of employees and increased capital spending'.[38] Afterwards, at a press conference, Almunia underlined that Greece's public finances had become a source of concern for the euro area as a whole, and that as a consequence the country needed not only 'a very ambitious and determined fiscal consolidation strategy over the medium-term' but also institutional reforms able to deliver 'structural and fiscal adjustments'.[39] Facing questions from the media, Papaconstantinou accepted that, when a timetable was revealed in the New Year, this would inevitably mean Greece falling under the second stage of the excessive deficit procedure (EDP) and being placed under supervision, but, like Alogoskoufis before him, he played down the consequences, denying that it would mean a review of EU funding to the country or the appointment of a commissioner in Athens. Nonetheless, when the draft budget was handed to the speaker of parliament on a USB stick rather than the traditional hard copy on 20 November, the figures had been further refined, so that the deficit would now be cut to 9.1 per cent of GDP, partly due to limiting public sector wage rises to 1.5 per cent, with the 40,000 earning more than €2,000 per month receiving nothing extra.[40] There was also to be a public sector hiring freeze in 2010 and a one recruitment for every five departures policy in 2011.

External pressure was mounting for the government to respond more decisively to the rising deficit and, when he unveiled the budget, Papaconstantinou mentioned that his European colleagues wanted to see deeper cuts in state expenditure to reduce it faster. However, the government was also faced with growing indications that domestic economic activity was again starting to slow, with the Purchasing Managers' Index (PMI) in November dropping to a six month low of 47.3. The European Commission in its autumn economic forecast was equally pessimistic, predicting negative growth of 1.1 per cent of GDP in 2009 and 0.3 per cent in 2010, and, as a consequence, that the budget deficit would remain above 12 per cent in 2010.[41] Papaconstantinou rejected this, saying the projection had been made 'without taking into account the change in policy' outlined in the budget, but the growth forecast led to a renewal of speculation that Greece might be unable to cope with its burgeoning debt levels.[42] These concerns were further reinforced on 13 November 2009 when the NSS announced that during the third quarter of the year the economy had contracted by 0.3 per cent of GDP compared with the second.[43] For the first time since the spring, the spread between Greek and German bonds began to widen, and it is possible that the divergence may have been amplified by a technical change made at this time which lengthened the settlement period for bond trading on the Bank of Greece's secondary trading platform in an effort to lessen the number of failed sales.[44] This extra time, it has been argued, gave greater opportunity for speculative short selling, which put pressure on bond yields at this key juncture. The issue became politically controversial and its impact cannot be easily separated from other factors present at this time, but a similar move in Italy two years later also reportedly produced a spike in yields.[45] However, in the autumn of 2009 the change in settlement dates went almost unnoticed by the media, which was far more preoccupied by growing indications that the European Central Bank (ECB) was determined to exit as soon as possible from the non-standard measures it had introduced the year before to try and alleviate the financial crisis.[46] This would mean that its minimum credit rating threshold for collateral would rise again from BBB– to A–, which could potentially pose particular problems for Greece, whose sovereign debt was already rated at this level by both Fitch and Standard & Poor's. The discussion about withdrawal from the non-standard measures might have been prompted, as was suggested, by the fact that the financial crisis appeared to be ebbing and the euro area as a whole was returning to growth but, as in 2005, it could also be interpreted as being part of a strategy to place pressure on states running high budget deficits. Certainly, Trichet in an interview at this time, without mentioning Greece by name, drew a clear distinction between those countries in a 'relatively favourable position because their past management was wise and prudent' and those 'already very close to losing their credibility' before pointedly continuing, 'The success of the recovery in Europe depends on the confidence of investors in the creditworthiness of sovereign issuers. If this confidence is lacking, investors will require higher market interest rates, which would penalise both the public and private sectors of the country concerned'.[47] Over the following weeks, this message was repeated by a stream of ECB governing council members, who stressed that Greece would ultimately be forced into a correction, if not by the other euro area governments, then, by the markets. And, as one Greek economist remarked in an interview, if that was to happen, the adjustment would be 'violent'.[48]

The possibility that the non-standard measure might come to an end caused particular concern because Greek banks, unable to access wholesale money markets, had become increasingly reliant on the ECB for capital. The Governor of the Bank of Greece, Provopoulos, who attended ECB governing council meetings every two weeks, had drawn attention to this situation, and now rumours started to circulate that the Greek central bank was advising local commercial banks to show restraint when applying for funds at the ECB's forthcoming 15 December 2009 one-year longer-term refinancing operation (LTRO), which it was said might be the last.[49] These rumours coupled with the news that the economy was contracting faster than expected and continuing doubts about the budget seem to have been sufficient to cause the ASE index to fall, with bank shares leading the way. To try and calm the markets the Bank of Greece issued a statement late on 16 November admitting that it had counselled the banks show restraint when participating in the LTRO, but stressing that 'in no way does this advice constitute a ban, and furthermore, it has nothing to do with the Greek government bonds which banks own or would like to purchase'.[50] Nonetheless, the doubts of earlier in the year were beginning to return. Provopoulos, addressing a parliamentary committee on 24 November, was quoted as saying that further downgrades could leave the Greek banks in the 'position of not drawing liquidity from the ECB because of the risk [Greek] bonds may not be accepted [as collateral]' and the next morning in its headlines a leading newspaper raised the possibility of bankruptcy.[51] This message was delivered to a local audience but overseas financial markets were also beginning to take note of events in Greece. A return more than double the euro area average had helped make Greek bonds especially attractive to foreign investors so far that year, and this had led the ten-year spread at one point in August 2009 to drop to 104 bps. However, in a matter of two weeks it had now risen by over 70 bps. This volatility caught the eye of foreign traders who thrive on such movements, leading one newspaper to report that Goldman Sachs had issued a research note which made a reference to the distress sign used by the Gotham City Police to summon Batman when it said, 'As far as the bond vigilantes are concerned, the Bat-Signal is up for Greece'.[52]

More fuel was then added to the mix from an unexpected source, when Dubai World, the state-run investment vehicle for Dubai, which had invested heavily in property development in the emirate, announced it was seeking a six-month standstill agreement with creditors and an extension of loan maturities on $59 billion of debt. The news led stock markets to fall across the world, but in Western Europe it was the ASE index which recorded the largest decline, with bank shares again recording the greatest losses. The next day the index recovered but the woes of Dubai World had helped rekindle speculation about sovereign default, as media coverage directly linked Dubai with Greece and Iceland, which had avoided defaulting on its debts in 2008 but left foreign creditors of its nationalised banks nursing large losses.[53] To try and stabilise the situation both Papaconstantinou and Provopoulos made statements stressing that the volatility in the bond markets had been due to the activities of speculators and that the domestic banks were solidly financed. However, more decisive than these soothing words was almost certainly continued purchasing of bonds by these banks, with the National Bank of Greece later admitting that it had bought €1.8 billion since the beginning of November, justifying its acquisitions by declaring that during 'the recent period of high volatility in spreads, the bank protected its large investment position in Greek government bonds and supported the market in the belief that fears concerning the Greek economy, banks and government were excessive'.[54] The actions of the banks helped stabilise the market and forced investors who had sold short Greek government securities to buy them back, and as a result the ten-year bond spread by 1 December had eased back to 172 bps. The immediate pressure had been, at least temporarily, stemmed but in its midst Deutsche Bank on 25 November 2009 had issued a note which suggested that the European Commission might recommend Greece apply to the IMF for assistance if normal funding mechanisms failed.[55] Until this point the general presumption had been that it would be the euro area that would come to Greece's aid if necessary, but now the mood was changing and this was caught in the title of an article in the *Financial Times* a few days later: 'Greece can expect no gifts from Europe'.[56] The picture was far from clear, with some leaders continuing to voice solidarity, but, after the controversy over the statistics, it seems that rather than any possible spill-over from a hypothetical Greek default, the chief problem for many had become moral hazard. This was largely perceived in terms of ensuring Greece did not escape from the adverse consequences of what was seen as ill-considered fiscal behaviour, by allowing it to pass on the costs to fellow euro area members. Hence, increasingly the refrain was that Greece's problems had to be 'resolved' by the Greek government, political parties and society, even if rumours continued to circulate that behind the scenes technical committees were working on an assistance programme, although, according to the IMF, both the European and Greek authorities ruled out the involvement of the Fund at this stage.[57]

On 2 December 2009 Moody's issued a report saying that it believed investors' fears that the Greek government faced a short-term liquidity crisis were misplaced.[58] There was some truth in this, since there was no talk of the ECB reversing its non-standard measures before the end of 2010. However, with various ECB governing council members continuing to stress that no country could be granted an exemption from the regulations the other agencies were not prepared to take such a relaxed view, and on 8 December Fitch announced a downgrade to BBB+ with negative outlook.[59] It was the first time in ten years that Greece's sovereign rating had fallen below A with any of the main agencies. Fitch's reasoning for the downgrade was couched in the formal language of the rating agencies but it was interpreted by market commentators as being due to the fact that the draft budget did not contain deeper and more lasting cuts in public expenditure. Similar sentiments were also traceable in a statement issued by Almunia on 8 December when, after noting that Greece had drawn 'the attention of financial markets and rating agencies' and acknowledging that the draft budget was an 'important step in the right direction', he added that 'more measures are required'.[60] The strategy of the government at this stage, though, seems to have been more focused on winning back the trust of both the markets and European colleagues through offering a series of candid and open appraisals of the problems confronting Greece. Indeed, for Papandreou the greatest obstacle facing the country was its lack of credibility, and in an effort to repair this he and Papaconstantinou were to give countless interviews to the media and to make some unusually frank speeches.[61] None more so than when Papandreou addressed the European Council on 10 December 2009 on the subject of corruption and, in the words of one account, delivered 'a short, blunt speech that said everything the rest of Europe had long known, or suspected, about Greek bureaucracy'.[62] The aim seems to have been to both persuade European partners that the new government could be trusted and also to make them aware that the country's many problems could only be solved through a deeper socio-economic transformation which had to be built on social consensus. This meant that there was little point in Greece following the same route as countries such as Ireland, which had just tabled a budget cutting public sector wages and welfare payments, and adopting what were portrayed in Greece as a few headline grabbing measures to reassure the markets. Instead, as Papandreou emphasised in a televised speech from the Zappeion Hall in Athens on 14 December 2009 the nation had to come together to solve the country's economic problems through dialogue. Speaking 'as a Greek' and 'a patriot', to repeated applause from his audience in his address he nonetheless mostly stuck to well-trodden themes, as he stressed the importance of protecting middle-income households and the most vulnerable, while declaring his willingness to tackle patron-client relations as well as vested interests, and to curb tax evasion and corruption. In contrast the few specifics were largely superficial, amounting to little more than the closure of some overseas press offices, which would be absorbed by Greek embassies, and a promise to freeze the bonuses paid to the high-ranking executives of banks controlled by the state and to tax those of private financial institutions at a rate of 90 per cent. Papandreou's caution was perhaps understandable given the fact that his speech was delivered so close to the first anniversary of the 2008 disturbances. More specific measures would also have undermined the budget then passing through parliament, and the government was already committed to outlining a fuller reform agenda in a forthcoming revised stability programme but, nonetheless, the speech can be seen as a missed opportunity. The Greek press predictably divided on party lines, but outside the country few seem to have been impressed, with one financial analyst in London remaking that the Greek premier had said 'too little new' and another lamenting his failure to outline explicit deficit reduction measures.[63] However, whether the announcement of these would have been sufficient to turn the tide of opinion at this time remains debatable, because the outside media and the financial markets, apparently already having decided that the Greek position was hopeless, were becoming increasingly fixated with the question of whether or not the country would be offered a package of assistance that, in keeping with the parlance of EU treaties, was usually referred to as a 'bail-out'.[64] Following the line of Moody's 2 December report, the problem for many outside observers was no longer one of short-term liquidity but long-term solvency.

Just two days after Papandreou's speech, on 16 December, Standard & Poor's joined Fitch in also downgrading Greece to BBB+ with credit watch negative.[65] This meant that if the third of the major agencies, Moody's, also lowered its rating, the country's bonds would become ineligible as collateral with the ECB if it reverted as planned to its pre-crisis requirements. One economist called it a 'bizarre and ultimately untenable situation', yet senior ECB governing council members continued to insist that no special exception could be made in the case of Greece and it was up to the country itself to take the necessary steps to regain the confidence of the markets and recover its A rating by the end of 2010.[66] In the end, the downgrade by Moody's on 22 December 2009 to A2, which is the equivalent of Standard & Poor's A, was less than expected and in response the bond spread eased. The company's lead sovereign analyst for Greece explained the decision by saying it had been made on the assumption that the ECB would change its rules on collateral if necessary and that the Greek government would shortly table more concrete proposals.[67] These appeared on 14 January 2010 as part of a revised 2010–2013 stability and growth programme. To forestall possible objections, this seems to have been drawn up with the aid of a team from the European Commission and the ECB, with an IMF delegation, which was in Athens at the time, apparently contributing technical advice and 'initial roadmaps for fiscal structural reforms'.[68] The new programme proposed a sharper reduction in the deficit, which would be lowered by 4.0 per cent of GDP from its latest projection of 12.7 per cent to 8.7 per cent in 2010, followed by further falls until 2013 by when it would stand at just 2.0 per cent. During this time debt would peak at 120.6 per cent of GDP in 2011. The document began by acknowledging that the crisis was predominantly endogenous and that the functioning of the state and civil administration was the 'main parameter of the "Greek problem".[69] It, then, detailed and quantified a series of fiscal consolidation measures for 2010 as well as a broad programme which was designed to curtail costs, enhance the efficiency of public spending and boost economic competitiveness by improving the functioning of labour and product markets. The new programme appeared to meet most of the concerns outlined by the European Commission but, as they left Athens, it was reported that its officials were still unhappy about the vagueness of the plan after the first year and that they were expecting the government to table further adjustment measures before it was approved.

The messages continued to be mixed. At one level, the outside political discourse was becoming in general more supportive or at least less critical. However, elsewhere, financial analysts were continuing to question the economic performance projections, suggesting they were over-optimistic, and to wonder if the country was solvent enough to survive without a financial assistance programme. There was also much speculation as to whether the European Commission's verdict on the programme would be positive, but at this point investors still appeared to be willing to suspend their doubts in the search for yield. This meant that Greece continued to be able to raise money through syndicated loans, with demand for a five-year bond on 25 January 2010 so high that the Public Debt Management Agency (PDMA) was able to place €8 billion rather than a planned €5 billion, with many of the orders coming from abroad. However, it was only with a yield of around 6.2 per cent, and with the media in Greece and abroad awash with speculation about a possible default or rescue packages involving not only the euro area and the IMF but also the Chinese, Russians or various sovereign wealth funds, the spread between the ten-year bonds continued to rise so that by 28 January it had reached 405 bps, the highest it had ever been since Greece joined the euro.[70]

Inside Greece opinion polls suggested most people supported the revised stability programme but there were also signs of mounting doubt and anxiety, with the vast majority expressing concern about deficit and debt levels and over half saying that they believed foreign assistance would be necessary. To a certain extent, the mounting pessimism was fed by stories in the media that a Plan B existed that would involve further austerity measures, and this seemed to be borne out on the eve of the Commission giving its verdict on the stability programme, when, after a day of consultations with other party leaders and amid talk of a cabinet split, Papandreou appeared in a live televised address to announce a freeze on all public sector wages as well as cuts in bonuses and a rise in fuel taxes.[71] This announcement paved the way for the Commission to give a broadly positive assessment of the programme. However, at the same time it also made a number of recommendations which were then further elaborated at a 11 February European Council and an Ecofin Council held shortly afterwards. For the first time the Commission adopted a recommendation under Article 126(9) of the Treaty on the Functioning of the European Union on the correction of an EDP and recommended action be taken under Article 121(4) to end what was judged to be Greece's divergence from the broad economic policy guidelines of the Commission on account of the risk this may jeopardise 'the proper functioning of the monetary union'.[72] This meant the country was expected to adopt a comprehensive package of structural reforms and, while noting that the outline of this was already contained within the Greek stability programme, the Commission also requested what it termed 'clarification' in some cases. To ensure the programme was followed there was also to be enhanced monitoring by the Commission 'in liaison with the ECB', and in framing additional measures 'the expertise of the IMF' would be drawn upon.[73] In effect, during the term of the stability programme Greece was expected to meet a tight deficit reduction timetable and implement major structural reforms under close supervision with the Commission holding a near veto over policymaking. It was, therefore, little wonder that afterwards Papandreou was quoted as saying, 'We have lost a part of our sovereignty because of this loss of credibility'.[74]

An outline of a possible solution to the crisis had been presented but there remained significant unanswered questions and it was around these that doubts now began to crystallise. Firstly, Greece had been given until 16 March to produce a timetable for the budgetary correction measures, with a clear expectation that more decisive action would be taken than hitherto. Until this point, though, the government had appeared reluctant to take measures, usually only doing so at the very last moment. There was therefore no certainty that agreement would be reached on taking further steps. Moreover, public opinion now also had to be taken into account, with the first indications of popular opposition beginning to appear. A general strike called jointly by the General Confederation of Workers of Greece (GSEE) and the Confederation of Civil Servants (ADEDY) on 24 February closed ports and grounded flights. Addressing the crowd, the President of the GSEE, Yiannis Panagopoulos, proclaimed his federation was participating in a 'major political strike' and, when they marched in a protest earlier in the month, the strikers had chanted 'We are not Ireland, we will resist'.[75] To a Greek audience this spectacle of banner waving strikers and rhetoric of militant resistance was not unexpected but, when it was projected to the outside world, it was interpreted as posing a potent obstacle to the passing of any future measures.[76] Secondly, although it was generally assumed that financial assistance would also be provided, the shape of any support mechanism was still far from clear. Amid much talk of agreed rules and shared responsibilities the member states had given a commitment to take 'determined and coordinated action', if needed, but only to safeguard the financial stability of the euro area as a whole. This may mostly have stemmed from continuing concerns about breaching treaty provisions but it was also because the woes of Greece had now become a global concern due to the turbulence they were credited with creating in international currency markets.[77] By the beginning of 2010 a combination of low interest rates and quantitative easing had helped diminish trading costs to such an extent that, as one London broker graphically explained, 'for the price of a cup of coffee at Starbucks I can short millions of euros'.[78] With stories of shadowy hedge fund managers meeting to plan raids on the euro adding spice to the mix, from a high of $1.51 on 3 December 2009 the value of the single currency had steadily declined against the US dollar, which some Greek politicians were quick to remark may not have been undesired by German exporters.[79] By the time the European leaders convened for the 11 February Council meeting, the media were speaking about the currency being under siege and Trichet having to leave a banking conference in Australia a day early in order to return home to address the crisis.[80] He denied this was the case, and the Council meeting was to disappoint those in the financial markets who had expected it would announce details of an assistance package. A brief one-page communiqué merely called on the Greek government to implement the measures it had announced in a rigorous and determined manner, before closing with the observation that it had 'not requested any financial support'.[81] The failure to confirm there would be an assistance package may have been because no agreement had been reached or to put further pressure on Greece to introduce more measures, but it gave space for the feverish speculation to continue, which left Papandreou complaining that his European colleagues had created 'a psychology of looming collapse', which could be self-fulfilling while at the same time making the country 'a laboratory animal' in a test of strength between the politicians and the financiers.[82]

The further measures were eventually announced on 3 March 2010, after a team from the European Commission visiting Athens had reportedly voiced 'fundamental objections' to the growth and revenue forecasts within the stability programme.[83] Expected to generate €4.8 billion in revenue and savings, they included an increase in VAT rates of up to 2.0 per cent, further rises in fuel, tobacco and alcohol duties, a tax on higher priced cars and boats and a 10 per cent reduction in supplementary income payments to civil servants, as well as cuts in the additional thirteenth and fourteenth months salaries which were paid beyond the normal twelve. For the first time, there was an enthusiastic response to the announcement from European leaders who showered Papandreou with praise. Even the ECB's governing council called the measures 'convincing' and on cue, a few days later, the President of the European Commission, José Manuel Barroso, speaking in the European Parliament, for the first time publicly acknowledged that a support mechanism was being prepared for Greece, although he was carefully to add it would fully conform with European treaties and include strict conditionality.[84] Taking advantage of the better atmosphere the PDMA issued a new bond which was again heavily oversubscribed. Seeking to place €5 billion of ten-year bonds it attracted €14.5

billion of bids at a spread of 327 bps above comparative German bonds, with 77 per cent of the offer being sold abroad, mostly in the UK and Germany.[85] In contrast to the warm plaudits from abroad, the reaction to the 3 March measures at home was sullen and sometimes angry. Opinion polls showed deep unhappiness with the measures, and, on the day they were due to be discussed by parliament, a one day general strike brought much of the public sector to a halt and a large crowd into Syntagma Square. In a pattern that was to become familiar over the coming months, some of the demonstrators hurled petrol bombs and other missiles at the riot police who countered with volleys of tear gas. Inside parliament unease was also visible, as PASOK members clashed among themselves, with one deputy telling a minister that the government was losing its soul.[86] The measures passed but the popular discontent, the unease in the ranks of PASOK, and their failure to have any lasting material impact on the dynamic of crisis were all to be harbingers of the future.

There had been some expectation that details of the Greek support mechanism would be announced when EU finance ministers met on 16 March, but they merely issued a bland statement about Greece reiterating the decisions taken in February and welcoming the 3 March measures.[87] In response the Commission began to show signs of impatience, with Barroso urging action as soon as possible because in his view the situation could not be prolonged.[88] The delay seems to have been caused by a series of disagreements. These concerned how assistance should be given, since the Eurogroup did not have sufficient 'legal personality' to issue its own debt; the interest rate that would be charged on the loans; and the extent to which the IMF should be involved. The latter seems to have been particularly contentious, with those in favour, including many in Germany, seeing IMF participation as not only lessening their own country's financial contribution but also giving credibility to any package. The low interest rates on loans from the Washington-based institution would also lessen the risk that lending from the euro area would be seen as a subsidy and thus in breach of EU treaties. Those more uneasy about IMF involvement, including the ECB, argued that its role should be limited to technical assistance otherwise its participation would not only undermine the standing of both European institutions and the euro as a world currency but also blunt the message that a state had to take responsibility for its own predicament.[89] For its part, the IMF, keen under the leadership of Strauss-Kahn to underline its continuing relevance as an organisation, had indicated it was willing to provide assistance to Greece, but in doing so it would be pushing its charter to its limits both as regards the rules it applied to its lending and the percentage of national quota that the country would be borrowing, which was eventually to amount to more than 3,200 per cent, the largest on record.[90] Within Greece itself IMF participation was in general viewed extremely negatively. It created expectations of an ideologically driven austerity programme and further polarised the local political environment, giving additional reason for most of the parties, including New Democracy, to oppose the support package. The KKE called the organisation 'imperialistic', while for SYRIZA, Tsipras spoke of the dissolution of the social contract of the *metapolitefsi* before prophesying that its participation would lead to the 'total looting' of the country.[91]

It was not until the spring European Council of 25–26 March that the final details of the support mechanism were reportedly agreed by Merkel, Sarkozy and Trichet, a few hours before the meeting convened, at a private gathering in the grey-walled office of the President of the European Council, Herman Van Rompuy, which was later joined by the Greek delegation led by Papandreou. The one-and-a-half page agreement carefully noted that Greece had not yet requested assistance but, if it was required to safeguard the financial stability of the euro area as a whole, it would be supplied through coordinated bilateral loans from fellow euro area members augmented by substantial IMF funding. Furthermore, not only would Eurogroup members have to unanimously agree to the granting of assistance but assessments recommending disbursement would also have to be carried out by both the Commission, working in conjunction with the ECB, and the IMF. The loans would not carry standard euro area interest rates but would have 'risk adequate pricing' to incentivise a return to the market and to make sure that they were seen as non-concessional.[92] Finally, it was announced that a task force would be formed under the chairmanship of Van Rompuy to consider how economic governance could be improved within the EU as a whole. The document, with its insistence on non-concessional interest rates and assistance only being given as a last resort, which could be read as both ensuring the loans did not breach EU treaties and guarding against moral hazard, bore a strong Germanic tone, but it had been drafted in conjunction with the French and seems to have been readily agreed by all parties. Northern European euro area states tended to share similar values, non-euro countries were relieved not to be involved, the other southern states, as well as the Irish, were all too aware of the precariousness of their own situation, and in the face of such unanimity the Commission acquiesced, allowing Barroso to seemingly overlook the involvement of the IMF when he triumphantly announced, 'We have solved this in the European family, in the euro area.'[93] At the same time, in what was to become a familiar pattern of carefully choreographed statements, Trichet, in a speech in the European parliament, reversed the ECB's previous position and announced that contrary to earlier assertions it would after all be keeping its minimum credit rating threshold for collateral at BBB– beyond the end of 2010, while also introducing a graded haircut schedule which 'will continue to adequately protect the Eurosystem.'[94] The organisation representing the larger international banks, the Institute of International Finance (IIF), headed by the CEO of Deutsche Bank, Josef Ackermann, under considerable pressure from euro area governments, also made a commitment that its members would retain their exposure to Greek bonds during the period of any support programme, although this met a mixed response. Some smaller public savings banks in Germany refused to participate and despite the agreement, by the end of the year, French financial institutions had reportedly cut their holdings by about half and Dutch banks by almost two-thirds.[95]

After the Council meeting, the Greek government said it would have preferred a purely EU deal but pronounced itself satisfied, and in the first flush of success sections of the domestic media presented the agreement as an example of Greek negotiating prowess. The response of the Greek administration was mirrored by European leaders who hailed the agreement as marking the end of the crisis. It was to be the first of many false dawns. In search of an explanation for the failure of the spreads to subsequently decline, the media focused upon a report that an unnamed Greek official had stated that the country wanted to renegotiate the deal to exclude the IMF. However, in reality, the downgrades by the rating agencies, endless speculation about default and general mood of uncertainty had combined to drive all but the most speculative of foreign buyers away from the bond market. Perhaps aware of this, counter to previous practice, there was no immediate attempt to capitalise on the Council meeting and issue more government debt. However, when the PDMA tried to place one bond and reopen another in the last days of March, the response was weak, perhaps because the coupon of the seven-year bond was too low.[96] The lack of market interest was noticed and it was not long after it was announced that the 2009 deficit might be higher than previously suspected, although it was predicted that it would rise by less than 1.0 per cent, that ten-year bond yields rose above the psychologically important 7.0 per cent, which increasingly had come to be seen as the level at which they became unsustainable. Significantly, the bond curve also inverted, so that short-dated issues yielded more than longer ones, a sign of stress which was exacerbated on

9 April when Fitch downgraded Greece's sovereign rating to the ECB's existing minimum credit rating threshold for collateral of BBB–.[97]

An 11 April 2010 teleconference of the Eurogroup agreed the details of the support mechanism and made it fully operational. The markets briefly settled and a placement of short maturity T-bills was judged to be a success, although yields were almost double those of January. However, in a by now familiar pattern, within days doubts were reported to be surfacing. Firstly, there was confusion over the size of the package, with it not being clear how much would be made available after the first year, with an indication of the final amount only coming on 15 April, when the German financial daily, *Handelsblatt*, citing sources in Berlin, said it would be around €105 billion. Secondly, there was a growing realisation that the high interest rates being demanded would make what was already a difficult fiscal correction almost impossible, especially since nearly every analyst expected an economic contraction in 2010 far deeper than the 0.35 per cent of GDP forecast by the Greek Finance Ministry, with Deutsche Bank suggesting it could be as much as 4.0 per cent. Lastly, speculation continued about the timing of any request for assistance. A 14 April meeting between Papandreou and Samaras was widely interpreted as paving the way for implementation, and a letter sent the next day by Papaconstantinou to Strauss-Kahn, Trichet and Olli Rehn, the newly appointed replacement for Almunia as commissioner for economic and monetary affairs and the euro, asking for discussions about the specifics of the programme, as making execution certain, but still no request had actually been made.[98] Indeed, the minister of finance was careful to stress he had not set a timeframe for activation, but popular feeling inside Greece at this time was caught by an opinion poll about the letter, which found that nearly half the respondents said it made them feel 'angry' and over a quarter 'fearful'.[99]

An informal meeting of the Eurogroup and Ecofin Council in Madrid passed, as did a gathering of Asian and European finance ministers, but by then nature had intervened in an unexpected way. The Eyjafjallajökull volcano in Iceland erupted, spewing such a plume of ash into the air that aeroplane flights across much of Europe were grounded for almost two weeks. This prevented officials from the EU institutions which were to participate in the troika from flying to Athens to carry out the inspection necessary for the activation of the support mechanism. The complete troika team eventually assembled on 21 April, but by this time the Greek secondary bond market had effectively frozen, as orders to sell far outstripped those to buy, allowing yields on ten-year bonds to rise to over 8.3 per cent in almost non-existent trading.

Until this point Greece had been able to secure sufficient funding to meet its current financing needs, but it still had to find the wherewithal to roll over a substantial amount of debt maturing in May and, as fears began to grow that the the country would not be able to meet its liabilities, panic began to fill the air. There were no queues in the streets but depositors started to withdraw their money from bank accounts in increasingly large amounts, while in a 'silent sovereign run' European and other foreign financial institutions, re-examining their exposure to Greece, started to pull credit lines amid a general resurgence of concern about the stability of the Greek banking sector.[100] On 22 April at a meeting in the Canadian Embassy in Washington, European finance ministers came under heavy pressure from representatives of the USA and other IMF members to act to prevent contagion spreading across the euro area like 'wildfire'.[101] On the same day Moody's also downgraded Greece from A2 to A3 and placed it on review for lowering further, and Eurostat revised the 2009 deficit to 13.6 per cent and warned that it might yet rise a little more.[102] Papandreou was later to say that the latter was what made 'the glass overflow' and push Greece to activate the support mechanism, but, in truth, it was a perfect storm of factors.[103]

A cabinet meeting stretching long into the evening revealed opinion was divided, with most being in favour of activating the mechanism but some wishing to wait until the full terms were known.[104] Characteristically, once the decision to activate was taken, instead of staying in Athens, Papandreou kept to his original schedule and left for the remote island of Kastellorizo to discuss regional development. His 23 April 2010 address to the nation announcing that Greece was requesting financial assistance was therefore made against the backdrop of the blue Aegean on an island that, according to the 2001 census, had a population of only 430. In his address Papandreou presented the package as a partnership between the EU and Greece, blaming the New Democracy government for leaving a 'sinking ship' and the financial markets which had not given Greece the time it needed either because they 'did not believe in the EU's determination' or because they continued to gain from speculation. Using classical imagery he described the journey ahead as a new 'Odyssey', finishing with a rousing call, 'Our final goal, our final desti-nation, is to liberate Greece from surveillance and guardianship, to liberate... every Greek, of perceptions, practices and systems that have been hindering them everywhere for decades, to give oxygen where there is asphyxiation, justice and rules where there is injustice, transparency where there is dark-ness, certainty where there is insecurity, and development for all'.[105] The next day, speaking in the small town of Kremasti in Rhodes, he is reported to have given a less rhetorical but more accurate assessment: 'Due to our budget deficits, the EU, along with the IMF, today, arrived here... It is a form of guardianship... and it is not at all pleasant'.[106]

Greece had requested assistance but as yet nothing was settled, with intensive talks still continuing across the globe. The package also needed to be ratified by euro area parliaments, and the position in Germany in particular was complicated, with an important regional election upcoming in North-Rhine Westphalia. Partly because of continuing doubts about the legality of the support mechanism but also due to growing public unease about the amount of assistance required, which had produced an outbreak of anti-Greek sentiment in parts of the German media, the tendency in Germany had been to emphasise the systemic risk posed by Greece to the euro area as a whole. Now, with the threat that Greece might be about to default continuing to hover in the air, attention turned to the issue of the exposure of northern European banks to Greek government debt. When few of these proved willing to divulge details, this only heightened speculation and, with concern mounting that other southern European states might need similar assistance, more and more voices were heard suggesting that in order to contain what was increasingly seen as a crisis in the euro zone as a whole a larger sum, perhaps up to €600 billion, was needed. With Standard & Poor's downgrading not only Greece by three notches to the non-investment grade BB+ but also Portugal and Spain as well and the media abuzz with stories about contagion, the focus now switched to Berlin where the heads of most of the world's leading economic organisations were involved in almost continuous talks with Merkel and members of the European leadership.[107] The sense of crisis was caught in a dramatic but cryptic metaphor by Ángel Gurría, the secretary general of the Organisation for Economic Co-operation and Development (OECD), who, comparing the problem to the deadly Ebola virus, added, 'When you realise you have it you have to cut your leg off in order to survive'.[108] On 2 May an extraordinary meeting of the Eurogroup in Brussels endorsed the Greek loan facility. The support mechanism in total was now priced at €110 billion over three years. The governments of the euro area, with the KfW development bank acting on behalf of Germany, were to provide €80 billion of loans. The remainder of the money was to come from the IMF. Together with the news that the negotiations in Athens between the teams from the Commission, ECB and IMF and the government had concluded and memorandums of understanding had been signed, the endorsement of the loan facility allowed the European political leadership to state that a decisive step had been taken towards putting the Greek economy back on track and ensuring the stability of the euro. In perfect coordination the ECB also did again what it had earlier said it would not do, and suspended the minimum credit rating threshold specifically for Greek bonds until further notice.[109]

On 2 May in Athens, Papandreou gave a televised address to his cabinet. He spoke in sombre tones about how it was a patriotic duty to take the necessary measures even if there would invariably be a high political cost.[110] Noting that the proposed wage and pension freeze together with the rise in VAT would suck demand out of the Greek economy, the economics editor of the London-based *Guardian* newspaper succinctly wrote, 'That is not a recovery plan. It is an economic death spiral'.[111] In Greece protesters took to the streets, as the unions proclaimed the 'mother of all battles'. A group draped banners over the side of the Acropolis calling on the people of Europe to rise up, while others entered the television studios of the Hellenic Broadcasting Organisation (ERT) and disrupted the news. Scuffles in Syntagma Square led to the firing of tear gas and on 5 May a huge demonstration snaked through the streets of Athens shouting slogans against the political elite. In Syntagma Square, where a crowd outside parliament was reported as chanting 'let the bordello burn', a rain of petrol bombs and other missiles fell on the police, tear gas was fired, windows were smashed and waste bins set ablaze.[112] The next day the press reported that the centre of Athens looked like a warzone, but the greatest tragedy had occurred earlier in the afternoon of 5 May, when a small group had broken away from the main body of demonstrators and thrown at least one petrol bomb into a branch of the Marfin Egnatia Bank on Stadiou Street. In the conflagration that followed three employees of the bank died. Amid general shock and revulsion, President Papoulias warned that with the country teetering on the brink of the abyss 'it is our collective responsibility to ensure that we don't go over the edge'.[113] The next day less than 5,000 appeared to demonstrate outside parliament. Inside, the legislation passed with 172 voting in favour and 121 against. Three PASOK deputies who simply voted 'present' rather than casting their ballot in favour were expelled from the parliamentary group.[114] LAOS was the only other party to support the government, with Karatzaferis explaining the decision by saying he could see no other option. New Democracy voted against, with Samaras in his speech declaring that the dose of medicine you are administering is in danger of killing the patient'.[115] Dora Bakoyanni was expelled from the party for voting in favour. The KKE and SYRIZA also voted against. The next day the German parliament ratified the deal, with Merkel declaring that it is 'about no more and no less than the future of Europe'.[116] However, many Social Democrat MPs abstained as Frank-Walter Steinmeier, their parliamentary leader, rebuked Merkel: 'You let things drift and only now are you calling the fire brigade when everything is ablaze'.[117]

The metaphors of fire were increasing because the warnings of contagion had become self-fulfilling. When stock markets opened on 4 May they fell across Europe, with the Spanish IBEX leading the way. The euro also declined against the US dollar to its lowest point in a year. The next day the sense of panic continued. In the graphic words of one analyst in the all-important London bond market, during these days 'we were close to staring into the abyss... The way spreads were going, you were looking at a situation where many of the European governments just wouldn't be able to borrow... It was like nothing we have ever seen. It's very interesting, it's stimulating. It's seeing history unfold. It's crazy and fun but at the same time it's really frightening'.[118] As both journalists and politicians started to make comparisons with the collapse of Lehman brothers, the crisis had been fully transmogrified from being a localised issue involving Greece to one bringing into question the very existence of the single currency, which even the French Minister of Finance, Christine Lagarde, later admitted she feared might not survive.[119] The European Commission backed by the finance ministers of the G7 urged quick action but publicly there was little sign of urgency.[120] Trichet made some remarks about the ECB being 'inflexibly attached to price stability' when ruling out bond purchases on the open market, while Merkel and Sarkozy contented themselves with issuing a joint letter calling for tighter economic governance within the euro area.[121] Indeed, when he had called a euro area summit for 7 May 2010 Van Rompuy had intended it to be little more than a chance to analyse the lessons to be learnt from the Greek crisis. However, in the morning before the meeting, Barroso reportedly called Merkel to discuss a 'worrisome development in the markets', and in the afternoon the finance ministers and central bank governors of the G7 together with Strauss-Kahn held a teleconference at which the US Secretary of the Treasury, Timothy Geithner, is reported to have urged a more decisive response.[122] The reasoning for this became apparent when the summit convened later that evening. After a short statement by Papandreou about the situation in Greece, to the evident surprise of some participants, it soon transpired that the focus of the discussions was going to be the destiny of the single currency itself, with Trichet warning that interbank lending had virtually ceased and that a potentially catastrophic financial crisis loomed.[123] The sometimes heated debate that followed seems to have ranged far and wide, with Sarkozy at one point reportedly banging the table and telling Merkel that Germany must face up to its responsibilities, but in the end the leaders produced a statement in which, amid a general commitment to consolidate public finances and increase regulation of the financial markets, they agreed to establish a European stabilisation mechanism.[124] The details, though, were left to the Ecofin Council to work out.

The Ecofin Council was due to meet on 9 May and, when he arrived at the Berlaymont building in Brussels, the Swedish Minister for Finance, Anders Borg immediately set the tone as he compared the financial markets to a pack of wolves, adding that if they were not stopped 'they will tear the weaker members [of the euro area] apart'.[125] The ministers were working to a tight deadline since it was generally accepted that they needed to formulate a package before the financial markets opened in the Far East in the early morning of Monday 10 May. At the same time, as the ministers were discussing the various options in Brussels, the main political leaders maintained contact with each other and with the board of the ECB in Frankfurt by telephone. A few days earlier at a meeting in Lisbon, the ECB seems to have taken the decision to introduce a scheme to purchase the bonds of troubled euro area states on secondary markets—something which was permitted within its charter, although not specifically to promote financial stability. This was now publicly announced under the title of the Securities Markets Programme (SMP) and, with the other euro area central banks following suit the next day, one important plank of the overall package was put in place.[126] The other was delivered by the finance ministers almost exactly as the financial markets opened in Tokyo. Together with the IMF they had agreed to establish a €750 billion safety net to provide assistance to any euro area member state that encountered difficulties similar to Greece. The €500 million to be raised from EU sources was to come from two instruments: the European Financial Stabilisation Mechanism (EFSM) and the European Financial Stability Facility (EFSF). The smaller of the two, the EFSM, would be run by the Commission and would raise money from investors against the spare capacity in the EU's budget. The larger mechanism, the EFSF, was to be established as a *société anonyme* under Luxembourg law. It was designed to be a temporary structure which would fund itself by issuing bonds and other debt instruments backed by guarantees from its shareholder member states. Its lending capacity of €440 billion was supposedly based on the amount thought necessary to cover the funding needs of Ireland, Portugal and Spain for three years. The finance minister after long discussions had created two mechanisms designed to stem the crisis in the euro area, but weaknesses still remained, particularly the fact that the EFSF was not prefunded but had to raise capital from the financial markets when it was required. This meant its fortunes were to a large extent tied to its member states with AAA credit ratings keeping this status and, when some of them were later downgraded, the credibility of the EFSF itself came into question, making it more difficult for it to raise money. Critics also charged that it was structured so as to minimise risk to the shareholder member states. This might have been to their satisfaction, but hardly gave an impression of confidence that borrowing states would be able to repay their loans. Nonetheless, with the activation of the support mechanism and the formation of the EFSM and EFSF a significant juncture had been reached in the crisis. The trajectory from PASOK's victory in the October 2009 election to the request for financial assistance in the spring of 2010 was not preordained. It took a certain configuration of events and factors to lead to the outcome. Any speculation as to whether the crisis could have been averted is by nature counterfactual since it is only suggesting what might have happened, but, as the preceding narrative has shown, at certain key points alternative actions by the Greek government, the ECB, leading players in the euro area, especially Germany, the Ecofin Council, the Eurogroup, and the Commission might have led to a different outcome. However, operating in an often highly pressured environment for a variety of reasons, the various actors chose to take the actions they did, and these all eventually interlocked to lead to the final outcome, although it is difficult to see any one incident or individual person as being decisive in this process.

5

FALTERING AT THE RUBICON

THE DIFFICULTIES OF THE MEMORANDUM

On 3 May 2010 Papaconstantinou and Provopoulos signed two letters of intent. One was addressed to Juncker, in his capacity as president of the Eurogroup, Rehn, as European commissioner for economic and monetary affairs and the euro, and Trichet, as president of the European Central Bank (ECB), and the other to Strauss-Kahn, as managing director of the International Monetary Fund (IMF). The letters formed the preamble to two sets of documentation which were copied to all recipients. These comprised of two generally similar versions of a Memorandum of Economic and Financial Policies which outlined the programme of fiscal consolidation and structural reform that the Greek government intended to follow until the agreed period of financial assistance ended in 2013. There were also two copies of a Technical Memorandum of Understanding providing definitions of many of the terms used, and within the European documentation a Memorandum of Understanding on Specific Economic Policy Conditionality detailing the measures to be taken. These would also serve as benchmarks when performance was assessed in a series of quarterly reviews to be carried out by a 'troika' of officials from the IMF, European Commission and the ECB, which would recommend the release of tranches of funding on 'observance of quantitative performance criteria, and a positive evaluation of the progress made with respect to policy criteria'.[1] Three weeks later, on 26 May 2010, the European versions of these memoranda appeared as annexes to a broader Economic Adjustment Programme for Greece which was published by the Directorate-General for

Economic and Financial Affairs of the European Commission.[2] Collectively all these documents as well as their later iterations came to be known in Greece simply as 'the memorandum' and throughout this book they will be referred to in this familiar singular form. The word, though, was always more than a simple description of some documents and a set of policies. It carried its own power and significance, defining the era in which it was applied and, for some, an ideology, able in its mere usage to conjure up a host of feelings and emotions.

The memorandum bore two Greek signatures and, in a press release welcoming the programme, Strauss-Kahn stated that it had been 'designed' by the domestic authorities.[3] However, while the memoranda of understanding in IMF programmes are handed over by the domestic authorities under their own responsibility, the standard practice is for them actually to be drafted by officials from the Fund after negotiations.[4] Greece was not a typical IMF mission, but most sources suggest that its procedures were broadly followed, and that the various memoranda were a product of just over a week of intense negotiations between the domestic authorities and around thirty officials from the three institutions making up the troika.[5] Later, one anonymous minister chose to label it a 'Frankenstein memorandum' and allege that it had been cobbled together in haste from previous IMF programmes, much as was said to have happened in the case of Latvia in 2009.[6] However, in reality its roots would seem to lie more in the stability programme drawn up earlier in the year, the policy guidelines of the European Commission and countless other documents produced by the Greek authorities, the IMF, Organisation for Economic Co-operation and Development (OECD) and other EU agencies over the years as well as academic research. This gave it both the strength of resting on accumulated knowledge and a degree of local expertise and the weakness, at least initially, of too often uncritically reflecting the assumptions and political beliefs of a relatively narrow policymaking elite upon whom the troika relied, since its consultations seldom seem to have broadened beyond a few ministers, senior administrators, banking officials and think tank staff. Thus, the document was not only marked by familiar references to the need to regain economic competitiveness, consult social partners, ensure equality of burden sharing and limit tax evasion, but also barely mentioned privatisation, talked about modernising the public administration and making it smaller without directly addressing the issue of redundancies, and contained economic growth forecasts, which in line with those made since the beginning of the crisis, were to prove unduly optimistic. In its relation to society as a whole, despite the references to the need for dialogue and consultation, the memorandum could also be seen as bearing links with the past, since it was essentially a state directed top-down imposition and, as such, at least in this regard, it could be seen as following in the footsteps of the modernisation programme of the Simitis era and the *dirigisme* of Konstantine Karamanlis, even if the prescriptions it offered, as testament to the fickleness of economic ideas, ran largely counter to the assumptions of that time.

In the short-term, the principal aim of the memorandum was to correct the fiscal imbalance so as to restore sufficient confidence in the county's finances to allow it to return to the international financial markets for funding. It also sought to ensure the stability of the local banking system. In the medium-term, it looked to correct the external imbalance by implementing a package of structural reforms designed to increase competitiveness and reorient the economy towards an investment, export-led model, so as to create the conditions for sustainable growth. Beyond these stated goals, it also had the unspoken aims of warding off insolvency and, at least on the Greek side, of keeping the country within the euro area. To correct the fiscal imbalance, the memorandum proposed a steeper reduction in the general government deficit, which would now be lowered to 8.1 per cent of GDP in 2010, followed by a further series of stepped reductions in subsequent years until it fell well below the Stability and Growth Pact's reference value in 2014. However, this reduction was to occur in an economy which, it was now recognised, would be shrinking faster than previously expected, with GDP forecast to decline by 4.0 per cent in 2010 and 2.5 per cent in 2011. At the same time, the public debt would also be growing, reaching a projected peak of about 155 per cent of GDP in 2013, before subsiding in 2020 to 120 per cent, which was deemed to be the maximum level at which it would be sustainable.[7] Within the euro area at least the debate about the relative merits of stimulus and austerity had been won by those who argued that only fiscal retrenchment could lay the foundations for sustainable growth.[8] However, from the outset, the uncertainty surrounding many of the forecasts about the Greek economy was also recognised. The debt projection in particular was sensitive to changes in levels of economic output and inflation, and, as a consequence, each IMF review of its Stand-By Arrangement contained a sustainability report detailing a variety of scenarios. The timetable for deficit reduction was also complicated by the fact that the 2009 budgetary data would almost certainly be further revised upwards by Eurostat and that lower cost borrowing, as it matured, would be replaced by non-concessional euro area loans. Indeed, when higher interest payments, negative real GDP growth and increased expenditure, due to projected rises in the public sector wage bill, pensions and unemployment benefit, were all taken into account, it meant that the total fiscal correction initially seen as being necessary during the period of the adjustment programme would be 18 per cent of GDP. This figure was well above the reduction needed to lower the budgetary deficit to the Stability and Growth Pact's reference level, and, according to the troika, was initially a source of misunderstanding with the Greek authorities.[9]

The tough targets had been set to bring the budgetary deficit below the reference value and the public debt to the level deemed sustainable within a relatively short timeframe. A more tapered rate of adjustment would have required a larger assistance package or the early restructuring of the national debt. The first solution, given the difficulty of putting the initial package together, was clearly politically impossible and the second, although it was discussed at the time, for a variety of reasons was not pursued. Firstly, not only was there still little agreement as to whether Greece was facing a liquidity or a solvency crisis but also the programme seems to have been seen as being achievable without resorting to restructuring, with one economist quoted as saying that it had 'priced in a large probability of slippage' and that there was a 'big cushion for deficit and debt targets'.[10] Secondly, due to the large number of Greek government bonds held by major Western European banks, restructuring risked bringing chaos to a European financial sector which was still recovering from the 2008 crisis. It would also lead to the total collapse of all the leading Greek banks, with potentially catastrophic consequences not only for the domestic economy but also for neighbouring states, where they had significant holdings. Thirdly, there were many, especially in Germany, who continued to see the crisis largely in terms of moral hazard and to believe that relieving Greece of some of its debt would be interpreted as rewarding profligacy. It would also provide a poor example for other states in the euro area at a time when many were preparing to embark on painful fiscal consolidation measures. As a consequence of these and other doubts, debt restructuring therefore does not seem to have been seriously considered. This left the level of fiscal adjustment required so high that the analysts at Barcap, the investment arm of Barclays Bank, were by no means alone in thinking it constituted a 'near-record', with Greece facing what a team at Deutsche Bank, falling back on a classical allusion, called a 'Herculean task'.[11] Indeed, one leading analyst estimated that the squeeze of government spending alone would be sufficient to cause total demand to fall by about a third of GDP and, according to another source, most economists at the IMF, European Commission and within the various euro area finance ministries harboured doubts as to whether the targets were feasible.[12] Yet, somehow none of this scepticism seems to have dented the confidence of the policymakers, who, at least in public, continued to voice faith in their prescriptions, although the existence of so much doubt was hardly an auspicious start for a programme that counted among its principal aims Greece regaining the confidence of global financial markets.

The goal of rekindling growth through 'modernising' the public administration, labour and product markets was also fraught with difficulties. In particular, as Strauss-Kahn made clear from the beginning and the memorandum reiterated, for Greece to regain competitiveness it was necessary to realign incomes to 'sustainable levels', although imposing wage cuts on the private sector workforce was initially ruled out, in the belief that a combination of lowering benchmark public sector pay and increasing job insecurity would be sufficient to achieve the same result.[13] Traditionally, IMF adjustment programmes have rested on three foundations: fiscal correction augmented by structural reforms, debt reduction, and a devaluation of the local currency to make exports more competitive on global markets. In the case of Greece the first occurred from the outset to be followed, eventually, by the second, although only after difficult and convoluted negotiations; but the last was impossible, due to the simple fact that Greece was part of a currency union. This meant that the lower prices needed to regain international competitiveness could only be obtained by boosting productivity or reducing costs. Since the troika had little control over commodity prices and reducing the high level of social security contributions would have derailed fiscal consolidation, the most immediate means of achieving the latter was through liberalising the domestic market to increase competition and curbing wages in order to effect an 'internal devaluation'.[14] The recessionary impact of this policy was recognised from the outset, with the memorandum, in what was to prove a masterly understatement, noting that initially 'growth is unlikely to be buoyant'. It was also accepted that it would lead to a reduction in government revenues, which would make the fiscal adjustment more challenging, and a worsening of debt dynamics, but, at least in public, ministers continued to express optimism that the economy could be rebalanced relatively quickly to make exports and foreign investment the locomotives of growth.[15] However, even a cursory glance at recent Greek history should have been sufficient to show that any moves to bring radical change to the public sector, including reducing wages and benefits, and to liberalise the product and labour markets were always likely to be bitterly contested by those standing to lose most from such actions. Moreover, although, theoretically, a combination of recession and reduced production costs should have pushed prices lower, thereby not only increasing economic competitiveness but also, to a certain extent, compensating employees for any loss in purchasing power resulting from wage cuts, for a variety of reasons these were to prove exceptionally 'sticky' in Greece. And, with so much of the economy dependent on domestic markets this meant that certain key sectors, especially retail and wholesale trade as well as construction, were likely to be particularly hard hit.

The implementation of the memorandum was to be monitored by a troika of officials drawn from the ranks of the IMF, European Commission and the ECB. The IMF and the Commission had worked together in Hungary, Latvia and Romania but Greece was to be the first country where the ECB was also involved. Its inclusion was probably due to the fact that no other institutional channels existed for its voice to be heard but, according to at least one source, its lack of experience limited its reach and it always remained something of a junior partner.[16] Indeed, the mission posed challenges for each of the institutions. For the IMF, it represented a departure from its normal procedures, since it was used to taking the lead in such missions, and it was occasionally criticised for being unduly accommodating to European and, especially German, points of view.[17] It was also working within a more restricted mandate than usual due to the rules and regulations of the EU as well as the constraints imposed by the single currency itself. The Commission was caught between two roles. It was acting both as an agent for member states, including Greece, and as an institution in its own right charged with enforcing the Stability and Growth Pact and other regulations. According to the IMF, this at times made it more concerned with ensuring measures complied with EU norms than assuring they were effective.[18] The need to ensure compliance also led to the Commission being involved in all the activities of the troika. This produced a certain amount of duplication, which increased documentation, but also introduced some checks and balances into policymaking, with, for instance, both the IMF and the Commission making separate calculations of Greece's financial needs.[19] In its assessment of the first programme, the IMF admits there were sometimes differences of opinion within the troika, especially as regards the prospects for economic growth, but these seem to have been worked out in private so a united front could be presented to the Greek authorities. Nonetheless, the IMF's conclusion that 'coordination seems to have been quite good under the circumstances' has a ring of damning the relationship with faint praise.[20] Even more telling was the lack of democratic accountability. Not one of the three bureaucratic institutions involved was accountable to a national parliament, and the Commission and the ECB only in limited ways to the European Parliament. This meant that, especially after the ending of the troika's press conferences in Greece, it rarely had to answer for policy failures, thereby removing a potential corrective mechanism which might have ameliorated some of the worst effects of the crisis on Greece and its society.

In its early reports the troika spoke of the Panhellenic Socialist Movement (PASOK) government's 'unwavering' resolve and praised its 'strong ownership' of the programme.[21] In other missions this has been seen as important in determining not only the eventual success of the programme but also the degree of conditionality that needs to be applied. However, in Greece the nature and extent of the ownership was always ambiguous. The government had little choice but to accept the memorandum, since, as one minister speaking at the time stressed the exigencies of the situation meant that there had been not only no desire but also no possibility to renegotiate.[22] This emphasis on the memorandum being the only option open to Greece was used to convey authority and, at least for a while, neutralised public opposition. However, at the same time, it also fuelled the polarisation which has long marked Greek politics, as figures from all sides of the political divide quickly enveloped the programme in a language of conflict and confrontation. Thus, Papandreou and the president of the General Confederation of Workers of Greece (GSEE) both spoke about fighting battles, while Samaras vowed he would 'declare war' against the government.[23] Papandreou also sought to give legitimacy to the reforms, just as Simitis had done in the period prior to entry into the Economic and Monetary Union (EMU), by presenting them as an escape route from the failures of the past, which he did not shy away from admitting derived in part from a time when his own party was in power.[24] In part this can be seen as a further element in the policy of candidness, but others within PASOK were less keen to dismiss the party's heritage; and the historical traditions of a socialist party that had many former union officials within its apparatus meant that it was always likely to be tepid to efforts to change labour laws, reduce the minimum wage and cut jobs in the public sector. Indeed, Papandreou, who was president of the Socialist International, and was not averse himself to attacking what he termed the 'conservative deification of the market', remained adamant throughout that 'zero jobs' would be shed in this area.[25] Within a Greek context this approach was to be expected. It was fully shared by New Democracy and even initially seems to have been accepted by the troika.[26] However, to a northern European world, more accustomed to equating austerity programmes with public sector layoffs, it appeared to be a stubborn restatement of principle and helped feed a perception that Greece, for better or worse, was not prepared to conform with expectations.

In the first months after the signing of the memorandum two incompatible narratives appeared. The first, which was largely articulated by government ministers and senior Greek, troika and European Commission officials but also sometimes by financial analysts, stressed the decisiveness of the administration and the successful fulfilment of programme targets. Their language was full of optimistic phrases about the programme having 'outpaced our expectations', its implementation being forceful and of Greece having 'crossed the Rubicon'.[27] The confidence stemmed partly from the fact that the fiscal correction appeared to be on track. Papaconstantinou constantly repeated the mantra that state finances were under control, citing figures that showed the central government deficit in cash terms had shrunk by around 40 per cent.[28] There were also signs that any contraction in the economy might be relatively short and shallow. Later seasonally adjusted year-on-year figures even showed that the economy grew slightly in the first quarter of the year and, although growth turned negative again in the second quarter, a rise in the Purchasing Managers' Index (PMI) in both June and July suggested that better times might lie ahead. Private consumption was also thought to be holding up better than expected. As a result, even as late as the autumn Papaconstantinou was still suggesting that the drop in GDP in 2010 would be less than the predicted 4.0 per cent. The government had also been able to raise some money from the financial markets, with the first T-bill sale in July achieving a reasonable bid-to-cover ratio, even if domestic banks had predominated and yields were slightly higher than before. Therefore, when Papaconstantinou and Provopoulos spoke of Greece returning to global financial markets for funding in 2011, their prediction did not seem unreasonable, especially since international sentiment also seemed to be changing, perhaps in part due to the policy of candidness being followed by the political leadership. At the October 2010 annual meeting of the IMF and World Bank in Washington, Papaconstantinou described the difference in attitude towards Greece from April of that year as being like night and day.[29] Signs could even be detected of a social consensus forming in favour of reform. A series of strikes at the end of June, including a general strike, had brought considerable disruption to transport links but had not attracted the same crowds as the May demonstrations, and opinion polls showed that many continued to support the notion of reform, even if the meaning of the term remained nebulous. Moreover, PASOK's persistent lead over New Democracy in the polls, with the party's support dipping little between May and September 2010, could even be read as an indication of public backing for the new adjustment programme.

However, in parallel to this optimistic discourse there was another that portrayed Greece as not emerging from the crisis but plunging deeper into its depths. The budget deficit figure might be declining but closer inspection revealed that this was largely due to cuts in the public investment programme. Revenues were rising less than planned and virtually every other economic indicator was also turning to the worse, as industrial and manufacturing production, retail and car sales, as well as housing starts all fell, while unemployment and inflation steadily rose. The first reports from the troika might have been sufficiently positive to ensure the second tranche of funding was released in September, but they also carried a subtext of concern over levels of expenditure in public enterprises as well as healthcare and social security, where lacunae in the data continued to plague attempts to establish reliable figures.[30] New taxes were also not yet bringing in as much income as expected. Public opinion remained downbeat as well, with almost every respondent in a poll released in August saying the economy was in a bad condition and, in a similar exercise in September, more judged the country likely to default than did not.[31] This was partly because the rating agencies were also showing little more confidence in Greece, with Moody's on 14 June dramatically downgrading the country by four notches to Ba1, citing macroeconomic and implementation risks.[32] This brought Moody's sovereign rating into line with the other agencies, but it unnerved the financial markets and, by putting Greek bonds firmly into junk territory, prompted many investment funds to divest their holdings, placing further pressure on yields. These remained high, despite reports of heavy ECB intervention in the secondary markets, perhaps, in part, because the support mechanism, by creating a new tier of debt held by euro area states and the IMF that was senior to privately held bonds, was already prompting some reassessment of risk.[33] The continuing high bond yields meant that the possibility of the country defaulting on its loans was still discussed in the media, although some have also suggested that such talk was encouraged in part to spur the Greek government into action. Even the prospect of Greece leaving the euro area continued to be raised, although, when questioned at a conference in Italy, Trichet said this would be 'the worst possible choice'.[34] Indeed, international comment was often far from positive, especially in

Germany, with the news magazine *Der Spiegel* writing about the onset of an economic depression, the head of a prominent private bank speaking of the return of fear as Greece suffocated under austerity, and most dramatically, Hans-Werner Sinn, the influential president of the leading Ifo Institute for Economic Research, warning that further measures could push the country to the brink of 'civil war'.[35]

The truth was that whatever the politicians said, people, especially those living in the major cities, could not ignore the growing signs of crisis around them. Adopting a Darwinist approach, the government had apparently accepted that up to a quarter of small businesses might close, but this overlooked the psychological impact that the rows of empty, dusty shop fronts would have on consumer confidence. Along with the rash of yellow stickers plastered across every public space, offering business premises and apartments for rent, they spoke of a rupture from the familiar and of continuing uncertainty. A failure of traffic lights in central Athens, which took several days to repair, as politicians and officials squabbled over competences, seemed to testify to deeper breakdowns in the fabric of society, accentuated by the growing number of strikes and stoppages. Almost daily, the television news broadcast images of protesters marching through the streets of Athens carrying makeshift banners emblazoned with slogans, voicing their opposition to measures being enacted in the name of the memorandum. Sometimes the protests ended in scuffles, as when the police fired tear gas to clear the Acropolis of public sector employees claiming back pay and demanding short-term contract staff be given full-time jobs.[36] At other times they were mutely symbolic as when striking truck drivers parked hundreds of lorries nose to tail for days along the sides of a motorway in Athens and left a giant teddy bear wearing a fluorescent vest hanging from a crane over the carriageways. The norms of life seemed to be crumbling and this impression was heightened by the growing number of stories circulating about burglaries and robberies, sometimes with fatal consequences, which were widely interpreted as arising from the desperate circumstances the crisis was creating. With political life outside the memorandum still dominated by scandals, the overall effect was to produce a sense of dysfunction and decay not dissimilar to that present in the last months of Kostas Karamanlis' administration, when similar circumstances led to an erosion of trust in the official narrative. In this atmosphere, as unemployment levels started to rise and the first measures hit wages and pension payments, the mood of the public began to darken, a change succinctly caught by a female employee of an accounting company who told a reporter 'I don't see hope for this country in the near future'.[37]

Public unease might be growing but the government was, nonetheless, making some progress in implementing the memorandum. Fiscal management legislation designed to increase accountability and transparency through a three-year strategy, which included imposing spending limits on ministries and requiring supplementary budgets in the case of overspending, had been adopted and a parliamentary budget office founded. Steps had also been taken to improve tax administration and increase absorption of EU structural funds as well as to establish a single payment authority for public sector workers.[38] Most of all, the government had been able to table, ahead of schedule, a pension reform bill that both it and the troika liked to call a 'landmark' piece of legislation.[39] The bill had its origins in a legal ruling that required Greece to harmonise its law with an EU requirement for male and female retirement ages to be equalised, but its chief aim was to secure the long-term sustainability of a system which was considered to be skewed in favour of certain professional groups and riddled with flaws.[40] The law, which aimed to produce a quasi-universal basic pension topped up by a contribution-related proportional one dependant on earnings and the number of days spent in the workforce, among its provisions merged some funds, removed state guarantees from others, and raised retirement ages by up to fifteen years to ensure pensions were only granted after forty years of contributions.[41] The public reaction was in general negative. The media tended to emphasise how much longer people would have to work before they retired, with the newspaper *Eleftherotypia* refashioning a national lottery slogan to declare 'three out of four are losers'.[42] However, a strike and protest march through Athens brought only 20,000 onto the streets, maybe because many seem to have seen the bill as a necessary evil, even if it was widely judged as unfair.[43] In its first review of the programme the IMF went so far as to state that the reform might be counted 'among the most ambitious undertaken by any country in one step', but important groups, including many professionals and some public sector workers, were excluded from its remit.[44] Significantly, it also failed to address the issue of supplementary pension funds which by 2012 were judged to be equally in crisis. Indeed, since 2010 many civil servants have continued to retire at a relatively young age, partly to meet workforce reduction targets but also to secure lump sum payments before they are withdrawn. By 2016, despite nearly a dozen further cuts which had reduced the average pension to around €700 per month, the collapse of the economy meant that the proportion of GDP spent on pensions was still among the highest in the EU, leaving the long-term sustainability of the system far from assured.[45]

Nonetheless, at the time, the passing of the pension reform legislation was seen as being indicative of the government's resolve, and this impression was further reinforced by its handling of a strike by truck and tanker drivers at the end of July, when civil mobilisation orders were issued to force the drivers back to work under threat of arrest. Poul Thomsen, the head of the IMF mission, expressed admiration at the government's decisiveness, but parts of the domestic media, even some generally supportive of the reform process, questioned whether its actions had been constitutional and if such a show of force had really been necessary.[46] These and other doubts were not just confined to the media, similar sentiments were also appearing within the ranks of PASOK, especially after the government attempted to change labour legislation to make it easier and less costly to dismiss staff from larger and medium sized companies.[47] The unease came to a head at a party conference held in the Olympic Tae Kwon Do hall by the sea in Paleo Faliro at the beginning of September. The immediate issue seems to have been the selection of candidates for the forthcoming local elections, especially the new regional governorships established during a recent reorganisation. The leadership wanted high profile candidates to contest these positions but few of PASOK's leading lights were initially willing to stand and, amid the usual personal rivalries and special pleadings, underlying concern centred on the extent to which the party was losing support due to its association with the memorandum. This, it was claimed, was leaving it open to attack not only from New Democracy but also from the Coalition of the Radical Left (SYRIZA) and the Communist Party of Greece (KKE), which were increasingly labelling PASOK as neo-liberal. With some speakers charging that the memorandum went against all the party's beliefs, Papandreou openly admitted there had been disagreement and almost immediately after the conference closed it was announced he would be reshuffling his cabinet.[48]

Such a reshuffle had been long anticipated despite denials that it was about to take place as late as the middle of August. In the end, most of the changes involved ministers swapping jobs, with only one leaving the cabinet altogether. This dismissal was presented as an example of the decisiveness of a premier prepared to take tough decisions, but in reality the reshuffle process had been so drawn out, with the names only emerging in the early hours of the morning, that the impression was more of indecision. The number of ministerial posts increased from thirty-six to forty-eight. Papandreou said this was necessary because of the weaknesses of the public administration but, with nearly a third of PASOK deputies now enjoying some ministerial status, the room for overlapping competences was high, with three ministers apparently being charged with securing foreign investment. The reshuffle could be interpreted as strengthening the government because it made the cabinet more representative of the mood of the party as a whole, but in the process it had introduced voices seen as being more critical of the memorandum, and the reappearance of a number of party stalwarts led an editorial in one newspaper to wonder ironically why it had taken Papandreou so long to abandon his fresh ideas and fall back on familiar faces. This cynical view also found echo within the general public, with two-thirds in an opinion poll saying they thought the reshuffle was mostly aimed at preserving the internal balances within PASOK.[49] The changes had made the cabinet potentially less unified, and to counteract this as well as the unwieldiness of the new body it was also announced that henceforth a smaller group would meet daily to tackle key issues and draft policy. In time this was to lead to accusations that Papandreou, who had always been presented as something of an outsider by some sections of the Greek media due, in part, to the amount of time he had spent in his early life outside Greece, was isolating himself with a small coterie of like minded colleagues, dismissed by detractors as 'gardeners' after a supposed remark by the former queen of Greece, Frederika, who is reputed to have said that she could appoint whoever she wanted as prime minister, even her gardener.[50]

After the cabinet reshuffle, Papaconstantinou wrote a letter to all government ministers involved in the memorandum's implementation reminding them of their obligations under the programme and asking them to both control expenditure and proceed with the necessary structural changes.[51] In his speech at the Thessaloniki International Fair that September, Papandreou also injected a new spirit of urgency when he spoke of a 'battle... for the survival of Greece' which 'we will either... all win... together or we will all sink together'.[52] Increasingly the rhetoric of the government was taking on a martial tone, with the stress being on the need to continue on the set path. However, this was legitimised not so much on the basis of the need to fulfil the demands of the adjustment programme but on a desire to justify the sacrifices society had already made—a line which was also increasingly followed by the troika institutions themselves and which still found echo half a decade later as they sought to prolong austerity. The change in rhetoric reflected the fact that a feeling of doubt seemed to be entering the air. Nothing was yet clear and the picture remained patchy, but, like a ban on smoking in public places introduced at this time which was widely flouted, it was easy to suspect that less was often being achieved than announced. The main focus remained on fiscal consolidation and, as with the previous New Democracy government, the priority was curbing expenditure within state owned enterprises. Indeed, it was commonly claimed that annual losses at the Hellenic Railways Organisation (OSE) were greater than in any other public enterprise in the EU, with a remark once made by a former minister that it would be cheaper to send passengers by taxi than subsidise the railways often being repeated.[53] The government's efforts to reorganise public enterprises and reduce wage costs brought it into direct confrontation with the unions. A series of 'revelations' appeared in the local media, presumably to try and gain the support of the public, which purported to show that much of the revenue earned by organisations such as OSE and the Electric Railway Athens-Piraeus (ISAP) was used to pay salaries that were far higher than the norm, with the average in the latter said to be €56,554 per annum.[54] In reply the unions countered with claims of managerial waste and ineffectiveness, which sometimes bordered on the corrupt. The various allegations inevitably became a major topic of conversation not only at home but also abroad due to the high degree of media coverage they received, helping further reinforce the image of Greece as a society of profligacy.[55] A series of strikes also brought tremendous disruption to transport links, grounding flights, leaving ferries berthed in harbour and creating gridlock across Athens as commuters took to the road. The economic costs of the chaos must have contributed to the deepening of the downturn but despite the protests the legislation passed through parliament. Salaries for those earning more than a certain amount were cut by approximately 10 per cent and wages capped but there were no job losses. Instead, those deemed surplus to requirements in organisations such as OSE were redeployed within the public sector, which, aside from the human costs it caused, produced a lingering suspicion that the exercise was merely transferring the problem of overmanning from one area to another.

Similar efforts to introduce greater competition into the road haulage sector in the early autumn of 2010 also met strong opposition. Tensions reached such levels that there were even reports of shots being fired and police escorts having to be brought in to protect convoys of vehicles belonging to freight operators who continued to work. With the government threatening ever more draconian penalties, the stand-off continued until late September, when a deal was reached postponing full deregulation and giving a form of compensation to those who were threatened with the greatest losses.[56] Faced with a strong challenge from a well organised professional group, the government had appeared willing to make concessions over structural reforms, providing fiscal consolidation targets were not challenged. The impact of such moves was not always easy to discern, but, sometimes, as with changes introduced into labour legislation designed to make it easier for companies to negotiate lower wages, the concessions seem to have been sufficient to render the law virtually inoperable. With the government also continuing to refine the pension legislation through additional amendments that appeared to lessen its effectiveness, the overall picture was becoming increasingly murky, especially as there were growing signs that even fiscal consolidation targets were being missed. The IMF had long noted that expenditure would rise in the second half of the year due to increased military spending and higher interest payments, but revenues were also dipping, due to the deepening recession and delays in tabling tax laws.[57] The government needed to make up the shortfall, but with local elections pending it seems to have been unwilling to table any tax rises that might alienate the electorate, resorting instead to an amnesty to gather extra funds.[58]

The local election campaign preoccupied the government for much of the autumn, partly due to the decision of New Democracy and much of the remainder of the opposition to cast it as an effective referendum on the memorandum.[59] At first PASOK had tried to counter this by focusing on local issues. However, after the party started to lose ground in the opinion polls, Papandreou in a rather roundabout way during a television interview had implied that he would call a fresh general election if PASOK did not perform well in the vote, although he conveniently failed to set any specific targets. This injected even more vigour into the campaign and in the first of the two rounds of elections the flyers of the various parties lay so thick on the ground outside some Athenian polling stations that the tarmac was barely visible below. Inside the polling booths voters were confronted with a list so long and complicated that most electors took at least five minutes to make their selection, but, in the end, PASOK performed creditably. It won the greatest share of the vote and fifteen of the new regions, as against New Democracy's eight. However, the scale of the socialists' success may have been exaggerated by the fact that their conservative opponents chose in general not to field high profile candidates, perhaps because Samaras wanted to minimise disruption within the party while he consolidated his hold on power.[60] Of the other parties, SYRIZA in particular performed poorly, gaining few councillors, despite the fact that it had shifted its strategy towards building a broad left-based anti-memorandum coalition, partly in the hope of picking up disaffected PASOK voters. The official rate of abstentions, which some authors have suggested is exaggerated due to inaccuracies in the voting lists, was also high, not only in the usual far flung islands and out of the way parts of northern Greece but also in more urban areas, with only just over a third of the registered electorate casting valid ballots in the second round of voting in Attica.[61] Rates of abstention varied across districts, and the reasoning of each voter cannot be known for sure, but post-election analysis seemed to show that up to a third of those who had voted for PASOK in 2009 had stayed away from the polls, and this fact does not seem to have been lost on the many deputies from this party representing the populous Athens B constituency, encompassing all the suburbs outside the city centre, who started to nervously consider their future.[62] As a result of the elections, suspicion of the memorandum seems to have deepened even further within the governing party, most visibly when ministers associated with its implementation faced hostile questioning from backbench groups.[63] Therefore, while Papandreou and the government's spokesperson might confidently assert that the local election results reflected a strong will for change in all sections of society and the 'complete legitimacy' of the government's policy for the 'country's salvation', others were more cautious in their appraisal, with Haris Kastanidis, the minister for justice, transparency and human rights, suggesting that the high level of abstentions demonstrated a loss of faith in the political system as a whole.[64]

At the same time as he was giving his judgement on the local election results, Kastanidis also mentioned that he thought that the terms of the memorandum should be renegotiated so as to lengthen the period of time over which the budgetary deficit was due to be reduced.[65] This was the first time a government minister had openly raised this prospect although in private meetings the possibility of changing some of the original terms of the agreement had been under discussion for some time.[66] Indeed, taken together with the tabling of a 2011 budget that suggested the government was still on track to meet its fiscal targets and continued rumours that the Chinese were prepared to step in and buy Greek government bonds once the country returned to the financial markets for funding, the possibility that the original targets might be changed in Greece's favour was sufficient to bolster international confidence in the adjustment programme well into the autumn.[67] As a result the spread on ten-year bonds dropped by 300 bps between September and mid-October to around 650 bps. Since late spring, events in Greece had not been an immediate concern for the other euro area states. As the sense of crisis waned, they had mostly been preoccupied with ensuring that their national parliaments ratified the legislation establishing the European

Financial Stability Facility (EFSF) and that stress tests were conducted on domestic banks to make sure they were able to weather any future upheavals. However, within the continuing speculation about Greece defaulting, a specific concern had grown about a hump in debt repayments at the end of the assistance programme, with the projection at the time being that these could rise from €53.2 billion in 2013 to €70.8 billion in 2014.[68] To make it easier for Greece to cope with this increase, the IMF had suggested that it might be necessary to either extend the repayment period or that a new programme could follow on from the old. Its European partners, still employing a language of moral hazard, showed little enthusiasm for these ideas, but within the broader debate on debt sustainability the notion of introducing a mechanism allowing for an orderly state insolvency within the euro area was starting to gain ground. It had been under discussion in Germany in particular since at least the beginning of 2009, as part of a debate about the creation of a European Monetary Fund, and was specifically mentioned in a speech by Merkel in the Bundestag in May 2010, although she still seems to have seen it primarily in terms of a further incentive encouraging states to keep their finances in order.[69] Others remained sceptical, with Lagarde maintaining that the idea was a diversion from immediate problems, and Thomas Mayer, the chief economist of Deutsche Bank, who had helped shape the idea of a European Monetary Fund, continued to insist that, when the creation of an insolvency mechanism had been suggested, it had not been envisaged that it would lead to the restructuring of the debts of Greece or any other country, let alone pave the way for an exit from the euro area. Instead he saw it as an attempt to defuse systemic risk because 'As long as we don't have a plan B, namely a plan for how to handle countries that are insolvent and not just suffering from a liquidity problem, the markets will doubt whether the policy approach is complete, whether it is convincing'.[70]

The issue was further pursued by the Van Rompuy task force which had been established in the spring of 2010 to strengthen economic governance within the EU. Along with its other findings this recommended that an 'improved crisis resolution framework' should be created, although no further details were outlined other than to note issues to be discussed 'may include the role of the private sector, the role of the IMF and the very strong conditionality under which such programmes should operate'.[71] The findings of the task force were endorsed by a 28–29 October European Council but not before a heated dispute had broken out over two points: the first was the extent to which any sanctions imposed under the new regime should be mandatory, and might even be extended to include suspension of voting rights within the EU; the second was whether private sector bondholders should be required to suffer losses if a state made a request for financial support from any new crisis resolution mechanism—something which, somewhat euphemistically, is termed private sector involvement (PSI). To try and iron out these differences, Merkel and Sarkozy had met on 18 October 2010 in the resort of Deauville on the north French coast during a summit with the Russian President Dmitry Medvedev. Pictures of the German chancellor and French president walking together in deep conversation on a boardwalk by the sea fed a growing narrative that presented them alone as deciding the destiny of the euro area and the meeting has come to be seen as a decisive moment in the crisis.[72] As a result of their talks and others between the finance ministers of the two states, the idea of imposing automatic sanctions was watered down, and it was agreed that in the event of a state requesting financial assistance from what was to become known as the European Stability Mechanism (ESM) the face value of its debt held by private bondholders would be reduced through a 'haircut'. To facilitate this legal caveats would be written into all post-2013 euro area sovereign bond contracts. Known as collective action clauses, these would make it easier to secure the necessary revision of terms to permit PSI because only a specified number of bond holders would have to agree to a change which would be binding on all.

Those who favoured PSI believed it would enhance financial rigour by making lenders more prudent and borrowers think twice before overextending themselves. However, others saw it holding considerable dangers, with Trichet on hearing of the agreement between the German and French leaders supposedly retorting, 'You're going to destroy the euro'.[73] Papandreou had argued against the provision for automatic sanctions and the suspension of voting rights at the 28–29 October European Council on the basis that it was impossible to expect Greece to accept that it would be allowed to participate in discussions on issues relating to Turkey without being able to cast a ballot, but he seems initially to have viewed decisions taken about the ESM in a positive light.[74] However, by the time he spoke at a Socialist International gathering in Paris in mid-November, he was warning that the insistence on PSI, in particular, could 'force some economies towards bankruptcy'.[75] His change of tone was almost certainly prompted by the reaction of the financial markets to the deal over PSI, which had spurred investors to deepen their reassessment of the levels of risk inherent in holding euro area sovereign bonds. The chief buyers of such bonds tend to be foreign central banks, commercial banks, insurance companies and pension funds seeking a safe and readily tradable investment with a steady yield.[76] Indeed, such is the size of the market, that large quantities of bonds can usually be traded with little perceptible change in price, allowing banks to hold them as an effective proxy for cash. Consequently they had previously been treated as virtually risk free collateral of the highest quality, but introducing the possibility of PSI had brought uncertainty into the forecasting of future yields and this was changing perceptions. As a result spreads began to rise across much of the euro area, but the movement was particularly pronounced in the case of Greece. This was partly due to its continuing poor public finances and the fact that the sustainability of its debt was already under question. However, coupled with this was now the fact that, under the projected timetable, the ESM would be activated and collective action clauses written into all new bonds at about the same time as Greece might be needing a new support programme to replace the old. As a result the spread on ten-year bonds now rose back over 900 bps, perhaps also driven by the fact that after the Council's decision on PSI many euro area commercial banks seem to have come to view the commitment they had made earlier in the year to retain their sovereign bond holdings as being null and void, and began to offload the government securities of Greece and other troubled euro area economies. Between December 2010 and February 2011 German banks are reported to have reduced their holdings of Greek sovereign debt by 40 per cent, although, according to one source, this was partly due to the fact that maturing bonds were not replaced.[77] Later, at the 28 November Economic and Financial Affairs (Ecofin) Council, the finance ministers revisited the whole question and decided that instead of any haircut being imposed automatically, private sector creditors would initially be required to participate in negotiations to establish debt sustainability. Trichet called this a 'useful clarification', but nonetheless the risk free status of euro area government debt had been called into question, and, as one unidentified European Commission official resignedly told a journalist at the time, 'Sometimes we in the EU are good at creating new difficulties just when we have overcome past difficulties'.[78]

The overall result was that by the end of November 2009 the notion that the country was in crisis had reappeared with renewed vigour both inside and outside Greece. This was not just due to the reaction of the financial markets to the decision regarding PSI. On 18 November, Ireland had joined Greece in seeking assistance from its euro area partners after continuing worries about the health of the country's banks led its sovereign bond yields to rise to what were seen as unsustainable levels. In the same period, Eurostat also revised the

Greek 2009 budget deficit even further upward to 15.4 per cent of GDP, and the national debt from 115.1 per cent of GDP to 126.8 per cent, largely because methodological changes had led to the incorporation of more debts from the wider public sector.[79] The new figures were widely interpreted as making fresh austerity measures and debt restructuring all but inevitable, especially after a troika inspection revealed that a combination of the deepening recession, expenditure overruns and revenue shortfalls meant programme targets were being missed. For the first time the talks between the troika and the government were described as tough, with the heads of the mission at one point reportedly spending twenty-four hours cloistered with Papaconstantinou.[80] There were also the first signs of frustration within the wider euro area, with the Austrian Vice Chancellor and Minister of Finance, Josef Pröll, under pressure at home to implement a cost-cutting budget and facing criticism from far-right groups opposed to giving more assistance to Greece, making some comments about the Greeks not keeping to their targets and suggesting that the next tranche of funding could be delayed.[81] The incident amounted to little more than a storm in a teacup, but signs of a new tone were apparent in the headlines of the newspaper *To Vima* on 17 November, when it declared, 'Merkel uses the third tranche of the loan as a blackmailing weapon'.[82] When they gave their customary post-inspection news conference, the comments of the heads of the troika mission were still broadly positive, but in a series of newspaper interviews afterwards they stressed the need for radical reform and this message was reinforced by Rehn during a visit to Athens, when he also dwelt on the importance of ensuring that legislation was fully implemented.[83] This now became the watchword of much of the external comment and was interpreted by many as criticism of the government, but implementation was not just a matter of political will. In the words of the IMF, Greece was embarking on a broad and deep agenda of reform 'unprecedented in Europe', and moves to establish a fast track approval process for investments and a one-stop shop for business start-ups were as much delayed by inadequate information technology and a shortage of skilled personnel as ministerial inaction.[84] Other reforms, such as the introduction of computer systems to curb pharmaceutical spending, which took a large proportion of the healthcare budget, were also complex and, necessarily, took time. Despite the passing of fiscal responsibility and management legislation, the Ministry of Finance was also continuing to encounter difficulties in controlling overspending in many government departments, with laws still being introduced into parliament without proper assessment of the implications for spending. Other key reforms, such as moving the

point of expenditure control from the time of spending to that of commitment, were even more challenging, since they involved transforming an entire
administrative culture.[85] The real reasons for reforms not being implemented
and objectives not being met were often as deep rooted and complex as the
external explanations tended to be simplistic, but the unavoidable fact was that
increasingly targets were being missed.

Despite the uncertainties of the autumn, as 2011 dawned echoes of the
narrative of success could still be heard. Looking at the euro zone as a whole,
some suggested the worst of the crisis was over. Ireland may have been forced
to ask for help but its woes were centred on its banks and were very different
from those of Greece. The nature of the loans it received, which were from the
EFSF and some non-euro area countries, such as the UK, was also different.
They carried slightly higher rates but were longer dated, and after the negotiations Papaconstantinou indicated that a decision had been taken to equalise
the terms of borrowing of the two countries, although this was not ratified, as
he had expected at a subsequent December meeting.[86] After the flurry of
recriminations in the autumn, when some comments by Merkel about former
Chancellor Gerhard Schröder being irresponsible when he agreed that Greece
could join the euro drew a sharp riposte from Papandreou, relations with
European partners also seemed to improve.[87] Merkel began the New Year by
declaring that Germany would 'support whatever is needed to support the
euro' and strategic bond buying by the ECB under its Securities Markets
Programme (SMP) had helped ease the pressure on a number of euro area
states.[88] The idea of issuing Eurobonds was even revived and Papandreou took
it so seriously that he established a committee to try and secure enough signatures on a petition to force the Commission to address the issue.[89] Public
opinion also appeared to be still broadly supportive of the government. In an
opinion poll taken at the time more saw austerity as being necessary than did
not, and over half viewed the crisis as being an opportunity for the country to
move forward.[90] A slew of figures also suggested that the economic situation
was improving. The downturn in the fourth quarter of 2010 had been less
than expected and even more encouragingly the initial indications were that
the economy had actually grown in the first quarter of 2011, driven by a strong
rise in exports to recovering euro area states.[91] Business turnover in January
2011 posted an increase on the year before, with gains in manufacturing and
the retail sector more than offsetting a continuing fall in services and construction. The Foundation for Economic and Industrial Research's (IOBE)
economic sentiment index perked up and, with business start-ups reported to

be exceeding closures, fewer employers were also said to be thinking of shedding labour.[92] Indeed, there were even signs that the policy of internal devaluation might be beginning to bear fruit, with hourly labour costs reported as decreasing by 6.5 per cent in the last quarter of 2010 compared with a year earlier.[93] Despite talk of the banks lacking liquidity, commercial lending was also holding up well, and earlier in the autumn EFG Eurobank Ergasias had even been able to raise a loan overseas using Greek government bonds as collateral, albeit at a premium.[94] Larger businesses, such as the Coca-Cola Hellenic Bottling Company, Hellenic Telecommunications Organisation (OTE) and Titan Cement, were continuing to tap international credit markets, and, at this point, it still seemed possible that the state itself might return to the financial markets for funding in the near future, even if this would be through bonds targeted specifically at the Greek diaspora.[95]

There were also signs that, after a lull over the autumn, momentum was picking up with structural reforms. Impressive targets were announced for slimming down the public sector workforce through natural wastage, with 150,000 jobs scheduled to go by 2015. Amid frequent strikes, key laws were also passing through parliament, with the public transport legislation being followed by another covering healthcare reform and a taxation bill with draconian penalties. After much debate, a draft bill for liberalising the closed professions was also published. However, when Andreas Loverdos, the minister for health and social solidarity, opened negotiations with pharmacists to try and bring changes to their profession, it only led to a series of strikes and in reality any feeling of optimism was little more than skin-deep. The passing of an omnibus bill containing measures required by the memorandum through parliament had been marked by the most violent protests since the signing of the document. Reports that the recession was beginning to bottom out hardly tallied with the news that nearly 100,000 jobs had been lost in the last quarter of 2010, and in November *Eleftherotypia*, under the headline 'Ten reasons for somebody not to live in Greece', had highlighted not only the collapsing economy and rising taxes but also growing unemployment.[96] It was therefore hardly surprising that just 22 per cent of the respondents in an opinion poll shared the view that the worst of the crisis had passed for the job market.[97] Furthermore, even some of the positive indicators were not as they seemed. Papandreou had attributed the 'export explosion' to the impact of the structural reforms but, in reality, it was driven more by turbulence in the Middle East, which led tourists to switch their holiday destination to Greece, and a recovery in world commodity markets boosting demand for Greek primary products.[98] Likewise, the rise in business start-ups—which was difficult to discern on the ground—at least in part seems to have been driven by efforts to bypass hiring restriction within the public sector, with individuals establishing companies which were then contracted to solely work for the state. Most importantly, it was becoming clear that the the fiscal adjustment of 8 per cent of GDP needed to reduce the 2010 budget deficit to 9.5 per cent of GDP was not sustainable in the longer-term. Revenues continued to lag seriously below target—the IMF blamed the tax administration but the recession was probably equally responsible—and expenditure above target, especially outside central government. As a result from early summer 2010 the government had only been balancing the books by holding back on military expenditure and accumulating over €4 billion of payment arrears.

On 27 January 2011 the officials of the troika arrived back in Athens for an inspection which was due to lead to the disbursement of the fourth tranche. The visit seems to have had its difficulties from the outset, with the troika identifying yet more shortfalls in the budget and unhappy about the non-implementation of legislation, with it being revealed during the course of their time in Athens that no OSE staff had been transferred prior to the expiry of an end of January deadline. Nevertheless, when they sat down for their customary press conference at the end of the visit, their message was at first familiar, as they reported that the programme was slowly gaining traction and progress was being made towards financial stabilisation, although they also noted that the pace of the structural reforms needed to be accelerated to gain a critical mass.[99] Then they dramatically veered off the expected script by suggesting that the Greek authorities through various means, including privatisation, could raise up to €50 billion by 2015. As the news spread around the globe, and the suggestion began to harden into a commitment, the authorities seemed to be caught off balance. It was only much later in the evening that a statement was released which complained of an 'unacceptable' interference in Greek domestic affairs.[100] The next day Papandreou rang both Strauss-Kahn and Rehn to pursue the issue and soon officials from the troika institutions were beginning to backtrack on the presentation, if not the substance of the announcement, with a statement confirming that the role of the mission was to advise and support the Greek government, and regret expressed 'if a different impression was perceived'.[101] At first confusion continued to reign but by the beginning of the next week the government was starting to take ownership of the proposal, suggesting that it had been after all its own idea, although it coupled this with a firm pledge that no public land would be transferred or sold in meeting the target.

The controversy sparked by the February 2011 press conference meant that it was the last given by the heads of the troika mission. They were never again required to answer questions from the media or to justify their decisions in public. At a stroke they became even more anonymous and alien to the people of Greece, their opinions in the future to be heard almost exclusively through government intermediaries or officials in distant Brussels or Washington. A gap was opened up in communications which was never to be bridged. The announcement had taken everybody by surprise, partly, because privatisation had hardly been mentioned in the original memorandum, which contented itself with the somewhat ungrammatical observation that the government would 'review the role for divesting state assets' and a brief mention of a plan being drawn up which would yield revenues of at least €1 billion a year between 2011 and 2013.[102] Nowhere was there a suggestion of €50 billion and this figure seems to have arisen in part from calculations made by the IMF, which in its second review under the Stand-By Arrangement, published in December 2010, had produced a table suggesting that the Greek state possessed share holdings worth 17 per cent of GDP, public sector capital stock worth half of GDP and property estimated to be worth between €200 and €300 billion.[103] However, the same report had been cautious about how readily these assets could be translated into cash, speaking only of €7 billion being raised over three years. The IMF had argued that a more ambitious privatisation programme was necessary to reduce public expenditure and to increase growth by releasing potential. However, with doubts continuing to be expressed about the sustainability of the country's debt and little sign of agreement on the need for restructuring, this new stress on divesting state assets can be seen as an attempt to outline an alternative debt reduction strategy, because, if the ambitious target had been met, it would have reduced the debt to GDP ratio by around 18 per cent by 2020. The extent to which the €50 billion was ever a feasible target, though, must be questioned, especially since actual privatization proceeds by 2015 only seem to have amounted to €3.1 billion. Possibly it was little more than a ploy by the IMF designed to put pressure on recalcitrant European partners to persuade them that they needed to seriously consider debt relief although the figure was not forgotten, being resurrected again by euro area leaders in the negotiations leading up to the signing of the third memorandum in the summer of 2015.[104]

Indeed, in some ways, it is possible to see the €50 billion target as merely being the troika's equivalent of a slew of stories emerging in Greece at the time suggesting alternative ways of paying off the debt. These arose partly as a by-product of fears of default and a desire to find less painful ways of resolving the crisis, and partly as a reaction to an increasing awareness of the powerlessness of local political actors. Some dwelt on familiar themes, like a story that appeared at this time saying that hundreds of billions had been stashed away by Greeks in Swiss bank accounts.[105] The assumption was that, if this money was returned to the country and properly taxed, enough would be raised to pay off a sizeable chunk of the debt. There was also renewed talk about presenting a formal demand for billions of euros of reparations from Germany for the damage it inflicted on the country during the Second World War, as well as requesting recompense for a forced loan extracted by the occupiers from the Bank of Greece at that time. The total by some calculations amounted to at least €162 billion.[106] Some approaches were more novel. Stories started to appear in the press detailing the mineral wealth of the country, with much speculation centring on possible offshore oil and gas reserves following a find in Cypriot territorial waters. There was also much talk of Greece borrowing money from the EFSF to buy back its own bonds at a heavily discounted price on the secondary market, although commentators in general thought this would have only a limited impact on debt levels. China was repeatedly said to be prepared to ride to the rescue and buy Greek bonds, and Russia was also cast in the mantle of providential saviour, with stories emerging that it was prepared to offer loans at a lower rate than the troika.[107] A campaign was even started to have part of the national debt declared odious.[108] This was in line with a contested legal concept which gives grounds for debts to be annulled if they are incurred by a regime, usually despotic, without the consent of the people, bring no public benefit and are knowingly made as such by the lenders.[109] In the aftermath of the Iraq War, it had been argued that the debts incurred by the regime of Saddam Hussein should be cancelled on these grounds and the concept had also been used by Ecuador to justify the repudiation of part of its borrowings in 2008.[110] Now, some wished to apply the notion to Greece, which they argued had also been systematically looted by its political elite, but, as with the idea that €50 billion could be raised from privatisation by 2015, neither this nor any of the other schemes have yet come to fruition, although many have continued to find favour, with talk of seeking reparations from Germany periodically resurfacing and SYRIZA establishing a Truth Committee on the Public Debt after its January 2015 election victory.

As the first blossoms of spring appeared in 2011, talk of a new general election filled the air but, with opinion polls showing the public rapidly losing faith in all the established political parties, other forms of opposition were also beginning to emerge. Some took a semi-traditional form, such as the fierce battles which raged at Keratea, just outside Athens, between the riot police and protesters trying to stop the construction of a landfill, while others were more innovatory, like the 'Won't Pay' movement, whose members refused to pay the ever rising motorway tolls.[111] As public discontent became more evident, politicians found it increasingly difficult to appear in public and there were noisy protest rallies outside the houses of former leaders, including Simitis.[112] Not only was the general public losing patience, stories also began to circulate that the troika considered the government to be suffering from 'reform fatigue' and incapable of instituting further change.[113] Some said this was because of a lack of collegiality, with too many ministers prepared to sit back allowing their colleagues to take the hard decisions. Others claimed it was due to inefficiency, with one newspaper editorial arguing that under the pressure of the memorandum the state apparatus had effectively stopped functioning.[114] This growing feeling that the government was losing control, coupled with the realisation that shortfalls still existed and that further austerity measures would be needed, as well as the constant speculation about default, shredded any optimism that the worst of the crisis was over and helped scotch any economic revival that may briefly have occurred. It also meant that eventual debt restructuring became more likely and this was underlined on 7 March by Moody's decision to downgrade Greece by three notches. The Greek Finance Ministry called the decision 'incomprehensible' and Papandreou responded by calling an extraordinary meeting of ministers.[115] A group of PASOK deputies were reported to be asking the government to sue Moody's for undermining the Greek position prior to a European summit, and there was much talk at the time about this being the decisive blow that derailed the programme, but, in reality, the first troika visit of the year and its aftermath had already punctured any remaining optimism. The furore over privatisation had also revealed publicly for the first time the extent to which domestic political actors were being marginalised, and perhaps in reaction the local media began to increasingly present the country as being at the mercy of the rest of the euro area and especially the Germans.[116] Domestic politics retreated into stories about past corruption scandals, a spat between Pangalos and SYRIZA, and renewed debates about immigration.[117] The narratives of success and failure were beginning to merge, and politically, as well as financially, the old system was increasingly looking bankrupt.

6

SURPRISED BY THE SURPRISE[1]

THE WIDER EURO ZONE CRISIS AND THE FALL
OF THE PAPANDREOU GOVERNMENT

The first troika reports of 2011 had still carried traces of optimism, with talk of targets being broadly fulfilled and reform momentum picking up, but inside Greece the popular perception was that the crisis was deepening. In the cities strikes were becoming ever more frequent, leaving huge piles of garbage accumulating on pavements across Athens, streets gridlocked for hours as commuters struggled to get to work and ferries stuck in harbours. Everyday talk was of business closures, redundancies and growing financial hardship, and, as sentiment at home became ever more pessimistic, with the encouragement of the political leadership, the local media began to increasingly dwell on a series of forthcoming EU meetings in the hope of a *deus ex machina*. However, Greece's euro area partners seemed to be unsure as to how to respond. The international media continued to be full of stories about default, debt restructuring and even exit from the euro but many among the European political leadership, especially in Germany, still seemed to see moral hazard as the greater peril. This led to another sustained period of uncertainty and doubt which fuelled market turbulence. After Portugal was forced to request financial assistance, fears were expressed that Spain and Italy might follow suit, breeding further concern about the soundness of the euro area banking system as a whole. Greece was to be at the centre of this turmoil but also only one constituent part. As yet, though, in the early days of the spring of 2011 the scale of this impending crisis was still far from apparent and when the government looked ahead to the forthcoming EU meetings its hopes did not rise above its euro area partners agreeing to some softening in the terms of its loan facility. It was a move that both the government and the troika had come to see as being necessary to persuade the financial markets that the adjustment programme remained viable.

Initially, little was expected when euro area leaders gathered for an informal meeting in Brussels on 11 March 2011, with the conflict in Libya the main point on the agenda. However, late in the evening, when they turned to the crisis in the euro zone, they made a series of decisions which caused analysts 'genuine surprise'.[2] As well as agreeing to proceed with the establishment of a framework for economic governance known as the Pact on the Euro and to raise the lending capacity of the European Financial Stability Facility (EFSF) to its full €440 billion to make it better able to meet future contingencies, the leaders also made some further decisions about the European Stability Mechanism (ESM). It would be allowed to purchase bonds on primary but not secondary markets, largely it seems because this would have required it to have a more elaborate structure and, in an atmosphere free from any concerns about moral hazard, it was also agreed that the cost of its loans would be little above the European Central Bank's (ECB's) base rate. This decision brought the interest rates on existing assistance package loans into focus and an agreement was reached that 'in principle' those of Greece should be lowered, but not of Ireland, apparently due to the obduracy of the new Taoiseach, Enda Kenny, who refused to increase the country's corporation tax rates to the chagrin of some European partners.[3] Although, as usual, it took some time and several other meetings before this decision was fully ratified, the interest rate on the Greek loans would be lowered by around 100 bps to 3.7 per cent on average and the grace and repayment periods lengthened, extending average maturities from three to seven-and-a-half years.[4] The International Monetary Fund (IMF) calculated that, in combination with some other measures, this would reduce future financing costs by around €47 billion during the period between 2012 and 2015, and in parts of the domestic media the agreement was presented as another example of Greek negotiating prowess.[5] Others, though, were more doubtful, with the main news programme of one of the main commercial television channels, on the day a deadly tsunami struck Japan, greeting the announcement with the headline 'Greece saved but the Greeks drowned'. It was widely assumed that agreement had only been reached upon promises of further austerity, and soon afterwards the domestic press again started to speculate about possible future measures.[6] As a result, the agreement brought little change in public sentiment and, when Papandreou visited the island of Syros later in the month, riot police had to intervene to shield him from angry protesters.[7]

The continuing optimism of the February troika reports was partly due to the fact that in the first quarter of 2011 the government had still more or less met its fiscal goals. However, a small shortfall of 0.75 per cent of GDP was only being held in check by a combination of expedited EU funds, lower than expected local government spending, as new administrations established themselves in office, and a continuing compression of central government expenditure coupled with a build-up of payment arrears.[8] This was no more sustainable than before and, after Eurostat had raised the projected 2010 budget deficit from 9.5 per cent of GDP to 10.5 per cent at the beginning of April, what had long been suspected was effectively confirmed. Greece would not be able to return to the financial markets for funding within the time span envisaged, making a new and more costly assistance package stretching beyond the existing period all but inevitable if the country was not to default. The granting of this new package, though, was far from a foregone conclusion. There was little obvious enthusiasm among European partners for providing further support to a country still seen as being responsible for creating its own ills, especially at a time when it was becoming increasingly apparent that further funds would be required to stem the wider crisis, with Portugal on the verge of requesting assistance and yields on Spanish and Italian bonds remaining high. 'Support fatigue', to use the apt term of Rehn, was evident in opinion polls conducted in many northern euro area members, and helped fuel the rise of right-wing parties sceptical about giving further assistance in the Netherlands, Austria and Finland.[9] These groups helped propel ruling administrations towards less accommodating positions, in the case of Finland even to demand that Greece provided collateral before it agreed further support. The same was also true for Germany where elements within both the junior parties of the ruling Christian Democratic Union (CDU), Christian Social Union and Free Democratic Party coalition began to adopt a markedly more sceptical tone. This was especially after public unhappiness with the assistance being given to Greece was used to explain poor showings in a string of regional elections, including the CDU losing power in Baden-Württemberg for the first time since the 1950s. Merkel, herself, insisted that the regional election results did not directly influence her euro area policy, but with elements of the German media continuing to voice hostility towards Greece the chancellor and some of her ministers were not averse to making disparaging remarks about the many public holidays and early retirement ages of the southern euro area states.[10] With the Federal Constitutional Court in Karlsruhe also considering the legality of some of the measures taken to stem the crisis, especially as regards the EFSF, the German position on Greece, whether from design or not, again appeared to be ambiguous and this fuelled the uncertainty, because without Teutonic finance there could be no new assistance package.[11]

The issue seems to have come to a head when finance ministers and central bank governors assembled in Washington for the spring meeting of the World Bank and IMF along with a concomitant G20 gathering. At a meeting with European colleagues in the French ambassador's residence in the city, Strauss-Kahn is reported to have given voice to continuing IMF unease over Greece's solvency and to have suggested that the Fund would find it difficult to carry on releasing its tranches of funding if the euro area states did not provide more support.[12] The warning, along with a series of leaks in the international media at the time about debt restructuring, seems to have been designed to concentrate minds, and a number of meetings were subsequently convened to address the issue.[13] Most notoriously a 'secret' gathering was held in an eighteenth century paper mill at the Château de Senningen in Luxembourg at the beginning of May. Here, at the invitation of Juncker, the finance ministers of the euro area G20 members, Germany, France and Italy, as well as Spain, as a permanent invitee at its meetings, together with Rehn and Trichet, assembled along with Papaconstantinou. News of the gathering was leaked in the German press and, on the basis of some briefing notes prepared for the German delegation, explosive claims were made that it would be discussing Greece's exit from the euro area, with the story being given added piquancy by the fact that the existence of the meeting was still being denied by Juncker's press secretary even as it was convening.[14] Afterwards, Greek and Commission sources combined to roundly dismiss the chance of any Greek exit, with Papaconstantinou reverting to the standard narrative, when he suggested that the consequences would be too catastrophic for it to be considered, since it would see public debt double, consumer spending power 'shattered' and the country sink into a 'war-like recession'.[15] However, perhaps stung into greater candour by the furore, Juncker in a subsequent press conference, for the first time, did admit that Greece would be needing a second assistance programme, although in public Merkel could still remain coy, stating that only when the full picture became apparent 'can I decide what, if anything, needs to be done'.[16] Indeed, it was only on 10 June 2011 that the Bundestag gave its non-binding approval to participation in the second package after Merkel, following a visit to the United States, had warned that an unruly default in the euro area would put the global economic recovery in jeopardy. In its vote, though, the German parliament had imposed a number of conditions, including that there should be 'adequate participation of private creditors'.[17]

By the time of the Senningen meeting most outside commentators had already come to the conclusion that some kind of debt restructuring was all but inevitable. Polls of investors found large majorities holding this view and Greek government bonds were already trading at prices that effectively discounted the possibility, with the spread between local and German two-year government securities exceeding 2650 bps. It also provided the rationale behind Standard & Poor's further downgrading the country's sovereign rating on 29 March to BB-.[18] Papandreou dismissed the downgrade, saying it was more a reflection of EU policymaking not being decisive enough than of Greece's current predicament.[19] However, putting debt restructuring into action, within an environment which until a few months previously had seen it as all but impossible, was always going to be a difficult exercise. At Senningen there had apparently been another heated exchange between the finance ministers and Trichet over the issue of private sector involvement (PSI) and besides the major political decisions there was also much fine detail to work out.[20] Moreover, there were still some outside Greece who continued to believe that it was only the threat of the 'horror story' of restructuring that was prodding the Greek government to accept fiscal consolidation.[21] In consequence the debate about debt restructuring was so full of doubt and confusion that for much of this period most political leaders and central bankers continued to declare it was off the agenda, calling it 'a huge mistake' that would lock Greece out of the financial markets for ten or fifteen years and more bluntly a 'nightmare'.[22] It was left to a few senior former politicians, like Simitis, who gave an extensive interview in favour, and a constant stream of leaks avidly reported in the media to suggest otherwise.[23]

In fact the idea of restructuring Greece's debts had been canvassed from at least the time the original support mechanism was being drawn up in 2010. The issue seems to have been broached at encounters between IMF officials and German and French finance ministry staff in the spring of 2010; and at the IMF board meeting called to agree the initial Stand-By Arrangement, representatives from Argentina, India, Russia and Switzerland all pressed for restructuring, with the board member from Brazil declaring that without PSI the loan would become 'a bailout of Greece's private-sector bondholders, mainly European financial institutions'.[24] However, there was no uniformity of view within the IMF and staff members deflected the criticism by saying that the issue had been discussed but ruled out by the Greek government on the grounds of its complexity due to the wide dispersal of the bonds and the fact that most lacked collective action clauses. As a result the matter does not seem to have been seriously pursued at this time, although it was apparently discussed behind the scenes at gatherings such as the meeting of G20 finance ministers in Seoul, South Korea, in November 2010 as well as in various private encounters. Nonetheless, when, at the beginning of April 2011, a German press agency carried a report that the IMF was pushing for restructuring, it was still officially denied by the Washington-based organisation.[25] Continuing to refute the possibility of restructuring, when it was becoming increasingly obvious that Greek debt levels were unsustainable, did little to stabilise the financial markets and seems largely to have been prompted by lack of agreement on the form the process should take, the degree to which it should be either voluntary or coercive and the timing. Many within the IMF consistently favoured an early date to maximise the benefits, but euro area partners such as France and Germany were far more wary, not least because some of their banks, which were only just recovering from the 2008 financial crisis, would have to take billions of euros of losses due to their extensive holdings of Greek government bonds.[26] Indeed, as the Brazilian IMF board member noted, the support mechanism by stopping the Greek state from defaulting on its loans, actually, protected its creditors, including the heavily exposed financial institutions of northern euro area countries. In this sense, the decision to lend money to Greece can be seen as being as much a rescue package for these institutions as it was for the country itself and, indeed, it has been suggested that in reality only about 10 per cent of the money provided has been used to finance Greek government activity, with most of the remainder being utilised to service the debt and shore up the banking sector after restructuring.[27] Indeed, this intertwining of the Greek sovereign debt crisis with the health of the financial institutions of the euro area as a whole was to make any restructuring particularly fraught with difficulty, because badly handled it could potentially lead to a disorderly default, which some were to suggest might cost a trillion euros and send not only the European but also the global economy spiralling into recession.

Even allowing for rhetorical excess, the perils were clearly considerable, and this was not least for Greece where any restructuring would inevitably lead to the failure of the larger domestic banks and leave such enormous financial holes in many social security funds that they too would collapse without assistance.

Perhaps as a consequence of these dangers, the first restructuring strategies suggested were relatively cautious. The most commonly mentioned were a debt rollover, which would have probably followed the lines of an IMF sponsored initiative through which a group of international banks had agreed to continue to support a number of East European countries in 2009, and a soft restructuring through the extension of maturities, as happened in the case of Uruguay in 2003. Both these options were, eventually, abandoned, partly because they were seen as offering insufficient debt relief. However, at the time, they were seen as attractive because they afforded the possibility that any restructuring could be considered voluntary, which meant it would almost certainly not be termed a 'credit event' and that credit default swaps (CDS) would not be triggered. CDS are complex financial instruments which in simplified terms are a private contract between a buyer and a seller that effectively insures a holder of a bond or security against a previously agreed credit event, such as bankruptcy or debt restructuring. Developed in the 1990s, they had subsequently gained some notoriety, partly due to the role they had played in the near collapse of the American insurance multinational AIG during the 2008 financial crisis, but also because of suggestions that speculation in the CDS market had been instrumental in pushing Greek bond yields to unsustainable levels.[28] This issue remains controversial but, when the German financial services regulator, BaFin (Bundesanstalt für Finanzdienstleistungsaufsicht), investigated, it found little evidence of 'speculative activity on a massive scale'.[29] Since 2008 considerable efforts had been made to make the market in CDS more transparent, but in 2011 concerns still remained as to how destabilising it might be if they were triggered by a Greek restructuring. However, in the end even these fears were not sufficient to stop policymakers from abandoning the more cautious restructuring options outlined above in favour of the application of a straightforward 'haircut' reducing the face value of the bonds.

The sheer number of actors involved and the often sharp differences that emerged between and within countries and institutions, let alone between them and financial analysts, made the debate about debt restructuring fluid and often highly contradictory. However, as the media obsessively picked over every utterance by the politicians and other officials, and the prospects of restructuring, more austerity measures, a new assistance package and even exit from the euro ebbed and flowed, the people of Greece were cast into a kind of purgatory, assailed daily by endless scenarios that bred nothing but uncertainty and fed economic and political paralysis. The situation, if anything, seemed to worsen after Portugal requested financial assistance at the beginning of April. According to one's point of view this could be interpreted as marking either the end of the assistance package process or the start of a wider contagion, but in both cases attitudes towards Greece seemed to harden, especially after Eurostat, in an emailed statement of 13 May 2011, raised the projected budget deficit for the year from 7.4 per cent to 9.5 per cent of GDP, it being considered 'neither feasible or desirable' to stick to the original target.[30] With signs that the programme might be unravelling, relations with the troika appeared to become more fraught, and in mid-May the mission heads even temporarily left the country, supposedly because the government had not been able to draw up a credible mid-term fiscal strategy and privatisation schedule. Some cryptic comments from Juncker about solidarity having its limits and Greece's sovereign rating being further downgraded by three notches by Fitch to B+ further helped rekindle a sense of crisis.[31] The troika officials returned but the feeling of uncertainty remained, and this intensified at the end of May when it was acknowledged that the IMF had warned that it would not be able to contribute further funds until it received sufficient commitments from members of the euro area that they were prepared to make up any shortfalls in the Greek budget detected by the troika.[32] The euro area states, however, made it be known that they were not prepared to do this until Greece itself had produced a credible mid-term fiscal strategy, broadly supported by all the mainstream political parties, and had made a firmer commitment to privatisation. It had all the trappings of a classic standoff and, with the three sides apparently waiting to see who would give ground first, the prospect of a disorderly default or even exit from the euro was once more invoked as the media began to speculate that Greece would be unable to meet a large bond redemption payment due in June.[33]

As the talk of crisis deepened, the government slowly edged towards finalising the mid-term strategy but even a privatisation programme hedged with provisos and restrictions was reported to have created dissension in the cabinet.[34] Papandreou again reached for martial metaphors as he tried to rally support, but an attempt to build the broader political consensus desired by the troika foundered, with Karatzaferis, after one five-hour-meeting of party leaders, taking his leave of waiting journalists with a parting reference to divisions before the Battle of Salamis in 480 BC.[35] As ministers issued dire warnings about the government running out of money, the rhetoric again became apocalyptic. The Greek European Commissioner, Maria Damanaki, bluntly stated the choice was between reform and the drachma, although the Commission later downplayed her remarks.[36] One foreign newspaper even carried a story which claimed that a CIA report was suggesting there might be a military coup.[37] When, a few days later, on 2 June, Moody's downgraded Greece's sovereign rating to the same level of Cuba, leaving only Ecuador lower, and said it thought that there was an even chance that the country would default in the foreseeable future, the sense of impending disaster became tangible.[38] Yet, beyond the immediate rhetoric, there was also a counterbalancing narrative hinting that solutions were close to being found. Perhaps as a consequence, the euro throughout this period remained relatively stable, with any dramatic headlines usually referring to relatively small movements against carefully selected currencies. Stock markets also continued to largely move to global and national economic rhythms. Only in the Greek secondary bond market were the fears highly visible. Until April banks had still been buying Greek bonds to use them as collateral with the ECB, with one trader recalling that he had been called an idiot for not doing so, but now, with the prospect of default looming anew, the market again started to freeze.[39] Turnover fell by over half in the month of May and in these thin trading conditions, which exacerbated volatility, ten-year bond spreads rose to 1400 bps. The growing fear of default once more raised the prospect of contagion, with Bloomberg carrying a good summary of the emerging scenario:

> Analysts say contagion following a Greek default could play out like this: Refinancing costs for Ireland, Portugal, Spain and possibly Italy and Belgium would soar, thwarting efforts to rein in public deficits and putting states under pressure to restructure their debt as well; banks in countries with weak finances could face a run by depositors, while other lenders would see their capital eroded by credit writedowns; investors would shun equity markets and the euro and seek the safest securities. In a worst-case scenario, panic could freeze credit markets, as happened after the bankruptcy of New York-based Lehman Brothers Holdings Inc. in September 2008.[40]

Perhaps concerned that the situation might be getting out of hand, in the evening after the Moody's downgrade, the troika published a statement.[41] Couched in provisos, it nevertheless suggested that the next tranche of funding could be released in early July, once the new mid-term fiscal strategy had been put in place, which led one media source to report the story under the headline 'the biggest gamble in IMF history'.[42] The situation inside Greece, though, remained highly fluid with rumours of a cabinet reshuffle and a possible referendum circulating. Outside parliament tens of thousands of people had started to gather for noisy nightly rallies organised by an 'indignant movement' (*aganaktismenoi*) which modelled itself on a Spanish grouping bearing a similar name. The protests were peaceful, aside from a few scuffles which broke out one night when at least twenty MPs were prevented from leaving parliament by the normal route and instead had to be escorted by torchlight across the closed National Gardens.[43] However, the sheer size of the gatherings introduced a new dynamic into the situation. Inside parliament, after days of speculation in the press about its contents, the government finally presented the mid-term fiscal strategy. Covering the period 2011–2015, it featured adjustment measures worth in total €28.3 billion or 12 per cent of GDP.[44] In the second half of 2011 alone, these amounted to €6.5 billion or 2.9 per cent of GDP, with just over half coming through higher duties and property taxes as well as adjustments in VAT brackets. Expenditure would be reduced through public sector wage cuts, the merging of state entities and efficiency gains as well as a reform of the health and social security systems designed to curb pharmaceutical and pension costs.[45] An extensive privatisation programme was also tabled, which included pledges to sell off part of Hellenic Postbank, Piraeus and Thessaloniki port authorities, the train operating system, TrainOSE, and the ferronickel producer, LARCO.[46] The cabinet approved the strategy, but at a meeting of the parliamentary group on the economy, after coming under criticism from a number of Panhellenic Socialist Movement (PASOK) deputies, Papaconstantinou agreed to consider alternatives to some of the revenue raising measures he had proposed.[47] This only heightened the air of uncertainty and weakened his own authority, with one PASOK deputy later openly calling for him to resign.[48] A meeting of PASOK's political council then stretched into the early hours of the morning, with delegates reported to be demanding from Papandreou assurances that the country's assets would not be put up as collateral and that foreign officials would not take control of the privatisation programme.[49] One parliamentary deputy resigned from the party but did not give up his seat, reducing PASOK's overall majority to the low single figures and, with several others publicly stating that they would not vote for the strategy, the media started to suggest that its passage through parliament might be in doubt.[50] The sense of crisis was then further exacerbated by Standard & Poor's on 13 June downgrading Greece's sovereign rating even further from B to CCC, making it according to Bloomberg the lowest in the world.[51] Before then, on 10 June, Papandreou had addressed the nation again calling for political consensus, but the other political parties continued to show little interest, with New Democracy calling the mid-term strategy 'unreliable, unfair and ineffective'.[52] In this increasingly fervid atmosphere strange rumours began to circulate, including a report that an escape tunnel was being cleared to allow deputies to flee parliament if it was occupied by protesters.[53]

A general strike to protest against the mid-term strategy had been called for 15 June 2011. After hearing news that the Eurogroup in an emergency session had failed to make headway on the debt restructuring issue, the mood at a European Commission meeting that morning was described as sombre, with participants said to be feeling that the markets were beginning to scent blood. In Athens the air was brittle, as for the first time a general strike coincided with the protests mounted by the indignant movement. As the *aganaktisme-noi* attempted to blockade parliament to stop the deputies attending to vote on the new measures, a huge crowd massed in the centre of Athens. To keep the protesters at bay the police erected a tall metal screen across Vassilissis Sofias Avenue running to the side of the parliament building. The barricade served to both emphasise the gulf between the people trapped on one side and the rulers secure on the other, as well as the impotence of the protesters who were left hammering at it with their bare fists. As tensions mounted in Syntagma Square, events suddenly took an unexpected turn when Papandreou announced that he was seeking an audience with President Papoulias. Expectations immediately arose that he was about to reshuffle his cabinet, announce the formation of a government of national unity or even resign. Thus, when he emerged only to say that he was going to continue as prime minister and try to build political consensus, the sense of anticlimax was palpable. In the lee of the parliament building black helmeted figures came into the open and began to throw missiles at the riot police who responded as usual with tear gas, marking the beginning of an afternoon of confused conflict in which small groups enveloped in huge clouds of choking chemicals struggled with the police for control of the square. At times the demonstrators seemed to be gaining the upper hand, and at others the riot police, but by the early evening the violence had run its course and calm had returned. Only a thin line of police stood guard in front of the parliament as thousands of demonstrators reoccupied the square, hurling abuse at the politicians inside and playing handheld green lasers across the surrounding facades, supposedly to blind the biases of the local media. Messages on Twitter, following the example of users in Spain, were increasingly employing the hashtag '#greekrevolution', but behind the scenes intense political negotiations were taking place to try and shape a new government.[54]

Searching for political advantage PASOK and New Democracy each put forward various scenarios involving new elections, the creation of a government of national unity and the replacement of Papaconstantinou by Papademos, but in the end, when a tired and drawn looking Papandreou appeared on television late in the evening of 15 June, he merely announced that he would be reshuffling his cabinet and seeking a vote of confidence. Afterwards PASOK was to claim that New Democracy had tried to bounce them into an agreement they could not accept, but Samaras, in a late night broadcast, merely said that his party could not cooperate with another that had 'lost the trust of both... Greek citizens and the markets'.[55] That night Greece dominated international headlines amid renewed talk of the country defaulting and Europe facing its own 'Lehman moment'.[56] As the world waited nearly two weeks for the final vote, time passed in a sea of speculation. Two PASOK deputies resigned but were replaced by party loyalists. The announcement of the new cabinet was delayed. An extraordinary meeting saw PASOK MPs rally behind Papandreou but the indecision and dithering had undercut his legitimacy. When it occurred, the reshuffle saw virtually all those associated with the prime minister removed from government, demoted or shifted sideways. The most significant change saw Papaconstantinou moved to the Ministry of Environment, Energy and Climate Change to be replaced by Venizelos as minister of finance. After all the talk of a fresh start just over eighteen months before, the new cabinet looked more like a journey into the past, since it was composed almost entirely of fifty and sixty-year-old men. The troika in its reports saw the changes as producing a more broadly based and consensual unit, but the possibility always existed that it would operate at the lowest common denominator of agreement and most domestic commentators agreed that the centre of power had shifted significantly towards Venizelos and his supporters. The next day, the new minister of finance flew to a Eurogroup meeting. According to reports, he began his presentation by suggesting that changes had to be made to the mid-term strategy to ensure its passage through parliament. However, his European colleagues seem not to have been persuaded. After seven hours, they emerged in the early hours of the morning, speaking about unity but making it clear that there could be no release of the next tranche of funding until the new government had secured a vote of confidence and the strategy had been approved by parliament.[57] The ball was firmly back in the Greek court and, amid reports that G7 finance ministers were discussing the potential impact of a Greek default on the world economy, the front cover of *Der Spiegel* personified the pressure, as under the headline 'Requiem for a Single Currency', it carried a photograph of a euro coin on top of a coffin draped with a Greek flag.[58] When the vote of confidence in the government was held, Papandreou survived, with PASOK deputies filing past him at the end, shaking hands amid warm smiles. With the party's poll rating dropping below that of New Democracy, it was hard not to believe they were voting for survival. However, as the parliamentary votes on the strategy drew nearer, uncertainty continued to reign, with every wavering in the ranks of PASOK being reported to a watching world amid constant speculation about imminent default.

As 29 June 2011 dawned, global media coverage of events in Greece remained intense. The day of the first vote on the mid-term strategy no formal trade union protest was planned, so the crowd in Syntagma Square gathered spontaneously. International news channels gripped by the Greek drama broadcast live pictures of the demonstration but only two local TV stations paid it similar attention. The violence began in the early afternoon and was particularly ferocious, with foreign correspondents in gas masks noting the sheer anger of the protesters. The police, coming under a relentless hail of missiles, fired endless salvos of tear gas and launched countless baton charges, leaving some of the protesters, choking for breath and bleeding from wounds, seeking shelter in a nearby metro station. Inside parliament the vote started dramatically with the blind PASOK deputy, Panayiotis Kouroublis, rebelling against the government but, when it became apparent that this was to be the limit of the dissent, a sense of anticlimax set in and deputies started to mill around the chamber. Kouroublis was summarily expelled from PASOK but was unrepentant and spoke about regaining the freedom to walk the streets. In contrast another deputy, who had previously spoken about rebelling but then voted in favour of the bill, was spotted as he was bundled out of the parliament by the police and surrounded by angry protesters who threw bottles and a chair at him. After the legislation was passed, paeans of congratulation soon issued forth from across Europe, with Merkel calling it a 'brave' vote.[59] However, outside in Syntagma Square the violence soon started again and before it petered out in the early hours of the morning the post office below the Ministry of Finance had been gutted by fire. The mindlessness and futility of the destruction was aptly caught in an image on a world wide web feed of a young girl repeatedly hitting a glass screen outside a cafe. Yet a little earlier, just a few miles away in a suburb of Athens, a police band, perhaps comprised of those who had been on duty that day, led a procession celebrating the festival of a patron saint of a local church through quiet neighbourhood streets. After the scenes from the centre, it seemed like a parallel universe, but the violence in Syntagma was always only a part of the Greek story, and opinion polls at this time showed that while 47.5 per cent of respondents wanted the mid-term strategy rejected, 34.8 per cent wanted it approved, with the rest undecided.[60]

A little after the mid-term strategy had passed through the Greek parliament, both the IMF and the Eurogroup signed off on the fifth tranche of funding, removing any fears of imminent default and allowing some to believe the crisis could be laid to rest for the summer. The financial markets, though, were to show little respect for the timetable of the political leaders. After a brief lull, commentary soon resumed about the fundamental weaknesses of the euro area. On 5 July Moody's downgraded Portuguese sovereign bonds to junk status, partly on the risk that the country's debt might also be subject to restructuring, and a few days later it did the same with Ireland.[61] With Spanish and, particularly, Italian spreads also coming under renewed pressure, the chaotic conditions on global financial markets were once again blamed on events in Europe. Willem Buiter, the influential chief economist at Citigroup, spoke of a 'systemic crisis' which 'is existential for the euro area and the EU'.[62] Expectation grew that a Eurogroup meeting on 11 July would take some decisive steps to stabilise the markets but when, after eight hours, Juncker and Rehn only appeared to read a ponderous statement, which among other things said the ministers had 'discussed the main parameters of a new multi-annual adjustment programme for Greece', the tired journalists could barely suppress their laughter.[63] The disconnect between the European political leadership and the world outside their meetings and conferences seemed total and, perhaps aware of this, a few days later Van Rompuy announced on Twitter that he was calling a special summit to discuss the financial stability of the euro area as a whole as well as the future financing of the Greek programme. This evinced a rather tetchy response from the Germans, who seem to have felt they had been bounced into a meeting before final agreement had been reached on either a second Greek programme or debt restructuring, but in the end a date of 21 July 2011 was agreed.[64]

After further intensive negotiations involving the Eurogroup working group and the Institute of International Finance (IIF), three proposals for cutting Greek debt levels eventually emerged. Two of the options, based on a debt rollover or a tax on financial transactions to pay for a buyback of bonds, were said to be favoured by the French and a third, which would involve a straight haircut, by the Germans.[65] However, debt restructuring was only one part of the broader package of measures that the euro area leaders were struggling to put in place, with proposed changes to the EFSF proving particularly divisive. Eventually, concessions were made by all sides but the final details were only hammered out hours before the heads of government and state convened in Brussels.[66] The Germans agreed to new more flexible powers for the EFSF, the French accepted restructuring would involve PSI, and the ECB, reassured by the new powers given the EFSF, accepted that a default might occur.[67] The package presented at the meeting was designed to address both the Greek and the wider euro zone crisis. It included a commitment to cover the Greek financing gap through a second programme which would involve the provision of €109 billion of additional funds. Adequate capital would also be provided to recapitalise Greek banks following debt restructuring and to underpin the quality of their collateral so they could continue to access the Eurosystem. There was also to be a further easing of the terms on the existing Greek, Irish and Portuguese loans, extending the maturities to at least fifteen years and cutting average interest rates to around 3.5 per cent. The loans of the new package would be made through the EFSF and be between fifteen and thirty years in duration with a grace period of ten years. They would also bear interest rates equivalent to those offered to non-euro area states under the EU's balance of payments facility, which would be close to, but not below, EFSF funding costs. A decision by the Commission to establish a Task Force to facilitate Greece's absorption of EU funds was also endorsed and welcomed amid a general pledge to mobilise funds and institutions, such as the European Investment Bank (EIB), to 'relaunch the Greek economy'.[68] To help tackle the wider euro zone crisis there was to be an enhancement of the powers of the EFSF. Contrary to previous decisions, it would be allowed to buy bonds in the secondary market, providing the member states had agreed and the ECB had established the existence of exceptional circumstances that posed a risk to financial stability. The Facility would also be permitted to lend money to recapitalise banks and to grant precautionary loans before countries lost access to credit markets. Last but by no means least, the framework of a complex debt restructuring, involving Greek sovereign and sovereign-guaranteed Hellenic Railways Organisation (OSE) bonds due to mature within the next nine years, was revealed. The final details had still to be agreed but this would feature four separate instruments imposing an average haircut of 21 per cent— the first proposal of 10 per cent having been rejected as too little—and in its statement the summit estimated that through this the net private sector contribution to the new package would be €37 billion.[69]

After the summit closed, a happy Papandreou was to declare that the new interest rates were so low that it was like Greece enjoying the benefits of Eurobonds. Outside commentators were also generally upbeat, although the economists at Barclays Bank voiced a note of caution, when they wrote that the package was 'more than expected but not enough to make us sleep comfortably'.[70] Initially the concerns focused on the failure to expand the EFSF sufficiently to give it the funds judged necessary for it to mount credible interventions in the secondary bond markets once it took over these duties from the ECB. The absence of a firm timetable was also noted and once Fitch Ratings ruled that the proposed bond deal would amount to a 'restricted default' and Moody's downgraded Greece to Ca—one notch above full default—the wider implications of the agreement were deemed sufficient to explain a new round of market volatility.[71] Yet, rather than Greece it was Italy that was to become the centre of attention that summer, as its bond yields climbed higher and the government of Silvio Berlusconi came under pressure from the ECB and its European partners to adopt ever deeper austerity measures. There was talk once more of a sense of panic infecting the bond markets, with this only being stemmed, at least temporarily, when the ECB's governing council, in a rare Sunday meeting, at the beginning of August agreed to begin buying Italian and Spanish bonds.[72] Indeed, in contrast, in Greece, the summer brought few alarms. However, a combination of the beginning of the holidays and the need for the new cabinet to settle into office seems to have been sufficient to not only cool the protests but also government activity, because, when the troika returned at the end of August, there was renewed talk of a fiscal shortfall. Venizelos said this was primarily due to the deepening recession, which had seen the economy, in comparison to the same period of the preceding year, contract by some 8.5 per cent of GDP in the second quarter of 2011, but the troika preferred to point to what they saw as a continuing failure to curb spending and gather taxes.[73]

Then, abruptly, on 2 September, the talks were suspended. Juncker said it was because the troika had been unable to secure credible figures from their Greek counterparts.[74] However, elements of the domestic media began to talk about the government seeking a higher level political solution to the crisis, and later Venizelos was to state that the break occurred after it had rejected some of the troika's proposals. Certainly, within days of the announcement of the suspension, senior German political figures began to openly talk about the possibility that Greece might have to leave the euro area.[75] This was presumably intended to put pressure on the Greek authorities, but it later emerged that at the time a proposal was made for something like 'a velvet exit from the euro', with the German Minister of Finance, Wolfgang Schäuble, and Venizelos meeting in the basement bar of a hotel during a Eurogroup meeting in Wrocław, Poland, in the middle of September to specifically discuss this possibility.[76] By many accounts Schäuble had by then become one of the more enthusiastic proponents of the idea of Greece at least suspending its membership of the euro, seeing it as being necessary to save the single currency as a whole, but nothing concrete appears to have come out of this meeting, perhaps because the possibility was rejected by the Greeks out of hand, as Venizelos has suggested.[77] Soon the European Commission was also vigorously discounting the idea. One analyst drew an analogy between the euro area and the lyric in the Eagles' song Hotel California ('you can check out anytime you like, but you can never leave') while another senior official told a journalist 'if you get 17 [states] minus one, you'll end up with 17 minus four, five, six or eight'.[78] Yet, this was an argument defending the single currency as a whole, and the ideals of the union rather than Greece's membership of the euro area per se, and some remarks by Merkel in a television interview at this time were couched in a similar vein. In this she argued that it was not in Germany's interest to allow Greece to leave, because, if it did, other states would come under pressure from speculators, leaving, in the end, only a small group of countries which, as she is reported to have remarked, would be 'deprived of the euro's advantages as the currency appreciates'.[79] Venizelos only revealed later in 2013 that the idea of a 'velvet divorce' from the euro had been raised, but there is as yet little evidence to suggest that the issue was pursued seriously at this time, although a certain amount of contingency planning does seems to have occurred. Other strategies would have to be employed in dealing with Greece and in the same television interview Merkel hinted at an alternative when she noted the importance of building a firewall around the country.

In the autumn of 2011, the Greek crisis still occupied the minds of the euro area leadership but it was no longer centre stage. It could create specific problems, as when two major French banks lost one third of their share value within a matter of weeks after their credit ratings had been downgraded, partly due to the liabilities of their Greek subsidiaries, but in general it had been subsumed within the wider euro zone crisis. This was taking different forms as continuing fears that Spain and Italy may be forced to seek assistance and renewed doubts about the soundness of the European banking system led interbank lending once again to tighten, promoting fears among policymakers of a wider collapse.[80] In a leaked report the Commission called the crisis 'systemic' and in response the rhetoric of the central bankers became ever more alarming, with Trichet in his final address to the European Parliament speaking of the worst crisis since the Second World War, and Mervyn King, the governor of the Bank of England, of possibly the worst financial crisis since the

1930s, if not ever.[81] US President Barack Obama declared the euro zone crisis was scaring the world and at the 23–25 September annual meeting of the World Bank and IMF in Washington euro area finance ministers came under sustained pressure to take more decisive action.[82] The influence of the Americans together with the deepening of the crisis seems to have been sufficient to move the debate away from the issue of moral hazard and, when the US Secretary of the Treasury, Timothy Geithner, attended the Eurogroup meeting in Wrocław, Poland, it was reported he also advocated some softening of austerity.[83] However, there was little sign of any change of heart on the part of his euro area counterparts in statements made after the meeting when he was publicly lectured by the Austrian finance minister about the dangers of debt.[84] By all accounts, there were divisions over Greece at the meeting, but it seems to have been agreed that more measures were required before another tranche of funding could be released. The seriousness of the situation was underlined when Papandreou, for the first time, abandoned one of his many trips abroad, this time to New York to attend the UN General Assembly, and flew back to Athens. After renewed talk of crisis, an emergency government meeting and further negotiations with the troika, a new raft of austerity measures was eventually announced on 21 September.[85] These included a further lowering of the individual tax-free threshold, the extension of a recently announced special property tax levied through electricity bills, more reductions in pensions and a pledge that 30,000 public sector workers would be placed in a newly created labour reserve.[86] They would remain in this for one year at 60 per cent of their previous pay, when, if no other job had become available, they would have to choose between resigning, retiring or being sacked. The government trumpeted that these measures would be sufficient to guide Greece out of the crisis, and on cue foreign leaders and officials also chimed in to offer their support and to state that the threat of an uncontrolled default and exit from the euro had receded. However, negotiations with the troika continued and a Eurogroup meeting at the beginning of October contrary to expectations failed to announce the release of the sixth tranche of funding. Indeed, if anything, there were signs that mistrust between the two sides was deepening, with talk of the Greek authorities having to sign a letter committing themselves to implementing the proposed measures. The meeting also announced that the Eurogroup would not gather again until its regular appointment in November.[87] There could be no prospect of the sixth tranche being released beforehand and this allowed talk once more to resume about Greece running out of money and defaulting.

In Greece the new measures brought fresh protests. A string of state premises were occupied by groups of angry workers. When Venizelos tried to address the press after a trip to Washington, the room in the Finance Ministry soon filled with protesting staff, while outside a large crowd chanted the old slogan from the Polytechnic uprising 'Bread, Education, Freedom'.[88] Strikes again paralysed public transport and thousands of tons of putrid rubbish piled up on the streets. To all intents and purposes much of the state sector appeared to be grinding to a halt. When the troika returned, they were met by protests wherever they went. Union leaders promised bloodshed on the streets if the government brought in private contractors to clear the rubbish, and the chairman of the federation of taxi owners pledged that they would 'not go to the cemetery' alone.[89] The government responded with equally bellicose language and issued civil mobilisation orders to force the rubbish collectors back to work, although putting this into practise proved difficult in the chaotic conditions prevailing at the time.[90] The crisis came to a head, as usual, when the unions called a two-day stoppage to coincide with the passage of the September measures through parliament. As before, the 'mother of all strikes' was promised and on 19 and 20 October vast crowds gathered in Syntagma Square. On the first day a sentry box guarding the Tomb of the Unknown Soldier was burned outside parliament but, on the second day, much of the violence was between the protesters themselves, as scuffles broke out between All-Workers Militant Front (PAME) activists and other demonstrators, possibly from the 'Won't Pay' movement.[91] More people quickly joined in, and soon a pitched battle was raging in the corner of the square by the Hotel Grande Bretagne. Amid exploding petrol bombs and flailing staves, a captive was dragged down a flight of steps into the square to be swallowed in a sea of pounding fists. Another protester crashed through the glass roof of a cafe and later it was reported that a fifty-three-year old PAME member had collapsed and died during the mêlée.[92] After standing aside and watching the mayhem for some time, the police eventually left their positions and moved in to quell the fighting with tear gas and stun grenades. The union members returned to their position at the top of the square, while the petrol bombers slinked away into side streets, where they set fire to rubbish piled up during the strike and continued to taunt the police who responded by firing more and more tear gas.

The measures passed through parliament and the Eurogroup duly endorsed the payment of the sixth tranche, as did the IMF. However, the money had again only been gained in the teeth of further civil unrest and, when the police stood watching while the protesters in Syntagma Square battled before them, they had appeared to act more as bodyguards of the elite than protectors of the citizen. It could be interpreted as not only being symptomatic of the gap that had come to exist between the wishes of a large swathe of the population and the policies the political leadership, however reluctantly, were trying to enforce, but also of a more general breakdown of the fabric of society and the body politic as a whole. Of the PASOK deputies, only one former minister voted against one of the measures and was immediately expelled from the party, but the strains of implementing the adjustment programme—with Venizelos warning deputies it was a straight choice between supporting the measures or a catastrophic Argentine style default—as one anonymous minister had suggested, were leading not only to the collapse of the country but also PASOK.[93] Different points of view increasingly came into the open. Three ministers published a letter backing Papandreou and calling for an acceleration of the pace of change.[94] Others were reported to be pressing for the formation of a government of national unity. And, when the premier asked Samaras if he was prepared to accompany him to the October European Council, the New Democracy leader is said to have dismissed the idea with the words, 'You can't even agree with your own ministers'.[95] Outside Greece, with details on strengthening the EFSF, the PSI process and other issues still to be finalised, the rhetoric again became dramatic. Merkel, following the lead of Trichet, spoke of the worst crisis in Europe since the Second World War and warned that what was at stake was not just the future of the euro but of Europe itself. To emphasise the point, the *Financial Times Deutschland* even appeared with its front cover priced in Deutsche Marks. The financial markets translated these warnings into fears that the banking crisis was accelerating and that other banks would follow the Franco-Belgian Dexia in seeking state assistance. It had run into trouble partly because of its large holding of euro area sovereign bonds, which led its CEO to publicly rue the fact that the bank had so naïvely acceded to government requests to maintain its exposure to Greek debt.[96] Rumours circulated that one of the major French banks was close to failure and, with the sense of crisis deepening by the day, the ECB on 6 October stepped in to announce that in order to strengthen bank liquidity it would be offering one-year and thirteen month longer-term refinancing operations (LTROs) and restarting covered bond purchases.[97]

The 23 October 2011 European Council was expected to finalise the second Greek assistance package, further enhance the EFSF and agree a plan to recapitalise euro area banks. The negotiations beforehand were feverish but then, suddenly, just days before it was scheduled to gather, the Council was downgraded to a working group meeting. The official reason was that the budget committee of the Bundestag had not had time to study the proposals for the EFSF in detail—and in a version translated into German—in time for the meeting, and without their endorsement Merkel would have been hamstrung in the negotiations. The unofficial reason was caught in the words of a senior EU official who was quoted as saying, 'We've lost the main parachute and we're on the reserve chute and we're not sure that will even work'.[98] The sense of discord and confusion was total, forcing Juncker to admit that the public image of the EU was 'disastrous', but the working group meeting took place and, contrary to expectations, the main talking point afterwards was not Greece, which was not even mentioned in the conclusions.[99] Instead, attention was focused on a growing rift between the UK and much of the rest of the EU, partly fuelled by resentment at criticism from the British Premier, David Cameron, who for some time had been calling for the euro area to take a more decisive stance and unleash a 'big bazooka' to resolve the crisis.[100]

A second meeting took place a few days later on 26 October in Brussels. Here the euro area leadership gathered in the Justus Lipsius building in another attempt to bring an end to the crisis. During the talks, Merkel and Sarkozy shuttled backwards and forwards between the main meeting room and the adjacent office of Van Rompuy, where representatives of the Institute of International Finance (IIF) were locked in negotiations with Lagarde, who had become managing director of the IMF after Strauss-Kahn had become enmeshed in a scandal involving alleged sexual impropriety. The agreement that emerged was broadly in line with the media speculation of the previous weeks. The second assistance package was confirmed at up to €100 billion of extra euro area funding scheduled to be disbursed until 2014. In line with Ireland, which had been required to contribute €17.5 billion to its own support package from the Irish National Pension Reserve Fund and other sources, Greece was expected to provide €15 billion to reduce its debt either from an ambitious, but economically questionable, export-oriented solar power project or privatisation proceeds in excess of those already included in the programme. Private bondholders would take a haircut of around 50 per cent on their holdings, although this was reportedly only agreed after the commercial banks had been threatened with the alternative of a disorderly default. According to the communiqué, at the request of Greece, it had also been decided that 'the Commission, in cooperation with the other Troika partners, would establish for the duration of the programme a monitoring capacity on the ground, including the involvement of national experts, to work in close and continuous cooperation with the Greek government and the Troika to advise and offer assistance in order to ensure the timely and full implementation of the reforms'.[101] The wording was vague but the idea of placing a permanent monitoring team in Greece had been mooted for some time, being particularly championed by the Dutch; but at least one external commentator saw the proposal as amounting to little less than a 'bureaucratic occupation force' and it has been claimed that, when it was first mooted, Papandreou threatened to leave the negotiations.[102] In addition to these measures specifically addressing the Greek crisis, the summit also took steps to strengthen the euro area as a whole. The 'firepower' of the EFSF was to be enhanced through a scheme similar to that proposed by the German financial services group Allianz, which would allow it to offer risk insurance to investors buying bonds on primary markets. Euro area banks, following emergency stress tests by the European Banking Authority, would be expected to take steps to meet a 9.0 per cent threshold for core tier one capital ratios, after marking to market sovereign bonds. Finally, there were also renewed commitments to strengthen economic governance, with it being decided that German-style debt brakes requiring a balanced budget would be written into constitutions or their legal equivalents.

Some of the domestic press reaction to the agreement was highly critical, with one newspaper talking of it bringing German tanks, but outside the country global stock markets in general responded positively, continuing a rally that had started earlier in the autumn, partly driven by news of the LTROs and a feeling that the euro area political leadership was finally taking control of the crisis.[103] However, as usual, it was not long before doubts started to set in. Firstly, once the calculations had been made, it soon became apparent that Greece's debt would only be cut by some 20 per cent in the proposed restructuring. This would leave it, at best, at much the same level as it had been in 2009 at the beginning of the crisis, when many had considered the country to be insolvent. Secondly, the final shape and size of the expanded EFSF was still to be decided, but the depth of the proposed Greek bond haircut raised questions about the effectiveness of any insurance model. It was also questioned whether sufficient money had been provided to allow for a credible intervention by the EFSF in secondary markets, since even the €90 billion the ECB had spent on buying bonds in August and September 2011 had produced little apparent effect.[104] Thirdly, the large amount seen as being needed to recapitalise the banks, which at €106.5 billion was nonetheless still less than suggested by the IMF, despite the stated request of the summit, which wanted to maintain credit flows and not put more pressure on the markets, was likely to be found not from raising extra capital but by internal cost-cutting, deleveraging and reducing dividends. The danger was not only that this would send the euro area once more into recession but that the large amounts that needed to be shrunk from balance sheets would drive Spanish and also possibly Italian banks to seek help from the EFSF.[105] And, in apparent confirmation of the inherent dangers lurking in the bond markets, the failure of the large US-based brokerage house, MF Global, at this time, was intimately linked to its exposure to European sovereign debt.[106]

However, before further comment could be passed, attention abruptly returned to Greece, when, in the evening of 31 October, Papandreou dramatically announced that he would be seeking a vote of confidence in his government and putting the 26 October package to a referendum, without being specific as to the exact question or date.[107] The reaction of the financial markets was swift. The next day, media headlines throughout the world talked of stocks and the euro being hammered. The Athens Stock Exchange (ASE) main index declined by 6.9 per cent and the Italian FTSE MIB by 6.8 per cent.[108] The euro slumped against most currencies, and bond spreads widened alarmingly, with the Italian reaching a euro era high. The fear was not only that the recent package was about to unravel but also that a disorderly Greek default was again on the cards. The mood was succinctly caught in the single Greek word *ΧΑΟΣ* [chaos] emblazoned across the front page of the French newspaper *Liberation*. As part of his vision of a participational democracy, Papandreou had long been an advocate of referenda and several times during the crisis it had been rumoured that he was toying with the idea of holding one, but his timing now brought expressions of surprise. He himself was to remark that he had been surprised by the surprise, in part because he seems to have felt he had given sufficient forewarning to other euro area leaders, although not all appear to have shared his point of view.[109] Trying to explain Papandreou's decision, sources inside Greece have long suggested that he was influenced by American academic advisors, but his motivations seem to have been more mixed. In part, he seems to have been seeking to shore up the legitimacy of his administration, especially after mass outbreaks of civil disobedience at the 28 October parades which are held every year to commemorate the rejection of an Italian ultimatum at the beginning of the Second World War. In Thessaloniki the main parade attended by President Papoulias was cancelled for the first time in its history amid a noisy demonstration by a mixed group of local football fans, angry at penalties imposed upon their club, former municipal workers and anti-austerity protesters; while in Larisa, in a widely publicised incident, a sixteen-year-old schoolboy had made the Greek open hand gesture of insult [*mountza*] at the dignitaries watching on the podium.[110] In this atmosphere and with weekend opinion polls also showing large majorities opposed to the latest package, Papandreou must have harboured doubts as to whether his slim parliamentary majority would hold in any vote. The proposal to hold a referendum can therefore be seen as an attempt to rekindle party loyalty and perhaps also to force Samaras into making a decision as to whether to support the package, as Papandreou later stated. However, at the time the government presented the decision as being little more than a declaration of national sovereignty designed to allow it to improve its bargaining position with the troika. In a similar vein, a number of foreign observers also interpreted it as an attempt to push the euro area into softening the terms of the package, perhaps in relation to the 'monitoring capacity on the ground', a view which is perhaps also supported by the frequent demand by European leaders in their speeches at this time that Greece should 'fulfil its obligations'.[111]

The domestic political reaction to Papandreou's decision was as dramatic as that of the global media and financial markets. Venizelos was admitted to hospital with an unspecified stomach ailment. Some other PASOK deputies announced they would not support the referendum bill when it came to parliament. One resigned from the party but did not give up her seat, thereby cutting Papandreou's slim majority even further. New Democracy called on the government to resign so it could be replaced by a caretaker administration tasked with guiding the second assistance programme through parliament before calling an early election. The cabinet, with Venizelos absent, appeared to back Papandreou but, with an emergency session lasting until three in the morning, rumours continued to circulate that the premier was about to resign. However, before this could happen, Papandreou had to deal with the reaction of the other euro area leaders. Sarkozy, who was about to host a G20 summit in Cannes, which would have allowed him to showcase his leadership skills prior to a presidential election, is reported to have gone 'ballistic' when he heard of the proposed referendum. He, then, agreed with Merkel a strategy built around a six point programme that had at its heart a demand that any referendum should be a simple 'yes' or 'no' question as to whether Greece should stay in the euro.[112] This was to be presented to Papandreou at a working dinner at the G20 summit in Cannes, which would also be attended by Merkel and the heads of the European Commission, Eurogroup, IMF and

ECB among others. Papandreou flew to the south of France accompanied by a discharged Venizelos and bitter jokes in the domestic media about Greece at last securing recognition as a G20 country. The encounter between the leaders took place in the Palais des Festivals et des Congrès. Reports of the meeting vary a little. Some suggest the talks were tense and at times heated, while others say they were conducted without argument or rancour.[113] However, all agree they were difficult and tough as Papandreou was interrogated about his plans. Watching officials thought that the Greek leader was surprised by the unanimity of the other participants and he was certainly left in no doubt that his actions were viewed as 'disloyal', to use the term employed by Juncker.[114] It was also made clear to him that the sixth tranche of funding would not be forthcoming until the issue of the referendum and Greece's acceptance of the terms of the new package was decided. The message was underlined by Sarkozy in a subsequent press conference when he declared, 'We wish to continue with the euro with our Greek friends... But there are rules that form the stability pact. It's up to Greece to decide if they want to continue the adventure with us', and afterwards the G20 meeting was said to have discussed what contingency plans should be put in place in the eventuality that Greece did leave the single currency.[115]

The atmosphere in the aeroplane back to Athens after the meeting was reportedly cold. Immediately the plane landed, Venizelos issued a public statement. In this, he not only distanced himself from the idea of a referendum but also pointedly stressed that joining the euro had been an historic achievement that could not be put in doubt and that the other European leaders had given assurances that the Greek banking system was safe.[116] He presumably felt this was necessary because there now arose across Europe a cacophony of voices speculating as to whether Greece would leave the euro. In this the Germans were noticeably joined by their French colleagues, with Jean Leonetti, the French European affairs minister, telling RTL radio that 'Greece is something we can get over, something we can manage without'.[117] Once again the rhetoric of crisis was being mobilised to achieve a political objective without any apparent thought for its impact on the lives of the population of the country as a whole. And, as the voices of dissent grew, the Papandreou administration began to collapse. The government survived the vote of confidence, but in a speech full of self-justification, in which he noted that he had received from his grandfather only a watch and from his father just his name, the premier stated that he was not attached to his position, which was interpreted as a general but not specific pledge to step down.[118] The Eurogroup had insisted that a new government be formed by the time it met on 7 November but the abiding mistrust between the parties was to make this a difficult task. After the first PASOK emissaries to New Democracy were reportedly turned away, the government seems to have initially tried to seek allies among some of the smaller parties, including the Popular Orthodox Rally (LAOS) and the Democratic Alliance. However, faced with backbench rebellions in both their parties, Papandreou and Samaras had little option but to begin talks. They were joined by Karatzaferis who had indicated his willingness to join a new administration. Eventually, on the eve of the Eurogroup deadline, in the late evening of Sunday 6 November, a communiqué was issued to the press waiting impatiently for the negotiations to conclude. Such was the mêlée that the copy grabbed by the state television channel, NET, was torn and the two reporters stumbled over the text as they read it to a watching nation. The contents were the bare minimum expected. It was announced that a new government would be formed with representatives from both the main parties as well as LAOS, that Papandreou would cease to be premier and that, in due course, a general election would be held. However, there was no mention of the identity of his successor and there then followed several days of chaos in which the political establishment struggled to nominate a new leader. At first, it had been widely presumed that Papademos would take the post but, as time progressed, a series of other names came to the fore, ranging from the veteran PASOK parliamentarian, Apostolos Kaklamanis, to the European Ombudsman, Nikiforos Diamandouros.[119] On 9 November Papandreou even appeared on television to resign but still no successor was named; and any expectations that somebody might be chosen at a meeting between the three party leaders afterwards were dashed when the LAOS leader stormed out of the presidential mansion and announced to the media assembled outside that he would not be part of PASOK's and New Democracy's games. His ire seems to have been roused by an attempt to install the PASOK MP and Parliamentary Speaker, Filippos Petsalnikos, as premier, which also sparked a widespread rebellion within the ranks of the socialist party itself. Finally, with the process appearing more and more farcical and patience wearing thin across the globe, the party leaders met again the next day, well over a week since Papandreou had returned from Cannes, and nominated Papademos, the man who had long been the favourite to take the post and whose appointment was welcome to the wider euro area leadership, as the new prime minister.

Despite the drama surrounding Papandreou's proposal to hold a referendum, Greece in many ways was a sideshow in the backstage discussions at the

Cannes summit. It was Italy that was most exercising the leaders' minds. Various options seem to have been proposed, with one discussion about increasing the size of the EFSF reportedly producing considerable dissension, but in the end it was agreed that the country would be subject to IMF monitoring without entering a full programme. On his return to Italy Berlusconi, having lost his parliamentary majority in a vote on public finance, resigned once an austerity budget had been approved. He was replaced by Mario Monti, a non-elected former European commissioner. In the space of a few days, in two troubled southern members of the euro area, technocrats had replaced democratically elected politicians as prime ministers. This was welcomed by their elected counterparts who heaped fulsome praise on the new incumbents. It was widely perceived that the European leaders had come to see Berlusconi as an embarrassment, with much being made of a shared smile between Sarkozy and Merkel when his name was mentioned at a press conference; and during the Cannes summit, the French leader is also reported to have remarked to Obama in an unguarded moment that it was no use attacking Papandreou over his sudden call for a referendum because it was just the act of a depressed man.[120] The hope was that technocrats, free from political impediment, might be able to hasten the pace of change in both countries. However, despite the fact that both premiers had endured difficult sessions with Merkel and Sarkozy in Cannes, their cases were not entirely analogous. There has been much speculation about the extent to which the ECB through tactical use of its bond buying programme applied pressure on Italy and discussions between senior figures in the Italian and German political establishments at this time have also attracted attention.[121] However, in the case of Greece, which was already ensconced in an adjustment programme, the outside world had possessed no such immediate levers. So, instead, it again resorted to suggesting the unthinkable—exit from the euro—to gain the required result, whether it was the withdrawal of the proposed referendum or the removal of the premier. Once again, both the formal limitations of European institutional power and the capabilities of informal bilateral power wielded in conjunction with the financial markets had become fully evident. Papandreou's referendum call, by threatening to derail the painstakingly crafted assistance package, did cause genuine consternation, but, unlike in Italy, where a government of technocrats took office, because the policy was identified with him alone, only he departed, and PASOK and New Democracy, finally working together, were able to maintain their hold on power.

7

MARATHON IS INDEED A GREEK WORD[1]

THE PAPADEMOS GOVERNMENT
AND THE RESTRUCTURING OF THE SOVEREIGN DEBT

In certain circumstances the Greek constitution can be interpreted as allowing for the appointment of an unelected premier.[2] Xenophon Zolotas had assumed the role at a time of crisis in 1989 and now on 11 November 2011 Loukas Papademos, another former governor of the Bank of Greece, followed in the footsteps of his predecessor and was sworn in as prime minister. Papademos had served as governor during the last administration of Andreas Papandreou and those of Kostas Simitis and afterwards as vice-president of the European Central Bank (ECB) under Jean-Claude Trichet, but from 2010, while teaching at Harvard University, had also acted as an adviser to Giorgos Papandreou. As somebody who had often been at the centre of the developing crisis, he possessed an excellent understanding of the issues and the workings of the institutions involved, but as a politician he appeared ill at ease, maintaining a somewhat wooden and stilted, if sincere, style of delivery. Like Mario Monti, the former EU commissioner and new leader of Italy, Papademos was essentially a technocrat but, unlike his Italian counterpart, he was not given the opportunity to head a like-minded government. The ministers in his administration were almost entirely seasoned political figures drawn from the ranks of the Panhellenic Socialist Movement (PASOK), New Democracy and the Popular Orthodox Rally (LAOS). The vast majority came from the socialists, with many, like Venizelos, retaining the portfolios they had held in the previous administration. New Democracy took control of a handful of positions, such as foreign affairs and defence, while LAOS secured transport. The new government was not a formal coalition. It was a tripartite creation with a limited mandate that centred on securing the next tranche of financing and overseeing the restructuring of the debt, before calling a general election.

The appointment of Papademos as prime minister took the immediate heat out of the political situation. Inside parliament the new government enjoyed a solid majority and outside most seemed to be prepared to give it the benefit of the doubt, with respondents in opinion polls expressing satisfaction that PASOK and New Democracy were at last working together, even if their verdicts on the new administration were somewhat variable.[3] However, it was still noticeable that no member of the government felt confident enough to attend the annual 17 November commemoration of the Polytechnic uprising to lay the customary wreath. A general strike on 1 December was less well attended than before, attracting only some 20,000 marchers, but there was little lull in other protests. Pharmacists, tax collectors, museum guards, hearse drivers, lawyers and doctors among others were all soon reported to be staging strikes, and a group from the power workers' union occupied the building containing the Public Power Corporation's (DEH) computer systems to try and prevent money gathered from the controversial property tax levied through electricity bills from being passed to the Ministry of Finance. The building was eventually cleared by a detachment of riot police but not before pictures of the struggling power workers' leader being thrust into a patrol car were shown live on television. With little sign of improvement in the economic situation, and the media full of dire predictions of future measures, not surprisingly an opinion poll found that 99 per cent of respondents thought the economic situation bad and 76 per cent believed it would become worse.[4] The long years of recession were beginning to take their toll and with austerity continuing to eat away at the social fabric of the nation around the time the government took power a spate of stories started to appear in the media highlighting the growing difficulties faced by the general population. With these also being taken up by the foreign press, a significant new narrative now began to appear, portraying the Greek crisis as a humanitarian tragedy.[5]

New Democracy participated in the tripartite government uneasily. Samaras had long resisted the outside pressure pushing him to come to an agreement with Papandreou and the party continued to harbour deep reservations about the adjustment programme. It insisted that its ministers were not serving deputies—one even resigned his parliamentary seat to enter office—and made sure that the posts they held were not directly associated with implementing the memorandum.[6] Nonetheless, participation in the administration created tensions within the party, fostering the formation of factional groups and reigniting old disputes about New Democracy's relationship with liberalism and new ones about its links with the broader anti-memorandum movement, including the indignant movement. Similar divides also appeared within the ranks of PASOK. There was general relief to be at last sharing the burden of implementing the memorandum, but a number of ministers could not hide their discomfort at having to participate in a cabinet with former rivals. The failure of Papandreou to immediately resign as president of PASOK was also a source of internal rancour, leading the party to turn inwards and focusing attention on the question of succession. At the time, it was widely said that his decision was prompted by a wish to secure his position as President of the Socialist International, but a desire to be in control of the selection of candidates for the forthcoming election was probably equally important. With many of the party's most senior figures also continuing to hold office, the result was that PASOK was unable to place any distance between itself and the previous government and, in consequence, its opinion poll rating continued to slide, so that sometimes it languished in fifth place among the parties. The most willing participant in the new government was probably LAOS since its leader Karatzaferis had long proposed the establishment of a national administration, and perhaps as a consequence he had consistently scored high ratings in opinion polls, frequently outstripping Papandreou and Samaras. The decision to participate in the government, however, led to the media placing the party under increased scrutiny, with allegations about the links some members had in the past with pro-dictatorship groups said to be causing discomfort for some of its partners in government, especially within PASOK.[7] Furthermore, many LAOS members do not seem to have shared the leadership's eagerness for office and the longer the administration lasted the more support leached away from the party.

The tripartite government was an unwieldy grouping between longstanding opponents who were well aware they would shortly be fighting each other again in a general election campaign. Tensions soon arose, with New Democracy clashing with PASOK over figures that seemed to show that the previous government had hired twice as many staff as permitted under the limits imposed by the memorandum, and the socialists arguing with LAOS over a draft law facilitating amicable divorce, which the right-wing party thought undermined the sanctity of marriage.[8] There was also no clear locus of power since, as in the earlier Zolotas administration, none of the party leaders were members of the government and Papademos had to meet them separately outside cabinet. In such conditions it was always going to be difficult for the government to move much beyond its limited mandate and push forward the reforms demanded by the troika. Some policies, such as the campaign against tax debtors, gained a higher profile. A list of 4,152 people, who owed nearly €15 billion to the state, was published and the sight of often elderly businessmen in handcuffs being escorted into police stations for the non-payment of taxes became a nightly feature of the television news.[9] However, more often the tendency was for contentious proposals to be revised. Thus, the new LAOS minister of transport tore up the proposals of his PASOK predecessor to liberalise the taxi profession and proffered instead a different framework establishing the number of licenses on the basis of density of population and social and economic need.[10] Likewise, the new PASOK minister in charge of the labour reserve ruled out any sackings, when he insisted that the scheme was 'bordering on the absurd and ridiculous' and that, for little financial gain, it risked making the administration inoperable due to the loss of key personnel.[11] Perhaps, as a consequence, it was not long before rumours began to circulate that the troika were again unhappy with the pace of reform and, following a dispute over the signing of a letter pledging to implement the October agreement, Karatzaferis after one meeting simply stated, 'I believe they have no trust in us at all'.[12]

When the Papademos government assumed office, the predominant narrative outside the country remained that the euro area's leaders had still not adequately dealt with the crisis and that as a consequence the threat of a disorderly Greek default remained. The politicians were cast as being bitterly divided and out of touch, often it seemed because they failed to immediately agree to adopt any of the many solutions advanced by the media and various other interested parties to resolve the crisis, such as Eurobonds, allowing the ECB to act as a lender of last resort for heavily indebted euro area states or turning the European Financial Stability Facility (EFSF) into bank and permitting it to borrow from the ECB.[13] Thus, the results of virtually every meeting were judged as disappointing, even when the Eurogroup agreed to release a sixth tranche of funding on 29 November. The story remained one of impending catastrophe and this was a view which many politicians, ably abetted by the media, for various reasons continued to promote. Rehn spoke of the crisis reaching the core of the euro zone, Monti warned that an Italian default would mean the end of the single currency and, alongside reports that British embassies and consulates had been told to ready themselves for the worst, William Hague, the British foreign secretary, made a dramatic analogy of the euro being a burning building with no exit.[14] As spreads rose across much of the euro area, a rash of stories suggested that the financial markets were preparing for the single currency's collapse. Central banks were said to be drawing up contingency plans, Nomura Holdings announced it had produced a report which it claimed was the first major study of what the splintering of the euro area would mean for investors, and the ICAP currency trading platform, the world's largest, was reported to have run tests with reinstated national currencies, including the drachma.[15] Capping it all, in one fell swoop Standard & Poor's put virtually the entire euro area on review for a downgrade, including Germany.[16] The prevailing mood was caught in a cover of the *Economist* magazine which had a picture of a flaming euro falling like a comet to earth alongside the headline 'Is this really the end?' and, when Rehn looked ahead to the next European Council meeting, he melodramatically warned the politicians that they had just ten days left to save the euro.[17]

Greece and the euro area again seemed to be teetering on the brink of disaster, yet at the same time another narrative could also be discerned, less prominently headlined but equally persuasive. The euro, after falling quite sharply in value in September against the US dollar, had rallied in October. Some suggested that this was only because of continuing demand for euros from European banks liquidating holdings abroad and repatriating the proceeds home to shore up their finances, but others noted there were signs of recovery in the economies of many euro area states, particularly Germany and France. Indeed, a general strengthening of economic sentiment, in part flowing from good Black Friday trading results in the USA, was beginning to generate a global sense of optimism which increasingly counteracted the localised gloom. There was also a feeling that policymakers were showing a new resolve in tackling the crisis. The central banks had responded to the threat of a liquidity crisis by taking concerted action to make dollars more easily available at low interest rates and the euro area's political leadership, in conjunction with the Commission and the ECB, seemed to be at last shaping a comprehensive response. As the German newspaper *Bild* proclaimed in mid-November, there was 'no grounds for hysteria'. Indeed, according to one point of view, the crisis was actually providing an opportunity to rectify the structural flaws in the euro area and introduce a new stability culture. High bond yields, rather than being a threat, could be seen, as some had argued all along, as a force pushing governments to introduce long needed reforms.[18] From this perspective the solution lay—in Merkel's words—with 'more Europe', perhaps

because, as the title of a Christian Democratic Union (CDU) policy document produced at the time had it, a 'Strong Europe' meant 'A Good Future for
Germany'.[19] 'More Europe' meant enhancing the economic governance of the
euro area in line with the findings of the Van Rompuy task force. Surveillance
would be strengthened, partly through an overhaul of the Stability and
Growth Pact. A European Semester process would provide a base for synchro-
nising fiscal policy across the euro area, giving the Commission, among other
powers, the right to request changes before domestic budgets were presented
in national legislatures. The European Stability Mechanism (ESM) would act
as a permanent crisis resolution mechanism, and a Euro Plus Pact would facilitate policy coordination and monitor competitiveness within what was stipulated to be a 'social market economy'.[20] The new structures were meant to
provide a remedy for what were generally considered, especially from a
German perspective, to be the weaknesses of the single currency regime, and,
when the limits of democratic accountability under the proposed system were
pointed out to a senior EU official, he defended the project by suggesting that
there was little alternative, since the markets had become so powerful, asking,
'which is more legitimate, the rule of the markets or economic governance by
representative institutions in which governments have a say?'[21]

With signs that economic sentiment was turning for the better, on
8 December 2011, the new President of the ECB, the Italian, Mario Draghi,
at a regular press conference announced a fresh package of measures. These
included the bank cutting its main refinancing rate by 0.25 per cent, relaxing
its collateral rules even further and reducing the reserve that commercial banks
were obliged to hold with central banks to 1.0 per cent. He also disclosed that
for the first time the ECB would be offering two three-year longer-term refinancing operations (LTROs). Analysts at the time were not overly impressed,
preferring to dwell on the lack of any announcement heralding an expansion
of the bond-buying programme or quantitative easing; but, in fact, the LTRO
was little less than a public invitation to reactivate the sovereign-bank loop. As
Christian Noyer, the governor of the Bank of France, noted the ECB was
helping the banks to 'continue to provide credit to the economy and... buy
sovereign debt'.[22] The change in strategy was in part driven by the fact that the
Securities Markets Programme (SMP) was failing to achieve its objectives.
Weekly limits had effectively been placed on the amount of bonds that could
be bought and, with some of the ECB governing council members' discomfort
with the policy well known, the bank's interventions had never been decisive
enough to quell market concerns. Instead, by reassuring sellers that there

would always be a buyer in the market, it may even have helped maintain yields at levels higher than they otherwise would have been. Indeed, there were some who suggested that in fact it had only really served as a ready buyer of the Greek and other southern European bond holdings of West European banks. As before, but now over a three-year timescale, the LTROs would allow commercial banks to borrow money from the ECB to buy short-term sovereign bonds. These could then be pledged as collateral with the ECB, which would impose a graduated haircut for credit risk, to borrow more money which could then be used to buy more bonds which could again be pledged with the ECB as the loop continued to play. In the process, the banks profited by pocketing the difference between the lending rate and the yield, sovereign issuers found buyers for their debt, and the ECB, while being relieved of the need to buy bonds, could still be seen as playing a role in solving the crisis. Indeed, by the end of February 2012 the 'Sarko trade', as it had come to be dubbed in parts of the British media, after the French president gave it his blessing, was working so well that the ECB was able to suspend its SMP.[23]

LTROs were not a permanent fix, and the reactivation of the sovereign-bank loop potentially bred its own dangers, but they gave a breathing space for the politicians to deal with both the crisis in Greece and the euro zone as a whole. This they attempted to do on the same day as Draghi made his announcement, when they met in Brussels in talks which, as so often in the past, stretched long into the night. However, eventually, in the early hours of 9 December, they emerged to announce a further strengthening of macroeconomic surveillance mechanisms designed in Merkel's words to lead to the establishment of 'a lastingly stable euro'. In future there was to be yet tighter fiscal governance, with balanced budget legislation enshrined in national laws, and automatic sanctions against malefactors unless a qualified majority decided otherwise.[24] Sections of the British press pointed out that a largely conservative group of leaders had placed restrictions on future economic policy which among other things potentially limited the prospect for Keynesian deficit financing during recessions.[25] This could have profound implications, not least for countries such as Greece, which had shown themselves to be particularly vulnerable during changes in the economic cycle, but the mechanisms were duly adopted and a Treaty on Stability, Coordination and Governance in the Economic and Monetary Union signed on 2 March 2012.[26] After the 9 December 2011 meeting divergent views of the future once again began to emerge. One, backed by the euro area political leadership but also some commentators, suggested that with a comprehensive package of economic governance now put in place, the global economy improving and the LTRO taking the pressure off bond yields, the situation would stabilise and the euro zone crisis draw to a close. The other held that the newly announced package was just another sticking plaster which failed to address fundamental problems. In this view the prospect that Portugal might join Greece and need debt restructuring, doubts that Monti would shape a credible austerity package in Italy and the continuing threat of renewed recession meant that the crisis could easily again intensify. The only common strand between these two discourses was a shared belief that Greece remained a 'special case', not only in terms of its need for debt restructuring and the possibility that it might be forced to leave the euro but also as regards the very exceptionality of its problems.

Like so much of the crisis, the details of the private sector involvement (PSI) were settled behind closed doors at meetings in Europe and even further afield, although the secretive nature of the discussions seemed at times to spur rather than curtail media speculation, which was full of talk of impasses, rebuffs and walkouts. One journalist described the room in the Hotel Grande Bretagne on the corner of Syntagma Square where the leader of the Institute of International Finance (IIF) delegation, the American banker, Charles Dallara, waited patiently to be summoned by the Greek authorities as a 'gilded prison'.[27] Dallara had experience of similar negotiations in the past but in his opinion none had been as complex. In some ways this is perhaps not surprising, given that the various parties were negotiating what was to prove the largest sovereign debt restructuring in history, both in terms of volume and aggregate creditor losses, as well as the first major event of its kind in Europe since the rescheduling of German debt in the London Agreement of 1953.[28] However, in Dallara's eyes what made the negotiations particularly difficult was the weakness of the Greek economy and the number of players involved. At an early December 2011 meeting, he and his colleague, Jean Lemierre, a senior adviser to the chairman at BNP Paribas, found themselves seated at a table with Petros Christodoulou of the Public Debt Management Agency (PDMA), representing the Greek government, representatives of their legal advisers, Cleary Gottlieb Steen & Hamilton LLP, and financial advisers, Lazard Ltd, as well as officials from the Commission, IMF, ECB and the German and French finance ministries. Finding a common position with so many actors was always going to be tricky, especially as some, such as the French, were faced with the dilemma of wanting to both secure the deepest possible PSI to lessen the amount they had to provide to the new assistance package, while at the same time protecting domestic banks heavily exposed to Greek debt. The bond holders themselves also had different priorities, with those possessing shorter-term debt having a vested interest in stretching out the process to allow as many bond redemptions as possible before the haircut was applied. Finally, behind Dallara, there was the chairman of the IIF and CEO of Deutsche Bank, Josef Ackermann, and, according to one person familiar with the talks, he was always 'the invisible man at the negotiation table'.[29] The issues to decide were also many, ranging from the depth of the haircut—with one hedge fund resigning from the negotiating committee at an early stage because it considered it to be too drastic—to the size of the coupon on the new bonds, with the Eurogroup vetoing one proposal because it considered it to be excessive.[30] Legal caveats, known as collective action clauses (CAC), that would make a restructuring agreed by a certain percentage of bondholders binding on all, and which were already present in the 10 per cent or so of bonds issued under English law, would also have to be added retroactively to Greek law bonds. Finally, the elephant in the room remained the question of what should happen to the bonds held by the ECB and other euro area central banks, with the Frankfurt-based institution arguing that they should not suffer a haircut. This was not just because it would be highly damaging to the reputation of both the euro area and the ECB, almost certainly forcing it to seek extra capital from member states to recapitalise its balance sheet, but also because, on its understanding, it would lead to an expansion of the monetary base, which it contended could lead to accusations that it was failing to fulfil its mandate of maintaining price stability.

By the beginning of February 2012 several key talks were taking place concomitantly: firstly, between the various parties involved about PSI; secondly, between employers and unions about changes in labour legislation, including a reduction in the minimum wage; thirdly, between the troika and the Greek government over a new package of measures to close a looming funding gap; and, fourthly, between the parties represented in the government and Papademos as he tried to form a common response to the troika's demands. The original idea had been that the leaders of these parties would meet to agree on a new package of measures on 4 February 2012, before they were presented to a Eurogroup meeting a couple of days later. However, when it became clear that no agreement was in sight, signs of external impatience began to appear, with Schäuble tetchily remarking that Greece could not become a 'bottomless pit'.[31] Papademos finally met with Papandreou, Samaras and Karatzaferis on Sunday 5 February but, when they left after over five hours of discussions without having secured agreement, and then failed to assemble the next day, the patience of the outside world began to wear even thinner. A deal had to be agreed and approved by the Eurogroup, ECB and IMF before 15 February in order to allow time for debt restructuring to be completed before a bond redemption of €14.5 billon due on 20 March. On Tuesday a planned meeting was again cancelled, apparently because there had not been time to translate the draft agreement into Greek, which led the prime minister of the Netherlands to pointedly note, 'We are currently so strong in the rest of the euro zone... that we can handle an exit of Greece'.[32] His sentiments were echoed in the financial world, with the chief economists at both Morgan Stanley and Citigroup circulating assessments that a Greek default and exit from the euro area were still on the cards. Indeed, the latter with a colleague is credited with coining the term 'Grexit' (Greek [euro] exit) at this time.[33] Yet, as before, the crisis was essentially one of political choices, because, beyond the speculation about default and Grexit, the euro itself, stock markets and wider euro area bond yields remained relatively stable. Outsiders accused the Greek side of brinkmanship, and certainly they were not unaware of the power they held, with Karatzaferis in an open letter to the EU authorities writing of the situation in Greece being 'a time bomb for the entire western world'.[34] With a general election upcoming, both he and Samaras had much to gain from presenting themselves as defenders of the national interest. And yet, Samaras' assertion in a televised address that they could not easily agree to a continuation of the policy of austerity after it had so abjectly failed also rings true, because the party leaders were faced with making a host of difficult and potentially divisive decisions, some of which were potentially of doubtful constitutionality.

The next day, 8 February 2012, Karatzaferis left the negotiations after seven and a half hours. Earlier, he had told the state broadcaster, ERT, that 'austerity measures are like shoes that are too tight. Sooner or later, you want to kick them off', and now, talking to reporters, he seemed to imply that his party was not prepared to support a deal, although it would continue to cooperate with the government.[35] Papademos then entered into a new round of negotiations with the troika, which reports suggest lasted virtually all night. However, when Venizelos left for a Eurogroup meeting in Brussels at seven o'clock the next morning, he suggested a deal had been done, although conflicting reports continued to circulate for some time. The new package of measures, which were included within an update of the memorandum, included €3.3 billion of expenditure cuts; a reduction in the minimum wage by nearly a quarter, and even more for those under twenty-five; an end to automatic wage indexation based on seniority; a further reduction in higher rate pensions; a restatement of the one-for-five hiring rule; a renewed target of 15,000 workers to be placed in the labour reserve; the liberalisation of a host of closed professions; and new fiscal targets established in terms of a primary surplus, which foresaw a more gradual decline in the budgetary deficit. The possibility was also raised that these targets might be extended until 2015 if economic growth was weaker than expected, with it now being accepted that there would be no recovery until 2013. Prior to the Eurogroup meeting, Schäuble had cautioned that no final agreement was likely, and indeed after six hours of discussions, described as pointed in the media, Juncker did emerge to announce that before signing off on the deal the finance ministers required further actions. The measures had to be approved by the Greek parliament, €325 million of spending cuts had to be specifically identified and the main party leaders had to give written assurances that they would keep to the programme. As Juncker stated: 'We can't live with this system while promises are repeated and repeated and repeated and implementation measures are sometimes too weak'.[36]

In response to the new package the main union federations immediately called a two day general strike. A PASOK deputy minister of labour, who was a former leader of the Confederation of Civil Servants (ADEDY), resigned, to be followed, the next day, by a colleague from the same party, who was the alternate minister of foreign affairs. The LAOS members of the government also quit office, although two of them signalled their displeasure at the party's official position by announcing they would support the package in the forthcoming vote. With three PASOK deputies choosing to resign from parliament rather than give the measures their support, it became clear that the party leaders would have to impose tight discipline to ensure the vote passed, and subsequently Samaras announced that any New Democracy deputy who did not follow the party line would not be selected as a candidate to fight the next election. The cabinet passed the package of measures without dissent on 10 February 2012, and Papademos then made two televised addresses to the nation. In the second, he appeared wearing a blue tie against a dark-blue backdrop, with only a red lampshade to one side breaking the sombre tone. He looked out of place and uncomfortable, perhaps also not entirely easy with what he had to say. In measured tones he offered two starkly contrasting visions of the world. One was if the package was not passed. This would lead to default, which would 'create conditions of uncontrollable economic chaos and a social explosion'. It would lead to exit from the euro and 'from the core of the euro zone, Greece would become a weak country on the fringes of Europe'. The other was if the package was approved. This would 'restore the competitiveness of the economy and return the country to growth, probably in the second half of the next year'. It would protect national interests and even enhance the country's position 'in Europe and the World'.[37] The citizens of Greece could not have been presented with a starker choice.

The two days of the general strike passed largely peacefully with little violence. There had been some brief clashes in the centre of Athens on the first day but nothing more. The next day, huge banners were draped over the side of the Acropolis by the All-Workers Militant Front (PAME), reading in English and Greek 'Down with the dictatorship/of the monopolies/European Union', but the demonstrations were limited and there was no repeat of the violence of the day before.[38] The vote on the new measures was due on Sunday evening and, although it was widely expected that they would pass, the extent of any rebellions within the various parties was still unknown. Indeed, on at least one occasion, there was a break in the debate to allow a new deputy to be sworn in to replace one who had just resigned. Outside parliament the demonstrators were so thick on the ground that it took hours to cross the centre of Athens. The very size of this crowd gave the protest an unpredictable dynamic. The disciplined cadre of PAME were out in force, red flagged staves on shoulders, crash helmets in hand, but sheer numbers placed the crowd far beyond their control. The first Molotov cocktails were thrown and tear gas fired in the late afternoon. By mid-evening, the local media was reporting that so much tear gas had been used that fresh supplies had been requested as the riot police struggled to quell larger groups of black-clad petrol bombers than usual. The gas dispersed the crowd, as was no doubt intended, but this spread the violence throughout the city centre. Groups began to attack buildings, especially banks. Iron bars prised open heavy-duty metal security shutters and ATMs were smashed or levered open, whether through vandalism or for financial gain it was impossible to say. Sledgehammers crashed against glass and, amid reports of looting, flames began to flicker. A red glow rose over large sections of the centre of the city as a thick pall of smoke spiralled into the night sky. The fires sprouted at different points in several streets, leaving, according to the police, a total of over forty buildings damaged, including a Starbucks coffee shop on Korai and the Asty Cinema next door, a nearby branch of Eurobank, a five-storey office block above the side entrance of an arcade on Harilaou Trikoupi, a row of banks on Athinas, the fine old Alpha Bank building on Panepistimiou, where the heat was so intense it left the metal shutters hanging buckled like the scales of an armadillo, and, most destructive of all, the grand neoclassical building housing the recently refurbished Attikon Cinema on Stadiou, which was left a gutted shell.[39] Against this backdrop the debate in parliament ground on remorselessly. The rhetoric was often heated and emotional but most telling were the images on television where several channels chose to shrink the pictures of deputies addressing the parliament to a small box in the corner of a screen showing the scene outside, full of billowing smoke and flames. The vote was eventually held shortly after midnight. The Communist Party of Greece (KKE) and the Coalition of the Radical Left (SYRIZA) were solidly against and a sizeable number of PASOK and New Democracy deputies also rebelled, but the legislation was carried easily. The reactions of the party leaders were, as usual, swift. Twenty-two PASOK, twenty-one New Democracy and two LAOS deputies were expelled from their parties, in the process effectively making those with no party allegiance the second largest group in parliament.[40] Some saw this as a positive development, arguing that the removal of the more populist elements from the main parties would make it easier for them to work together in the future to implement reforms, while others saw it as merely laying the ground for further uncertainty. One thing the violence did make certain, though, even if it was not obvious beforehand, was that there would be no extension of the Papademos government. A general election would take place in the spring.

Overseas reaction to the vote, partly due to the fact that the other conditions demanded by the Eurogroup had yet to be fulfilled, was more muted than usual, with a new stress on it being part of a process rather than a defining moment. Technical discussions on what was known as the 'PSI consideration' were still ongoing and the Eurogroup was also waiting for an IMF debt sustainability report. This was to be crucial because it would not only help decide whether the IMF could contribute to the new package but would also determine the size of the PSI and, in the blunt observation of Dutch Finance Minister Jan Kees de Jager, what chance the creditors would have of getting their money back. When the report dated 15 February 2011 appeared, it made a series of 'creative' suggestions as to how the public debt could be reduced to a level at which it would be deemed sustainable. These included proposals to restructure the accrued interest on government bonds and lower further the interest rates on the bilateral loans, each of which it was estimated would knock some 1.5 per cent of GDP off the debt in 2020.[41] To avoid being subject to retroactive CACs, the ECB would simply swap its €42.7 billion of Greek government bonds for new ones with identical payment terms and maturity dates but different International Securities Identification Numbers; and this seems to have happened around the 20 February, with a similar procedure being followed a few days later with the €13.5 billion of bonds held by the national central banks of the euro area and the €315 million in the possession of the European Investment Bank.[42] Samaras and Papandreou then duly signed the letters requested by the Eurogroup committing themselves to implementing the package, and Venizelos reported that the necessary €325 million of cuts had been identified. However, these were not approved by the cabinet until 18 February, and this delay, in combination with the uncertainties unleashed by the splintering of the Greek political establishment, provided the backdrop for another outburst of hostilities between Greece and Germany. Schäuble in a wide ranging interview with a celebrity chef in a German Sunday newspaper spoke of his frustration at what he saw as the Greek government's broken promises, and a low-circulation Athenian daily drew plenty of attention with a front page montage of Merkel wearing a uniform bearing a Nazi armband in front of a Swastika emblazoned banner.[43] Indeed, a polling of Greek attitudes towards Germany at this time found 77 per cent agreeing with a statement that the country was trying to forge a Fourth Reich.[44] This was much to the bemusement of *Bild* which thought that the Greeks and other European recipients of assistance packages 'should put flowers outside our embassies and send the chancellor thank-you notes'.[45] Venizelos claimed that there were forces in Europe which did not want Greece to remain in the euro and, when asked about the possibility of this happening, Alexander Stubb, Finland's minister for European affairs and foreign trade, told the *Financial Times*, 'Europe is prepared. A hell of a lot better prepared than it was on May 9 2010—and a hell of a lot better prepared than it was last year, so I think we've taken the necessary measures'.[46] Meanwhile, though, as so often during the crisis, parallel to the often dramatic headlines a dialogue was also continuing. Papademos was reported to be spending long hours on the telephone with Merkel, Monti and other leaders, and on 19 February he flew to Brussels to hold a string of face-to-face meetings with officials. The next day he accompanied Venizelos to a Eurogroup meeting, his attendance being explained by the fact that the breadth of items under discussion placed them beyond the remit of the finance minister. The talks started in the early afternoon on the seventh floor of the Justus Lipsius building in Brussels. In one room were the ministers together with Lagarde and Draghi, in another room the bankers of the IIF. A small contact group shuttled between the two, struggling to secure a deal which would bring the debt down to a level which the IMF judged to be sustainable. According to one official present, at times the talks stalled but there was never a feeling that they were going to totally implode.[47] Eventually, after fourteen hours, at five in the morning on 21 February, Rehn, Juncker, Lagarde and Draghi assembled before the press. Rehn quipped, 'In the past two years and again tonight, I've learnt that "marathon" is indeed a Greek word', but they had managed to reach agreement on a new programme and put in place what was to be the largest ever restructuring of sovereign debt.[48]

This covered all privately held Hellenic Republic bonds issued prior to 2012, which had a total face value of €195.7 billion, together with thirty-six sovereign guaranteed bonds issued by the likes of the Hellenic Railways Organisation (OSE) and the Athenian public transport authorities worth €10 billion. Under the terms of the PSI consideration, investors would swap their existing bonds for new ones worth 31.5 per cent of the face value of their past investment.[49] The new bonds, which were issued under English law, had a maturity of up to thirty years and a variable coupon that started at 2.0 per cent and increased over time. Investors also received what was termed a 'cash sweetener'. This was a bond from the EFSF amounting to 15 per cent of the face value of their original holding which matured within twenty-four months. As in the 2005 settlement after an Argentine default, each bondholder also received a warrant with the new bonds which could be detached for trading. The value of these was difficult to calculate, but they would make a payment if the country's nominal GDP level rose above 'a defined threshold' and the growth rate continued above a 'specified target'. The nominal haircut imposed by the PSI consideration was 53.5 per cent and the Net Present Value (NPV) loss—the loss to investors after factors such as future interest payments were taken into account—at the time was stated to be around 75 per cent, although others, including, Goldman Sachs, argued it was, in reality, several percentage points higher.[50] However, other computations, based on a notion of present value calculated on the differential in exit yield between new and old bonds immediately after the exchange, later suggested losses were somewhat lower. Depending on the date of maturity, according to these calculations it was more in the range of 59–65 per cent, with longer dated bonds losing much less than shorter ones.[51] It was also agreed that certain 'profits' arising from the SMP, which the ECB would distribute to national central banks, would be allocated to 'further improve sustainability of the Greek public debt'. Until 2020 these banks would also pass on to Greece an amount equal to the income accruing from their holdings of Greek sovereign bonds, which the IMF estimated could lower the GDP to debt ratio by that date by up to 5.5 per cent.[52] Through a combination of the debt exchange, a retroactive reduction of the interest rates on the bilateral loans of the first package and these actions taken by the ECB and national central banks, the IMF's sustainable debt target of 120 per cent of GDP by 2020 was only raised to 120.5 per cent.[53] Taken together with the new measures agreed in Athens, the additional funding for the next adjustment programme was also held to €130 billion, a figure that seems to have become set in stone to avoid Greece being cast as Schäuble's 'bottomless pit'.

To avoid some of the uncertainties of the past and meet some of the concerns about trust, the agreement also mandated the establishment of a segregated escrow account which would hold three months of debt payment funds. If it fell below the required amount, it would be topped up from general expenditure. Greece was also to introduce a legal provision, later to be made part of the constitution, that would give priority to debt servicing rather than domestic expenditure. There was also to be a beefed up monitoring presence, although a suggestion that the Greek authorities should no longer have control over budgetary decisions, which had been floated by the Germans, had been roundly condemned and rejected not only by the Greeks but by other European leaders at an end of January 2012 informal European Council.[54] Lastly, before any funds could be disbursed, a prior action plan also had to be activated. News of the agreement prompted the expected response. The Greek government feted it with accolades, with Venizelos calling it perhaps the most important in Greece's post-war history and Samaras saying it secured the country's place in Europe.[55] Papariga and Tsipras were hostile, the latter arguing it was an agreement signed by a government with no democratic legitimacy. A hint of the prevailing popular sentiment was caught by the response of a fifty-five-year-old passerby on the streets of Athens who replied when asked to comment on the deal by a journalist: 'They don't want to kill us but keep us down on our knees so we can keep paying them indefinitely'.[56] European politicians were also generally upbeat, with Leonetti quoted as saying it had been a political and moral duty to help Greece before reportedly adding, with seemingly little awareness of the difficulties faced by many Greeks, 'Saving a country from bankruptcy, that's also saving the population from misery'.[57] Others were less sanguine, with Juncker referring again to the need for implementation and de Jager carefully specifying all the measures that had been taken, some beyond what was usual in IMF programmes, to limit the risk of non-implementation: the surveillance mechanism, the escrow account, the strengthening of the monitoring mission and the continuation of the tranche payment system.[58]

The remainder of the process more or less passed as expected, although the media continued to speculate about the possibility of derailment until the very end. The assistance package was ratified by various euro area parliaments, but not before Merkel fell short of a so-called chancellor's majority in the Bundestag and had to rely on the support of the opposition Social Democratic Party. In her speech Merkel looked to the future, arguing that a strong EU was necessary to ensure the security of coming generations, but Gregor Gysi, of the left-wing *Die Linke* turned to the past. He compared the demands made on Greece to the reparations required from Germany after the First World War, telling parliament, 'You're giving Greece Versailles when it needs a Marshall Plan'.[59] The Greek parliament voted through legislation making collective action clauses applicable to all Greek law bonds on 21 February 2012 but did not activate it. A few days later, on 24 February 2012, the debt exchange process was officially launched and, as expected, the rating agencies proceeded to downgrade Greece, beginning with Standard & Poor's which placed it in 'selective default'.[60] In the days before the deadline, rumours started to circulate that participation had been too low to allow it to proceed and that hedge funds had built blocking stakes in some bonds. Except in the case of a few minor foreign law bonds, this did not happen but prior to the deadline there was a last rush of stories highlighting the dangers of a disorderly Greek default, with a leaked IIF report suggesting that this could cost the wider euro zone one trillion euros.[61] To shore up support, the body representing the main creditors, the Private Creditor-Investor Committee for Greece (PCIC), announced that its members were supporting the deal, although the chairman of the board of managing directors of Commerzbank, which reportedly lost €942 million due to its holdings of Greek government bonds and related interest rate derivatives in the fourth quarter of 2011, was widely quoted as having said that his bank's participation had been about as voluntary as a confession to the Spanish Inquisition.[62]

Under the rules of exchange, the holders of half the eligible Greek law bonds had to vote on the swap and 66 per cent had to agree to amend the bonds for the government to be able to impose retroactive CACs. When the results were announced on 9 March 2012, 85.8 per cent of Greek law bond holders had accepted the deal but only 69 per cent of those who held foreign law bonds. This was sufficient to pass the necessary thresholds but not enough to meet the suggestion in the IMF debt sustainability report that 95 per cent of bond holders had to participate, so the deadline for foreign acceptances was further extended twice into April, although the final figure rose only slightly to 71 per cent.[63] Among those not agreeing to the debt swap were a number of Greek pension funds, including one belonging to the workers at the finance ministry and another to the police.[64] *Bild*, which had bought €10,000 of bonds at a heavy discount on the secondary market, also baulked at losing just under €2,000 on its investment.[65] Most of these holdings were forced to participate once the collective action clause legislation was activated, but about €6.4 billion of largely foreign law sovereign or sovereign guaranteed bonds, which was 3.1 per cent of the total eligible debt, remained as holdouts, giving the government a dilemma that it decided to meet by continuing to make repayments in full.[66] The high level of private bondholder participation was greeted with enthusiasm by both the Greek government and mainstream media, with *Ta Nea* claiming it exceed all expectations. Foreign leaders were also positive, with Merkel adding that it was not just a case that Greece should not leave the euro, but that it could not do so, because of its treaty obligations.[67] This may have been part of a concerted attempt to draw a line under the Greek crisis by removing once and for all the possibility of euro exit. However, it did not stop Karatzaferis from stating that he had been correct all along in arguing that there had never been any real danger of Greece being forced out of the euro and that the Germans had just been bluffing to force deeper austerity cuts.[68] Once the extent of private sector participation was known, the Eurogroup held a mid-morning teleconference and issued a statement confirming that the CAC legislation would be activated, although the decision was officially made at a late afternoon cabinet meeting in Athens. Following the activation, the International Swaps and Derivatives Association (ISDA) determinations committee met to rule whether a credit event had occurred. After an afternoon of deliberation, a statement was issued confirming that this would be the case once the activation had been officially announced in the government gazette. When this appeared it triggered the 4,369 outstanding CDS contracts, which at that point insured a net $3.2 billion of debt, and, following the establishment of a recovery price for the bonds at an auction on 19 March, a total of $2.89 billion was paid against losses, which amounted to only some 2.0 per cent of the total restructured debt.[69] The notorious CDS had been triggered but the effect on global markets was negligible, although it was rumoured there were some major losers, including one state-controlled Austrian bank.[70] With the activation of the CAC legislation, the participation rate in the debt swap rose to 96.9 per cent, and it then just remained for the Eurogroup and the IMF to give their final approval to the second support package.[71]

The gains for Greece from the restructuring of its debt were not as great as first appeared. The face value reduction in the debt was around €107 billion, but, when the cost of recapitalising the domestic banks and the losses sustained by many social security funds as well as various interest payments were taken into account, one estimate was that the real figure was nearer €58 billion.[72] To achieve this the euro area had endured a year of such turbulence and discord that many came to feel the policy had been a mistake. Once the decision had been made to proceed with PSI, the chief benefactors of the prevarication had probably been the main commercial banks of the euro area, since it had given them an opportunity to reduce their exposure to Greek sovereign debt. This had fallen from $68 billion in May 2010 to $31 billion at the time of the debt exchange. This decline was in part due to bonds maturing but others had been offloaded on the market. How much was saved from avoiding the haircut is difficult to say, since many of these had presumably been sold for less than they had been bought.[73] Greece also gained because of a reduction in its debt servicing costs. Prior to the crisis, these had averaged 4.5 per cent but with the new low coupon bonds and the reduction in the loan facility rate they now fell to close to 3.0 per cent. On some estimates this brought a total saving of around €15 billon per annum.[74] Most importantly, though, restructuring created Merkel's firewall. Henceforth, Greece's main creditors were not to be private sector commercial banks and insurance funds but its partner states within the euro area and official institutions such as the EFSF, ECB and IMF. They effectively controlled the debt and, providing the Greek government kept to the programme and continued to receive funding, through the escrow account they were able to make sure that it was serviced. €4.9 billion of the first tranche of €5.9 billion handed out by the EFSF went straight into this account, from which €4.66 billion then passed to the ECB and other euro area central banks to cover the 20 March 2012 bond redemption.[75] The flow of money, as in many ways it always had been, was largely circular, and, with Germany and the USA, through its influence over the IMF, now effectively in control of the debt, the threat of a disorderly default to all intents and purposes seemed to have been removed. The ECB's new LTROs; the coming to power of governments in Spain and, particularly, Italy, perceived as being more committed to introducing reforms; a growing belief that both the Portuguese and Irish economies were responding to their programmes; a feeling that the new structures of economic governance gave a long-term framework for resolving the problems of the single currency and that the EFSF and ESM provided a reasonably credible backstop; all combined to produce a sense that, even if the new Greek assistance programme did not solve the problems of Greece, they at least might have been quarantined. As Swedish

Finance Minister Anders Borg remarked after the debt exchange, 'The Greeks remain stuck in their tragedy' but we have 'reduced the Greek problem to just a Greek problem'.[76]

Following the restructuring of the debt, the Eurogroup met on 12 March 2012 and authorised the euro area funding for the new adjustment programme which was slated to last until the end of 2014. A few days later the IMF board granted Greece a longer four year €28bn arrangement under the Extended Fund Facility (EFF) amounting to 2,159 per cent of the country's quota. However, Brazil refused to support the proposal and a number of other board members were said to have voiced concern that the credibility of future IMF intervention programmes might be undermined if Greece continued to miss targets, as it had during the first period of assistance.[77] The Greek parliament then duly voted 213 to 79 in favour of the new programme on 21 March 2012, with the deputies backing the government broadly following their party's line, while the KKE, SYRIZA and many of the new independents voted against. In response, the outside world began to adopt a more confident tone, with Draghi speaking of the worst of the crisis being over and Schäuble saying that Greece should now be left in peace to introduce the necessary reforms. Inside Greece, with the major objectives of the government achieved, the political parties began to prepare for the forthcoming election. Early opinion polls gave New Democracy a clear lead and, with PASOK still presumed to be the main challenger, the twin behemoths of Greek politics began to trade blows as if the landscape was unchanged.

The election had been called for 6 May 2012 and on that day polling stations hummed with a mixture of expectation and uncertainty. Opinion polls had been showing that voters saw the ballot as a chance to express their feelings not just about the memorandum and the economy but about the two party system in general, and this became fully apparent when the results were announced. New Democracy came first, but it had obtained only 18.9 per cent of the vote, which was nearly 15 percentage points less than in its previous poorest performance in 2009. However, PASOK fared far worse, with its vote collapsing by more than 30 percentage points to just 13.2 per cent. In the process, it dropped to third place in the polls. Together the two parties which had dominated the Greek political landscape for so long, sometimes winning a combined total of over 80 per cent of the votes cast, had gained the support of less than a third of those who had gone to the polls. The electorate had given its verdict. The biggest 'winner' was SYRIZA, which came second with a vote of 16.8 per cent, but the Independent Greeks, an anti-memorandum party centred on deputies expelled from New Democracy, the right-wing Golden Dawn and a group which had split from SYRIZA, the Democratic Left, all entered parliament for the first time. The chief casualty was LAOS, which failed to gain enough votes to gain representation. Samaras, who had long been seen as a controversial and divisive figure by many Greeks due to his chequered political career, nonetheless, had appeared confident during the election campaign that his party would emerge victorious and he would be the next prime minister. This failed to happen because, for all its tactical manoeuvring within the Papademos government, New Democracy too had become associated with the memorandum. The Independent Greeks had also taken with them much support, and the departure of the liberal-leaning Bakoyanni as well as a reversion to a more pronounced right-wing rhetoric had allowed the left to once more brand the party as reactionary. Despite pressing for elections for so long, when the time came, New Democracy also seemed oddly unprepared for the polls, failing to effectively mobilise voters, perhaps in part due to the fact that fear of public disorder meant that its message was largely confined to the television. This lack of contact with the voters also seems to have left the party largely reliant on opinion polls when trying to gauge the public mood, and this meant it failed to detect the surge of support for SYRIZA, leaving it fighting the campaign as though PASOK was still the main foe.[78]

Even with the extra seats granted to the party gathering the most votes, New Democracy's tally in parliament only stood at 108, which was well short of a majority. Moreover, even if its partner in the Papademos government, PASOK, could be persuaded to give its support, the two parties together would still only control 149 votes in the 300 seat parliament. Additional backing would also be required. As was stipulated under the constitution, each of the leaders of the main parties were handed a mandate to try and form a government, but with none having a realistic chance of success, as the negotiations ground on, a sense of acute crisis once more filled the air. Talk of Greece leaving the euro reappeared, and, pressed by journalists international brokerage companies admitted they were preparing for the reintroduction of the drachma, with the code 'XGD curncy' at one point appearing on Bloomberg screens.[79] This was soon removed, but subsequently stories emerged suggesting that, after the turbulence of the autumn, small groups within the institutions of the troika had begun to look in detail at the implications of a possible Greek exit from the single currency.[80] The plans were kept secret for fear of market reaction, with apparently not even the Greek authorities being informed; but, nonetheless, the strong showing of openly anti-memorandum parties such as SYRIZA in the election as well as continuing doubts about New Democracy's commitment to the adjustment programme led to volatility on global markets once more being attributed to events in Greece. Some supporters of the existing government freely played on these fears. An anonymous source was quoted as warning that repudiating the memorandum would bring massive food shortages, petrol rationing and runs on the banks, leading to the freezing of deposits and ultimately no option but Greece leaving the euro; while, speaking on a local radio station, a PASOK minister was even more explicit when he reportedly declared, 'What will prevail are armed gangs with Kalashnikovs and which one has the greatest number of Kalashnikovs will count... We will end up in civil war'.[81]

For several more days Papoulias convened meetings to try to secure agreement on a government but, when a final attempt broke up amid petty political infighting, a new election became inevitable.[82] There was initial discussion about Papademos remaining in office in the meantime, but with some party leaders objecting, it was eventually decided that in line with constitutional procedures, the President of the supreme administrative court, the Council of State, Panayiotis Pikrammenos, would become prime minister in a caretaker administration.[83] The swearing in of the new cabinet on 17 May 2012 was a low key affair, with the ministers being largely technocrats.[84] The formation of the new government and the setting of a date for a fresh election introduced a sense of process. The news initially took on a less frantic character but apprehension remained close to the surface, with talk of the country leaving the euro abating little; and, as the new election approached and the old worries reappeared, people once again began to hurry to the banks to safeguard their savings. In the week before the new election, €2 billion was said to have been withdrawn in one single day.[85] The number of banknotes in circulation again rose sharply, as the Bank of Greece employed a fleet of trucks to keep ATMs constantly replenished to avoid any hint of panic.[86] The open fear was that a bank run would lead not only to the collapse of the local banking system but also a de facto disorderly default and exit from the single currency. Indeed, according to one seasoned observer, the single currency was never more at risk of 'blowing apart' than in this period of 2012, although, before this assessment is accepted entirely at face value, it should be placed within the context of an election in which the rhetoric of fear was being freely evoked in an effort to prevent voters turning to SYRIZA.[87]

The continuous electoral activity also wreaked havoc with the implementation of the memorandum, leaving the troika little option but to postpone any further visits until after the vote.[88] The campaign itself boiled down to a straight fight between New Democracy and SYRIZA. Initial polls gave the advantage to the left-wing party but, as time went on, the picture became increasingly blurred. Faced with a clearer ideological challenge, New Democracy began to project a more inclusive image, helped by the reintegration of Bakoyanni, who had dissolved the Democratic Alliance party which she had founded in 2010. It also toned down its nationalist rhetoric, replacing flag-waving political commercials with some polished productions highlighting the dangers of leaving the euro. One of the most striking showed a teacher slowly intoning the countries of Europe. When a small girl asked him why he had not included Greece, his face became despondent and the closing caption warned voters not to play with the future of their children.[89] Increasingly the political debate was again being cast in terms of absolutes, with SYRIZA presenting the election as a straight fight between anti and pro-memorandum forces, while New Democracy and PASOK portrayed it as a struggle between those who wanted to stay in the euro and those who wanted to return to the drachma. Both, though, were false dilemmas. Firstly, none of those dubbed as being pro-memorandum, whether it be New Democracy, PASOK or even the Democratic Left, were actually in favour of the document. All campaigned for some degree of renegotiation, with Fotis Kouvelis, the leader of the Democratic Left, talking about 'gradual withdrawal' from the adjustment programme being a 'red line' over which his party would not cross.[90] This meant that whichever party won the election, relations with the troika were likely to remain fraught, with a high likelihood that tranches would continue to be withheld, as subsequently did happen. Secondly, with the exception of the KKE, no party was advocating a return to the drachma, and, indeed, SYRIZA and its leadership were explicit in their insistence that Greece should stay within the euro; although less addressed was the question of how this could be squared with its pledge to renegotiate or even repudiate the memorandum.[91]

Billed as being of crucial importance not only for the future of Greece but also for the EU and the global economy as a whole, the 17 June 2012 election attracted enormous international media coverage. To deal with any potential fallout, it was reported that Rehn and Draghi remained at their respective desks in Brussels and Frankfurt instead of setting out for a G20 Summit in Los Cabos, Mexico. Yet, in the polling stations the atmosphere was markedly more subdued than in May, with the turnout even more sparse, as, at least according to the official figures, many more chose to abstain than vote for the winning party.[92] Until the last minute many electors remained undecided but, when the result was announced, New Democracy, by almost three percentage points, had managed to hold off the challenge of SYRIZA, with both parties gaining about 10 per cent more of the vote than they had in May. However, with 129 seats New Democracy was still not able to form a government on its own. Of the other parties, the number of votes cast for PASOK, the Democratic Left and Golden Dawn remained broadly the same, while the Independent Greeks fell back slightly, as did the KKE. In the new poll, SYRIZA seems to have picked up extra votes in the countryside and smaller centres but to have lost a little ground in its strongholds in the cities, where New Democracy strengthened its position, perhaps due to its organisational base. A strong age bias was also again present, with SYRIZA easily outperforming New Democracy among all groups, except the over fifty-fives, among whom it trailed badly. The memorandum and the path to the future it offered had been rejected most overwhelmingly not by the elderly, who it might be presumed would shun its message of change in favour of the preservation of existing norms, but by the young, who had turned their back on its prescriptions in search of a different left-leaning and, for many, more radical future, free from the encumbrance of the parties that had for so long dominated the Greek political scene. However, away from the relatively narrow ranks of the converted, many of those who voted for SYRIZA seem to have done so largely on the basis that it was the main alternative to the hopelessly compromised PASOK. They were voting out of hope but not yet commitment.

The day after the election, Samaras was handed an exploratory mandate to form a government, but it took several more days of negotiations with other party leaders before, in the late afternoon of 20 June 2012, he was finally installed as prime minister of the Hellenic Republic. The new government was supported by PASOK and the Democratic Left but no deputies from these parties took ministerial posts. Instead, a scattering of technocrats took their place alongside the New Democracy ministers. This decision was broadly supported by the deputies of the Democratic Left but brought heated discussion within the ranks of PASOK. After weeks of uncertainty, Greece once again had a government with a democratic mandate, and yet the same formation could have emerged after the 6 May election. At that time, though, it had not been widely accepted that the democratic process had been exhausted. Now, a third election was generally held to be out of the question. Compromises had to be reached and, with New Democracy having a considerable electoral advantage vis-à-vis PASOK, Samaras seems to have become more open to forging an agreement with his former rivals.[93] Indeed, with New

Democracy and PASOK together now holding 162 seats, they could have formed a coalition government without any further support. The inclusion of the Democratic Left, though, not only made it easier for the socialists to participate in the government but also gave it additional legitimacy both in terms of the breadth of representation and the share of votes the coalition had gained. In explaining its change of heart the spokesman of the Democratic Left merely remarked, 'Everyone has to put water in their wine', but no longer the potential kingmaker, when faced with the choice of joining the new government or staying outside, the party had chosen the former.[94] The 17 June 2012 general election had given some democratic legitimacy to the memorandum and the process of change unfolding in Greece and helped concentrate external minds. Taken together with the restructuring of the debt, it was an important step bringing this intense phase of the crisis to a close. This would not happen overnight. The memorandum was to remain heavily contested, the economic crisis was to continue and, indeed, in many ways deepen, and political life remained turbulent, but Greece had stepped back from the edge of the abyss. The possibility that the country might be forced to leave the euro was not to entirely disappear, and it was to take several more months of contemplation before most, but by no means all, of those in favour of this option, in Germany and elsewhere, were to come round to the opinion that the costs would probably outweigh the advantages; but the crisis was once again becoming a largely internal matter, and this allowed it to slip, at least for a while, from the international news headlines.

8

REFORM AND RESISTANCE

POLITICS DURING THE CRISIS

In May 2010 Papandreou in conversation with the Archbishop of Athens and all Greece, Ieronymos II, pinpointed the public sector as the 'sick man' of Greece.[1] Indeed, just a few months before, in the country's revised 2010 stability and growth programme, it had been named as one of the chief causes of what the document called the 'Greek problem'.[2] Such depictions of the Greek bureaucracy are by no means new. They can be traced back to the origins of the modern state and have been voiced by followers of more than one ideological persuasion.[3] In part they are based on an understanding which sees the state as being historically both influential and feeble. In this view, it gained extraordinary influence because of the slow development of local industry and the small size of the bourgeoisie, while at the same time remaining feeble because of political interference, limited efficiency and low popular legitimacy due to a lack of trust. Given the ubiquity of this view, it was hardly surprising that the memorandum contained references to an 'ambitious' programme of change designed to modernise the public sector at both the national and local levels, including reorganising recruitment procedures, revising procurement policies and restructuring management practices. Indeed, almost 40 per cent of the measures stipulated within the first two adjustment programmes were concerned with administrative change, a process that was usually termed 'reform' by the troika and the Greek authorities, presumably because this word carries connotations of improvement.[4] These reforms took many different forms, from relatively simple measures to complex attempts to change paradigms and ways

213

of thinking. The breadth and depth of the endeavour makes it difficult to draw firm conclusions as to its success, but the general tendency seems to have been for form to often change more than content, as institutional structures and patterns of behaviour have frequently reproduced themselves in different shapes and guises. This has created a curious mixture of change, stagnation and at times even reversion. The reasons for this are many and by no means rest with the authorities alone. There has been considerable resistance to change from elements within both the public sector as well as society at large, and the strains of introducing the reforms also put enormous pressures on existing party alignments, leading to a fracturing of the political landscape. Indeed, so much emphasis has been placed on the deficiencies of the public administration that it has led some to present Greece as being little more than a failed state.[5] This in turn prompted calls for ever more radical reform, with, for instance, the Organisation for Economic Co-operation and Development (OECD) advocating a single 'big bang' as being the only solution to reorganising the civil administration, and, as the list of reforms within the second adjustment programme grew and became more detailed, it, indeed, came to be seen by some as resembling an exercise in state building.

Greece, for much of its immediate, post-independence history, operated within a system of constrained sovereignty in which so-called 'guaranteeing powers' retained considerable influence.[6] Together with American intervention after the Second World War, this helped encourage the creation of a narrative that has often been suspicious of external prescriptions for what are perceived to be local problems, casting them as uncalled for interferences in domestic affairs. At one level, the memorandum can be placed within this narrative, allowing it to be presented as an alien intrusion that runs counter to local values and practices, especially when it was labelled as neo-liberal. However, it also belongs to a wider story of Europeanisation through which the norms of the EU have been infused into Greece. This theoretically should have been a mutually informed process, with all the member states contributing to the creation of a common set of European values. However, in reality, the voices of longstanding EU members in the north of the continent have often been more readily heard, and the perception both inside and outside Greece seems to be that, overall, the country has played only a limited part in this process.[7] Indeed, sometimes Europeanisation appears to have been seen as little more than an opportunity for the local elite to impose ideas and discipline on a reluctant society to erase practices that it viewed as being backward. It is thus hardly surprising that claims have been made that some wider reform measures were introduced into the memorandum by local policymakers solely to take advantage of the leverage it offered. However, in the process the focus of the adjustment programme may have been diluted and the chance of failure increased, since it gave opponents of the document an opportunity to use unhappiness with specific measures to fashion a general narrative of resistance to virtually any change. The leaders of the Panhellenic Socialist Movement (PASOK) administration tried to neutralise this by emphasising both the failures of the past, which Papandreou spared no words in painting in the direst terms, and the better future which reform was held to bring. The message was also reinforced by the appearance of an argument that, if the memorandum was not properly implemented, then Greece risked being cast out of the euro leaving it permanently marooned on the margins of Europe. However, the cost of the economic downturn associated with the memorandum was such that these arguments were increasingly challenged by even deeper rooted counter-narratives stressing the importance of reasserting national sovereignty. Indeed, even though Europeanisation was expected to lead to a gradual convergence of values and norms across the EU, it has necessarily been an uneven process, largely because policies have to be implemented within specific local socio-economic contexts, which in the case of Greece have arguably differed more than most from core models. Over the years this has produced patchy results, with the general rule seeming to be that changes have been more fully implemented and accepted if they fitted easily with local norms. At other times, they have been met by requests for derogation from regulations, prevarication and sometimes a blind eye being turned to breaches—the most obvious example being the reluctance to impose a ban on smoking in public spaces such as cafes.[8] However, in the past the cost of non-compliance was generally judged to be tolerable, even if, well before 2010, it often led to Greece being seen as something of an outsider within the EU, facing almost as many infringement proceedings as Italy. Adopting similar strategies to the measures contained in the memorandum may have proved to be more costly, particularly in terms of the economic consequences, but it is unsurprising that it occurred.

In the past, and during the crisis, the failure of reforms to achieve their expected goals has often been ascribed to a lack of political will. Indeed, politicians themselves, perhaps to cast aspersions at rivals and express their frustration at not being able to transform the world as much as they would wish, have often tended to blame reform failure on insufficient commitment. This reluctance to act has usually been traced to an unwillingness to bear the political costs in terms of both the reaction of voters as well as the divisions which might be engendered within the ranks of their own parties and associated groups, such as trade unions. However, at least initially, the troika publicly exhibited few qualms about the will of the Papandreou government, believing it was fully committed to the memorandum, and, indeed, at times it could appear resolute when dealing with strikers and passing legislation. Increasingly, though, the gap between enactment and implementation came to be highlighted. At times this seems to have been because the consequences of some legislation does not appear to have been foreseen. This may have been because a measure was poorly conceived, badly drafted or amendments introduced which effectively prevented it from meeting its objectives, as seems to have happened with some early labour legislation. These problems were compounded by the pressures of the crisis which often did not allow for proper scrutiny of new legislation. One minister serving under Papandreou plausibly spoke of the government facing relentless dilemmas with no time to weigh decisions, although it is also noticeable that there was a sharp increase in activity after 2012 when measures long urged by the troika were enacted to control spending and improve administrative performance.[9] The pressure to introduce legislation led to the perpetuation of methods much criticised in the past, such as fast-tracking bills with little chance for debate, presenting an array of measures within single omnibus bills and tacking others on as amendments to totally unrelated laws.[10] As a result it is perhaps not surprising that primary bills often had to be followed by supplementary legislation, adding to a flood of laws that left the country's legal and administrative framework in a state of almost permanent flux. A situation which prolonged and deepened the sense of crisis, as the absence of stable rules of the game in fields such as taxation created even greater uncertainty. In theory, implementation should have been eased by the heavily centralised nature of the Greek political system in which executive power rests almost exclusively with the prime minister who in the popular imagination bestrides the political landscape. Moreover, as party leader, the premier is also responsible for drawing up candidate lists for elections, giving him a power to make and break political careers, which, it has been suggested, may in part explain the high levels of party discipline displayed in even the most difficult parliamentary votes throughout much of the crisis. Yet, in reality, the prime minister's power is not so absolute.[11] In the absence of clearly elucidated party manifestos, policymaking has tended to reflect the priorities of individual ministers, each of which have their own influential political bureau. Indeed, such is the importance of these that a cabinet reshuffle can bring as many changes of personnel within the adminis-tration as a new government. This dispersal of power to individual ministers, when combined with the absence of a powerful cabinet office to coordinate and oversee policy implementation, perhaps naturally meant that measures tended to be most successful when they were introduced by a small like-minded group in a relatively narrow area to meet specific goals—the best example of this being the successful quest to meet the Maastricht convergence criteria to join the Economic and Monetary Union (EMU). In that case, for-eign policymakers were also able to exert a high degree of leverage on their Greek counterparts due to a real threat of exclusion if the criteria were not met. In relation to fiscal consolidation during the crisis, somewhat similar conditions have also existed and this may help explain why these goals have been broadly achieved. In contrast, in other areas where a more diverse con-stituency has been involved in implementing changes, which perhaps posed specific threats to powerful interest groups, introducing reforms has often been more difficult, leaving the adjustment process, at best, incremental.

Any consideration of Greece's reform capacity inevitably focuses heavily on its civil administration.[12] This, like other areas of the public realm, has itself been the subject of frequent reform over the years, however, with limited apparent gain, perhaps because it has usually focused on areas such as organisa-tion, recruitment and grade rather than effectiveness or evaluation.[13] The defi-ciencies of the administration to a certain extent depend on viewpoint. Politicians have emphasised its inability to enact substantive policy initiatives, while citizens have dwelt on the time needed to fulfil what often appear to be pointless bureaucratic requirements as well as the inadequate provision of ser-vices—the different points of view being obviously closely interrelated but not necessarily coincident. In English language press reports, references to the Greek public administration have regularly been paired with the words 'bloated' and 'byzantine' to underline both the large number of people it employed and its convoluted working practices. Indeed, it has often been sug-gested that it was the unchecked squandering of resources on the civil admin-istration that gave rise to the persistent fiscal imbalances which plunged the country into crisis. This was especially in the years after entry into the euro when salaries and other forms of remuneration as well as pension payments to former employees rose sharply. During this period, it was suggested that the number of state employees, including uniformed staff and clergy, had reached one million but, when the Papandreou government held a census in 2010 to establish a more precise number, a smaller figure of 768,009 emerged.[14]

However, the existence of many different forms of contract and phenomena such as 'disguised workers' left even this figure open to question, and it is noticeable that a detailed discussion within an OECD report was qualified with the observation that the issue was surrounded by an 'unusually high degree of uncertainty'.[15] Indeed, on the basis of some criteria it has been argued that Greece had no more civil servants than the average for EU or OECD states.[16] However, it is not just an issue of numbers. According to many sources, structural problems also inhibited efficiency. These included the irrational distribution of personnel across ministries, with there being considerable over-manning in some areas and shortages in others. This situation had been exacerbated over the years by a tendency of personnel in front-line services, such as rubbish collectors and nursing staff, to seek a transfer to a desk post after a couple of years of employment. This invariably led to the recruitment of another batch of temporary workers, who were then, eventually, also given permanent status because they fulfilled a vital service. Of the 7,000 nurses and paramedics employed between 2004 and 2009, 3,000 were reported to have been quickly transferred to other posts at the discretion of the relevant ministry, with many decisions said to have been made on the basis of personal intervention or party allegiance.[17] In marked contrast, top-down attempts to move staff to alleviate shortages in key areas and effect a more rational redistribution of resources in general proved problematic, in large part due to the rigidity of the branch system within the administration.

The number of employees within the civil administration tended to steadily grow over the years, partly in response to the growing number of tasks it was asked to perform but also due to patronage appointments made to gain electoral support and lessen the number of unemployed. Few will openly accept they have obtained their jobs through such means, but research published in 2012 suggested that, despite the existence of an evaluation process run by the Supreme Council for Civil Personnel Selection (ASEP), this mode of appointment remained pervasive in many ministries, with the exceptions generally being those more reliant on meritocratic examination, such as those concerned with the police and foreign affairs.[18] Once a person is appointed to an established public sector job, in most cases they can expect to hold it for life. Permanently contracted civil servants have long enjoyed tenure under the constitution provided their statutory position continues to exist, and this state of affairs gradually came to apply to the public sector in general. The troika was keen to challenge this right and eventually under the Samaras government a number of lower-grade employees lost their jobs, including some school janitors, municipal policemen and a group of cleaners from the Ministry of Finance who set up a camp protesting their dismissal outside the ministry in Athens. However, all the major political parties continued to oppose any radical change, in part because they believed that talk of redundancies only lowered morale and efficiency even further and that the culture of meritocracy was so weakly embedded that it would quickly lead to a return to the damaging cycles of the past, when a change of government was marked by wholesale expulsions and appointments.[19] Indeed, one of the campaign promises of the Coalition of the Radical Left (SYRIZA) during the January 2015 general election was that it would reinstate most of those who had been fired from the public sector; and instead of compulsory redundancies successive governments during the crisis have argued that the requisite number of jobs could be lost largely through natural wastage. This was possible because various recruitment freezes over the years had produced a disproportionately elderly workforce. Over a third of civil servants were over fifty-years-old in 2011, with this figure rising to more than half in ministries such as finance. Indeed, according to the troika, by the end of 2012 around 80,000 had already left the public sector and figures later released by the Greek government were even higher, suggesting that the overall number employed diminished by at least 200,000 during the period 2009–2013.[20] However, this downsizing by attrition was largely unplanned, leading officials to suggest that it has further impaired efficiency, as key personnel have not been replaced. Perhaps in recognition of this, as time progressed, the troika came to stress the need for improvements in the quality of administration and in certain priority areas such as tax collection the rules were relaxed to allow replacements to be hired at a ratio of one for one departure.[21]

Tenure, higher pay than in comparable jobs in the private sector, at least at lower levels, generally lax working conditions and the possibility of a substantial pension, often at a relatively young age, have long made public sector jobs highly desirable in Greece, with ASEP in the past on average receiving 350,000 applications for the 6,000 jobs it tended to advertise each year.[22] During the crisis the public sector has suffered salary cuts but these have been cumulatively less than in the private sector, which has also endured the vast bulk of job losses. The result is that the tendency for public sector jobs to be privileged over the private has if anything been reinforced, with lower income families in particular often speaking enviously of others who have at least one member working for the state. However, set against this, such jobs also tend to be monotonous and highly regulated, with little room for initiative and, if they also involve face-to-face relations with the general public, frequently mutual aggravation. Talented young people in particular tend to become buried within the system, perhaps having to wait twenty years until they are in sufficient position of authority to influence policy, by which time many have become disillusioned and disaffected.[23] The overall result is that people who have gained what are generally seen as highly desired jobs, and which, partly on account of this, can sometimes appear aloof and arrogant, at a personal level often express considerable unhappiness with their work environment. This state of affairs has been exacerbated by the existence of political clientelism. This not only undermines workplace cohesion and notions of meritocracy but also, it has been argued, led the parties in power to drag out and delay the reforms required by the memorandum so as to protect the interests of their clients in the public sector and ensure their continuing electoral support.[24] Moreover, patronage does not only relate to obtaining a job. It also pervades areas such as promotion, making this a particularly opaque process. It is factors such as this, as much as the constantly heard complaint that political appointees are able to shirk work to the detriment of colleagues employed through more regular channels, that helps explain the low morale and weak work ethos that has been noted throughout much of the civil administration. This was compounded during the crisis by falling wages and constant fears that ways would be found to shed jobs either through the abolition of statutory positions or alternative measures, such as the labour reserve. However, political patronage and low morale are only two factors explaining weak reform capacity. Structural reasons also need to be taken into account. The administration was top heavy with a disproportionate number of senior managerial staff. About a fifth of departments had only a director with no other personnel. This led to talk about 'ghost departments' as part of a general phenomenon in which 'every government official builds a power structure around him, which often serves to undermine the natural hierarchy or operates in parallel to it'. Indeed, the administration can probably best be understood as a zone of continuous negotiation in which individuals engage in complex power relationships in order to either exploit a situation for their own ends or prevent others gaining advantage. In such a situation managerial functions easily wither away, as the higher echelons effectively lose control over the lower, allowing the system to malfunction or be manipulated for personal interest. Indeed, it has been frequently charged that the public sector in Greece is characterised by excessive rent seeking, which in this context means that its resources, both human and other, are appropriated for personal political, economic or social advantage, leaving it generating no added value for the economy or society as a whole.

A combination of attempting to bypass blockages within a highly hierarchical system as well as a continuing need to create more jobs has led governments over the years to establish numerous agencies which lie outside regular structures. Free to adopt contemporary work practices and recruit younger, more highly trained staff, these can be more efficient and effective. However, within a system already prone to a high degree of fragmentation, frequently due to political pressures—there is, for instance, hardly a major urban centre in Greece without a higher education institution—this process has led to a duplication of services as well as a weakening of coordination.[27] In the case of the administration, fragmentation was seen both in terms of space—with a 2011 survey revealing that the central bureaucracy was spread over 1552 buildings, half of which were leased, sometimes in the past at high rents— and also structure. In 2011 each ministry had on average 302 departments at a central as well as a further 137 at a regional level, and a constant theme has been the need for rationalisation, with a target set at that time of reducing the total of 5,427 to 3,567. However, the extent to which lessening the number would in itself improve efficiency is unclear, given the number of single person departments and the tendency over the years to leave empty statutory positions that are described in competences but no longer relevant. In the Ministry of Finance these apparently accounted for 36 per cent of all positions. Indeed, the need to address the lack of coordination was as important as rationalisation. Scheduled meetings between officials from different ministries were apparently rare and problems with information technology were often due not so much to lack of equipment as to the incompatibility of different departmental systems. Administrative activity has also tended to be highly structured, operating within a rigid, rule-based framework in which no action is possible without proper authorisation. This has given rise to a culture stressing bureaucratic procedure that is replete with myriads of forms, most of which have to be rubber stamped several times. Plenty of opportunities have also been created for officials to evade responsibility, accountability being difficult to establish by the time a document has passed through so many hands. However, aside from providing excuses for obstruction and inaction, rigid compartmentalisation at other times has made laws not limits to be respected but obstacles to be overcome. In such a situation those able to bypass the system gained a special status and this, ultimately, facilitated the growth of informal practices and corruption, which is popularly considered to be rife in certain sections of the administration. More generally, though, this culture of bureaucratic process, when coupled with security of tenure and automatic seniority payments, fed an expectation of stasis. The result has been that most civil servants seem to have felt that there was no real need for change beyond, perhaps, the replacement of some political appointees within their department—a state of affairs caught in a 2011 OECD report which strongly argued that reforms had been rejected not because they threaten rent seeking but because they challenge a way of life established by legal contract that was expected to be unchanging.[28]

Many of these issues surfaced within the budgetary process, the failure of which to control expenditure can be seen as lying at the heart of the causes of the crisis. As with so much else, this was also fragmented, with the budget divided between ordinary and investment categories, and highly complex, containing 14,000 distinct lines of expenditure.[29] This simultaneously made it both highly prescriptive and difficult to control. In part, this was due to the existence of 130 special budgets, totalling around €5 billion, created partly to bypass regulations that required even modest reallocations of less than €5,000 to follow lengthy authorisation processes. Despite various attempts to bring change over the years, prior to the crisis, the budget was still formulated through what was essentially a bottom-up process, with each ministry making a bid for funds on the basis of its own assessment of its needs rather than limits being imposed from above. This built in a tendency to overspend and, if the Stability and Growth Pact's reference value was then threatened, one-off measures were introduced to fill funding gaps. The budget was presented to parliament, but scrutiny tended to be formalistic, with the relevant subcommittee lacking independent research facilities to allow detailed examination.[30] Afterwards, expenditure was monitored by various bodies, including a Court of Audit, but these tended to be concerned more with legality and process than judging whether funds were used efficiently and identifying wastage, and certain areas, such as defence procurement, were totally excluded. Under the adjustment programmes considerable attention has been paid to establishing a new framework for executing the budget which is now established on the basis of fixed targets. All ministries have set up internal directorates for financial services, with accounting officers supervising expenditure, and a parliamentary office has also been established to scrutinise the budget as it is being applied. The aim is not just to prevent overspending, as in the past, but to ensure that Greece continues to post a high primary surplus in the future to allow it to pare down its considerable public debt.

Others, in searching for a reason for the failure of reforms to bring the desired results, have looked not just at the weaknesses of the state administration but have also pointed to the absence of an informed citizen body willing to support change, suggesting this might be due to a weak civil society, lack of social capital or the existence of an obstructive underdog culture. However, within popular narratives the most commonly advanced societal explanation revolves around the malign effects imputed to certain vested interests. Drawing on longstanding historical narratives, the term 'vested interest' is most frequently equated with the existence of a small elite deemed sufficiently powerful to control the destiny of the country. In the period after 1974, this idea was powerfully articulated by both Andreas Papandreou in the concept of 'the privileged' and by the opponents of PASOK in the notion that Greece had fallen into the hands of a corrupt socialist *nomenklatura*. Nowadays, these two elements are often fused into a narrative that holds that the fortunes of the country are manipulated by a narrow party-state-media-business elite who live in a rarefied world far distant from everyday society, receiving treatment in special hospital units and sending their children to expensive private schools.[31] In the comment he allegedly made about five pimps controlling Greece, Kostas Karamanlis was merely articulating a variant of this discourse, which has tended to focus on the owners of construction and media companies.[32] However, more broadly, special interest groups can be traced across society as a whole, and in many ways they are little different from pressure groups encountered elsewhere in the world. Indeed, from this perspective they need not be seen as a negative phenomenon at all, as they can act as agencies for social advancement, and locally, in the past, they have been seen as a source of stability, especially during the *metapolitefsi*.[33] The numerous interest groups that exist within Greek society have been divided according to various typologies, but among the most important are employers groups; unions, especially those from the public sector; professional groups, such as lawyers, doctors and pharmacists, as well as lorry and taxi drivers; and also the clergy and the army.[34] Each during the crisis has defended its own particularities. In particular, public sector employees, and especially their union representatives, who were among the chief beneficiaries of the existing system, standing to gain little from any change, have tended to oppose all aspects of the memorandum. Likewise, members of professional groups, often well represented in parliament, have been generally reluctant to shed their protective regulations and lose their privileged status in areas such as tax. Other groups, such as taxi and lorry drivers, may have been less well represented, but through their very numbers they remained electorally important, allowing them to find advocates willing to aid them in their struggle to maintain existing regulations. Even business groups, which tend to be dominated by large corporations that sometimes had previously been under state ownership, while embracing the rhetoric of the free market, have often been less than keen to see a weakening of the protective measures that in the past enhanced their profits. Organisations representing smaller traders have also battled to keep restrictions that protect the vast majority rather than endorse reforms which would empower a minority who sense opportunity in change. The balance throughout has therefore been overwhelmingly tilted towards inertia rather than change.

The various interest groups were able to gain significance partly due to the high degree of politicisation within Greek society. This had long been reflected in recruitment policies in the civil service and strategies adopted towards the trade unions, particularly in the aftermath of the Civil War, when measures were taken to limit the influence of the left. However, from 1974 onwards, PASOK and New Democracy had both adopted a strategy of 'colonising' the public space, leading myriads of national and local professional, business, and social organisations to exhibit an overtly political hue. However, this process not only allowed the political parties to reach deep into society, it also permitted these groups to penetrate the parties. Andreas Papandreou had warned of the danger of the civil administration taking over PASOK, but as jobs and career prospects came to be increasingly associated with party membership, it was natural that the composition of the party—and presumably New Democracy as well, since by 2005 the two parties claimed to have between them 600,000 members—became skewed towards public sector employees, leading it to increasingly reflect their interests and consolidating the position of the state at the centre of political thinking.[35] Under the quasi-corporatist environment envisaged by both PASOK and New Democracy, various employer and employee groups, generally known as 'social partners', were expected to work harmoniously with the government to pursue common objectives that would benefit all. However, attempts to establish social consensus were often less than successful, and there emerged instead a series of fragmented and intermittent processes in which the rhetoric tended to echo hostility and mistrust more than compromise. In this deeply politicised environment, in which relations were often symbiotic and balances of power difficult to divine, informal corridor exchanges frequently became more important than formal negotiations, leading to the production of a series of imperfect compromises rather than harmonious consensus.[36] Leaving none either entirely satisfied or completely dissatisfied, this process gave plenty of space for begrudging acceptance, cementing a tendency for any change to occur incrementally at the lowest common denominator of agreement. In the process inequalities were often introduced into the system, with powerful groups in the public sector, such as transport and oil refinery workers, being able to extract relatively high pay and pensions, with the costs being effectively carried by the reminder of society. This potentially undermined social solidarity. However, by employing a rhetoric, full of references to earned and historic rights, and casting any change from the status quo as a return to medieval conditions, some groups, particularly within the public sector unions, were able to link the defence of their interests with the upholding of values such as egalitarianism and social solidarity that are seen as being integral to Greek society. This has made it very difficult to introduce change even if the politicians, many of whom have strong links to the various interest groups, have the desire to do so.

The political culture which allowed interest groups to play such an important role evolved, in part, because the agendas of PASOK and New Democracy, despite a rhetoric of intense rivalry, had broadly converged over the years. In the absence of clear ideological and policy differences, to attract support both parties had largely come to rely on outbidding their rivals with promises of benefits, denying the legitimacy of their opponents to rule through charges of incompetence, and playing upon their audience's response to recent national history. Outbidding involved promising sizeable increases in wages and pensions, keeping tax rates low and giving pledges of jobs in the public sector. This usually produced a pronounced fiscal-electoral cycle in which government spending increased and tax revenue decreased as elections approached, placing the budget under extra pressure at these times.[37] To maintain their hold on power the two parties also relied on ample public funding topped up by borrowing from state-controlled banks. However, as this diminished and the adjustment programme restricted the granting of state largesse, the established patronage system also started to contract, until it was only those judged to have exemplary connections who were said to still be able to benefit. This produced a sense of bitterness and betrayal among those who had become used to profiting from such patronage over the years, leading them to abandon en masse the parties that had previously supported them, especially PASOK, but also New Democracy.[38] However, at the same time, because stories continued to circulate about preference being given on political grounds, claims by the proponents of the memorandum that it would cleanse Greece from such practices were also undercut, removing a key source of potential legitimacy.

Aside from plying the electorate with benefits, the parties also stressed their right to rule. Apart from any residual claims to legitimacy through resistance to the dictatorship, which was important for internal self-belief within PASOK, this right to rule was often put forward through assertions of expertise, frequently expressed in terms of academic qualifications rather than practical experience. Indeed, few European nations can have drawn on so many professors to provide ministers as Greece has over the years. In this environment, there was a general tendency to suggest that opponents were ineligible to rule not due to a lack of expertise but because of moral failings, especially as regards susceptibility to corruption. Indeed, it would be relatively easy to produce a narrative which reduces the contemporary history of Greece to little more than a succession of corruption scandals and such a presentation would almost certainly accord well with popular perceptions.[39] The various scandals obviously differed but they have tended to share some common characteristics. They were usually complex, often involved a large number of actors drawn from various walks of public life and received exhaustive coverage in the local media, partly because it was able to claim a privileged position as chief interpreter of the many intricacies amid endless scoops and opportunities to besmirch political rivals. For the parties the political gains came not only from undermining the standing of opponents but, in the absence of strong ideological ties, also from the opportunity provided to foster internal cohesion, as colleagues were forced to close ranks to ward off accusations. Moreover, the scandals, usually, posed limited real risk to the political class, given the generous statutes of limitations legislation and the consummate ability various administrations showed over the years to drag out proceedings by appointing a succession of committees to investigate the claims. However, during the crisis there were some signs that this may be changing, with the former PASOK Defence Minister, Akis Tsochatzopoulos, who had once challenged for the leadership of the party, being sentenced in 2013 to a long prison term for money laundering, and a former mayor of Thessaloniki jailed for embezzlement, initially for life, although he was later released on medical grounds.[40] Nonetheless, the effect of the scandals in general was to weaken the legitimacy of both the traditional ruling parties and a large part of the Greek political class as a whole, which came to be seen in the public eye as incorrigibly corrupt, distant from society, opportunistic and obsessed with personal gain. This left PASOK and New Democracy with little claim to authority when called upon to implement the memorandum, especially since most people held them responsible for creating the crisis in the first place.

Differentiation between PASOK and New Democracy was also created through constant reiteration of the ideological positions they had historically occupied. This was principally through making frequent references to key events in recent Greek history, especially the Civil War and its aftermath, the dictatorship and, more recently, the first PASOK government of 1981, with Samaras at one point during the crisis leading the New Democracy deputies out of the debating chamber after Pangalos had called it the first democratic administration in the country's history. Through this tactic the parties were able to create an acute political polarisation that left little space, at least formally, for compromise, as became apparent within the initial years of the crisis, when, despite the best efforts of the outside world, PASOK and New Democracy resisted all attempts to push them towards agreement.[41] However, this tactic of fostering division through reference to the past was so successful because, as much as it was imposed, it also reflected a Greek society in which political identity has long been shaped through a complex amalgam of ideological beliefs and personal and family histories, as well as sometimes a more practical need to gain access to resources for oneself and immediate relatives. In particular, a tendency exists to place families either on the political left or right although such attributions are to a large extent self-selected, since ideological leanings seldom seem to prohibit marital unions, leaving many a choice between identifying with the left or the right.[42] The overall result is not only a general tendency to partition society along these lines, which the political parties both use and reinforce, but also a near universal belief that society should be ordered in this way. The strength and depth of this understanding is evident from the fact that, after initially appearing to fragment into pro- and anti-memorandum forces, the political arena by the general election of January 2015 had more or less reconsolidated itself along the familiar divide, permitting the intense and divisive politics of absolutes to be reproduced once again, but with SYRIZA occupying the place previously held by PASOK.[43]

Along with the rise of SYRIZA, one of the most striking and commented upon aspects of the political realignment brought about by the crisis was the appearance of Golden Dawn (*Chrysi Avgi*) on the national stage. The party traces its origins back to the publication of a pamphlet in 1980 but it languished in relative obscurity until the crisis. In the October 2010 local elections it polled well in Athens, when its leader, Nikolaos Michaloliakos, gained a seat on the city council, probably benefiting from a decision by LAOS not to field a candidate. However, at the same time it was also building grassroots citizen movements in areas of the city with large immigrant populations and these tactics brought further reward in the May 2012 general election.[44] In these it gained 6.97 per cent of the national vote which gave it twenty-one seats in parliament. It gathered support throughout much of the country, but particularly in the Athens-Piraeus area and parts of the Peloponnese traditionally associated with the political right, such as Laconia. Since 1974, nationalist parties to the right of New Democracy have often obtained enough votes to gain representation in the Greek parliament, and Golden Dawn with its insistence that it is 'the secret voice of the blood that passes unchanged through thousands and thousands of years of history until today', charged with 'making the Greek rise up, waking his conscience and leading him to his destiny', can in some ways be seen as part of this tradition.[45] However, others have pointed to its stress on action, racial purity, the need to build a new society and the individual only becoming a person through the collective 'we'. When taken with the party's ambiguous attitude to traditional democratic structures, quasi-cult of an all-powerful leader and flaming torch lit marches by black-shirted, shaven haired youths, this has prompted commentators to term the party neo-fascist or neo-Nazi, although Golden Dawn itself denies it is such and, when asked in surveys, its deputies and supporters alike declared they did not see themselves as extreme.[46] According to a statement of its ideology published in 2012, when Golden Dawn achieves power Greece will be freed from ineffective 'sinful' rule by parties peddling 'failed liberalism' and 'failed Marxism'. Instead, patriotism will replace the tyranny of profit, spiritual values the tyranny of materialism and the 'fighters of virtue' the tyranny of the privileged 'chosen'. This rhetoric skilfully positions the party within longstanding narratives, leading some to suggest that it is the attractiveness of its nationalist message to a society facing an influx of migrants rather than the malign effects of the economic downturn that best explains its rise.[47] In Golden Dawn's vision of the future, all immigrants will be expelled from the country so as to give employment to Greeks, a detailed audit of the debt will determine which parts are odious and 'a thunderous extraction of national resources' will ensure economic autarky and 'true national liberty'.

Golden Dawn sees itself as an organised and disciplined body, with Michaloliakos in the past making allusions to a formation based on military lines.[48] Recruitment is said to be highly selective with aspiring members having to be recommended by two existing members, receive the approval of a relevant committee and serve one year of probation before being inducted with full voting rights.[49] Perhaps because of its lack of access to the conventional media, Golden Dawn has focused on alternative ways of propagating its message through the world wide web and local activism, building a tight cell-based organisational structure that may in part explain its resilience.[50]

Through the activities of local supporters and the circulation of tales, such as the story that it was escorting those fearful of being robbed to take money out of ATMs in inner city areas, the party was able to establish an effective narrative that it was helping those affected by austerity.[51] This social activism, which included the establishment of medical centres and distributing free clothing and food, although only to those deemed to be true Hellenes, as well as a 'jobs for Greeks' campaign, however, seems to have played better to a young audience than old. During the 2012 elections, Golden Dawn's share of the youth vote was high enough to almost be on a par with that of SYRIZA, but its support among older electors was limited. The party was also disproportionately overrepresented among male voters, the self-employed and the unemployed. It had some following among university students, although by and large it attracted the moderately schooled, being underrepresented among the least educated voters. Most of its supporters had either previously voted for other right-wing parties or had never voted before, with Golden Dawn only narrowly trailing SYRIZA in this group. To win support, the party also made skilful use of publicity, happily courting controversy. Its opinion poll rating apparently rose when the party spokesman threw a glass of water over a female SYRIZA deputy and came to blows with another from the Communist Party of Greece (KKE) during a 2012 television debate.[52] Indeed, according to Golden Dawn's programme, a person only has ideological consciousness if they act out of belief rather than personal gain and if this is then transformed into action. Such ideas proved attractive to many of those who felt they had been excluded from the benefits of the two-party system which had dominated Greece for so long, perhaps because they reflected their own sense of rage and impotence, even if it was often at the expense of the most marginalised group in society, migrants both legal and illegal. The nation became accustomed to seeing television footage of Golden Dawn supporters clashing with the police around immigrant shelters or overturning the stalls of migrant vendors said not to possess the correct papers at local markets.[53] With accusations regularly being made that the party had infiltrated the police and that the two were collaborating in activities against immigrants, a clamour grew for action to be taken.[54] The New Democracy dominated government at first appeared uncertain, but after a man associated with the party was implicated in the murder of the rapper Pavlos Fyssas in September 2013, charges that Golden Dawn was a criminal organisation were levied and much of its leadership arrested, including Michaloliakos.[55] This, however, apparently did little to diminish its support in the eyes of the electorate. In the European

Parliament elections of May 2014 it garnered 9.4 per cent of the vote and, although in the January 2015 general election this fell to 6.3 per cent, it came third in the poll and retained all but one of its seats in parliament.[56]

Under the pressure of the memorandum not only the political right fragmented but also the left. A number of groups broke from PASOK, but most made little impact, although a more distinct centre-left grouping, The River (*To Potami*), attracted 6.0 per cent of the vote in the January 2015 general election and won seventeen seats in parliament.[57] Likewise, the KKE, despite its consistent opposition to all aspects of the memorandum, its disciplined presence in demonstrations, support of strikes and high profile of a number of its deputies, was unable to expand its vote, which in the June 2012 poll tumbled to 4.5 per cent.[58] This has usually been explained through reference to its doctrinaire position, which ruled out any coalition with other left-wing parties and foresaw the only solution to the crisis being an exit from the euro and the EU. This stance was in part driven by an interpretation of its participation in the 1989–1990 governments, which saw them as an ideological dilution that weakened the party and eventually lost it votes. As a consequence, the party had instituted a policy of 'internal fortification' that saw it emphasise ideological purity and the recruitment of a disciplined cadre over winning electoral support.[59] Extra stress instead was placed on union activity, leading in 1999 to the formation of the All-Workers Militant Front (PAME) to coordinate the activity of trade unions controlled by KKE members, although it was not formally linked with the party, partly to allow the recruitment of a more diverse and less ideologically committed membership.[60] As a result of these policies the electoral appeal of the KKE remained limited, and its rallies during the 2012 general elections, even in the working-class suburbs of western Athens, often gave the appearance of being little more than private gatherings for the converted.

Instead of the KKE, it was SYRIZA that attracted the support which was to eventually lead it to power. Created in 2004, SYRIZA held its first founding congress as a unitary party in July 2013.[61] Prior to this, it was a broad alliance of different entities with Synaspismos (The Coalition of the Left Movement and Ecology), which traces its lineage in part back to the post-1968 Communist Party of Greece-Interior, as its main constituent, alongside various other Marxist, Trotskyist, Maoist and leftist ecological groups as well as the Democratic Social Movement (DIKKI), which had split from PASOK.[62] Since its formation, SYRIZA has suffered various splits, including the departure in June 2010 of a former minister in the 1989 government, Fotis

Kouvelis, and a number of other deputies, who subsequently founded the Democratic Left (DIMAR), followed shortly afterwards by the former President of Synaspismos and parliamentary leader of SYRIZA, Alekos Alavanos.[63] SYRIZA gained support because of its consistent opposition to the troika-inspired adjustment programme and its promise to repudiate it if elected to office. In doing so, it not only became a voice for those opposed to the memorandum but also rejected the assumption, which it saw as being propagated at home and abroad, that the Greek people as a nation bore a 'collective guilt' for the crisis.[64] Instead, it firmly blamed it on the excesses and corruption of the main parties and the wealthy elite.[65] In the process, it not only tapped into the popular anger with the ruling elite but was also able to draw a contrast with its own clean hands which, it stressed, had never been corrupted by power, despite the presence of a number of ex-PASOK members in its ranks. Seeing the population of Greece as being traditionally left-wing, SYRIZA skilfully employed a number of discourses to appeal to popular sentiment. At one level it suggested that the crisis in Greece was merely part of a wider systemic crisis of capitalism. Utilising a language full of references to class, colonialism, state planning and monopoly capitalism, it promised to place people above profits, and spoke of empowering the powerless. It argued its policies, based on solidarity, social justice and equality, stood in diametric opposition to those of the troika and its creed of neo-liberalism, which SYRIZA claimed only redistributed resources to the detriment of the weak. These were familiar themes from a discourse which has long dominated the domestic public space and bore direct comparison with the language of early PASOK, not least because of the widespread use of a rhetoric of blame and frequent stress on the divide that exists between the people and elite.[66] However, SYRIZA was by no means alone in adopting such a discourse so at the same time it was also careful to stipulate that the path to the future lay in moving both against and beyond familiar left currents and traditions.[67] In particular the radical transformation of Greek society was to come not from social democratic reformism or even revolution but through changes rooted in everyday struggle. In keeping with this, SYRIZA adopted a strategy of associating itself with protest movements and other grassroots phenomena. However, at least in theory, rather than seeking to dominate these, it saw itself as learning from their experiences. The youth group, in particular, became an important intermediary with the protest movement that arose against New Democracy's education reforms prior to the crisis as well as the participants in the 2008 December disturbances. SYRIZA also interpreted the indignant movement as being another example of a new kind of direct democracy with potential transformative powers, believing that in an enhanced dialogue between itself and similar groups that have appeared as a result of the crisis a model of democracy could emerge which would allow Greece to 'become a driving force for change in Europe' as a whole.[68]

In contrast to the KKE, SYRIZA actively engaged with the political system and sought to build links with existing structures, especially the trade unions in the public sector and former state utilities. As a result, not without qualms, many previous PASOK voters switched to support the party, but it would be wrong to see SYRIZA's rise entirely in this light.[69] Tsipras in his speeches reached out to all those 'wronged' by the memorandum which, he suggested, might amount to much of the electorate, and party documents spoke of appealing to the youth of the country as well as the workers and intellectuals. Indeed, in 2012 SYRIZA was particularly successful in attracting younger voters, whether they be employed or unemployed, perhaps in part due to the appeal of Tsipras.[70] By far the youngest of the party leaders, his passionate but non-demagogic oratorical style, in which he talked of restoring dignity to the country, directly engaged with audiences in a way which won him many converts. He also personified the idea that SYRIZA was a voice for the future, a supposition reinforced by its energetic use of social media. However, at the time of the 2012 elections, SYRIZA only had 15,000 members and there were few banners in evidence at Tsipras' small town rallies and certainly none of the fervour that had surrounded the leaders of PASOK and New Democracy in past years.[71] In the years afterwards, the party doubled in size but in the idea that it represented a new kind of connective politics, in which it would act as an umbrella organisation, allowing smaller groupings to develop their capacities, there was always a risk that it might be seen as speaking with more than one voice.[72] Indeed, within the party there remained significant ideological currents, including the radical Left Platform, some of whose members were to split and form their own grouping, Popular Unity, in August 2015. Its leftist origins also led to the party being initially marginalised within the wider European political environment, with Tsipras being shunned prior to the 2012 elections by the socialist French presidential candidate, François Hollande, who preferred to see Venizelos instead. Its closest allies instead have been the likes of the French communists, Sinn Féin and the German *Die Linke* party, which traces its lineage in part from the old East German Socialist Unity Party.[73] Partly as a result, New Democracy and PASOK in the general elections of 2012 were able to effectively play on fears that a SYRIZA government would mean not only a catastrophic exit from the euro but complete ostracism from the EU.

The growing influence of SYRIZA was partly due to the links it had forged with the wider protest movement. At one time or another during the crisis perhaps a third of the population has participated in strikes and other protests against the memorandum and the austerity regime, with there being around 7,000 of these in 2010 alone.[74] These occurred across Greece but the main focus was Athens and particularly Syntagma Square. Here the larger protests were frequently associated with marches organised by the trade union federations during general strikes. By no means all of these ended in violence, and even when clashes did occur, they usually happened within a well sequenced pattern. Typically on the days of general strikes, the main union groupings first met in downtown Athens, usually the General Confederation of Workers of Greece (GSEE) and Confederation of Civil Servants (ADEDY) in Pedion tou Areos and the All-Workers Militant Front (PAME) in Omonia Square. The PAME march was invariably headed by ranks of disciplined cadres shouldering pickaxe handles draped with red flags. Behind them marched KKE supporters, many well versed through years of protest. Once the marchers of all descriptions reached Syntagma Square, they assembled in front of parliament, which was protected by detachments of white helmeted riot police in defensive positions that tended to vary little. The street to the side of parliament was usually blocked by a steel barricade but other roads remained open. The demonstration would be noisy but peaceful, until small clusters of individuals emerged, generally on the corner of the square by the Hotel Grande Bretagne. Often termed 'anarchists' by the local media, these were usually portrayed as being a coherent group. However, they seem to see themselves not as a structured movement, but as a series of loose formations drawn together by a shared idea of politics as a performance of direct action. Around these core actors gathered other groupings of varying degrees of organisation attracted by the violence of the anarchists but not necessarily their ideology. They ranged from the well-prepared, clad in black with backpacks and full-face gas masks, to those with only their faces painted white with Maalox suspension and simple kerchiefs to ward off the worst effects of the tear gas.[75] Scenes made familiar by thousands of news photographs then started to unfold, as a hail of missiles poured down on the police positions and exploding petrol bombs threw up gouts of flame. The heavily protected and gas mask clad riot police responded with salvo after salvo of tear gas which left the square and surrounding area wreathed in a thick, choking cloud of chemicals.

Many protesters retreated but others remained, holding their ground and wielding any weapons that came to hand to retaliate. The violent clashes could then spread across the square, drawing in parts of the crowd and sometimes even bystanders, who might be left struggling for breath from the tear gas or clutching bleeding wounds, as the police sallied forth. The level of violence was often shocking and the hatred between the two sides seemed visceral, but, just a few streets away, other groups of police might be chatting to people leaving the march or buying takeaway coffees from cafes without a hint of menace in the air. Even if Syntagma Square itself was covered in a thick cloud of tear gas and smoke from burning kiosks or, on at least two occasions, a blazing television transmission truck, the small shops in the side streets leading off the square remained open. Files of tourists passed by almost oblivious to the violence, except when they halted to grab a quick photograph. Only the larger boulevards, the hunting grounds of packs of police motorbikes, with officers riding pillion wielding truncheons, remained deserted. Usually the confrontation lasted for an hour or so and then petered out. The petrol bombers, having hurled their last Molotov cocktail, faded away; the demonstrators, clasping their rolled up banners, trudged home; and the riot police, having taken off their protective armour, returned once more to the tedium of life on their specially equipped buses. The anarchists and their followers might be marginal figures in Greek political life, but their production of violence was an important element in the crisis. The drama of the scenes from Syntagma became a key ingredient in the narrative for the watching world, allowing media commentators to easily raise fears that the country was on the verge of slipping into anarchy, which would lead to the unravelling of the adjustment programme, disorderly default and even exit from the euro. The troika in its reports expressed concern about the civil unrest and the protesters themselves, in pairing Syntagma with Tahrir Square in Cairo, were not slow to suggest there might be parallels between events in Greece and the concurrent uprisings of the Arab Spring.[76] For its part, the PASOK government could use the violence and civil unrest to raise questions about the soundness of the troika's prescriptions and to argue that it should proceed with caution. However, with the sounds of the clashes audible in parliament, the violence also placed increasing strains on party loyalties and, in particular, the self-belief of the PASOK administration and its right not only to impose new measures but also, ultimately, to rule.

The protests which ended in violence were relatively few. Most of the many thousands of demonstrations were peaceful. They were by no means all made up of youthful protesters. Many, particularly the participants in the general strikes organised by the public sector unions, were older protestors, with the greatest number being in late middle-age or even older. Most were still male but, as the crisis continued, a growing number of women also began to participate. The vast majority of these strikers were employed by the state and were members of unions or associations espousing a left-wing ideology, which led to them mostly identifying themselves in party political terms with either SYRIZA or the KKE. Indeed, this background may help explain why four out of five in a poll taken at the end of 2010 stated that they had taken part in similar activities in the past.[77] This also meant that they tended to perceive protest as an effective means of airing their views, since it had brought changes in policy in the past at relatively little cost. In general, therefore, the general strikes and the protests associated with them can be seen as a continuation of past patterns. However, there were also others on the streets who were less identified with any political groups, and these were to become particularly visible in the 2011 demonstrations organised by the indignant movement or *aganaktismenoi* as they were called in Greek.[78] These began at the end of May 2011, mostly in Athens but also to a lesser extent in other towns and cities, and continued in various guises until 1 August 2011, when Syntagma Square was cleared of its encampment of demonstrators by the police in an early morning raid. The indignant movement derived its appellation, and it appears some of its organisational forms, from the similarly minded Spanish *indignados* who occupied the Puerta del Sol in Madrid in May 2011.[79] They in turn had, at least in part, drawn their inspiration from a slim booklet *Time for Outrage* [*Indignez-vous!*] written by a ninety-three-year old French resistance hero, Stéphane Hessel, in which he excoriated indifference and urged non-violent action against the ills of contemporary society.[80] At the time, it was said that the *aganaktismenoi* had been spurred into action by banners held up in the protests in Spain saying, 'Don't be too noisy, you might wake the Greeks up.'[81] However, the story is probably apocryphal since the banners seem to have related to a sporting event.[82] Organised through social media, the movement drew large numbers to nightly gatherings in Syntagma Square in which the protesters, playing green lasers along the facades of the surrounding buildings, supposedly to blind the biases of the traditional media, expressed their outrage at both the measures being imposed and those who had brought the country to such a state of crisis. As in Spain, a makeshift encampment also appeared. Amid a scattering of tents, banners strung from the trees in the square offered support for causes as varied as the rights of asylum seekers and the return of the Elgin marbles from the British Museum. These reflected the diversity at the heart of the movement, which some, especially on the left, chose to divide into distinct upper and lower squares.[83] In the upper, they placed nationalists and religious groups as well as the politically uncommitted who came to pour abuse at the parliament in an expression of pure rage, while, in the lower, they located left-leaning groups who tended to see the protests as something akin to the anti-globalisation Occupy movement active in this period in the USA and elsewhere. Yet, within this new indignant movement some also traced older practices, because there were clear classical allusions in the organisation of a popular assembly, where some speakers were invited but most were selected by lot.[84] As one participant noted, this made the act of speaking almost as important as what was said, describing the experience of addressing thousands who listened in 'church-like silence' and then contributed fully to the debate as 'life changing'.[85] During the day, when the square bustled with tourists and shoppers, street vendors sold snacks and national flags while protesters sat idling away the hours on benches outside their tents or gathered in small groups. Sometimes this would be to hear a speaker, at other times they would just talk, breaking off occasionally to listen to a loudspeaker announcing forthcoming events, such as a workshop teaching children how to write protest banners supporting democracy. The diversity among the *aganaktismenoi* created tensions, with some on the political left uneasy with the slogans and boorish behaviour of other protesters. However, in general, a spirit of coexistence seems to have reigned, with the demonstrators being united by their contempt of the privileged establishment and the political class. Witty posters mocked the 'Greek Parliament Circus' and two large banners hoisted directly in front of the building cast Papandreou as 'IMF employee of the year' and Papaconstantinou as 'Goldman Sachs employee of the decade'. Some, such as Pangalos, dismissed the *aganaktismenoi* as an inchoate movement without ideology that could only articulate rage.[86] However, in their rejection of the adjustment programme and its attendant austerity, their desire to see a reassertion of national independence in the face of what was widely perceived to be a state of humiliating neo-colonialist subservience and their condemnation of what was seen as a deeply flawed political system riddled with corruption, the *aganaktismenoi* in their peaceful and noisy protests could, indeed, be seen as the voice of many within the country. It was, therefore, hardly surprising that the movement garnered considerable support in various opinion polls, although at the same time there were also plenty who were willing to disparage the 'gypsy encampment' in the square.[87]

Some on the left invested the *aganaktismenoi* with the mantle of being the precursors of a new form of bottom-up direct democracy, and it is possible to see the demonstrations as being a visible example of a wider civic mobilisation which was, in part, triggered by the crisis but also spoke of changing values in general. Partly in response to the rise in the price of petrol but also as a lifestyle choice, cycling became more popular, with new bike shops opening across Athens. Mass groups of cyclists met to ride together and protest about the poor facilities for those on bicycles. A rash of community self-help groups also emerged, such as *borume*, whose members offered to trade skills with each other.[88] Others formed part of a broader anti-middleman initiative designed to allow producers to sell directly to consumers. There were even reports of alternative currencies appearing, some of which were traded electronically on the model of Bitcoin. Free or low cost events attracted growing crowds, encouraging Athenians to rediscover their city.[89] Much of this activity was coordinated through social media, and, therefore, arguably did not reach many of those in most need, but other movements were more inclusive. In 2011 potato growers from the Nevrokopi region in northern Greece began selling their products directly to consumers at prices far lower than those to be found in shops or local markets.[90] Soon pictures of people carrying large sacks of potatoes away from parked lorries became commonplace on the television news, leading the government to even talk of setting up its own parallel online scheme.[91] The story was used to highlight what were seen as the excessive profits of middlemen, but the economics of the movement were always a little opaque, and within months it had withered and died, leaving potatoes selling at the same price as usual. No doubt many initiatives will follow a similar fate and, just as the old nongovernmental organisation sector became heavily reliant on state largesse, even if some blossom, they may be co-opted, as arguably the government tried to do with the potato movement before it expired. Nonetheless, the broader picture would seem to be one of the crisis producing a growing civic consciousness, especially among the educated young and middle-aged, which sometimes is politically orientated towards the left, although how this will be translated into society as a whole remains yet to be fully seen.[92]

Aside from the protests by groups like the *aganaktismenoi*, the crisis was also marked by a huge number of smaller strikes and demonstrations, with the police recording over 27,000 of these in Athens alone between 2011 and 2015. Almost nightly pictures were shown on the news of groups marching behind slogan daubed banners through the centre of the city, which, according to shop owners, caused so much disruption that they lost millions of euros in trade. However, most attention was focused on a series of general strikes called periodically throughout the crisis by the main union federations. Despite their appellation, these were far from being general, largely involving public sector workers. Usually lasting only one day, for all the obvious anger of the protesters they, in reality, drew varying degrees of support. Occasionally many thousands poured onto the streets of Athens and there was a genuine widespread shut down of public services but more frequently the protests were relatively limited in scale, and most schools and the like continued to function as normal. Even within institutions that joined the strike, participation could be half-hearted, with some employees feeling they had been intimidated into taking action by more militant colleagues. The shuttered facades of shops in downtown Athens on strike days also seem to have reflected as much a desire to protect businesses as show solidarity. The ambivalence about taking strike action, however, did not necessarily arise because of any great difference of opinion with the strikers. It was driven more by a personal dislike of such actions, distrust of the unions and perhaps, most importantly, a desire to see already falling wages not docked further because of participation in industrial action. Arguably those striking, as well as being those threatened with the greatest losses in terms of wages and benefits, such as public transport workers, were often also those still able to bear the costs of their action.

Relatively few private sector workers belong to unions, the figure cited is usually around twenty per cent. The small size of many companies, fragmented union structures, a general trajectory away from industrial conflict throughout Europe in recent years due to growing job uncertainty, and heavy politicisation have all combined to keep unions weak in this area of the economy. So, for example, at the beginning of the crisis, the Bookshop Workers' Union of Athens represented only about 16 per cent of staff working in the sector and, even though it was regarded as being particularly active, less than a third of its members participated in its internal elections and even fewer attended its weekly meetings.[93] Yet, it is in the private sector that the vast bulk of job losses have occurred during the crisis, and even if work has been retained the cuts in salaries and benefits have often been swingeing, with it not being unknown for employees to work for months without being paid. The relatively low level of union representation in the private sector may have been a factor in dampening industrial action but, nonetheless, according to figures from the GSEE, which are probably incomplete, of the 445 work stoppages recorded in 2011, 240 occurred in this area of the economy.[94] Aside from the pages of a few newspapers, such as the communist *Rizospastis*, most of these strikes evolved outside the public gaze but, among others, there were disputes at Alter TV, Hellenic Coca-Cola in Thessaloniki and the Elefsina Shipyards. The most high profile was probably the strike at the Elliniki Halyvourgia steel works in Aspropyrgos near Athens, where over 350 workers downed tools for 272 days in a dispute over pay and working hours.[95] The strikers, who declared they were defending the interests of the working class in general, received backing from PAME and expressions of public support. The union and the management made conflicting claims about the company's financial viability, but after the company shifted production to a sister plant at Volos, which had accepted the management's terms, amid growing divisions among the workforce following a legal judgment, police activity led the strike to eventually fold. The workers did not gain the support of the metalworking union's federation and although the dispute became something of a cause célèbre for the left, perhaps because of the relatively few workers involved, public consciousness of the strike in general remained relatively low.[96] Indeed, more obvious than these industrial disputes, were those involving professional groups, such as pharmacists, lawyers, taxi and lorry drivers. Some of these were prolonged and caused considerable disruption.

Yet, in spite of the aggravation caused by many of the disputes, with traffic frequently gridlocked in Athens, and islands periodically left isolated, public opinion appeared in general to remain favourable to the strikers. With many of those on strike being associated with PASOK, the Papandreou government's response was also a measured mixture of carrot and stick. Disputes with public sector workers and significant interest groups, as has long been the case, usually led to discussions with the relevant minister and in some instances concessions being made and changes in the proposed legislation. However, at other times, when industrial action threatened disruption which was judged harmful to the country's economic interests and the goal of fiscal consolidation, civil mobilisation orders were issued forcing the strikers back to work on pain of legal action. These could sometimes be implemented with alacrity, as in the case of the lorry drivers, seamen, and Athenian transport workers. Likewise, an occupation of the Acropolis by public sector workers was broken up before the eyes of tourists by baton wielding police. Indeed, at times, the firmness of the government's actions during the crisis left some commentators questioning if they were opportune or even legal. The administration's tactics, political infiltration and the general fragmentation of organised labour, meant that, despite the obvious anger felt by many individuals, the union movement as a whole was not able or willing to build on this hostility to seriously challenge the authority of the government. Indeed, while public opinion surveys in the past have often shown that unions are held in a higher regard in Greece than in many other European countries, more focused polling among union members has revealed considerable levels of disillusionment with the GSEE, and during the crisis this antipathy at times led to popular outpourings of anger against its leaders.[97] In places it also seems to have led to the formation of new groups sometimes operating outside established frameworks more committed to rank and file activism.[98]

Outside the realms of the street demonstrations and strikes, broader based citizens' protest groups also appeared, particularly the 'Won't Pay' movement, which drew inspiration for its name from a play by Dario Fo. This emerged in 2010 and was initially directed at rises in motorway tolls, which were felt as being particularly unjust given the poor state of some roads. Supporters of the organisation refused to pay tolls when requested and also, along with similar groups, periodically intervened to allow other motorists to pass for free.[99] Although it was portrayed as an anti-memorandum movement, the situation was actually more ambiguous, because many of the tolls were collected by construction companies, which had acquired the right to gather them in return for building the roads. Ministers complained about the breaking of the law and the withholding of revenues. However, other commentators defended the protesters through reference to the American civil rights movement, arguing that their actions were valid in a malfunctioning state in which the democratic legitimacy of the government was in question and few alternative avenues existed to express grievances.[100] When public transport fares were raised in Athens, the 'Won't Pay' movement briefly spread to the metro and the Electric Railway Athens-Piraeus (ISAP), with bags being placed over ticket validating machines to prevent them being used. However, afterwards it seemed to gradually lose steam and failed to translate into a distinct political voice when it stood in the 2012 elections. The 'Won't Pay' movement faded from the public eye, but in one reading it can be seen as just a highly visible example of a wider societal response to the measures of the memorandum which has often been interpreted in terms of resistance. This could occur at all levels from large companies to individual citizens, but was often, at least partially, grounded in existing informal practices. Thus, when an increase in the tax on cigarettes led consumers to switch to widely available cheaper contraband imports, the big domestic manufacturers, to try and reclaim market share, cut prices. The overall result was that the government in the end gained little from the tax increase since fewer legal packets were sold at a lower price, leading one commentator to see the drop in prices in terms of the industry taking revenge on the government for its policy.[101] Some measures were seen as being particularly unjust, such as the equalisation of the tax on diesel fuel and heating oil, which raised the cost of the latter by nearly a third. In reaction, partly driven by a popular and media driven notion that it was always going to be cheaper than using heating oil, people switched to burning wood in fireplaces and stoves. Dozens of wood yards sprang up around Athens and other cities selling timber by the tonne, and the results included a rise in illegal logging in forests, as well as reports of a deterioration of air quality in Athens and other cities, partly due to the burning of unsuitable materials, such as medium-density fibreboard (MDF), which led to a rise in those seeking medical help for respiratory problems. There were also occasional reports of fatalities due to fires in flats, but far more common were the prolonged, and often bitter, social conflicts that broke out in the many apartment blocks with communal boiler systems, as occupants argued over the length of time heating systems should be used and even whether oil should be bought at all.[102] Sales of alternative heating devices boomed, with shops piled high with oil filled radiators, and there was a massive decline in heating oil sales which may have lessened imports but also cut the extra revenue raised by the tax to a fraction of the expected amount.[103] One measure had spawned multiple consequences, with perhaps the most poisonous being the least foreseen, as previously harmonious residential blocks became near battlegrounds split between the 'capitalists' who had money for oil and those who did not. The only fortunate thing was that, in the years immediately after the tax increase, the winters were remarkably mild, so less heating than usual was actually needed. Ideas of rebelliousness and resistance have long occupied a central place in Greek self-conception. Indeed, some have even been able to see the indifference that civil servants show towards members of the public as a resistance to modernisation.[104] However, to cast all these actions in this mould is not so easy, since, in reality, they appear to be motivated by mixed emotions, even if, when asked, individuals often chose to ascribe political significance to their behaviour. The response to the increase in fuel duty was driven by both anger and outrage at what was seen as another injustice as well as a practical need to lessen the economic impact on household budgets. In the process, as with so much else, society evolved ways of coping with the crisis within familiar frameworks. However, this was often only by subverting the measures, sometimes in unexpected ways, through informality.

9

INTERNAL DEVALUATION AND DEPRESSION

THE ECONOMY DURING THE CRISIS

During the crisis the Greek economy has shrunk to such an extent that one parliamentarian has described it as the greatest downturn in recent world history.[1] After many years in which Greece consistently registered one of the highest annual rates of increase of GDP in the EU, economic growth began to falter at the end of 2007 before turning negative in the second quarter of 2008. This process then continued almost without a break until, by the first quarter of 2014, Greece had endured six years of negative growth, during which time the country's real GDP had declined from its pre-crisis peak by a cumulative total of around 26 per cent, with the sharpest falls being recorded in 2011.[2] Other European countries in the wake of the 2008 financial crisis experienced sharp downturns, with GDP in Latvia falling by 18 per cent in 2009 alone, but no other economy in the Organisation for Economic Co-operation and Development (OECD) has endured such a sustained period of contraction as Greece. Even fellow support package recipient Portugal experienced a far lesser downturn, recording reasonable phases of positive growth during its period of fiscal consolidation. Yet, when the initial adjustment programme was being shaped in the spring of 2010, none of this was apparently foreseen.[3] Instead, the official projections were relatively benign, suggesting that the downturn would be moderately short and shallow, the rise in unemployment controllable and any decline in living standards limited. Beyond the political uncertainty covered in previous chapters and the decline in confidence, which is considered in the next, this chapter will explore some of the reasons why these projections proved to be so wayward and why the economic downturn was so deep and prolonged.

One of the most abiding impressions left by the crisis was the scores of empty shops lining the streets of the capital and other cities. In the Athenian suburbs most tended to lie on side streets. However, in the city centre, where rents on some thoroughfares had been among the highest in the world prior to the crisis and disruption from civil protests was greatest, major boulevards like Stadiou were left an eerie shadow of their former selves, with 42 per cent of its businesses said to have ceased trading by 2012.[4] The circumstances surrounding closure varied in each case. Some chose to prominently post signs in their windows declaring their demise was due to retirement. Others seemed to almost slink away, abandoning their premises with all the fittings left intact, as if on the spur of the moment. Closures were particularly pronounced in fields such as clothing, footwear and furniture, where enterprises carrying debt and often relying on a business model of high margins on low sales were barely viable at the best of times. In 2009 almost half of all the 221,363 firms filing tax returns were already reporting they were making no profits. This figure was not entirely out of line with those of countries such as the UK at that time, but in Greece under the pressures of the crisis, for a variety of reasons, many businesses did close.[5] Figures vary considerably according to source, but the consensus seems to be that between a fifth and a third of all businesses had already ceased trading by 2014, and even prior to the imposition of capital controls in 2015, which increased their difficulties further, many of those that had survived were expressing fears that they may yet be forced to shut down.[6]

The demise of so many small companies may not have been mourned by all. There has long been a tendency among some Greek policymakers and academics to view such enterprises as a facet of backwardness, preventing the development of a modern economy. Yet, the Greek small and medium size business sector is unique within the EU. It is exceptionally large, accounting for nearly all the companies in the country, almost entirely at the micro level, and such large scale closures were bound to have a profound effect on the economy as a whole. Moreover, many rested on proud family traditions, which not only gave employment and a living but also meaning to lives, so that when they were deprived of the social interaction of work many owners and former employees all too readily slipped into depression and despair. The impact on society as a whole was also considerable, since the dusty, empty windows and ubiquitous yellow stickers offering premises for rent remained a perpetual sore, constantly reminding passers-by of the depth of the crisis. Indeed, such was the scale of closures, that most knew somebody connected with a business that had folded. This reinforced a collective sense of precariousness and gave the crisis a human face. Yet, such large scale closures are not without precedent. Similar numbers are reported to have gone out of business in the recession at the beginning of the 1990s. In the years afterwards the small and medium sized business sector rebounded to become once again a mainstay of the economy and, even during the crisis, there have been signs of resilience in some areas. Many of the shops, after standing empty awhile, have found new occupiers, often after the negotiation of markedly lower rents, with reports that on the prime shopping thoroughfare of Ermou in the heart of Athens they at first roughly halved.[7] The same has also happened in the Athenian suburbs although here the new shops have tended to be those selling goods at cheaper prices, such as chain delicatessens, or niche crisis industries, including workshops converting cars to run on cheaper Liquid Petroleum Gas.

Most of the new start-ups have been in familiar retail and service trades like fast food and cafes. Indeed, with few other jobs available, self-employment for many remains a necessity rather than an opportunity. There are only limited signs of the creation of companies in more innovative areas and, in general, the business strategy of the authorities, perhaps understandably given the depth of the downturn, has appeared to focus mostly on the further development of sectors such as tourism, in which Greece has had a longstanding comparative advantage, rather than what can be seen as more future-orientated alternatives. However, in doing this they are perpetuating an overreliance for which the country has been criticised in the past.[8] Likewise, although the number of part-time jobs, which was previously negligible, has risen sharply during the crisis, the fact that the vast majority continue to see these as a second best to full employment speaks more of an evolution driven by necessity rather than a change of culture.[9]

The closure of so many businesses was bound to have an impact on jobs, but the rise in unemployment during the crisis was still far greater than expected. By the close of 2013, 1,363,137 people were registered as jobless. Amounting to 27.5 per cent of the workforce, this was proportionately a far greater number than in Portugal and Ireland, being matched only by Spain within the EU.[10] As demand for goods and services fell, employers laid off workers and then, as the downturn continued, a lack of investment meant that few new jobs were created. As a result, the unemployment figure after 2013 has stabilised at a very high level.[11] Many of these are long-term unemployed, with 71.6 per cent at the beginning of 2015 having had no job for over a year, and some for far longer, with an estimated quarter of a million at the beginning of the previous year not having worked for over four years.[12] Indeed, it is possible that real unemployment levels may be higher than stated because many registered as self-employed are languishing in a permanent state of underemployment, although, counterbalancing this, it also seems likely that some of the jobless do a certain amount of work in the shadow economy.[13] Initiatives from the Manpower Employment Organisation (OAED) have also helped keep the figures lower than they might otherwise have been, perhaps by as much as five percentage points. and after a new round of measures in 2014 in the second quarter of that year the rate fell to 26.6 per cent, the first statistically significant decline since the fourth quarter of 2008.[14] However, critics charged that the new measures followed an agenda driven more by foreign concerns about the headline youth unemployment figure than a desire to tackle deeper rooted problems. Indeed, the much cited youth rate, which at times reached nearly 60 per cent among young men and was even greater among women of the same age, was slightly deceptive, since it was based on the number of people aged between fifteen and twenty-four who were out of education and available for employment, and this is a relatively small proportion of this age group as a whole.[15] Some jobs have been created by official programmes, which has brought the youth unemployment figure down, but these are frequently short-term posts on the minimum wage. Finding jobs for the many older people, who form the growing body of long-term unemployed, poses just as great a challenge because the length of the downturn and the dislocation it has brought makes it possible that, even if new jobs are created, many of these more elderly workers may not have the necessary skills to fill them.[16]

The rise in unemployment has skewed work participation rates within the population in general to such an extent that even among those aged from fifteen to seventy-four only a bare majority have been left gainfully employed. In the population as a whole far more are economically inactive than active but this must be set against the fact that Greece has long had one of the lowest rates of work participation in the EU, largely due to the many women engaged in domestic duties. Indeed, the steady rise in those entering paid employment over recent years means that, despite the large numbers losing their jobs at the beginning of the crisis, the actual number gainfully employed in 2011 was little less than in 2000, although by 2015 the figure had slipped below 1995 levels.[17] Nevertheless, the fall in the number in work has been disastrous for the adjustment programmes, reducing the spending power of consumers and lowering tax and social security revenues, while at the same time boosting government expenditure on unemployment benefit. First and foremost, though, it has been a tragedy for the people concerned. Its impact might vary depending on personal circumstance. It makes a difference whether unemployment stems from the closure of a whole company or if just a handful of employees are dismissed, but also, crucially, if other members of the household continue to work. Rigid labour legislation in the past protected the jobs of 'primary-earners' who were almost always married men. This perpetuated a socially conservative pattern of employment which gave fewer opportunities to women and unmarried youngsters but it also meant that lack of a job rarely translated into poverty.[18] The crisis has broken this rule, creating many households in which both partners are unemployed and in such cases research has found that poverty is widespread, especially if there are dependent children. However, even if one partner remains in work, it does not necessarily bring an escape from a life of isolation at home for the other, feelings of inferiority and possibly even mental health problems.[19]

Unemployment has long ranked as a particularly high social concern in Greece, partly because of the lack of a comprehensive social security net but also due to the sheer difficulty of obtaining a job in a society where the general understanding is that few opportunities are available in either the public or private sector to those without personal connections. Indeed, one of the consequences of the mass unemployment of the crisis has been the narrowing of this range of contacts, and, as a result, hunting for anything but the most low paid of positions in sectors such as the catering trade has become a herculean task.

In the early years of the crisis the greatest loss of jobs was in the construction sector. From an estimated 400,000 workers employed in 2008, by the third quarter of 2011 this figure had already fallen to 242,000 and subsequently it was to decline even further.[20] Greece experienced something of a construction boom in the 2000s, so that within the EU this sector of the economy was only more important in Spain and Ireland as a percentage of GDP. However, unlike these countries the boom in Greece was not the cause of the crisis. There was no spillover into the banking sector and, despite the fact that in 2009 there were an estimated 200,000 unsold flats in Athens, there was no precipitate fall in prices. This was largely due to the fact that most companies working in the field were small family developers which usually adopted a conservative strategy of funding the construction of one block of flats by selling another. As a result, most had sufficient capital reserves or enough alternative sources of income to keep empty flats on their books during the first years of the crisis in the hope there would eventually be an upturn in demand. This helped keep prices high, and with the government passing legislation stopping the banks foreclosing on some 200,000 family homes because of mortgage arrears, there was no sudden rise in supply.[21] As a result, housing prices during the crisis have declined very unevenly, although by 2014, they were said to have fallen on average from their peak by about 40 per cent. However, by then demand had also collapsed, with appraisals involving financial institutions, including not only property transactions but also procedures such as the renegotiation of existing loans, falling to only 17,044 in the country as a whole in that year.[22] This was due not just to the fall in household incomes and an unwillingness to take on credit obligations in such an uncertain environment, even if the money was available to borrow. Tax rises have also led to a questioning of the old assumption that property is always the best investment, and a belief that prices could yet fall further has made investors wary of entering the market. The relatively high professional charges of lawyers, solicitors, architects and estate agents have also been cited as an obstacle, but more important probably is the fact that, partly due to the complexity of building regulations, many homes are at least in part technically illegal.[23] The authorities have made use of this during the crisis to raise money by offering property owners the chance to purchase immunity from prosecution for a certain number of years on payment of a fine. However, while in the past buyers may have been prepared to overlook any infringements in their eagerness to make a purchase, this is not such an appealing prospect in the new framework of tighter regulation introduced by the austerity regime. As a consequence, sales have stalled and the overall result of this collapse in the housing market coupled with the cuts in the public investment budget has been that one of the key sectors of the Greek economy, despite a renewal of the motorway construction programme, remains in the doldrums, and this was a significant factor in deepening and lengthening the depression.[24]

Indeed, as noted at the beginning of this chapter, a deviation from economic growth projections as great as has occurred in Greece has rarely been seen in International Monetary Fund (IMF) programmes in the past, and nothing similar happened in the cases of either Ireland or Portugal.[25] The reasons for this would seem to lie both in the structure of the Greek economy and a failure to correctly foresee the impact of fiscal consolidation measures. Prior to the crisis consumption was generally held to account for a greater percentage of GDP in Greece than in most other euro area economies, with retail sales accounting for almost half of this. During the crisis these have plummeted by over a third in volume, as Greeks have dramatically cut spending on almost all non-essential items.[26] Car sales, for instance, shrank considerably. New registrations fell from an average of 265,312 in the years between 2004 and 2009 to just 58,165 in 2013 before recovering somewhat in 2014 to 70,188.[27] The overall result was that between 2009 and 2013 monthly average household spending at constant prices decreased by 31.5 per cent to just €1,509.[28] This steep decline in household expenditure occurred within the context of an adjustment of state finances which saw measures in gross terms amounting to more than 30 per cent of GDP enacted between 2010 and 2014, as the primary budget balance moved from a deficit of 10.5 per cent in 2009 to a surplus of 0.8 per cent in 2013, according to the adjustment programme's definition.[29] This was a far deeper fiscal consolidation than seen in Portugal and Ireland and from the outset it was accepted by the troika that the expenditure cuts and tax rises required would be recessionary. However, higher than expected budget deficits and a failure to readjust targets in the face of the deeper than anticipated economic downturn meant that the adjustment of the structural deficit between 2009 and 2012 was nearly half as much again as projected in the original adjustment programme for the whole period up until 2014.[30] Aside from being driven by the need of Greece's euro area partners to minimise the size of the assistance package and avoid debt restructuring, it can be argued that such a deep frontloaded consolidation was also intended in part to accelerate the policy of internal devaluation, since by suppressing demand it should have speeded the lowering of prices and wages. However, in truth, such an aggressive tightening, when the economy was already in recession, credit difficult to find and significant trading partners were following similar policies, was always most likely to only produce an even deeper downturn.

The initial projections of the impact of the fiscal consolidation measures also seem to have been flawed. In particular, the IMF has suggested that the fiscal multiplier used to forecast the impact of the measures on the economy was too low since it implied that economic activity would decrease by only half the amount it eventually did. The European Commission and the European Central Bank (ECB) have both challenged this view but, according to the IMF, later iterations of the adjustment programme did use a multiplier twice the size of the initial figure.[31] The issue remains contentious and the debate is primarily concerned with explaining the failure of forecasting rather than the depth of the depression, although, since policy was shaped by the projections, the two are obviously intimately linked. However, it generally seems to be accepted that multipliers can differ over time and space and that in the case of Greece the relatively closed nature of the economy, which meant that any decline in demand would disproportionately hit domestic manufacturers, and the lack of exchange rate flexibility, which meant that no attempt could be made to boost exports through a devaluation of the currency, amplified the effects of the adjustment measures, leading to a far greater fall in economic activity than expected. Indeed, not only may the fiscal multiplier used have been wrong but the IMF has also suggested that other policy choices may have deepened the downturn. In its opinion, the initial adjustment by the Greek government focused too much on raising revenue instead of cutting expenditure.[32] It would have preferred it to have followed the example of Ireland and to have cut the public sector wage bill more sharply, probably through redundancies, and to have taken earlier steps to rein in social protection programmes and curb healthcare costs. According to the troika it was only with the second assistance programme that the Greek authorities moved to a more expenditure based adjustment, making deeper cuts, although these also contributed to keeping demand depressed and may have heightened income inequalities.[33] Indeed, just as much as the type of measures, the sequence in which they were applied may also have been important, with it being suggested that the downturn might have been mitigated if some decisions had been taken earlier. For instance, it may have been better if the measures to ensure greater price competition had been enacted at the same time as those designed to free labour markets.[34]

Indeed, the policy of internal devaluation was meant to see a lowering of both wages and prices but, as the IMF ruefully admitted in an early report, the latter proved remarkably unresponsive to market stimulus. Recessions are caused by a decline in demand and, theoretically, in response companies should reduce prices until they reach a level at which consumers start to buy again. However, in Greece this was slow to happen, and, instead, prices initially rose, partly because many companies seem to have chosen to pass on the full cost of increases in VAT and other duties rather than cut profit margins.[35] Indeed, four years into the recession, in 2011, prices in Greece were still only slightly below average EU levels, and were actually higher in areas such as food, non-alcoholic beverages and clothing. Only in the energy sector, where the price of electricity was influenced by the state, were they much lower.[36] This general failure of prices to move downwards more speedily not only exacerbated the economic downturn by keeping demand depressed but also contributed to public alienation from the adjustment programme, since it prevented it from delivering what could have been an early tangible benefit. The reasons for the failure of prices to adjust are many and stretch beyond companies protecting profit margins. Local explanations have often focused upon market inflexibilities arising from the perceived domination of cartels, particularly in areas such as fuel supplies, but also within the supermarket sector, where 40 per cent of business rested in the hands of four companies.[37] In a similar vein, much has also been written on the tendency of foreign multinationals to pass goods through various subsidiary companies, which, it is said, allowed them to lower tax payments and keep prices high for the likes of household cleaning products. As time progressed, though, attention began to focus on bureaucratic regulation, with the New Democracy led government committing itself to implementing the findings of an OECD report designed to cut administrative burden, which by some estimates added up to 7.0 per cent to prices.[38] These include elaborate rules concerning storage and the shelf-life of products such as milk, which was shorter than in many countries. However, an attempt to lengthen this sparked so much controversy that a deputy minister resigned, and, when it did occur, contrary to expectations, at least initially, there seems to have been a small price rise rather than a decrease.[39]

In explaining the high prices, the manufacturing companies themselves would probably point to the relatively small size of the local market and the difficulties of achieving economies of scale, as well as the lengthy supply chains that allow middlemen and importers to seek their own profits. The tendency of many local companies to retain practices judged as inefficient elsewhere, such as maintaining high stock levels as well as relatively loose inventory control, no doubt also played a role as almost certainly did manning levels in some firms. Indeed, perhaps the initial inability of prices to respond to market stimulus is not so surprising given the culture of regulation that has long prevailed in Greece. Even after formal controls were removed, prices at times continued to be manipulated through informal 'gentleman's agreements' concluded between manufacturers, retailers and the government. During the crisis, there was talk about these being resurrected, with the authorities said to be in discussions with the major supermarkets about reducing prices on key staples. Powerful trade associations have also continued to control opening hours, price discounts and sales periods, as part of this culture which remains suspicious of the open market. Staff of smaller shops have long been sent to check the prices of competitors, but in the past this was not so they could be undercut and sales boosted, but more to ensure that profits were not being lost by selling goods too cheaply. Opinion polls have also continued to show that far more view businesses and, especially big companies, as having a negative influence on society than a positive, and perhaps as a consequence consumer groups rather than campaigning for greater competition within the market have tended to press governments for tighter controls to lower prices across the board.[40] Indeed, prices different from the norm, in the past, would often be treated as a source of suspicion by shoppers, being seen as an indication of lower quality or shoddy manufacturing. Under the pressure of the crisis some of these attitudes seemed to change, with surveys showing that consumers started to look for better value, embracing supermarket own brands and happily patronising cheaper chain delicatessens and coffee shops, which maintained standards through tight quality control.[41] Hosts of special offers, some more transparent than others, flooded a market little accustomed to such things, with internet coupon companies offering everything from theatre tickets to face creams and wine, accompanied by a no quibble return policy which set new standards for Greek customer care. These were only available to the computer literate but they were part of a trend that saw prices in certain areas of the economy which proved more sensitive to market forces than others drop considerably. Initially most visible within service sector industries such as private healthcare and tourism, from early 2013 these price reductions led the economy into a sustained period of negative inflation or, as it is more frequently termed, deflation. The troika had long stressed the necessity of such a decline in prices as part of its plan to help the economy regain competitiveness. By restoring some of the purchasing power lost due to wage and pension cuts it also assisted consumers. However, the sustained period of negative inflation that then followed was more in keeping with an economy falling into a deflationary spiral in which price and wage cuts become mutually supporting. Indicative of high unemployment, limited purchasing power and low demand, deflation in Greece may have not only deepened and prolonged the economic downturn but also, by reducing revenues, made it more difficult to meet fiscal consolidation targets as well as further eroded debt sustainability.[42]

Indeed, for many years the IMF and other commentators have argued that Greek producers have effectively priced themselves out of both domestic and international markets leading to a surfeit of imports and few merchandise exports. The reasons for this have been much debated, but relatively high labour costs per unit of output have frequently been held as being responsible.[43] Despite this, initially, the troika decided not to press for a reduction of wages in the private sector, believing it would only deepen the recession and heighten income inequalities. Instead, it was decided to allow wage levels to be set by market forces, with a clear expectation that the recession would be sufficient to lead them to fall. However, as time progressed, with little sign of the economy recovering, exports stagnating and the number of jobless growing, policy switched towards actively encouraging wage reduction. This, it was hoped, would not only increase competitiveness but also slow the rise in unemployment and speed job creation, possibly by attracting overseas investment. Therefore, at the beginning of 2012, the lowest minimum monthly wage was cut for those over twenty-five by 22 per cent to €684 over twelve salary payments, with the figures being reduced even further for those under that age. Previously the absolute minimum had been €877. This was towards the lower end of the Western European spectrum but it was far higher than in Portugal, where it stood at €566, and neighbouring south-eastern European states, such as Bulgaria, where at this time it was just €159 per month.[44] In fact, the reduction in the minimum wage was just the culmination of a series of measures designed to reduce wage costs by allowing companies to negotiate agreements outside wider sectoral arrangements. These were initially stymied by regulations but, after new legislation was passed, by the end of December 2012 over one thousand agreements had been signed covering more than 140,700 employees. Typically, these seem to have brought wage reductions of around 22 per cent.[45]

According to OECD statistics the average wage per annum in Greece declined from €20,917 in 2008 to €17,642 in 2015.[46] However, other sources have suggested that for many it may have fallen by considerably more. In 2013 there were frequent claims that around one third of workers in the private sector were being paid no more than the minimum wage, with young graduates working at major companies said to be receiving under €500 a month for a forty-hour week. The tendency has been for the greatest decline in wages to occur in sectors where pay was already low and in general, despite the cuts in public sector salaries, the differential in their favour still seems to persist.[47] Indeed, in parts of the private sector the situation frequently appeared to be anarchic, with stories abounding of workers being palmed off with fifty or at best a hundred euros at the end of the week, with the excuse that the employer could not afford to pay more. In early 2012 it was widely reported that at any one time nearly half a million employees had received no wages for up to five months.[48] It has been argued that, without the wage cuts, job losses would have been even greater, but the new salary levels in many cases cannot be taken as living wages and, as one former minister pertinently remarked, there is little point lowering prices to boost competitiveness if nobody has any money to buy anything. As might be expected in these circumstances, there have been growing indications that workplace morale is breaking down, which has not only economic but also longer-term social implications. A survey produced by the European Commission in 2014, which was not specifically concerned with remuneration, showed levels of unhappiness far higher in Greece than anywhere else in the EU. Nearly two-thirds of the respondents said they felt their own working conditions were bad, as opposed to less than half in every other country. Workload and the length of working hours were particular issues but many also showed concern about health and safety and the lack of consultation between management and workforce.[49]

The reduction in wages further depressed domestic demand, which deepened the downturn, but it was seen by the troika as being necessary to regain international competitiveness.[50] The exact relationship between this and wage levels has long been contested in Greece. As noted above, wages have in general remained low in comparison with EU norms, leading many to contend that the problem lies more with productivity than earnings. Nonetheless, the wage reductions during the crisis have been sufficient to allow some to argue that Greece has been able to regain much of the international competitiveness lost since the introduction of the euro, but this, as yet, has not translated into the hoped for surge in exports.[51] This may in part be because in certain key sectors, such as tourism, price competitiveness seems to have been broadly maintained throughout the years. This was partly because, while formally wages were high, with large payments prescribed for weekend work and the like, many employees were actually working outside official bounds in the informal economy.[52] A series of inspections in 2012 led to suggestions that up to half of migrant workers and about a third of Greeks were working without the employer contributing to social security payments, with the catering trade the worst offender.[53] Add in the consistently higher inflation rate in Greece than European partners in the years since the introduction of the euro, which some contend accounted for two-thirds of any loss of competitiveness, shifting employment patterns that may have adversely impacted on productivity, and the tendency for local company profit margins to increase in the period prior to the crisis, while they were declining in trading rivals, as well as the high level of social security contributions, and it becomes clear that any loss of competitiveness may have had multiple causes.[54]

As noted above, the translation of lower wages and the increased economic competitiveness they are presumed to have brought into higher exports has not been pronounced. This has led to some puzzlement among analysts, especially when Greece is compared to the performance of fellow assistance package recipient Portugal.[55] Increasing exports was a key plank of the adjustment programme and to support this aim the Panhellenic Socialist Movement (PASOK) government of Giorgos Papandreou produced a National Trade Facilitation Strategy and Road Map. However, in setting this goal it was working against an entrenched trend which has seen merchandise exports steadily diminish as a percentage of GDP since the 1970s, so that they are currently among the lowest in the EU and far less than in Portugal. It is only through the inclusion of services, such as shipping and tourism, that Greece moves closer to EU norms for external earnings as whole, although it is still somewhat below average. Among the reasons for the low levels of merchandise exports is probably the structure of the economy, with nearly all the myriad of small and medium sized enterprises being solely oriented towards the home market—a tendency that has been compounded over the years by government regulation, which has often acted as a closet form of protectionism. The geographic location of the country, which until recently lacked strong neighbouring markets, is probably also a factor and, although trade increased with the remainder of south-eastern Europe during the years prior to the crisis, this market remains relatively undeveloped and is prone to instability. As a result of these patterns, only a small fraction of Greek companies export, and many of those who do are trading in relatively low-value-added primary goods. Towards the beginning of the crisis, in 2010, it was quickly claimed that the reforms introduced under the adjustment programme were leading patterns to change, but the rise in merchandise exports at this time seems to have reflected more a pickup in demand for commodities after the global financial crisis and afterwards a certain amount of reassignment of categories, so that items such as fuel supplied to foreign-flagged ships using Greek ports were included.[56] After reaching new highs in 2012, in terms of value, merchandise exports by 2013 were dipping again and, if a longer-term timeframe is taken, the picture looks broadly flat, although there is anecdotal evidence that Greek companies in general are showing growing interest in exporting. Moreover, a 2014 study suggested that the country is still utilising only half of its export potential, which could be considerable given its geopolitical position and its dominance of international shipping, where it controls 16 per cent of the market.[57]

Indeed, an argument has been advanced that non-price factors may be equally important in explaining the low level of merchandise exports, since even when Greece was supposedly fast losing economic competitiveness in the years prior to the crisis, its share of EU and US markets remained remarkably stable, albeit at a low level.[58] Non-price factors highlighted by business owners in surveys include a continuously changing tax code, rigid employment legislation and high social security contributions, as well as the more nebulous 'market psychology'. As a result, for years the country has performed badly in studies surveying the ease of doing business and, although under the memorandum Greece topped the OECD reform index, this was in part because it was starting from a very low base. Among the key factors responsible for leaving Greece languishing among the lowest placed EU states in such tables have been the requirements of the bureaucracy and, as an example of this, during the crisis, a story about the difficulties faced by a group of entrepreneurs trying to establish an online business selling olive oil based products went viral. Their travails resulted not only from a bureaucratic system, which required, as well as countless forms, to general consternation, a request to supply stool samples for medical analysis, but also from banks unable to establish payment procedures for foreign credit cards.[59] From these and other accounts, as well as official reports, a picture has emerged of exporting being a fraught and time-consuming process marked by unpredictability and informality. Typically, exporters have had to contend with the limited opening hours of many government offices and the need to often be personally present when filing documentation, as well as delays in VAT clearance processes. Indeed, such was the complexity of the procedures they faced that many exporters employed intermediaries to facilitate matters, which merely raised costs further. The total value of exports increases by 1 per cent every day the export process is shortened according to some calculations and this led the Samaras government to set a target of halving times.[60] However, when setting this goal, which required extensive computerisation of the export process, it also acknowledged that, as in so many other areas, problems relating to skill shortages and low morale within the workforce had to be tackled as well as the remarkable ability of the Greek bureaucratic system to reproduce itself.

Exports have been slow to materialise but so also has investment, another key plank in the reorienting of the economy identified in the initial adjustment programme. Domestically, this can largely be attributed to the crisis, which has left many local industries working at low capacity, giving companies neither incentive to invest in a weak market nor the available funds to do so. The latter was partly due to declining profitability, although the picture in this field has by no means been uniform, but also because of increased taxation. A tendency to hold back payments to suppliers as governments chose to prioritise meeting fiscal consolidation targets also contributed, as did a shortage of credit, especially, from the beginning of 2012 onwards, reflecting the increasing difficulties of the local banking sector. The crisis in Greece, unlike Ireland, did not originate with the banks. Indeed, prior to 2010, financial services were considered one of the great success stories of the Greek economy, with the major banks consistently posting higher annual profit figures and expanding throughout south-eastern Europe. Indeed, even after the onset of the global financial turmoil in 2007, such was the standing of Greek financial institutions that they continued to attract deposit inflows, so that these stood at record levels at the end of 2009.[61] The subsequent problems of the sector were caused partly by a steady reversal of this flow, with some €80 billion of deposits being withdrawn between the end of 2009 and June 2012.[62] Some of this money was sent abroad, some was stored under the proverbial mattress, partly explaining the doubling of the number of banknotes in circulation between February 2010 and June 2012, and some was spent, as people struggled to maintain living standards while paying higher taxes and meeting other financial demands.[63] Aside from losing deposits, the banks were also struggling with an increasing number of non-performing loans. These started to grow sharply after 2011, until they reached around 44 per cent of all loans by the beginning of 2016 by which time over half of all households said they were finding the repayment of debts difficult.[64] These growing problems started to eat away not only at profits but also at capital ratios. Nonetheless, all the major banks, except ATEBank and, narrowly, EFG Eurobank Ergasias, were able to pass the July 2011 EU-wide stress tests.[65] It was the 2012 debt exchange, in which the Greek banking sector collectively lost €37.7 billion, that was to bring the banks to the point of total collapse and cause a major restructuring of the industry.[66]

To help secure the second aim of the memorandum, which was the stability of the local banking system, the Hellenic Financial Stability Fund (HFSF) had been established in July 2010 as a private entity.[67] Prior to the restructuring of the debt, it had attracted most attention when it had intervened to deal with the collapse of a couple of smaller banks. However, after the restructuring of the debt it became the main vehicle for recapitalising local financial institutions. In the process the Greek financial sector was divided into core and non-core banks. Of the four core banks the HFSF took effective control of one, Eurobank, and substantial stakes in the other three, Piraeus, the National Bank of Greece (NBG) and Alpha, which were all allowed to remain in the hands of private management after they had raised 10 per cent of the recapitalisation amount from outside sources. Of the other dozen or so banks existing before the crisis just two remained as sizeable independent entities in 2014.[68] The others were all folded into the core banks, with the biggest mergers involving Alpha Bank, which acquired Emboriki for a symbolic €1 from

Crédit Agricole, and Piraeus Bank, which acquired Geniki from Société Générale on similar terms. Piraeus also took over the good assets of the previously state-controlled ATEBank, (whose break up constituted the largest bank resolution ever seen in Europe), Millennium Bank and the Greek assets of three Cypriot banks to make it, by many measures, the largest of the Greek banks.[69] It continues to hold this status as of 2016 partly because the proposed merger of two of the other core banks, the NBG and Eurobank, was blocked by the troika on the grounds it would create a group deemed 'too big to fail'.[70] Indeed, the concentration of the banking sector has raised concerns about competition within the European Commission, but it seems to be supported by local policymakers, perhaps because it falls within long-term goals. The mergers were the prelude to a period of rationalisation in which branches were closed and jobs shed.[71] Non-core assets, including property and insurance portfolios were sold, as were some of the extensive foreign holdings of the banks, which, until 2015, aside from Eurobank's Polish subsidiary and a few other smaller investments, had mostly been retained.[72] The European Commission had pressed for an immediate sale of East European assets on the basis that the capital injections by the HFSF constituted state aid, giving the Greek banks an unfair advantage against local competition. The banks protested that this would effectively amount to a fire-sale and they were given longer to divest on agreement that there would be no transfer of funds to subsidiaries during this period.[73] With the NBG in 2016 announcing that it had sold its substantial holding in the Turkish Finansbank, the international expansion of the 2000s, which spearheaded the development of the economy during that period, has been thrown into reverse, and a programme that was designed to make Greece a more outward facing economy will end up making it more introverted, at least in the sphere of banking.[74]

The restructuring of the public debt also changed the dynamics of the local credit supply. This had fallen in 2009 either from a lack of demand or supply, as effectively frozen out of interbank money markets the local banks had increasingly come to rely on the ECB for funding, which reluctantly lowered its collateral rules to accommodate their needs. Eventually, though, with their remaining collateral impaired by the recession unacceptable to the ECB, the banks were forced to turn to the Bank of Greece for assistance. In response this began to issue Emergency Liquidity Assistance (ELA). This process was still closely supervised by the ECB which retained the right to set a threshold and restrict provision if sufficient board members considered it would interfere with the 'objectives and tasks of the Eurosystem'.[75] However, ELA could be issued against collateral that was of a lower quality than that acceptable to the ECB, although only after a substantial haircut, and this allowed funds to continue to flow to the banks. Any costs or risks arising from the provision of ELA lie with the local central bank. The funding also carries an interest rate that is above regular ECB levels, which reportedly by 2012 was adding around €2 billion per annum to bank costs. As a result of these initiatives, the supply of credit initially appeared to remain relatively strong, even possibly increasing in the commercial sector, as companies sought funding for restructuring.[76] However, after the rescheduling of the public debt, it started to decline, with nearly a third of all bank loan applications reportedly rejected between October 2012 and March 2013, and in 2014 it was still contracting by about 4.0 per cent per year.[77] Equally significant, though, has been the large number of non-performing loans, about a third of which were owed by commercial clients. Yet even though some sectors such as steel making were hard hit by the crisis and many businesses have filed for protection under the bankruptcy code few, at least initially, were allowed to fail.[78] The issue is far from straight-forward but it has been argued that by continuing to prop up these moribund companies the banking sector was not only distorting the market but also stopping credit flowing to more dynamic business start-ups.[79] Under pressure from the institutions of the troika the government and the banks have begun to address the issue, changing the bankruptcy laws so the state is no longer privileged over banks when it comes to asset recovery and taking the first steps towards the creation of a secondary market in distressed debt.[80] To help fill the gap in funding for small and medium sized businesses, a guarantee fund was founded as a joint venture between the Greek authorities, the European Commission and the European Investment Bank (EIB). Using €500 million from unabsorbed structural funds, this channelled EIB loans to small and medium sized enterprises via partner banks in Greece, although reports, at least at first, spoke of the money being slow to appear.[81] Moreover, smaller businesses faced not just difficulties in securing credit but also high domestic interest rates, which on new private sector loans in April 2016 averaged 6.1 per cent as opposed to a ECB refinancing rate of zero per cent at that time.

The weakness in the domestic investment climate resulting from the travails of the banks was partly filled by EU funding, as various measures were taken to make it easier for Greece to tap existing avenues of assistance. Matching fund-ing limits were adjusted to the country's benefit and problems of absorption tackled by a European Commission Task Force. As a result, in 2013, Greece surpassed the rate required by the adjustment programme, taking in over €3.89

billon of funds.[82] Funding has also come from the EIB and the European Investment Fund (EIF), although new lending from the EIB tended to reflect the cycles of the crisis, reaching a high in 2010 and then falling away before reviving again in 2013 to €965 million.[83] Most importantly, to help alleviate some of the worst effects of the crisis, a new partnership agreement also foresees Greece receiving €15.35 billion in Cohesion Policy funding from the EU during the period 2014–2020, as well as additional money from other sources.[84] This money will be spent on supporting small and medium sized companies, alleviating unemployment and further developing the country's infrastructure. These EU funds to a certain extent have compensated for the continuing lack of foreign direct investment. Despite frequent speculation about inflows from China and the Middle East foreign investments continue to be mostly held by companies originating from countries such as Germany, the USA and the UK; and during the crisis money has continued to flow into the country from these sources, albeit at a relatively low rate. There were occasional takeovers, such as the American group Actavis' acquisition of the local pharmaceutical company Specifar for €400 million, but most was used to recapitalise local subsidiaries, sometimes in preparation for sale, as with the French owned banks, Emboriki and Geniki, or to further consolidate existing holdings, as when Deutsche Telekom raised its stake in the Hellenic Telecommunications Organisation (OTE).[85] To try and facilitate the inflow of foreign funds a new investment law was passed and the Invest in Greece agency created as a one-stop-shop that has the ability to fast-track investments, with eleven projects falling under its remit in 2013. However, in the same year, a US government assessment still finished with the observation that 'Greece provides a challenging climate for investment, both foreign and domestic'.[86] The lack of investment has also been stressed by the IMF, which holds that it deepened the downturn created by the austerity measures and contributed to the fact that 'Greece has adjusted mainly through recession, rather than through productivity-enhancing reforms.'[87]

In its reference to 'productivity-enhancing reforms' the IMF was primarily implying the liberalisation of labour and product markets and, in the understanding of the troika, it was the failure of the Greek government to fully implement these which was the primary reason for the length of the downturn. Some of the difficulties involved in enacting reforms in these areas have been mentioned elsewhere in this book and the discussion of consensual pricing earlier in this chapter has also suggested that the instillation of a culture of competition will need much more than the passing of a few laws. Moreover, while the restricted professions and their like undoubtedly limited competition, market forces were not entirely absent within the many rules and regulations that protected their positions. There were at least 343 restricted or 'closed' professions in Greece, including lawyers, civil engineers and pharmacists but also lorry drivers and even ballet school owners and beekeepers. They were not unique to Greece. Similar institutions existed in other Mediterranean countries, including Italy, and in certain trades and professions, such as taxi drivers, almost worldwide. However, while the tendency in most other EU countries had been for the rules and regulations surrounding such professions to be relaxed over the years, this process in Greece was more haphazard. The various restrictions were usually defended on the grounds that they preserved professional standards but they essentially served as a form of protectionism, often by setting minimum prices and limiting ability to practice, frequently on the basis of location. Drawing upon international studies, proponents of change argued that the restrictions only led to higher profit margins and that gradual liberalisation could boost economic output in the long term by up to 13.0 per cent.[88] Yet, a 2011 law intended to open up the professions was criticised even by those in favour of reform for being ill-thought-out and designed more to satisfy the demands of the troika than foster genuine competition.[89] The myriad of rules and regulations were generally thought to favour the numerically predominant weaker members of the professions. However, even the more dynamic could argue strongly for the benefits of their professional associations, pointing out that in many cases the restrictions were designed to regulate the large numbers wishing to practice, with Greece having among the highest numbers of lawyers, pharmacists and doctors per capita in the world. In some cases, the restrictions produced situations in which members of a profession gained a strong vested economic interest in maintaining existing practices. For instance, the fact that no new taxi or haulage licenses had been issued for many years led to these reportedly changing hands for large sums of money.[90] This undoubtedly restricted entry to these professions, but its actual effect on competition is more difficult to evaluate. In the case of taxis, it seems to have worked to keep supply constant, even though demand dropped, due to major improvements in public transport. The result was that fares, which are fixed by the state, in general in cities such as Athens remained low, with taxi drivers partly compensating for this by adopting the practice of accepting more than one passenger at a time so as to boost income. Similar forces were also present in the road haulage sector, with some lorry drivers choosing to register their vehicles in Bulgaria and other neighbouring states to escape domestic regulation and increase price competitiveness.[91] As a result, deregulation has sometimes brought fewer gains than expected, although in the case of road haulage the OECD initially blamed this on the continuing existence of restrictions as well as the general economic downturn.[92] Many of the restrictions have now been removed or relaxed but even when this has occurred, if cultural norms dictate otherwise, changes have often been hard to detect, as in the opening hours of petrol stations.[93]

In the eyes of the IMF far more successful than the faltering structural reform programme has been the fiscal readjustment which, it regularly notes, has been one of the largest on record.[94] This correction has been produced by curbing government expenditure but also by raising revenue, especially taxes, often to high levels. Indeed, the issue of taxation has been a perpetual sore in contemporary Greece, with the issue of evasion featuring regularly in the political discourse. Tax evasion cannot be separated from, but is distinct from, the issue of the informal economy. This may be defined as both legal and illegal economic activity that is not detected by the state and recorded in official output figures. Since the first serious research on the subject in 1980s, Greece has often been held as being paradigmatic of a state with a large informal economy.[95] A number of methodologies have been employed over the years to try and assess its size but, by the most commonly accepted international computation, in 2012 it probably amounted to about 24 per cent of GDP.[96] This made it slightly larger than the informal economies of other southern EU states, such as Italy, and slightly smaller than many East European members. However, local estimates have often held it to be considerably bigger, suggesting it might be around 45 per cent of GDP or even more and, perhaps equally importantly, the stories that constantly circulate in everyday life about tax evasion, bribery, corruption and people playing 'the system' to their benefit have created a widespread popular impression that it is all-pervasive.[97] These stories, though, can be ambiguous in their morality. The cunning and guile frequently attributed to the protagonists may provoke admiration as much as censure, perhaps in part because the tale is often placed within a familiar environment, with the storyteller frequently claiming personal knowledge. True malpractice instead is reserved largely for those working outside such familiar bounds, and this typically includes the likes of politicians, business oligarchs and others seen as belonging to a privileged elite as well as elements of the self-employed nouveaux riches. In a narrative with deep roots in the popular moral universe they are regularly excoriated for a lifestyle seen as being full of excess replete with villas, swimming pools, boats, expensive Swiss watches, children in private schools, lavish displays in tavernas and nightclubs and even particular tastes in breeds of dog.[98] Cars, as in the past, have often featured prominently, particularly the top-of-the-range Porsche Cayenne, which came to be seen as being almost synonymous with this class. An early pronouncement by the Coalition of the Radical Left (SYRIZA) Finance Minister, Yanis Varoufakis, that 'growth does not mean having Porsche Cayennes in the narrow streets of Greece' attracted much attention, as did an earlier story claiming that there were more of these expensive vehicles on the road in Greece than taxpayers declaring incomes of €50,000 per year, with the city of Larisa said to have more per capita than anywhere else on the globe.[99] When journalists investigated the matter more closely, they found that the number of Cayennes imported by official distributors were relatively small and that, at least superficially, the claim had little base.[100] However, the story so neatly fitted the accepted popular narrative about the size and wealth of this social group that it seems to have been widely believed, even apparently in senior policymaking circles. Indeed, in many ways such stories are merely the popular expression of an influential intellectual narrative that has long traced many of the problems of the country, including some of the roots of the crisis, to the activities of a 'comprador-cum-financial oligarchy'.[101] In this understanding of Greek society it is this elite, who 'profit through their special linkage with authority' that is rent seeking and not the civil administration.[102] More specifically, it is the failure of this elite through evasion, avoidance or political connivance to pay what most see as a fair amount of tax that is widely held as being one of the root causes of the crisis and, in keeping with this, the SYRIZA dominated coalition government came to power in January 2015 pledging to curb what it termed 'a network that viciously sucks the energy and the economic power from everybody else in society'.[103]

The size of the informal sector imparts certain characteristics to the Greek economy. Most obviously it cuts state revenue due to the non-payment of taxes and social security contributions. It also tends to encourage short-term thinking and a mentality of quick turnover, rapid profit, and, at least in the past, investment in property rather than more productive areas. However, as previously mentioned, it has also been a significant factor in allowing the economy to remain competitive in key sectors such as tourism, keeping unemployment in check and enabling some of those on the margins of society to maintain an acceptable standard of living. Within the context of the crisis, it seems to have particularly influenced assumptions about economic growth made in the adjustment programme. Thus, when IMF board members at the meeting approving the original Stand-By Arrangement questioned the optimistic assumptions about growth made in the memorandum, staff members appear not to have been unduly perturbed, saying that in fact the economy might perform better than expected because of what they termed 'upside risks... related to the uncertain size of the informal economy'.[104] And this view seems to have been shared by their Greek colleagues who considered 'the informal economy and unrevealed pockets of wealth [would] act as a buffer and underpin private consumption data'.[105] Much about the behaviour of the underground economy during the crisis remains a matter of conjecture but recent calculations seem to suggest that it has not changed much in size. The general propensity is for such phenomena to grow during economic contractions but in the case of Greece this has probably been counteracted by a tendency for informality to be grounded in marginal areas of activity that have been hardest hit by the downturn. However, in contrast to the mid-1980s, when the informal economy was credited, perhaps erroneously, with mitigating the worst of the recession created by that stabilisation programme, the depth of the economic depression suggests it did not play the same role during this crisis. Indeed, by early August 2010, the IMF was already voicing scepticism that the informal economy and unrevealed pockets of wealth mentioned by the Greek authorities would be sufficient to support 'economic activity in a sustainable way'. However, it is possible the original assumptions that seem to have been made about the informal economy and its potential to support economic growth may have been as important as any errors in calculating the fiscal multiplier in rendering the targets of the memorandum impossible. Why these assumptions proved so wrong is not easy to comprehend. It may be that the informal economy was not as large as many, perhaps influenced by the prevailing popular narrative, thought; that it was not distributed in such a way as to sustain consumption; or it could have been due to some other factor altogether. Yet it would be wrong to discount its impact completely since it does seem to have played a role in buttressing incomes and, as such, it has been an important factor in allowing many of the population of the country to 'muddle through' the crisis as best they can.[106]

Large informal economies are usually associated with countries with high direct or indirect tax rates, excessive bureaucratic regulation and corruption.[107] Greece exhibits elements of all three of these traits and, as regards the latter, it regularly languishes among the worst placed EU states in Transparency International surveys measuring corruption.[108] In his pronouncements Papandreou highlighted the issue as being a root cause of the country's problems, without being specific as to what he exactly implied or how it related to the crisis.[109] The incoming SYRIZA led coalition in January 2015 in its rhetoric also dwelt heavily on the issue and many Greeks seem to share its view. Nearly three-quarters of the respondents in a 2010 opinion poll held corruption to be greatly responsible for the crisis, and in 2013 virtually everybody questioned in another poll said that they felt Greece as a country was 'very' or 'fairly' corrupt. Indeed, almost two-thirds went as far as to say that corruption impacted directly on their everyday lives, although only 13 per cent said they had actually witnessed it during the past year.[110] Media headlines, often drawing on research, have also tended to support the narrative by suggesting that corruption costs the country vast amounts of money every year, but as with the informal economy in general these must, at best, be estimates.[111] Stories surrounding scandals, such as Vatopedi and Siemens, often mentioned many millions of euros but, when prosecutions for corruption were mounted, the amounts involved were usually considerably less. Indeed, perceptions of bribery and corruption are malleable and no more so than in the case of the infamous 'little envelopes' or *fakelakia*, which pass hands to facilitate services, including operations in hospitals.[112] During the crisis the decline in disposable income has contributed to a fall in the size of these payments, although offsetting this in certain sectors, such as healthcare, the same factor has also led to an increase in the use of state facilities. This has presumably led to more 'little envelopes' passing hands, although, when asked about their experiences in a single year, only about one in ten of those using such facilities admitted to having paid something resembling a bribe.[113] Indeed, at this lower level, it is possible to make some comparisons between such exchanges and wider patterns of favours and obligations encountered elsewhere in south-eastern Europe and further afield.[114] Seen in this light, corruption then becomes just another part of the informality and personalisation of exchange that allows the complex rules and regulations of the administrative system to be bypassed. However, at the same time, it reduces taxation revenue, distorts market mechanisms, wastes resources and undermines both official institutions and cohesion within society. Moreover, the early publicity given to the issue means that it now also forms an important part of the narrative explaining the origins of the crisis to the outside world, with one 2011 British television documentary telling its audience that 'tax evasion, corruption and mismanagement' had combined 'to sink the Greek economy'.[115]

Corruption is most likely to occur when public employees enjoy a degree of autonomy or powers of discretion and this is most obviously found in places such as hospitals, planning departments and tax offices, with Transparency International suggesting that, prior to the crisis, a building permit might require a bribe of up to €9,000 and the verification and auditing of a company's books €300 to €15,000.[116] Indeed, the issue of tax evasion is so deeply embedded in local narratives that it has frequently been termed a national sport, with the popular perception both at home and abroad being that it is particularly widespread in Greece.[117] A 2013 EU report surveying the gap between theoretical liability for VAT and actual collection rates produced somewhat contradictory results depending on the methodology used. Overall, though, as with the informal economy in general, it seemed to suggest that the gap is greater in Greece than in other southern European countries but less than in some East European states, such as Romania.[118] However, as with taxation in general, the picture was clouded by the fact that the VAT system, according to the IMF, was 'riddled with preferential rates and exemptions that distort consumption choices and provide poorly-targeted subsidies'.[119] This suggests that a failure to gather sufficient revenues was often about political choices as well as evasion. As with the informal economy and corruption, by its very nature tax evasion is difficult to measure and, as others have noted, much of the work on the issue has been subject to *a priori* assumptions.[120] Various methodologies have been used over the years to try and assess the extent to which taxes are withheld, ranging from comparisons with the performance of other EU states and the extent to which Greece deviates from international norms to a well-publicised 2012 study using information supplied by a leading bank relating to the payment of interest on loans. This led the authors to suggest that evasion, which they claimed amounted to perhaps €28 billion in 2009 alone, is rampant among the professional classes in particular.[121] Other research, though, has tended to point the finger at farmers as well, while suggesting the phenomenon may be particularly located at the two ends of the income scale amongst both the lowest and highest earners.[122] While carefully noting that their research, which was based on a selection of anonymised returns supplied by the tax authorities, rests on various assumptions, the authors of this 2012 study suggest that it produces a relatively small rise in income of 4.5 per cent but a large shortfall in revenue of some 27.8 per cent. With other research producing a slightly lower, but still substantial, figure of €12 billion per annum, the general conclusion is that evasion continues to be widespread.[123] This perception is then amplified in the local popular narrative through a tendency to use the term broadly to reflect what has been termed the 'tax gap' as a whole, encompassing not only illegal evasion but also the legal but often morally questionable avoidance, as well as those who for one reason or another owe taxes to the state. According to the IMF, in 2011 the latter amounted to the equivalent of 72.2 per cent of annual net tax revenue, far more than the OECD average and, despite various efforts to lessen the amount, in 2015 the state was still said to be owed arrears of €76 billion.[124] Indeed, many of the news reports about tax evasion during the early part of the crisis tended to focus on these debtors, although it was noticeable that, once the media began to scrutinise the cases brought to light by the authorities, they found that some of those cast in this mantle in fact appeared to be owed money by the state, and that in one case it was the ordinary employees of the finance department of a company who were being threatened with prosecution for taxes owed by the firm as a whole.[125] In fact, the authorities seem to have accepted that only about €9 billion of such debts were probably recoverable, since much of the rest were owed by companies that have ceased trading. Moreover, as with VAT, the continuing existence of multiple exemptions and preferential rates within a highly complex system gave plenty of scope for an industry of skilled accountants and tax advisors to keep taxpaying to a minimum.[126] As a result even high net worth individuals expected to pay relatively little tax.

Indeed, until the onset of the crisis, Greece in relation to average incomes had a particularly high taxpaying threshold. This left over half of those filing a tax form paying no tax, with there being a conspicuous spike in the number of incomes reported just under the limit.[127] In 2009 almost 90 per cent of individuals were reporting incomes below €28,000, with the result that just 30 per cent of registered tax payers paid 95 per cent of direct taxes, which was an extremely high concentration in European terms.[128] The choice to pursue what was a limited direct tax regime for most of the population was essentially political, although it was presented in terms of promoting administrative efficiency. The relatively small group of taxpayers included higher salaried staff, often those working in the public sector, as well as many self-employed, with there always remaining a strong suspicion among the former that the latter were underreporting their incomes and not paying as much tax as they should. The decision to follow such a tax regime had several consequences. Firstly, by allowing most people to pay little or no direct tax, it engrained the idea that only the wealthy paid taxes, and this was a socio-economic group to which even those who others consider to be well-off did not tend to think that they belonged. The fact that taxpaying was perceived as being only something done by the rich also made it politically costly to re-impose taxes on those lying below the threshold. Secondly, it left the small number of direct tax payers feeling they were unfairly carrying the costs of the system, offering them a justification for avoidance, if not evasion. Thirdly, it left the state budget perpetually compromised and put a greater onus on indirect taxes such as VAT. As a result, the system was detrimental to the very poor, who would have paid no direct tax anyway but were faced with high indirect taxes, and beneficial to the middle classes, whose vote the politicians sought. The crisis to a certain extent reversed these policies. A blizzard of tax legislation widened the taxation net by first reducing the tax-free threshold and then, in 2014, removing it altogether and replacing it for all but the self-employed by a rebate scheme.[129] However, it also brought increases in indirect taxes, such as VAT, which disproportionately hit the poorest in society. Taxes and duties were raised to increase revenue but at the same time this not only diminished the spending power of consumers, deepening the economic downturn and reducing potential state income, but also, as in the past, reportedly spurred further avoidance, with yacht owners in 2010 apparently preferring to register their vessels in Turkey to escape paying new levies rather than Italy, as they had under the dictatorship.[130] In the quest for revenue all too easily retroactive taxes have been applied, gross rather than net income taxed, fundamental exemptions scrapped and perhaps, most crucially of all, the ability of the citizens of the country to pay overlooked.[131] Indeed, taxes have risen to such levels that large numbers of people are reportedly unable to pay what is demanded.[132] Arrears continue to grow apace and with increasing numbers of people falling behind with their tax payments governments have been forced to offer ever easier payment options, with even small amounts being spread over dozens of instalments.[133] The property tax levied through electricity bills, in particular, was widely resented, with the feeling it lacked legitimacy reflected in the fact that it was popularly known by the Ottoman term *haratsi*.[134] Often due to inheritance, a surprisingly large number of Greeks within all income brackets own more than one property, and as a consequence this tax was onerous for many, especially since large numbers of tenants, both residential and commercial, had negotiated lower rents during the crisis or frequently ceased to pay them at all.[135] This has added to a chain of debt that stretches across the economy. The government owes money to businesses; companies to employees, each other and the banks, as do ordinary individuals, who might also owe money to businesses as well as friends and relatives.[136] This complex and intermeshing network of debt, which entraps much of the population as either creditors or debtors, is almost impossible to map and potentially highly unstable. It has eroded the idea that payments have to be made on time or, indeed, at all, and further delayed the return to growth, increasing uncertainty and trapping resources.

Various technical reasons may also be advanced to explain the problems encountered with gathering revenue. Public perception of the tax authorities is unremittingly negative. A visit to a tax office is invariably viewed with trepidation, amid fears that many hours will be spent waiting in long queues to satisfy petty bureaucratic needs in an atmosphere that has been evocatively described as being 'thick with hostility and existential despair'.[137] The morale of tax office staff is reported to have declined during the crisis due to pay cuts. At least initially, they were also said to be badly allocated both from a geographic and a functional point of view and to have a propensity to carry out time-consuming blanket audits rather than targeted inspections of suspect individuals and companies. Add as well a tendency to legal formalism, inefficient working practices and continuing issues surrounding transparency, with stories appearing in the media alleging that tax officers when striking deals pocketed part of the proceeds, and it is little surprise that the 2 per cent of GDP saving predicted to come from revenue administration reform consistently failed to appear.[138] These deficiencies compound the many problems inherent in gathering revenues in what is already a challenging environment with a weak culture of tax compliance. In particular, the large number of micro-businesses make tax auditing difficult and give the many self-employed ample opportunity to underreport their incomes. As a consequence the government over the years has relied more on indirect taxes such as VAT as well as social security contributions for revenue but both of these are easier to evade than direct taxes. Nonetheless, evaluations in 2014 were talking of 'real progress' being made as the Samaras government simplified tax legislation and procedures, put in place measures limiting the possibility of corruption and introduced a much disliked consolidated property tax.[139] Indeed, in terms of broader policy, governments over the years have tended to adopt two strategies to deal with the problem. The first is to offer a series of tax settlements through which citizens are allowed to correct past irregularities. This tactic has been used during the crisis with reference to breaches of planning laws. The idea with such schemes is that they will both raise revenue and create a clean slate, allowing taxpayers and tax collectors to build a new more trusting relationship, although there have been few attempts to change the fundamental presumption of guilt upon which an assessment system based on imputed expenditure is ultimately founded.[140] The IMF and OECD have both opposed this strategy, arguing that it undermines compliance, because taxpayers stop paying if they think that later they will pay less without penalties.[141] The other strategy is to pursue those who have not paid their fair share of taxes vigorously, to both encourage compliance in general and to produce exemplary punishments in the belief that, if tax evaders are seen to be punished, it will enhance social solidarity and make ordinary citizens more willing to pay their own taxes. Legitimised through a discourse of fairness, this approach led to arrests, with stories emerging of people being given prison terms for tax debts of €10,000 or less. How successful this policy was in increasing revenue remains unknown, but in conjunction with the constantly changing tax code it created a climate of considerable uncertainty and, at times, fear.[142] Taxpayers were frequently unsure as to whether they were fully complying with the new requirements and could not predict with certainty how much tax they would be paying in the future, which obviously made planning and investment difficult. Moreover, research also suggests that, while in the shorter term such a strategy might reduce evasion, in the longer run it will do little to create a culture of compliance in which correctly declaring income becomes a social norm and citizens begin to trust the tax authorities and other formal institutions to provide the expected services.[143]

Indeed, despite the widening of the exemplary net, the predominant narrative at virtually all levels of society has remained that real tax evasion is largely the preserve of a small wealthy elite. The veracity of this claim is almost impossible to establish, but it does have certain consequences. Firstly, it provides a shield for lesser income earners who protest that any minor peccadilloes they commit are nothing in comparison. Indeed, the more society believes tax evasion is rife, the less legitimate taxes become, and any imposition over the bare minimum merely prompts more avoidance, since it is seen as lacking fairness. Secondly, it has distorted policymaking, because the constant belief that large sums of money were available, if only arrears could be gathered and evasion curbed, in the past allowed politicians to avoid making more painful decisions. Thirdly, it has legitimised the granting of extra resources and powers to the tax authorities with the result that Greece has a greater density of people working within tax offices per taxpayer than many higher-income countries.[144] Lastly, such is the strength of the narrative that during the crisis it has been readily taken up by the outside world, further reinforcing the discourse of dysfunction and the theme of profligacy. Indeed, throughout northern Europe and elsewhere it has come to be widely believed that the root cause of the crisis is the failure of the citizens of Greece in general to pay their taxes, and this has at times been used by the political leadership of countries such as Germany to justify the taking of an uncompromising stance when facing requests to lessen the austerity measures imposed on the Greek people.[145]

Economic policy after 2010 has been shaped within the framework of the adjustment programmes but, although it was widely accepted that the fiscal consolidation targets set by these were demanding and recessionary, it does not follow that they alone were responsible for the depth and severity of the depression. The economic downturn began nearly two years prior to the introduction of the first adjustment programme and the various structural problems outlined in this chapter, coupled with the ongoing political uncertainty at the local and European levels—which drained consumer confidence and removed any incentive to invest—all contributed to make it exceptionally deep, as did policy choices made by the various governments and the troika. Of the aims of the original adjustment programme the events of 2015 covered in the epilogue showed that any achievements were at best precarious. Previously, commentators had been pointing to growing investment in local banks to suggest that stability had returned to this sector but it was not long before doubts about solvency returned, as the extent of their continued reliance on ELA and ECB funding became fully apparent; and in 2017 limits still remained on the amount of money that customers could withdraw in any one week. Likewise, the IMF had been full of praise regarding the country's efforts at fiscal consolidation, noting that 'Greece has gone from having the weakest to the strongest cyclically-adjusted fiscal position within the euro area in just four years' before concluding, 'This is an extraordinary achievement by any international comparison'.[146] Yet, the public debt as a percentage of GDP remains at a level which the IMF considers to be unsustainable and after the installation of the SYRIZA-led coalition in office in January 2015 it was only a matter of days before talk of default and even exit from the euro reemerged. This ebbed for a while after the agreement of a third adjustment programme but still periodically reappeared in the headlines into 2017. Most of all, though, the core objective of creating the conditions for sustainable economic growth has yet to be achieved. The brief return to growth in 2014 subsequently petered out and while the economy is projected to expand again in 2017 any recovery will have to be built on the base of an extraordinary economic collapse that by 2012 had already seen GDP levels at purchasing power parity fall back almost to those of 2002. Indeed, if comparison is made with other purchasing power parities, where Greece has fallen from 96 per cent of the EU average to 75 per cent, then it may be argued that under the austerity regime the country in some ways has returned to levels last seen in the mid-1990s.[147]

10

THE GREAT CRISIS

The crisis has left its mark on the physical fabric of Greece. In the winter of 2011 shop after shop on once thriving boulevards in the centre of Athens lay empty. Their windows were hidden behind battered facades of corrugated iron while outside on the streets the scattering of shoppers made the hustle and bustle of yesteryear a nostalgic memory. Graffiti, sometimes witty and often bitter, had crept from abandoned buildings and parking lots onto private walls and even public monuments. The call for 'Revolt Now' emblazoned on the statue of the poet Kostis Palamas on Akadimias Street was quickly removed but the large 'Fuck the Euro' on the wall of the adjacent cultural centre remained untouched, perhaps in sneaking sympathy with the more witty Anglophone graffitist who contributed, 'Blank walls make blank people'. On the wide pavements of the main thoroughfares whole families sat together begging but they were only the most visible indigents. It was the smartly dressed young man who sidled up to ask if you could buy him a cheese pie, and the passing moped rider who stopped his vehicle on the roadside, turned and stretched out a hand asking for cash, which caught you by surprise. Meanwhile, out in the middle of the road young men drawn from countries across Asia brazenly weaved their way through the traffic, pushing supermarket trolleys piled high with scrap scavenged from rubbish bins. These became the centre of a whole parallel economy, providing many with a means of subsistence and, sometimes it seemed, sustenance. A creased paper attached to a bin in a moderately well-to-do suburb pleaded in disjointed letters, 'Please do not throw your leftovers in the bin, leave them in this little container'.[1] Some scavenged the bins openly but others were more awkward and cast their eyes down as they passed. It was as if they did not want their story known, and, indeed, there was always a strange anonymity about the crisis, partly because it became so everyday. After a while, the trolleys parked in the corner of supermarkets to receive donations to feed the hungry and even the old ladies picking over the discarded fruit and vegetables in local markets just became part of the furniture.

The bare statistics tell how the crisis has left most Greeks poorer. Average household disposable income in real terms has tumbled by at least 36 per cent since its onset and by 2014 the best part of 2.5 million people or 22 per cent of the population were judged to be at risk-of-poverty in a society in which the poverty threshold was defined as an annual income of just €4,608 for a single person household.[2] This meant that a greater percentage of the population were deemed to be at-risk-of poverty or social exclusion in Greece than nearly everywhere else in the EU, other than Romania and Bulgaria. The most vulnerable social categories have tended to be foreign nationals, with nearly 70 per cent of those aged between eighteen and sixty-four within this group falling under this heading, the unemployed, the elderly living alone, students, and younger people in general, including children.[3] This partly reflects the difficulty young parents have in finding jobs but also the inadequacy of social security benefits, which in the past generally favoured larger families irrespective of need, leaving nearly three-quarters of single parent households highly vulnerable. Indeed, the social security system by most accounts was woefully unprepared for the crisis. Other than in fields such as pensions and healthcare, benefits were limited and often badly targeted. Only half went to the poorest third of the population and although subsequently there was some re-targeting to the benefit of families with children, gaps still seem to remain.[4] In particular, unemployment benefit was circumscribed by a series of restrictions. It was dependent, among other things, on the number of insured work days completed within a specified period and was only paid for a limited amount of time.[5] A follow-on benefit was hedged with so many restrictions that many of the unemployed received no assistance at all, and as the crisis deepened this not only led to growing poverty but also to increasing numbers falling outside the welfare net, until changes in the law provided more comprehensive coverage for Greek citizens.[6] Moreover, beyond the large number deemed poor, 43 per cent of the remainder of the population in 2014 said they would find it difficult to cope if asked to make an extraordinary payment of around €550. Taken in total this would seem to indicate that around two-thirds of the population, if not more, are probably living with constant concerns about whether they have enough money to meet day-to-day expenses.[7] All these figures, though, are only rough aggregates and within the country there are variations, with certain areas, such as Perama on the edge of Piraeus, where the decline of the shipbuilding industry has left many unemployed, being particularly blighted. However, even in the wealthier northern suburbs of Athens, by 2012 there were signs that people were being forced to turn to the Orthodox Church and charities for assistance.[8] Moreover, poverty thresholds have diminished considerably over the years and if the figure from 2008 is used, when the threshold for a single person household was established at €6,480 a year, to measure those at-risk-of-poverty in 2014 then the number rises to almost half the population.[9] Indeed, by 2014 the number classified as suffering from material deprivation in terms of lacking four out of nine key indicators, which ranged from being able to afford a meal including meat or fish every second day to providing adequate heating for the home and possessing a telephone, colour television or car, had almost doubled since 2009 to encompass about a fifth of the population.[10]

Yet, many middle-age and older Greeks will also admit that privation is not something unknown in their lives, and the reaction of society to the hardship of the crisis can in many ways only be understood in reference to the poverty that bound much of the country for a large part of the twentieth century. This in equal measure seems to have bred both a fear of a return to this past and a sense of resilience.[11] The poverty of yesteryear had eased for most, but the country, like many others in southern Europe, still exhibits income disparities greater than average in the EU-15, although the tendency prior to 2008 was for these to diminish.[12] During the crisis itself, this trend seems to have initially continued, perhaps due to the pay cuts in the public sector, where three-quarters of civil servants and two-thirds of public utility workers were within the top third of earners, but by 2013 there were signs that it was widening again, as ever greater numbers were thrust towards absolute poverty.[13] This helped feed a political narrative stressing the socio-economic divisions within society which has been so widely accepted that much of the population with some justification believes that the burden of the austerity measures has not been evenly shared and that many of the middle classes, as well as the poorer members of society, have suffered disproportionately.[14] However, in contrast to income inequalities, wealth differentials have tended to remain lower than in many countries, largely due to relatively high levels of property ownership.[15] A long running tendency to view land and bricks and mortar as the only sound investment, and a corresponding reluctance to sell anything inherited unless in dire circumstances, has left a surprisingly large number of Greeks holding diverse property portfolios. As a result, household income has often tended to be made up not just of salaries, which in the past, especially in the public sector, were augmented by a bewildering range of perks and bonuses, the earnings of the self-employed, pensions and benefits, but also rents. The crisis has seen all these sources squeezed, including rental incomes, which have declined sharply, not only because of falling rents but also the inability of increasing numbers of tenants to pay and, as a consequence of this, as the crisis has lengthened, it has not only deepened and extended existing patterns of poverty but also sometimes created hardship in places where it is not always suspected.[16]

Prior to the crisis, poverty was not particularly obvious in Greece, mostly being associated in popular perceptions with Roma or migrant populations. Beggars could always be seen on the streets, and at times in the past their numbers grew, especially during the Yugoslav wars, when many held notices declaring they were Bosnian Serb refugees, but during the crisis they became even more visible, with the signs this time proclaiming hunger and homelessness.[17] In 2009, on the basis of incomplete and contested figures, the government suggested there might be 7,720 homeless people in Greece but they were not particularly visible and the issue received little media attention.[18] However, by 2012 this was changing, as a scattering of mattresses were laid out on the streets of central Athens with signs declaring that the owners had nowhere else to live, and stories began to appear in the media about people living in caves on Philopappos Hill opposite the Acropolis.[19] Local nongovernmental organisations claimed that the issue was becoming more pressing because the poorly socially integrated 'traditional homeless', who often had mental health and drug related problems, had been joined by a 'new homeless', impoverished by the crisis due to the loss of a job or the collapse of a businesses.[20] However, with only limited indications of the extent of the problem prior to the crisis, and issues of definition persisting, despite the government passing legislation to this effect, the extent to which homelessness has actually risen during the crisis remains uncertain. One charity working in the field, though, has suggested that about 1,500 people, both Greeks and immigrants, were sleeping rough in Athens in 2012, with perhaps another 11,500 living in squats, often in squalid conditions without electricity or running water; and by 2015 the total was reported to have risen to 17,700.[21]

For sustenance the homeless and many others have been able to turn to the growing number of soup kitchens that have sprung up, especially in Athens.

Some of these have been established by the municipal authorities but many are run by the churches, largely the Orthodox but the Anglican and Catholic also play an important role, as do the Red Cross and other voluntary groups.[22] One soup kitchen in the heart of the old commercial quarter of Athens served over 1,000 meals each day, but there were reportedly over a hundred others spread across the city and its suburbs.[23] So much so that in 2011 the Orthodox Church alone through its various forms of food aid was reported to be providing daily sustenance to around a quarter-of-a-million people, including 10,000 in Athens.[24] To meet this demand existing facilities have often been expanded, with, in one case, the kitchens of a Church-run home for the elderly being utilised to provide takeaway meals to families in the neighbourhood deemed, after a thorough assessment, to be in need of assistance.[25] Turning to charity, though, has not not easy for those used to the dignity of fending for themselves, and, as important in staving off hunger, if not more so, have been the social networks which exist everywhere, not just within families but also between neighbours and friends. People cook for each other and share food as well as sometimes other items in need, such as medicines, in gestures of common humanity.[26] The overall result has been that, although there have been persistent media reports of people not having enough money to buy food and a service providing free school meals in some of the most deprived areas of the country found that about a tenth of the children it served lacked even basic nutrition, cases of real hunger have not been particularly visible.[27] However, many families have shifted their diet towards cheaper, sometimes less nutritious foodstuffs, and this lack of wide-scale destitution should hardly be taken as a matter of congratulation for a euro area which comprises some of the wealthiest nations on earth.[28]

Soup kitchens and homelessness have attracted attention, however, for many more Greeks the crisis has not brought destitution but a more general decline into poverty. Through ingenuity and adaptability most people have been able to find enough money from somewhere to muddle through, but the difficulties of making ends meet, amid the challenges of everyday life and the uncertainties of both the present and the future, have combined to create a potent narrative of hardship and tribulation. Whether it is in the cafe or at the kitchen table, talk inevitably seems to come back to money, or more usually the lack of it, as notions of social cohesion are constructed around a discourse of mutual suffering and shared poverty. Initially few were openly willing to declare they were poor although even this taboo eventually seemed to breakdown, but the effect in general has been to produce an environment in which suspicion tinged with envy sits alongside solidarity. It is a world in which it is seen as necessary to explain any expenditure beyond the expected to family, friends and even the wider world on social media such as Facebook for fear it might attract criticism and be seen as transgressing the new social norms. In reality, the state of family finances are known to few and each person carries their own private definition of what constitutes impoverishment. This is frequently based more on relative decline in income than actual penury, although this is by no means unknown. However, this collective assumption of hardship, even among those who might not normally be seen as poor, extended the crisis deep into society and, at least in the early years, was a powerful factor inhibiting consumer spending and thereby economic recovery. As time has progressed, however, and household resources have dwindled, the crisis from being an aberration has become a way of life in which straightened circumstances and low expectations are increasingly the norm. In the process, the value of money has also again been redefined, with the €50 note giving way as the ubiquitous point of reference to the €20 or even €10. To ward off the decline in incomes people have adopted various strategies. The most obvious and widely followed has been to spend less although readjusting living standards has been harder for some than others. Many have also tried to take extra jobs, if they can find them, although, since these were often within the informal economy, they do not necessarily show up in official statistics. This was part of a general strategy adopted by many of trying to diversify sources of family income, a practice long followed by the self-employed on the margins of the system. Canny and industrious, for years they have balanced a variety of jobs, like helping in a family shop, maintaining buildings and running a market store, and in their case the crisis has just posed another challenge and an opportunity to deploy skills already well-honed in the art of survival.

The lack of money has also led to the appearance of chains of debt, not just tabs run up in the local shop, as in the past, although these did reappear, but between friends and business colleagues, and ultimately banks and their borrowers, with 800,000 customers by 2012 reported to have rescheduled their debts.[29] In search of cash many others pawned goods in a host of brokers which sprang up across the country. Urbane voices in radio advertisements promised fair evaluations for gold and jewellery and the ubiquitous leaflets scattered through the streets pledged 'honesty', 'absolute secrecy' and European priced evaluations—one finishing with the admonition, 'Do not throw me away. You will need me'.[30] Nonetheless, the chief foil against poverty for most, remained the family, which in concept extends beyond the nuclear grouping to embrace grandparents and grandchildren, if not great-grandchildren, and potentially also siblings and their families.[31] A tendency to pool family resources has been a longstanding facet of Greek society, but in the face of the crisis the practice has deepened, as food has been shared, health and other costs divided, and money given as gifts and loans, often with little expectation on either side of eventual repayment.[32] This, it has been suggested, can be traced to deeply embedded senses of obligation in which the roles of creditor and debtor are seen as transient and easily reversible. Such an understanding provides little space for the concept of one-way indebtedness in which dues have to be paid.[33] Indeed, extrapolated further it might even be suggested that this has helped give an ambiguity to the notion of debt in Greek society in general. The idea has been reinforced over the years by the tendency of governments to waive debts, especially those of farmers, and to allow citizens to petition for their alleviation in the courts. This state of affairs would seem to contrast sharply with Germanic understandings of debt based on guilt and wrong-doing.[34]

Particularly important in staving off the worst effects of the crisis have been pensions, which keep at least a fifth of the population above the poverty line, and in the absence of a comprehensive social security system have long served as an income support mechanism by which the elderly assist not only children but also grandchildren.[35] In the past this was possible not only because payments were often relatively generous but also because the fractured nature of the system meant that many people received more than one pension. Indeed, the death of a pensioner can have a substantial impact on family income, especially if they did not own a house which can be subsequently rented. The cuts in pensions have therefore had a significant impact on household incomes in general and not just among the elderly, because along with a public sector salary they remain a vital safety net. As one person reflected:

> The crisis in Greece would have been so much worse if it hadn't been for the family. There is always a pension, a civil servant in the family... This is the only thing that holds us together. I mean, we are not poor, but... we eat food that other people, family, friends, neighbours are giving us. We eat for free through this network, which, however, has always existed.[36]

This propensity to pool family income is increased by the tendency of children to live at home until they are married. Men in particular often stay until their mid-thirties or later.[37] This not only gives the potential for a greater income to enter the household but also in the past allowed many to maintain a lifestyle which at first glance might be seen as extravagant, marked as it was by long nights in bars and clubs. Saving was rarely considered, not only because of the ready availability of credit in the years before the crisis for purchases such as cars but also because it was frequently presumed that separate accommodation would be provided at an appropriate juncture, often on a different floor of the same apartment block which was owned by parents or grandparents. In such situations, rents rarely pass hands or, if they do, it is often at a heavily subsidised rate and even utility bills can be paid by older members of the family, especially if services like electricity and water remain registered in their name. The main day-to-day living expense then becomes food but even the cost of this is frequently shared, with the various members of the family household coming together to eat meals, and, as the quote above indicates, it is these patterns more than anything else which have kept the crisis at bay for many, including the unemployed.

The growth in poverty lies at the heart of the crisis in Greece. Yet, although it is obvious from the statistics, in reality it is not so easy to measure or even see. It is played out not in the official figures and reports but in millions of individual lives behind closed doors. It was caught in the look of delight that crossed the face of a nun working in one of the poorer areas of the city when handed a pair of worn old shoes to give to those in need; in the eyes of the middle-aged man from somewhere far away as thin as a waif begging for alms on the side of the road; in the photographs of a homeless former dance troupe member and a drug addict thrown together by the crisis and living alongside rats under a bridge in Athens; in the novel about three children struggling to survive the crisis with a septuagenarian father; even in the ghoul-like figures etched in lurid orange on a wall, who reassured passers-by that, although they were hungry, they would not resort to cannibalism and use the utensils in their hands to eat one another.[38] Here, though, however expressive and cleverly executed the image may be, hardship and suffering were beginning to stray into the path of politics. This was most brazenly obvious when Golden Dawn organised food handouts only to those who produced identity documents showing themselves to be ethnically Greek, but even the homeless at times could be heard complaining that their cause was being usurped to further the objectives of those who purported to help them.[39] To dwell on the political use of suffering, though, can lead to the overlooking of the other side of the coin, because the hardships of the crisis have also produced innumerable acts of charity and more than anything else it is these deeds of personal kindness that have blunted the worst of the crisis for both Greeks and immigrants.[40] Indeed, as destructive as the crisis has often been, it has also given these chances for charitable giving, reinforced social solidarity and provided opportunities to build new relationships with family, friends, neighbours and other members of the community, leading some to hope it might eventually even leave a more cohesive society in its wake.

The family has provided a backbone of support for many throughout the crisis, allowing them to weather its exigencies. In this, it can be seen as confirming with the longstanding national narrative, caught in the slogan 'Country, Religion, Family', which has elevated it to be one of the key building blocks of Greek society, projected as a source of security, mutual support, moral values and even work in what is often a hostile and difficult socio-economic environment.[41] However, beside this eulogising of the family a counter narrative also exists within Greek artistic expression which dwells on its darker side, perhaps most visibly in recent years in Giorgos Lanthimos' 2009 film *Dogtooth*.[42] In this a patriarchal father and his wife completely control the lives of their grown-up children, keeping them in such isolation that even words can take on different meanings. In this alternative vision families are not sites of harmony and support but the source of the ills of Greek society and cauldrons of strife. Indeed, according to some even the origins of the crisis itself lie in the corruption, tax evasion and anti-meritocratic culture engendered by the nepotism and clientelism unleashed in a ceaseless search to further the interest of family members.[43] Instead of solidarity and social cohesion, the family in this counter-narrative embodies discord and rancour. Obsessive mulling over money breeds envy and distrust. Past behaviour is raked over to fuel present day justifications, and even when assistance is given, it provokes resentment rather than gratitude. This alternative universe is insular and closed behind four walls, but in it cash-strapped children push elderly parents to hand over pension money as well as other goods, and hatreds fester as revenges are plotted.[44] It sometimes echoes in arguments heard in the streets by passers-by, but it is difficult to penetrate and almost impossible to quantify. Some have tried by pointing to a rise in domestic violence, with a helpline which opened in 2012 reporting a steady number of calls, with the assumption being that the increase was due to the crisis.[45] However, greater attention to the issue following the launch of a publicity campaign may also have been a cause, and a case study, while pointing to unemployment being a factor contributing to the onset of abuse, stopped short of directly linking it to the crisis.[46]

Instead, in attempting to quantify the social consequences of the crisis, attention has tended to focus on measurements from the beginning and end of life. Various reports have purported to show that the crisis has had an effect on sex lives, but more contentious has proved the issue of still-births, with the newspaper *Eleftherotypia* in July 2013 carrying an article on the subject bearing the headline, 'The troika eats our children'.[47] Drawing on medical research, this highlighted the fact that there had been an increase of a little over 20 per cent in the number of still-births recorded after 2008, and suggested that the crisis was directly to blame, because unemployed, uninsured women had not been able to undergo vital tests during pregnancy. Some brief findings published in the *British Medical Journal* seemed to broadly confirm this picture, although the caution present in the authors' concluding statement that the rise was 'probably' associated with the economic downturn was removed in most media reporting.[48] However, other research published in the *Lancet* comparing stillbirth rates over a longer period of time, while agreeing there had been an increase since 2008, found it more difficult to draw conclusions when looking at the decade 2003–2012 as a whole and, indeed, the number did start to fall again in 2013 and this trend has continued.[49] With other figures relating to infant and child mortality showing little change between the pre-crisis and crisis periods, conclusions remain difficult to draw and the issue is probably best placed within an ongoing debate about the impact of the adjustment programmes on the Greek health service in general. This has led to a spate of sometimes contradictory articles appearing in academic journals, although the general conclusion seems to be that change, which has mostly been driven by a need to curb expenditure, has often been implemented clumsily and that the longer-term consequences of the crisis for healthcare may be detrimental.[50] A finding amply backed by the scores of stories circulating about people finding it difficult to secure healthcare or the necessary drugs for treatment.[51] The national birth rate has also been in a state of decline for some time, although there were signs of a reversal in this trend immediately prior to the crisis. Since 2008, though, the rate has fallen sharply, so that by 2013 it was nearly 20 per cent below the immediate pre-crisis figure.[52] The fall seems to have been due to fewer younger women giving birth, perhaps because declining living standards make it difficult for them to consider starting families.[53] However, the rate among foreign citizens has noticeably declined far faster than among the native population, perhaps because many young migrants, who previously might have given birth in Greece, have returned home. With the number of deaths rising as well, which some researchers also in part ascribe to the crisis, the natural change figure has once again turned negative. There were 17,660 more deaths than births in Greece in 2013 and the overall pattern seems to be that the crisis, as in so much else, has amplified existing trends: in this case the creation of a demographically ageing society with some projections suggesting that by 2050 a third of the population might be over sixty-five-years-old.[54]

At the other extremity of life from birth, death, and in particular the rise in the number of suicides, has also received much comment, although there is little agreement on figures, with sources differing and one researcher in a media interview explicitly arguing that official statistics underestimate the phenomenon.[55] Historically the suicide rate in Greece has been low. This is probably partly due to the influence of the Orthodox Church, which teaches that it is wrong, although this may also have been a reason for underreporting over the years, as families often preferred to give other causes of death to ensure priests performed funeral rites. During the crisis, the general trend has been for the suicide rate to rise, although, as noted, this is from a low base and in 2015 the figure for Greece was still the lowest in the EU, and considerably less than in other countries receiving assistance packages, such as Portugal and Ireland, as well as northern European states like Germany.[56] Causation is not always easy to establish in suicide, although in some cases the crisis was undoubtedly foremost in the mind of the victim, most notably in the public death of the retired pharmacist, Dimitris Christoulas, who shot himself in the head in broad daylight on the fringes of Syntagma Square in April 2012. In his pocket he left a note in which he compared the rulers of Greece at that time to collaborators during the German occupation of the country in the Second World War and declared that he had chosen suicide to provide a dignified end to his life rather than fishing through rubbish bins for sustenance.[57] Afterwards reports began to appear in the media suggesting that other people were also taking their lives due to the financial pressures arising from the crisis, but a series of academic studies based on Crete, which has the highest suicide rate in Greece, seemed to find that it was not a key factor.[58] However, other research based on the rest of the country paints another picture, with one study dating from 2014 suggesting that several hundred additional suicides may be attributed to the unemployment and uncertainties created by austerity, with men in mid and later life at the highest risk.[59] As with the issue of stillbirths, conclusions are not easy to draw and too much discussion about statistics risks diminishing the real tragedy of suicide, but it seems plausible to say, as a psychiatrist interviewed by a journalist suggested, that the crisis, even if it had no direct causal effect, created 'conditions that push vulnerable people who would otherwise not resort to such action to the edge'.[60]

Suicides are only the most extreme sign of a more general societal anxiety. Antidepressant usage figures, depending on sources, seem contradictory, but, even so, they would give little indication of the worries, fears and feelings of hopelessness that have reached deep into every family and workplace. Greek ratings on wellbeing indexes are invariably abysmal, with the country recording considerable falls in subjective happiness and large numbers of respondents saying they are experiencing stress.[61] Indeed, the ratings for Greece have fallen further than other assistance programme countries and more than might be expected from loss of income alone, which left a UN report speculating that the drop may be explained not only by the rise in unemployment but also by a general loss of trust in bodies such as the police and judiciary. In reality, the true causes of the collapse in wellbeing can only be found in myriads of personal stories but, as with suicides, it is probably best to say that it is those most vulnerable who have succumbed to despair, as the crisis burrows deep to exploit existing weaknesses. Nonetheless, a shortage of money places obvious strains on any household and, when coupled with a fear of unemployment, which has constantly stalked many of those working in the public as well as the private sector, it has bred widespread anxiety and insecurity.[62] Occasionally, when a job has been lost, the reaction has been marked by desperation, as when an aggrieved fifty-two-year-old former employee of a small factory took a gun to his old workplace, shot two and held three others hostage for eleven hours.[63] Yet, for far more it has meant descent into a futureless life, in which the present has been stripped of its customary meaning and the past is either cast as a golden ideal or the root of all current woes.[64] This is especially true of those pushed into early retirement. Often long desired, this has turned for many into a prison of low expectations, as slashed pensions offer few opportunities beyond the mundane. Most of all, it strikes at the hope that often highly educated children will have a better future. Indeed, from being overwhelmingly optimistic in 2007, only a bare quarter of young people by 2011 could muster any enthusiasm about their prospects.[65] The talk was increasingly of a lost generation and in this narrative Greece lay at a dead end, destined to endure almost perpetual misery and torment. It was a sentiment caught at the height of the crisis in the single haunting phrase, 'I'm tortured', that appeared painted in spindly black letters of varying size on walls throughout the city centre and suburbs of Athens. The message was both anonymous—it may have been the work of a single graffitist or have spawned a host of copycats—and also recognisable, since it was a sentiment that could be shared by so many.[66] The cafes of Greece might still have been crowded on warm summer nights, as was often observed, but this dark underside of the crisis brought much hidden misery in its wake.

Indeed, rather than offering a route to the future, the memorandum in many ways seemed to be reinforcing patterns of the past, not only in its consolidation of the centrality of the state, mentioned in previous chapters, but also in terms of social behaviour that has often been portrayed as traditional, such as women returning to domestic duties and grandparents more than ever looking after youngsters to lessen childcare costs. As wages fell and unemployment increased, the tendency for children, not just men but also women, to live at home until later in life seemed to grow, producing a suspicion that marriage was increasingly prompted only by the ticking of the biological clock and a desire for children, and certainly the number of weddings declined by 13 per cent between 2009 and 2013. In the opposite direction, although official statistics for average household size showed little variation, there also seemed to be a tendency for the elderly to leave their own homes and move in with their children to cut costs and further integrate pensions into family budgets.[67] While providing company, this can also lead to a loss of independence and sometimes overcrowding, but as a result, at least in some of the poorer areas of Athens, scores of properties were left uninhabited. The situation was exacerbated by a tendency for people to leave what was increasingly seen as a high cost and crime ridden urban environment for provincial towns and villages.[68] Again this phenomenon is difficult to quantify, with aspiration not necessarily leading to action, and media coverage tending to dwell on a few well publicised cases.[69] However, the proclivity for families living in the city to retain strong connections with their locales of origin made it relatively easy for some who had lost their jobs to seek a rural alternative and, as a result, the number of people engaged in agriculture has actually grown during the crisis. Perhaps even more common, though, has been the further extension of what might be seen as a modern transhumant lifestyle, in which older people, in particular, to cut down on expenses and take advantage of local food supplies choose to spend not only the summer but many other months, if not all their time, living away from their residences in Athens and the other major cities in old family homes in villages, not all of which are in good repair.

In a similar vein, opinion polls throughout the crisis have also shown large numbers, particularly young people, expressing a wish to emigrate. Again, though, putting this aspiration into practice is not easy and, when more pointed questions were asked, the number actually taking active steps to move abroad often turned out to be far smaller.[70] Still, undoubtedly many have left and others are thinking about joining them or preparing their children for the likelihood that they will have to live outside Greece. There has been a surge in

German language learning, which now ranks second to English in popularity, and an increasing number of advertisements offer opportunities to learn Swedish, Finnish, Dutch and other north European tongues.[71] Of those who have left, some seem to have held dual nationality and to have returned to counties such as Australia, the United States, and Canada where they were born.[72] Others, though, are new emigrants and the vast majority of these seem to have chosen to stay in the EU, although the few leaving for Turkey attracted much publicity.[73] Often skilled graduates, they have frequently eschewed the traditional pattern of moving to live with family members abroad, in favour of striking out on their own to look for jobs in northern European countries.[74] Due to the popularity of English language learning, many still looked to the UK, with 17,310 Greeks reported to have registered for national insurance numbers in 2012 and 2013, but others have turned to the Netherlands, Denmark and especially Germany.[75] It was reported that 34,109 Greeks moved to that country in 2012, with a possibility that the figure might have been even higher, since not all the new arrivals may have registered with the authorities.[76] Indeed, as the crisis drags on the figures, if anything, are rising even faster, with the number moving to the UK jumping by a third in just one year. However, whether these new migrants travel with the intention of permanently staying abroad is still far from clear. Most seem to journey with an expectation that one day, if opportunity permits, they will return to Greece. By no means all the emigrants are young. In the new transnational Europe single mothers take their children abroad when they go in search of work and fathers speak to their children through Skype, but the loss of so many highly educated and skilled workers undoubtedly has considerable longer-term social and economic implications for Greece. These new emigrants are not the only ones leaving the country. Many immigrants, especially from south-east European states, have also returned home, with around a fifth of Albanians reported to have departed by 2012, partly because, lacking stable work and social security contributions, many were unable to renew their residence permits.[77] Others, though, especially second generation immigrants, seem to have stayed, perhaps because the economies of neighbouring countries like Albania still do not offer the same opportunities, but also because, for many, Greece has become home.[78] However, growing competition for jobs has also meant that the crisis in places seems to have not only renewed tensions between Albanians and Greeks but also to have created new ones within the immigrant community itself.[79]

Indeed, it is immigrants and those outside family support networks who seem to have fared particularly badly in the crisis, especially those who have arrived from Asia and Africa. The geographic position of Greece means they have been trickling into the country for many years, but they have become more noticeable in recent times, partly due to the adoption of the Dublin Regulations, which lay down that those who seek political asylum must do so in the first EU country in which they arrive. This resulted in so many applications for asylum that the processing system effectively collapsed, leading to interminable queues outside the main registration centre and the UN General Assembly special rapporteur in 2013 describing it as 'dysfunctional'.[80] Faced with truly wretched conditions inside Greece, some migrants have chosen to return home. The International Organization for Migration has arranged a constant flow of repatriations, but others, often deeply in debt to the traffickers who arranged their journey to the West, remained trapped in an alien land. Along with other migrants of all kinds of status, they moved into areas of the centre of Athens, especially off Patission Street, which until only a decade or so ago, were seen as desirable addresses by their Greek residents. The social standing of these neighbourhoods began to decline before the new migrants arrived, but the gap between an idealised vision of the local past and the present uneasy population mix, forms a potent part of the discourse of racial division propagated by right-wing groups.[81] It is in these areas of the city that poverty and destitution are most readily encountered and images of crisis easily conjured. In an uneasy mix, often elderly Greeks, marooned in their once fashionable apartments, live cheek-by-jowl with drug addicts and others on the margins of society as well as the many migrants, who having survived an often arduous and dangerous passage to the country, squeeze into overcrowded flats. With limited access to social welfare and largely dependent on clinics of local branches of international charities like Médecins du Monde for healthcare, they try to survive in a land which economically, politically and socially has become increasingly unwelcoming, with reports of racial attacks growing during the crisis along with persistent stories of police collusion or indifference.[82] Mirroring the Greeks who moved from the countryside to the city in the 1950s and 1960s, migrants could be found huddling over the metal grills of the metro in Omonia Square at night to keep warm.[83] During the day many also imitated their Greek predecessors by hawking goods on the streets or clustering at busy road junctions to peddle their wares to passing motorists. Others found low-paid work in small workshops and service industries or joined the scrap metal collectors. These have long toured the suburbs of the cities in battered pickups, with tinny loudspeakers mounted on cab roofs screeching for 'any old iron', but the newcomers not having the funds to buy a vehicle were forced to start on foot with supermarket trolleys. The more successful then graduated to little tricycle trucks, which disappeared in times of plenty but during the crisis returned to the streets, or mopeds with crates strapped to the pillion, drawing skilfully up to the sides of the bins so as to rifle the contents with a long metal hook without having to dismount. Once gathered, the metals passed to smelters, which could be little more than primitive hole-in-the-floor workshops in rundown suburbs such as Tavros, where noxious fumes from power cables burnt to extract the copper inside blighted public health. Most, though, ended up at the bigger steelworks, where it was melted down to produce reinforcing rods for the construction trade and, in the absence of a market in Greece, shipped to Beirut and other overseas destinations as a valuable export.[84]

Not all the metals came from bins. The railways and power companies have been plagued by thefts, although this in itself is not new. Around €10 million of cabling was reportedly stolen each year, and at least one thief lost his life through electrocution.[85] Hundreds of metal gratings were also plundered from roadways in Athens. Indeed, crime in general formed another important narrative strand within the crisis. Some incidents, such as the 2011 stabbing to death in plain daylight of a man for a video camera with which he was about to film the birth of his child, were particularly shocking but they only seemed to personify what was judged to be a general rise in crime.[86] Surveys of inner city residents found most maintaining that they had been the victim of crime of some type in recent years and, especially at night, many, and not just the elderly, said they feared to leave their homes. Yet, official statistics suggest that crime as a whole actually decreased quite dramatically between 2007 and 2011, with recorded criminal offences falling by 55 per cent during this period.[87] Within this trend, though, certain categories, such as robbery and theft, did initially see sharp increases, growing by up to a half. However, this still left them considerably lower than in many EU-15 states, and by 2013 even in these areas the figures were falling back towards previous levels.[88] This discrepancy between perceptions and reality is more easily noted than explained. However, it is not unknown for crime to be underreported elsewhere in the world and it may be that in Greece many people do not inform the authorities because of the widely held belief that the police will take little, if any, action.[89] Most of the many stories of crime spread by word of mouth involved domestic burglaries or raids on small businesses. A surprising number were reported to be violent, with even attacks on kiosks and petrol stations involving Kalashnikov rifles and sometimes deaths. For some businesses the robberies became so frequent that the owners seemed almost blasé when describing a new incident, even if it involved being held up at gunpoint. Most held non-Greeks responsible for the crime and this assumption appears to be supported by the statistics, which suggest that in 2009 in cases in which the police could identify the offenders around half of all thefts and burglaries were committed by foreigners, although it could be that this merely reflected the fact that the attention of the authorities was more concentrated on this group.[90]

A previous study, looking at the period between 1991 and 1998, which was also characterised by a rhetoric of austerity and economic restructuring, but not by and large recession, suggested that a rise in unemployment at that time led to an increase in property crime.[91] However, although it is widely presumed that the growing impoverishment of both Greeks and migrants during the crisis has similarly encouraged crime, a direct causal link can rarely be presumed or established other than in incidents such as a series of 'Robin Hood raids' carried out on supermarkets in 2011. These saw young people bursting into stores, seizing goods from the shelves and then afterwards distributing them for free in local markets.[92] Strangely, though, these times of austerity presented richer pickings for thieves, because, fearing the solvency of financial institutions and exit from the euro, many people withdrew their savings from bank accounts and took to squirrelling them away at home, particularly since safe deposit boxes proved to be in short supply. Jewellery also proved a tempting target, perhaps in part because the rash of new pawn shops made it even easier to fence stolen goods. Elsewhere, in the countryside, away from the cities, isolated holiday homes continued to provide tempting and relatively simple targets as well, and this helped spread the perception that the crisis was producing lawlessness throughout the country. The main response on the part of the government to this concern about crime seems to have been to raise the visibility of the police, with pairs of patrolling motorbikes frequently evident, especially in the wealthier Athenian suburbs. For their part, citizens turned home security into one of the few growth areas of the economy, with sales of alarms and safes reportedly rising sharply. In many blocks first-floor residents installed expensive armoured glass or placed iron bars across their windows, turning their homes either into fortresses or prisons, depending on one's point of view. Elsewhere others said they resorted to firing hunting rifles into the air every now and again to remind those around that they were armed or mounted vigilante patrols with neighbours, a practice frowned upon by the government.[93]

Fear of crime has heightened levels of mistrust and produced a feeling of insecurity in society. This has compounded the lack of faith in official institutions and raised tensions with migrant communities. Yet, there is a discrepancy between fear of crime, which has long been high, and actual felony levels that have in general been low when compared with other EU-15 states.[94] As noted above, this may have been in part because of underreporting of incidents due to lack of faith in the police. However, the discrepancy is so great that various other causes have also been posited. These include an accentuated awareness of illegal drug use, which is perceived as being a major problem, and a general unease resulting from social change, financial uncertainty and an urban environment, especially in the inner cities, that is often seen as deprived, with graffiti encrusted walls, litter, vandalism and beggars and homeless people present on the streets. All these, it is argued, have served to heighten public awareness of crime over the years and the crisis has intensified this process. To this must also be added the constant stories of wrongdoing circulating by word of mouth and media coverage of the phenomenon which sometimes tends to be sensationalised.[95] The need for editors to keep audiences engaged during the chief news programme, which on the most popular channels normally lasts one hour, has long led them to dwell on crime stories, with some also choosing to play dramatic and eerie music in the background to heighten the sense of tension. Indeed, the same needs can also be seen influencing reporting of the crisis in general on television, which for most Greeks remains the predominant source of information and entertainment. Throughout the crisis news programmes were naturally dominated by the unfolding events. Pictures of, mostly male, grey-suited politicians and officials scurrying from one meeting to another, were regularly augmented by screens of financial data. These were joined by images of marching strikers, protesting about wage and benefit cuts, and countless interviews with ordinary people as they went about their daily business on how aspects of the crisis were affecting their own lives or those of their families, which almost inevitably brought forth anguished expressions of complaint. Complementing these, the news shows were also full of interviews with experts and other commentators, who, while dissecting every sinew of the crisis, often bamboozled their audience with a technical lexicon of bewildering complexity. On the more popular channels the technique of sub-dividing the screen into small 'windows' was frequently used to allow up to six of these pundits the opportunity to give their views on a subject at any one time. It has been argued this procedure is essentially democratic, but too often it degenerated into a shouting match, as the various participants struggled to make their voices heard. At best, this could be seen as entertaining, but in practice it helped feed the prevailing mood of pessimism and uncertainty because, with so many conflicting views, it was almost impossible to establish any sense of authority. The memorandum and its reforms had always found few public champions within Greek society and this cacophony of critical voices weakened still further any legitimacy the document might have held in the eyes of the public. Indeed, in the face of this barrage of bewildering information the natural reaction of many was to ignore the experts, and, instead, feel empathy with the views expressed by their fellow citizens in the vox pop interviews. Prevailing sentiments of powerlessness and hopelessness were reinforced, and, as the expert panellists endlessly speculated on the prospects of default, euro exit or the need for further austerity measures, the regular complaint became that the news was 'too hard to bear'.

Even before the crisis, surveys showed that public trust in television as a source of information was lower in Greece than anywhere else in the EU, largely due to a perception that it was hopelessly politically compromised and did little more than echo the party lines of either PASOK or New Democracy.[96] This lack of trust has translated into a generalised belief that the mainstream media feeds the population lies and withholds important information. Such an interpretation gives plenty of space for alternative narratives to flourish and the crisis has brought no shortage of these. Some followed familiar conspiratorial forms to explain apparent submission, such as the oft heard story that aeroplanes were criss-crossing the skies spraying chemicals to keep the population quiescent.[97] Others offered alternative outcomes to the crisis, many of a providential nature. One that received much publicity was a story that a rich benefactor was prepared to provide soft loans on the basis of old bank bonds deposited in a Canadian account, which were reported to be worth €600 billion.[98] The story seems at first to have been accepted by many at face value, with any doubts usually being reserved for the government whose curmudgeonly attitude was said to be the only factor inhibiting the donor's munificence. In propagating such stories the media, both old and new, may have been guilty of not always subjecting them to the critical examination they deserved, but they were at the same time accurately mirroring narrative currents within society as a whole. These could be heard not only in conversations at home, in the workplace and the cafe but were also expressed in written form through devices like blogs and the numerous chain emails sent by one recipient to another. Frequently laced with a bittersweet humour, these reflected the many moods of the crisis from anger with the political class—after it was announced that Papandreou would be teaching at Harvard University, a photograph circulated purporting to show a homeless beggar holding a piece of cardboard on which was scribbled, 'Please help!!! My teacher in Harvard was George Papandreou. I have no future'—to affirmations of national pride and even invocations to optimism.[99] The perceived failings of the more traditional media also gave space for new voices that ranged from what were effectively shadow mainstream outlets to the likes of Athens Indymedia that termed itself an 'open collective of people offering grassroots, non-corporate, non-commercial coverage', but which caught the attention of the authorities for its anti-establishment links, and the cooperative Radio Bubble, with its citizen journalists.[100] The stated goal of many of these new media outlets, as well as some of the more professionally produced blogs, was to bridge what they saw as an information gap left by the traditional media. Initially this was seen in terms of Greece itself but, as the crisis progressed, some by writing in English sought also to fill what they saw as deficiencies in external reporting of events within the country. The idea of an information gap helped give legitimacy to the new media, which could present itself as the antithesis of what was seen as a hopelessly compromised old media enmeshed within vested interests. However, in reality, a lack of resources usually prevented it from offering extensive news reporting, so it more often came to reflect the preoccupations and narratives of society, often within the framework of a leftist, anti-globalisation discourse with deep roots in Greece.

The same currents of thought have also driven other forms of self-expression, including the street artists, whose work has been highly visible throughout the centre of Athens and adorned many international stories about the crisis, especially online.[101] Thus, according to the artist who operates under the name Bleeps, the existing system served only the interests of the bourgeoisie and Greece could not be considered a democracy because the 'consciousness of the citizen is manipulated... the notion of free will is a utopia'.[102] The street artists saw the crisis as providing not just inspiration but also an audience for their work, which furnished a sardonic commentary on the age of austerity in images such as 'Greece's Next Economic Model', which playing on the title of a television series, showed a dark-haired girl strutting a catwalk in a bikini with one leg amputated below the knee. The political class was also seen as fair game, as one artist explained: 'These people take my fate into their own hands, so I take their public image in my own hands'.[103] Thus an impassively faced Papademos stared out from one wall, threatening passers-by with a gun like a bank robber, while on another Samaras and Merkel stood in solidarity bearing blindfolds inscribed with the words 'no future'. The artists saw their work as being a dialogue with the people, but one in his blog noted how it was often foreigners who seemed more interested in his art and openly aired his disappointment that at the time he was actively producing antifascist propaganda, Golden Dawn continued to gain votes.[104] Nevertheless, the street artists along with the cartoonists in the mainstream media, the satirists on television and many other voices in society as a whole did succeed in producing an alternative, highly critical commentary on the crisis. Through its ubiquity this not only undermined what was always a weak official narrative but also reinforced what had come to be the prevailing view which was that the memorandum was a disaster for Greece.

The street art has shared the walls with enormous quantities of graffiti which seem in places to cover every available space. Many are just tags or proclaim loyalty to a football team but others respond to the crisis. Outside the headquarters of the country's central bank an Anglophone graffitist transposed the Bank of Greece to the Bank of Berlin, while also cleverly circling the 'EEC' of Greece as a reminder of the origins of the EU and adding some extra letters to give either 'heel', presumably referring to the jackboot of austerity, or 'hell', depending on interpretation. Some were ironic, like, 'My love, you are so beautiful, like a bank on fire', or the seasonal greeting of 'Merry Crisis and a Happy New Fear', but others were couched in the same mixture of humour tinged with anger seen in much of the street art and other popular commentary, as the passer-by was admonished, 'Do not kill mosquitoes, others suck your blood', or called upon to 'vote for Ali Baba, he has only forty thieves'. Indeed, perhaps, most of all the slogans and street art provided a vivid daily reminder of the sense of outrage and anger that penetrated so deeply into society and fuelled so much of the popular response to the crisis. This was most visible in the protests in Syntagma Square, but it seemed to infiltrate almost every aspect of life, even being caught in the lyrics of songs by popular singers such as Nikos Karvelas, who in 'Smash Everything' urged people to 'wake up, don't believe them, don't vote for them, it has to be done now, smash everything... Nothing should be left... it has to be done... NOW.'[105] Transcending political alignments, it was an all-pervasive anger with the political class, the system they had created, tax evaders, the banks, capitalism, the troika, the Germans, the outside world but, most of all, it was an expression of rage against the austerity regime and the degradation and shame it had brought to the country and its citizens. In the song 'Crisis' by Dimitris Mentzelos, Tiny Jackal and Pavlos Fyssas, who appeared under the stage name Killah P., the performers dressed in white coats stand in a butcher's shop beating out a rhythm with meat cleavers while proclaiming: 'I eat one meal and five tear gas canisters a day... Soon we will be breaking into people's houses for broccoli... The ads on buses are not about *frontistiria* [private tuition centres] but pawn shops... I rap for food.'[106] In these lyrics the essence of popular feeling was caught. The crisis had stripped life to its existential core and similar sentiments were also evoked in Ektoras Lygizos' 2013 film *Boy Eating the Bird's Food*, which is loosely based on the Norwegian author Knut Hamsun's study of physical and psychological decay *Hunger*.[107] In this a young man with a beautiful singing voice wanders through Athens. Estranged from his family and unable to earn a living, despite his talents, but determined to exist without seeking help, he steals food or scavenges from bins. As he drifts towards starvation and insanity, the film could easily be read, and perhaps is intended to be, as a metaphor for the suffering of the country as a whole. However, the message is not so simple, because, according to Lygizos, he wanted more to show that his protagonist is a victim of his own choices and, especially, his decision not to reveal his weaknesses to others.[108] The film, thus, moves beyond mere notions of fate, to suggest that even in the midst of the crisis individuals, and presumably countries, are still in charge of their own destiny even if this is only to ensure survival. Humiliation does not necessarily have to be equated with impotence; it can also lead to action.

Indeed, other artists wanted to read into the anger more than blind rage. Investing it with political meaning, they traced a direct lineage between the protests of the crisis and a venerable and, according to some, occasionally romanticised Greek tradition of resistance, stretching from the Ottoman era through the Second World War to the dictatorship and the Polytechnic uprising.[109] In this view the artists and slogan writers, like their predecessors, often working clandestinely in fear of the police, were producing acts of defiance and calls to action—a sentiment caught in a banner draped over the entrance to Syntagma metro station in the early summer of 2011 which read, 'You got the disease. We got the solution. Revolution.' To encourage resistance past acts were sometimes evoked. A leaflet circulating in Athens paralleled the December disturbances of 2008 with the *Dekemvriana* of 1944, and the leader of the power workers' union was interviewed with a photo of the Second World War Greek People's Liberation Army (ELAS) leader, Aris Velouchiotis, who occupies a talismanic status in leftist circles in Greece, prominently displayed on the wall beside him. The music of Mikis Theodorakis, which had formed the soundtrack to the fall of the dictatorship and the restoration of democracy, could be regularly heard from concert halls to street corner demonstrations, where tinny loudspeakers broadcast lyrics such as, 'If tonight you do not take stock, to read your heart's hidden message, tomorrow you'll find yourself a cheap manager, in the hands of foreign powers', which were seen as having lost little relevance over the years.[110] More contemporary artists spoke in a harsher, abrasive language reflecting the anger of many of the younger protesters. The group Psychodrama in their song 'Fuck the Police', which was written as a response to the December 2008 disturbances, warned, 'I'll set the city alight so you do not sleep, pimp, the worst is coming, you can't imagine the human revolution, which will come and wreck the order of things—prime, ignite, throw—so you uniformed monsters would burn like insects'.[111] Even the singers of *laika*, the pre-eminent popular music of lost loves and broken hearts sung in countless night clubs across the country reflected the mood, with Notis Sfakianakis over images drawn from Syntagma in 'The Square' singing, 'If they bolt our souls and tape our mouths there are the streets and squares'.[112]

The story told was of popular resistance to the dictates of the troika and this was not entirely without justification, given the numbers who participated in the protests. However, these calls for action were also so persistent because other sentiments were equally prevalent. For all the widespread anger and rage there was also resignation, the greatest enemy of resistance, as well as fear. When questioned many said it was fear that stopped them from protesting, and this led to claims that the violence was being deliberately fomented by the authorities to secure public quiescence, but fear was also present in many forms in everyday life. It ranged from fear of poverty, of losing a job, of crime, of 'the other' or just fear of the future.[113] As much as anger mobilised society, fear paralysed it, making it passive and defensive, as people slipped into a mode of subsistence just waiting for the crisis to end. Perhaps in response the need for participation, or as some termed it 'solidarity', increasingly came to be stressed. Citizens were urged not to be onlookers on the margin of society, like the two siblings watching the spectacle in Loula Anagnostaki's play, *The Parade*, which was staged during the crisis, but to actively engage in the unfolding events and play a part in shaping history. Potentially serving as exemplars, countless articles and stories appeared in the media highlighting the activities of various self-help initiatives and other civic groups giving the impression that they were flourishing throughout the country. However, the extent to which they enjoyed mass support was never entirely clear and there was always a suspicion that the stories were more often describing an ideal than a reality. Indeed, running counter to this narrative there was always another that stressed the weakness of Greek civil society and the absence of active participation, which for some translated into a reluctance to take responsibility. The philosopher Stelios Ramfos in his analysis cast society in psychoanalytical terms as infantile, suggesting that its citizens behave like small children when they seek security in the embrace of the state or a political party.[114] Cocooned in a world of illusions, he argues, society is able to see itself as the perpetual victim of circumstances, ready to blame but not to accept that it makes its own choices for which it must bear responsibility. In this view, the crisis is located in the shortcomings of a national culture which is unable to act against the pathogens of society. The reasons given for this are many, but for Ramfos they are grounded in the persistence of residues of past cultural forms and a deficiency of logic and rationality, especially within an education system that does little to foster the critical thinking that might allow Greece to diverge from the patterns of the past and exit crisis.

On all sides the discourse echoed with confrontation. In the lyrics of the songs, the slogans on the walls and the words of the politicians, but the enemy was far from clear. For some it might be the police, for others the troika, the Germans or even the capitalist system itself but for most Greeks it seems also to have been the immediate past prior to the crisis, as embodied by the corruption and failings of the political class and those perceived to be their accomplices, the 'sharks with jeeps who are still out of prison'.[115] It was caught in the endless chants of 'thieves' by the crowd on the streets and the revival of practices such as throwing yoghurt at those in authority, although, unlike in the past, this was not now the preserve of the young but of all ages, with a pensioner at one point tipping a pot over Venizelos.[116] Other politicians were attacked while eating in restaurants or watching films and in Corfu a group had to leave by boat after their dining place was surrounded by raucous protesters.[117] Indeed, such was the vehemence of the reaction that the political class was effectively driven from the public stage at one point in the crisis. This narrative about the past is eloquently examined within the novels of Petros Markaris, whose explorations of modern Greece so closely map its contours that he has been called the 'anatomist' of the crisis. In a series of detective stories, Markaris has spent years exploring the pathogenesis of the ills that trouble the Greek state, and, in a trilogy of books directly concerned with the crisis, he returned to many familiar themes.[118] In *Overdue Loans* he paints a picture of a culture of exploitation within the banks, in which loans were given to people unable to pay, allowing the financial institutions, as he has one ex-banker explain, 'to keep hostage half the Greek population'. In *Closure* a killer starts to murder those in arrears with their tax payments. This makes others who owe money pay up quickly but, when the state refuses to give the tax-collector-cum-killer the 10 per cent cut he demands, he turns his sights on 'all those who enriched themselves due to their connections with the Greek political system'. The third book, entitled *Bread, Education, Freedom*, after the old slogan of the Polytechnic uprising, is set in a future in which Greece has left the euro and returned to the drachma but this has created no utopia. Strict limits have been placed on the amount people can withdraw from cash machines, salaries go unpaid and pensioners march in the streets chanting, 'Bring back the euro'. The plot again revolves around a series of murders but, as the title suggests, the real villains, as in an earlier book *Che Committed Suicide*, are not the killers but their victims, who are influential members of the Polytechnic generation.[119] In Markaris' story they have long ago cast aside their youthful idealism and now see power, in whatever guise it comes, as an entitlement. The sentiment is caught perfectly when one late middle-aged character, after he lists the privations he suffered as a youth, tells another 'the country owes us', and this has led Markaris elsewhere to argue:[120]

> The Polytechnic generation has devastated this country. They wanted to build a new Greece with the jargon of the left and failed. The ones with any integrity have withdrawn to take care of themselves. The others have gone into politics or collared themselves a lucrative job in business with the patronage system or a rewarding position in the state bureaucracy. In the beginning of the '80s this leftist jargon was crucial if you wanted to enter politics under the banner of PASOK or secure a position in the state bureaucracy. Anyone without a good grasp of the jargon was part of the old, reactionary system. In the meantime some of these people have become filthy rich. They still use the same leftist terms. But it's a masquerade. They were yesterday's winners. The children are among the lost generation of today. And tomorrow the fathers will come to feel the wrath of the children.[121]

In Markaris' view the Polytechnic generation are the profiteers of the Greek system and alongside them he also places their business cronies, the tax evaders of the professional classes and the farmers, who have plundered EU subsidies to buy themselves Jeep Cherokees.[122] These are also joined by the 'Molochs' of the civil service and trade unions, who have gained their posts due to political patronage and require regular sacrifices from the people to satisfy their needs. Yet, these are only a minority because, like so many others, Markaris divides society into opposing forces, and on the other side he places 'the righteous' or the 'martyrs'. Among these he includes those he calls the honest small and medium sized business owners, taxi drivers and other professionals, as well as the civil servants who acquired their jobs legitimately through meritocratic exams and are then punished by having to do the work of political appointees. For Markaris this group are not reactionary underdogs derailing the project of modernisation but the bedrock of Greek society. Lastly, and presumably to a certain extent overlapping with this group, he also adds the 'hopeless', those who have simply lost faith in the future, including the young forced to seek work abroad.

The typology is straightforward and like Markaris' novels highly persuasive. It reflects both the world he creates in his books and the narratives of society. Like these, however, the typology is a construction and it is a moot point as to how much it represents reality or just fulfils expectations. Indeed, arguably equally important as the activities of the members of the Polytechnic generation themselves are the narratives that they and their successors have tried to impose on Greece. Many at root are stories of unfulfilled expectations and give voice to a disappointment that Greece has not been transformed in the ways they had hoped. For Markaris the reason for this failure seems to be corruption. Not just in terms of actual corruption, although this is often writ large in his work, but in terms of the erosion of hopes and ideals. The message once again returns to the idea that Greece is somehow held back by human fallibility from fulfilling the high expectations that have been invested in it by so many both now and in the past. Yet Markaris is not alone in seeing the roots of the crisis in these terms. It was nowhere more eloquently put than by Papandreou himself when he lamented to his audience in Thessaloniki in 2010, 'We built a world of bureaucracy and lust for power. A world of corruption, of small and big privileges and interests for anyone who could take advantage of other people. We managed to drown the hopes and dreams of a whole generation.'[123] The same themes can also be traced in the writings of a host of commentators, from Theodosis Tassios, who speaks of a generation of pimps who have exploited their children and are now forcing them to pay back the loans they shamelessly lived on, to Nikiforos Diamandouros, who talks of the 'submerged realities' of post-authoritarian Greece which includes the 'sense of omnipotence, invulnerability, and, ultimately arrogance' that the ability to dispense almost unlimited patronage gave to the elite.[124] Aside from human fallibility, the common strand within all these expositions is a rejection of the past and its practices or, it might be better to say, a certain understanding of the past, but what is not yet clear is the path that should be taken from this past to the future and, in particular, the extent to which this future should reflect the past. How clean should the break be and according to whose understanding?

The past has also been referenced as Greeks within the context of the crisis have continued to explore the place of their country in the world, with the issue of national identity, as might be expected, given the extensive literature on the subject, forming a strong subtext. This has been particularly obvious in the rhetoric of political groups such as Golden Dawn, but it has also underlain much of the general commentary on the crisis. In part it arose in reaction to differences between the Greek and foreign, especially German, media and an external narrative that portrayed Greece as being the 'sick man' or 'basket case' of Europe.[125] In response, the national flag was waved as a symbol of defiance at demonstrations—and the German flag burnt—and reports appeared that protesters were chanting the old Spartan cry of defiance, 'Come and take them' (Μολὼν λαβέ), said to have been uttered by King Leonidas in response to the demand by the Persians at the Battle of Thermopylae that his troops lay down their arms. There were also practical campaigns encouraging consumers to purchase Greek goods, with supermarkets prominently marking domestic products, usually with the national flag, and long lists circulated via email dictating which products and retailers should be patronised. The campaign made inroads into perceptions, with a large majority in opinion polls saying they favoured buying Greek products, but under questioning most admitted that price, availability and special offers were still the main determinants when it came to making a purchase. Yet, more than just an inspiration for defiance and national pride, as Greece teetered on the brink of exit from the euro, the past, and particularly the Ancient Greeks, also served to bind the country to a European future. Was not the very symbol of the euro derived from the Greek letter epsilon and are the new euro banknotes not called the Europa series after the ancient myth which provides the very name for the continent itself?[126] Numerous blog entries and chain emails repeatedly stressed the significance of the Greek language as the bedrock of many European tongues, with a speech once given by Zolotas in English in which every word is derived from Ancient Greek circulating widely. In this counter-narrative Greece stood not as a failed state on the margins of Europe but proudly as the fount of European civilisation at the heart of the continent. But even here ambiguities lurked. An imaginative staging of Aristophanes' *The Birds* in 2011 featured black-suited officials bestriding the stage to the lyrics of Laurie Anderson's song, 'Only an expert'.[127] The obvious inference was that the Athenians of today were seeking a better life outside the clutches of the Olympian Gods of the troika, but were their aspirations any more realistic than the Cloud Cuckoo Land of Pisthetaerus and Euelpides?

National symbolism was used to signal opposition to the memorandum and also to reaffirm the significance of Greece and the Greeks to the European story, even if it was only sometimes voiced in terms of mutual incomprehension as in Goin' Through's 2011 song, 'I don't understand', which asked 'which language they speak? Are they looking at me? The weeping are laughing? I don't understand what they say... Ask Europe why so much hatred? I am Europe too, like you, a bordello.'[128] However, the same narrative, in an alternative reading, could also be seen as exclusive, stressing the uniqueness of the Greeks, their difference from others and the importance of maintaining the purity of the national strain. This was mostly visibly expressed by Golden Dawn, with its party symbol derived from antiquity, which depicts the twists and turns of the Meander River, its flag waving parades and its nationalist rhetoric. Instead of reaffirming Greece's place in the community of nations, the Ancient Greek past was drawn upon by this group and others on the right, including a clutch of punk and heavy metal groups—a form of music with which Golden Dawn has been closely associated—to spread a message of distinction, with lyrics pressing for a racially pure, Greek speaking homeland. The crisis in conjunction with new technology has allowed what previously was more hidden to be openly articulated and widely disseminated. 'Patriotic' videos attract hundreds of thousands of 'hits' on YouTube, as do the speeches of the previous dictator Giorgos Papadopoulos, while blogs rage against what is seen as the moral degeneration of Greek society, especially homosexuality and a perceived decline in religious values and patriotism. Such ideas do not fit the narrative of crisis which stresses social solidarity and inclusion. Instead, they speak of division and a quest to apportion responsibility which, fanned by the words of the politicians and the media, has too often consumed society in a search for scapegoats, whether they be individuals, the political class as a whole or those who 'ate' the money of state largesse.[129] In such narratives the past is allowed to dominate not only the present, which remains for many little more than a continuous struggle for survival, but also the future and in the process the memorandum became not an instrument for building a new and better Greece, but in its unleashing of anger, hatred, envy and jealousy, one for tearing the country apart.

In this vision Greece is lost, cast adrift with little hope for the future and perhaps the strongest narrative to come out of the crisis has been that of despair, with surveys showing that half of Greeks see little purpose in life. This is the Greece of bleak anomie caught in the 2011 black and white film *Tungsten*, which is set in a wasteland that stretch from Tavros to Aegaleo in Athens.[130] The film interweaves the separate stories of a bus ticket inspector deeply indebted to loan sharks, a violent security company employee who beats up his girlfriend, and a couple of young drifters, one of whom is vainly trying to find a job. In a landscape of scars and dereliction, the stories slide towards despair, as the ticket inspector is beaten up by debt collectors and one of the young drifters is murdered by Sri Lankan migrants, after he sets fire to a moped, leading the other to take revenge with an old pistol. There is little hope in this world and the same sentiments occur frequently elsewhere, as in the film *Wasted Youth*, which is centred on the parallel lives of a sixteen-year-old school boy and a middle-aged policeman.[131] However, in this case it interacts directly with the crisis, cutting between the lives of the two protagonists until they come together in a denouement which is clearly a reworking of the death of Alexis Grigoropoulos. In both films the characters are trapped within their lives, and this can be easily extrapolated to stand as a metaphor for Greece in the hands of the troika, with the country a victim of wider forces it cannot control. In this conception there is an almost fatalistic acceptance that Greece and its people are powerless to determine their future. As one author wrote, the crisis has transformed 'our consciousness into an inability to dream', leaving a world in which 'nobody can look to the future' and 'our vision... [is] blurred'.[132] Stripped of the belief that the future will be better, hope can all too easily fade, and perhaps more than anything else it is the eroding of this virtue and its replacement by disillusion and despair that explains the particular depth and intensity of the crisis in Greece. The giant pair of inverted hands, praying downwards, painted on a wall on Pireos Street in the centre of Athens might be inspired by a work of Albrecht Dürer but the question it asks is very much inspired by the Greece of today: Is God praying for the Greeks rather than the Greeks to God?[133] With tomorrow becoming a source of anxiety and fear, and not hope, society turned in on itself, seeking solace whenever it could. Those previously immune to such rituals now crossed themselves as they passed a church or stepped inside to light a candle and offer a quick prayer for intercession. Lives more than ever have become determined by superstition, as the omnipresent evil eye, cast by known rivals and unknown strangers alike, came to be held responsible for all reversals, even illness. In this time of troubles life was something to be endured rather than constructed, and such patterns are not easy to reverse, since they require not just a rebuilding of confidence but also trust in society and fellow citizens as well as the government and the state.[134]

Yet pessimism, as much as the evil eye, is not new. It regularly seeped into opinion polls even before the crisis.[135] In part it was grounded in an economic reality in which some always found it difficult to make ends meet and many more struggled and failed to reach the material standards that the media had helped establish as the supposed norms of society. However, it also seems to stem from a widely held belief that Greece is essentially a dysfunctional state.[136] Such a view reaches deep into modern Greek history and the revival of a string of plays during the crisis appears in part to have been driven by a desire to remind of the strength of this narrative and its continuities, although synchronisation between the views of the directors and the audience cannot be taken for granted. Nonetheless, it is not difficult to trace parallels in works such as Alexandros Papadiamantis' novella *The Country Wreckers*, originally written in 1892, just a year before the Prime Minister, Charilaos Trikoupis, famously admitted the country was bankrupt, which caustically comments on the problem of 'buying' and 'selling' votes during an election campaign; and Alexandros Ragavis' 1845 *Koutrouli's Wedding*, which is filled with complaints about lack of meritocracy, clientelism and corruption. Through these works life in Greece can be read as a continuity, with the country trapped in an almost permanent state of crisis, which stretches far beyond the economy deep into the social fabric of the nation. This narrative permeates almost every understanding of public life from the allegations of corruption in the political arena to the stories of abuse of public funds reported with such relish in the media, with thousands said to have received disability benefits without cause and farmers falsifying certificates to gain subsidies, with cotton growers in Thessaly even said to have raised plants in flower pots to maximise their claims.[137] More insidiously this narrative is enacted in everyday encounters with an often inefficient public sector from the post office to the hospital and is heard in a myriad of tales circulating about people exploiting the 'system'. Whether it be the DEH employee who used his personal allowance to provide free electricity to a chain of shops; the motorist who always parks his car wherever he wants, secure in the knowledge that his friend in the traffic office will annul his fines; and the doctor, who unable to match the earnings of his colleagues working as surgeons, took to issuing fake disability certificates for a fee. Due to the fact they are relayed in person, often by people who claim first-hand knowledge, these tales acquire a particular truth, but how much they reflect the exception or the rule it is impossible to say, because after all they are just stories. However, taken together, they have created a narrative of systemic corruption, favouritism and greed, and this is so firmly rooted that the tendency has been for everything to be read to support this understanding. A news report on increased fare evasion on the metro during the crisis dwelt on what has almost come to be seen as the inherent dishonesty of Greek society rather than pointing out that even in these straitened times the vast majority of travellers still paid on a system which at that point had no real ticket barriers and little apparent means of inspection. The crisis has given an added twist of bitterness to this story of dysfunction as society struggles for dwindling resources and looks for culprits to blame. Perhaps as a result in one reading this time of crisis can only really come to an end through a radical caesura, which will decisively break with the past and set the country on a new path to the future.[138] Previously this has been sought through various local interpretations of modernisation and socialism but now it is the prescriptions of the institutions of the troika. Several times in the past, such a vision of radical change, which has sometimes been voiced in almost messianic terms, has been embraced by much of Greek society, but in the era of the memorandum belief that it offers a path to a better future seldom seemed to stretch beyond the bounds of a handful of government ministers and EU officials. Instead, running directly counter to this first reading another has come to prevail that holds that bureaucratic mismanagement, tax evasion, political clientelism and the tendency to abuse public funds is so deeply engrained in Greek society that nothing can be done to set things right. This feeds the narrative of despair and disillusionment that has permeated society throughout the crisis. A third reading, though, might try to look beyond both of these and argue that, as much as the narrative of dysfunction is grounded in realities, it is still only a construction. In its vivid description of the deficiencies of Greek life it might at times be a useful tool for analysis, suggesting what needs to be done, but at the same time it has also established a pattern of understanding that legitimises certain prescriptions and renders illegitimate others. Understanding that it is only a construction, allows for the possibility of moving beyond such a narrative and the idea of perpetual crisis that accompanies it, as well as the endless comparisons with other countries upon which it so readily feeds. Instead, another story may be permitted to emerge, as it has at times in the past, which posits that an exit from crisis can occur within the framework of existing institutional structures and norms without a radical caesura, which in its desire to expunge what are seen as the failures of the collective self may bring anomie instead of salvation. However, such is the strength of the narrative of perpetual crisis within the crisis that it seems to have become an unquestionable truth—and this makes it potentially destined to endless repetition.

EPILOGUE

The vote of 17 June 2012 might have given Greece a new elected government, but the partnership of New Democracy with the Panhellenic Socialist Movement (PASOK) and the Democratic Left (DIMAR) was uneasy. The remainder of the summer and early autumn was to be marked by constant horse-trading, as the parties squabbled among themselves and with the troika over further adjustment measures. As a result, even by late autumn, no further funding had been released. Yet, the election also seemed to herald a change of mood. Maybe it was just the warm weather, which continued long into the autumn, but the acute feeling of crisis which had gripped the country in the first part of the year began to slowly recede. There were still to be plenty of protests in the years to come. Indeed, 2013 was to see a record number, with over 6,000 in Athens alone, but the violent incidents after a general strike in the autumn of 2012 were relatively short lived and the 28 October parades of that year were not marked by the disruption of twelve months previously. The picture abroad was also changing. Initially the euro zone crisis seemed to be continuing as before, with Spain being forced to request €100 billion of financial assistance to recapitalise its banking sector. However, after Draghi had made a speech in London declaring that the European Central Bank (ECB) would do whatever was necessary to preserve the euro and the bank had unveiled a new programme for purchasing government securities on the secondary bond market known as Outright Monetary Transactions (OMT), the pressure on both Spanish and Italian bonds started to lessen. OMT did not fully deal with fundamental issues relating to the interdependence of states and banks, but its announcement has been credited with defusing the wider euro zone crisis as a whole, allowing Draghi, a year later, to call it 'probably the most successful monetary policy measure undertaken in recent time'.[1] The issue of interdependence was approached more directly within plans for a banking union which, after being endorsed in a June 2012 euro area summit, were finally agreed at a December 2013 Economic and Financial Affairs (Ecofin) Council meeting. This gave the ECB powers to supervise, rescue and even close banks, but doubts were voiced about its overall effectiveness, particularly since mutualisation was only to occur gradually and supervisory mechanisms remained largely rooted in national institutions. The single currency states, once the immediate pressures had passed, appeared to be no more ready than Greece to make deeper commitments to change, and underlining this a December 2012 European Council refrained from endorsing moves towards greater euro area integration. Nonetheless, despite the fact that Cyprus had been forced to seek financial assistance in March 2013, the wider crisis seemed to be ebbing. Economic uncertainties might continue, with concerns about deflation and a return to recession sparking much debate about whether the ECB should embark on its own programme of quantitative easing, but by the middle of that year the words 'euro zone crisis' had begun to recede from international headlines until they disappeared altogether.

As far as Greece's relationship with its euro area partners was concerned, there had also been a change for the better, underlined by an unexpected six-hour visit to Athens by Merkel in October 2012. This change had not come overnight. Merkel is said to have pondered the matter long and hard before being persuaded that it would be better for Greece to stay within the single currency than leave but, with so much of the country's debt in official hands, the costs involved in exit were now seen as being greater than those associated with remaining, especially at a time when the crisis was ebbing in the euro zone as a whole. The rhetoric of threat began to fade and shortly after Merkel's visit a euro area summit reinforced the message that the coalition government was to be supported and that exit from the euro, at least for the time being, was no longer considered a possibility. Yet, in reality, little was different as the government and troika held endless meetings and supposed deadlines came and went. Eventually, amid further strikes and mass demonstrations, in a late-night sitting early in November 2012, parliament narrowly passed an extensive package of measures and, a few days later, a budget for the next year with another substantial amount of frontloaded fiscal consolidation. With the government now judged to be showing the necessary resolve, the Eurogroup met and decided to endorse an adjustment of fiscal targets. However, no agreement was reached on releasing the funds that had been held back since the summer, in part, it seems, because of continuing differences over the issue of debt sustainability; and, with talk of crisis once more in the air, Greece was forced to hold a special auction of T-Bills to raise the funding for the redemption of a bond. Finally, at a further meeting of the Eurogroup at the end of November an agreement was brokered in which an adjusted debt sustainability target of 124 per cent of GDP in 2020 was coupled with a projection that it would be 'substantially' lower than 110 per cent in 2022. To make this feasible, the Eurogroup intimated that it would be 'prepared to consider' a further lowering of the interest rate on the loans provided under the original facility; the extension of maturities on both these and the European Financial Stability Facility (EFSF) loans by fifteen years, with interest payments on the latter also being deferred for ten years; as well as the transfer into the segregated escrow account of an amount equivalent to the income generated by Greek government bonds bought under the SMP programme by the central banks of the other euro area states. However, at the same time it also stressed that these measures would only 'accrue to Greece in a phased manner and conditional upon a strong implementation by the country of the agreed reform measures'.[2] To lower the debt more immediately, it was therefore also announced that the Greek authorities would be launching a bond buyback scheme using EFSF funding. As with the earlier debt exchange, this was by no means assured of success but, with domestic banks having little option other than to participate, the government was eventually able to purchase €31.9 billion of bonds at about a third of their nominal value. This was still above the level they had been trading in the market but, nonetheless, the face value of the debt was reduced by €20.6 billion. As a result, on 12 December 2012 the Eurogroup finally authorised the release of €34.3 billion in loans and sanctioned further payments of €14.8 billion provided prior actions were met. A few days later the ECB also revealed it was lifting a suspension of July 2012 and that it would once more accept collateral issued or guaranteed by the Greek state, paving the way for the banks to gradually reduce their dependence on Emergency Liquidity Assistance (ELA).

Greece and its crisis were moving out of the headlines in international media. In January 2013 the government passed a bill which simplified the structure of tax bands but also raised rates and lowered thresholds. Following this and some adjustments to the price of electricity, both the Eurogroup and the IMF agreed to release tranches of funding, but soon there were reports of another fiscal gap emerging and, although further money was disbursed after a revised medium-term fiscal strategy was endorsed by parliament in February 2013, talks once more ground to a halt. A general dispute over whether targets could be met without further austerity took more specific form over the perennial problem of public sector lay-offs. After further protracted negotiations, an agreement was eventually reached formalising civil service redundancies. It was supposedly to help meet these targets and the wider goal of improving public sector efficiency that a decision was made to close the state-run Hellenic Broadcasting Corporation (ERT). This was dramatically taken off-air in June 2013 while still transmitting, in a late-night police operation that prompted mass protests and an expression of 'profound dismay' by the European Broadcasting Union.[3] The abrupt closure of ERT reignited the volatile local political environment and led DIMAR to withdraw its support from the government. In the subsequent cabinet reshuffle prominent members of PASOK accepted posts, with Venizelos becoming deputy prime minister and minister of foreign affairs. The government's overall majority in parliament had been reduced to single figures but PASOK was now fully integrated into its structures and, subsequently, Samaras and Venizelos signed a forty-three point programme reiterating and strengthening points made in a July 2012 statement of aims. The new alignment further polarised the political arena, leaving the two parties willing to still work with the troika on one side and the remainder dominated by the Coalition of the Radical Left (SYRIZA) on the other.

Meanwhile, on 8 July 2013, the Eurogroup had agreed a further disbursement of funds but only after parliament had passed another lengthy omnibus bill. This proposed to place 12,500 public sector staff, mostly school employees and members of municipal police forces, in a new mobility programme that had replaced the old labour reserve. This prompted more prolonged strikes but only 3,000 gathered outside parliament to demonstrate on the night of the vote. The long years of austerity might have ground down the will to protest, but this did not mean the adjustment programme was any closer to being accepted. When the troika embarked on a further review, the chief points of dispute remained familiar, as the international officials pressed for the closure or restructuring of state-owned companies as well as the settlement of the debts of others to facilitate privatisation, the activation of the mobility scheme and further liberalisation of the restricted professions. Eventually a settlement was reached, allowing the release of a further €0.5 billion of funding on 17 December 2013 but, as the second adjustment programme entered what was scheduled to be its last year, its implementation remained as fraught and protracted as ever. After what one journalist termed the 'deepest strains' since the height of the crisis, on 1 April 2014 the Eurogroup agreed to disburse more funds once further conditions were met, but only after another omnibus bill had passed through parliament in a highly charged debate which at one point saw Tsipras pull SYRIZA MPs out of the chamber amid accusations that the government was 'selling the country piece by piece'.[4]

As ever the narratives continued to point in different directions. With the IMF talking of 'reform fatigue' and casting doubts about the government's commitment to tackling vested interests and freeing product markets, familiar accusations also surfaced that public sector redundancies, supposedly to be made on the basis of performance, were actually being decided by political criteria. Yet, at the same time progress was apparently being made on rebalancing the economy, with Greece in 2013 posting a current account surplus, reportedly for the first time since 1948. This was not, however, fuelled by any great surge in the export of merchandise due to improving international competitiveness, although the service sector, particularly tourism, continued to perform strongly. Instead, it was due more to a decline in imports, especially petroleum products, partly because of falling demand for petrol and heating oil. Nevertheless, by the end of 2013 there were more signs of economic recovery. In November the volume of retail trade rose for the first time since March 2010 and this trend was broadly sustained throughout most of 2014 although the rise in turnover was more muted as prices continued to fall. By September 2013 the unemployment rate was also dipping as government schemes created more jobs, especially for younger people, with the rate for the fifteen-to-twenty-four-year-old age group falling below 50 per cent. Most importantly, the long contraction of the economy also came to an end, with revised seasonally adjusted figures calculated under ESA 2010 methodology showing real year-on-year growth of 0.6 per cent of GDP in the first quarter of 2014. This was the first positive figure in this series since the first quarter of 2010 and, although a neutral figure was posted in the next quarter, when further positive figures were posted for the third and fourth quarters, this was the first time Greece had posted two consecutive quarters of positive growth on this basis since the winter of 2007–2008.

Equally significantly the European Commission in April 2014 also declared that in 2013 Greece had posted a primary surplus. This was trumpeted as being 'well ahead' of target but was only achieved by stripping out bank recapitalisation costs, which brought some criticism and a reminder from a Commission spokesperson that it was based on a 'country specific definition'.[5] Taken in combination with the upturn in other indicators the news reinforced growing investor confidence, which had seen the stock market rebound strongly since its low point in July 2012, allowing the government in April

2014 to return to the international financial markets with a placement of five-year bonds. The bond sale was accompanied by a car bomb exploding outside the Bank of Greece in the centre of Athens but was generally seen as a success. Buying in a market long stabilised by the OMT announcement, investors seem to have judged that there was little chance that they would be asked to take a further haircut. However, the yield on the bonds was still appreciably higher than the interest rate Greece was paying on its official loans and, while Ireland and Portugal by this time had exited their adjustment programmes, the picture regarding Greece was far from clear, with the troika still needing to conclude a fifth review before the final disbursements of funds from the EFSF could be made. However, when the mission heads arrived back in Athens at the end of September 2014, they left after only a little over a week, with Greek media sources again suggesting their departure had been precipitate. This was denied by the authorities but in reality the adjustment programme was already petering out.

Earlier in the year New Democracy had performed relatively poorly in the May 2014 European Parliament elections in which SYRIZA had emerged in front. The results prompted Samaras to reshuffle his cabinet and sparked renewed talk of an early general election. In an attempt to curb this, a parliamentary vote of confidence was called in October 2014. The government won the vote but not by a sufficient margin to stop speculation mounting that it would not be able to garner the required support to ensure the choice of its preferred candidate as president in a parliamentary vote due in the spring of 2015. If this was to happen, it would automatically trigger a general election, and to stand any chance of reversing the lead SYRIZA held in the opinion polls Samaras needed a successful conclusion to the adjustment programme and the disbursement of the remaining €1.8 billion of EFSF funds. However, after what was seen by the Greek side as a positive Eurogroup meeting at the beginning of November 2014, the troika sent an email to the Greek minister of finance intimating that a series of difficult measures would have to be implemented before the final, fifth, review could be concluded. The troika's stance reflected not only the outside world's increasing impatience with the pace of reform but also a growing belief that New Democracy's days in power were limited. Nonetheless, after the 2015 budget passed through parliament at the beginning of December 2014, the Eurogroup agreed to extended the adjustment programme by two months, until the end of February 2015, so the troika could complete its mission. Realising that rather than a swift end to the fifth review he faced the prospect of having to announce further unpopular austerity measures, Samaras, then, much like Papandreou with his decision to call a referendum, took almost everybody by surprise by announcing that the vote for a new president would be brought forward. It would now take place before the end of the year, but with the government only controlling 155 votes in parliament it always seemed unlikely that it would gain the two-fifths of votes needed to secure the election of its preferred candidate in the last of three possible ballots, let alone the two-thirds required in the first two. With fears again being stoked that a SYRIZA victory in any subsequent election might lead to Greece defaulting on its loans, outside voices weighed in to urge caution. Juncker, who had succeeded Barroso as president of the European Commission, publicly warned Greek parliamentarians against making the 'wrong' choice.[6] Outside media interest was rekindled in Greece. Bloomberg talked of a Greek crisis 'Mark 2' and, as share prices on the Athens Stock Exchange (ASE) began to fall and bond yields rise, the votes for the presidency took place over the Christmas period. The result was as most had foreseen, with the government, even on the third ballot, falling short of the votes required, leaving Samaras, having seen his gamble fail, no option but to call an early general election for 25 January 2015.

The main issue in the short and fiercely contested election campaign was the state of the economy. New Democracy touted the return to growth but this had still to bring tangible rewards for most ordinary citizens. So, instead, as in 2012, it relied more on stoking fears about what a SYRIZA victory would bring. However, this time the message failed to sway the increasingly jaded electorate and as a result New Democracy was left largely reacting to an agenda set by its left-wing opponents. This had already been in large part mapped out by Tsipras in a speech in Thessaloniki in September 2014. At its centre this speech contained a pledge that on entering office SYRIZA would replace the memorandum with a national reconstruction plan built on a number of pillars, including one addressing what were termed the 'humanitarian' aspects of the crisis which would introduce food vouchers for the poorest and an annual quota of free electricity to those unable to pay the normal tariff. Under the plan the new unified property tax would be replaced, labour legislation that had been introduced under the memorandum rescinded, hundreds of thousands of new jobs created, many in the public and what was termed the 'social sector', and what was seen as a democratic deficit addressed through legislation allowing citizens to sponsor referendums. ERT would also be re-established, and during the election campaign pledges were made that other staff dismissed from the public sector, including a group of cleaners from the ministry of finance who had mounted a high-profile campaign to regain their jobs, would be rehired.

When the election was held, SYRIZA increased its vote by over half a million to gain 36.3 per cent of the total, a figure greater than projected as opinion pollsters once again failed to track the underlying support for the party. Many of these new voters were former supporters of PASOK, which found itself relegated to seventh place, with just 4.7 per cent of the vote. Others came from DIMAR, which failed to garner enough support to enter parliament, the Communist Party of Greece (KKE) and various other parties of the left. During the campaign SYRIZA made many extravagant promises, but much of the electorate, including its own supporters, seems to have viewed these with a healthy degree of scepticism. Indeed, survey evidence suggests many of those voting for SYRIZA were less radical than the party's parliamentary deputies when it came to issues such as immigration and even austerity.[7] When this was combined with the goodwill that a new government often receives upon entering office and the distrust many continued to harbour for New Democracy and PASOK, it was to help the party retain popular backing in the coming months even after pressure from its European partners had forced it to abandon many of its promises. Perhaps most of all, though, the party won support through its pledge to end what was seen as the national humiliation of the memorandum. It was the party's slogan 'Hope is on the way' that spoke directly to the electorate, bringing it large majorities in areas such as the western suburbs of Athens and Piraeus where New Democracy found few supporters. Elsewhere the vote for the conservative party held steady, leaving it overall just over 100,000 lower than in June 2012. Yet, uninspired by a tired looking Samaras, who seemed to lack belief in policies he had so long opposed, and worn out by the years of crisis, many of those, especially among the middle class, who might previously have turned to New Democracy to prevent the radical left from gaining power seem to have lost the will to vote, a fact reflected in the continuing high levels of abstention. Thus, although the rhetoric might have been as uncompromising as ever, the polarisation was limited, with only some 40 per cent of the total registered electorate voting for one of the two leading parties. The sharp divisions of the past, when the vast majority had either voted for PASOK or New Democracy, had not been reproduced, and with around half of SYRIZA voters stating they felt no strong identity with the party and Golden Dawn failing to increase its share of the vote but remaining in third place, the political scene still appeared fluid.

In the end, when the bonus given to the winning party was added, SYRIZA gained a total of 149 seats in parliament, a figure still shy of an overall majority. However, in contrast to 2012, a new government was formed almost immediately, as Tsipras swiftly concluded a coalition agreement with Panos Kammenos, the leader of the Independent Greeks party (ANEL), which had entered parliament with thirteen seats. The fact that Tsipras chose as a partner a right-wing party with which SYRIZA had virtually nothing in common other than a shared desire to see the end of austerity was interpreted as a signal that there would be no softening of the party's position regarding the memorandum, the troika, debt restructuring or even seeking Second World War reparations from Germany. Indeed, Tsipras' first action after being sworn into office was to visit the Kaisariani firing range which has a deep symbolic importance for the Greek left as a memorial to executions by the Germans during the Second World War. The gesture was open to multiple interpretations. Aside from honouring the sacrifice of those on the left in the past and symbolically reaffirming the party's link with the national resistance of the Second World War, it was also inevitably read as a statement of intent regarding the stance that SYRIZA would be taking when dealing with the most powerful member of the euro area. However, at this point external reaction to the new government remained muted. Like Samaras' initial calling of the election, SYRIZA's victory had brought little reaction on foreign financial markets. Encouraged by the ECB's almost simultaneous announcement of its own quantitative easing programme, most European stock exchanges took the change of government in their stride and even posted a small gain on the first day of post-election trading. Only the ASE index faltered, with the value of bank shares falling by nearly a quarter in just two days. The response of the European political leadership was also in general circumspect. Suggestions from the new government that 'the greater part' of Greece's public debt might be written off were firmly rejected by its European partners, but they did intimate that they were open to the idea of extending the adjustment programme beyond the end of February to allow the troika review to be completed.

Virtually none of the ministers in the new government had previous experience of office, but, buoyed by their democratic mandate, during their first days in office, they struck a confident and at times combative pose. There was talk of quickly raising the minimum wage, halting privatisations and reemploying sacked public sector staff. The adjustment programme with its troika-inspired policies of austerity would be allowed to lapse and in its place the government would seek to agree a bridging loan with its euro area partners to allow what was termed a new 'contract' to be put in place by the beginning of June. This, it was believed, should include a reduction of the national debt, but rather than an outright write-off 'smart debt engineering' would see future interest payments linked to levels of economic growth. To sell this idea and to win support for the new government's programme in general, the Minister of Finance, Yanis Varoufakis, embarked on a whistle-stop tour of Europe, as did Tsipras. The new finance minister in particular, partly because of his informal clothing style, polished English and penchant for witty quips, attracted considerable attention and was able to dominate the outside media agenda, making it appear that his ideas were gaining traction. However, by the end of January there were clear signs that he was having less success with some of his European colleagues. Varoufakis held an awkward press conference in Athens with Jeroen Dijsselbloem, the Dutch finance minister, who had succeeded Juncker as president of the Eurogroup, and, at a meeting with Schäuble in Berlin, while the German finance minister noted that the two 'agreed to disagree', his Greek counterpart was reported to have more bluntly observed that they 'didn't even agree to disagree'.[8] This meeting was to be the prelude to a further deepening of the war of words between the two countries, as amid much petty name calling a more serious claim was advanced that Germany owed Greece hundreds of billions of euros in compensation for its actions during the Second World War.

In an increasingly difficult atmosphere the Eurogroup met on 11 February 2015 for what were afterwards termed 'intense' but also 'constructive' talks. Many of the ministers, including Schäuble, seem to have believed they had even agreed a statement, but for one reason or another this was not endorsed by Varoufakis. As a result, media coverage afterwards was negative, but the meeting had brought indications that the Greek authorities might after all be willing to request some kind of extension to the adjustment programme. Dijsselbloem has said that, when he met Tsipras the next day, they agreed that representatives from the bodies that had made up the troika, which were henceforth to be termed the 'institutions', would meet the Greek authorities to try and find a way forward. In the opinion of the Dutch finance minister the Greek side had been pushed into adopting a more accommodating position by the growing difficulties of the local banks. Deposit withdrawals, which had been running at a high level before the election, continued at a similar rate afterwards, so that by May €30 billion or 19 per cent of the total amount held by the banks at the beginning of the year had left the system. With the rate of non-performing loans also increasing, the banks had again been compelled to turn to the Bank of Greece, which under the sanction of the ECB once more began to issue ELA; from zero in December 2014 this rose to €78 billion in May 2015. The hand of the banks had also been forced by the fact that, the day before Varoufakis and Schäuble had met, the ECB's governing council on a split decision had voted to again stop accepting collateral issued or guaranteed by the Greek state on the basis that a successful conclusion of the adjustment programme could no longer be assumed. In the absence of any extension to the programme this waiver would have expired at the end of the month anyway, but the announcement that it would now terminate on the same day as the Eurogroup was due to meet was read by many as an attempt to put pressure on the Greek authorities, even prompting a demonstration in Syntagma Square in support of the government. Draghi defended the decision by reiterating once again that the ECB was a rule-based and not a political institution and, by acting before the Eurogroup was due to gather, it can be argued that the bank was merely ensuring it would not be associated with the outcome of its deliberations. However, when the head of the Bundesbank in a newspaper interview published the next day called for strict controls over the issuing of ELA, memories of the suggestion that this form of funding could be withheld from Cyprus in 2013 if the country's parliament failed to endorse an agreement were easily evoked.[9]

The woes of the banks were also in part caused by a renewal of concerns about state finances. As in the past, during the election campaign, some taxpayers seem to have held back from paying their dues in the belief that an incoming SYRIZA administration, which had pledged to rescind the unified property tax and once again raise tax thresholds, might lighten their burden, and as a result revenues again started to fall short of projections. With access to further adjustment programme funding ruled out until the successful completion of the fifth review, the government had hoped to tide itself over by drawing on money remaining within the Hellenic Financial Stability Fund (HFSF), the 'profits' accruing from the Securities Markets Programme (SMP) and issuing some more T-bills. However, the Eurogroup insisted that the HFSF money could only be used for its original purpose; the redistribution of the SMP 'profits' remained dependent on the successful conclusion of the review; and the ECB was unwilling to allow the domestic banks, who were the only ready buyers, to increase their purchases of T-bills, arguing that due to their reliance on ELA this would mean that the central bank was effectively financing the Greek state. Indeed, rumours soon began to circulate that the Bank of Greece was only managing to cover these sales by bidding for some of the bills itself, using the cash reserves of state entities. The circumstances were driving the various parties towards a compromise. However, this was not to come without several extended periods of high drama, with renewed speculation about Grexit being augmented by increasing discussion about the possibility of a 'Grexident', which would see the country depart from the single currency not by design but by accident, perhaps after a run on its banks.

A 16 February Eurogroup meeting was heralded as a final showdown, but amid claims and counterclaims about statements the gathering ended in such confusion that no communiqué was issued. Beyond the rhetoric, though, as usual, intensive discussions were taking place behind the scenes and, after some further confusion, which led to German accusations that the Greek authorities were trying to introduce a 'Trojan Horse', a document was finally presented at another Eurogroup meeting on 20 February. This proposed a further four month extension of the existing programme to enable the 'successful completion of the [fifth] review on the basis of the conditions in the current arrangement, making best use of the given flexibility which will be considered jointly with the Greek authorities and the institutions', providing the Greek government presented a preliminary set of proposals by the end of the following Monday that was acceptable to both the institutions and the Eurogroup.[10] These proposals were duly presented just before the deadline and, after the institutions had given a provisional assessment, they were accepted by the Eurogroup in a teleconference the day afterwards. Varoufakis suggested that the agreement was full of 'creative ambiguity' to allow passage of the extension through euro area parliaments, but outside Greece it was widely interpreted as little less than a capitulation by the Greek government.[11]

This interpretation stressed that the Greek authorities had been forced to accept an extension of a programme they had pledged to end; that the institutions would continue to evaluate and give judgement on their policies; and that they had committed themselves 'to refrain from any rollback of measures and unilateral changes to the policies and structural reforms that would negatively impact fiscal targets, economic recovery or financial stability, as assessed by the institutions'.[12] The veteran SYRIZA member of the European Parliament, Manolis Glezos, was quoted as saying the agreement was little more than 'renaming fish as meat', and at a meeting which lasted for over ten hours Tsipras faced criticism from the party's parliamentary deputies, with a number reportedly refusing to back the deal. Defending the agreement the prime minister, though, spoke of the government winning a battle, if not the war. He talked of a 'new framework' and stressed that the extension was for the funding arrangement, the Master Financial Assistance Facility Agreement, rather than the adjustment programme itself. The fact that Greece had secured the right to put forward its own proposals in his view also meant that the period of troika-enforced austerity had effectively come to an end. Indeed, according to the Greek premier, the very fact that the agreement had been reached at the Eurogroup level was an indication that normal interstate relations were again prevailing and that the power of the institutions to dictate events in Greece had been eroded. The institutions, though, were to take a different view. Like the Eurogroup they believed that the Greek proposals were merely a base for further negotiations, and that any future discussions should primarily be concerned with determining how much the adjustment programme was off-track and the drawing up of new measures to allow the fifth review to be successfully concluded. The meeting of minds was clearly far from total.

Both the managing director of the IMF and the president of the ECB penned letters voicing reservations about the 20 February agreement. Indeed it was to be the mere prelude to a new period of crisis, which, as one journalist remarked after a late-night euro area mini-summit, was 'just like the old days'. In many ways, with its succession of high-level negotiations, elapsed deadlines, alarmist headlines, leaked proposals, bland official statements and rumour and counter-rumour, it did seem like a return to the height of the crisis, although there were also important differences, most notably the lack of any real reaction within global financial markets. There was no return to the turmoil of 2011, partly because the fiscal position of the other weaker euro area states had since improved, but also because, with so much of the Greek debt in official hands, the risks were perceived to now largely lie with the states of the euro area rather than private bondholders. The initial target had been for the talks to be concluded by the end of April, but a Eurogroup meeting in Riga laid bare the continuing failure of the parties to agree. Donald Tusk, the former prime minister of Poland, who had succeeded Van Rompuy as president of the European Council, later admitted that a failure to insist on adherence to deadlines had been a mistake, but each side blamed the other for the lack of progress. European Commission officials spoke of the Greek authorities doing nothing for many months and rejecting the assistance of 'anyone who tried to help them', while Varoufakis complained of the institutions constantly raising new points, leaving the negotiators 'like a cat chasing its own tail'.[13] In trying to divine the Greek government's strategy much was made of Varoufakis' academic work on game theory, and it has been suggested that he was following a deliberate strategy of spinning out the negotiations in the belief that Greece's euro area partners would eventually offer better terms, although in reality the pattern of events that followed differed little from that seen previously in the crisis.[14] Some of his European colleagues also seem to have resented what they saw as the Greek finance minister's lecturing tone and, when it was announced that henceforth the Alternate Minister for International Economic Relations, Euclid Tsakalotos, who retains much of the understated demeanour of his English public school upbringing, would be taking the lead in the negotiations, it was held to be sufficient to explain a rise in global stock markets. However, for their part, both Varoufakis and Tsakalotos, who also comes from an academic background, openly rued the fact that their well briefed presentations cognisant of the particularities of the Greek economy, which they believed provided a constructive base for further discussion, were too readily swept aside by their negotiating partners in favour of arguments dwelling on the need to adhere to rules and establish verifiable fiscal outcomes.[15] Indeed, it was reportedly when the institutions reduced a lengthy Greek document to a mere five pages at the beginning of June, delivering what Tsakalotos was quoted as saying was a 'slap in the face' to the Greek negotiators, that the talks seriously began to flounder.[16]

The negotiating position of SYRIZA was circumscribed by its determination to ensure that its period in office would not be what it termed a 'left parenthesis'—a short interregnum before more centrist parties reassumed power. This meant that it was constantly balancing the demands of its negotiating partners against a need to consolidate its voter base at home and preserve unity within a fractious party that previously had been a coalition used to open debate. During the talks themselves, it is reported that several times the Greek negotiators in Brussels appeared willing to agree a deal only to withdraw and return after consulting colleagues in Athens with a changed stance, much to the irritation of the country's partners. Maintaining the balance between these demands meant that, while the leaders of SYRIZA continued to employ a strident anti-austerity rhetoric at home, more contentious policies, such as rapidly raising the minimum wage and scrapping the unified property tax, were quietly postponed, which led some within the party to talk of it being the subject of a 'soft coup' by its opponents in the worlds of finance and media. Instead, stress tended to be placed on more symbolic actions, such as reopening ERT, rehiring the ministry of finance cleaners, and passing a humanitarian crisis law that had only a limited financial impact but a compelling moral legitimacy. In particular the visits of the institutions of the troika to Athens, which personified for many the country's loss of sovereignty, were downplayed and, even after the 20 February agreement had stipulated that the officials should be made 'welcome' in the city, the talks were reported to be proceeding at a 'glacial' pace. This reluctance to engage with the institutions was also driven by a broader policy aim of seeking to bring an end to the crisis through what was again termed a 'higher level political agreement'. In attempting to achieve this, the Greek authorities focused their attention on a series of meetings involving Tsipras, Merkel, Hollande and the heads of the institutions, but the German chancellor retained the cautious rule-based approach she had adopted throughout the crisis and proved reluctant to move beyond the position of her negotiating partners or what she considered was acceptable to either her party or the German electorate. To bolster its argument for a political solution, SYRIZA also continued to insist that the Greek crisis had to be treated as part of a wider European problem. This led it initially to champion the idea of a euro area debt conference, and afterwards it persisted in projecting itself as the representative of the workers and youth of the continent as a whole in what it saw as their struggle against neo-liberal orthodoxy. Indeed, the idea that it was engaged in an ideological conflict was particularly played upon by SYRIZA's leadership, which frequently charged that conservative political forces elsewhere in Europe were deliberately fomenting the crisis to force the radical left party from office; and, in truth, the prevailing economic discourse within the euro area with its emphasis on continuing liberalisation did run counter to many of SYRIZA's stated beliefs. More specifically, within the context of the negotiations, Tsipras laid down a number of red lines on issues such as labour market and pension reform, changes in the rate of VAT and the sale of public property, which he repeatedly reiterated he was not prepared to cross, and, while providing transparency, these were also to limit the room for manoeuvre. Indeed, at its heart the Greek negotiating position seems to have continued to rest on two propositions: firstly, a belief that the country exiting the single currency would be a step into the unknown that carried as many perils for the remainder of the euro area as it did for Greece; and secondly, that the monetary union was irrevocable and that Greece's place within it could not legally be challenged. This, it was claimed, was what distinguished the euro area from a fixed exchange system with a shared currency. If Greece was to leave the single currency, it would not only set a precedent which other euro area members might be tempted to follow in future crises but it would also undermine the integration ideology underlying the wider European project.

For their part Greece's euro area partners and the IMF also at times seemed divided, especially over the issue of debt restructuring. However, there seems to have been a general consensus that the fifth review should be properly completed and, as the negotiations dragged on, a growing emphasis was placed on the lack of trust between the sides to provide space for demands that Greece should take more and more prior actions as confidence building measures. Especially in the Greek media, where it was often given a strong moral twist, the confrontation was presented as being between Germany and Greece, but in reality the picture was more confused. Other northern European states, such as Finland, Austria and the Netherlands, to a greater or lesser extent shared German concerns and in some cases had coalition governments which included parties opposed to giving Greece further assistance. East European members tended to feel little sympathy for a country which, in relation to their own, was relatively wealthy. Portugal and Ireland, having undergone their own programmes of austerity, seem to have felt that any relaxation of Greek conditions might cast into doubt the legitimacy of their own experiences. And the same was also true of Spain where the rise of a party ideologically allied to SYRIZA, Podemos, made the ruling People's Party particularly wary. Countering Greek reasoning, an argument was also increasingly advanced that the euro area was now in a position to weather any Grexit. After so many years of economic depression, by 2015 Greece accounted for less than 2.0 per cent of euro area GDP, and the exposure of the wider zone's commercial banks to the country was only a fraction of what it had been in 2010. Government finances in most of the more vulnerable states were also much stronger than in the past; the European Stability Mechanism (ESM) was in place as were the OMT and quantitative easing programmes of the ECB. Grexit could thus be perceived as being broadly manageable, although as a proportion of GDP the greatest cost would be borne by east and southern European states, such as Malta and Estonia. Cyprus also remained particularly vulnerable. Even the argument that Greece was legally unable to leave the euro area was increasingly being challenged, especially if the departure was voluntary.

Not only did the view seem to be growing that any contagion within the financial markets in the case of a Greek exit from the euro would be containable but the growing weakness of the country's financial situation also gave it little option but to compromise. The ECB continued to permit the amount of ELA the Bank of Greece could issue to rise only little by little, leading Tsipras to complain that it was effectively placing a rope around the government's neck.[17] However, the ECB contended that it was doing as much as it was permitted under its rules, with Draghi stressing in July that in the six months since the election it had more than doubled its lending to Greece. With revenues stalling, the Greek authorities were also only able to continue to post a small primary surplus by cutting back on payments, leading arrears to again rise sharply. As its coffers started to run dry, the government turned to social security funds and other state entities for finance, requiring them to place their reserves in a common fund to help it fill any gaps, although some initially were said to have refused for fear of legal challenge if the state was to default on its borrowing. A law was eventually passed obligating such transfers for all but pension funds, although reports suggested many local authorities still refused to comply, with the notable exception of Thessaloniki. A payment to the IMF in May was only met by Greece taking the unusual step of tapping its reserve fund for the institution and, with rumours circulating that the government was finding it difficult to meet wage and pension payments, amid a new wave of rating agency downgrades, speculation mounted that the country would be unable to meet a series of forthcoming payments to the Washington-based institution as well as one to the ECB to cover the redemption of a bond.

Indeed two crucial deadlines loomed at the end of June. The first, long known, was that the four month extension of the adjustment programme would expire, when the Greek authorities would not only lose the chance of tapping undisbursed funds but also, it was widely presumed, the country's banks would cease being eligible to draw ELA, which in all probability would lead to their collapse. The second had just arisen at the beginning of June when the Greek authorities, using a little-known provision previously only employed by Zambia in the 1980s, had elected to bundle together the various sums it owed the IMF that month into a single payment to be made at its close. If the country failed to make this payment, it would be the first time a Western state had ever fallen into arrears with the IMF. The rating agencies had declared they would not categorise this as a default since it involved an official lender, but, nonetheless, it was expected to be read as evidence of insolvency, which could lead to both the ECB applying a deeper haircut to Greek collateral and the board of the EFSF asking for the immediate repayment of its loans. With time running out, the various sides entered into an increasingly frantic round of negotiations. The Eurogroup and euro area leaders, either as a small group or in a full summit, met repeatedly amid headlines proclaiming that the crisis had reached its apogee and disaster awaited not only Greece but also possibly the euro zone as a whole. As the sense of crisis intensified, so did the war of words. One Greek minister was quoted as complaining that every time a solution was almost reached the institutions asked for a few more pensioners to be executed, while Tsipras openly accused the IMF of bearing 'criminal responsibility' for the situation in the country.[18] For their part, IMF officials were said to be willing to cut off their little fingers rather than extend their relationship with Greece, and after one Eurogroup meeting Lagarde was reported to have spoken of the need for dialogue with 'adults in the room' in what was widely taken to be a thinly veiled jibe at the Greek negotiators.[19] By the middle of the month the Greek financial system was showing signs of increasing strain. The ASE index fell nearly 15 per cent in three days, and deposits were reported to be leaving the banks at such a rate that the ECB's governing council started to assess Greece's ELA needs on a daily basis. Amid increased speculation that capital controls might soon be imposed, a new document was presented by the Greek authorities on 22 June with what, Tusk declared, were the first 'real proposals' in many weeks. Nonetheless, after the institutions had scrutinised the document, it was returned covered in comments in red ink as they rejected government proposals for a special tax on companies and other measures seen as potentially curtailing economic growth, and proposed instead the abolition of subsidies on diesel oil for farmers and cuts in military spending. Amid a flurry of proposals and counter-proposals, a succession of Eurogroup meetings attempted to break the deadlock and the two sides appeared to be edging towards a compromise when, in the evening of 26 June, the Greek delegation unexpectedly withdrew from the talks in Brussels. A few hours later in the early hours of the morning, looking tired and drawn after a lengthy cabinet meeting, Tsipras appeared on television and, just as Papandreou had four years before him, announced that he was putting the latest proposals to a referendum, with the vote scheduled to take place in just over one week's time on 5 July 2015.

When he announced the referendum, the Greek premier's language was emotive as he talked of the latest proposals being an ultimatum bringing unbearable new burdens designed to humiliate the entire Greek nation.[20] Yet, in reality, his choice to hold a referendum seems to have been determined by the fact that, in the face of growing unease within the ranks of SYRIZA, he had come to realise that, when the latest proposals from the institutions were presented to parliament, he would either face a party rebellion and possible defeat, prompting a new election, or win the vote but then lack sufficient legitimacy to carry out measures which differed so radically from his previous programme.[21] The referendum was apparently seen as a relatively low cost strategy to resolve this conundrum and to strengthen his position both inside Greece and in his negotiations with euro area partners. Perhaps as a consequence of this, when the question upon which the electorate was called to pronounce a simple 'yes' or 'no' was revealed, it was lengthy and convoluted. The Greek people were asked whether or not they wanted the authorities to accept two documents. The first was a long text bearing the imprint of SYRIZA in its stress on the need to tackle the social crisis and strengthen fairness across society but which at its core had a series of measures required by the institutions.[22] It was a negotiating outline rather than a final text endorsed by the Eurogroup, and when the second programme lapsed prior to the referendum, it effectively ceased to have any validity. The second document was a debt sustainability analysis containing a number of scenarios, a technical exercise which the institutions were still in the process of reconciling. It was therefore perhaps not altogether surprising that the secretary general of the Council of Europe suggested the referendum fell short of its standards due to both the brevity of the campaign and the complexity of the question.

At least some of those taking part in the negotiations seem to have been taken by surprise by the announcement of the referendum. Merkel was warned beforehand but Dijsselbloem was not, and within the European Commission talk of betrayal once more emerged. Once it became clear that SYRIZA would be urging a 'no' vote, signifying rejection of the documents, a barrage of criticism followed, with Juncker in a particularly emotional speech urging the country to vote 'yes'.[23] Indeed, the message of the political leadership of the EU was unequivocal, as one after another they warned that a 'no' vote could only mean Greece's exit from the euro. For some this appeared to be foreshadowed when the statement of a Eurogroup meeting, which was held as scheduled on 27 June despite the calling of the referendum, carried a footnote recording that it had been supported by all members except the Greek.[24] Inside Greece, within hours of the referendum being announced, photographs started to circulate on social media showing queues forming outside cash machines. By Sunday morning these were becoming longer and, on the same day that the ECB's governing council convened and decided not to authorise any increase in ELA, the Hellenic Systemic Stability Council met in Athens and decided to recommend the imposition of capital controls. The doors of the banks were closed and withdrawals from ATMs limited to €60 per debit card per day.[25] Credit cards could be used as normal but nearly all foreign transfers were prohibited except for those authorised by a special committee. The restrictions on the banks opening were soon eased slightly to allow pensioners who did not possess debit cards to withdraw money over the counter, but the capital controls themselves remained in place, which meant that the referendum campaign was conducted amidst queues outside banks that were constantly rumoured to be running out of money and close to collapse. Yet the impact of the move was essentially limited to Greece. The controls had been imposed at the weekend, but, when global markets reopened on Monday, the reaction was muted; and this continued to be the case on 30 June when the IMF payment was missed and the second adjustment programme was allowed to lapse. At least for the time being, to all intents and purposes, market pressures had ceased to be a driving force within the crisis.

Having called the referendum, the Greek government broadly followed a two-pronged strategy. On the one hand, it sought to keep open channels of negotiation with its European partners. Therefore, after Varoufakis' request for a short extension of the adjustment programme beyond the end of June to allow the referendum to be held was rebuffed at a Eurogroup meeting, supposedly on the grounds that national parliaments within the euro area would be unable to pass the required legislation, on 30 June Tsipras sent a letter to the European Commission as part of a request for both an extension of the existing programme and a new one under the provisions of the ESM.[26] On the other hand, the government sought to harness and channel to its cause the popular enthusiasm unleashed by the calling of the referendum, the result of which increasingly seemed in doubt because of the appearance of a vocal 'yes' campaign backed by much of the local mainstream media. The 'no' campaign was fronted by SYRIZA with its coalition partner ANEL. Golden Dawn also encouraged its supporters to cast their vote in this way. In phrasing the question to make its preferred option 'no' the government was clearly playing upon the rejection of an ultimatum presented by Mussolini at the beginning of the Second World War, which is celebrated in Greece as the annual *okhi* (no) day national holiday. This link was further evoked by ministers referring to the last negotiating document of the institutions as an ultimatum as well as in claims that casting a 'no' vote would amount to a reassertion of national sovereignty. Within the 'no' campaign there was also much play on other themes and narratives which had featured prominently within the crisis, including resistance, suffering and victimisation. Tsipras spoke of Greeks regaining their dignity and one poster bearing a picture of Schäuble carried the slogan 'For five years he has drunk your blood—now tell him no'.[27] Indeed, the discourse had been so internalised within Greek society that many of those interviewed on the street by journalists echoed the same sentiments as the politicians almost word for word. The 'yes' campaign was backed by New Democracy, PASOK and *To Potami*. It was fronted by the popular mayors of Athens and Thessaloniki rather than a national politician, presumably in recognition of the limited appeal Samaras was thought to hold for many voters. Nonetheless, its campaign followed a pattern familiar from those of New Democracy as it pointed to what it called the broken promises of SYRIZA and the dangers of exit from the euro. Yet, as previously during the crisis, the dilemma posed was essentially false. Relatively few of those who supported the 'no' campaign wanted to leave the single currency and the vast majority expected that Greece would not only stay in the euro but also that the negotiations with its partners would continue afterwards.[28] Likewise, a 'yes' vote did not mean support for continuing austerity. It just reflected a fear that a 'no' might really herald exit from the single currency.

After a week of intensive campaigning that saw huge mass rallies reminiscent of the heyday of PASOK and New Democracy, the opinion polls, which had showed the two camps as being neck and neck, again proved flawed as the 'no' campaign secured an easy victory winning 61.3 per cent of the vote as opposed to 38.7 per cent by its opponents. Despite the passions evoked by the campaign, the turnout was just 62.5 per cent, although this relatively low figure presumably reflected not only any deficiencies within the official registers but also the fact that many people on the electoral roll had left the country during the long years of crisis. The partisan nature of the campaign meant that the vote broadly reflected party preferences, but in general 'no' supporters seem to have been the young, the unemployed, those living in the countryside, perhaps because of the growing strength of SYRIZA in many rural areas, where it seems to have taken over the organisational structures of PASOK, and those battered to such an extent by the crisis that they felt they had little left to lose. Those who voted 'yes' tended to be the elderly fearing that rejection of the negotiating documents would put in jeopardy their pension payments, live in urban centres and, it was generally assumed, still had savings to lose in the chaos that might be unleashed if Greece was to leave the euro. Afterwards the referendum was seen by many, especially in the 'yes' camp, as being largely pointless, since its result was subsequently in effect ignored. However, it strengthened the position of both Tsipras and SYRIZA, effectively polarising the electorate, which had been forced to take a decision along essentially party political lines. It also weakened the opposition and prompted the resignation of Samaras. Indeed, the sheer scale of the 'no' victory facilitated a coming together of the parliamentary parties. With the exception of Golden Dawn, the leaders of these met the following day and, aside from the head of the KKE, agreed a short statement in which they accepted that the referendum was not the basis for a rift with Europe but a chance to achieve a socially just and economic sustainable accord to which each party leader would 'contribute within the context of their institutional and political role'.[29] This newly found sense of consensus strengthened Tsipras' position in relation to his own party, allowing him to marginalise those discontented with the negotiations. These also included Varoufakis who quickly resigned. As questionable as SYRIZA's handling of the external negotiations may have been, Tsipras' political strategy inside the country was proving highly effective.

The result of the referendum had been greeted with exuberant celebrations in the centre of Athens, but Tsipras in his statement afterwards was circumspect, dwelling on the need to build national unity and return to the negotiating table. Around the time capital controls had been imposed, at a meeting with senior colleagues, Varoufakis seems to have advocated a combative response to the pressure he felt the ECB was applying on Greece that, nonetheless, stopped short of the country leaving the euro. Specifically, he proposed that the government should either issue IOUs or declare that it was going to issue some form of euro-denominated liquidity, announce or impose a haircut on Greek government bonds held by the ECB and take control of the Bank of Greece.[30] If Varoufakis' advice had been followed it would have led to an escalation of the crisis, but it was rejected by most of the others present and now in the wake of the referendum the Greek premier continued to adopt a conciliatory approach. Likewise, although some euro area politicians were open in their dismay at the outcome, with Dijsselbloem speaking of a result 'very regrettable for the future of Greece', most seem to have been content to allow their response to be shaped by a series of meetings which were now rapidly scheduled. Again unwilling to be seen as pre-empting any decisions, by a majority rather than unanimously, the ECB's governing council also voted to maintain ELA at existing levels but adjusted the haircut on Greek collateral. As a result, the banks remained effectively closed but retained sufficient capital to continue to allow ATM withdrawals at the same level. At the first Eurogroup meeting after the referendum on 7 July, the new Minister of Finance, Tsakalotos, was expected to table further proposals but instead gave a verbal presentation which was said to be well received. It was only at the summit that followed immediately afterwards that the euro area response to the referendum result became clear. Amid media headlines of the EU facing the most critical moment in its history, Tusk warning of the possibility of Greece going bankrupt, Juncker admitting that the Commission had prepared a scenario for the country's exit from the euro, which included providing humanitarian aid, and members of the ECB's governing council cautioning that if the leaders did not reach an agreement the bank would be unable to continue to sanction the provision of ELA, the Greek authorities were given an ultimatum of 9 July to produce new proposals.

As this deadline approached, unverified rumours circulated in Athens that French officials were helping draft new proposals and Hollande, who had a meeting with Merkel immediately after the referendum, led a chorus of French politicians insisting that Greece had to stay in the euro. However, when the proposals were presented, a couple of hours before the deadline, they bore a remarkable resemblance to the final negotiating paper released by the European Commission prior to the referendum. There was a slight softening of some conditions relating to farmers, VAT on distant islands, over the counter medicines, ferry charges, privatisation of the electricity grid, the minimum wage, labour market reforms and cuts in military expenditure, as well as some additional passages on controlling government expenditure and combating tax evasion. Otherwise the documents were nearly identical, with, crucially, the same budgetary targets, starting with a primary surplus of 1.0 per cent of GDP in 2015. While the new proposals were being scrutinised by the institutions, they were put before the Greek parliament for approval as a negotiating position. With the support of the mainstream opposition parties they passed after an all-night debate by 251 votes to 32. The ANEL deputies eventually gave their approval, but foreshadowing future dissent two SYRIZA parliamentarians voted against and fifteen others either abstained or were absent. Afterwards the French and Italian governments suggested that the proposals formed a good basis for negotiations, but little was heard from German sources and the external media narrative continued to suggest that Grexit remained imminent. The Eurogroup met on 11 July but, after what many sources say was a bad tempered encounter, the ministers adjourned at midnight to allow further modification of the proposals. In particular, the fate of a short paper from the German finance ministry was unclear. This included two options, the second of which proposed giving Greece what was termed a 'time-out' from the euro zone of at least five years, ostensibly to give time for its debt to be restructured within an informal framework similar to what is known as the Paris Club.[31] Although ministers denied it had been discussed, and it is possible that it was merely a negotiating ploy, the option of some kind of Greek exit from the euro area had nevertheless been tabled. Eventually, after fourteen hours of discussions, as the euro area leaders assembled for their own summit, on 12 July the Eurogroup agreed a four page document. As

Dijsselbloem noted, they had come a long way in their discussions but key issues still needed to be resolved.

As so often in the past, the fate of Greece was to be decided during a mammoth summit, although this time it exceeded all records by lasting seventeen hours, perhaps partly because the leaders were no longer governed by the deadlines of the financial markets. At times the meeting was interrupted so that a smaller group including Tsipras, Merkel, Hollande and Tusk could gather, and, after one of these encounters, there were reports that the talks nearly faltered, but in the end the blurry-eyed leaders emerged in mid-morning on 13 July to announce a deal had been struck. Afterwards, the general tone of the media commentary was that Germany had gained the agreement it wanted and that Greece had been humiliated, with some reports even talking about Tsipras being 'crucified'.[32] However, the path had been opened for Greece to gain the €7.16 billion of short-term bridging finance it needed to clear its arrears with the IMF and cover the redemption of a bond held by the ECB. Furthermore, it had also been effectively accepted that Greece would require a mid-term financing package worth up to €86 billion, with the agreement suggesting funding might come from the ESM, IMF and, rather optimistically, privatisation proceeds and market sources. Indeed, given the fact that only a year before it had been regularly suggested that Greece might only require precautionary credit lines after the end of the second programme, this was sufficient to allow some to argue that it was in fact the German authorities who had capitulated since they had been forced to accept there would be an expensive third adjustment programme with no guarantee that it would have a better outcome than the previous two.[33]

Under the agreement the Greek parliament was required to pass four laws by 15 July and a further two by 22 July. The first laws broadly implemented the VAT and pension provisions included in the 9 July document, gave full legal independence to the national statistics authority and mandated 'quasi-automatic' cuts in expenditure if there were deviations from the 'ambitious' primary surplus targets. This enforced a provision of the previously signed Treaty on Stability, Coordination and Governance in the Economic and Monetary Union but it still led one observer to comment that it meant that 'If Greece is in a hole, the rest of the euro zone will hand it a spade and tell it to keep digging'.[34] The quasi-automatic cuts had been a key part of the first set of options outlined in the German finance ministry paper and a number of other features of this now appeared in the remainder of the agreement alongside familiar measures drawn from previous negotiating positions relating to pension reform and product and labour market liberalisation. There was also talk of reducing the cost of the civil service within a general capacity building and de-politicisation programme which, in words that could be read as echoing previous plans, would be 'under the auspices of the European Commission'.[35] Relations with the institutions were also to be normalised, which meant not only the resumption of monitoring visits in Athens but also that they would retain an effective veto over any legislation which could be interpreted as relating to the programme. Indeed, aside from the humanitarian crisis law, the document raised the possibility that any legislation passed since the government had taken power running counter to the memorandum could be rescinded. Equally controversially, in another partial resurrection of previous ideas, €50 billion of state assets would be placed in an independently managed fund, which through outright sale and other means would raise money to recapitalise the banks, pare down the public debt and invest in the economy. Long advocated by some of Greece's partners, including Germany, which had established a similar agency to divest East German assets after unification, the establishment of this body was designed to both end political interference in the privatisation process and to reassure other euro area states that Greece would contribute to the assistance package and not leave them bearing all the costs. Initially the assets were scheduled to be transferred to the Luxembourg-based Institution for Growth in Greece, a fund established by the Samaras government with the 'guidance and support' of the German KfW development bank, the European Investment Bank (EIB) and other investors. However, after protests from Tsipras it was agreed they would remain under independent Greek management in Athens but be under the 'supervision' of the institutions.

Condemnation of the agreement surfaced on Twitter even during the negotiations and afterwards it was widely attacked by commentators both inside and outside Greece on the grounds of the harshness of its conditions, its morality and the damage it inflicted not only to the wider European project but even to the concept of democracy. The Nobel laureate, Paul Krugman, termed it 'pure vindictiveness' and even *Der Spiegel* called it a 'catalogue of cruelties', although an opinion poll suggested that most Germans viewed the agreement as fair or even too lenient on Greece.[36] Yet, Tsipras had little option but to conclude an agreement. In talks before and during the summit Juncker, Lagarde and Draghi had all stressed the severity of the situation and the extent to which Greece had become reliant on the support of their institutions. Under capital controls the Greek economy was faltering. The banks had been closed for two weeks, with little sign that they would soon reopen. Some medicines were said to be running short as well as foodstuffs, with the import of meat coming to a virtual halt. Perhaps most importantly of all, though, the Greek premier had no real alternative. Some members of SYRIZA had been advocating what they termed a 'progressive' exit from the euro involving the nationalisation of the banks within a broader programme of increased public ownership and state control of the economy. However, even under this scenario assets and liabilities would have to be redenominated into the new currency—which would be a challenging task given the level of integration within the euro area—and considerable technical difficulties surmounted. Nonetheless, preliminary planning for some sort of disengagement from the Eurosystem does seem to have taken place, with Varoufakis forming a small committee under the coordination of an American academic in March 2015. This produced a lengthy memorandum that foresaw, among other steps, any withdrawal from the euro necessitating the nationalising of all banks, including the Bank of Greece, and even the possible establishment of a new institution to replace the latter, the imposition of capital controls and the introduction of a new currency, which in the absence of printed banknotes might, as was suggested at one point, have at first circulated as over-stamped euro notes. However, this contingency planning never seems to have extended beyond the bounds of this highly secret committee and with even the memorandum it produced admitting that abandoning the euro would be a leap into the unknown a more general lack of foreign reserves and tangible support from countries such as Russia seems to have combined to effectively rule it out as an option.[37] Indeed, if anything, it was the European Commission that appears to have been better prepared for such an eventuality, since over the years it seems to have drawn up detailed plans in case Greece was to leave the single currency, as presumably had other euro area finance ministries.

The first set of prior measures passed the Greek parliament on 15 July although not without a further rebellion in the ranks of SYRIZA inside the building and the resumption of street protests and violence outside, as riot police again clashed with petrol bomb throwing protesters. This was followed the next day by the ECB sanctioning a €900 million rise in the amount of ELA that could be issued, which was sufficient to allow the banks to reopen on 20 July after three weeks of effective closure, although this initially did little more than move the queues from the ATMs inside the buildings. The passing of the measures also cleared the way for the Commission to issue an implementing decision releasing the €7.16 billion bridging loan which, it had been agreed, would be funded by the European Financial Stabilisation Mechanism (EFSM) once the interests of non-euro area countries had been safeguarded, although some reports later suggested the money actually came from the ESM. The money was used to pay first the arrears of the IMF as senior creditor and then the ECB and other euro area central banks, including the Bank of Greece. Once this had occurred, the board of the ESM chaired by Dijsselbloem agreed that negotiations on a new programme could begin. The mission heads duly returned to Athens and the talks proceeded smoothly, allowing the institutions and the Greek authorities to conclude a technical agreement on 11 August. This was subsequently endorsed by the Greek parliament on 14 August and by the Eurogroup as well as other euro area national assemblies, including the German, although there were again signs of dissent within Merkel's parliamentary group. With it being judged that Greece had largely complied with the fifty-three prior actions required by the 12 July agreement, on 19 August, one day before a €3 billion payment was due to the ECB to cover another bond redemption, the Greek authorities signed a Financial Assistance Facility Agreement specifying the terms of the loan and a new Memorandum of Understanding with the European Commission acting on behalf of the ESM, detailing the conditions that needed to be met to permit disbursement of future funds. This paved the way for the release of a substantial part of a first tranche of funding totalling €26 billion. Half of this sum was mostly used to repay the bridging loan and cover the redemption of the bond held by the ECB, while €10 billion of the remainder was placed in a segregated account at the ESM for bank recapitalisation and resolution purposes.

The new memorandum covering the period 2015–2018 was a dense thirty-two page text. With its extensive lists of reforms designed to restore fiscal sustainability, safeguard financial stability, enhance competitiveness and growth, and modernise the public administration, it bore many similarities with previous documents and also according to its critics many of their flaws.[38] However, in comparison to pre-referendum negotiating papers there were also signs of greater pragmatism. Budgetary targets had been substantially reduced, so that instead of a primary surplus it was now accepted that Greece would post a primary deficit in 2015 before running a small surplus in 2016. Only the 2018 target of a primary surplus of 3.5 per cent of GDP remained unchanged. These lower targets, which required a relatively small amount of further fiscal consolidation, were largely prompted by sharply reduced growth forecasts, with the country now expected to only return to positive growth in 2017. Likewise, although the overall €50 billion 'target' for the asset fund was retained, a more modest privatisation goal was established of €6.4 billion in the period 2015–2017. The modernisation of the state administration would also probably be hardly more intrusive than before since it would occur under the auspices of the Commission's recently established Structural Reform Support Service, which was basically a permanent enhanced Task Force. Significantly it was also accepted that all the funding for the programme might have to come from the ESM. It was still hoped that the IMF would make further contributions and that privatisation proceeds and market funding might be tapped as well, but it was no longer taken for granted.

Inside Greece, the 12 July agreement was roundly condemned by some sections of the governing parties. Varoufakis termed it a 'new Versailles treaty', while others spoke of the euro area leaders as 'brutal blackmailers' who had launched a coup.[39] It was therefore hardly surprising that the passage of the various pieces of legislation associated with the agreement saw increasing numbers of SYRIZA MPs rebelling against the government, until forty-three failed to give it their support in the 14 August vote. The growing dissent placed the government's parliamentary majority in question and so, the day after the new memorandum was signed, Tsipras resigned as prime minister to force a general election. Eventually, on 27 August, the President of the Supreme Court, Vassiliki Thanou, was sworn in as the first female prime minister of Greece; but, prior to this, constitutional provisions relating to the calling of an election so soon after a previous one had dictated that the leaders of the two biggest opposition parties both be given an opportunity to form new governments. The first of these had been the president of New Democracy, but rather than the head of Golden Dawn the second had been the leader of a new grouping based on the dissident voices in SYRIZA called Popular Unity. Twenty-five SYRIZA MPs initially joined the party which, in its explicit rejection of austerity and the memorandum, and its openness to a possible return to the drachma, sought to be a voice for those who had voted 'no' in the referendum. In the general election of 20 September SYRIZA again confounded the pollsters, who had predicted a tight race. For all the drama of the previous months, with its endless negotiations, policy shifts, capital controls and splits within the main ruling party, the result of the January election was almost exactly replicated, with SYRIZA enjoying a clear lead over New Democracy, although little more than half the registered electorate voted. Popular Unity failed to enter parliament. Tsipras quickly announced SYRIZA would be reforming its coalition with ANEL, but, alongside saluting the resistance and dignity of the Greek people, he also stressed that the road ahead would be hard as, in words that echoed many of those before him, he declared his victory was a mandate to curb vested interests and put an end to systemic corruption.

Following the general election, SYRIZA looked set fair to dominate the Greek political landscape for some time to come. Yet, only a year later, few could be found who were willing to declare themselves content with the performance of the government, and a resurgent New Democracy under a new leader, Kyriakos Mitsotakis, the son of the former premier, was consistently ahead of its rival in opinion polls. Instead of hope and renewal, the SYRIZA-led government for too many electors had brought little more than disappointment and continuity with the recent past, as the supervising institutions continued to play a powerful role in the country's life. At the end of 2016, when the government decided to use some of its greater than projected primary surplus to postpone a requirement to increase VAT rates on some islands and reinstitute a small Christmas bonus for poorer pensioners without consulting the institutions beforehand, voices in Germany were quick to express their irritation at such unilateral actions and a short-term debt relief plan, announced by the Eurogroup just days before, was put on hold, it was said, until the institutions had been able to fully consider the implications of the new measures.

Nevertheless, after the general election the government's relations with the institutions and Greece's euro area partners did improve. Perhaps in part this was because all sides felt that little had been gained during the previous months of tense negotiations but there was also a new need to buttress political stability at a time when hundreds of thousands of displaced people from the Middle East were crossing into Greece from Turkey in a bid to reach Germany and other countries in western Europe. This 'migrant crisis' placed considerable additional strain on both the Greek economy, costing the country perhaps €600 million, and the social fabric of the nation. It also once more placed Greece at the heart of both world media attention and a major EU crisis, underlining again the tendency of this state of the so-called 'periphery' to frequently stand centre stage in significant European events.[40] Yet, in spite of this, the disbursement of further tranches of funding under the third programme continued to be a fraught process, with the institutions insisting on new measures to close funding gaps which resulted in yet more tax hikes. With significant differences in key areas such as privatisation and labour reform also remaining, even if relations were less tense, there was little change in the familiar narrative which told of a Greek government struggling—effectively or ineffectively depending on viewpoint—to ameliorate the worst consequences of an adjustment programme which was being foisted onto the country by outside forces, with little attention being paid to any potential longer-term gains that might accrue.

Adding even further complications were continuing disagreements between the institutions themselves over the thorny issue of debt sustainability. The Eurogroup's assertion that this could be achieved through a combined strategy of further lowering debt servicing costs and Greece continuing to maintain a high enough primary surplus to gradually pare down its borrowing was rejected by the IMF, partly on the basis that it believed that the primary surplus targets were unsustainable over the longer term. Instead the Washington-based institution, which needed to judge the debt was sustainable before it could draw up a new Greek programme to replace the one that had lapsed at the beginning of 2016, argued that there should be a further haircut of Greece's borrowing. This was an approach which, in turn, its European partners who held the greatest part of this debt continued to rule out as they had in the 12 July 2015 agreement, largely on the grounds that it was incompatible with Article 125 of the Treaty on the Functioning of the European Union. For its part, the Greek government, while seeking to secure a substantial reduction in the debt, implacably opposed the imposition of any further austerity measures. The result was another standoff and in the early part of 2017 attempts to break this logjam by setting another largely artificial deadline led to a further spate of international headlines suggesting Greece was on the verge of another crisis. The Greek government had no need of any extra funding until summer and outside commentators, showing signs of weariness with what seemed like a never-ending Hellenic drama, tended to presume that the dispute would again end in the familiar pattern of compromises being reached just before or even after any deadlines had passed. However, at the beginning of 2017 the international environment was changing. Already in 2016, the United Kingdom had voted to leave the EU and the United States had elected a new President, Donald J. Trump, who had publicly signalled his reluctance to intervene in any resumption of the Greek debt crisis, and now, in 2017, a string of forthcoming elections in the Netherlands, Germany and France offered plenty of opportunities for shifts in European political balances. At the time of writing, the end of this latest dispute has yet to be scripted and, although it still seems most likely that a compromise agreement will again be reached, these changes in the wider international environment raise the possibility that the outcome may yet not be as entirely expected.

The situation inside Greece in early 2017 also had a depressing familiarity. As so often in the years since 2010, two narratives could be traced. The first, mostly emanating from official sources, stressed the changes that had occurred in many areas, with the OECD suggesting that the various liberalisation measures within the economy had already added billions of euros to the country's GDP. As a result, both the European Commission and the IMF were forecasting that the economy would grow strongly, with the latter suggesting this could be by up to 2.8 per cent of GDP in 2017. There were also some signs of greater consumer spending on items such as cars although this also contributed to an increase in imports, and, with a lack of any concomitant rise in exports, this meant that the balance of trade again deteriorated. For alongside this narrative of success there, as always, lay another of despair. With nearly a quarter of the workforce without a job the unemployment rate in Greece at the beginning of 2017 is still the highest in the EU; for most of those in work wages remain paltry; and with tax rates rising above EU averages more than 70 per cent of respondents in a survey declared that they feared they would be unable to meet the state's demands. Economic growth remains patchy, with provisional seasonally adjusted data for the fourth quarter of 2016 suggesting that it has again turned negative, and capital controls remain in place. These have been gradually loosened since they were first imposed and it can be argued that a €420 a week bank withdrawal limit is more than adequate in a country where the average salaried income has dropped to under €1,000 per month; but psychologically the persistence of the controls marks Greece out as still living through exceptional times. Even if, after the passage of so many years, it is not always easy to continue to describe Greece as being in the throes of a crisis, it is also clear that both the country and the lives of its inhabitants are still far from returning to anything close to the normality of yesteryear.

At the beginning of 2017, with little sign of the country recovering from the effects of the crisis, it would be all too easy to view the problems that beset Greece as being intractable, destined to constantly reproduce themselves across time. As far back as 1854 the French essayist and novelist Edmond About was writing of Greece being 'the only known example of a country living in full bankruptcy since the day of its birth', adding 'All budgets, from first to last, are in deficit'.[41] Equally pertinently he also remarked that, while in France or England such a situation would have quickly resulted in catastrophe, Greece had somehow managed to live peaceably with bankruptcy for many years; but more recent authors have tended to highlight the endemic weakness of state finances, noting the country was in an almost continuous state of default from the war of independence until after the Second World War.[42] Certainly parallels can easily be drawn between the crisis of the twenty-first century and past events such as the bankruptcy of 1893, especially since it was followed a few years later by the establishment of an International (Financial) Control Commission made up of representatives of the Great Powers that had the right to intervene in the civil administration to ensure sufficient taxes were collected to allow the state to meet its liabilities to its creditors. Through such parallels not only has there been a tendency to reflect the past onto the present but also, it sometimes seems, even the future. This is because the causes of crisis are also often portrayed as constant, with About's comments on the inefficiency of the civil administration and the tax collecting service finding ready recognition in many of the commentaries of today. And yet, the origins of the 1893 bankruptcy, at least from a short-term perspective, actually lay outside the country in a collapse of world currant prices. This was caused by both a recovery in global production levels after disease had devastated crops and a decision by France to impose high import tariffs, which effectively closed this important market to Greek exporters. However, looking at the issue from a more long-term point of view, it could be argued that the 1893 crisis was actually caused by a fragile domestic ecology which had produced an overdependence on a single export that made the country vulnerable to external shock. Viewed from different timeframes and perspectives either internal or external factors can be seen as predominating and the same would also seem to be true today. It is a similar intermingling of factors that provides the best explanation for the causes of crisis. In truth, however, the past rarely maps comfortably onto the present, and rather than searching for historical analogies it may be more productive to consider the importance of the popular narratives that have been constructed over the years around these issues of bureaucratic efficiency and tax evasion, as well as others relating to clientelism, vested interests, profligacy and resistance. Occupying a central place in popular understandings of everyday life, these narratives have been constantly reproduced to meet current needs, whether it be domestic actors arguing that only a radical caesura can wrest Greece from its pre-modern attributes or outside politicians citing an inability to clamp down on tax evasion to justify the imposition of further austerity measures. No real understanding of the crisis in Greece is possible without grasping the importance of these narratives and not just the power and significance they command within the domestic discourse but also the limits they place on meaningful debate.

In the past the role of the outside world in the region has often been viewed negatively, from the nineteenth century essayist who saw the western powers as deliberately keeping Greece emasculated to the scholars associated with the world systems school of thought in the twentieth century. Within a core-periphery framework they argued that what was frequently termed the 'backwardness' of the south-east European states was mostly due to exploitative activity by external capitalist powers. Others, though, have suggested that the terms of trade were not so skewed as they argued, and that connections with the West provided the conduit through which modern rational forms were introduced into what at the time were still essentially pre-modern societies. The end result of this process was meant to be the transformation of the countries of the region into quintessential modern states. However, in the face of a more prosaic reality such ideals remained unfulfilled, and this has reinforced a narrative of incompleteness that for some of those on the left in Greece stretches as far back as the nineteenth century revolution, which is viewed as unfinished due to the failure of popular social forces to consolidate their victory.[43] This notion of incomplete modernisation lies at the heart of many explanations of the crisis. It is the product of a discourse which, in seeing progress as inevitable, has imposed its own definitions of pre-modern and modern on Greek society, most recently in the moderniser/underdog dichotomy discussed in Chapter One. However, in real life such neat categorisations can rarely be made. Instead, traits are subsumed within more fluid identities which enable both ordinary citizens and members of the domestic elite to be as 'modern' as they want in their own particular ways.[44] Even before the recent crisis the morality of a domestic elite, let alone a foreign one, imposing significant costs on society to effect its transformation had been questioned, but beyond this in their binary outlook these categorisations also both impose simplicity on complexity and produce a tendency to see everything that differentiates the periphery from the core as a weakness. Indeed, arguably at one level the crisis has been about how or, indeed, if, diversity can be valued and accommodated within the rigidities of modernity as it is defined by the euro project.

The crisis in Greece and the wider euro zone has posed a considerable challenge to the EU. When a large part of Athens had to be cleared to ensure the security of the visiting chancellor of the most powerful member of a group of countries bound closely together within a common currency, the pictures of eerily deserted streets stood testament to a European project whose wider consequences had yet to be fully understood. In particular, the crisis brought into question the idea that the EU and its common currency were intrinsically forces for progress and social and economic development, not just within Greece but also the union as a whole, where it helped fuel the voice of those more sceptical of their value. After the creation of the single currency it was presumed that the process of European integration would deepen further, leading ultimately to political union, but instead diversity and imbalance as much as convergence remained the order of the day. No joint crisis resolution mechanism was developed and the euro area response to the turmoil within the global financial system in 2008 remained uncoordinated and incomplete. By one calculation, if the maturities of Greek government bonds had been extended in 2010, the cost of assistance to the country might have been kept to less than €45 billion.[45] In part this lack of coordination may have been because the response to the crisis was frequently based on national rather than common European interests, with even the ESM designed not as a traditional EU institution but rather as a 'sort of credit cooperative'.[46] However, the re-emergence of the notion of periphery and core as part of the everyday lexicon of the crisis suggests that problems foreseen at the time of Greece's entry into the EEC in 1981 remain far from solved. Indeed, the advent of the euro has, if anything, made the distribution of resources within the union an even more pressing issue, as it has contributed to a reduction in international competitiveness and therefore, over the years, in economic growth in states such as Greece while at the same time speeding a process of agglomeration which appears to be working in favour of the area's core. Aside from the narrower issue of how an optimum currency area should be constructed, the crisis in Greece has therefore also helped feed a more fundamental debate about how smaller countries away from the core and populations that feel they are marginalised within that core can flourish in a globalised world in which universal rules are expected to predominate. This debate has contributed to the rise of powerful, more nationally orientated, political movements in both Europe as well as the United States and has raised the possibility that there may yet be a protectionist backlash against globalisation.

Perhaps as a result of the role of the European Commission within the troika, an autumn 2016 opinion poll found that in Greece more people had a negative opinion of the EU than in any other member state.[47] However, at the same time, well over two-thirds of Greek respondents also said they supported the euro, perhaps in part because of their internalisation of the long-standing discourse emphasising the catastrophic consequences that exit from the single currency would bring. The consensus in Greece, where the balance between security and sovereignty remains as ever at the heart of political calculations, still seems to be that participation in the single currency in the long-term will be beneficial and that it is in the country's national interest to remain a member. And yet, as noted above, it still is far from clear how this desire can be squared with building a successful modern economy. The institutions maintain this can come with the completion of liberalising reforms but their prescriptions continue to be viewed with mistrust in a Greece where almost the entirety of the population in 2016 considered the economic situation to be 'bad'. Instead many both within and without Greece continue to believe that the more pressing need is to resolve systemic weaknesses within the architecture of the single currency, if not the global capitalist system itself. As it stands, no sure forecasts can be made about the future, and in general this book has shied away from constructing an overarching narrative which might have allowed such a projection to be made.[48] It has instead tried to draw a picture of a complex interlocking matrix of economic, political and social factors which only when they are taken as a whole can provide an explanation for both the crisis and the failure of the Greek economy to as yet stage any sustained recovery. Any simplification of this matrix to favour one explanation or another runs the risk that not only the wrong conclusions will be drawn but also, since the crisis and its malign consequences have far from disappeared, that the wrong solutions might be applied. Since the causes of the crisis in Greece were complex and multifaceted so must ultimately be the solutions.

ABBREVIATIONS

ADEDY   Confederation of Civil Servants [Ανώτατη Διοίκηση Ενώσεων Δημοσίων Υπαλλήλων, ΑΔΕΔΥ]

ANEL   Independent Greeks [Ανεξάρτητοι Έλληνες]

ASE   Athens Stock Exchange

ASEP   Supreme Council For Civil Personnel Selection [Ανώτατο Συμβούλιο Επιλογής Προσωπικού, ΑΣΕΠ]

ATM   Automated Teller Machine

bps   Basis points

CAC   Collective Action Clause

CDS   Credit Default Swaps

CDU   Christian Democratic Union of Germany

CEO   Chief Executive Officer

DEH   Public Power Corporation [Δημόσια Επιχείρηση Ηλεκτρισμού, ΔΕΗ]

DIMAR   Democratic Left [Δημοκρατική Αριστερά, ΔΗΜ.ΑΡ]

ECB   European Central Bank

Ecofin   Economic and Financial Affairs (Council)

ECU   European Currency Unit

EDP   Excessive Deficit Procedure

EEC   European Economic Community

EFSF   European Financial Stability Facility

EFSM   European Financial Stabilisation Mechanism

EIB   European Investment Bank

ELA   Emergency Liquidity Assistance

EMU   Economic and Monetary Union

ERM   Exchange Rate Mechanism

ERT	Hellenic Broadcasting Corporation [Ελληνική Ραδιοφωνία Τηλεόραση, ΕΡΤ]
ESA95	European System of Accounts 1995
ESA 2010	European System of Accounts 2010
ESM	European Stability Mechanism
EU	European Union
EU-15	The 15 member countries of the EU prior to the accession of ten candidate countries on 1 May 2004
GDP	Gross Domestic Product
GNP	Gross National Product
GSEE	General Confederation of Workers of Greece [Γενική Συνομοσπονδία Εργατών Ελλάδας, ΓΣΕΕ]
HFSF	Hellenic Financial Stability Fund [Ταμείου Χρηματοπιστωτικής Σταθερότητας]
IIF	Institute of International Finance
IMF	International Monetary Fund
IOBE	Foundation for Economic and Industrial Research [Ίδρυμα Οικονομικών και Βιομηχανικών Ερευνών, IOBE]
IRI	Institute for Industrial Reconstruction [Istituto per la Ricostruzione Industriale]
KKE	Communist Party of Greece [Κομμουνιστικό Κόμμα Ελλάδας]
LAOS	Popular Orthodox Rally [Λαϊκός Ορθόδοξος Συναγερμός, ΛΑ.Ο.Σ]
LTRO	Longer-Term Refinancing Operation
NBG	National Bank of Greece [Εθνική Τράπεζα της Ελλάδος, ΕΤΕ]
NSS	National Statistical Service [Εθνική Στατιστική Υπηρεσία της Ελλάδος, Ε.Σ.Υ.Ε.]
OAE	Organisation for Rehabilitation of Business Firms [Οργανισμός Ανασυγκρότησης Επιχειρήσεων, ΟΑΕ]
OECD	Organisation for Economic Co-operation and Development
OMT	Outright Monetary Transactions
OSE	Hellenic Railways Organisation [Οργανισμός Σιδηροδρόμων Ελλάδος, ΟΣΕ]
OTE	Hellenic Telecommunications Organisation [Οργανισμός Τηλεπικοινωνιών Ελλάδος, ΟΤΕ]
PAME	All-Workers Militant Front [Πανεργατικό Αγωνιστικό Μέτωπο, ΠΑΜΕ]
PASOK	Panhellenic Socialist Movement [Πανελλήνιο Σοσιαλιστικό Κίνημα, ΠΑΣΟΚ]

ABBREVIATIONS

PDMA	Public Debt Management Agency
PMI	Purchasing Managers' Index
PSBR	Public Sector Borrowing Requirement
PSI	Private Sector Involvement
SMP	Securities Markets Programme
SYRIZA	Coalition of the Radical Left [Συνασπισμός Ριζοσπαστικής Αριστεράς]
T-Bill	Treasury Bill
VAT	Value Added Tax [Φόρος προστιθέμενης αξίας, ΦΠΑ]

NOTES

INTRODUCTION

1. Tsoucalas (1969); Clogg (1986).
2. For the 1980s see Vergopoulos (1988) and for crisis in the 1990s see Keridis (1997) and the other essays in Allison & Nicolaïdis (1997); see also Pirounakis (1997) and the tenor of many of the contributions in Constas & Stavrou (1995).
3. See, for instance, references to crisis in 'Tackling the fiscal crisis', *ekathimerini.com*, 15 May 2004, available https://goo.gl/XbmbrD; 'Summer holidays 2005: many Greeks planning to stay at home; most will not venture very far away', *ekathimerini.com*, 30 July 2005, available https://goo.gl/WX83Pu; as far as can be ascertained, as of the end of 2016 the electronic resources cited in this book remain accessible. However, the crisis has already led to the disappearance of some electronic archives and it is entirely possible that others may yet follow. The propensity for media organisations and the European Union to change URLs regularly also presents additional problems and for this reason sufficient information has been given, when possible, to allow references to be identified through search engines or paper copy if necessary.
4. 'Μαύρη λίστα για όσες εταιρείες επιμένουν...ακριβά', *Kathimerini*, 30 May 2008, available http://goo.gl/KIGXUU
5. 'Η κρίση χτυπά την πόρτα μας', *Kathimerini*, 19 Sep. 2008, available http://goo.gl/DkhrWr
6. 'Βιομηχανία, οικοδομή, λιανεμπόριο και τουρισμός στη δίνη της κρίσης', *Kathimerini*, 22 Feb. 2009, available http://goo.gl/cPLuBH
7. See 'Πλήττονται από την κρίση ένδυση, υπόδηση, έπιπλο', *Kathimerini*, 12 Apr. 2009, available http://goo.gl/rL6hr2
8. The figure is drawn from the work of Metron Analysis, available http://goo.gl/apA3Mg
9. Layoun (2011).
10. 'Πρόσωπα και απόψεις', *Skai*, 27 Mar. 2011, available http://goo.gl/gzn9KH
11. 'Christine Lagarde: can the head of the IMF save the euro?', *Guardian*, 25 May 2012, available http://goo.gl/19BdVC
12. See, for instance, 'L'Allemagne au coeur du débat français', *Le Monde*, 23 Apr. 1997, available http://goo.gl/FDJykX; it sporadically appeared in 2008, as in a BNP Paribas report

quoted in 'Euro suffering from "reserve currency curse" as investors pull out', *Daily Telegraph*, 30 May 2008, available http://goo.gl/QTGa9x; 'Why PIGS can't fly', *Newsweek* (Atlantic edition), 152: 1/2, p. 467; and *Financial Times*, 1 Sep. 2008, where the Lex Column carried the headline 'PIGS in muck'. This brought a reprimand from a Portuguese minister; see 'Pigs in muck and lipstick', *AFP*, 15 Sep. 2008, available http://goo.gl/0UJK0t; 'Media monkey's diary', *Guardian*, 8 Sep. 2008, available http://goo.gl/uxOLHc; when 'PIGS to S&P slaughter', *FTAlphaville*, 19 Jan. 2009, available http://goo.gl/UBMSdk; appeared the journalist who wrote the piece stated in the comments that she believed she was just using a widely accepted acronym but subsequently the term was barred within the *Financial Times* and some investment banks. See 'Anything but porcine at Barcap', *FTAlphaville*, 5 Feb. 2010, available http://goo.gl/7zfoSk; by 2010 Ireland had entered the acronym either replacing Italy or becoming an extra I in PIIGS. See 'Acronym acrimony: the problem with Pigs', *Guardian*, 12 Feb. 2010, available http://goo.gl/Zgjpgu; 'Europe's PIGS: country by country', *BBC News*, 11 Feb. 2010, available http://goo.gl/3ssWFR; for an academic discussion of the issue see Brazys & Hardiman (2013).

13. 'Greece acknowledges debt concerns', BBC News, 30 Nov. 2009, available http://goo.gl/oPfxk9

14. 'Understanding the eurozone crisis', *Forbes*, 17 May 2010, available http://goo.gl/XWOsRV

15. Lynn (2011); Manolopoulos (2011).

16. D. Kontogiannis in noting that the memorandum followed the line that it was a liquidity crisis suggests that this was partly due to the need for haste and the inexperience of the officials involved. 'Soft and hard default scenarios draw closer for Greece', ekathimerini.com, 4 Sep. 2011, available http://goo.gl/KhN66d

17. Montiel (2014), p. 11, defines a solvency crisis as when 'the present value of the government's projected future primary surpluses falls short of the face value of the government's outstanding net debt'.

18. Alcidi, Giovannini & Gros (2011) argue that most independent analysts considered Greece faced a solvency problem from the beginning of the crisis

19. Bastasin (2012), p. 148.

20. For examples of some different approaches see Kouvelakis (2011); Mitsopoulos & Pelagidis (2011); Featherstone (2011); Lapavitsas, Kaltenbrunner & Labrinidis et al. (2013); Katrougalos (2012); Mitropoulos (2012); Karamouzis & Hardouvelis (2011); Veremis, Kalyvas, Kouloumbis et al. (2011).

21. OECD (2016); 'Annual National Accounts', *Hellenic Statistical Authority*, 10 Oct. 2014, available http://goo.gl/M1LYoc this figure is widely cited but other accounting methodologies give slightly different results. See 'Greek GDP nowcasting model update', *Eurobank Global Markets Research*, 22 Oct. 2014, available http://goo.gl/mGf030; few statistical figures regarding the crisis can yet be treated as sacrosanct. Statistics are prone to revision for several years after they are first announced and over an even longer period if accounting methodologies change or important subsets are introduced, as with seasonally adjusted growth figures. In many cases, as here, the figure quoted is the one widely accepted at the beginning of 2017 but elsewhere initially released figures are used when the need is to explain political and market reactions.

22. Laskos & Tsakalotos (2013), pp. 104–105; Pelagidis & Mitsopoulos (2014), p. 81 talk of a

Greek 'Great Depression'. The initial phase of the Great Depression was followed by a second decline between a peak in May 1937 and a trough in June 1938 and, if depression is judged in terms of a return to previous pre-depression output levels, it can be said to have lasted until 1940 or 1941.

23. For an attempt to distinguish various meanings in Greek see D. Ioannou, 'Η «διαρθρωτική κατάρρευση» της ελληνικής οικονομίας', *Foreign Affairs: The Hellenic Edition*, 17 May 2013, available http://goo.gl/3VfkHR

24. As regards other analogous events: Argentina is said to have suffered a similar decline in GDP between 1998–2002 and Finland to have seen a fall of 11 per cent between 1990–1993, while in Russia economic output collapsed by 45 per cent between 1990–1998, although this was at a time of high inflation.

25. Kehoe (2007) uses the term 'depression' in relation to Argentina but note that in the title of an earlier version of the same paper Kehoe (2003) he had preferred the word 'crisis', merely mentioning that the Argentine government was using the term 'depression'. In Conesa, Kehoe & Ruhl (2007) the same author writing with two co-authors uses the word 'depression' in relation to Finland as do Gorodnichenko, Mendoza & Tesar (2012), who suggest that it was the largest slump in an industrial country since the 1930s. For examples of the use of the term in relation to Greece see 'Update 1-Greece sinks deeper into depression in third quarter', *Reuters*, 14 Nov. 2012, available http://goo.gl/N9bjQS; Pelagidis & Mitsopoulos (2014), who entitle a chapter of their book 'The depression of the century'.

26. OECD (2013), pp. 10, 19, 53; OECD (2016).

27. Bank of Greece (2014) and Palaiologos (2014). From another perspective, Kornelius (2013) gives a chapter of his book the same title. For examples of the use of the term 'Great Recession' see Jenkins, Brandolini, Micklewright et al. (2013); Chorafas (2014).

28. This approach follows arguments developed in the conclusion of Siani-Davies (2005).

29. Το βίντεο με τη δήλωση Πάγκαλου: "μαζί τα φάγαμε"', *YouTube*, 29 Oct. 2010, available http://goo.gl/YXuWtR; eating can serve as a metaphor for the appropriation of public funds by both politicians and civil servants. See Theodossopoulos (2013), p. 202.

30. The line came from the 1960 film *Τρεις κούκλες κι 'γω*, available http://goo.gl/GzqEKM; for examples of spoofs see 'Μαζί τα φάγαμε—το τραγούδι', *YouTube*, 14 July 2011, available http://goo.gl/tWKIY8; 'Μαζί τα φάγαμε—Aomatoi Productions', *YouTube*, 13 Nov. 2011, available http://goo.gl/rEqjrK. In a 2010 opinion poll only 20 per cent of respondents felt that society as a whole should take full responsibility for the crisis. See Karyotis & Rüdig (2015).

31. The figures come from various polls by Metron Analysis.

32. Knight (2012).

1. THE TEMPEST OF PROGRESS: THE SEARCH FOR ECONOMIC STABILITY AFTER THE DICTATORSHIP

1. Economist Intelligence Unit (henceforth EIU), *Greece: Quarterly Economic Review*, 1, 1973, p. 9.

2. Dragoumis (2004), pp. 30–42; Thomadakis (1995), p. 102; Freris (1986), pp. 155–200 more prosaically calls it 'the take-off that never was'.

3. For the economy in general at this time see Pesmazoglu (1972); OECD (1972).

4. Halikias (1978), p. 63.

5. 'Employers, workers protest price rises', *Athens News*, 3 Nov. 1973.

6. 'Markezinis takes over', *Athens News*, 9 Oct. 1973.

7. For the Polytechnic uprising see Kornetis (2013), pp. 253–80.

8. McDonald (1983), p. 82.

9. UK National Archives, Foreign and Commonwealth Office (henceforth FCO) 9/2003.

10. Diamandouros (1984), p. 53.

11. FCO 9/2734.

12. Arvanitopoulos (1994), 76; 'Premier, "I am a socialist BUT"...', *Athens News*, 21 June 1975.

13. FCO 9/2831; see also in general Katsoudas (1978); Pappas (1999).

14. Pagoulatos (2003), p. 29; Psalidopoulos (1996).

15. 'Κώστα, θα σε παρασύρουν στην καταστροφή!', *To Vima*, 1 Apr. 2012, available http://goo.gl/VNnE3R

16. 'Greece V: labour relations', *Financial Times*, 7 June 1978.

17. Vergopoulos (1988), p. 108.

18. Psomiades (1982), p. 255; Dragoumis (2004), p. 58.

19. Clogg (1987), pp. 59–81.

20. Siani-Davies & Katsikas (2009), p. 567.

21. Samatas (1993).

22. FCO 9/2831.

23. Kalyvas (1997).

24. Thomadakis (1995), pp. 106–110.

25. Spourdalakis (1988), pp. 74–81.

26. Dimitras (1987), p. 70.

27. Ioannou (1986).

28. Kyriazis (1995), pp. 275–80.

29. See in general Kornetis (2013).

30. Freris (1986), p. 158.

31. See in general Halikias (1978).

32. EIU, *Greece: Quarterly Economic Review*, 1, 1980, p. 9.

33. FCO 9/2001.

34. Pesmazoglu (1972), p. 78.

35. For industralisation see Mouzelis (1980), pp. 253–56.

36. Dimitras (1987), pp. 70–71.

37. EIU, *Greece: Quarterly Economic Review*, 4, 1974, p. 6; Clogg (1987), pp. 157–58.

38. Strogylis (1995), pp. 169–74.

39. Karakousis (2006), p. 22.

40. 'The Andreadis banks affair', *Athens News*, 18 Dec. 1975. The story is discounted by Nikolaou (2008), pp. 40–45.

41. On the importance attached to state control of credit at this time see Pagoulatos (2003), p. 199.
42. 'Bureaucracy in Greece is "shocking" industry undersecretary charges', *Athens News*, 20 Jan. 1978.
43. 'Mitsotakis addresses OPIC mission', *Athens News*, 26 Oct. 1979.
44. On the contrast between the 'grand gestures' of political leaders and the difficulties of every-day negotiations see Wallace (1979).
45. Wallace (1979), p. 24; Alogoskoufis (1995), p. 157.
46. Verney (2011), 59–60; 'Greeks are pre-occupied with post-Junta feelings of guilt', *Athens News*, 14 Apr. 1976.
47. FCO 9/2734.
48. Freris (1986), p. 165.
49. Spraos (1991), p. 178.
50. Fouskas (1997), p. 68 quoting Angelos Angelopoulos.
51. For the economy in general at this time see Katseli (1990).
52. 'Economy out of control PASOK leader claims', *Athens News*, 10 June 80.
53. On this issue see Alogoskoufis & Philippopoulos (1992); Paleologos (1993).
54. Vergopoulos (1988), p. 108.
55. Arvanitopoulos (1994), p. 66. Karamanlis was addressing an international forum but his remarks reflected his concerns about Greece.
56. 'Premier calls for self-restraint', *Athens News*, 7 May 1977.
57. Theodossopoulos (2013), p. 204.
58. 'Excessive consumption and waste', *Athens News*, 27 July 1979.
59. Vergopoulos (1988), p. 113.
60. Dimitras (1987), pp. 71–72.
61. EIU, *Greece: Quarterly Economic Review*, 1, 1980, p. 8.
62. 'Europe's bankers rate Greece's credit highly', *Athens News*, 14 Sep. 1979.
63. Spourdalakis (1988), p. 212.
64. FCO 9/2732.
65. Spourdalakis (1988), p. 199.
66. Lakopoulos (1999), p. 71.
67. Karakousis (2006), p. 422.
68. FCO 9/2732.
69. 'Greek socialists win a landslide victory', *Multinational Monitor*, 2:11, Nov. 1981, available http://goo.gl/daxuFx; Kourvetaris & Dobratz (1999), p. 294.
70. For the development of PASOK's ideology see Spourdalakis (1988).
71. Vamvakas & Panagiotopoulos (2010), pp. 328–30.
72. Vasilopoulou, Halikiopoulou & Exadaktylos (2014), pp. 390–92; Pappas (2014) in general.
73. See the comments in Theodossopoulos (2013), p. 202.
74. OECD (1992), p. 58.
75. Dimitras (1987), p. 72; Tsoukalas (1995), p. 203.
76. Spourdalakis (1988), p. 249.

77. Stavrou (1988), p. 32.

78. Papandreou & Wheeler (1954); Kariotis (1997).

79. EIU, *Greece: Quarterly Economic Review*, 1, 1983, p. 7.

80. See Axt (1984) in general.

81. For policy at this time see Axt (1984), 197; Kleinman (1988), 194–95.

82. Spourdalakis (1988), p. 226.

83. EIU, *Greece: Quarterly Economic Review*, 2, 1984, p. 5.

84. Tsakalotos (1991), p. 270.

85. Spraos (1991), pp. 176–77.

86. EIU, *Greece: Quarterly Economic Review*, 2, 1985, p. 3.

87. EIU, *Greece: Quarterly Economic Review*, 4, 1985, p. 7.

88. Vamvakas & Panagiotopoulos (2010), pp. 557–60.

89. On the impact of devaluation in general at this time see Alogoskoufis (1992).

90. Kleinman (1988), p. 207.

91. Jouganatos (1992), pp. 140–42.

92. As with all statistics relating to this period, various figures are given in different sources. See, for instance, Antzoulatos (2011), p. 253.

93. For the impact of the programme see Kleinman (1988), pp. 208–13.

94. OECD (1990), p. 9.

95. Ibid.; for alternative figures see Alogoskoufis (1992).

96. EIU, *Greece: Quarterly Economic Review*, 3, 1987, p. 21.

97. Karakousis (2006), pp. 104, 140, 244.

98. Jouganatos (1992), p. 141.

99. Pavlopoulos (1987).

100. EIU, *Greece: Quarterly Economic Review*, 3, 1988, p. 20.

101. Tsoukalis (1991), pp. 200–202.

102. Verney (2011), pp. 64–67.

103. 'Scandals the looting of Greece', *Time Magazine*, 13 Mar. 1989, available http://goo.gl/lebiu8

104. Nikolaou (2008), pp. 180–81.

105. 'Τι είναι ο εκσυγχρονισμός', *To Vima*, 10 Apr. 1992.

106. Diamandouros, (1993), p. 4.

107. On the concept of the developmental state see Pagoulatos (2003).

108. For an introduction to this issue see Triandafyllidou, Gropas & Kouki (2013).

109. See Xenakis (2013).

110. Diamandouros (2013), p. 225; Katrougalos (2013), p. 89.

111. Axt (1997); Koliopoulos & Veremis (2002), p. 317.

112. Wallace (1979), p. 34.

113. Featherstone, Kazamias & Papadimitriou (2000), p. 396.

114. Marsh (2009), p. 153.

115. Karakousis (2006), pp. 136–40.

116. EIU, *Greece: Quarterly Economic Review*, 2, 1990, p. 17.

117. Ibid., p. 22.

118. Ibid., p. 9.

119. Clogg (1987), p. 158. Our thanks to Andreas Andrianopoulos who was helpful in clarifying these points.

120. EIU, *Greece: Quarterly Economic Review*, 2, 1991, pp. 16–18.

121. EIU, *Greece: Quarterly Economic Review*, 2, 1991, p. 20; EIU, *Greece: Quarterly Economic Review*, 1, 1992, p. 17.

122. Trantidis (2014), p. 225.

123. EIU, *Greece: Quarterly Economic Review*, 2, 1993, p. 16.

124. EIU, *Greece: Quarterly Economic Review*, 4, 1992, p. 17.

125. Ibid., p. 7.

126. Trantidis (2014), p. 227.

127. Pelagidis (1997), p. 67; for an example of reporting of measures see 'Νέο πακέτο μέτρων', *To Vima*, 15 Mar. 1992.

128. OECD (1992), pp. 14–15.

129. OECD (1993), p. 53; EIU, *Greece: Quarterly Economic Review*, 4, 1991, p. 20.

130. EIU, *Greece: Quarterly Economic Review*, 1, 1994, p. 20.

131. Karakousis (2006), p. 244; EIU, *Greece Quarterly Economic* Review, 1, 1994, p. 19.

132. 'Premier defends modernization policy', *Athens News Agency: Daily News Bulletin in English (henceforth ANA)*, 13 Mar. 1997, available http://goo.gl/0wDwXK

133. EIU, *Greece: Quarterly Economic Review*, 2, 1998, p. 19.

134. Mourmouras & Arghyrou (1998), p. 12, draw on OECD research but others suggest a smaller figure.

135. Knight (2012).

136. Quoted in Panagopoulos & Marantzidis (2006), p. 405.

137. EIU, *Greece: Quarterly Economic Review*, 3, 1999, p. 26.

138. EIU, *Greece: Quarterly Economic Review*, 3, 1998, p. 12.

139. Bitros (1992), p. 25.

140. Note there is little agreement on what level of public debt is sustainable.

141. 'Presidency conclusions, Santa Maria da Feira European Council', *Europa.eu*, 19–20 June 2000, available http://goo.gl/o10OwW

142. 'Round of applause for Simitis from EU leaders over EMU entry', *ANA*, 21 June 2000, available http://goo.gl/RVmMg5

143. 'Greece becomes 12th EMU member, PM Simitis says entry marks new historic era for country', *ANA*, 20 June 2000, available http://goo.gl/lHgCvG

144. 'Greece ready to contribute to the creation of 21st century Europe, Simitis says', *ANA*, 20 June 2000, available http://goo.gl/H96cBM

145. Most famously the German Finance Minister, Theo Waigel, disputed whether Greece would ever join the euro with his Greek counterpart, Yiannos Papantoniou, at an informal Ecofin council meeting in Verona in April 1996. See 'Euro breakup talk increases as Germany loses proxy', *Bloomberg*, 14 May 2010, available http://goo.gl/93bckS

146. '2275th Council meeting in the composition of the heads of state or government, and

2274th and 2277th Council meetings Ecofin, Sta Maria da Feira', *Europa.eu*, 18–20 June 2000, available http://goo.gl/CydG48

147. See, for instance, Bayoumi & Eichengreen (1993); Krugman (1993); Bayoumi & Masson (1995); Varoufakis (2011).
148. Marsh (2009), p. 256.
149. For a discussion see Pisani-Ferry (2014), pp. 21–22.
150. Pagoulatos (2003), p. 170; see also Pisani-Ferry (1998), p. 156, where he suggests Portugal, Spain and Ireland are also vulnerable.
151. Andreou & Koutsiaras (2004), p. 91.
152. 'Greece: 2000 Article IV Consultation: conclusions of the IMF Mission', *IMF.org*, 20 Nov. 2000, available http://goo.gl/UL4wV9
153. 'ECB, Convergence report 2000', *Europa.eu*, available http://goo.gl/xdzdoO

2. THESE GAMES WITH NUMBERS HAVE TO STOP: GREECE IN THE EURO AREA

1. This comment relating to the Simitis government's economic statistics is attributed to Alogoskoufis. See 'New gov't disputes predecessor's account of economic indicators', *ANA*, 23 Mar. 2004, available http://goo.gl/xeEPw0
2. Marsh (2009), p. 213.
3. Kalaitzidis (2010); Karakousis (2006) and Featherstone (2008) all finish on broadly positive notes.
4. Buti & Pench (2004).
5. 'Rating action: Moody's upgrades Greece to A1 from A2', *Moodys.com*, 4 Nov. 2002, available http://goo.gl/ldaP0A
6. 'Papandreou again', *Financial Times*, 9 Jan. 2004.
7. 'Communication from the Commission to the European Parliament, the European Council, the Council, the European Central Bank, the Economic and Social Committee and the Committee of the Regions: reinforcing economic policy coordination', *Europa.eu*, 12 May 2010, available http://goo.gl/NR1Lw0
8. Marsh (2009), p. 218. This quote relates to economists throughout Europe and not just in Germany.
9. For a general failure to consider the implications of joining the euro see Pisani-Ferry (2014), p. 42.
10. 'Ομιλία στο επίσημο δείπνο της Διεθνούς Έκθεσης Θεσσαλονίκης', *costas-simitis.gr*, 8 Sep. 2001, available http://goo.gl/7MdKvs
11. See, for instance: '2000 broad economic policy guidelines', *Europa.eu*, 2000, pp. 71–72, available http://goo.gl/2m3unU; '2407th Council meeting Ecofin, Brussels', *Europa.eu*, 12 Feb. 2002, available http://goo.gl/zkgQJ0; 'IMF report calls for further reforms to Greek pension system, labor market', *ANA*, 14 Sep. 2004, available http://goo.gl/Pm7SL8.
12. 'For a good discussion of pension reform at this time see K. Featherstone, 'The politics of pension reform in Greece: modernization defeated by gridlock', *lse.ac.uk*, Oct. 2003, available http://goo.gl/G3ahB4

13. On pension reform in general see Tinios (2012).

14. 'Industrialists from Greece hit at reform delay', *Financial Times*, 1 June 2001.

15. 'Details on those other Greek debt deals', *FTAlphaville*, 25 Feb. 2010, available http://goo.gl/11Q4f8

16. 'Greece had 13 currency swaps with Goldman, Eurostat says', *Bloomberg*, 12 May 2011, available http://goo.gl/h8bXHz; 'How to borrow €1bn without adding to your public debt figures', *FTAlphaville*, 15 Feb. 2010, http://goo.gl/CFVSCg; 'Report on the EDP methodological visits to Greece in 2010', *Europa.eu*, n.d., available http://goo.gl/bGPLDc

17. Dunbar (2011), pp. 22, 258 n.10.

18. 'Wall St. helped to mask debt fueling Europe's crisis', *The New York Times*, 13 Feb. 2010, available http://goo.gl/UTna7m

19. 'Goldman Sachs, Greece didn't disclose swap contract (Update1)', *Bloomberg*, 17 Feb. 2010, available http://goo.gl/FQnTzW

20. 'Revealed: Goldman Sachs' mega-deal for Greece', *Risk Magazine*, 1 July 2003, available http://goo.gl/jKIEAk; 'How Goldman Sachs helped mask Greece's debt', *BBC News*, 20 Feb. 2012, available http://goo.gl/Cfv5a1

21. Piga (2001).

22. 'New decisions of Eurostat on deficit and debt: securitisation operations undertaken by general government', *Europa.eu*, 3 July 2002, available http://goo.gl/UjeS7i

23. 'Article IV consultation—staff report; staff supplement; public information notice on the Executive Board discussion; and statement by the Executive Director for Greece', *IMF.org*, June 2003, available http://goo.gl/ifC091

24. Dellas & Tavlas (2013), p. 514; for comparisons see Lapavitsas, Kaltenbrunner, Labrinidis et al. (2013), pp. 79–84.

25. Christodoulakis (2010), p. 92.

26. EIU, *Country Report: Greece*, Jan. 2003, p. 20.

27. Immediately afterwards the government denied he had made the comment: 'Gov't dismisses press reports attributing slang reference to PM; efforts to curb vested interests remain', *ANA*, 8 Oct. 2004, available http://goo.gl/98vqh9 but it continues to circulate widely. See, for instance, 'Special report: Greece's triangle of power', *Reuters*, 17 Dec. 2012, available http://goo.gl/NSVIiD; 'Politics, media and pimps', *whenthecrisishitthefan.wordpress.com*, 5 Jan. 2012, available https://goo.gl/cWIe00

28. EIU, *Country Report: Greece*, Apr. 2002, p. 15; EIU, *Country Report: Greece*, Oct. 2003, pp. 14–15.

29. Panagopoulos & Marantzidis (2006); Verney (2004); Kassimeris (2004).

30. 'Athens bids farewell to the Games', *CNN*, 30 Aug. 2004, available http://goo.gl/JtcYml

31. Beyond the headlines many articles gave a more balanced view. See the opinions in 'Olympics "may cost Greece dear"', *BBC News*, 2 June 2004, available http://goo.gl/gnIUI8; 'Rogge: Athens 2004 weighed on debt', *ekathimerini.com*, 26 Dec. 2011, available http://goo.gl/6YtNP5; 'How the 2004 Olympics triggered Greece's decline', *Bloomberg*, 2 Aug. 2012, available http://goo.gl/HiRCTE

32. However, see the comments in Christodoulakis (2012), pp. 102–103.

33. Kottakis (2011), p. 367, notes that public spending rose at this time because of pay increases in state entities and expenditure on social programmes rather than due to patronage appointments.

34. '"Mild adjustment" over three years for fiscal policy, Finmin says', *ANA*, 14 Sep. 2004, available http://goo.gl/oO60Ts; 'Government will stick to policy of "mild adjustment" in fiscal issues, finmin reiterates', *ANA*, 3 Dec. 2004, available http://goo.gl/EJVW65

35. EIU, *Country Report: Greece*, Apr. 2004, p. 15.

36. Featherstone (2008), p. 179.

37. Tsoukas (2012), pp. 88–89.

38. Arghyrou (2007), p. 24.

39. 'New gov't disputes predecessor's account of economic indicators', *ANA*, 23 Mar. 2004, available http://goo.gl/xeEPw0; 'Greek fiscal deficit reached 3.2 pct in 2003', *ANA*, 8 May 2004, available http://goo.gl/PftiXh

40. 'Premier calls for off-the-agenda discussion on economy in parliament', *ANA*, 17 Apr. 2004, available http://goo.gl/smtMDK

41. '2594th Council meeting Economic and Financial Affairs, Brussels', *Europa.eu*, 5 July 2004, available http://goo.gl/zphvT3

42. EIU, *Country Report: Greece*, Jan. 2005, pp. 19–20.

43. '2634th Council meeting Economic and Financial Affairs, Brussels', *Europa.eu*, 18 Jan. 2005, available http://goo.gl/ob7gRL

44. '2638th Council meeting Economic and Financial Affairs, Brussels', *Europa.eu*, 17 Feb. 2005, available http://goo.gl/DZFYjv

45. 'Main opposition sees economy under EU supervision', *ANA*, 18 Feb. 2005, available http://goo.gl/VzYKyX

46. EIU, *Country Report: Greece*, Apr. 2004, p. 19. The audit was subsequently viewed as a mistake by New Democracy: 'Mihelakis: "ND 'state audit' a mistake"', *Protothema News in English*, 28 Apr. 2011, available http://goo.gl/zGMtGr

47. Koen & van den Noord (2005), p. 6 n. 2.

48. 'Greek fiscal deficit to fall to 2.8 pct in 2005, FinMin says', *ANA*, 13 Sep. 2004, available http://goo.gl/5u0s8N; 'EU Commission publishes updated figures for Greek economy', *ANA*, 24 Oct. 2004, available http://goo.gl/kkSpMj; '2612th Council Meeting Economic and Financial Affairs, Luxembourg', *Europa.eu*, 21 Oct. 2004, available http://goo.gl/we2CKs

49. 'Finmin to present results of gov't fiscal audit at Eurogroup meeting, plays down risks for Greece's credit rating', *ANA*, 10 Sep. 2004, available http://goo.gl/29Hy0W

50. 'Greece escapes expulsion from the euro', *Financial Times*, 15 Nov. 2004, available http://goo.gl/4RZdIc

51. 'Four EU countries risk breaking stability pact in 2005', *Financial Times*, 22 Oct. 2004.

52. 'Report by Eurostat on the revision of the Greek government deficit and debt figures', *Europa.eu*, 22 Nov. 2004, available http://goo.gl/eMoVMa

53. 'EU raps Greece over deficit', *Guardian*, 2 Dec. 2004, available http://goo.gl/GQYQGZ; 'Report on the EDP methodological visit to Greece 29 May—2 June 2006', *Europa.eu*, 27–29 Sep. 2006, available http://goo.gl/ITaJuI

54. 'Euro-indicators: news release 54/2008', *Europa.eu*, 18 Apr. 2008, available http://goo.gl/cLLe9e

55. 'EU raps Greece over deficit', *Guardian*, 2 Dec. 2004, available http://goo.gl/GQYQGZ; see also the comments in EIU, *Country Report: Greece*, Jan. 2005, pp. 13–14.

56. 'Greece's deficit revision damaged EU', *Financial Times*, 21 Dec. 2004, available http://goo.gl/X2IW7t

57. 'Eurostat takes issue with former Greek PM on reasons for the revision of economic data', *Financial Times*, 28 Dec. 2004, available http://goo.gl/rTznWZ.

58. 'EU launches infringement procedure against Greece over erroneous fiscal statistics; Athens responds', *ANA*, 2 Dec. 2004, available http://goo.gl/sQ8Zwv

59. 'Complicit in corruption: how German companies bribed their way to Greek deals', *Spiegel Online International*, 11 May 2010, available http://goo.gl/CRpZ8C

60. 'JP Morgan Greek tragedy sets "hero" banker against old bosses', *Bloomberg*, 25 Oct. 2007, available http://goo.gl/QNVOdj

61. Telloglou (2009).

62. An entertaining account in English can be found in M. Lewis, 'Beware of Greeks bearing bonds', *Vanity Fair*, 1 Oct. 2010, available http://goo.gl/MpxUuS; for an earlier example of similar practices see 'Monks buying industries', *Athens News*, 18 Dec. 1979.

63. 'PM's speech carries burden of expectation', *Athens Plus*, 4 Sep. 2009.

64. 'A Trojan Horse?', *The Wall Street Journal*, 27 Sep. 2004, available http://goo.gl/4sOjTN

65. 'Finmin to present results of gov't fiscal audit at Eurogroup meeting, plays down risks for Greece's credit rating', *ANA*, 10 Sep. 2004, available http://goo.gl/Ih9hI8; 'Standard & Poor's lowers long-term ratings on Greece', *ANA*, 18 Nov. 2004, available http://goo.gl/9Eulnk; 'Fitch downgrades Greece's currency ratings', *ANA*, 17 Dec. 2004, available http://goo.gl/mHxpNb

66. 'Greece set to issue 30-year-bond', *Financial Times*, 1 Mar. 2005.

67. 'ECB targets its problem nations', *Financial Times*, 9 Nov. 2005; 'ECB sends powerful signal on debt. Some governments could face having their bonds rejected as collateral', *Financial Times*, 10 Nov. 2005.

68. See on this issue Arghyrou & Kontonikas (2011); Gibson, Hall & Tavlas (2012).

69. For the euro area in general at this time see Marsh (2009); Pisani-Ferry (2014).

70. 'EU raps Greece over deficit', *Guardian*, 2 Dec. 2004, available http://goo.gl/GQYQGZ; 'EU launches infringement procedure against Greece over erroneous fiscal statistics; Athens responds', *ANA*, 2 Dec. 2004, available http://goo.gl/PHtfPu

71. 'Presidency conclusions, European Council, Brussels', *Europa.eu*, 22–23 Mar. 2005, available http://goo.gl/GB8sLP

72. 'Greek fiscal deficit to fall to 2.8 pct in 2005, FinMin says', *ANA*, 13 Sep. 2004, available http://goo.gl/5u0s8N

73. Pisani-Ferry (2014), p. 54.

74. Featherstone (2008), p. 167; 'Greece "cheated" to join euro, former ECB economist Issing says', *Bloomberg*, 26 May 2011, available http://goo.gl/ofs59b

75. 'Commission recommends abrogation of excessive deficit procedure for Germany, Greece and Malta', *Europa.eu*, 16 May 2007, available http://goo.gl/PSi8py

76. 'Finmin to present results of gov't fiscal audit at Eurogroup meeting, plays down risks for Greece's credit rating', *ANA*, 10 Sep. 2004, available http://goo.gl/zzdDbX

77. 'Greece faces up to taxing times', *Financial Times*, 12 Oct. 2005; 'Greeks drop €1.5bn securitisation plan for budget', *Financial Times*, 16 Dec. 2005, available http://goo.gl/L5ujF6

78. 'Some idea of the complexity of the Olympic Airways issue can be gauged from the 'Commission decision of 17/09/2008 on state aid C 61/2007 (ex NN 71/2007)—Greece Olympic Airways Services/Olympic Airlines', *Europa.eu*, 17 Sep. 2008, available http://goo.gl/I75KsG

79. 'Oldest profession helps boost Greek national output by 25%', *Financial Times*, 29 Sep. 2006; 'Greek GDP (base year 2000) revised growth rate 9.6 pct, report', *ANA*, 9 Oct. 2007, available http://goo.gl/Hxmlt9; the revision made the list of CNN's '101 dumbest moments in business', available http://goo.gl/iTVfpJ because it lowered receipts from the EU.

80. 'Eurozone finance ministers', *Financial Times*, 15 Nov. 2007, available http://goo.gl/L60lC0

81. 'Rising prosperity brings feel-good factor', *Financial Times*, 13 July 2007.

82. 'Buy now, try to pay later', *Athens News*, 20 Feb. 2004.

83. Arghyrou (2007), p. 21; Antzoulatos (2011), p. 249.

84. Dziuda & Mastrobuoni (2009).

85. Featherstone (2008), p. 170.

86. The quote widely reproduced at the time was attributed to the then Chairman and CEO of LVMH Moët Hennessy—Louis Vuitton S.A's Celine fashion brand, Serge Brunschwig. It appears in 'Apparel chains struggle as Greek crisis takes toll', *ekathimerini.com*, 10 Aug. 2012, available http://goo.gl/EIT8Pv

87. 'OECD obesity update', *OECD.org*, June 2014, available http://goo.gl/regRDq

88. 'Θεολογική θεώρηση της οικονομικής κρίσεως', The Church of Greece, *Encyclical no. 2894*, 15 Mar. 2010, available http://goo.gl/2DuyY1

89. 'Papandreou, Venizelos address PASOK pre-congress meeting', *ANA*, 21 Jan. 2008, available http://goo.gl/4HPWKF

90. See 'Pay developments—2005', *Europa.eu*, 9 July 2006, available http://goo.gl/mM2EY5; 'Pay developments—2006', *Europa.eu*, 1 July 2007, available http://goo.gl/WVqAtD; 'Pay developments—2007', *Europa.eu*, 3 Aug. 2008, available http://goo.gl/zVIhsC

91. 'Minimum wages', *Europa.eu*, n.d., available http://goo.gl/MQiytX

92. Manolopoulos (2011), p. 86; on the issue in general see Christopoulou & Monastiriotis (2014); Papapetrou (2006); Patronis & Liargovas (2004).

93. 'Αφαίμαξη 650.000 ευρώ από τα golden boys του Εθνικού Ιδρύματος Αγροτικών Ερευνών', *enet.gr*, 13 Apr. 2011, available http://goo.gl/qIdArV; 'Govt on election speculation, state utilities, OA', *ANA*, 14 Jan. 2009, available http://goo.gl/cy3Rgt; but see also 'Οι τράπεζες ευθύνονται για την κρίση τους', *Kathimerini*, 2 Nov. 2008, available http://goo.gl/Mv7dEu

94. Typical is the chapter in Manolopoulos (2011) entitled, 'The looting of Greece: scandals, corruption and a monstrous public sector', but see also the tone of parts of McDonald (2005); Tsimas (2011); Palaiologos (2014).

95. Pisani-Ferry (2014).

96. Arghyrou (2007), p. 22, stresses the appreciation of the Greek real exchange rate due to pre-existing inflationary pressures and the incompatibility of euro area monetary policy.

97. On this issue in general see Antzoulatos (2011), pp. 251–55.
98. Lapavitsas, Kaltenbrunner, Lindo et al. (2010), p. 344.
99. See in general Cholezas & Tsakloglou (2009).
100. OECD (2009), p. 20.
101. Zombanakis, Stylianou & Andreou (2009), pp. 5–8 give a survey of the literature.
102. Gibson, Palivos & Tavlas (2014).
103. 'Greece urged to reduce deficit', *Financial Times*, 9 May 2008; Provopoulos (2014) also stresses the fiscal imbalance.
104. 'EMU@10: successes and challenges after ten years of economic and monetary union', *Europa.eu*, 2008, available http://goo.gl/gpoQc0
105. Pisani-Ferry (2014), p. 36.
106. This was largely due to Germany. Indeed, in real (price-deflated) terms Greek exports can be seen as growing during this period at close to the euro area average. Jones (2012), pp. 30–31.
107. M. Higgins & T. Klitgaard, 'The balance of payments crisis in the euro area periphery', *Federal Reserve Bank of New York: Current Issues in Economics and Finance*, 20:2, 2014, available http://goo.gl/xFgLpb; see also Christodoulakis (2010), p. 91.
108. W.H. Buiter, E. Rahbari & J. Michels, 'The implications of intra-euro area imbalances in credit flows', *CEPR Policy Insight*, 57, Aug. 2011, available http://goo.gl/wQl9B0; 'What has the ECB done in the crisis? The role of TARGET balances', *Financial Times*, 28 Dec. 2011, available http://goo.gl/rTdT1z; 'Merkozy failed to save the eurozone', *Financial Times*, 6 Dec. 2011, available http://goo.gl/kTb2gg
109. Sinn & Wollmershäuser (2012); Lapavitsas, Kaltenbrunner, Labrinidis et al. (2013), pp. 198–99.
110. Gemenis (2008); Patrikios & Karyotis (2008); Spourdalakis (2008).
111. EIU, '*Country Report: Greece*', Oct. 2007.
112. 'The rise and fall of George Alogoskoufis', *Reuters*, 7 Jan. 2009, available http://goo.gl/mXYVnS
113. For LAOS see Ellinas (2010).
114. EIU, *Country Report: Greece*, Sep. 2008.
115. 'Inflation fears fail to dent confidence about growth', *Financial Times*, 2 June 2008.
116. 'Μαύρη λίστα για όσες εταιρείες επιμένουν... ακριβά', *Kathimerini*, 30 May 2008, available http://goo.gl/UXalS2
117. 'Quarterly National Accounts', *Hellenic Statistical Authority*, 28 Nov. 2014, available http://goo.gl/OcI3Z4

3. AN UNPRECEDENTED CRISIS: THE SECOND KOSTAS KARAMANLIS GOVERNMENT, GLOBAL FINANCIAL TURMOIL AND A LOCAL ECONOMIC DOWNTURN

1. The crisis was described in these terms by Papandreou. See 'Papandreou refers to "unprecedented crisis"', *ANA*, 7 Oct. 2008, available http://goo.gl/agkRym

2. Trichet (2010), p. 8.

3. 'PM: int'l developments need "steady course, solid steps"', *ANA*, 6 Sep. 2008, available http://goo.gl/5A7sQv

4. OECD (2009).

5. 'Papandreou: "red line" separates PASOK from ND on economic policy', *ANA*, 18 Apr. 2008, available http://goo.gl/vV6jcN

6. Ibid.; 'Papandreou: time has come to overcome crisis of values', *ANA*, 16 Aug. 2009, available http://goo.gl/4awZK8

7. For movements in the ASE index at this time see Pasiouras (2012), pp. 43–45.

8. On this issue see Gibson, Hall & Tavlas (2012); Arghyrou & Kontonikas (2011).

9. 'Iceland contagion may spread far and wide', *Daily Telegraph*, 27 Mar. 2008, available http://goo.gl/67RjsC

10. There has been much discussion of this issue. See, for instance, OECD (2009), pp. 30–31; S. Sgherri & E. Zoli, 'Euro area sovereign risk during the crisis', *IMF.org*, 2009, available http://goo.gl/WavS38

11. 'PM Karamanlis to ruling party: "nothing will obstruct truth"', *ANA*, 27 Sep. 2008, available http://goo.gl/7bFTXr

12. 'Δέσμευση για κρατική «ομπρέλα» στις καταθέσεις', *Kathimerini*, 3 Oct. 2008, available http://goo.gl/cO7adh

13. 'Greece joins bailout stampede as Germany vows no blank cheques', *Daily Telegraph*, 2 Oct. 2008, available http://goo.gl/KzLSYV

14. 'Papandreou refers to "unprecedented crisis"', *ANA*, 7 Oct. 2008, available http://goo.gl/agkRym; 'ND parliamentary group meeting', *ANA*, 6 Oct. 2008, available http://goo.gl/JA7PpB

15. Mason (2009), p. 48.

16. 'Greek, Maltese PMs discuss credit crisis, migration', *ANA*, 10 Oct. 2008, available http://goo.gl/QjK1hm

17. 'Changes in tender procedure and in the standing facilities corridor', *Europa.eu*, 8 Oct. 2008, available http://goo.gl/QjRo2b

18. 'Measures to further expand the collateral framework and enhance the provision of liquidity', *Europa.eu*, 15 Oct. 2008, available http://goo.gl/v7c0DM;

19. Lapavitsas, Kaltenbrunner, Lindo et al. (2010), p. 360, suggest the easing of collateral requirements may also have affected the markets.

20. '2894th Council meeting Economic and Financial Affairs, Luxembourg', *Europa.eu*, 7 Oct. 2008, available http://goo.gl/o9SzYM

21. The saying is generally attributed to Mervyn King. See for instance 'Can banking regulation go global?', *BBC News*, 18 Mar. 2009, available http://goo.gl/AcvIHd

22. 'Presidency conclusions, European Council, Brussels', *Europa.eu*, 15–16 Oct. 2008, available http://goo.gl/eLLkGJ

23. '2894th Council meeting Economic and Financial Affairs, Luxembourg', *Europa.eu*, 7 Oct. 2008, available http://goo.gl/YFBTff

24. 'Communication from the Commission to the European Council: a European economic recovery plan', *Europa.eu*, 26 Nov. 2008, available http://goo.gl/tr5gUx

25. Blyth (2013), p. 83.

26. Hardie & Howarth (2009).

27. Pisani-Ferry (2014), p. 88 notes how after its bail-out by the German government Hypo Real Estate bought Greek government bonds.

28. Merkel speaking on Deutsche Welle, 6 Oct. 2008; see also Bastasin (2012), pp. 30–35; Crawford & Czuczka (2013), pp. 41–57.

29. Pasiouras (2012), p. 64.

30. 'Οι τράπεζες ευθύνονται για την κρίση τους', *Kathimerini*, 2 Nov. 2008, available http://goo.gl/Mv7dEu

31. 'Marfin Egnatia opts out of gov't plan to boost bank liquidity', *ANA*, 27 Nov. 2008, available http://goo.gl/TBaM2n

32. 'PM issues stern warning for banks', *ANA*, 11 Nov. 2008, available http://goo.gl/qmf6oZ

33. Panayotakis (2009), p. 98.

34. 'Gov't: bank plan to boost growth', *ANA*, 31 Oct. 2008, available http://goo.gl/9fTLLO

35. 'BoG on bank support plan', *ANA*, 13 Nov. 2008, available http://goo.gl/xvF8Pn

36. Quaglia, Eastwood & Holmes (2009), p. 64.

37. Statistics from OECD database and 'Regional economic outlook. Europe: building confidence', *IMF.org*, Oct. 2010, available http://goo.gl/O4zS85

38. 'IMF in talks on loans to countries hit by financial crisis', *IMF.org*, 22 Oct. 2008, available http://goo.gl/JyXF2G

39. Csáki (2013); 'Council Regulation (EC) No 332/2002 of 18 February 2002 establishing a facility providing medium-term financial assistance for Member States' balances of payments', *Official Journal of the European Communities*, L 53/1, 23 Feb. 2002, available http://goo.gl/Ai5Nhd

40. 'Greece cuts deficit target', *Financial Times*, 7 Oct. 2008; 'Gov't tables draft 2009 state budget', *ANA*, 7 Oct. 2008, available http://goo.gl/1zawPO

41. The overall index is based on a series of sub-indices covering the fields of industry, construction, retail trade, services and consumer confidence.

42. 'Eurobarometer 70: Public opinion in the European Union. National report executive summary Greece', *Europa.eu*, autumn 2008, available https://goo.gl/7mULpo

43. Barda & Sardianou (2010); 'Quarterly national accounts: 3rd quarter 2014 (provisional data)', *Hellenic Statistical Authority*, 28 Nov. 2014, available http://goo.gl/OcI3Z4

44. Kretsos (2011), p. 267.

45. 'PM on real needs of financially weaker', *ANA*, 15 Nov. 2008, available http://goo.gl/eGw9hH; 'ΣΕΒΑΘ: Οδηγείται σε εκκαθάριση', *imerisia.gr*, 26 Nov. 2008, available http://goo.gl/jgfBs7; see also 'Government promises jobs for BIAMYL workers', *ANA*, 8 Sep. 2008, available http://goo.gl/Yu9R86

46. 'FinMin: there are no easy solutions', *ANA*, 11 Aug. 2008, available http://goo.gl/GSyg59

47. Exceptions include: 'Investors shun Greek debt as shipping crisis deepens', *Daily Telegraph*, 28 Oct. 2008, available http://goo.gl/JDHTSo; 'Recession hits Europe as Club Med debt worries grow', *Daily Telegraph*, 3 Nov. 2008, available http://goo.gl/yvpNOQ

48. 'Οι ειδικοί φρουροί δεν υπάκουσαν στις εντολές', *Kathimerini*, 13 Dec. 2008, available http://goo.gl/ADQkBv

49. Some insights into the impact of the media can be found in Hugh-Jones, Katsanidou & Riener (2009).

50. On visibility and invisibility see Pourgouris (2010).

51. Andronikidou & Kovras (2012), p. 721.

52. 'Γκάλοπ: κοινωνική εξέγερση, χαμένη η Ν.Δ.', *Eleftherotypia*,15 Dec. 2008.

53. 'Rebellion deeply embedded in Greece', *BBC News*, 9 Dec. 2008, available http://goo.gl/sJRx1c

54. Pagoulatos (2009a), p. 48.

55. 'Why Athens is burning', *The New York Times*, 11 Dec. 2008, available http://goo.gl/2t3aLg

56. For a rebuttal of the idea it was a new *Dekemvriana* see 'Τα Δεκεμβριανά ως φάρσα', *To Vima*, 21 Dec. 2008; for anarchist orientated views of the disturbances see Schwarz, Sagris & Void Network (2010).

57. Andronikidou & Kovras (2012) discuss the culture of resistance.

58. There was also a conservative discourse in the UK which saw the disturbances as a harbinger of the collapse of the euro system. See 'Greek fighting: the eurozone's weakest link starts to crack', *Daily Telegraph*, 10 Dec. 2008, available http://goo.gl/F3kvXk

59. Astrinaki (2009), p. 104.

60. Kambouri & Zavos (2010).

61. Dalakoglou (2012), p. 537; Kandylis & Kavoulakos (2011).

62. 'Sarkozy drops reform amid fears of riot', *Sunday Times*, 21 Dec. 2008; 'Greek police teargas youths in 2nd week of protests', *Reuters*, 15 Dec. 2008, available http://goo.gl/Vz4Omr

63. Kalyvas (2010), p. 361. n. 7.

64. For terrorism in general during this period see Kassimeris (2013), pp. 77–113.

65. 'Greece's most wanted man who gives to the poor', *BBC News*, 25 Sep. 2014, available http://goo.gl/Ne6jqc

66. 'Καίγεται η Ελλάδα: η κραυγή της γενιάς των 0 ευρώ!', *zalmoxis.wordpress.com*, 8 Dec. 2008, available http://goo.gl/Zqc8XS

67. Kornetis (2010), p. 179.

68. The size of this elite group depended entirely on perspective. For some it could stretch to encompass the hundreds of thousands or even more they believed possessed luxurious summer villas, large cars, boats and swimming pools.

69. 'Αιχμές και οι πρώτες δυσλειτουργίες', *Kathimerini*, 9 Jan. 2009, available http://goo.gl/Jk64Iu

70. 'Papandreou: yes to consensus—with conditions', *ANA*, 9 Mar. 2009, available http://goo.gl/6VsPrP

71. 'Greece unravelled', *Financial Times*, 11 Dec. 2008; 'Greek riots unnerve investors', *The Wall Street Journal*, 12 Dec. 2008, available http://goo.gl/odqd01; see also 'When times are hard, the weakest link comes under strain', *Financial Times*, 7 Jan. 2009.

72. Fender, Ho & Hördahl, (March 2009), p. 9.

73. Lapavitsas, Kaltenbrunner, Lindo et al. (2010), p. 325.

74. 'FinMin defends economic policy', *ANA*, 15 Jan. 2009, available http://goo.gl/iMaJ1t

75. A list of ratings actions at this time can be found in R. Arezki, B. Candelon & A.N.R. Sy, 'Sovereign rating news and financial markets spillovers: evidence from the European debt crisis', *IMF.org*, 2011, available http://goo.gl/IynDha

76. For some thoughts on how the one transformed into the other see A. Mody, 'From Bear Stearns to Anglo Irish: how eurozone sovereign spreads related to financial sector vulnerability', *IMF.org*, May 2009, available http://goo.gl/DFw5mA

77. 'Once a boon, euro now burdens some nations', *The New York Times*, 23 Jan. 2009, available http://goo.gl/VS572v

78. 'Euro zone can bail out members if needed: Almunia', *Reuters*, 3 Mar. 2009, available http://goo.gl/pBFIPq

79. 'Λιτότητα σοκ αλλιώς χρεοκοπούμε: Προβόπουλος αδειάζει Παπαθανασίου', *Ta Nea*, 17 Feb. 2009. 'Τέσσερα χρόνια λιτότητα! και μάλιστα ξεκινώντας από εφέτος—Η βόμβα Προβόπουλου και η αναμενόμενη οδηγία της Ευρωπαϊκής Ένωσης', *To Vima*, 17 Feb. 2009, available http://goo.gl/MRqn3Y

80. 'PM to seek meetings with party leaders on crisis', *ANA*, 20 Feb. 2009, available http://goo.gl/zBgJpA

81. 'A test for Europe's common currency: support for wobbly euro economies', *Spiegel International Online*, 20 Feb. 2009, available http://goo.gl/XZ1c7d

82. Ryvkin (2012).

83. 'Euro zone can bail out members if needed: Almunia', *Reuters*, 3 Mar. 2009, available http://goo.gl/pBFIPq

84. 'Gov't: growth will deflect int'l crisis', *ANA*, 5 Feb. 2009, available http://goo.gl/836j68

85. 'Commission opinion on the existence of an excessive deficit in Greece', *Europa.eu*, 24 Mar. 2009, available http://goo.gl/qjVQAh; 'Council decision of 27 April 2009 on the existence of an excessive deficit in Greece (2009/415/EC)', *Official Journal of the European Union*, L 135/21, 30 May 2009, available http://goo.gl/EjYYlu

86. Christodoulakis (2010), pp. 92–93.

87. 'NBG ups share in Greek state securities', *ANA*, 18 Feb. 2009, available http://goo.gl/n6vp4h

88. Lapavitsas, Kaltenbrunner, Labrinidis et al. (2013), pp. 194–95.

89. 'Charting Europe's grim sovereign-bank loop', *FTAlpahville*, 15 June 2010, available http://goo.gl/hTqbJ6; 'How do you say vicious circle in Greek?', *FTAlphaville*, 8 Dec. 2009, available http://goo.gl/52JJml which draws on research from UBS.

90. Bastasin (2012), p. 111.

91. Pasiouras (2012), p. 47.

92. 'Small, very small enterprises mostly hit by crisis, survey', *ANA*, 24 July 2009, available http://goo.gl/7o2W01

93. 'Draft bill introduces tax breaks to boost auto market', *ANA*, 4 Apr. 2009, available http://goo.gl/Yud5KJ

94. 'Economy to shrink 1.3 pct', *ANA*, 31 July 2009, available http://goo.gl/HDGRIE; 'GDP down 0.2pct down in Q2', *ANA*, 12 Aug. 2009, available http://goo.gl/BamgEW; 'World economic outlook: sustaining the recovery', *IMF.org*, Oct. 2009, available http://goo.gl/HyAEo8

95. This followed the publication of 'Commission opinion on the existence of an excessive deficit in Greece', *Europa.eu*, 24 Mar. 2009, available http://goo.gl/pkhsPu.

96. 'Finmin: public debt the biggest worry', *ANA*, 27 Apr. 2009, available http://goo.gl/RAe4Lm; 'Eurozone call to rein in deficits', *Financial Times*, 4 Apr. 2009.

97. Papathanassiou (2011), 21; 'Brussels knew about staggering Greek budget deficit in July', *nrc.nl*, 20 Dec. 2009, available http://goo.gl/OcNyWc; 'Eurostat chief, Almunia support Georgiou in parliament probe of 2009 deficit figure', *ANA*, 28 Mar. 2012, available http://goo.gl/gSGWNu

98. 'Greece: 2009 article IV consultation', *IMF.org*, Aug. 2009, available http://goo.gl/9Fmkf9

99. 'State borrowing derailing debt targets, PASOK asserts', *ANA*, 7 Mar. 2009, available http://goo.gl/uVjPwA; 'IOBE: Fiscal targets for 2009 unfeasible', *ANA*, 3 Aug. 2009, available http://goo.gl/dRegZs

100. 'No incentive to be good in eurozone', *Financial Times*, 25 Mar. 2009, available http://goo.gl/OtEvMR

101. Cited in 'The rise and fall of George Alogoskoufis', *Reuters*, 7 Jan. 2009, available http://goo.gl/Iw0DmY

102. 'Papandreou: Euro-elections a "referendum"', *ANA*, 27 Apr. 2009, available http://goo.gl/uOx8lD

103. 'Eurobarometer 71: Public opinion in the European Union', *Europa.eu*, Sep. 2009, available http://goo.gl/3GKlsv

4. EVEN IN OUR WORST NIGHTMARES: THE PAPANDREOU GOVERNMENT, THE SOVEREIGN DEBT CRISIS AND THE SIGNING OF THE MEMORANDUM

1. Sentiments attributed to Papaconstantinou when discussing the size of the 2009 general government deficit in '«Μας είπε τη μισή αλήθεια»', *tanea.gr*, 26 Nov. 2009, available https://goo.gl/mytWj7; see also 'FinMin on monetary situation', *ANA*, 26 Nov. 2009, available http://goo.gl/6QquEK

2. 'ECOFIN meeting in Brussels', *ANA*, 3 Sep. 2009, available http://goo.gl/PKS9gg

3. Dinas (2010); Kovras (2010); Pappas (2010).

4. 'Three opinion polls on post-elections developments', *ANA*, 12 Oct. 2009, available http://goo.gl/zfoAvR

5. 'Greece's socialists win snap poll', *BBC News*, 5 Oct. 2009, available http://goo.gl/mzCo4W

6. 'Greek economic sentiment index jumped in October', *ANA*, 5 Nov. 2009, available http://goo.gl/tUeISx

7. On this see Patrikios & Chatzikonstantinou (2015).

8. 'Rating agencies warn Greece's socialists on spending', *Reuters*, 5 Oct. 2009, available http://goo.gl/FAlxux

9. 'Papandreou unveils economic policy, foreign policy goals', *ANA*, 14 Sep. 2009, available http://goo.gl/e5gEk0

10. See also the extensive interview 'Γιώργος Παπανδρέου στην «Κ»: «Το έργο μας θα είναι δύσκολο» (I)', *Kathimerini*, 20 Sep. 2009, available, http://goo.gl/JSkWrU

11. See 'PASOK leader: "time for the people to speak"', *ANA*, 19 Mar. 2007, available http://goo.gl/FJeBtK; in this speech he continued 'it's only that Mr. Karamanlis prefers to give it to the few and powerful'.

12. 'Papandreou presents government policy statement', *ANA*, 17 Oct. 2009, available http://goo.gl/TpF2vb

13. 'Greek deficit will be double EU limit, minister says (Update1)', *Bloomberg*, 17 Sep. 2009 available http://goo.gl/7t1j8v; see also Papathanasiou (2011).

14. 'Στο 8% το έλλειμμα αν δεν αποδώσουν τα εισπρακτικά μέτρα', *Kathimerini*, 29 Sep. 2009, available http://goo.gl/5FNOgn; it is unclear as to whether this is referring to the central or general government deficit.

15. 'FinMin on monetary situation', *ANA*, 26 Nov. 2009, available http://goo.gl/6QquEK

16. 'Transformed by Greece, Eurostat bares its teeth', *Reuters*, 16 Oct. 2012, available http://goo.gl/BW03Fh; later it was raised even higher to 15.8 per cent of GDP. However, under ESA 2010 methodology it would probably have been around 15.2 per cent of GDP.

17. Papaconstantinou (2016); 'FinMin briefs ECOFIN on Greek econ situation; "concerns" aired by Almunia', *ANA*, 21 Oct. 2009, available http://goo.gl/cZFhDm; more or less the same line was repeated in 'The Hellenic Stability and Growth Programme executive summary', *wsj.com*, available http://goo.gl/B2cywh; 'Finmin promises single-digit deficit in letter to Almunia', *ANA*, 31 Oct. 2009, available http://goo.gl/eAOT4Y

18. 'Value-added tax may help Greece find road to fiscal recovery soon', *ekathimerini.com*, 26 Oct. 2009, available http://goo.gl/Ocdik8

19. 'Sick man of Europe seeks remedy from wary neighbours', *Independent*, 11 Feb. 2010, available http://goo.gl/iYvN62; for the continuing controversy see, for instance, 'Statistics probe hears from accuser over 2009 figures', *ekathimerini.com*, 8 Mar. 2012, available http://goo.gl/GLP16z; 'MPs blame ND for 2009 deficit', *ekathimerini.com*, 30 Mar. 2012, available http://goo.gl/GqD2vo; 'Greece's statistics chief faces charges over claims of inflated 2009 deficit figure', *ekathimerini.com*, 22 Jan. 2013, available http://goo.gl/ggEwHi; 'Prosecutor says probe into 2009 deficit should stop', *ekathimerini.com*, 26 May 2015, available http://goo.gl/wmRDWv

20. Hewitt (2013), p. 56.

21. 'Highlights: Eurogroup finance ministers' meeting', *Reuters*, 19 Oct. 2009, available http://goo.gl/kM0wGm; Lapavitsas, Kaltenbrunner, Labrinidis et al. (2013), p. 210 call it 'holy anger'.

22. 'Report on Greek government deficit and debt statistics', *Europa.eu*, 8 Jan. 2010, available http://goo.gl/MrJdy3

23. Ibid.

24. 'Euroindicators 170/2010', *Europa.eu*, 15 Nov. 2010, available http://goo.gl/AoEuBo

25. 'Update 1-ECB's Trichet: euro zone states must be more responsible', *Reuters*, 25 Mar. 2010, available http://goo.gl/jRkloQ

26. '2967th Council meeting Economic and Financial Affairs, Luxembourg', *Europa.eu*, 20 Oct. 2009, available http://goo.gl/pv4QfS

27. 'Plan outlined for return to growth', *ekathimerini.com*, 29 Oct. 2009, available http://goo.gl/Vw38MH; 'Gov't blames ND for "credibility deficit" at EU', *ANA*, 22 Oct. 2009, available http://goo.gl/eusUzA

28. The quote is from a Citigroup note cited in 'Markets live transcript', *FTAlphaville*, 26 Nov. 2009, available http://goo.gl/eNmGV7

29. 'In brief', *ekathimerini.com*, 4 Nov. 2009, available http://goo.gl/ic13VU

30. 'The economy a top priority for the government', *ANA*, 9 Nov. 2009, available http://goo.gl/2ldZZJ

31. 'Wall St. helped to mask debt fueling Europe's crisis', *The New York Times*, 13 Feb. 2010 available http://goo.gl/UGnsz3; '«Ήμασταν σαν τις πόρνες μετά την πρώτη τους φορά» Το δραματικό παρασκήνιο των δύο ετών του μνημονίου', *To Vima*, 16 Oct. 2011, available http://goo.gl/rfaSO3; 'Athens hopes that Beijing will buy €25bn in government debt', *Financial Times*, 27 Jan. 2010, available http://goo.gl/wgTbPV

32. 'Finmin promises single-digit deficit in letter to Almunia', *ANA*, 31 Oct. 2009, available http://goo.gl/jL61zJ; 'Petalotis repeats aim for single-digit deficit in 2010', *ANA*, 5 Nov. 2009, available http://goo.gl/KGAvQL

33. 'Προειδοποιητικό καμπανάκι για την κυβέρνηση', *Kathimerini*, 14 Nov. 2009, available http://goo.gl/et4aVG

34. 'Less noise, more real reform', *ekathimerini.com*, 26 Nov. 2009, available http://goo.gl/ik1bF

35. 'Απέσυραν υπό πίεση και τα ημίμετρα', *Kathimerini*, 20 Nov. 2009, available http://goo.gl/bPdy07; 'Κυβερνητικές «διευκρινίσεις» περί μισθών', *Kathimerini*, 20 Nov. 2009, available http://goo.gl/UyZcl8

36. 'Gov't unveils 2010 draft budget', *ANA*, 6 Nov. 2009, available http://goo.gl/KYw2ip

37. '2972nd Council meeting Economic and Financial Affairs, Brussels', *Europa.eu*, 10 Nov. 2009, available http://goo.gl/4mSF80

38. 'Excessive deficit procedure steps: the Stability and Growth Pact as the anchor for fiscal exit strategies', *Europa.eu*, 11 Nov. 2009, available http://goo.gl/DiLq1p

39. 'Almunia: Greece needs strong structural adjustments', *ANA*, 12 Nov. 2009, available http://goo.gl/tijoPe

40. "Budget serves up spending cuts', *ekathimerini.com*, 21 Nov. 2009, available http://goo.gl/ZeaS57

41. 'European economic forecast—autumn 2009', *Europa.eu*, Oct. 2009, pp. 92–94, available http://goo.gl/fbXkWW

42. 'Greece determined to cut deficit, improve stats—finmin', *FinanzNachrichten.de*, 11 Nov. 2009, available http://goo.gl/cybA8S

43. 'Econ shrinks 1.6% in Q3', *ANA*, 14 Nov. 2009, available http://goo.gl/0TluFB

44. 'Greek central bank faces short selling claims', *Financial Times*, 19 May 2010, available http://goo.gl/TTJ2SR; 'Frozen in the Greek repo markets', *FTAlphaville*, 19 July 2010, available http://goo.gl/NkiyfK

45. 'Italian settlement fail penalty, bond sell-off—causation or correlation?', *FTAlphaville*, 4 Nov. 2011, available http://goo.gl/Qqw74K; 'Why Italy is "Oh, so special!"', *FTAlphaville*, 10 Nov. 2011, available http://goo.gl/0vYmUb

46. 'Lessons from the financial crisis', keynote address by Jean-Claude Trichet, president of the European Central Bank, at the 'Wirtschaftstag 2009' organised by the Volksbanken and Raiffeisenbanken, Frankfurt am Main, *Europa.eu*, 15 Oct. 2009, available http://goo.gl/AXLgof; 'Monetary policy before, during and after the financial crisis', speech by Jürgen Stark, member of the executive board of the ECB, University Tübingen, Tübingen, *Europa.eu*, 9 Nov. 2009, available http://goo.gl/wlZEsX; 'ECB spurns IMF with early exit strategy', *Financial Times*, 29 Nov. 2009, available http://goo.gl/TQneys

47. 'Interview with Jean-Claude Trichet', *Le Monde*, 17 Nov. 2009, available http://goo.gl/qPYndc; Bastasin (2012), p. 159 argues that Germany cultivated uncertainty to pressurise Greece.

48. 'Warning to Greece over bond markets', *Financial Times*, 14 Dec. 2009, available http://goo.gl/yGBz5p

49. 'ΤτΕ: ζητά "φρένο" στη χρηματοδότηση από ΕΚΤ', *Euro2day*, 16 Nov. 2009, available http://goo.gl/5PhC8S

50. 'Greek cenbank advises banks to limit ECB funding', *Reuters*, 16 Nov. 2009, available http://goo.gl/s2Rwn2

51. 'Funding concerns hit equities', *ekathimerini.com*, 26 Nov. 2009, available http://goo.gl/XIidxP; 'Ιός χρεοκοπίας προ των πυλών', *Ta Nea*, 25 Nov. 2009, available http://goo.gl/Bijvah

52. 'Greece tests the limit of sovereign debt as it grinds towards slump', *Daily Telegraph*, 22 Nov. 2009, available http://goo.gl/0jPyxQ

53. 'The new Iceland? Greece fights to rein in debt', *Guardian*, 30 Nov. 2009, available http://goo.gl/crSxIZ; 'Greece acknowledges debt concerns', *BBC News*, 30 Nov. 2009, available http://goo.gl/oPfxk9; 'Credit agencies downgrade debt linked to Greece and Dubai', *The New York Times*, 8 Dec. 2009, available http://goo.gl/dDCI9c

54. 'NBG justifies move to buy govt bonds', *ekathimerini.com*, 2 Dec. 2009, available http://goo.gl/owiUyi; 'Key to Greece's economic recovery may lie in terse orders from Brussels', *ekathimerini.com*, 30 Nov. 2011, available http://goo.gl/Zm44AN

55. 'Commission declines comment on bank forecast', *ANA*, 27 Nov. 2009, available http://goo.gl/k2Wx8G

56. 'Greece can expect no gifts from Europe', *Financial Times*, 29 Nov. 2009, available http://goo.gl/ZkOcp1

57. 'Euro zone cannot solve Greek problems-Almunia', *FinanzNachrichten.de*, 13 Dec. 2009, available http://goo.gl/WSHcsG; 'Greece: ex post evaluation of exceptional access under the 2010 Stand-By Arrangement', *IMF.org*, 20 May 2013, available http://goo.gl/jx7hSD; Pisani-Ferry (2014), p. 77 says that Papandreou approached Strauss-Kahn seeking assistance but was told that before the IMF could act the other euro area members had to give their consent.

58. 'Investor fears over Greek government liquidity misplaced', *Moodys.com*, 2 Dec. 2009, available http://goo.gl/s7pFrd

59. 'Greek stocks, bonds slide for second day on downgrade concern', *Bloomberg*, 8 Dec. 2009, available http://goo.gl/nmUv1E

60. 'Statement by Commissioner Almunia on Greece', *Europa.eu*, 8 Dec. 2009, available http://goo.gl/vGIObq

61. 'Spiegel interview with Greek Prime Minister Papandreou: "It's a question of survival for Greece"', *Spiegel International Online*, 22 Feb. 2010, available http://goo.gl/AQ72hh; 'Please have confidence in us!', *FTAlphaville*, 17 Dec. 2009, available http://goo.gl/4JtWSr; 'PM Papandreou: state of Greek economy symptom of chronic problems', *ANA*, 13 Jan. 2010, available http://goo.gl/KeJ7mi; Tzogopoulos (2013), p. 5 says Papaconstantinou gave approximately 400 interviews to the press in a little over a year.

62. 'Papandreou says Greece is corrupt', *Financial Times*, 12 Dec. 2009, available http://goo.gl/JNwM38

63. 'Greek bonds fall as Papandreou fails to ease deficit concern', *Bloomberg*, 15 Dec. 2009, available http://goo.gl/X7X4KV

64. See for instance the use of the term 'bail-out' within the 'Treaty of Nice amending the Treaty on European Union', *Official Journal of the European Communities*, C 80/1, 10 Mar. 2001, pp. 1–87, available http://goo.gl/Ht6EBd

65. 'Another downgrade for Greece—S&P cuts to BBB+', *FTAlphaville*, 16 Dec. 2009, available http://goo.gl/QRnTS4

66. 'ECB must end Moody's veto on Greek debt, Goldman says (Update1)', *Bloomberg*, 18 Dec. 2009, available http://goo.gl/g3oX5f; 'ECB's Papademos says ECB will not change collateral rules', *capital.gr*, 18 Dec. 2009, available http://goo.gl/roQxwq; 'Introductory statement with Q&A: Jean-Claude Trichet, president of the ECB, Lucas Papademos, vice president of the ECB, Frankfurt', *Europa.eu*, 14 Jan. 2010, available http://goo.gl/cicJbi; 'ECB's Smaghi warns that Greece has one year to tackle rating problems', *capital.gr*, 14 Dec. 2009, available http://goo.gl/OoGLkO

67. 'Rating action: Moody's downgrades Greece to A2 from A1', *Moodys.com*, 22 Dec. 2009, available http://goo.gl/kqPpwo; 'Moodys: Τα δύσκολα για την Ελλάδα είναι μπροστά', *Kathimerini*, 25 Dec. 2009, available http://goo.gl/rSuO7q

68. 'Greece: ex post evaluation of exceptional access under the 2010 Stand-By Arrangement', *IMF.org*, 20 May 2013, available http://goo.gl/jx7hSD

69. 'The Hellenic Stability and Growth Programme: executive summary', *wsj.com*, available http://goo.gl/B2cywh

70. 'Update 2-Greece turns to Beijing for 25 bln-euro bond sale-FT', *Reuters*, 27 Jan. 2010, available http://goo.gl/rGPRA9

71. 'Report to the implementation of the Hellenic Stability and Growth Programme and additional measures in response to Council decision 6147/10', *Europa.eu*, Mar. 2010, available http://goo.gl/v7KzRB

72. 'Commission assesses stability programme of Greece; makes recommendations to correct the excessive budget deficit, improve competitiveness through structural reforms and provide reliable statistics', *Europa.eu*, 3 Feb. 2010, available http://goo.gl/iWH2qc

73. 'Statement by the heads of state or government of the European Union', *Europa.eu*, 11 Feb. 2010, available http://goo.gl/cks3gA

74. 'EU leaders deploy "bazooka" to repel attack on Greece (Update2)', *Bloomberg*, 12 Feb. 2010, available http://goo.gl/MgqKKR

75. 'Wednesday's nationwide strike', *ANA*, 25 Feb. 2010, available http://goo.gl/KzLq0S; 'Athens protest: "We are at war with them, as they are with us"', *Guardian*, 10 Feb. 2010, available http://goo.gl/C1BHZM

76. Lynn (2011), pp. 134–35.

77. See, for instance, 'Euro weakens to five-month low versus dollar on Greece concerns', *Bloomberg*, 20 Jan. 2010, available http://goo.gl/TEJrsM

78. 'Traders can gamble on the euro for the price of a cup of coffee in Starbucks', *Guardian*, 19 Feb. 2010, available http://goo.gl/IY4QP1

79. 'Hedge funds try "career trade" against euro', *The Wall Street Journal*, 26 Feb. 2010, available http://goo.gl/GXgP5G; the story is debunked in Bastasin (2012), pp. 160–62.

80. 'Trichet leaves early to attend crisis meeting', *ABC*, 8 Feb. 2010, available http://goo.gl/eO584X

81. 'Statement by the heads of state or government of the European Union', *Europa.eu*, 11 Feb. 2010, available http://goo.gl/cks3gA

82. 'Greece turns on EU critics', *Financial Times*, 12 Feb. 2010, available http://goo.gl/eyhmk0

83. 'Rehn in Athens on Mon.', *ANA*, 25 Feb. 2010, available http://goo.gl/Ur9D8c

84. 'Statement by the ECB's governing council on the additional measures of the Greek government', *Europa.eu*, 3 Mar. 2010, available http://goo.gl/wtTCPc; 'Debates of the European Parliament', *Europa.eu*, 9 Mar. 2010, pp. 92–93, available http://goo.gl/hwisSF

85. 'Greece's bond offer gets good response', *The Wall Street Journal*, 4 Mar. 2010, available http://goo.gl/OeL3Wk

86. 'Ελλείμματα, χρέος και spreads στις καφετέριες της περιφέρειας', *Kathimerini*, 9 Mar. 2010, available http://goo.gl/9KXpQv

87. '3003rd council meeting economic and financial affairs, Brussels', *Europa.eu*, 16 Mar. 2010, available http://goo.gl/UjkIYo

88. 'Statement of President Barroso on the creation of a euro area instrument for coordinated assistance to Greece', *Europa.eu*, 19 Mar. 2009, available http://goo.gl/DPLdm7

89. 'Update 1-ECB's Trichet: euro zone states must be more responsible', *Reuters*, 25 Mar. 2010, available http://goo.gl/m5JeEN; 'Juncker says "absurd" to talk of IMF aid for Greece (Update1)', *Bloomberg*, 16 Feb. 2010, available http://goo.gl/z96QVI

90. 'IMF reaches staff-level agreement with Greece on €30 Billion Stand-By Arrangement', *IMF. org*, 2 May 2010, available http://goo.gl/RpCKtZ

91. 'Samaras: "IMF gun" was PM's idea', *ANA*, 17 Apr. 2010, available http://goo.gl/xJw2Xo; 'Tsipras sees dire consequences from resort to IMF', *ANA*, 19 Apr. 2010, available http://goo.gl/STgNWu

92. 'Statement by the heads of state and government of the euro area', *Europa.eu*, 25 Mar. 2010, available http://goo.gl/OSB57N

93. 'José Manuel Durão Barroso, statement at the press conference following the first day of the spring European Council', *Europa.eu*, 25 Mar. 2010, available http://goo.gl/jr7oTW

94. 'Introductory statement before the plenary of the European Parliament: speech by Jean-Claude Trichet, president of the ECB', *Europa.eu*, 25 Mar. 2010, available http://goo.gl/LCwW0X

95. Bastasin (2012), pp. 217, 270.

96. 'Greece tries hand at short-term debt', *ekathimerini.com*, 31 Mar. 2010, available http://goo.gl/EgHGHq; 'Greece may raise cash needed in May but banks finding things tough', *ekathimerini.com*, 6 Apr. 2010, available http://goo.gl/qc459m

97. 'Crisis-hit Greece downgraded by Fitch', *Guardian*, 9 Apr. 2010, available http://goo.gl/dRo72A

98. 'Letter from the Ministry of Finance to the European Commission, to the European Central Bank and to the International Monetary Fund', *nrc.nl*, 15 Apr. 2010, available

http://goo.gl/GRvfIj; 'Greece asks for official talks', *Reuters*, 15 Apr. 2010, available http://goo.gl/PGMgsj

99. 'Poll reveals anger, fear over IMF involvement', *ANA*, 19 Apr. 2010, available http://goo.gl/ezB5tJ

100. 'Greece steps in to shore up banks', *Daily Telegraph*, 7 Apr. 2010, available http://goo.gl/EGuQ5z; 'Götterdämmerung for Greek banks', *FTAlphaville*, 14 June 2010, available http://goo.gl/ZJgya0

101. 'How Washington pushed Europe to save the euro', *Financial Times*, 10 Oct. 2010, available http://goo.gl/K6bD1l

102. 'Rating action: Moody's downgrades Greece's sovereign ratings to A3; on review for further possible downgrade', *Moodys.com*, 22 Apr. 2010, available http://goo.gl/0221v2; 'Euroindicators, 55/2010', *Europa.eu*, 22 Apr. 2010, available http://goo.gl/sxLza6

103. 'PM on activation of support mechanism', *ANA*, 24 Apr. 2010, available http://goo.gl/I3LrRY

104. Papaconstantinou (2016); 'Πώς και γιατί ερρίφθη ο κύβος του ΔΝΤ', *Kathimerini*, 24 Apr. 2010, available http://goo.gl/TklzSP

105. 'PM Papandreou: Greece formally asks activation of EU support mechanism', *ANA*, 24 Apr. 2010, available http://goo.gl/vWxnD3

106. 'PM from Rhodes on eurozone-IMF support', *ANA*, 26 Apr. 2010, available http://goo.gl/FvIQPk

107. 'S&P downgrades Greece ratings into junk status', *Reuters*, 27 Apr. 2010, available http://goo.gl/UJvW3n

108. 'OECD's Gurria warns Greek crisis spreading "like Ebola"', *Bloomberg Business*, 28 Apr. 2010, available https://goo.gl/CmVN6T

109. 'ECB announces change in eligibility of debt instruments issued or guaranteed by the Greek government', *Europa.eu*, 3 May 2010, available http://goo.gl/fcpfZJ

110. 'PM Papandreou: big feat ahead', *ANA*, 3 May 2010, available http://goo.gl/GlCvo1

111. 'This Greek bailout is not a recovery plan—it is an economic death spiral', *Guardian*, 4 May 2010, available http://goo.gl/wJthzc

112. 'Greek bailout: Athens burns—and crisis strikes at heart of the EU', *Guardian*, 5 May 2010, available http://goo.gl/6a7wIi

113. 'Greece approves sweeping austerity measures', *Guardian*, 6 May 2010, available http://goo.gl/yZUHNG

114. Verney (2012), p. 201.

115. 'Greece agrees to austerity plan to secure European Union, IMF rescue loans', *The Washington Post*, 7 May 2010, available http://goo.gl/9Amkyx

116. 'Crisis in Greece leaves EU future in balance, warns Angela Merkel', *Guardian*, 5 May 2010, available http://goo.gl/D3xcnD

117. 'Germany's MPs rage at Merkel over bailout plan', *Independent*, 6 May 2010, available http://goo.gl/7UIIdw

118. 'Bond traders who could decide Portugal's fate tell of a "crazy, fun" week', *Guardian*, 30 Apr. 2010, available http://goo.gl/chjcac

119. 'Christine Lagarde: "there should never be too much testosterone in one room"', *Independent*, 7 Feb. 2011, http://goo.gl/MJfqlu

120. On the various pressures within the financial system at this time see Lapavitsas, Kaltenbrunner, Labrinidis, et al. (2013), pp. 103–111.

121. 'ECB paralysis rattles markets as debt costs hit new highs', *Daily Telegraph*, 6 May 2010, available http://goo.gl/AiEIlm; 'Franco-German show of unity ahead of eurozone summit', *Euractiv.com*, 7 May 2010, available http://goo.gl/30iIlr

122. '"We only have one shot": how the euro rescue package came together', *Spiegel International Online*, 17 May 2010, available http://goo.gl/ESvCys

123. Lynn (2011), pp. 149–82; 'Papandreou: "We can do this. We must do this. We will do this together"', *FTAlphaville*, 7 May 2010, available http://goo.gl/lqI2I6

124. 'Statement of the heads of state or government of the euro area', *Europa.eu*, 7 May 2010, available http://goo.gl/74nNva

125. 'EU to fend off market "wolves" in Greek crisis', *Reuters*, 9 May 2010, available http://goo.gl/N0RssZ

126. Bastasin (2012), pp. 201–202; 'ECB decides on measures to address severe tensions in financial markets', *Europa.eu*, 10 May 2010, available http://goo.gl/nbW8lz

5. FALTERING AT THE RUBICON: THE DIFFICULTIES OF THE MEMORANDUM

1. 'Greece: request for Stand-By Arrangement', *IMF.org*, 10 May 2010, available http://goo.gl/uXKJLz

2. 'The Economic Adjustment Programme for Greece', *Europa.eu*, May 2010, available http://goo.gl/B7u4gw

3. 'IMF reaches staff-level agreement with Greece on €30 Billion Stand-By Arrangement', *IMF. org*, 2 May 2010, available http://goo.gl/NQn2nV

4. Pisani-Ferry, Sapir & Wolff (2013).

5. 'PM: rebirth of Greece, now or never', *ANA*, 28 Apr. 2010, available http://goo.gl/JFALcJ

6. '«Ήμασταν σαν τις πόρνες μετά την πρώτη τους φορά»', *To Vima*, 16 Oct. 2011, available http://goo.gl/hrYWWF; 'Why is Germany talking about a European Monetary Fund?', *The Economist*, 9 Mar. 2010, available http://goo.gl/aU6r2J

7. 'Greece: ex post evaluation of exceptional access under the 2010 Stand-By Arrangement', *IMF.org*, 20 May 2013, available http://goo.gl/jx7hSD

8. See in general Blyth (2013) but in relation to 2010 especially pp. 173–77.

9. 'The Economic Adjustment Programme for Greece', *Europa.eu*, May 2010, available http://goo.gl/KW2mjy

10. 'Shock therapy may smother Greek economy, extend crisis', *Reuters*, 9 May 2010, available http://goo.gl/W9XVd9

11. 'Grim Greek austerity arithmetic', *FTAlphaville*, 5 May 2010, available http://goo.gl/9XRTmR; 'Greece faces a Herculean adjustment task', *FTAlphaville*, 11 May 2010, available http://goo.gl/eEbDMC

12. 'It's not about Greece anymore', *The New York Times Economix Blog*, 6 May 2010, available http://goo.gl/IFn8vA; Pisani-Ferry (2014), p. 88.

13. 'Greece—memorandum of economic and financial policies', *IMF.org*, 3 May 2010, available http://goo.gl/uXKJLz
14. On some of the potential pitfalls see Antzoulatos (2011), p. 253.
15. 'Greece needs investment to exit crisis: minister', *Reuters*, 28 May 2010, available http://goo.gl/akCJbD
16. It was probably also unwilling to move beyond what it considered to be its remit.
17. 'The IMF should heed this resignation', *Financial Times*, 25 July 2012, available http://goo.gl/0nrFxf; the IMF had taken the lead in Hungary and Romania but this was not the case in Latvia.
18. 'Greece: ex post evaluation of exceptional access under the 2010 Stand-By Arrangement', *IMF.org*, 20 May 2013, available http://goo.gl/jx7hSD
19. Pisani-Ferry, Sapir & Wolff (2013).
20. 'Greece: ex post evaluation of exceptional access under the 2010 Stand-By Arrangement', *IMF.org*, 20 May 2013, available http://goo.gl/jx7hSD
21. 'The Economic Adjustment Programme for Greece', *Europa.eu*, May 2010, available http://goo.gl/KW2mjy; 'Greece: first review under the Stand-By Arrangement', *IMF.org*, 26 Aug. 2010, available http://goo.gl/vLgqp5
22. 'Greece needs investment to exit crisis: minister', *Reuters*, 28 May 2010, available http://goo.gl/akCJbD
23. 'GSEE president: no margins for bargaining, negotiation', *ANA*, 28 May 2010, available http://goo.gl/6o7bmy; *Athens News*, 4 July 2010.
24. 'Greek PM calls for collective efforts to change the country', *ANA*, 13 Sep. 2010, available http://goo.gl/tHl0Pm
25. From a Stephen Sackur interview with George A. Papandreou at the OECD headquarters in Paris, 16 Nov. 2010, broadcast on BBC HARDtalk, transcript available http://goo.gl/A8LjUB
26. 'EC-IMF: more still to be done', *ANA*, 8 Aug. 2010, available http://goo.gl/5gCOSo
27. 'Update 1-euro zone lauds Greek effort to cut budget deficit', *Reuters*, 12 July 2010 available http://goo.gl/QvrcGU; 'Central bank chief optimistic', *ANA*, 23 July 2010, available http://goo.gl/6wSzES
28. See, for instance, 'Update 2-Greek PM urges banks to regroup to cope with crisis', *Reuters*, 24 June 2010, available http://goo.gl/tjq7Wh; 'Update 1-Greek first-half budget deficit down 46 pct y/y', *Reuters*, 12 June 2010, available http://goo.gl/zDfKqb
29. 'FinMin Papaconstantinou ascertains considerable change in climate at IMF, World Bank annual conference', *ANA*, 11 Oct. 2010, available http://goo.gl/JbwX8u
30. 'Letter of intent, memorandum of economic and financial policies, technical memorandum of understanding, and memorandum of understanding on specific economic policy conditionality (European Commission and European Central Bank)', *IMF.org*, 6 Aug. 2010, available http://goo.gl/c90JHT
31. 'Ευρωβαρόμετρο. Καταχνιά για νοικοκυριά, εργαζόμενους', *enet.gr*, 27 Aug. 2010, available http://goo.gl/kZIf4D; 'Table of results: standard Eurobarometer 73', *Europa.eu*, Nov. 2010, available http://goo.gl/kd7JN5

32. 'Rating action: Moody's downgrades Greece to Ba1 from A3, stable outlook', *Moodys.com*, 14 June 2010, available http://goo.gl/DA1tMV

33. C. Chamley & B. Pinto, 'Why official bailouts tend not to work: an example motivated by Greece 2010', *The Economists' Voice*, Feb. 2011, available http://goo.gl/rFEXV3

34. 'Trichet: no euro exit for Athens', *ANA*, 6 Sep. 2010, available http://goo.gl/90I2VD

35. 'EU austerity policies risk civil war in Greece, warns top German economist Dr Sinn', *Daily Telegraph*, 3 Sep. 2010, available http://goo.gl/XvYhhQ; 'Entering a death spiral? Tensions rise in Greece as austerity measures backfire', *Spiegel Online International*, 18 Aug. 2010, available http://goo.gl/jF10EX

36. 'Police, workers clash at Acropolis', *Reuters*, 14 Oct. 2010, available http://goo.gl/C8FU87

37. *Athens News*, 12 July 2010.

38. 'Greece: first review under the Stand-By Arrangement', *IMF.org*, 26 Aug. 2010, available http://goo.gl/vLgqp5

39. 'The Economic Adjustment Programme for Greece first review—summer 2010', *Europa.eu*, Aug. 2010, available http://goo.gl/RzoY2X

40. Matsaganis (2012), pp. 159–60.

41. Ibid., pp. 166–67.

42. Από 5.000.000 ασφαλισμένους, ζήτημα αν γλιτώσουν 1.250.000', *enet.gr*, 28 June 2010, available, http://goo.gl/YEO1rK

43. 'Update 2-Greek PM urges waverers to vote for pension bill', *Reuters*, 3 July 2010, available http://goo.gl/DxcnLv

44. 'Greece: first review under the Stand-By Arrangement', *IMF.org*, 26 Aug. 2010, available http://goo.gl/YTREYW

45. 'Pensions at a glance', *OECD.org*, 2013, available http://goo.gl/MOn3fe; Palaiologos (2014).

46. 'Greece will become more competitive', interview with Poul Tomsen published in *Kathimerini*, *IMF*.org, 8 Aug. 2010, available http://goo.gl/pCAYFh; 'Barbarism at the gates', *Inside Greece*, 7 Oct. 2010, available http://goo.gl/zOR9O8

47. For the legislation see Koukiadaki & Kretsos (2012).

48. 'PM: upcoming elections a "yes" vote for a new Greece', *ANA*, 6 Sep. 2010, available http://goo.gl/UIlEFL

49. 'Οι πολίτες αποδοκιμάζουν την «αντιμνημονιακή» στρατηγική της Ρηγίλλης, αλλά συσπειρώνονται και πάλι γύρω από τα δύο μεγαλύτερα κόμματα. Η ΝΔ δεν πείθει για το μνημόνιο', *To Vima*, 12 Sep. 2010, available http://goo.gl/s55aJa

50. 'Άγριο κλάδεμα στους «κηπουρούς»', *enet.gr*, 5 June 2011, available http://goo.gl/dfAklx

51. 'FinMin addresses letters to ministers on memorandum's implementation', *ANA*, 9 Sep. 2010, available http://goo.gl/uO83ep

52. 'Greek PM offers some tax relief, but no handouts', *Reuters*, 11 Sep. 2010, available http://goo.gl/w5BCXo

53. 'Is it cheaper to put Greek train passengers in taxis?', *BBC News*, 13 May 2012, available http://goo.gl/G1MfmY

54. 'Greek strikers halt flights, buses as bailout bites', *Bloomberg*, 15 Dec. 2010, available http://goo.gl/o3kOTI; a lower figure of €35,111 is mentioned in 'Public sector enterprises' pay-

roll costs down 15% in Jan-Sep', *ANA*, 30 Dec. 2010, available http://goo.gl/nCV2Sc; after the wage reductions, in 2013 taking into account overtime, night shifts and bonuses the average monthly salary was said to be €4,095 before tax. See 'Χατζηδάκης σε εργαζόμενους του μετρό: η κοινωνία είναι απέναντι σας, δεν υπάρχουν άλλα περιθώρια', *Star.gr*, 23 Jan. 2011, available http://goo.gl/NHK7oF

55. 'Greek strikers halt flights, buses as bailout bites', *Bloomberg*, 15 Dec. 2010, available http://goo.gl/anrTdr

56. For road transport see Mitsopoulos & Pelagidis (2011), pp. 264–67; 'Greece's dilemma: which way to the future?', *ekathimerini.com*, 8 Oct. 2010, available http://goo.gl/VfCsbA; 'Κονδύλι 30 εκατ. στους φορτηγατζήδες από το αναπτυξιακό', *enet.gr*, 7 June 2011, available http://goo.gl/A4CVOk

57. 'Greece: first review under the Stand-By Arrangement', *IMF.org*, 26 Aug. 2010, available http://goo.gl/YTREYW

58. 'Greece unveils tax amnesty bill to boost revenues', *Reuters*, 27 Sep. 2010, available http://goo.gl/0B0gZb;

59. For some idea of what was said to be delayed see 'Οι «διαρθρωτικές» αλλαγές αρχίζουν μετά τις εκλογές', *enet.gr*, 31 Oct. 2011, available http://goo.gl/wpMKun

60. Gemenis (2012).

61. Verney (2012), p. 211.

62. Karyotis & Rüdig (2015). The abstention rate was 39.1 per cent with an additional 5.5 per cent of ballots being blank or spoilt.

63. 'Διαφώνησαν μεμονωμένα...', *enet.gr*, 14 Dec. 2010, available http://goo.gl/M3OXGi

64. 'Government rules out default, says third tranche secure', *ANA*, 23 Nov. 2010, available http://goo.gl/G1PyUJ; 'Minister Kastanidis: memorandum terms should be renegotiated', *ANA*, 10 Nov. 2010, available http://goo.gl/If3kaJ

65. 'Minister Kastanidis: memorandum terms should be renegotiated', *ANA*, 10 Nov. 2010, available http://goo.gl/If3kaJ

66. A copy of the Eur 80 000 000 000 loan facility agreement dated 8 May 2010 can be found on the Irish Statute Book, available http://goo.gl/TgZ2h5

67. 'Update 6-China's Wen offers to buy Greek debt', *Reuters*, 2 Oct. 2010, available http://goo.gl/Mi1Dsy

68. 'Greece: first review under the Stand-By Arrangement', *IMF.org*, 26 Aug. 2010, available http://goo.gl/vLgqp5

69. 'Merkel urges action against market "extortion"', *Reuters*, 19 May 2010, available http://goo.gl/yuQ3ln

70. 'Germany prepares for worst in euro zone crisis', *Reuters*, 26 May 2010, available http://goo.gl/U5JhNk; D. Gros in collaboration with T. Mayer, 'How to deal with sovereign default in Europe: towards a Euro(pean) Monetary Fund', *Europa.eu*, 8 Mar. 2010, available http://goo.gl/0pkoh1

71. 'Strengthening economic governance in the EU: report of the task force to the European Council', *Europa.eu*, 21 Oct. 2010, available http://goo.gl/FUKVwO

72. 'Brussels summit: EU agrees to Merkel's controversial euro reforms', *Spiegel International Online*, 29 Oct. 2010, available http://goo.gl/sXzZbP

NOTES pp. [150–154]

73. 'As Ireland flails, Europe lurches across the Rubicon', *The Wall Street Journal*, 27 Dec. 2010, available http://goo.gl/u9XkG7

73. 'As Ireland flails, Europe lurches across the Rubicon', *The Wall Street Journal*, 27 Dec. 2010, available http://goo.gl/u9XkG7

74. Έβαλαν τους «δανειστές» στην Ε.Ε., *enet.gr*, 29 Oct. 2010, available http://goo.gl/23d5NQ

75. 'Update 1-German stance may push nations to bankruptcy-Greek PM', *Reuters*, 15 Nov. 2010, available http://goo.gl/XQyik4

76. On the characteristics of the bond market see Pisani-Ferry (2014), p. 70.

77. Bastasin (2012), p. 270; 'Greek default spells "havoc" for banks a year after bailout', *Bloomberg*, 20 June 2011, available http://goo.gl/rWNQ0U

78. 'Trichet tries to calm nerves over default mechanism', *The Wall Street Journal*, 30 Nov. 2010, available http://goo.gl/dX3jhI; 'Angela Merkel forces Europe to protect euro from future collapse', *Guardian*, 29 Oct. 2010, available http://goo.gl/dBKOOU

79. 'Focus Greece. Fiscal data revisions: assessment & implications', *eurobank.gr*, 15 Nov. 2010, available http://goo.gl/ceYs9X

80. 'Greece to conclude EU/IMF talks on Monday—finmin', *Reuters*, 22 Nov. 2010, available http://goo.gl/kgY9w8

81. 'Update 2-Austria: Greece has not met aid commitments', *Reuters*, 16 Nov. 2010, available http://goo.gl/wtJPpZ

82. 'Δήλωση Σόιμπλε—Η αλληλεγγύη δεν είναι μονόδρομος. Εκβιάζει η Μέρκελ με όπλο την τρίτη δόση', *To Vima*, 17 Nov. 2010, available http://goo.gl/ly78oc

83. '«Επιμήκυνση έχετε μόνο αν μας πείσετε»', *enet.gr*, 30 Nov. 2010, available http://goo.gl/tV4dRM; 'Greece: second review under the Stand-By Arrangement', *IMF.org*, 6 Dec. 2010, available http://goo.gl/Fkd1dT

84. 'Greece: third review under the Stand-By Arrangement', *IMF.org*, 28 Feb. 2011, available http://goo.gl/eP42TK

85. Ibid.

86. 'Update 2-Greece gets repayment extension to 2021—finmin', *Reuters*, 29 Nov. 2010, available http://goo.gl/7a7syg

87. '«Επιπόλαιη η ένταξη της Ελλάδας στο ευρώ»', *enet.gr*, 16 Nov. 2010, available http://goo.gl/byd8JP

88. 'Merkel ready to do "whatever needed" to save euro', *Bloomberg*, 12 Jan. 2011, available http://goo.gl/UhP3O2

89. 'E-bonds would end the crisis', *Financial Times*, 5 Oct. 2010, available http://goo.gl/saNRQV

90. Karyotis & Rüdig (2015).

91. 'Greek economy returns to growth amid push for new EU-led bailout', *Bloomberg*, 13 May 2011, available http://goo.gl/K6fKdB

92. 'Business mood improves for second month', *ekathimerini.com*, 3 Mar. 2011, available http://goo.gl/zuaCJI; Ένα στα δύο στελέχη αισιοδοξούν ότι δεν θα χρεοκοπήσουμε', *enet.gr*, 12 Apr. 2011, available http://goo.gl/dpt1T5

93. 'Euroindicators, STAT/11/42', *Europa.eu*, 16 Mar. 2011, available http://goo.gl/L5RSGQ

94. 'Corrected—(official)-update 1-Eurobank puts up Greek bonds to tap markets', *Reuters*, 18 Oct. 2010, available http://goo.gl/HWIeeI

95. 'OTE successful in 500 mln euro bond deal', *ekathimerini.com*, 5 Apr. 2011, available http://goo.gl/wjQri4; 'Strapped Greece taps U.S. diaspora', *The Wall Street Journal*, 10 Mar. 2011, available http://goo.gl/KbpEyR

96. '10 λόγοι για να μη ζει κάποιος στην Ελλάδα', *Eleftherotypia*, 21 Nov. 2010, available http://goo.gl/cEL6vY

97. 'Eurobarometer 74', *Europa.eu*, Feb. 2011, available http://goo.gl/SCK2PE

98. 'Greek exports surge but don't pop the champagne', *Reuters*, 7 Mar. 2011, available http://goo.gl/qrmMyE

99. 'Greece: third review under the Stand-By Arrangement', *IMF.org*, 28 Feb. 2011, available http://goo.gl/LVaIcs

100. 'Update 2-Greece slams EU, IMF officials after inspection visit', *Reuters*, 12 Feb. 2010, available http://goo.gl/WcPUWh

101. 'Troika: regret, "deep respect"', *ANA*, 13 Feb. 2011, available http://goo.gl/vS9AD2

102. 'Greece: request for Stand-By Arrangement', *IMF.org*, 10 May 2010, available http://goo.gl/uXKJLz

103. 'Greece: second review under the Stand-By Arrangement', *IMF.org*, 6 Dec. 2010, available http://goo.gl/Dl0885

104. For the 2015 negotiations see the Epilogue.

105. Palaiologos (2014); a figure of €600 billion originally circulated but see also 'Στα 280 δισ. ευρώ οι ελληνικές καταθέσεις στην Ελβετία', *imerisia.gr*, 11 Mar. 2011, available http://goo.gl/kR46El

106. 'Οσα μας χρωστούν οι Γερμανοί…Το πόρισμα του υπουργείου οικονομικών και η ιστορική ευθύνη της κυβέρνησης', *To Vima*, 7 Apr. 2013, available http://goo.gl/bLXbOH; 'Secret Athens report: Berlin owes Greece billions in WWII reparations', *Spiegel International Online*, 8 Apr. 2013, available http://goo.gl/RRcBn2; subsequent claims were even higher see 'Finance ministry officials put Germany's WWII debt at 280 to 340 bln', *ekathimerini.com*, 4 June 2015, available http://goo.gl/WhtXtu

107. For Russia see '«Η Ρωσία έδινε δάνειο, η Ελλάδα αδιαφόρησε»', *enet.gr*, 14 July 2011, available http://goo.gl/ml44qA; for a detailed rebuttal, 'Дайте, пожалуйста self-aggrandising bullcrap?', *LOL Greece Blog*, 1 Aug. 2011, available http://goo.gl/333AZN

108. See, for instance, *DebtOcracy*, edited/written by K. Kitidi & A. Chatzistefanou, 75 mins, 2011, available http://goo.gl/rFd5XP; '«Το ΔΝΤ παραβιάζει τα ανθρώπινα δικαιώματα»', *To Vima*, 17 Apr. 2011, available http://goo.gl/fU3QVb

109. Buchheit, Gulati & Thompson (2007); Ludington & Gulati (2008); Ludington, Gulati & Brophy (2010).

110. 'Lessons from Ecuador's bond default', *Reuters*, 29 May 2009, available http://goo.gl/buiXE5

111. Palaiologos (2014); 'En Grèce, la lutte contre les décharges s'organise à Kératéa', *Le Monde*, 11 Apr. 2011, available http://goo.gl/04zcD5

112. 'Συγκέντρωση διαμαρτυρίας έξω από το σπίτι του Κ. Σημίτη', *enet.gr*, 3 Mar. 2011, available http://goo.gl/CdthzF

113. '«Μετά τον έλεγχο βαλτώσατε»', *To Vima*, 6 Mar. 2011, available http://goo.gl/novTt6

114. 'The day after', *ekathimerini.com*, 8 Mar. 2011, available http://goo.gl/mcZjwB

115. 'Greece downgrade by Moody's sends default risk to record', *Bloomberg*, 7 Mar. 2011, available http://goo.gl/pyA3T6

116. 'MPs looking to take Moody's to court', *ekathimerini.com*, 9 Mar. 2011, available http://goo.gl/AAL1vV

117. 'Deputy prime minister hits out at SYRIZA', *ekathimerini.com*, 18 Mar. 2011, available http://goo.gl/ihz7pj

6. SURPRISED BY THE SURPRISE: THE WIDER EURO ZONE CRISIS AND THE FALL OF THE PAPANDREOU GOVERNMENT

1. A paraphrase of a comment made by Papandreou about his decision to hold a referendum. See his speech in the cabinet meeting room, parliament, 3 Nov. 2011, available http://goo.gl/VMhwA3

2. 'EU debt-relief pact puts pressure on nations to cut deficits: euro credit', *Bloomberg*, 14 Mar. 2011, available http://goo.gl/RjWy1C

3. 'Irish "bad boys" vow to keep tax rate after Sarkozy summit spat', *Bloomberg*, 14 Mar. 2011, available http://goo.gl/EakEQI

4. 'Good news, but targets remain elusive', *ekathimerini.com*, 13 Mar. 2010, available http://goo.gl/vhNAW0

5. 'Greece: fourth review under the Stand-By Arrangement and request for modification and waiver of applicability of performance criteria', *IMF.org*, 4 July 2011, available http://goo.gl/n5dLK

6. See, for instance, 'Ασήκωτη η βαλίτσα της επιστροφής', *enet.gr*, 13 Mar. 2011, available http://goo.gl/n5nZSj

7. 'Students protest against PM on Syros', *ekathimerini.com*, 21 Mar. 2011, available http://goo.gl/evLZ7v

8. 'The Economic Adjustment Programme for Greece: third review—winter 2011', *Europa.eu*, Feb. 2011, available http://goo.gl/S23iPt

9. 'Eurogroup meeting/European Stability Mechanism meeting: extracts from the press conference by Jean-Claude Juncker, president of the Eurogroup and Olli Rehn, European commissioner for economic and monetary affairs', *Europa.eu*, 20 June 2011, available http://goo.gl/iay7uX

10. 'German chancellor on the offensive: Merkel blasts Greece over retirement age, vacation', *Spiegel Online International*, 18 May 2011, available http://goo.gl/jckvxf

11. 'German court reins in Berlin on euro crisis', *Reuters*, 7 Sep. 2011, available http://goo.gl/xxc5FU

12. 'Dithering at the top turned EU crisis to global threat', *The Wall Street Journal*, 29 Dec. 2011, available http://goo.gl/Dcl4jO

13. 'Greek-out culminates in talk of euro zone exit [updated]', *FTAlphaville*, 6 May 2011, available http://goo.gl/iL5Z8b

14. 'Luxembourg lies on secret meeting', *The Wall Street Journal*, 9 May 2011, available http://goo.gl/t6qkk9

15. 'Atene non esce dall' euro, sarebbe un disastro', *La Stampa*, 7 May 2011, available http://goo.gl/9pYwbA

16. 'Merkel pushes off Greek aid decision in replay of last year', *Bloomberg*, 10 May 2011, available http://goo.gl/XFF4Wg

17. 'Schaeuble defies ECB to insist bondholders share Greek aid', *Bloomberg*, 10 June 2011, available http://goo.gl/KTf1OC

18. 'Standard & Poor's downgrades Greece, Portugal', *Reuters*, 29 Mar. 2011, available http://goo.gl/pxmN3S

19. 'PM dismisses debt downgrade, looks forward', *ekathimerini.com*, 29 Mar. 2011, available http://goo.gl/Pq1NOx

20. 'Dithering at the top turned EU crisis to global threat', *The Wall Street Journal*, 29 Dec. 2011, available http://goo.gl/Dcl4jO

21. 'ECB may have more scope for Greek leeway than talk suggests', *Bloomberg*, 26 May 2011, available http://goo.gl/DXSler

22. 'Οι 8 εφιάλτες του σεναρίου της αναναδιάρθρωσης', *imerisia.gr*, 2 Apr. 2011, available http://goo.gl/SPfmXh; 'Greece sells bills at almost 5% as bailout talk lifts bonds', *Bloomberg*, 10 May 2011, available http://goo.gl/cgUcOl; 'Papademos says losses on Greek debt neither desirable nor needed', *Bloomberg*, 8 Apr. 2011, available http://goo.gl/pEohkb

23. 'Πρόταση-σοκ από Σημίτη για αναδιάρθρωση', *To Vima*, 17 Apr. 2011, available http://goo.gl/HDhwPL

24. 'IMF board meeting on Greece's request for an SBA', *wsj.com*, 9 May, 2010, available http://goo.gl/KT5gwh

25. 'IMF denies pressing Greece to restructure debt', *Reuters*, 2 Apr. 2011, available http://goo.gl/WsFNRi

26. Blundell-Wignall & Slovik (2010).

27. 'Greek debt and a default of statesmanship', *Financial Times*, 28 Jan. 2015, available http://goo.gl/ivGjBL

28. 'Bruxelles veut interdire des opérations spéculatives sur la dette des Etats', *Le Monde*, 9 Mar. 2010, available http://goo.gl/bYWUs6; 'Banks bet Greece defaults on debt they helped hide', *The New York Times*, 24 Feb. 2010, available http://goo.gl/swoyms; 'Athens dinner that led to political indigestion', *Financial Times*, 4 Mar. 2010, available http://goo.gl/yR209P; 'Why is Germany talking about a European Monetary Fund?' *The Economist*, 9 Mar. 2010, available http://goo.gl/BA9xLk

29. 'BaFin clarifies: so far no evidence of massive speculation against Greek bonds', *BaFin.de*, 8 Mar. 2010, available http://goo.gl/Mx0IHC; see also 'ISDA survey shows continued improvement in OTC derivatives infrastructure', *DTTC Connection*, 3 May 2010, available http://goo.gl/BlnzOU; but also 'Credit Default Swaps on government debt: potential implications of the Greek debt crisis. Hearing before the Subcommittee on Capital Markets, Insurance, and Government Sponsored Enterprises of the Committee on Financial Services', *U.S. House Of Representatives*, 29 Apr. 2010, available http://goo.gl/5wAqY2; it was claimed that the partly Greek government-owned TT bank made a profit of some €35 million by buying CDS in August 2009 and selling them in December. The allegation is reproduced in

'Trojan speculators, or, one headache for the Greek authorities', *FTAlphaville*, 23 May 2010, available http://goo.gl/2udAqj

30. 'EU raises Greek deficit forecast amid calls for new bailout', *Bloomberg*, 13 May 2011, available http://goo.gl/3vZxRq; 'Greece: fifth review under the Stand-By Arrangement', *IMF. org*, 30 Nov. 2011, available http://goo.gl/gUL0ck

31. 'Fitch cuts Greece to B+, says voluntary maturity extension is default', *Bloomberg*, 20 May 2011, available http://goo.gl/LtcENE

32. 'Greek debt maturity lengthening possible—Juncker', *Reuters*, 24 May 2011, available http://goo.gl/NJu6WN; 'Juncker says EU cannot help Greece without IMF', *ekathimerini.com*, 26 May 2011, available http://goo.gl/mPBQNp

33. 'Greek austerity standoff rattles euro zone', *Reuters*, 25 May 2011, available http://goo.gl/x859qs

34. 'Midterm economic program eyes taxes, pensions', *ekathimerini.com*, 23 May 2011, available http://goo.gl/88zRZY

35. 'Έσκασε η φούσκα της συναίνεσης στις επιταγές του μνημονίου', *enet.gr*, 27 May 2011, available http://goo.gl/DqKvmD; 'Greek politicians fail to forge deal', *The Wall Street Journal*, 28 May 2011, available http://goo.gl/m8GCN2

36. 'EU's Damanaki tells Greece euro membership at risk', *Reuters*, 25 May 2011, available http://goo.gl/pBljhM; '«Έπνιξαν» τη δήλωση Δαμανάκη περί δραχμής', *enet.gr*, 27 May 2011, available http://goo.gl/W8LC0Y

37. 'Report: military coup possible in Greece', *Hurriyet Daily News*, 29 May 2011, available http://goo.gl/SDSuLz; see also 'Greece: don't discount the role of the military', *The Wall Street Journal*, 19 Sep. 2011, available http://goo.gl/vqZSGd; the story reportedly originally came from *Bild*.

38. 'Moody's latest cut puts Greece in debt rating hall of shame', *Bloomberg*, 2 June 2011, available http://goo.gl/4MLfOk

39. 'Greece's 100 billion-euro shadow over banks', *Reuters*, 25 May 2011, available http://goo.gl/GddnFC

40. 'Greek default spells "havoc" for banks a year after bailout', *Bloomberg*, 20 June 2011, available http://goo.gl/jrvZjl

41. 'Statement by the European Commission, the ECB and IMF on the fourth review mission to Greece', *IMF.org*, 3 June 2011 available http://goo.gl/m00eR8

42. 'The biggest gamble in IMF history', *FTAlphaville*, 3 June 2011, available http://goo.gl/i3U1gw

43. '«Από πού θα φύγετε;»', *enet.gr*, 1 June 2011, available http://goo.gl/biK436

44. 'Greece: medium-term fiscal strategy 2012–15', *minfin.gr*, June 2011, available http://goo.gl/Ky2uZV

45. See 'Box 1. The medium term fiscal strategy (MTFS), 2011–14' in 'Greece: fourth review under the Stand-By Arrangement', *IMF.org*, 4 July 2011, available http://goo.gl/sBgHb7

46. Note the reporting in 'Πάρε, πάρε: ακίνητα, δρόμους, αεροδρόμια, λιμάνια, πετρέλαια, τράπεζες, οργανισμούς!', *enet.gr*, 7 June 2011, available http://goo.gl/FPwUEq

47. '«Αγανάκτησαν» και εκτονώθηκαν με το βλέμμα στην πλατεία', *enet.gr*, 8 June 2011, available

http://goo.gl/QvPF1L; 'Ruling party MPs slam austerity plan', *ekathimerini.com*, 7 June 2011, available http://goo.gl/WyQc7U

48. 'PASOK MP calls for Papaconstantinou to go', *ekathimerini.com*, 12 June 2011, available http://goo.gl/ngKSmW

49. 'Cabinet approves fiscal plan, new tax hikes', *ekathimerini.com*, 9 June 2011, available http://goo.gl/wAb1Jo

50. 'PASOK's majority slips as MPs resist measures', *ekathimerini.com*, 14 June 2011, available http://goo.gl/UnfwPI

51. 'Greece gets world's lowest rating from S&P as default risk rises', *Bloomberg*, 14 June 2011, available http://goo.gl/TW2TNH

52. 'PM seeks backing on new measures', *ekathimerini.com*, 10 June 2011, available http://goo.gl/FH1V3m

53. 'Οι εθνοπροδότες σκάβουν λαγούμια για να την κοπανήσουν', *Kontra TV*, 11 June 2011, available http://goo.gl/OH1HbM

54. #spanishrevolution had already been used by the movement in Spain; see Jiménez & Estalella (2011).

55. 'PM opts for reshuffle, vote of confidence', *ekathimerini.com*, 15 June 2011, available http://goo.gl/1FDQdc

56. 'Europe faces "Lehman moment" as Greece unravels: euro credit', *Bloomberg*, 16 June 2011, available http://goo.gl/IFUIk5

57. 'Ramping up pressure on Athens: Euro group postpones decision on Greek aid', *Spiegel Online International*, 20 June 2011 available http://goo.gl/rQxMQf

58. *Der Spiegel*, 20 June 2011, available http://goo.gl/5yp5xi

59. 'Greece backs first austerity package, violence worsens', *Reuters*, 29 June 2011, available http://goo.gl/Sjm5zd; Hewitt (2013).

60. 'Greeks protest, almost half oppose austerity', *Reuters*, 18 June 2011, available http://goo.gl/iLRA60

61. 'Rating action: Moody's downgrades Portugal to Ba2 with a negative outlook from Baa1', *Moodys.com*, 5 July 2011, available http://goo.gl/173ch9; 'Rating action: Moody's downgrades Ireland to Ba1; outlook remains negative', *Moodys.com*, 12 July 2011, available http://goo.gl/1LsbwE

62. 'Europe considers Greek default, leaders to meet', *Reuters*, 12 July 2011, available http://goo.gl/0aqOTM

63. 'Statement by the Eurogroup', *Europa.eu*, 11 July 2011, available http://goo.gl/iVVNXn; 'Special report—Europe's debilitating deja vu', *Reuters*, 5 Oct. 2011, available http://goo.gl/hJ7pJo

64. 'Germany: Van Rompuy must trust in Greek deal by summit', *Reuters*, 15 July 2011, available http://goo.gl/pmjbos

65. 'Special report—Europe's debilitating deja vu', *Reuters*, 5 Oct. 2011, available http://goo.gl/3EbCkx

66. 'Dithering at the top turned EU crisis to global threat', *The Wall Street Journal*, 29 Dec. 2011, available http://goo.gl/STG4tF

67. 'Europe agrees sweeping new action on debt crisis', *Reuters*, 22 July 2011, available http://goo.gl/jfaUzt

68. 'Factbox—new euro zone steps on debt crisis', *Reuters*, 22 July 2011, available http://goo.gl/7kaS3b

69. 'Statement by the heads of state or government of the euro area and EU institutions', *Europa.eu*, 21 July 2011, available http://goo.gl/wxQs0G

70. 'Fitch calls default, Greece pledges no let-up on debt', *Reuters*, 22 July 2011, available http://goo.gl/z0wxfs

71. 'Rating action: Moody's downgrades Greece to Ca from Caa1, developing outlook', *Moodys.com*, 25 July 2011, available http://goo.gl/9dG58Z; 'Fitch to consider Greece in temporary default', *ekathimerini.com*, 22 July 2011, available http://goo.gl/UW186I

72. 'Statement by the president of the ECB', *Europa.eu*, 7 Aug. 2011, available http://goo.gl/VhQqgN

73. The figure is from 'Quarterly national accounts: 2nd quarter 2015 (provisional)', *Hellenic Statistical Authority*, 28 Aug. 2015, available http://goo.gl/hCxEkl

74. 'Greece, EU/IMF talks on hold, at odds over deficit', *Reuters*, 2 Sep. 2011, available http://goo.gl/cwjWkX

75. 'Greek backsliding sparks euro exit talk', *Reuters*, 8 Sep. 2011, available http://goo.gl/deq14M

76. See 'Lenders gave Greece option of "velvet exit" from euro, says Venizelos', *ekathimerini.com*, 1 Mar. 2013, available http://goo.gl/dNTXk4; Papaconstantinou (2016).

77. 'Inside Europe's plan Z', *Financial Times*, 14 May 2014, available http://goo.gl/H6SddQ

78. 'Greek backsliding sparks euro exit talk', *Reuters*, 8 Sep. 2011, available http://goo.gl/e5qHbb

79. 'Merkel says Greece needs "barrier" erected to stave off default', *Bloomberg*, 25 Sep. 2011, available http://goo.gl/nBRntA

80. Pisani-Ferry (2014), 12; 'Eurozone banks nearly collapsed, says ECB director', *Guardian*, 17 May 2012, available http://goo.gl/YCKr1A

81. 'EU preparing bank rescues amid Greece doubts', *Reuters*, 4 Oct. 2009, available http://goo.gl/9llIhN; 'Quantitative easing boosted by £75bn by Bank of England', *Guardian*, 6 Oct. 2011, available http://goo.gl/rthGUh

82. 'Obama: Europe's debt crisis is "scaring the world"—video', *Guardian*, 27 Sep. 2011, available http://goo.gl/vStfke

83. 'Europe rules out stimulus, shunning Geithner plea on crisis fix', *Bloomberg*, 16 Sep. 2011, available http://goo.gl/aE9BC0

84. 'Geithner warns EU against infighting over Greece', *BBC News*, 16 Sep. 2011, available http://goo.gl/Gz8ub5

85. 'Statement of the deputy prime minister and minister of finance, Mr. Evangelos Venizelos, after the meeting of the governmental committee', *wsj.com*, 18 Sep. 2011, available http://goo.gl/kOWsB0

86. 'With eye on loan, Greece unveils austerity measures', *ekathimerini.com*, 21 Sep. 2011, available http://goo.gl/80jPtF

87. 'European debt crisis live: world markets slide as EU meeting stalls', *Guardian*, 4 Oct. 2011, available http://goo.gl/amMC0j

88. 'European debt crisis: Greece vows to "fight back to prosperity"—as it happened', *Guardian*, 27 Sep. 2011, available http://goo.gl/hDttS1

89. 'Lords of trash', *ekathimerini.com*, 16 Oct. 2011, available http://goo.gl/6kX5eT

90. 'Γκάφες και κουκουλώματα σε δύσοσμο κλίμα', *enet.gr*, 20 Oct. 2011, available http://goo.gl/Q7QzPF

91. 'ΚΡΑΝΙΟΥ τόπος το Σύνταγμα', *enet.gr*, 21 Oct. 2011, available http://goo.gl/9L4fCJ

92. 'Man killed in Greek austerity protests—20 October 2011', *Guardian*, 20 Oct. 2011, available http://goo.gl/dUhNuk

93. 'Μπούμερανγκ γίνεται το χαράτσι στ' ακίνητα', *enet.gr*, 18 Sep. 2011, available http://goo.gl/b7LCRT

94. 'Διαδικτυακή στήριξη του πρωθυπουργού από Λοβέρδο-Διαμαντοπούλου-Ραγκούση', *enet.gr*, 16 Oct. 2011, available http://goo.gl/nNwAFF

95. 'ND leader says there is no consensus [update]', *ekathimerini.com*, 19 Oct. 2011, available http://goo.gl/nb9j7q 8

96. 'Dexia CEO defends track record amid bailout', *Reuters*, 10 Oct. 2011, available http://goo.gl/NHPwG1

97. 'ECB announces details of refinancing operations from October 2011 to 10 July 2012', *Europa.eu*, 6 Oct. 2011, available http://goo.gl/vodSIj; 'ECB announces new covered bond purchase programme', *Europa.eu*, 6 Oct. 2011, available http://goo.gl/O9REgw

98. 'Europe on edge as rescue talks stall', *Financial Times*, 20 Oct. 2011, available http://goo.gl/vDf6p0

99. 'Euro leaders begin "tough" six-day marathon on Greece, banks', *Bloomberg*, 21 Oct. 2011, available http://goo.gl/vQFWnE; 'European Council conclusions', *Europa.eu*, 23 Oct. 2011, available http://goo.gl/omP6qD

100. 'David Cameron's "big bazooka" idea leaves big questions unanswered', *Guardian*, 10 Oct. 2011, available http://goo.gl/HWbc3L; 'Nicolas Sarkozy tells David Cameron: shut up over the euro', *Guardian*, 23 Oct. 2011, available http://goo.gl/uIXNaK

101. 'Euro summit statement', *Europa.eu*, 26 Oct. 2011, available http://goo.gl/wprnzv

102. Bastasin (2012), p. 334. Similar stories had been circulating in Greece since at least May; see 'Στα χέρια της τρόικας η κρατική μηχανή', *enet.gr*, 15 May 2011, available http://goo.gl/YN6Fa2

103. 'Γερμανικό τανκς φέρνει νέο Μνημόνιο', *enet.gr*, 27 Oct. 2011, available http://goo.gl/ZJIpW5

104. On the weaknesses of the SMP in general see Pisani-Ferry (2014), p. 96.

105. 'Banks' extra cash needs put at €106bn—recapitalisation', *Financial Times*, 26 Oct. 2011.

106. 'What happened at MF Global', *Reuters*, 1 Nov. 2011, available http://goo.gl/ritDT2

107. 'Greece calls referendum on EU bail-out', *Financial Times*, 31 Oct. 2011, available http://goo.gl/O1kxoO

108. 'European stocks sink as Greece calls referendum; banks tumble', *Bloomberg*, 1 Nov. 2011, available http://goo.gl/cw3iPg

109. G. A. Papandreou, 'Speech in the cabinet meeting', *papandreou.gr*, 3 Nov. 2011, available http://goo.gl/VMhwA3; 'It was the point where the eurozone could have exploded', *Financial Times*, 12 May 2014, available http://goo.gl/3t8SIl

110. 'Αποβολή 1,5 μήνα μετά, για τη μούντζα', *enet.gr*, 19 Dec. 2011, available http://goo.gl/kuvZtn

111. 'Working on Greek exit from euro zone: Juncker', *Reuters*, 3 Nov. 2011, available http://goo.gl/3Di0D9

112. 'Inside Europe's plan Z', *Financial Times*, 14 May 2014, available http://goo.gl/H6SddQ

113. 'It was the point where the eurozone could have exploded', *Financial Times*, 12 May 2014, available http://goo.gl/3t8SIl

114. 'Insight—grave mood, straight talk at historic EU meeting', *Reuters*, 3 Nov. 2011, available http://goo.gl/q6rVWy

115. 'Highlights-comments by policymakers at G20 in Cannes', *Reuters*, 2 Nov. 2011, available http://goo.gl/TU4X2T

116. 'Evangelos Venizelos' statement upon arrival from Cannes', *evenizelos.gr*, 3 Nov. 2011, available http://goo.gl/6Rc1as; 'Venizelos breaks ranks, challenges euro referendum', *ekathimerini.com*, 3 Nov. 2011, available http://goo.gl/KYk9Lm

117. 'Euro can live on without Greece: French minister', *Reuters*, 3 Nov. 2011, available http://goo.gl/x8abws

118. 'Analysis—EU-prescribed coalition gives Greece short-term relief', *Reuters*, 7 Nov. 2011, available http://goo.gl/9cdJGk

119. For a description of the negotiations see 'Πρωθυπουργός σε τέσσερις νύχτες', *enet.gr*, 13 Nov. 2011, available http://goo.gl/mjIXI3

120. 'Sarkozy told Obama Greek PM too down to take to task', *Reuters*, 9 Nov. 2011, http://goo.gl/1gGCek

121. 'Deepening crisis over euro pits leader against leader', *The Wall Street Journal*, 30 Dec. 2011, available http://goo.gl/VDrfdg

7. MARATHON IS INDEED A GREEK WORD: THE PAPADEMOS GOVERNMENT AND THE RESTRUCTURING OF THE SOVEREIGN DEBT

1. The words are attributed to Rehn. See 'Eurozone seals second Greek bailout after "marathon" talks', *Daily Telegraph*, 21 Feb. 2012, available http://goo.gl/3Q7Fx4

2. The relevant articles are 37 and 38.

3. 'Most back new PM, coalition, poll shows', *ekathimerini.com*, 13 Nov. 2011, available http://goo.gl/I19MxB; 'Greeks strongly back Papademos unity coalition—polls', *Reuters*, 12 Nov. 2011, available http://goo.gl/LZIsCq; 'Greece's opposition leader gives government three-month lifespan', *Bloomberg*, 14 Nov. 2011, available http://goo.gl/1INEVx

4. 'Most Greeks say worst yet to come', *ekathimerini.com*, 22 Dec. 2011, available http://goo.gl/NNP6CD; 'Στο τραπέζι 8 πακέτα περικοπών', *enet.gr*, 17 Dec. 2011, available http://goo.gl/YD02Io

5. See for instance 'NICHTS ZU ESSEN! Griechen geben ihre Kinder im Heim ab', *Bild*, 11 Nov. 2011, available http://goo.gl/XwXZRa

6. It has been suggested this was also to avoid the leader of the KKE gaining the privileges associated with being the main opposition party; see "Η επιλογή της Συγγρού και το... KKE', *Kathimerini*, 12 Nov. 2011, available http://goo.gl/00jxdZ

7. See, for instance, 'The far right in the new Greek government', *whenthecrisishitthefan.word-press.com*, 14 Nov. 2011, available https://goo.gl/uWbUzo

8. 'Rifts appear within coalition', *ekathimerini.com*, 1 Dec. 2011, available http://goo.gl/Iqyjxs; 'Fresh clash between ND, Reppas on civil service', *ekathimerini.com*, 2 Dec. 2011, available http://goo.gl/oH15Gm; 'Voridis vs. Venizelos: arguments erupt and things get personal', *Greekreporter.com*, 23 Dec. 2011, available http://goo.gl/uxb4di

9. 'Government launches name and shame campaign [update]', *ekathimerini.com*, 23 Jan. 2012, available http://goo.gl/ZPZp0B

10. 'Υπό εκκόλαψη συμφωνία για ταξί, με βολές κατά Ραγκούση', *enet.gr*, 15 Dec. 2011, available http://goo.gl/zIxTEi

11. 'Minister admits civil service failure', *ekathimerini.com*, 10 Jan. 2012, available http://goo.gl/XGj9qM

12. 'Greece's Samaras told to quit "political games" for EU aid', *Bloomberg*, 21 Nov. 2011, available http://goo.gl/0OF4dE

13. D. Gross & T. Mayer, 'August 2011: what to do when the euro crisis reaches the core', *CEPS Commentary*, 18 Aug. 2011, available http://goo.gl/cjlGwp

14. 'Monti says Merkel, Sarkozy agree Italy fall would end euro', *Bloomberg*, 25 Nov. 2011, available http://goo.gl/WC6k2r; 'William Hague raises doubts about future of the euro', *Daily Telegraph*, 20 Nov. 2011, available http://goo.gl/x9rfmC; 'Euro is a burning building with no exits, says Hague as his warning of 13 years ago is proved right', *Mailonline*, 30 Sep. 2011, available http://goo.gl/7L0MGo

15. 'Icap tests systems for eurozone collapse', *Financial Times*, 27 Nov. 2011, available http://goo.gl/vcoIz1

16. 'S&P jumps into politics warning EU downgrades before summit', *Bloomberg*, 6 Dec. 2011, available http://goo.gl/ILm27v

17. 'Is this really the end?', *The Economist*, 24 Nov. 2011, available http://goo.gl/BRhJt7

18. 'France, Germany to press euro zone treaty change', *Reuters*, 22 Nov. 2011, available http://goo.gl/a7jUFw

19. 'Merkel to walk fine line on euro at party congress', *Reuters*, 13 Nov. 2011, available http://goo.gl/hwm9US

20. 'Conclusions of the European Council', *Europa.eu*, 24/25 Mar. 2011, available http://goo.gl/7M9CdK

21. 'Eurozone crisis: European Union prepares for the "great leap forward"', *Guardian*, 20 Nov. 2011, available http://goo.gl/e6egLr

22. 'Noyer-ECB liquidity will allow banks to buy debt, lower rates', *Reuters*, 9 Dec. 2011, available http://goo.gl/EqSdIq

23. 'The Sarko and Corzine trade', *FTAlphaville*, 12 Dec. 2012, available http://goo.gl/1YPWx1; 'Exclusive—ECB limits bond buying, eurozone looks to banks', *Reuters*, 9 Dec. 2011, available http://goo.gl/XNrJql; 'ECB keeps bond buys dormant for second week', *Reuters*, 27 Feb. 2012, available http://goo.gl/TjP7YZ

24. 'Conclusions of the European Council, 9 December 2011', *Europa.eu*, 25 Jan. 2012, available http://goo.gl/fdDL7G; 'Decisive steps towards more discipline, integration and convergence', *Europa.eu*, 15 Dec. 2011, available http://goo.gl/5UqgNB

25. 'As the dust settles, a cold new Europe with Germany in charge will emerge', *Guardian*, 9 Dec. 2011, available http://goo.gl/eULBgX

26. 'Treaty On Stability, Coordination and Governance In the Economic and Monetary Union', *Europa.eu*, available http://goo.gl/WmRda5

27. 'Insight—How the Greek debt puzzle was solved', *Reuters*, 29 Feb. 2012, available http://goo.gl/ztYfyf

28. Zettelmyer, Trebesch & Gulati (2013).

29. 'Refile-Profile Dallara the helmsman for banks on Greek rocks', *Reuters*, 25 Jan. 2012, available http://goo.gl/10AeeE

30. 'Greece's creditors said to resist IMF push for more losses', *Bloomberg*, 22 Dec. 2011, available http://goo.gl/I6cr53

31. 'Greece seeking second rescue faces battle to stay in euro', *Bloomberg*, 3 Feb. 2012, available http://goo.gl/U5IvT7

32. 'Greek parties delay bailout talks despite EU threats', *Reuters*, 7 Feb. 2012, available http://goo.gl/bhEoK7

33. 'Grexit', *FTAlphaville*, 7 Feb. 2012, available http://goo.gl/aAZ5Og

34. 'Feuding Greek leaders united by desire to avoid blame', *Reuters*, 7 Feb. 2012, available http://goo.gl/0FdXT8

35. 'Eurozone crisis live: Greek bailout talks finally begin', *Guardian*, 8 Feb. 2012, available http://goo.gl/EBFxLq

36. 'Papademos tells Greek ministers to back bailout demands or quit', *Bloomberg*, 10 Feb. 12, available http://goo.gl/SbZffq

37. 'Papademos: it's either this program or chaos', *ekathimerini.com*, 11 Feb. 2012, available http://goo.gl/TvXjaU; 'Εισήγηση του Πρωθυπουργού Λουκά Παπαδήμου στο υπουργικό συμβούλιο', *To Vima*, 10 Feb. 2012, available http://goo.gl/qksrnu

38. 'Climax nears in Greek drama', *Reuters*, 11 Feb. 2012, available http://goo.gl/naQcQP

39. 'Officials take stock of riot damage; politicians ask for calm', *ekathimerini.com*, 13 Feb. 2012, available http://goo.gl/26lFJN

40. 'More than 40 MPs ousted as Greece approves EU-IMF deal', *ekathimerini.com*, 13 Feb. 2012, available http://goo.gl/Gvl1BL

41. 'Greece: preliminary debt sustainability analysis', *IMF.org*, 15 Feb. 2012, available http://goo.gl/WQTPI9

42. All figures as of February 2012; see Zettelmyer, Trebesch & Gulati (2013).

43. 'Ich hoffe, wir schaffen das im Laufe des Jahres', *Welt am Sonntag*, 22 Feb. 2012, available http://goo.gl/EvvSlZ

44. 'Eurozone crisis live: EU commission predicts "mild recession"', *Guardian*, 23 Feb. 2012, available http://goo.gl/lBSw1X

45. 'Chafing at insults, Germany loses patience with Greece', *Reuters*, 13 Feb. 2012, available http://goo.gl/JGohsj

46. 'Athens rehearses the nightmare of default', *Financial Times*, 17 Feb. 2012, http://goo.gl/CKMIVG

47. 'Insight—How the Greek debt puzzle was solved', *Reuters*, 29 Feb. 2012, available http://goo.gl/ztYfyf

48. 'Eurozone seals second Greek bailout after "marathon" talks', *Daily Telegraph*, 21 Feb. 2012, available http://goo.gl/3Q7Fx4; 'Eurogroup statement', *Europa.eu*, 21 Feb. 2012, available http://goo.gl/ow8VYU

49. 'Hellenic Republic, Ministry of Finance, PSI launch press release', *tovima.gr*, 21 Feb. 2012, available http://goo.gl/5xAFjC

50. 'Eurogroup statement', *Europa.eu*, 21 Feb. 2012, available http://goo.gl/SnVp1O; 'EU govts—Greece PSI looking at actual 78% NPV loss', *Reuters*, 9 Mar. 2012, available http://goo.gl/UZiwqx

51. Zettelmyer, Trebesch & Gulati (2013).

52. 'Eurogroup statement', *Europa.eu*, 21 Feb. 2012, available http://goo.gl/SnVp1O

53. Pisani-Ferry (2014), p. 95, notes the essential arbitrariness of the target.

54. 'Germany to set the terms for saving the euro', *Guardian*, 31 Jan. 2012, available http://goo.gl/ebRuH4

55. 'Highlights—Greek finance minister on EU/IMF bailout', *Reuters*, 21 Feb. 2012, available http://goo.gl/1hQLZE; 'Samaras upbeat over deal for new Greek bailout', *ekathimerini.com*, 21 Feb. 2012, available http://goo.gl/ADqooB

56. 'Growing air of concern in Greece over new bailout', *The New York Times*, 21 Feb. 2012, available http://goo.gl/UXaZH7

57. 'Debt crisis and Greek bailout deal: as it happened', *Daily Telegraph*, 21 Feb. 2012, available http://goo.gl/HSd5Zb

58. 'Highlights-Comments from meeting of EU finance ministers', *Reuters*, 21 Feb. 2012, available http://goo.gl/A0YUBG

59. 'Eurozone crisis live: German parliament approves Greek package—as it happened', *Guardian*, 27 Feb. 2012, available http://goo.gl/FRUFQs; 'Big majority for unpopular Greek rescue', *Deutsche Welle*, 27 Feb. 2012, available http://goo.gl/OBZVZa

60. 'Hellenic Republic, Ministry of Finance, press release', *Reuters*, 24 Feb. 2012, available http://goo.gl/n6c3Tv; 'S&P downgrades Greece to selective default', *Reuters*, 27 Feb. 2012, available http://goo.gl/iBQHco

61. 'IIF warns on €1tn cost of Greek euro exit', *Financial Times*, 6 Mar. 2012, available http://goo.gl/UaH402

62. 'Private investors with 20% of Greek debt to join swap', *Bloomberg*, 6 Mar. 2012, available http://goo.gl/GwCDUy; 'Commerzbank boss rues Greek write-down', *The Wall Street Journal*, 23 Feb. 2012, available http://goo.gl/OE147J; 'Europe's banks bleed from Greek debt crisis', *Reuters*, 23 Feb. 2012, available http://goo.gl/smufvI

63. 'Hellenic Republic, Ministry of Finance, press release', *pdma.gr*, 9 Mar. 2012, available https://goo.gl/mPNPhQ; 'Hellenic Republic, Ministry of Finance, press release', *pdma.gr*, 4 Apr. 2012, available https://goo.gl/4PjzpO; Zettelmyer, Trebesch & Gulati (2013).

64. 'Eurozone crisis: live blog', *FT.com*, 8 Mar. 2012, available http://goo.gl/oJ2wiQ

65. 'Griechenland will von BILD 7000 Euro Schulden-Erlass', *Bild*, 7 Mar. 2012, available http://goo.gl/svHR6u

66. Zettelmyer, Trebesch & Gulati (2013).

67. On this issue see Athanassiou (2009).

68. 'Eurozone crisis as it happened: Spain in the spotlight as troika returns to Greece', *Guardian*, 26 Mar. 2012, available http://goo.gl/rSOTGT

69. 'Greek swaps sellers to pay $2.5 billion to settle contracts', *Bloomberg*, 19 Mar. 2012, available http://goo.gl/Ydwe0K; 'Greece bond protection pays out $2.89 billion after swap: DTCC', *Reuters*, 27 Mar. 2012, available http://goo.gl/lYVuHK

70. 'Austria faces bank injection after ISDA triggers Greek CDS', *Bloomberg*, 10 Mar. 2012, available http://goo.gl/JgFJMl

71. 'Hellenic Republic, Ministry of Finance, press release', *pdma.gr*, 4 Apr. 2012, available https://goo.gl/4PjzpO; 'Greece says final participation rate in PSI is 96.9 pct', *ekathimerini.com*, 25 Apr. 2012, available http://goo.gl/aHTDcJ

72. Zettelmyer, Trebesch & Gulati (2013); 'Deal too tough to help growth', *ekathimerini.com*, 12 Feb. 2012, available http://goo.gl/mgWCbA

73. 'Greek restructuring delay helps banks as risks shift', *Bloomberg*, 15 Mar. 2012, available http://goo.gl/WDJ9SD

74. 'PSI: gift horse or Trojan horse?', *ekathimerini.com*, 9 Mar. 2012, available http://goo.gl/g0NDY2

75. 'Greece receives first tranche of new bailout aid', *Reuters*, 20 Mar. 2012, available http://goo.gl/alVJuY

76. 'Highlights—comments from meeting of EU finance ministers', *Reuters*, 21 Feb. 2012, available http://goo.gl/L4ItZ6

77. 'IMF Executive Board approves €28 billion arrangement under Extended Fund Facility for Greece', *IMF.org*, 15 Mar. 2012, available http://goo.gl/f2pOf6; 'IMF approves new Greek bailout, warns on missteps', *Reuters*, 15 Mar. 2012, available http://goo.gl/bfAvWC

78. 'Η ώρα του λογαριασμού στη Νέα Δημοκρατία', *To Vima*, 7 May 2012, available http://goo.gl/NjF3SJ

79. 'Eurozone banks nearly collapsed, says ECB director', *Guardian*, 17 May 2012, available http://goo.gl/lRA5Lv; 'Bloomberg tests post-euro Greek drachma code', *The Wall Street Journal*, 1 June 2012, available http://goo.gl/1L66HX

80. 'Inside Europe's plan Z', *Financial Times*, 14 May 2014, available http://goo.gl/H6SddQ

81. 'Eurozone crisis live: markets slide as Greek euro exit looms', *Guardian*, 14 May 2012, available http://goo.gl/2oGqxS

82. 'The meetings between the president of the republic and political party leaders', *radiobubble.gr*, 13 May 2012, available http://goo.gl/vzAarp; 'The minute men', *ekathimerini.com*, 22 May 2012, available http://goo.gl/dXe8Wt

83. Under Article 37 of the constitution the prime minister can be the president of the Supreme Administrative Court or the Supreme Civil and Criminal Court or the Court of Auditors.

84. 'Greek deadlock: caretaker PM Panagiotis Pikrammenos', *YouTube*, 16 May 2012, available http://goo.gl/8AqvuX

85. 'George Provopoulos: facing a run on Greek banks, he never blinked', *The Globe and Mail*, 19 Apr. 2013, available http://goo.gl/9pVzZT; see also 'Plug-pulling in Athens', *FTAlphaville*, 16 May 2012, available http://goo.gl/Vo76my

86. Bank of Greece (2014).

87. 'Inside Europe's plan Z', *Financial Times*, 14 May 2014, available http://goo.gl/H6SddQ
88. 'Greek asset sales program to be delayed months, chief says', *Bloomberg*, 17 May 2012, available http://goo.gl/RC4hXH
89. The advert with the teacher and the child can be found on *YouTube* at http://goo.gl/bcha4w; a number of spoofs soon appeared including http://goo.gl/xqooWb and http://goo.gl/oL1xz8; two other adverts can be found on *YouTube* at http://goo.gl/z9K8Eq and http://goo.gl/jHdhm0; they too attracted spoofs, including http://goo.gl/1BVb0G
90. 'Greek election: bid to build coalition government begins', *Guardian*, 18 June 2012, available http://goo.gl/ZYKNRQ
91. 'I will keep Greece in the eurozone', *Financial Times*, 12 June 2012, available http://goo.gl/v8uskX but see also 'Τσίπρας: «Το ευρώ δεν είναι φετίχ»...', *Kathimerini*, 14 June 2012, available http://goo.gl/0AwmwQ
92. Vasilopoulou & Halikiopoulou (2013), p. 533 suggest the rate of abstention was actually only 24 per cent.
93. 'Samaras takes office as Greece's prime minister, facing major challenges', *The New York Times*, 20 June 2012, available http://goo.gl/fp2D4R
94. 'Eurozone crisis live: Greece announces new government', *Guardian*, 20 June 2012, available http://goo.gl/tpvDgr

8. REFORM AND RESISTANCE: POLITICS DURING THE CRISIS

1. 'PM meets Archbishop Ieronymos, discusses Church welfare work', *ANA*, 5 May 2010, available http://goo.gl/r5eYb8
2. 'The Hellenic Stability and Growth Programme: executive summary', *wsj.com*, n.d., available http://goo.gl/B2cywh
3. See, for instance, About (1858) and more recently Langrod (1965).
4. Featherstone (2015).
5. 'Deutsche Bank's Fitschen says failed Greece lacks leaders', *Bloomberg*, 25 May 2012, available http://goo.gl/qzyufe; see also the comments in M. Lewis, 'Beware of Greeks bearing bonds', *Vanity Fair*, 1 Oct. 2010, available http://goo.gl/MpxUuS
6. Siani-Davies (2003).
7. 'Is Greece drowning in Europe's fruit salad?', *ekathimerini.com*, 3 June 2011, available http://goo.gl/NxbVNY
8. See Pappas (2014), p. 67 on anti-social behaviour in general; 'Greece: refusing to quit', *Guardian*, 2 Sep. 2010, available http://goo.gl/BMd8rQ
9. Featherstone (2015).
10. Alexopoulos (2011).
11. Featherstone & Papadimitriou (2013).
12. See in general Featherstone & Papadimitriou (2012); Monastiriotis & Antoniades (2012); Sotiropoulos (2012); Tsoukas (2012); Featherstone & Papadimitriou (2008); Herzfeld (1992).
13. Featherstone (2015).

14. Ἐνημερωτικό σημείωμα: αποτελέσματα απογραφής', *apografi.gov.gr*, 30 July 2010, available https://goo.gl/zPVabC

15. OECD (2011); see also 'State service evaluation to be completed by end of this year, minister says', *ANA*, 16 Mar. 2012, available http://goo.gl/UCICo9

16. Katrougalos (2013), p. 98.

17. Pappas & Assimakopoulou (2012), p. 152.

18. Ibid., p. 150.

19. Spanou (2013), p. 180.

20. 'A figure of 79,923 is given in 'Commission staff working document, assessment of the 2013 national reform programme for Greece', *Europa.eu*, 29 May 2013, available http://goo.gl/A17bhC; but compare with 'The Second Economic Adjustment Programme for Greece fourth review', *Europa.eu*, Apr. 2014, available http://goo.gl/cqg2eK; which seems to suggest the number had already been reduced from 907,531 in 2009 to 747,356 by the end of 2011. For the issue in general see Zahariadis (2014).

21. 'Commission staff working document, assessment of the 2013 national reform programme for Greece', *Europa.eu*, 29 May 2013, available http://goo.gl/A17bhC

22. 'The institution of ASEP and its contribution to public administration', *ASEP.org*, available http://goo.gl/r2JjXW

23. Palaiologos (2014).

24. Afonso, Zartaloudis & Papadopoulos (2014).

25. 'Public overhaul tasked to French', *ekathimerini.com*, 8 June 2012, available http://goo.gl/600YPQ

26. This draws on Crozier (1964).

27. Pappas (2014), p. 62.

28. OECD (2011).

29. For budgetary practices in general see Hawkesworth, Bergvall, Emery et al. (2008).

30. Alexopoulos, (2011).

31. 'In the populist view the very existence of elites and hierarchies smacks of oligarchy and embodies an intolerable injustice against "The People"'. Mavrogordatos (1997), p. 19.

32. For the media see Leandros (2010).

33. Fakiolas (1987), p. 178.

34. See in general Mavrogordatos (2001).

35. Spourdalakis (1988), p. 249; Afonso, Zartaloudis & Papadopoulos (2014).

36. Varoufakis (2013), p. 96 from a slightly different viewpoint appears to move towards the same conclusions.

37. Thomadakis (1995), pp. 106–110.

38. Afonso, Zartaloudis & Papadopoulos (2014); Teperoglou & Tsatsanis (2014), pp. 225–26; 'Πιπιλή για ΝΔ: Στροφή προς το κέντρο—Ὅσοι ψήφισαν ΧΑ, ταυτισμένοι με τη βία', *Skai.gr*, 29 May 2014, available http://goo.gl/o3m3wd

39. For an investigation of one scandal see Telloglou (2009).

40. 'Former Greek defense minister convicted of graft', *The Wall Street Journal*, 7 Oct. 2013, available http://goo.gl/zddBFh; 'Ex-mayor in Greece gets life in prison for embezzlement', *The New York Times*, 27 Feb. 2013, available http://goo.gl/bAzufT

41. Kalyvas (1997); Alivizatos (1990), p. 145; Lyrintzis (2011), p. 13.
42. For a short discussion of families and political identity see Kornetis (2013), pp. 106–107.
43. Pappas (2014), pp. 99–106, suggests a classification.
44. Dinas, Georgiadou, Konstantinidis et al. (2013).
45. All quotations from 'Χρυσή Αυγή: ένα κίνημα ιδεολογικό', *xryshaygh.com*, summer 2012, available http://goo.gl/DJyzwR
46. Karyotis, Rüdig & Judge (2014); The party is frequently called neo-fascist or neo-Nazi in both Greek and English sources see, for instance, Palaiologos (2014); 'Greece's neo-Nazis were scarier than anyone imagined', *Foreign Policy*, 13 Nov. 2014, available http://goo.gl/dFG2vh; 'SS songs and antisemitism: the week Golden Dawn turned openly Nazi', *Guardian*, 7 June 2014, available http://goo.gl/q6idJV
47. Koronaiou, Lagos, Sakellariou et al. (2015).
48. Ellinas (2015).
49. Ellinas (2013).
50. Ellinas (2015). On the strength of the movement see also Palaiologos (2014).
51. 'Hundreds flock to Golden Dawn food handout despite ban', *ekathimerini.com*, 24 July 2013, available http://goo.gl/TKzVOK
52. 'Fight breaks out on Greek TV talk show', *Bloomberg TV*, 7 June 2012, available http://goo.gl/wxMEqK
53. 'Case closed over Golden Dawn's street market raid', *ekathimerini.com*, 5 Dec. 2014, available http://goo.gl/VY4e8x
54. 'Golden Dawn performs well at polling stations used by police', *ekathimerini.com*, 26 May 2014, available http://goo.gl/MCBQdT; 'Alarm at Greek police "collusion" with far-right Golden Dawn', *BBC News*, 17 Oct. 2012, available http://goo.gl/slTGqs
55. 'Golden Dawn leader jailed ahead of Greek criminal trial', *Guardian*, 3 Oct. 2013, available http://goo.gl/cpU059
56. 'Greece moves to ban far-right Golden Dawn party', *Guardian*, 18 Sep. 2013, available http://goo.gl/GVhzi9; 'Golden dawn drops its black shirts to win votes', *Guardian*, 24 May 2014.
57. 'Stavros Theodorakis's "river" party aims to get Greek politics flowing in the right direction', *Guardian*, 13 Mar. 2014, available http://goo.gl/HvwnJx
58. It rose slightly to 5.5 per cent in January 2015.
59. On the strategy of the KKE see 'Understanding the Greek Communist Party', *Greece@LSE*, 2 Sep. 2012, http://goo.gl/MUEV8f
60. Tsakatika & Eleftheriou (2013). The acronym PAME also plays upon the Greek for 'let's go'.
61. 'Tsipras hails "historic" moment as he is elected leader of unified SYRIZA', *ekathimerini.com*, 15 July 2013, available http://goo.gl/Uyc6sD
62. On the origins of the movement see Kalyvas & Marantzidis (2002). Some of the original constituents of the coalition, including DIKKI, did not support the formation of a unitary party and remained categorized as allied groups.
63. Moschonas (2013).
64. Traces of this line of arguing could be found in early articles in the foreign press see, for instance, 'Party's over for Greek graspers', *Sunday Times*, 20 Dec. 2009, available http://goo.

gl/T95Lwk; 'European Union: A coalition of irresponsibility', *The Washington Post*, 16 May 2010, available http://goo.gl/XCYswY

65. 'The economic program of SYRIZA-USF (Coalition of the Radical Left—United Social Front)', *syn.gr*, available http://goo.gl/UUYqMs

66. Vasilopoulou, Halikiopoulou & Exadaktylos (2014).

67. Spourdalakis (2013).

68. Ibid.

69. 'Το παλαιό ΠΑΣΟΚ πάει στον ΣΥΡΙΖΑ', *Kathimerini*, 27 May 2012, available http://goo.gl/D9LOkC

70. Vasilopoulou & Halikiopoulou (2013), p. 536.

71. 'Greek result buys Europe time', *BBC News*, 18 June 2012, available http://goo.gl/tXK2bt; Tsakatika & Eleftheriou (2013) give a figure of 16,000.

72. 'Greece: phase one', *Jacobin*, 22 Jan. 2015, available http://goo.gl/nVM1x0

73. They sit together in the European Parliament as members of the Party of the European Left.

74. This estimate is based on a poll of 1,014 adults taken in December 2010 (before the major demonstrations of 2011) which showed that 29 per cent of respondents had participated in some sort of anti-austerity protest. See Rüdig & Karyotis (2014).

75. 'Protestor chic: how Greeks prepare for tear gas', *globalpost.com*, 20 Oct. 2011, available http://goo.gl/uJIYhh

76. 'Greek austerity plan draws 80,000 to Athens square', *Reuters*, 5 June 2011, available http://goo.gl/tDhn89

77. Rüdig & Karyotis (2014).

78. Rüdig & Karyotis (2013) describe the characteristics of new protesters; for a discussion about the appropriate translation of *aganaktismenoi* see Theodossopoulos (2013), p. 201, n.4.

79. Jiménez & Estalella (2011).

80. Hessel (2011).

81. Theodossopoulos (2013), p. 200; 'The paradox of the "Indignant"', *ekathimerini.com*, 27 May 2011, available http://goo.gl/XDCSrR

82. 'Κοιμάται, ωρέ, ο «ομφαλός της γης»', *protagon.gr*, 26 May 2011, available http://goo.gl/yOGNl6

83. 'Το άνω και το κάτω Σύνταγμα', *enet.gr*, 5 June 2011, available http://goo.gl/tAwLhK

84. N. Panourgia, 'The squared constitution of dissent', *Cultural Anthropology Online*, 29 Oct. 2011, available http://goo.gl/OCgvQB; 'Ψάχνοντας το νόημα της γεμάτης πλατείας', *enet.gr*, 5 June 2011, available http://goo.gl/YDoWWg; a similar popular assembly had also appeared in Madrid.

85. Douzinas (2013), p. 148.

86. 'Record turnout for "indignant" protesters in Athens', *ekathimerini.com*, 29 May 2011, available http://goo.gl/DrIVbK

87. Tzogopoulos (2013), pp. 54–55 cites a poll showing 74 per cent supported the movement. For those indignant with the indignant see Theodossopoulos (2013).

88. For examples see the websites of Τοπικό Δίκτυο Ανταλλαγών και Αλληλεγγύης Μαγνησίας

available http://goo.gl/MhQABw; Τράπεζα Χρόνου Αθήνας, available http://goo.gl/s0vq5J; Φασούλι, available http://goo.gl/cBxOU1

89. 'The silent revolution of self-aware Athenians', *ekathimerini.com*, 19 Mar. 2012, available http://goo.gl/2PqIAf

90. 'Potato wars', *whenthecrisishitthefan.wordpress.com*, 8 Mar. 2012, available https://goo.gl/8TskUD

91. 'Government to launch e-grocery store', *ekathimerini.com*, 29 Feb. 2012, available http://goo.gl/5yT2Ps

92. Rakopoulos (2014).

93. Kretsos (2011).

94. 'Greece: industrial relations profile', *Europa.eu*, 15 Apr. 2013, available http://goo.gl/XNKIuU

95. Palaiologos, (2014); *Μέρες απεργίας—Days of Strike*, directed by K. Kallergis, 10 mins, 2012, available http://goo.gl/o6Msb8; Στις πύλες της φωτιάς (*Ελληνική Χαλυβουργία*), 29 mins, 2012, available https://goo.gl/5DUxUn; 'Greek steelworks strikers still holding out after 228 days', *Guardian*, 14 June 2012, available http://goo.gl/XSH3gM; in May 2012 the strike was deemed illegal in a court decision. See 'Court finds steelworkers' strike illegal [update]', *ekathimerini.com*, 6 June 2012, available http://goo.gl/SWPCls

96. See, for instance, 'Ελληνική Χαλυβουργία—μες την καλή χαρά', *YouTube*, 3 Dec. 2011, available http://goo.gl/XQKXVZ

97. Kretsos (2011), pp. 274–75.

98. Kretsos (2012), pp. 522–23.

99. Exadaktylos & Zahariadis (2014), pp. 170–72.

100. 'Greek protests show democracy in action', *Guardian*, 7 Feb. 2011, available http://goo.gl/K4yEdy

101. 'Two goals behind the reduction in cigarette prices', *ekathimerini.com*, 2 Mar. 2012, available http://goo.gl/yzJGqM

102. 'Greece's financial crisis produces dangerous air quality', *UPI*, 27 Dec. 2013, available http://goo.gl/aeENJi

103. Palaiologos (2014).

104. Noted in Xenakis (2013), p. 174.

9. INTERNAL DEVALUATION AND DEPRESSION: THE ECONOMY DURING THE CRISIS

1. 'Is Greece's the longest recession in history?', *BBC News*, 1 Mar. 2012, available http://goo.gl/JcnW0c

2. OECD (2016); 'Annual National Accounts', *Hellenic Statistical Authority*, 10 Oct. 2014, available http://goo.gl/YboKeL; 'Quarterly National Accounts', *Hellenic Statistical Authority*, 28 Nov. 2014, available http://goo.gl/OcI3Z4; this figure is widely cited but other accounting methodologies give slightly different results. See 'Greek GDP nowcasting model update', *Eurobank Global Markets Research*, 22 Oct. 2014, available http://goo.gl/mGf030

3. Pisani-Ferry, Sapir & Wolff (2013), p. 49.

4. By the spring of 2012 the overall figure for the city centre was around 30 per cent. Vlamis (2013), p. 17.

5. Vasardani (2011), p. 19; Kotsios & Mitsios (2013), p. 36 quote a figure just over 100,000 but others suggest it is more than double this amount. See 'Greece macro view July 2014', *National Bank of Greece*, July 2014, available https://goo.gl/AHi29B

6. 'Economic Climate Trends Survey', *IME GSEVEE*, Feb. 2014, available http://goo.gl/hpcI3d; 'Crisis wipes out a quarter of Greece's SMEs', *ekathimerini.com*, 8 May 2015, available http://goo.gl/wRBym3

7. 'Nike gets prime central Athens space for 43% less than last tenant', *Bloomberg*, 19 Jan. 2012, available http://goo.gl/mTJYdZ

8. Pitelis (2012).

9. 'Labour force survey 4th quarter 2013', *Hellenic Statistical Authority*, 13 Mar. 2014, available http://goo.gl/6yWClW

10. Ibid.

11. 'Labour force survey, 1st quarter 2015', *Hellenic Statistical Authority*, 11 June 2015, available http://goo.gl/ix6NVS

12. R. Antonopoulos, 'The problem of unemployment in Greece', *The Multiplier Effect: The Levy Economics Institute Blog*, 12 Feb. 2014, available http://goo.gl/YQjImk; T. Klitgaard & A. Şahin, 'The different paths of Greece and Spain to high unemployment', *Liberty Street Economics Blog*, 28 Nov. 2012, available http://goo.gl/g145Ny

13. But note the observations of Kannellopoulos (2012).

14. 'Labour force survey 3rd quarter 2014', *Hellenic Statistical Authority*, 18 Dec. 2014, available http://goo.gl/FKUTvo

15. 'Labour force survey 4th quarter 2013', *Hellenic Statistical Authority*, 13 Mar. 2014, available http://goo.gl/MVqZOb

16. 'More than 4 in 10 employers cannot find the right workers', *ekathimerini.com*, 18 June 2014, available http://goo.gl/jMrTSG

17. 'Employment by sex, age and nationality figures', *Europa.eu*, available http://goo.gl/SMkNvG

18. Matsaganis (2012), p. 156.

19. Chletsos, Mazetas, Kotrotsiou et al. (2013).

20. 'Problems build up for construction sector', *ekathimerini.com*, 16 Feb. 2012, available http://goo.gl/M9omr1; and for alternative figures Pelagidis & Mitsopoulos (2016), p.193 n.4.

21. 'MPs voice concerns about plans to lift ban on home repossessions and auctions', *ekathimerini.com*, 1 Aug. 2012, available http://goo.gl/JiR6NG

22. 'Indices of residential property prices: Q1 2015', *Bank of Greece*, 14 May 2015, available http://goo.gl/riQyvW; 'House price decline is biggest in the eurozone', *ekathimerini.com*, 10 July 2014, available http://goo.gl/ji33aa

23. 'Athens mosque gets green light', *ekathimerini.com*, 7 Sep. 2011, available http://goo.gl/oR88pz

24. 'Major highway projects get green light from EC', *ekathimerini.com*, 16 Dec. 2013, available http://goo.gl/Bt1b8G

25. 'Box 1: why has the recession in Greece been so deep?' in 'Greece: 2013 Article IV Consultation', *IMF.org*, 20 May 2013, available http://goo.gl/CuzrmK

26. 'Greece macro view July 2014', *National Bank of Greece*, July 2014, available https://goo.gl/AHi29B

27. 'Motor vehicles, both new and used, put into circulation for the first time by region in Greece (cumulative 2013)', *Hellenic Statistical Authority*, available http://goo.gl/Xhl5YJ; 'Motor vehicles, both new and used, put into circulation for the first time by region in Greece (cumulative 2014)', *Hellenic Statistical Authority*, available http://goo.gl/kbHIIV

28. 'Household budget survey 2013', *Hellenic Statistical Authority*, 12 Sep. 2014, available http://goo.gl/d81MwX

29. Provopoulos (2014). The primary surplus is according to the definition of the adjustment programme.

30. OECD (2013), p. 60.

31. A. Spilimbergo, S. Symansky, & M. Schindler, 'IMF Staff Position Note SPN/09/11, Fiscal Multipliers', *IMF.org*, 20 May 2009, available http://goo.gl/qauhvM; for a good introduction to the debate see the sheet produced by the European Parliament, 'The Fiscal multiplier in forecast models: a short summary of the recent debate', *Europa.eu*, n.d., available http://goo.gl/y5tuRu; see also 'Box 1.1, Are we underestimating short term fiscal multipliers?' in *World economic outlook: coping with high debt and sluggish growth*, IMF: Washington D.C., 2012, pp. 41–43, available http://goo.gl/3QbWuX; 'Box 1.5, Forecast errors and multiplier uncertainty', *European Economic Forecast*, European Economy, 7, autumn 2012, pp. 41–44, available http://goo.gl/Fs1vBB; 'Box 6: The role of fiscal multipliers in the current consolidation debate', *ECB Monthly Bulletin*, Dec. 2012, pp. 82–85 available http://goo.gl/VrR45b.

32. 'Greece: ex post evaluation of exceptional access under the 2010 Stand-By Arrangement', *IMF.org*, 20 May 2013, available http://goo.gl/jx7hSD; Pelagidis & Mitsopoulos (2014), p. 41 also broadly follow this line as does the Bank of Greece (2011). See also Provopoulos (2014), p. 246.

33. 'The Second Economic Adjustment Programme for Greece', *Europa.eu*, Mar. 2012, available http://goo.gl/IQ2FdO

34. See Pagoulatos (2012), p. 257 for sequencing and other factors.

35. Petrakis (2011), p. 383; Christodoulakis (2010), p. 96.

36. 'Major dispersion in consumer prices across Europe', *Europa.eu*, 2012, available http://goo.gl/KLNYtG

37. Petrakis (2011), pp. 168–69.

38. 'Measurement and reduction of administrative burdens in Greece: an overview of 13 sectors', *OECD.org*, 2014, available http://goo.gl/mQ3GGb

39. 'Price of fresh milk has risen after reform', *ekathimerini.com*, 20 July 2014, available http://goo.gl/DQwxGQ

40. 'Flash Eurobarometer 363, how companies influence our society', *Europa.eu*, 2012, available http://goo.gl/6sAFZ0

41. 'Spending per supermarket trip drops 11.2 percent', *ekathimerini.com*, 28 Mar. 2012, available http://goo.gl/dF3Tbn; 'Shoppers save 160 euros per year through offers', *ekathimerini.com*, 24 Feb. 2015, available http://goo.gl/o0qxg8

42. 'Is deflation a risk for Greece?', *Eurobank Research*, Apr. 2014, available http://goo.gl/gLEzlw

43. See the discussion of the literature in Demekas & Kontolemis (1997); Seferiades (1999); the comments in Ioakimoglou & Milios (1993); Wallace (1979), p. 32, where the loss of competitiveness is linked to the democratic transition.

44. 'Minimum wages', *Europa.eu*, available http://goo.gl/SSDveE

45. Koutsogeorgopoulou, Matsaganis, Leventi et al. (2014).

46. 'Average annual wages', *OECD.org*, available http://goo.gl/rWTptG

47. Pelagidis & Mitsopoulos (2014), p. 56.

48. *Athens News*, 14 Mar. 2012.

49. 'Flash Eurobarometer 398, working conditions', *Europa.eu*, Apr. 2014, available http://goo.gl/jYkCQu

50. See the discussion in Chapter Five.

51. Bank of Greece (2013); Provopoulos (2014).

52. Pelagidis & Mitsopoulos (2014), pp. 42–43.

53. There seems little consensus with some reports suggesting informality continues to grow while others suggest the economic downturn has cut opportunities for such work.

54. In general see 'Competitiveness and external imbalances within the euro area', *Europa.eu*, 2012, available http://goo.gl/5jqFNB

55. D. Gros, 'What Makes Greece Special?', *Project Syndicate Blog*, 6 Mar. 2014, available http://goo.gl/hDa01j

56. 'Exports break 20-bln-euro barrier', *ekathimerini.com*, 25 Jan. 2012, available http://goo.gl/GcwZc3

57. U. Böwer, V. Michou & C. Ungerer, 'The puzzle of the missing Greek exports', *Europa.eu*, June 2014, available http://goo.gl/1GfvSt; see also Hausmann, Hidalgo, Bustos et al. 2013.

58. Jones (2010).

59. 'Starting an online store is no easy business', *ekathimerini.com*, 21 Feb. 2012, available http://goo.gl/UvC5J9

60. S. Ioannides, 'The microeconomic effects of business environment reforms', *Europa.eu*, 31 Jan. 2014, available http://goo.gl/m9hFzV

61. Pasiouras (2012), pp. 102–106.

62. 'Financial crises and bank funding: recent experiences in the euro area', *bis.org*, Mar. 2013, available http://goo.gl/lDPAHi

63. For the circulation of banknotes see Bank of Greece (2014).

64. 'Material deprivation & living conditions', *Hellenic Statistical Authority*, 23 June 2016, available https://goo.gl/jXDsLv

65. 'Stress tests put pressure on 24 European banks to raise capital', *Bloomberg*, 15 July 2011, available http://goo.gl/MgTO5b

66. 'Report on the recapitalisation and restructuring of the Greek banking sector', *bankofgreece.gr*, Dec. 2012, available http://goo.gl/l9Xkr8

67. 'What we do', *Hellenic Financial Stability Fund*, n.d., available http://goo.gl/1o8PXf

68. There were also 16 small cooperative banks; see Provopoulos (2014).

69. 'Report of the Hellenic Financial Stability Fund for the period January—June 2013', *Hellenic Financial Stability Fund*, available http://goo.gl/AvAy8W; 'Société Générale announces the sale of Geniki Bank to Piraeus Bank', *societegenerale.com*, 19 Oct. 2012, available http://goo.

gl/6AJzjn; 'State aid: Commission approves liquidation aid for Greek ATE Bank', *Europa. eu*, 3 May 2013, available http://goo.gl/ZO0m3V

70. 'Eurobank: from nationalisation to re-privatisation', *MacroPolis*, 6 May 2014, available http://goo.gl/uWvAXj

71. 'Banks continue to face major challenges', *Economist Intelligence Unit*, 13 Nov. 2013.

72. 'Polbank sale shows pressure on Greek lenders', *Financial Times*, 4 Feb. 2011, available http://goo.gl/X7h211

73. 'Banks continue to face major challenges', *Economist Intelligence Unit*, 13 Nov. 2013.

74. 'NBG Group announces the completion of sale of Finansbank A. Ş.', *nbg.gr*, 15 June 2016, available https://goo.gl/o4HQQY

75. 'ELA procedures', *Europa.eu*, available http://goo.gl/eSb3Fl

76. The figure to a certain extent was influenced by technical changes. See Lapavitsas, Kaltenbrunner, Labrinidis et al. (2013), pp. 203–205.

77. 'Greece: fifth review under the extended arrangement under the Extended Fund Facility', *IMF.org*, 16 May 2014, available http://goo.gl/cbxd4k

78. 'Once powerful Greek businessman arrested for unpaid taxes & insurance contributions', *keeptalkinggreece.com*, 28 Nov. 2012, available http://goo.gl/JSJepH

79. 'Greece's central bank governor makes case for consolidation', *Financial Times*, 6 May 2014, available http://goo.gl/HEH6f1

80. A 2014 study suggested that around a fifth of larger Greek companies were effectively 'zombies'. See 'Stars & Zombies: Οι ελληνικές επιχειρήσεις βγαίνοντας από την κρίση', *PWC.com*, May 2014, available http://goo.gl/LBvTzH

81. 'EIB starts channeling EUR 100 million to Greek SMEs via Eurobank under the guarantee fund for Greek SMEs', *Europa.eu*, 21 Dec. 2012, available http://goo.gl/e41cnc

82. 'Greece beats target for taking up EU co-financing funds', *Reuters*, 2 Jan. 2014, available http://goo.gl/eumjiV

83. 'EIB bolsters key investments in Greece with EUR 2 billion loan', *Europa.eu*, 1 July 2010, available http://goo.gl/Ndslsu; 'The EIB in Greece in 2014', *eib.org*, Apr. 2015, available http://goo.gl/rnjD9b

84. 'European Commission adopts "Partnership Agreement" with Greece on using EU Structural and Investment Funds for growth and jobs in 2014–2020', *Europa.eu*, 23 May 2014, available https://goo.gl/jP1FvV; 'Cohesion Policy and Greece', *Europa.eu*, Mar. 2014, available http://goo.gl/nPGCMH

85. 'Watson acquires Specifar Pharmaceuticals', *actavis.com*, 25 May 2011, available http://goo.gl/DZOCOF; 'Greece sells 10 per cent OTE stake to Deutsche Telekom', *Reuters*, 6 June 2011, available http://goo.gl/lcFrB1

86. '2013 investment climate statement-Greece', *US Bureau Of Economic And Business Affairs*, Apr. 2013, available http://goo.gl/6GZTCf

87. 'Greece: 2013 Article IV Consultation', *IMF.org*, 20 May 2013, available http://goo.gl/e5NSA3

88. Zohios (2011) drawing on research by IOBE.

89. Zohios (2011).

90. For taxis see Exadaktylos & Zahariadis (2014), pp. 172–74.

91. 'Greek trucks head north', *ekathimerini.com*, 7 Mar. 2012, available http://goo.gl/19VvM0

92. OECD (2013), pp. 32, 100–101.

93. 'Greece makes progress in opening restricted professions', *The New York Times*, 9 May 2013, available http://goo.gl/yi78kZ; 'Fill 'er up at any time', *ekathimerini.com*, 16 Mar. 2012, http://goo.gl/2D8qZc

94. See, for instance, 'Greece: fifth review under the extended arrangement under the Extended Fund Facility', *IMF.org*, 16 May 2014, available http://goo.gl/cbxd4k

95. In general see Manolas, Rontos, Sfakianakis et al. (2013); Katsios (2006).

96. F. Schneider, 'Size and development of the shadow economy of 31 European and 5 other OECD countries from 2003 to 2013: a further decline', *jku.at*, 5 Apr. 2013, available http://goo.gl/Jytrjm

97. Fouskas & Dimoulas (2013), p. 175; Vasardani (2011) notes a figure around 30 per cent has often been suggested.

98. See also the discussion in Chapter Two.

99. 'Unyielding truth', *ekathimerini.com*, 30 Jan. 2015, available http://goo.gl/rIwH9d; 'Fast cars and loose fiscal morals: there are more Porsches in Greece than taxpayers declaring 50,000 euro incomes', *Daily Telegraph*, 31 Oct. 2011, available http://goo.gl/mbdzrw; Tzogopoulos (2013), p. 18, reproduces the story.

100. It is of course possible that cars were imported directly by some purchasers; 'The truth about the number of Porsche Cayennes in Greece', *Business Insider*, 4 Nov. 2011, available http://goo.gl/UmsDDC; 'The truth about Greek Porsche owners', *BBC News*, 16 Apr. 2012, available http://goo.gl/wEn6zN

101. See, for instance, V. Fouskas, 'A Greek tragedy: the making of the Greek and Euro-Atlantic ruling classes', *OpenDemocracy*, 5 Dec. 2011, available http://goo.gl/9w7W9c

102. Katrougalos (2013), p. 91 speaks of a rent seeking elite.

103. 'Rpt-update 1- "Accidental economist" and scourge of austerity tipped for Greek finance post', *Reuters*, 27 Jan. 2015, available http://goo.gl/UZXjA9

104. 'Board meeting on Greece's request for an SBA', *wsj.com*, 10 May 2010, available http://goo.gl/Kso4lF

105. 'Greece: first review under the Stand-By Arrangement', *IMF.org*, 27 Aug. 2010, available http://goo.gl/Cjx9ss; 'No incentive to be good in eurozone', *Financial Times*, 25 Mar. 2009, available http://goo.gl/OtEvMR

106. The concept of 'muddling through' comes from Sampson (1981–1983).

107. On the nature of the relationship see Buehn & Schneider (2009).

108. Transparency International (2012).

109. 'Papandreou says Greece is corrupt', *Financial Times*, 12 Dec. 2009, available http://goo.gl/JNwM38

110. 'Eurobarometer: corruption', *Europa.eu*, Feb.-Mar. 2013, available http://goo.gl/dXCQX5

111. 'Graft costing public sector millions of euros', *ekathimerini.com*, 3 Apr. 2012, available http://goo.gl/uKmHTk; 'Corruption costs Greece 10% of GDP', *Greek Reporter*, 17 Feb. 2013, available http://goo.gl/UuHkaO

112. 'Greek crisis spurs war on health fraud rooted in gifts', *Bloomberg*, 1 Apr. 2012, available http://goo.gl/2gQ49I

113. 'Eurobarometer, corruption', *Europa.eu*, Feb.-Mar. 2013, available http://goo.gl/dXCQX5

114. For a good discussion see Ledeneva (1998), although she chooses to argue there are distinctions.

115. 'Tragic flaw: graft feeds Greek crisis', *The Wall Street Journal*, 15 Apr. 2011, available http://goo.gl/bBEqd2; 'In Greece, "corruption pervades every corner of life"', *Guardian*, 20 Oct. 2011, available http://goo.gl/dDrNTu; *Go Greek for a Week*, Channel 4, broadcast 7 Nov. 2011, available http://goo.gl/siADmI

116. Transparency International (2012), p. 26; for an example of reporting see 'Οι εφορίες παίζουν ακόμη 4–4–2...', *Ta Nea*, 14 Dec. 2011, available http://goo.gl/5TxBYW

117. Malaby (2003); Manolopoulos (2011); Tzogopoulos (2013); Palaiologos (2014); see also 'Greek wealth is everywhere but tax forms', *The New York Times*, 1 May 2010, available http://goo.gl/HbyP0z; 'Athènes s'attaque à l'évasion fiscale, sport national', *Le Monde*, 13 May 2010, available http://goo.gl/rbLRht

118. 'Study to quantify and analyse the VAT Gap in the EU-27 Member States: final report', *Europa.eu*, July 2013, available http://goo.gl/EpndG4

119. 'Greece: fifth review under the extended arrangement under the Extended Fund Facility', *IMF.org*, 16 May 2014, available http://goo.gl/cbxd4k

120. Vasardani (2011).

121. Artavanis, Morse & Tsoutsoura (2012).

122. Matsaganis, Leventi & Flevotomou (2012).

123. Tzogopoulos (2013), p. 31; 'Greece struggles to address its tax evasion problem', *Guardian*, 24 Feb. 2015, available http://goo.gl/kUUIqV

124. 'Greece: request for extended arrangement under the Extended Fund Facility', *IMF.org*, Mar. 2012, available http://goo.gl/cEnMlu; 'Gov't vindicates those who chose not to pay their taxes before it took office', *ekathimerini.com*, 20 Feb. 2015, available http://goo.gl/HEHxvx

125. 'Και απλήρωτοι και απειλούνται με σύλληψη για χρέη στο Δημόσιο', *enet.gr*, 6 Dec. 2011, available http://goo.gl/Z0ZmI0; 'Συνελήφθη ο διευθύνων για χρέη 725.000 ευρώ, το Δημόσιο χρωστά 7,3 εκατ.!', *enet.gr*, 7 Dec. 2011, available http://goo.gl/Z5E8qC

126. 'Tax exemptions deprive state budget of over 3.5 bln euros', *ekathimerini.com*, 21 Dec. 2014, available http://goo.gl/2DNCLl

127. See the lengthy discussion of taxation in Mitsopoulos & Pelagidis (2011).

128. Kaplanoglou & Rapanos (2013), p. 290.

129. The system has also been simplified so that there are now three basic tax bands.

130. Visvizi (2012), p. 32.

131. Palaiologos (2014).

132. 'Greece's weary taxpayers are exhausted, report warns', *Financial Times*, 29 Jan. 2014, available http://goo.gl/1Fk2Ps

133. 'Expired debts to the state soar to more than 72 bln euros', *ekathimerini.com*, 22 Dec. 2014, available http://goo.gl/w3a5SI

134. Zahariadis (2013a), pp. 655–56.

135. 'Rental rates continue their slide across the country', *ekathimerini.com*, 9 Dec. 2014, available http://goo.gl/p8xy47

136. 'Firms write off a tenth of turnover in bad debts', *ekathimerini.com*, 25 May 2015, available http://goo.gl/2eD8nE

137. Palaiologos (2014).

138. 'Greece, selected issues', *IMF.org*, 21 May 2013, available http://goo.gl/Z3Qzwe; Zahariadis (2013b) suggests that if Greece matches the efficiency of its partners in tax administration it would boost revenues by about 4.5 per cent per annum; see also Palaiologos (2014).

139. 'Task Force for Greece, seventh activity report', *Europa.eu*, July 2014, available http://goo.gl/MSwhH1; Featherstone (2015).

140. However, an interviewee in Palaiologos (2014) suggests that reforms under the Samaras government were underpinned by a philosophical argument that regards tax payers as being fundamentally honest.

141. 'Greece, selected issues', *IMF.org*, 21 May 2013, available http://goo.gl/Z3Qzwe

142. Pryce (2012), p. 58 calls the tax system 'unfair, paranoid and contradictory' and likens it to 'gang-extortion'; Visvizi (2014), pp. 336, 339 talks of a 'fiscal witch-hunt' and suggests the problem of tax evasion is largely 'constructed'.

143. On the importance of such a culture see Kaplanoglou & Rapanos (2013), pp. 294–98.

144. Kaplanoglou & Rapanos (2013), p. 293.

145. See also the comments of Lagarde in 'Christine Lagarde: can the head of the IMF save the euro?', *Guardian*, 25 May 2012, available http://goo.gl/mUn2me; interview with Martin Schulz, the president of the European Parliament, *BBC Radio 4*, 5 Feb. 2015, available http://goo.gl/51Eu3S

146. 'Greece: fifth review under the extended arrangement under the Extended Fund Facility', *IMF.org*, 16 May 2014, available http://goo.gl/cbxd4k

147. OECD (2013), p. 55.

10. THE GREAT CRISIS

1. The sign was seen in Ambelokipi. The image of people scavenging for food from bins has become a familiar theme within writings about the crisis, although it is not so easy to detect on the ground. See, for instance, 'Hier kramt eine Onassis-Erbin im Müll', *Bild*, 20 Oct. 2011, available http://goo.gl/YjAdvm; P. Markaris, 'In Athen gehen die Lichter aus', *Zeitonline*, 5 Dec. 2011, available http://goo.gl/Bw5sWK; Makris & Bekridakis (2013), p. 116.

2. 'Risk of poverty: 2014 survey on income and living conditions', *Hellenic Statistical Authority*, 8 July 2015, available http://goo.gl/V8lJPH; These figures should probably be treated with some caution given the discrepancies that are widely held to exist between real and declared incomes.

3. For children in general see Daskalakis (2014).

4. For social protection in general see Koutsogeorgopoulou, Matsaganis, Leventi et al. (2014); Matsaganis & Leventi (2014); Mitrakos (2014); Matsaganis (2012).

5. 'Your social security rights in Greece', *Europa.eu*, July 2013, available http://goo.gl/PJWt8F

6. 'Uninsured mother unable to afford medication loses her life', *enetenglish.gr*, 23 Apr. 2014, available http://goo.gl/MxhCL9; 'Amid cutbacks, Greek doctors offer message to poor: you

are not alone', *The New York Times*, 24 Oct. 2014, available http://goo.gl/wjxYGf; Palaiologos (2014).

7. 'Material deprivation & living conditions', *Hellenic Statistical Authority*, 8 July 2015, available http://goo.gl/f5jRYx

8. 'Soup kitchens for the Greek middle class', *Deutsche Welle*, 13 Jan. 2014, available http://goo.gl/0Bo2UF

9. 'Risk of poverty: 2014 survey on income and living conditions', *Hellenic Statistical Authority*, 8 July 2015, available http://goo.gl/V8lJPH

10. 'Material deprivation & living conditions', *Hellenic Statistical Authority*, 8 July 2015, available http://goo.gl/f5jRYx

11. See the 85-year-old-man quoted in Theodossopoulos (2013), p. 204.

12. Fredriksen (2012).

13. Koutsogeorgopoulou, Matsaganis, Leventi et al. (2014).

14. Rüdig & Karyotis (2013), p. 326.

15. 'Distribution of population by tenure status, type of household and income group (source: SILC)', n.d., *Europa.eu*, available http://goo.gl/qWtTy9

16. 'Rental rates continue their slide across the country', *ekathimerini.com*, 9 Dec. 2014, available http://goo.gl/MAFVEO

17. 'Το εμπόριο ζητιάνων στα χέρια του οργανωμένου εγκλήματος', *enet.gr*, 7 Apr. 2011, available http://goo.gl/2pTbgI

18. 'Country fiche, Greece', *FEANTSA*, updated Nov. 2016, available https://goo.gl/GS0uMu

19. 'What would Socrates think of homeless Greeks in caves today?', *euronews*, 10 Oct. 2013, available http://goo.gl/pNgYYW; 'Filopappos: sacred hill of muses and homeless', *Greek Reporter*, 11 Apr. 2013, available http://goo.gl/Tkdokl

20. 'Greek rise in homelessness creates a new poor: debt crisis forces many on to the streets through bankruptcy and job loss', *Guardian*, 3 Aug. 2011, available http://goo.gl/Hm6PaA; other sources suggest that even prior to the crisis homelessness was largely due to financial circumstances. See N. Fondeville & T. Ward, 'Homelessness during the crisis', *Europa.eu*, Nov. 2011, available http://goo.gl/k3Kbvj

21. On the issue see Stamatis (2012); Theodorikakou, Alamanou & Katsadoros (2013); 'NGO reassesses city's homeless', *ekathimerini.com*, 23 May 2012, available http://goo.gl/QDt8qS; 'Misery in Athens: "new poor" grows from Greek middle class', *Spiegel Online International*, 14 Feb. 2012, available http://goo.gl/AqpFNi; 'Attica's 17,700 homeless to get mobile showers, laundries', *ekathimerini.com*, 11 June 2015, available http://goo.gl/TkkoNU

22. 'Election brings no hope to Athens soup kitchens', *Reuters*, 27 Apr. 2012, available http://goo.gl/UONWGX; 'Greece's food crisis: families face going hungry during summer shutdown', *Guardian*, 6 Aug. 2013, available http://goo.gl/ysEorc

23. City of Athens homeless shelter (KYADA), *cityofathens.gr*, n.d., available https://goo.gl/Kgxxmy

24. Makris & Bekridakis (2013), p. 122; the figures seem to be derived from 'Περίπου 250.000 άτομα τρέφονται καθημερινά από τα συσσίτια της εκκλησίας', *skai.gr*, 27 Dec. 2011, available http://goo.gl/Mo6rlg; see also 'Ουρές στα συσσίτια για ένα πιάτο φαγητό', *iefimerida*, 12 Feb. 2012 available http://goo.gl/QUxGHT

25. Makris & Bekridakis (2013), p. 124.
26. The concept of *philotimo* may have some relevance. See the discussion in Xenakis (2013), p. 180.
27. Petralias, Papadimitriou, Riza et al. (2016); 'More children in Greece are going hungry', *The New York Times*, 17 Apr. 2013, available http://goo.gl/VZslTZ; 'Half of schoolchildren in poor areas face "food insecurity"', *ekathimerini.com*, 23 Dec. 2014, available http://goo.gl/4TcSxB
28. Vlontzos & Duquenne (2013). The appearance of a book of wartime recipes also drew much attention. Nikolaidou (2011).
29. See D. Sutton, 'Eating in times of financial crisis', *FoodAnthropology*, 27 June 2011, available http://goo.gl/zOq8RH; 'PASOK says 800,000 bank loans have been rescheduled', *ekathimerini.com*, 31 Mar. 2012, available http://goo.gl/pi737m
30. 'In Greece's sour economy, some shops are thriving', *The New York Times*, 2 Jan. 2012, available http://goo.gl/Mao8Tw
31. Papadopoulos (2006).
32. 'IME/GSEVEE survey shows Greeks reduce food expenditures to pay bills', *Greek Reporter*, 12 Jan. 2012, available http://goo.gl/6BqLUK
33. Herzfeld (2011), p. 24. For obligation see Campbell (1964).
34. 'As we forgive our debtors', *economist.com*, 16 July 2015, available http://goo.gl/YLiklC
35. 'Risk of poverty: 2014 survey on income and living conditions', *Hellenic Statistical Authority*, 8 July 2015, available http://goo.gl/V8lJPH
36. Gkartzios (2013).
37. 'Young Greek adults are not the only homebirds', *enetenglish.gr*, 27 Mar. 2014, available http://goo.gl/2kIWMJ
38. Nissaris (2013); 'Rejecting cannibalism', *whenthecrisishitthefan.wordpress.com*, 13 Feb. 2014, available https://goo.gl/wAkTdB
39. 'Hundreds flock to Golden Dawn food handout despite ban', *ekathimerini.com*, 24 July 2013, available http://goo.gl/3L26zc; 'Golden Dawn plays Nazi anthem at food handout', *enetenglish.gr*, 25 July 2013, available http://goo.gl/S3oi9t
40. 'Greek crisis prompts new spirit of humanitarianism', *Guardian*, 15 June 2012, available http://goo.gl/BTzmEX
41. Gazi (2011). Article 21 of the constitution speaks of the family as the cornerstone of the preservation and the advancement of the nation.
42. *Dogtooth* (original title Κυνόδοντας), directed by Giorgos Lanthimos, 94 mins, 2009.
43. Xenakis (2013), p. 175, notes the argument.
44. Knight (2012) includes some stories in this vein.
45. 'Women violence helpline receives 5,089 calls', *amna.gr*, 16 Mar. 2012, available at http://goo.gl/GVZncO; 'One in three women victim of domestic violence', *Greek Reporter*, 1 Nov. 2013, available http://goo.gl/kl87gL; on levels of domestic violence before the crisis see Chatzifotiou (2005).
46. 'Greek police report spike in domestic abuse cases', *Thomson Reuters Foundation*, 2 Dec. 2013, available http://goo.gl/NQTduA
47. 'Η τρόικα... τρώει τα παιδιά μας', *enet.gr*, 14 July 2013, available http://goo.gl/Mxf7Cd

48. Vlachadis & Kornarou (2013).
49. Michas, Varytimiadi, Chasiotis et al. (2014); 'Vital statistics 2013', *Hellenic Statistical Authority*, 30 Sep. 2014, available http://goo.gl/UnUPXC
50. See, for instance, Kentikelenis, Karanikolos, Papanicolas et al. (2011); Kondilis, Giannakopoulos, Gavana, et al. (2013); Kentikelenis, Karanikolos, Reeves et al. (2014); Simou & Koutsogeorgou (2014).
51. See, for instance, the accounts in Palaiologos (2014).
52. 'Greece birthrate drops further', *ekathimerini.com*, 26 June 2013, available http://goo.gl/Skt7KB
53. 'Towards a "baby recession" in Europe? Differential fertility trends during the economic crisis', *Europa.eu*, 7 May 2013, available http://goo.gl/8RL3CH; note the figures appear to be different to those given by EL.STAT.
54. 'Vital statistics 2013', *Hellenic Statistical Authority*, 30 Sep. 2014, available http://goo.gl/UnUPXC; 'Vital statistics 2012', *Hellenic Statistical Authority*, 1 Aug. 2013, available http://goo.gl/V1cu0L; Vrachnis, Vlachadis, Iliodromiti et al. (2014); 'Greece's dismal demographics', *The New York Times*, 9 Dec. 2013, available http://goo.gl/X8zVzS
55. 'Study finds link between austerity cuts and male suicide', *enetenglish.gr*, 22 Apr. 2014, available http://goo.gl/kZ2zQI
56. 'Death due to suicide, by sex: standardised death rate by 100 000 inhabitants', *Europa.eu*, available at http://goo.gl/1jQwVM
57. 'Pensioner's note reveals financial pressure drove him to Syntagma suicide', *ekathimerini.com*, 4 Apr. 2012, available http://goo.gl/Nkz3KY
58. Vgontzas, Kastanaki, Michalodimitrakis et al. (2013); Stefanakis, Vgontzas, Basta, et al. (2013).
59. Antonakakis & Collins (2014) using complex modelling seem to suggest there were somewhere between 262 and 551 additional suicides during the period 2009–2010. Media reporting of their research tended to use a figure of 500. See 'Austerity in Greece caused more than 500 male suicides, say researchers', *Guardian*, 21 Apr. 2014, available http://goo.gl/uYmN8B
60. 'Suicides double in Greece in 2009–2011 period', *ekathimerini.com*, 9 Sep. 2013, available http://goo.gl/oRVPNf
61. 'Well-being and the global financial crisis' in *How's life? 2013: measuring well-being*, OECD Publishing, 2013, available http://goo.gl/mFMPqO; Helliwell, Layard & Sachs (2012); Helliwell, Layard & Sachs (2013).
62. Economou, Madianos, Peppou et al. (2013); Mazetas, Gouva, Kotrotsiou et al. (2013).
63. 'Hostage-taker is "no criminal," says policeman', *ekathimerini.com*, 2 Mar. 2012, available http://goo.gl/utNWVC; 'Hostage-taker at northern Greece factory surrenders', *ekathimerini.com*, 2 Mar. 2012, available http://goo.gl/MFxqMy; 'In Greece, redundancy tips factory worker over the edge', *Reuters*, 3 Mar. 2012, available http://goo.gl/bkaUco; 'Greek town withers as boom turns to bust', *Reuters*, 4 Mar. 2012, available http://goo.gl/NtNA6y
64. Interview with Stelios Ramfos by Elli Stai, *Net Week*, 22 May 2012, available http://goo.gl/bNcsox
65. 'Social situation of young people in Europe', *Europa.eu*, 2014, available http://goo.gl/mMlO1k

66. It even gave rise to a play, *Βασανίζομαι*, by Antonis Tsipianitis; see 'Η ιστορία του «βασανίζομαι»', *To Vima*, 13 June 2012, available http://goo.gl/Op1f68

67. 'Average household size', *Europa.eu*, 13 Aug. 2015, available http://goo.gl/r6r5e2

68. Gkartzios (2013); 'Greeks go green thumb to fight recession. Some urbanites are returning to their rural roots to farm the land', *Aljazeera*, 18 June 2013, available http://goo.gl/sqglZW; 'Pensioners turn back to living off the land', *ekathimerini.com*, 1 Sep. 2011, available http://goo.gl/IY6p4D

69. 'With work scarce in Athens, Greeks go back to the land', *The New York Times*, 8 Jan. 2012, available http://goo.gl/EJU2cR; 'Greeks drawn by village life', *ekathimerini.com*, 27 Mar. 2012, available http://goo.gl/qUw5g3

70. 'One in four Greeks wants to leave country, EU finds', *ekathimerini.com*, 25 June 2013, available http://goo.gl/EYbWXj; 'Young Greeks hesitant about moving abroad', *ekathimerini. com*, 25 Apr. 2012, available http://goo.gl/W5msTp; See also Labrianidis & Vogiatzis (2013).

71. 'Junge Griechen-elite verlässt ihr land', *Handelsblatt*, 29 Oct. 2011, available http://goo.gl/vjvxSU

72. 'Battling economic woes at home, Greeks look to NY for new prospects', *WNYC News*, 6 Jan. 2012, available http://goo.gl/OJCGty; 'Μόνο 12 Έλληνες μετανάστες ήρθαν στην Αυστραλία', *protothema.gr*, 31 Dec. 2011, available http://goo.gl/r98xQ6; 'New wave of migrants follows earlier exodus for a life Down Under', *Financial Times*, 1 July 2015.

73. 'Tough times see Greeks moving to former rival Turkey', *BBC News*, 25 Mar. 2014, available http://goo.gl/Uma3mg

74. 'Φεύγει η «αφρόκρεμα» των νέων Ελλήνων', *Kathimerini*, 30 Nov. 2013, available http://goo.gl/ZUJ6vB

75. 'Migration statistics quarterly report', *UK Office for National Statistics*, Feb. 2014, available http://goo.gl/iHxBHo; 'Germany sees sharp rise in Greek immigration', *enet.gr*, 7 May 2013, available http://goo.gl/SBPvYE

76. 'Few opportunities: young Greeks struggle to gain foothold in Berlin', *Spiegel Online International*, 17 Apr. 2012, available http://goo.gl/6vqDUC; 'Adiós Alemania: many immigrants leave Germany within a year', *Spiegel Online International*, 13 June 2013, available http://goo.gl/oz6qSO

77. The Albanian Centre for Competitiveness and International Trade (2012).

78. For those going home life could be difficult. See 'For Albanians, taste of capitalism turns sour in Greece', *Reuters*, 6 Apr. 2012, available http://goo.gl/Im24gT

79. Michail (2013).

80. 'Report of the special rapporteur on the human rights of migrants, François Crépeau, addendum: mission to Greece', *UN General Assembly Human Rights Council*, 17 Apr. 2013, available http://goo.gl/eM14u8; Palaiologos (2014).

81. Kandylis & Kavoulakos (2011); Dinas, Georgiadou, Konstantinidis et al. (2013).

82. Amnesty International (2012); *Into the Fire—The Hidden Victims of Austerity in Greece*, Reel News, 39 mins., 20 Apr. 2013, available http://goo.gl/oDyuBy and http://goo.gl/DHOSVw

83. For the plight of migrants see *Impossible Biographies*, produced by Ross Domoney and Christos Filippidis, 12 mins, 2013, available http://goo.gl/YkNmIy and the mapping

project 'The city at the time of crisis', available http://goo.gl/rB5PZZ; Ἄστεγοι, υπό το μηδέν, *Athens Voice*, 2–8 Feb. 2012, available http://goo.gl/3F7Os9

84. *Raw Material*, (original title Πρώτη Ύλη), directed by C. Karakepelis, 78 mins, 2012; see also the interview with Karakepelis by V. McMahon, available http://goo.gl/bY2zKL; 'Ode on a Grecian pile of crap', *Vice*, 1 Feb. 2010, available http://goo.gl/23s8N3

85. 'Αθήνα: η πόλη του scrap metal', *Lifo*, 31 Oct. 2012, available http://goo.gl/EJix94; 'Scavengers stripping Greece of metals', *Greek Reporter*, 11 Feb. 2013, available http://goo.gl/pfN46t

86. 'Murder fuels fears of rising city crime', *ekathimerini.com*, 10 May 2011, available http://goo.gl/zjHF4M

87. 'European sourcebook of crime and criminal justice statistics, 2014', *heuni.fi*, 2014, available http://goo.gl/OTOvbd; Xenakis & Cheliotis (2013b).

88. 'Στατιστικά στοιχεία—απολογισμός συνολικής δραστηριότητας της Ελληνικής Αστυνομίας για το έτος 2013', *astynomia.gr*, 14 Feb. 2014, available http://goo.gl/48AE7k; 'Στατιστικά στοιχεία—απολογισμός συνολικής δραστηριότητας της Ελληνικής Αστυνομίας για το έτος 2014', *astynomia.gr*, 21 Jan. 2015, available http://goo.gl/TXxlhZ

89. 'Greeks confront crime wave amid austerity', *BBC News*, 16 Aug. 2012, available http://goo.gl/Am02mX

90. Xenakis & Cheliotis (2013b), p. 731; see also Herzfeld (2011).

91. Saridakis & Spengler (2012).

92. '«Ρομπέν των σουπερμάρκετ» σε Αθήνα και Πάτρα', *enet.gr*, 5 Nov. 2011, available http://goo.gl/PDyiWg; 'Τρίτη φορά χτύπησαν οι «Ρομπέν των σουπερμάρκετ»' *enet.gr*, 7 Nov. 2011, available http://goo.gl/HKbEch; '"Robin of the Supermarket" group acquitted in Larisa', *enetenglish.gr*, 18 June 2013, available http://goo.gl/jsyYg9

93. 'Minister warns he will not "tolerate" vigilantism', *ekathimerini.com*, 15 Mar. 2012, available http://goo.gl/ih6SQf

94. Zarafonitou (2009).

95. Zarafonitou (2011), p. 60 argues that while it is widely acknowledged that coverage is sensationalised, this is less evident among those who fear crime most, suggesting that there might be an association between the two.

96. 'Eurobarometer 67: Public opinion in the European Union', *Europa.eu*, Nov. 2007, available http://goo.gl/7IwzRH shows public trust in television in Greece to be the lowest in the EU at 39 per cent.

97. This would seem to be a variant of the chemtrails theory, see Cairns (2014).

98. 'Magical ponies and Greek debt: how Greeks around the world were conned into false hope', *Hellenic American Leadership Council Blog*, 5 Oct. 2012, available http://goo.gl/cQ88L7

99. Ὁ μεγάλος δάσκαλος !!!!', *greekpayback.com*, n.d., available http://goo.gl/tXrb9e

100. 'Athens Indymedia shut down', *enetenglish.gr*, 12 Apr. 2013, available http://goo.gl/8PRTFP; 'Declaration of principles', *Radiobubble.gr*, n.d., available http://goo.gl/WCbd9K

101. 'Across Athens, graffiti worth a thousand words of malaise', *The New York Times*, 15 Apr. 2014, available http://goo.gl/0csdHm; 'Η αισθητική της κρίσης', Deutsche Welle, 26 July 2013, available http://goo.gl/7U4Gbk; but see also 'Το πρωί καθαρίζουν τους τοίχους, το βράδυ τους ξαναγράφουν', *Kathimerini*, 10 Sep. 2013, available http://goo.gl/qfnRfD

102. Quoted in *The Wake Up Call*, directed by K. Kallergis, 16 mins, 2012, available https://goo.gl/gfE3cn; see also the images at *bleeps.gr*, available http://goo.gl/SknOgw

103. Ibid.

104. '116th post', *mapetstencils*, 22 July 2013, available http://goo.gl/95pZX8

105. The title of the song in Greek is 'Ντου από παντού' and the lyrics can be found at http://goo.gl/kgRRrd

106. D. Mentzelos, Killah P, Tiny Jackal, 'Κρίση', *Riseout Productions*, 23 Apr. 2012, available http://goo.gl/jqFgEu; the full title of the song in translation is 'Crisis (flight-erection)'.

107. *Boy Eating the Bird's Food* (original title *Το Αγόρι Τρώει το Φαγητό του Πουλιού*), directed by E. Lygizos, 80 mins, 2012.

108. 'Boy eating the bird's food Q&A– TIFF12', *YouTube*, 10 Sep. 2012, available http://goo.gl/f2MRvh and http://goo.gl/0Qbx0F and http://goo.gl/GCYAYM

109. On attitudes to resistance see Andronikidou & Kovras (2012); Rüdig & Karyotis (2014).

110. Taken from an extended extract of A. Maratou, *Ουτοπία κρυμμένη στο σώμα της πόλης. Ο μουσικός κόσμος του Μίκη Θεοδωράκη και η εποχή του*, Athens: Ianos, 2013, published by *unfollow.com.gr*, 14 Jan. 2014, available http://goo.gl/mcsrjN

111. 'Δ.Ι.A, dust rhymes, flowjob, Ψυχόδραμα 07—Fuck the police 061208', *Pure Rap Lyrics*, 19 July 2012, available http://goo.gl/WXFxPG

112. N. Sfakianakis, 'Η πλατεία', *YouTube*, 2012, available http://goo.gl/I5tiSj

113. 'Fear itself', *ekathimerini.com*, 8 June 2012, available http://goo.gl/nlQOgK

114. Ramfos' views on the crisis in Greek can be found at *steliosramfosgr.wordpress.com* and several of his television interviews with English subtitles at *steliosramfos.wordpress.com*; 'Κίνημα 10: η ευκαιρία της κρίσεως', *protagon.gr*, 30 May 2011, available http://goo.gl/8xRMfS; Y. Mylonas & P. Kompatsiaris, 'Pathologizing politics: the making of the neoliberal subject during the Greek crisis', n.d., available http://goo.gl/yMfvMy

115. Markaris (2011), p. 261.

116. L. Vournelis, 'Strained yogurt and people in Greece', *Food Anthropology*, 12 Oct. 2011, available http://goo.gl/lSUtk5; 'On yogurts as a form of political protest in Greece', *whenthecrisishitthefan.wordpress.com*, 10 Mar. 2012, available https://goo.gl/ERbifT

117. 'Protestors block PACE MPs in restaurant on Corfu', *newpost.gr*, 3 June 2011, available http://goo.gl/TsQha5

118. Markaris (2010); Markaris (2011); Markaris (2012).

119. Markaris (2009).

120. Markaris (2012), p. 205.

121. P. Markaris, 'In Athen gehen die Lichter aus', *Zeitonline*, 5 Dec. 2011, available http://goo.gl/Bw5sWK; for a translation into English see 'Petros Markaris' "The Lights Are Going Out in Athens"', *Breach of Close Blog*, 26 Dec. 2011, available http://goo.gl/nidGJn

122. This typology is outlined in P. Markaris, 'In Athen gehen die Lichter aus', *Zeitonline*, 5 Dec. 2011, available http://goo.gl/Bw5sWK

123. 'Greek PM calls for collective efforts to change the country', *ANA*, 13 Sep. 2010, available http://goo.gl/y7g3Zb

124. Diamandouros (2013), pp. 220–25; 'Μεσοπρόθεσμη θεραπεία εθελοτυφλίας', *To Vima*, 10 June 2012, available http://goo.gl/5lCjMP

125. Beyond the headlines the articles are usually more thoughtful, but see, for instance, J. Kakissis, 'Europe's basket case: has Greece's dysfunction reached the point of permanent crisis?', *Foreign Policy*, 24 June 2013, available http://goo.gl/L9KrEA

126. 'How to use the euro name and symbol', *Europa.eu*, n.d., available http://goo.gl/1sd404

127. The production, directed by Yiannis Kakleas, toured Greece.

128. Goin Through, 'Δεν καταλαβαίνω', *YouTube*, 3 Apr. 2014, available http://goo.gl/44jYgn

129. See the discussion of Pangalos' remarks in the Introduction.

130. *Tungsten*, directed by Giorgos Georgopoulos, 100 mins, 2011.

131. *Wasted Youth*, directed by Argyris Papademetropoulos & Jan Vogel, 120 mins, 2011.

132. '17 Συγγραφείς + 1 κρίση', *Athens Voice*, 6 Mar. 2013, available http://goo.gl/2Ba5ia

133. 'Προσεύχεται για εμάς', *Athens Voice*, 28 Sep. 2011, available http://goo.gl/KL5L6h

134. See the discussion of trust in M. Katsimi, T. Moutos, G. Pagoulatos & D. Sotiropoulos, 'Growing inequalities and their impacts in Greece', *gini-research.org*, 2013, available http://goo.gl/m8FqA0.

135. When asked in 2011 whether they expected their lives in five years to be worse than they were at the present time, Greeks were found to be the most pessimistic people in the world, even more than Syrians enduring a civil war. See 'Worldwide, Greeks most pessimistic about their lives', *Gallup*, 25 July 2012, available http://goo.gl/N6u4Qe

136. See the discussion in Theodossopoulos (2013), p. 208.

137. Tsimas (2011), p. 103.

138. Tsoukalis (2013), p. 41 speaks of a 'peaceful revolution'.

EPILOGUE

1. 'Introductory statement to the press conference (with Q&A)', *Europa.eu*, 6 June 2013, available http://goo.gl/8WeHGk

2. 'Eurogroup statement on Greece', *Europa.eu*, 27 Nov. 2012, available https://goo.gl/pNg-HOR

3. 'EBU urges Greek government to reverse decision on ERT', *ebu.ch*, 11 June 2013, available http://goo.gl/UQ7v3G

4. 'Greece reforms clear way for €8.3bn aid', *ft.com*, 31 Mar. 2014, available http://goo.gl/1RJHqy

5. 'More Greek statistics? Troika confirms primary surplus', *The Wall Street Journal*, 23 Apr. 2014, available http://goo.gl/pqM23n; 'Greek statistics are back: primary deficit presented as surplus, with Eurostat's seal of approval', *yanisvaroufakis.eu*, 24 Apr. 2014, available http://goo.gl/TBWLkR

6. 'Don't vote "wrong" way, EU's Juncker urges Greeks', *Reuters*, 12 Dec. 2014, available http://goo.gl/qm85PE

7. Karyotis, Rüdig & Judge (2014).

8. 'Wolfgang Schäuble and Yanis Varoufakis press conference', *bundesfinanzministerium.de*, 5 Feb. 2015, available http://goo.gl/fcyRdN; 'Schaeuble "agrees to disagree" with Greece's Varoufakis', *Bloomberg*, 5 Feb. 2015, available http://goo.gl/hnE40M

9. 'ECB should be strict with emergency liquidity—Weidmann', *Reuters*, 5 Feb. 2015, available http://goo.gl/48H2xL

10. 'Eurogroup statement on Greece', *Europa.eu*, 20 Feb. 2015, available http://goo.gl/V7vdYp

11. 'Greece's "creative ambiguity" won extra lifeline, says finance minister', *Reuters*, 27 Feb. 2015, available http://goo.gl/RjzP9P

12. 'Eurogroup statement on Greece', *Europa.eu*, 20 Feb. 2015, available http://goo.gl/V7vdYp; the institutions were also sometimes termed the Brussels Group and could involve representatives from the ESM.

13. 'Insight—darkness at dawn: the fragile plan to rescue Greece', *Reuters*, 13 July 2015, available http://goo.gl/nTwv8F; 'Exclusive: Yanis Varoufakis opens up about his five month battle to save Greece', *New Statesman*, 13 July 2015, available http://goo.gl/FBCEkp

14. 'Greece: the struggle continues', *Jacobin*, 14 July 2015, available https://goo.gl/6KiXnY

15. 'Grèce: «Nous présentons nos arguments, on nous répond par des règles»' *mediapart.fr*, 27 Apr. 2015, available http://goo.gl/NhL7Go

16. 'Defiant Greeks reject EU demands as Syriza readies IOU currency', *Daily Telegraph*, 5 July 2015, available http://goo.gl/rcZhWj

17. 'Spiegel interview with Greek prime minister Tsipras: "we don't want to go on borrowing forever"', *Spiegel Online International*, 7 Mar. 2015, available http://goo.gl/KcxpGf

18. 'Prime minister Alexis Tsipras' speech in the parliamentary group of SYRIZA', *primeminister.gov.gr*, 17 June 2015, available http://goo.gl/1T8fDH; 'Skourletis: "little chance of reaching an agreement with the creditors"', *To Vima English*, 26 June 2015, available http://goo.gl/s2iU1E

19. 'Creditors, Greece need to talk like adults—IMF's Lagarde', *Reuters*, 18 June 2015, available http://goo.gl/NOvJal; 'Greece's proposals to end the crisis: my intervention at today's Eurogroup', *yanisvaroufakis.eu*, 18 June 2015, http://goo.gl/bHpDoi

20. 'Prime minister Alexis Tsipras' address concerning the referendum to be held on the 5th of July', *primeminister.gov.gr*, 27 June 2015, available http://goo.gl/0uN0eV

21. This interpretation draws on 'Greece: the struggle continues', *Jacobin*, 14 July 2015, available https://goo.gl/6KiXnY

22. The documents were 'Reforms for the completion of the current programme and beyond', *wsj.com*, available http://goo.gl/hBFHdp; 'Preliminary debt sustainability analysis for Greece', *wsj.com*, 25 June 2015, available http://goo.gl/CEnBAp; on the referendum website the government also posted 'Greece—financing needed and draft disbursement schedule linked to the completion of the fifth review', *ft.com*, 25 June 2015, available http://goo.gl/9SP7Sl

23. 'Transcript of President Jean-Claude Juncker's press conference on Greece', *Europa.eu*, 29 June 2015, available http://goo.gl/um1xtn

24. 'Eurogroup statement on Greece', *Europa.eu*, 27 June 2015, available http://goo.gl/Rxstbd

25. The controls were published in Εφημερις της κυβερνησεως της Ελληνικης Δημοκρατιας, Αρ. Φύλλου 65, 28 June 2015, a detailed description in English can be found at 'Bank holiday in Greece: restrictions on bank transactions envisaged in the respective legislative act', *eurobank.gr*, 29 June 2015, available http://goo.gl/Wgmq3L

26. 'Government's new proposal to the institutions', *amna.gr*, 1 July 2015, available http://goo.gl/psdwhM

27. 'Prime Minister Alexis Tsipras' address at the NO rally in Syntagma Square', *primeminister.*

gov.gr, 4 July 2015, available http://goo.gl/bz6uY4; the poster is reproduced in 'Wolfgang Schaeuble: Germany's man with a Grexit plan', *BBC News*, 14 July 2015, available http://goo.gl/GdFQFJ

28. I. Jurado, N. Konstantinidis and S. Walter, 'Why Greeks voted the way they did in the bailout referendum', *blogs.lse.ac.uk*, 20 July 2015, available http://goo.gl/iPi0pO

29. 'Greek party leaders issue joint statement', *ekathimerini.com*, 6 July 2015, available http://goo.gl/GdLr2X

30. 'Yanis Varoufakis full transcript: our battle to save Greece', *New Statesman*, 13 July 2015, available http://goo.gl/kzCbAb

31. On the time-out document, which was dated 10 July 2015, see 'Schäuble bringt „Grexit" auf Zeit ins Gespräch', *faz.net*, 11 July 2015, available http://goo.gl/HLP67X; a photograph of the proposal can be found in 'Greek debt crisis: eurozone finance ministers fail to reach agreement—as it happened', *Guardian*, 12 July 2015, available http://goo.gl/9x5LBc

32. '"Sorry, but there is no way you are leaving the room"', *Financial Times*, 14 July 2015.

33. 'Germany's conditional surrender', *Financial Times*, 14 July 2015.

34. 'With Europe behind it, Greece is being pushed into further peril', *Guardian*, 13 July 2015, available http://goo.gl/HlSXmR

35. 'Euro summit statement', *Europa.eu*, 12 July 2015, available http://goo.gl/cejZbU

36. 'Killing the European project', *The New York Times*, 12 July 2015, available http://goo.gl/q37jxp; 'Vorschläge der Euro-Gruppe: Der Katalog der Grausamkeiten', *Spiegel Online*, 12 July 2015, available http://goo.gl/GH1AfD; 'Klares Votum für Athen im Euro', *tagesschau.de*, 13 July 2015, available http://goo.gl/QzSvTr

37. See Galbraith (2016), pp. 155–60, 189–98, and also 'Syriza's covert plot during crisis talks to return to drachma', *ft.com*, 24 July 2015, available http://goo.gl/ay96cC; 'Varoufakis unplugged: the London call transcript', *ft.com*, 27 July 2015, available http://goo.gl/JpiQB5; Varoufakis has also stated the Bank of Greece had contingency plans, see 'Statement by Yanis Varoufakis on the FinMin's Plan B working group & the parallel payment system', *yanisvaroufakis.eu*, 27 July 2015, available http://goo.gl/UCGH8g

38. 'Greece's Third MoU (Memorandum of Understanding) annotated by Yanis Varoufakis', *yanisvaroufakis.eu*, 17 Aug. 2015, available http://goo.gl/OqP3lK

39. 'Greek bailout "a new Versailles Treaty", says former finance minister Yanis Varoufakis', *ABC*, 13 July 2015, available http://goo.gl/ZV0rsl; 'Greece's Alexis Tsipras faces Syriza rebellion over "humiliation"', *ft.com*, 14 July 2015, available http://goo.gl/dUrCLz; "Συμφωνια νεο μνημονιο καταστροφης της χωρας', *ethnos.gr*, 13 July 2015, available https://goo.gl/sgvMkI; 'Λαφαζάνης σε Τσίπρα: απόσυρε έστω και στο «και πέντε» την συμφωνία', *To Vima*, 14 July 2015, http://goo.gl/0GstAH

40. See also M. Mazower, 'Democracy's cradle, rocking the world', *The New York Times*, 29 June 2011, available https://goo.gl/hv1ZbK

41. About (1858), p. 297.

42. Reinhart & Rogoff (2010), p. xxx.

43. Liakos (2004). We would like to thank Professor Liakos for taking the time to discuss his ideas.

44. Tzanelli (2008), p. 188.

45. M. Brooke, R. Mendes, A. Pienkowski & E. Santor, 'Sovereign default and state-contingent debt', *Bank of England Financial Stability Paper*, no. 27, Nov. 2013, available http://goo.gl/xdjuyF

46. Pisani-Ferry (2014), p. 168.

47. 'Standard Eurobarometer 86. Public opinion in the European Union, first results', *Europa. eu*, autumn 2016, available https://goo.gl/sAzAKE

48. For some thoughts on what the future may hold see Kalyvas (2015).

BIBLIOGRAPHY

About, E. 1858. *La Grèce Contemporaine*, 3rd edition. Paris: Hachette.

Afonso, A., S. Zartaloudis and Y. Papadopoulos. 2014. 'How party linkages shape austerity politics: clientelism and fiscal adjustment in Greece and Portugal during the eurozone crisis', *Journal of European Public Policy*, 22:3, pp. 315–34.

Alcidi, C., A. Giovannini and D. Gros. 2011. *History Repeating Itself: from the Argentine Default to the Greek Tragedy?*, Brussels: Centre for European Policy Studies.

Alexopoulos, A. 2011. 'Greece: government as the dominant player', in B.E. Rasch and G. Tsebelis (eds), *The Role of Governments in Legislative Agenda Setting*, Abingdon: Routledge, pp. 145–63.

Alivizatos, N. 1990. 'The difficulties of "rationalization" in a polarized political system: the Greek chamber of deputies', in U. Liebert and M. Cotta (eds), *Parliament and Democratic Consolidation in Southern Europe: Greece, Italy, Portugal, Spain and Turkey*, London: Pinter, pp. 131–53.

Allison, G.T. and K. Nicolaïdis (eds). 1997. *The Greek Paradox: Promise Vs. Performance*, Cambridge, Mass.: The MIT Press.

Alogoskoufis, G. 1992. 'Fiscal policies, devaluations and exchange rate regimes: the stabilisation programmes of Ireland and Greece', *The Economic and Social Review*, 23:3, pp. 225–46.

——— 1995. 'The two faces of Janus: institutions, policy regimes and macroeconomic performance in Greece', *Economic Policy*, 10:20, pp. 149–93.

Alogoskoufis, G. and N. Christodoulakis. 1991. 'Fiscal deficits, seigniorage and external debt: the case of Greece', in G. Alogoskoufis, L. Papademos and R. Portes (eds), *External Constraints on Macroeconomic Policy: The European Experience*, Cambridge: Cambridge University Press, pp. 264–301.

Alogoskoufis, G. and A. Philippopoulos, 1992. 'Inflationary expectations, political parties and the exchange rate regime: Greece 1958–1989', *European Journal of Political Economy*, 8:3, pp. 375–99.

Amnesty International. 2012. *Police Violence in Greece: Not Just 'Isolated Incidents'*, 2012, London: Amnesty International.

Andreou, G. and N. Koutsiaras. 2004. 'Greece and economic and monetary union: whither europeanisation?', in D. Dimitrakopoulos and A. Passas (eds), *Greece in the European Union*, London: Routledge, pp. 86–109.

Andronikidou, A. and I. Kovras. 2012. 'Cultures of rioting and anti-systemic politics in southern Europe', *West European Politics*, 35:4 pp. 707–25.

Antonakakis, N. and A. Collins. 2014. 'The impact of fiscal austerity on suicide: on the empirics of a modern Greek tragedy', *Social Science and Medicine*, 112, pp. 39–50.

Antzoulatos, A.A. 2011. 'Greece in 2010: A tragedy without(?) catharsis', *International Advances in Economic Research*, 17, pp. 241–57

Arghyrou, M.G. 2007. 'The accession of Greece to the EMU: initial estimates and lessons for the new EU countries', *Liverpool Macroeconomic Research Ltd Quarterly Economic Bulletin*, 28:1, pp. 19–30.

Arghyrou, M.G. and A. Kontonikas. 2011. *The EMU Sovereign-Debt Crisis: Fundamentals, Expectations and Contagion*, Brussels: Economic and Financial Affairs Directorate Economic Papers.

Artavanis, N., A. Morse and M. Tsoutsoura. 2012. *Tax Evasion Across Industries: Soft Credit Evidence from Greece*, Chicago Booth Research Paper no. 12–25; Fama-Miller Working Paper.

Arvanitopoulos, C. 1994. 'The belief system of Constantine Karamanlis', *Mediterranean Quarterly*, 5:2, pp. 61–83.

Astrinaki, R. 2009. '"(Un)hooding" a rebellion: the December 2008 events in Athens', *Social Text*, 27: 4, pp. 97–107.

Athanassiou, P. 2009. *Withdrawal and Expulsion from the EU and EMU: Some Reflections*, ECB Legal Working Paper Series, no. 10, Frankfurt: ECB.

Attinasi, M.-G., C. Checherita and C. Nickel. 2009. *What Explains the Surge in Euro Area Sovereign Spreads during the Financial Crisis of 2007–09?*, ECB Working Paper Series, no. 1131, Frankfurt: ECB.

Axt, H-J. 1984. 'On the way to self-reliance? PASOK's government policy in Greece', *Journal of Modern Greek Studies*, 2:2, pp. 189–208.

—— 1997. 'Financial transfers and security: why Greece favoured the Maastricht Treaty on European Union', in H-J. Axt (ed.), *Greece and the European Union: Stranger Among Partners?*, Baden-Baden: Nomos Verlagsgesellschaft, pp. 99–134.

Bank of Greece. 2011. *Annual Report 2010*, Athens: Bank of Greece.

—— 2013. *Annual Report 2012*, Athens: Bank of Greece.

—— 2014. *The Chronicle of the Great Crisis: The Bank of Greece 2008–2013. Public Interventions and Institutional Actions to Safeguard Financial Stability and Overcome the Crisis*, Athens: Bank of Greece.

Barda, C. and E. Sardianou. 2010. 'Analysing consumers' "activism" in response to rising prices', *International Journal of Consumer Studies*, 34:2, pp. 133–40.

Barrell, R., D. Holland and I. Hurst. 2012. *Fiscal Consolidation: Part 2. Fiscal Multipliers and Fiscal Consolidations*, OECD Economics Department Working Papers, no. 933, Paris: OECD Publishing.

Bastasin, C. 2012. *Saving Europe: How National Politics Nearly Destroyed the Euro*, Washington, DC: Brookings Institution Press.

Bayoumi, T. and B. Eichengreen. 1993. 'Shocking aspects of European monetary integration', in

BIBLIOGRAPHY

F. Torres and F. Giavazzi (eds), *Adjustment and Growth in the European Monetary Union*, Cambridge: Cambridge University Press, pp. 193–229.

Bayoumi, T and P. Masson. 1995. 'Fiscal flows in the United States and Canada: lessons for monetary union in Europe', *European Economic Review*, 39:2, pp. 253–74.

Bitros, G.C. 1992. 'Structural policies to unwind the Greek fiscal tangle', in T.S. Kouras (ed.), *Issues in Contemporary Economics. Proceedings of the Ninth World Congress of the International Economic Association, Athens, Greece. Volume 5. The Greek Economy: Economic Policy for the 1990s*, Basingstoke, England: Macmillan, 23–29.

Blundell-Wignall, A. and P. Slovik. 2010. *The EU Stress Test and Sovereign Debt Exposures*, OECD Working Papers on Finance, Insurance and Private Pensions, no. 4, Paris: OECD Publishing.

Blyth, M. 2013. *Austerity: the History of a Dangerous Idea*, Oxford: Oxford University Press.

Bratsis, P. 2010. 'Legitimation crisis and the Greek explosion', *International Journal of Urban and Regional Research*, 34:1, pp. 190–96.

Brazys, S. and N. Hardiman. 2013. *From 'Tiger' to 'PIIGS': Ireland and the Use of Heuristics in Comparative Political Economy*, Dublin: UCD Geary Institute, UCD School of Politics and International Relations.

Buchheit, L.C., G.M. Gulati, and R.B. Thompson. 2007. 'The dilemma of odious debts', *Duke Law Journal*, 56:5, pp. 1201–62.

Buehn, A., F.G. Schneider. 2009. *Corruption and the Shadow Economy: a Structural Equation Model Approach*, IZA Discussion Papers, no. 4182, Bonn: Forschungsinstitut zur Zukunft der Arbeit.

Buti, M. and L.R. Pench. 2004. 'Why do large countries flout the Stability Pact? And what can be done about it?', *Journal of Common Market Studies*, 42:5, pp. 1025–32.

Cairns, R. 2016. 'Climates of suspicion: "chemtrail" conspiracy narratives and the international politics of geoengineering', *The Geographical Journal*, 182:1, pp. 70–84.

Campbell, J.K. 1964. *Honour, Family, and Patronage: a Study of Institutions and Moral Values in a Greek Mountain Community*, Oxford: Clarendon Press.

Chang, S-S., D. Stuckler, P. Yip and D. Gunnell. 2013. 'Impact of 2008 global economic crisis on suicide: time trend study in 54 countries', *British Medical Journal*, 347:f5239.

Chatzifotiou, S. 2005. 'Family violence against women in Greece', in W. Smeenk and M. Malsch (eds), *Family Violence and Police Response: Learning from the Research, Policy and Practice in European Countries*, Aldershot: Ashgate, pp. 139–59.

Cheliotis, L. K. and S. Xenakis (eds). 2011. *Crime and Punishment in Contemporary Greece*, Oxford: Peter Lang.

Chletsos, M., D. Mazetas, E. Kotrotsiou and M. Gouva. 2013. 'The effect of unemployment on mental health', *European Psychiatry*, 28, Supplement 1, 1.

Cholezas, I and P. Tsakloglou. 2009. 'The economic impact of immigration in Greece: taking stock of the existing evidence', *Southeast European and Black Sea Studies*, 9:1–2, pp. 77–104.

Chorafas, D.N. 2014. *Banks, Bankers, and Bankruptcies Under Crisis: Understanding Failure and Mergers During the Great Recession*, Basingstoke, England: Palgrave Macmillan.

Christodoulakis, N. 2010. 'Crisis, threats and ways out for the Greek economy', *Cyprus Economic Policy Review*, 4:1, pp. 89–96.

———— 2012. 'Market reforms in Greece, 1990–2008: external constraints and domestic limitations', in S. Kalyvas, G. Pagoulatos and H. Tsoukas (eds), *From Stagnation to Forced Adjustment: Reforms in Greece, 1974–2010*, London: Hurst, pp. 91–116.

Christopoulou, R. and V. Monastiriotis. 2014. 'The Greek public sector wage premium before the crisis: size, selection and relative valuation of characteristics', *British Journal of Industrial Relations*, 52:3, pp. 579–602.

Clements, B., K. Nanou and S. Verney. 2014. '"We no longer love you, but we don't want to leave you": the Eurozone crisis and popular euroscepticism in Greece', *Journal of European Integration*, 36:3, pp. 247–65.

Clogg, R. 1986. *A Short History of Modern Greece*, 2nd Edition. Cambridge: Cambridge University Press.

——— 1987. *Parties and Elections in Greece*, Durham, NC: Duke University Press.

Close, D.H. 2002. *Greece Since 1945: Politics, Economy and Society*. Harlow, England: Longman.

Conesa, J.C., T.J. Kehoe and K.J. Ruhl. 2007. 'Modelling great depressions: the depression in Finland in the 1990s', in T.J. Kehoe and E.C. Prescott (eds), *Great Depressions of the Twentieth Century*, Minneapolis, MN: Federal Reserve Bank of Minneapolis, pp. 427–75.

Constas, D. and T.G. Stavrou (eds). 1995. *Greece Prepares for the Twenty-First Century*, Washington, DC: The Woodrow Wilson Center Press.

Crawford, A. and T. Czuczka. 2013. *Angela Merkel: a Chancellorship Forged in Crisis*, Chichester, England: John Wiley.

Crozier, M. 1964. *The Bureaucratic Phenomenon*, Chicago: University of Chicago Press.

Csáki, G. 2013. 'IMF loans to Hungary, 1996–2008', *Public Finance Quarterly*, 58:1, pp. 95–110.

Dalakoglou, D. 2012. 'Beyond spontaneity: crisis, violence and collective action in Athens', *City*, 16:5, pp. 535–45.

Daskalakis, D. 2014. Ἔκθεση: η Κατάσταση των Παιδιών στην Ελλάδα, οι Επιπτώσεις της Οικονομικής Κρίσης στα Παιδιά, Athens: UNICEF.

Debrun, X., L. Moulin, A. Turrini, J. Ayuso-i-Casals and M. Kumar. 2008. 'Tied to the mast? National fiscal rules in the European Union', *Economic Policy*, 23:54, pp. 299–362.

Dellas, H. and G.S. Tavlas. 2013. 'The Gold Standard, the euro, and the origins of the Greek sovereign debt crisis', *Cato Journal*, 33:3, pp. 491–520.

Demekas, D.G. and Z.G. Kontolemis. 1997. *Unemployment in Greece: a Survey of the Issues*, Florence, European University Institute.

Demertzis, N. 1997. 'Greece', in R. Eatwell (ed.), *European Political Cultures: Conflict or Convergence?*, London: Routledge, pp. 107–121.

Diamandouros, P.N. 1984. 'Transition to, and consolidation of, democratic politics in Greece, 1974–1983: a tentative assessment', *West European Politics*, 7:2, pp. 50–71.

——— 1993. 'Politics and culture in Greece, 1974–91: an interpretation', in R. Clogg (ed.), *Greece, 1981–89: the Populist Decade*, London: Macmillan, pp. 1–25.

——— 2013. 'Postscript: cultural dualism revisited', in A. Triandafyllidou, R. Gropas and H. Kouki (eds), *The Greek Crisis and European Modernity*, Basingstoke, England: Palgrave Macmillan, pp. 208–33.

Dimitras, P. 1987. 'Changes in public attitudes', in K. Featherstone and D.K. Katsoudas (eds),

BIBLIOGRAPHY

Political Change in Greece: Before and After the Colonels, New York: St Martin's Press, pp. 64–84.

Dinas, E. 2010. 'The Greek general election of 2009: PASOK—the third generation', *West European Politics*, 33:2, pp. 389–98.

Dinas, E., V. Georgiadou, I. Konstantinidis and L. Rori. 2016. 'From dusk to dawn: local party organization and party success of right-wing extremism', *Party Politics*, 22:1, pp. 80–92.

Djankov, S., C. L. Freund and C. S. Pham. 2006. *Trading on Time*, World Bank Policy Research, Working Paper no. 3909, Washington DC: World Bank.

Douzinas, C. 2013. *Philosophy and Resistance in the Crisis: Greece and the Future of Europe*, Cambridge: Polity.

Dragoumis, M. 2004. *The Greek Economy 1940–2004*, Athens: Athens News.

Du Boulay, J. 1974. *Portrait of a Greek Mountain Village*, Oxford: Clarendon.

Dunbar, N. 2011. *The Devil's Derivatives: the Untold Story of the Slick Traders and Hapless Regulators Who Almost Blew Up Wall Street… and Are Ready to Do It Again*, Boston, MA: Harvard Business Review Press.

Dziuda, W. and G. Mastrobuoni. 2009. 'The euro changeover and its effects on price transparency and inflation', *Journal of Money, Credit and Banking*, 41:1, pp. 101–29.

Economou, M., M. Madianos, L.E. Peppou, A. Patelakis, and C.N. Stefanis. 2013. 'Major depression in the era of economic crisis: a replication of a cross-sectional study across Greece', *Journal of Affective Disorders*, 145:3, pp. 308–14.

Ellinas, A.A. 2010. *The Media and the Far Right in Western Europe: Playing the Nationalist Card*, Cambridge: Cambridge University Press.

——— 2013. 'The rise of Golden Dawn: the new face of the far right in Greece', *South European Society and Politics*, 18:4, pp. 543–65.

——— 2015. 'Neo-nazism in an established democracy: the persistence of Golden Dawn in Greece', *South European Society and Politics*, 20:1, pp. 1–20.

Exadaktylos, T. and N. Zahariadis. 2014. '*Quid pro quo*: political trust and policy implementation in Greece during the age of austerity', *Politics and Policy*, 42:1, pp. 160–83.

Fakiolas, R. 1987. 'Interest groups—an overview', in K. Featherstone and D.K. Katsoudas (eds), *Political Change in Greece: Before and After the Colonels*, New York: St Martin's Press, pp. 174–88.

Featherstone, K. and D. Papadimitriou. 2008. *The Limits of Europeanization: Reform Capacity and Policy Conflict in Greece*, Basingstoke, England: Palgrave Macmillan.

——— 2012. 'Assessing reform capacity in Greece: applying political economy perspectives', in S. Kalyvas, G. Pagoulatos and H. Tsoukas (eds), *From Stagnation to Forced Adjustment: Reforms in Greece, 1974–2010*, London: Hurst, pp. 31–46.

——— 2013. 'The emperor has no clothes! Power and resources within the Greek core executive', *Governance*, 26:3, pp. 523–45.

Featherstone, K. 2008. 'Greece and EMU: a suitable accommodation?', In K. Dyson (ed.), *The Euro at Ten: Europeanization, Power, and Convergence*, Oxford: Oxford University Press, pp. 165–81.

——— 2011. 'The Greek sovereign debt crisis and EMU: a failing state in a skewed regime', *Journal of Common Market Studies*, 49:2, pp. 193–217.

———— 2015. 'External conditionality and the debt crisis: the "troika" and public administration reform in Greece', *Journal of European Public Policy*, 22:3, pp. 295–314.

Featherstone, K., G. Kazamias, and D. Papadimitriou. 2000. 'Greece and the negotiation of Economic and Monetary Union: preferences, strategies, and institutions', *Journal of Modern Greek Studies*, 18:2, pp. 393–414.

Fender, I., C. Ho and P. Hördahl. 2009. 'Overview: investors ponder depth and duration of global downturn', *BIS Quarterly Review*, March 2009, pp. 1–17.

Fountoulakis, K.N., I.A. Grammatikopoulos, S.A. Koupidis, M. Siamouli and P.N. Theodorakis. 2012. 'Health and the financial crisis in Greece', *The Lancet*, 379:9820, pp. 1001–1002.

Fouskas, V. 1997. 'The left and the crisis of the third Hellenic Republic, 1989–97', in D. Sassoon (ed.), *Looking Left: European Socialism after the Cold War*, London: I.B. Tauris, pp. 64–87.

Fouskas, V.K. and C. Dimoulas. 2012. 'The Greek workshop of debt and the failure of the European project', *Journal of Balkan and Near Eastern Studies*, 14:1, pp. 1–31.

———— 2013. *Greece, Financialization and the EU: the Political Economy of Debt and Destruction*, Basingstoke, England: Palgrave Macmillan.

Fredriksen, K.B. 2012. *Income Inequality in the European Union*, OECD Economics Department Working Papers, no. 952, Paris: OECD Publications.

Freris, A. 1986. *The Greek Economy in the Twentieth Century*, London: Croom Helm.

Galbraith, J.K. 2016. *Welcome to the Poisoned Chalice: the Destruction of Greece and the Future of Europe*, New Haven: Yale University Press.

Gavriilidis, A. 2009. '[Greek riots 2008:]—a mobile Tiananmen' in S. Economides and V. Monastiriotis (eds), *The Return of Street Politics? Essays on the December Riots in Greece*, London: The Hellenic Observatory, LSE, pp. 15–19.

Gazi, E. 2011. *Πατρίς, Θρησκεία, Οικογένεια: η Ιστορία ενός Συνθήματος (1880–1930)*, Athens: Polis.

Gemenis, K. 2008. 'The 2007 parliamentary election in Greece', *Mediterranean Politics*, 13:1, pp. 95–101.

———— 2012. 'The 2010 regional elections in Greece: voting for regional governance or protesting the IMF?', *Regional and Federal Studies*, 22:1, pp. 107–15.

Gibson, H.D., S.G. Hall and G.S. Tavlas. 2012. 'The Greek financial crisis: growing imbalances and sovereign spreads', *Journal of International Money and Finance*, 31:3, pp. 498–516.

———— 2014. 'Fundamentally wrong: market pricing of sovereigns and the Greek financial crisis', *Journal of Macroeconomics*, 39, Part B, pp. 405–19.

Gibson, H.D., T. Palivos and G.S. Tavlas. 2014. 'The crisis in the euro area: an analytic overview', *Journal of Macroeconomics*, 39, Part B, pp. 233–39.

Gkartzios, M. 2013. '"Leaving Athens": narratives of counterurbanisation in times of crisis', *Journal of Rural Studies*, 32, pp. 158–67.

Gorodnichenko, Y., E.G. Mendoza and L.L. Tesar. 2012. 'The Finnish great depression: from Russia with love', *American Economic Review*, 102:4, pp. 1619–44.

Halikias, D. 1978. *Money and Credit in a Developing Economy: the Greek Case*, New York: New York University Press.

———— 1993. 'Economic stabilization and growth: the case of Greece', *Greek Economic Review*, 15, pp. 97–136.

Hardie, I. and D. Howarth. 2009. '*Die krise* but not *la crise*? The financial crisis and the transfor-

BIBLIOGRAPHY

mation of German and French banking systems', *Journal of Common Market Studies*, 47:5, pp. 1017–39.

Haugh, D., P. Ollivaud, and D. Turner. 2009. *What Drives Sovereign Risk Premiums? An Analysis of Recent Evidence from the Euro Area*, OECD Economics Department Working Papers, no. 718, Paris: OECD Publishing.

Hausmann, R., C.A. Hidalgo, S. Bustos, M. Coscia, A. Simoes and M.A. Yildirim. 2013. *The Atlas of Economic Complexity: Mapping Paths to Prosperity*, Cambridge, Mass: MIT Press.

Hawkesworth, I., D. Bergvall, R. Emery and J. Wehner. 2008. 'Budgeting in Greece', *OECD Journal on Budgeting*, 8:3, pp. 70–119.

Helliwell, J., R. Layard and J. Sachs (eds). 2012. *World Happiness Report 2012*, New York: Earth Institute.

——— 2013. *World Happiness Report 2013*, New York: UN Sustainable Development Solutions Network.

Herzfeld, M. 1985. *The Poetics of Manhood: Contest and Identity in a Cretan Mountain Village*, Princeton, NJ: Princeton University Press.

——— 1992. *The Social Production of Indifference: Exploring the Symbolic Roots of Western Bureaucracy*, Chicago: University of Chicago Press.

——— 2011. 'Crisis attack: impromptu ethnography in the Greek maelstrom', *Anthropology Today*, 27:5, pp. 22–26.

Hessel, S. 2011. *Time for Outrage!*, London: Quartet.

Hewitt, G. 2013. *The Lost Continent*, London: Hodder and Stoughton.

Hugh-Jones, D., A. Katsanidou and G. Riener. 2009. *Political discrimination in the aftermath of violence: the case of the Greek riots*, Hellenic Observatory Papers on Greece and Southeast Europe, no. 30, London: The Hellenic Observatory, LSE.

Ioakimoglou, E. and J. Milios. 1993. 'Capital accumulation and over-accumulation crisis: the case of Greece (1960–1989)', *Review of Radical Political Economics*, 25:2, pp. 81–107.

Ioannou, C. 1986. 'Η βιομηχανική εργατική τάξη στο συνδικαλιστικό κίνημα 1974–1984' in N. Palaiologos and D. Charalambis (eds), *Κοινωνικές Τάξεις, Κοινωνική Αλλαγή και Οικονομική Ανάπτυξη στη Μεσόγειο*, vol. A., Athens: Foundation for Mediterranean Studies, pp. 31–56.

Jenkins, S.P., A. Brandolini, J. Micklewright and B. Nolan. 2013. *The Great Recession and the Distribution of Household Income*, Oxford: Oxford University Press.

Jiménez, A.C. and A. Estalella. 2011. '#spanishrevolution', *Anthropology Today*, 27:4, pp. 19–23.

Jones, E. 2010. 'Merkel's folly', *Survival*, 52:3, pp. 21–38.

Jouganatos, G.A. 1992. *The Development of the Greek Economy, 1950–1991: an Historical, Empirical, and Econometric Analysis*, Westport, Conn: Greenwood Press.

Kalaitzidis, A. 2010. *Europe's Greece: a Giant in the Making*, London: Palgrave Macmillan.

Kalyvas, A. 2010. 'An anomaly? Some reflections on the Greek December 2008', *Constellations*, 17:2, pp. 351–65.

Kalyvas, S.N. 1997. 'Polarization in Greek politics: PASOK's first four years, 1981–1985', *Journal of the Hellenic Diaspora*, 23:1, pp. 83–104.

——— 2015. *Modern Greece: What Everyone Needs to Know*, New York: Oxford University Press.

BIBLIOGRAPHY

Kalyvas, S.N. and N. Marantzidis. 2002. 'Greek communism, 1968–2001', *East European Politics and Societies*, 16:3. pp. 665–90.

Kambouri, N. and A. Zavos. 2010. 'On the frontiers of citizenship: considering the case of Konstantina Kuneva and the intersections between gender, migration and labour in Greece', *Feminist Review*, 94, pp. 148–55.

Kandylis, G. and K.I. Kavoulakos. 2011. 'Framing urban inequalities: racist mobilization against immigrants in Athens', *The Greek Review of Social Research*, 136, pp. 157–76.

Kannellopoulos, C. N. 2012. *The Size and Structure of Uninsured Employment*, Athens: Bank of Greece.

Kaplanoglou, G. and V. T. Rapanos. 2013. 'Tax and trust: the fiscal crisis in Greece', *South European Society and Politics*, 18:3, pp. 283–304.

Karakousis, A. 2006. *Μετέωρη Χώρα: από την Κοινωνία της Ανάγκης στην Κοινωνία της Επιθυμίας 1975–2005*, Athens: Estia.

Karamichas, J. 2009. 'The December 2008 riots in Greece', *Social Movement Studies*, 8:3, pp. 289–93.

Karamouzis, N. and G. Hardouvelis (eds). 2011. *Από τη Διεθνή Κρίση στην Κρίση της Ευρωζώνης και της Ελλάδας: τι μας Επιφυλάσσει το Μέλλον*; Athens: Livanis.

Karantinos, D. 2012. *EEO Review: Long-term Unemployment, Greece*, Brussels: European Employment Policy Observatory.

Kariotis, T.C. 1997. 'Andreas G. Papandreou: the economist', *Journal of the Hellenic Diaspora*, 23:1, pp. 33–58.

Karyotis, G and W. Rudig. 2015. 'Blame and punishment? The electoral politics of extreme austerity in Greece', *Political Studies*, 63:1, pp. 2–24.

Karyotis, G., W. Rüdig and D. Judge. 2014. 'Representation and austerity politics: attitudes of Greek voters and elites compared', *South European Society and Politics*, 19:4, pp. 435–56.

Kassimeris, G. 2004. 'The 2004 Greek election: PASOK's monopoly ends', *West European Politics*, 27:5, pp. 943–53.

——— 2013. *Inside Greek Terrorism*, London: Hurst.

Katrougalos, G. 2012. *Η Κρίση και η Διέξοδος*, Athens: Livanis.

——— 2013. 'Memoranda: Greek exceptionalism or the mirror of Europe's future?', in A. Triandafyllidou, R. Gropas and H. Kouki (eds), *The Greek Crisis and European Modernity*, Basingstoke, England: Palgrave Macmillan, pp. 89–109.

Katseli, L.T. 1990. 'Economic integration in the enlarged European Community: structural adjustment of the Greek economy', in C. Bliss and J.B. de Macedo (eds), *Unity with Diversity in the European Economy: the Community's Southern Frontier*, Cambridge: Cambridge University Press, pp. 235–309.

Katsios, S. 2006. 'The shadow economy and corruption in Greece', *South-Eastern Europe Journal of Economics*, 1, pp. 61–80.

Katsoudas, D.K. 1978. 'The conservative movement and New Democracy: from past to present', in K. Featherstone and D.K. Katsoudas (eds), *Political Change in Greece: Before and After the Colonels*, New York: St Martin's Press, pp. 85–111.

Kay, J. 2004. *The Truth About Markets: Why Some Nations are Rich but Most Remain Poor*, London: Penguin.

BIBLIOGRAPHY

Kehoe, T.J. 2003. 'What can we learn from the current crisis in Argentina?', *Scottish Journal of Political Economy*, 50:5, pp. 609–33.

——— 2007. 'What can we learn from the 1998–2002 depression in Argentina?', in T.J. Kehoe and E.C. Prescott (eds), *Great Depressions Of The Twentieth Century*, Minneapolis, MN: Federal Reserve Bank of Minneapolis, pp. 373–402.

Kentikelenis, A., M. Karanikolos, I. Papanicolas, S. Basu, M. McKee and D. Stuckler. 2011. 'Health effects of financial crisis: omens of a Greek tragedy', *The Lancet*, 378:9801, pp. 1457–58.

Kentikelenis, A., M. Karanikolos, A. Reeves, M. McKee and D. Stuckler. 2014. 'Greece's health crisis: from austerity to denialism', *The Lancet*, 383:9918, pp. 748–53.

Keridis, D. 1997. 'Greece in the 1990s: the challenge of reform', in G.T. Allison and K. Nicolaidis (eds), *The Greek Paradox: Promise Vs. Performance*, Cambridge, Mass.: The MIT Press, pp. 85–96.

Kleinman, J. 1988. 'Socialist policies and the free market: an evaluation of PASOK's economic performance', in N. A. Stavrou (ed.), *Greece Under Socialism: a NATO Ally Adrift*, New Rochelle, NY: Caratzas, pp. 187–219.

Knight, D.M. 2012. 'Turn of the screw: narratives of history and economy in the Greek crisis', *Journal of Mediterranean Studies*, 21:1, pp. 53–76.

Koen, V. and P. van den Noord. 2005. *Fiscal Gimmickry in Europe: One-Off Measures and Creative Accounting*, OECD Economics Department Working Papers, no. 417, Paris: OECD Publications.

Kofas, J.V. 2005. *Independence from America: Global Integration and Inequality*, Aldershot, England: Ashgate.

Koliopoulos, J.S. and T.M. Veremis. 2002. *Greece: the Modern Sequel. From 1831 to the present*, London: Hurst.

Kondilis, E., S. Giannakopoulos, M. Gavana, I. Ierodiakonou, H. Waitzkin and A. Benos. 2013. 'Economic crisis, restrictive policies, and the population's health and health care: the Greek case', *American Journal of Public Health*, 103:6, pp. 973–79.

Kornelius, S. 2013. *Angela Merkel: the Chancellor and her World*, London: Alma.

Kornetis, K. 2010. 'No more heroes? Rejection and reverberation of the past in the 2008 events in Greece', *Journal of Modern Greek Studies*, 28:2, pp. 173–97.

——— 2013. Children of the Dictatorship: Student Resistance, Cultural Politics and the 'Long 1960s' in Greece, New York: Berghahn.

Koronaiou, A., E. Lagos, A. Sakellariou, S. Kymionis and I. Chiotaki-Poulou. 2015. 'Golden Dawn, austerity and young people: the rise of fascist extremism among young people in contemporary Greek society', *The Sociological Review*, 63:S2, pp. 231–49.

Kotsios, P. and V. Mitsios. 2013. 'Entrepreneurship in Greece: a way out of the crisis or a dive in?', *Research in Applied Economics*, 5:1, pp. 22–44.

Kottakis, M. 2011. *Καραμανλής off the Record*, Athens: Livanis.

Koukiadaki, A. and L. Kretsos. 2012. 'Opening Pandora's Box: the sovereign debt crisis and labour market regulation in Greece', *Industrial Law Journal*, 41:3, pp. 276–304.

Kourvetaris, G.A. and B.A. Dobratz. 1999. 'Public perception of the influence of dominant

BIBLIOGRAPHY

groups on politics in Athens, Greece' in G.A. Kourvetaris (ed.), *Studies on Modern Greek Society and Politics*, Boulder, Col.: East European Monographs, pp. 287–301.

Koutsogeorgopoulou, V., M. Matsaganis, C. Leventi and J.-D. Schneider. 2014. *Fairly Sharing the Social Impact of the Crisis in Greece*, OECD Economics Department Working Papers, no. 1106, Paris: OECD Publishing.

Kouvelakis, S. 2010. 'The Greek crisis—politics, economics, ethics', *Journal of Modern Greek Studies*, 28:2, pp. 303–306.

—— 2011. 'The Greek cauldron', *New Left Review*, 72, Nov.-Dec., pp. 17–32.

Kovras, I. 2010. 'The parliamentary election in Greece, October 2009', *Electoral Studies*, 29:2, pp. 293–96.

Kretsos, L. 2011. 'Grassroots unionism in the context of economic crisis in Greece', *Labor History*, 52:3, pp. 265–86.

—— 2012. 'Greece's neoliberal experiment and working class resistance', *WorkingUSA: The Journal of Labor and Society*, 15:4, pp. 517–27.

Krugman, P. 1993. 'Lessons of Massachusetts for EMU', in F. Torres and F. Giavazzi (eds), *Adjustment and Growth in the European Monetary Union*, Cambridge: Cambridge University Press, pp. 241–66.

Kyriazis, N. 1995. 'Feminism and the status of women in Greece', in D. Constas and T.G. Stavrou (eds), *Greece Prepares for the Twenty-First Century*, Washington DC: The Woodrow Wilson Center Press, pp. 267–301.

Labrianidis, L. and N. Vogiatzis. 2013. 'The mutually reinforcing relation between international migration of highly educated labour force and economic crisis: the case of Greece', *Southeast European and Black Sea Studies*, 13:4, pp. 525–51.

Lakopoulos, G. 1999. *Το Μυθιστόρημα του ΠΑΣΟΚ: Πολιτικό Αφήγημα*, Athens: Kastaniotis.

Langrod, G. 1965. *Reorganisation of Public Administration in Greece*, Paris: OECD Publications.

Lapavitsas, C., A. Kaltenbrunner, D. Lindo, J. Michell, J.P. Painceira, E. Pires, J. Powell, A. Stenfors and N. Teles. 2010. 'Eurozone crisis: beggar thyself and thy neighbour', *Journal of Balkan and Near Eastern Studies*, 12:4, pp. 321–73.

Lapavitsas, C., A. Kaltenbrunner, G. Labrinidis, D. Lindo, J. Meadway, J. Michell, J.P. Painceira, E. Pires, J. Powell, A. Stenfors and N. Teles. 2013. *Crisis in the Eurozone*, London: Verso.

Laskos, C. and E. Tsakalotos. 2013. *Crucible of Resistance: Greece, the Eurozone and the World Economic Crisis*, London: Pluto Press.

Layoun, M.N. 2011. 'Locating crisis', *Journal of Modern Greek Studies*, 29:1, pp. 121–25.

Leandros, N. 2010. 'Media concentration and systemic failures in Greece', *International Journal of Communication*, 4, pp. 886–905.

Ledeneva, A.V. 1998. *Russia's Economy of Favours: Blat, Networking and Informal Exchange*, Cambridge: Cambridge University Press.

Liakos, A. 2004. 'Modern Greek historiography (1974–2000): the era of tradition from dictatorship to democracy', in U. Brunbauer (ed.), *(Re)writing History: Historiography in Southeast Europe After Socialism*, Münster: LIT Verlag, pp. 351–78.

Ludington, S. and M. Gulati. 2008. 'A convenient untruth: fact and fantasy in the doctrine of odious debts', *Virginia Journal of International Law*, 48:3, pp. 595–639.

BIBLIOGRAPHY

Ludington, S., M. Gulati and A.L. Brophy. 2010. 'Applied legal history: demystifying the doctrine of odious debts', *Theoretical Inquiries in Law*, 11, pp. 247–81.

Lynn, M. 2011. *Bust: Greece, the Euro, and the Sovereign Debt Crisis*, Hoboken, NJ: Bloomberg Press.

Lyrintzis, C. 2011. *Greek Politics in the Era of Economic Crisis: Reassessing Causes and Effects*, Hellenic Observatory Papers on Greece and Southeast Europe, no. 45, London: The Hellenic Observatory, LSE.

Makris, G., and D. Bekridakis. 2013. 'The Greek Orthodox Church and the economic crisis since 2009', *International Journal for the Study of the Christian Church*, 13:2, pp. 111–32.

Malaby, T. M. 2003. *Gambling Life: Dealing in Contingency in a Greek City*, Urbana, IL: University of Illinois Press.

Malakos, T. 2013. 'Greece facing herself: the past and present as fate', *Journal of Balkan and Near Eastern Studies*, 15:1, pp. 1–15.

Manolas, G., K. Rontos, G. Sfakianakis and I. Vavouras. 2013. 'The determinants of the shadow economy: the case of Greece', *International Journal of Criminology and Sociological Theory*, 6:1, pp. 1036–47.

Manolopoulos, J. 2011. *Greece's 'Odious' Debt: The Looting of the Hellenic Republic by the Euro, the Political Elite and the Investment Community*, London: Anthem.

Markaris, P. 2009. *Che Committed Suicide*, London: Eurocrime.

―――― 2010. *Ληξιπρόθεσμα Δάνεια*, Athens: Gavriilides.

―――― 2011. *Περαίωση*, Athens: Gavriilides.

―――― 2012. *Ψωμί, Παιδεία, Ελευθερία*, Athens: Gavriilides.

Marsh, D. 2009. *The Euro: the Battle for the New Global Currency*, New Haven: Yale.

Mason, P. 2009. *Meltdown: the End of the Age of Greed*, London: Verso.

Matsaganis, M. 2012. 'The crisis and the welfare state in Greece: a complex relationship', in A. Triandafyllidou, R. Gropas and H. Kouki (eds), *The Greek Crisis and European Modernity*, Basingstoke, England: Palgrave Macmillan, pp. 152–77.

Matsaganis, M., and C. Leventi. 2014. 'The distributional impact of austerity and the recession in southern Europe', *South European Society and Politics*, 19:3, pp. 393–412.

Matsaganis, M., C. Leventi and M. Flevotomou. 2012. 'The crisis and tax evasion in Greece: what are the distributional implications?', *CESifo Forum*, 13:2, pp. 26–32.

Mavris, Y. 2012. 'Greece's austerity election', *New Left Review*, 76, pp. 95–107.

Mavrogordatos, G. 1984. 'The Greek party system: a case of "limited but polarised pluralism?"', *West European Politics*, 7:4, 156–69.

―――― 1997. 'From traditional clientelism to machine politics: the impact of PASOK populism in Greece', *South European Society and Politics*, 2:3, pp. 1–26.

―――― 2001. *Ομάδες Πίεσης και Δημοκρατία*, Athens: Patakis.

Mazetas D., M. Gouva, E. Kotrotsiou and M. Chletsos. 2013. 'The effect of borrowing on mental health', *European Psychiatry*, 28, Supplement 1, 1.

McDonald, R. 1983. *Pillar and Tinderbox: the Greek Press and the Dictatorship*, New York: Marion Boyars.

―――― 2005. *The Competitiveness of the Greek Economy*, Athens: Athens News.

Michail, D. 2013. 'Social development and transnational households: resilience and motivation

BIBLIOGRAPHY

for Albanian immigrants in Greece in the era of economic crisis', *Southeast European and Black Sea Studies*, 13:2, pp. 265–79.

Michas, G., A. Varytimiadi, I. Chasiotis and R. Micha. 2014. 'Maternal and child mortality in Greece', *The Lancet*, 383:9918, pp. 691–92.

Mitrakos, T. 2014. *Inequality, Poverty and Social Welfare in Greece: Distributional Effects of Austerity*, Bank of Greece Working Papers 174, Athens: Bank of Greece.

Mitropoulos, A. 2012. *Στο Έλεος του Μνημονίου: η Πολιτική της Χρεοκοπίας και η Υπέρβασή της*, Athens: Livanis.

Mitsopoulos, M. and T. Pelagidis. 2011. *Understanding the Crisis in Greece: from Boom to Bust*, London: Palgrave Macmillan.

Monastiriotis, V. and A. Antoniades. 2012. 'Reform that! Greece's failing reform technology: beyond "vested interests" and "political exchange"', in S. Kalyvas, G. Pagoulatos and H. Tsoukas (eds), *From Stagnation to Forced Adjustment: Reforms in Greece, 1974–2010*, London: Hurst, pp. 47–65.

Montiel, P.J. 2014. *Ten Crises*, London: Routledge.

Moschonas, G. 2013. 'A new left in Greece: PASOK's fall and SYRIZA's rise', *Dissent*, 60:4, pp. 33–37.

Mourmouras, I.A. and M.G. Arghyrou. 1998. 'Greece and the European Monetary Union: a bottle half-empty or half-full?', *Synthesis: Review of Modern Greek Studies*, 2:2, pp. 1–16.

Mouzelis, N. 1980. 'Capitalism and the development of the Greek state', in R. Scase (ed.), *The State in Western Europe*, Paris: Maison des Sciences de l'Homme, pp. 241–73.

———— 1987. 'Continuities and discontinuities in Greek politics: from Elefterios Venizelos to Andreas Papandreou', in K. Featherstone and D.K. Katsoudas (eds), *Political Change in Greece: Before and After the Colonels*, New York: St Martin's, pp. 271–87.

———— 1995. 'Greece in the twenty-first century: institutions and political culture', in D. Constas and T.G. Stavrou (eds), *Greece Prepares for the Twenty-First Century*, Washington DC: Woodrow Wilson Centre Press, pp. 17–34.

Nikolaidou, E. 2011. *Οι Συνταγές...της Πείνας: η Ζωή στην Αθήνα την Περίοδο της Κατοχής*, Athens: Oxygono.

Nikolaou, N. 2008. *Πρόσωπα της Οικονομίας*, Athens: Livanis.

Nissaris, E. 2013. *Ελληνική Ασφυξία: Μυθιστόρημα για την Κρίση*, Athens: Oi Ekdoseis ton Synadelfon.

OECD. 1972. *OECD Economic Surveys: Greece 1972*, Paris: OECD Publications.

———— 1990. *OECD Economic Surveys: Greece 1989–1990*, Paris: OECD Publications.

———— 1992. *OECD Economic Surveys: Greece 1991–92*, Paris: OECD Publications.

———— 1993. *OECD Economic Surveys: Greece 1993*, Paris: OECD Publications.

———— 2009. *Economic Surveys: Greece*, Paris: OECD Publications.

———— 2011. *Greece: Review of the Central Administration*, OECD Public Governance Reviews, Paris: OECD Publishing.

———— 2013. *Economic Survey of Greece*, Paris: OECD Publications.

———— 2016. *Economic Survey of Greece*, Paris: OECD Publications.

Pagoulatos, G. 2003. *Greece's New Political Economy: State, Finance, and Growth*, London: Palgrave Macmillan.

BIBLIOGRAPHY

——— 2009a. 'Some thoughts on the 2008 riots in Greece', in S. Economides and
V. Monastiriotis (eds), *The Return of Street Politics? Essays on the December Riots in Greece*,
London: The Hellenic Observatory, LSE, pp. 45–49.

——— 2009b. 'The return of the Greek patient: Greece and the 2008 global financial Crisis',
Southern European Societies and Politics, 14:1, pp. 35–54.

——— 2012. 'The political economy of forced reform and the 2010 Greek economic adjustment
programme', in S. Kalyvas, G. Pagoulatos and H. Tsoukas (eds), *From Stagnation to Forced
Adjustment: Reforms in Greece 1974–2010*, London: Hurst, pp. 247–74.

Palaiologos, Y. 2014. *The 13th Labour of Hercules: Inside the Greek Crisis*, London: Portobello.

Paleologos, J. M. 1993. 'An investigation on the effectiveness of the devaluation policy in the case
of the Greek economy: 1975–1991', *Economia Internazionale*, 46:2–3, pp. 247–56.

Panagiotarea, E. 2013. *Greece in the Euro: Economic Delinquency or System Failure?*, Colchester,
England: ECPR.

Panagopoulos, C. and N. Marantzidis. 2006. 'The parliamentary election in Greece, March
2004', *Electoral Studies*, 25:2, pp. 404–09.

Panayotakis, C. 2009. 'Reflections on the Greek uprising', *Capitalism Nature Socialism*, 20:2,
pp. 97–101.

Papaconstantinou, G. 2016. *Game Over: The Inside Story of the Greek Crisis*, CreateSpace
Independent Publishing Platform.

Papadopoulos, T. 2006. 'Support for the unemployed in a familistic welfare regime', in
M. Petmesidou and E. Mossialos (eds), *Social Policy Developments in Greece*, Aldershot:
Ashgate, pp. 219–38

Papandreou, A.G and J.T. Wheeler. 1954. *Competition and its Regulation*, New York:
Prentice-Hall.

Papapetrou, E. 2006. 'The public-private sector pay differential in Greece', *Public Finance Review*,
34:4, pp. 450–73.

Papathanassiou, Y. 2011. *Με τη Γλώσσα των Αριθμών: η Αλήθεια για την Οικονομία*, Athens, available http://www.papathanassiou.gr/numbers.pdf

Pappas, T.S. 1999. *Making Party Democracy in Greece*, London: Palgrave Macmillan.

——— 2010. 'Winning by default: the Greek election of 2009', *South European Society and
Politics*, 15:2, pp. 273–87.

——— 2014. *Populism and Crisis Politics in Greece*, Basingstoke, England: Palgrave Macmillan.

Pappas, T. and. Z. Assimakopoulou. 2012. 'Party patronage in Greece. Political entrepreneurship
in a party patronage democracy: Greece' in P. Kopecký, P. Mair and M. Spirova (eds), *Party,
Patronage and Party Government in European Democracies*, Oxford: Oxford University Press,
pp. 144–64.

Paraschackis, A., D. Konstantinidou, I. Michopoulos, A. Douzenis, C. Christodoulou,
F. Koutsaftis, L. Lykouras. 2012. 'Stressful life events the year before suicide in a sample of
suicide victims from Greece', *European Psychiatry*, 27, Supplement 1, 1.

Pasiouras, F. 2012. *Greek Banking: from the Pre-Euro Reforms to the Financial Crisis and Beyond*,
Basingstoke, England: Palgrave Macmillan.

Patrikios, S. and G. Karyotis. 2008. 'The Greek parliamentary election of 2007', *Electoral Studies*,
27:2, pp. 356–59.

BIBLIOGRAPHY

Patrikios, S. and M. Chatzikonstantinou. 2015. 'Dynastic politics: family ties in the Greek parliament, 2000–12', *South European Society and Politics*, 20:1, pp. 93–111.

Patronis, V. and P. Liargovas. 2004. 'Economic policy in Greece, 1974–2000: nationalization, state's intervention or market forces?', *Entreprises et Histoire*, 37, pp. 120–34.

Pavlopoulos, P. 1987. *Η Παραοικονομία στην Ελλάδα: μια Πρώτη Ποσοτική Οριοθέτηση*, Athens: IOBE.

Pelagidis, T. 1997. 'Economic policies in Greece during 1990–1993: an assessment', *Journal of Modern Greek Studies*, 15:1, pp. 67–85.

Pelagidis, T. and M. Mitsopoulos. 2014. *Greece from Exit to Recovery?*, Washington D.C.: Brookings Institute Press.

——— 2016. *Who's to Blame for Greece? Austerity in Charge of Saving a Broken Economy*, London: Palgrave, Macmillan.

Pescatori, A. and A.N.R. Sy. 2007. 'Are debt crises adequately defined?', *IMF Staff Papers*, 54:2, pp. 306–37.

Pesmazoglu, J. 1972. 'The Greek economy', in R. Clogg and G. Yannopoulos (eds), *Greece under Military Rule*, New York: Basic Books, pp. 75–108.

Petralias, A., E. Papadimitriou, E. Riza, M.R. Karagas, A.B.A. Zagouras and A. Linos, on behalf of the DIATROFI Program Research Team. 2016. 'The impact of a school food aid program on household food insecurity', *European Journal of Public Health*, 26:2, pp. 290–96.

Petrakis, P. 2011. *The Greek Economy and the Crisis: Challenges and Responses*, New York and Heidelberg: Springer.

Piga, G. 2001. *Derivatives and Public Debt Management*, New York: International Securities Market Association (ISMA) in cooperation with the Council on Foreign Relations.

Pirounakis, N.G. 1997. *The Greek Economy: Past, Present and Future*, Basingstoke, England: Palgrave Macmillan.

Pisani-Ferry, J. 1998. 'Monetary union with variable geometry', in J.A. Frieden, D. Gros and E. Jones, (eds), *The New Political Economy of EMU: Governance in Europe*, Lanham, MD: Rowman and Littlefield, pp. 125–62.

——— 2014. *The Euro Crisis and its Aftermath*, New York: Oxford University Press.

Pisani-Ferry, J., A. Sapir and G.B. Wolff. 2013. *EU-IMF Assistance to Euro-Area Countries: an Early Assessment*, Bruegel Blueprint Series 19, Brussels: Bruegel.

Pitelis, C.N. 2012. 'On PIIGS, GAFFS and BRICS: an insider-outsider's perspective on structural and institutional foundations of the Greek crisis', *Contributions to Political Economy*, 31:1, pp. 77–89.

Pourgouris, M. 2010. 'The phenomenology of hoods: some reflections on the 2008 violence in Greece', *Journal of Modern Greek Studies*, 28:2, pp. 225–45.

Provopoulos, G. 2014. 'The Greek economy and banking system: recent developments and the way forward', *Journal of Macroeconomics*, 39, Part B, pp. 240–49.

Pryce, V. 2012. *Greekonomics: the Euro Crisis and Why Politicians Don't Get It*, London: Biteback Publications.

Psalidopoulos, M. 1996. 'Keynesianism across nations: the case of Greece', *The European Journal of the History of Economic Thought*, 3:3, pp. 449–62.

Psomiades, H.J. 1982. 'Greece from the colonels' rule to democracy', in J.H. Herz (ed.), *From*

BIBLIOGRAPHY

Dictatorship to Democracy: Coping with the Legacies of Authoritarianism and Totalitarianism, Westport, CT: Greenwood, pp. 251–73.

Quaglia, L., R. Eastwood and P. Holmes. 2009. 'The financial turmoil and EU policy co-operation in 2008', *Journal of Common Market Studies*, 47, Annual Review, pp. 63–87.

Rakopoulos, T. 2014. 'Resonance of solidarity: meanings of a local concept in anti-austerity Greece', *Journal of Modern Greek Studies*, 32:2, pp. 313–37.

Reinhart, C.M. and K.S. Rogoff. 2008. *This Time is Different: Eight Centuries of Financial Folly*, Princeton: Princeton University Press.

Roumeliotis, P. 2012. *Προσωπική μαρτυρία: το Άγνωστο Παρασκήνιο της Προσφυγής στο ΔΝΤ. Πώς και γιατί Φτάσαμε στο Μνημόνιο*, Athens: Livanis.

Rüdig, W. and G. Karyotis. 2013. 'Beyond the usual suspects? New participants in anti-austerity protests in Greece', *Mobilization*, 18:3, pp. 313–30.

———— 2014. 'Who protests in Greece? Mass opposition to austerity', *British Journal of Political Science*, 44:3, pp. 487–513.

Ryvkin, B. 2012. 'Saving the euro: tensions with European treaty law in the European Union's efforts to protect the common currency', *Cornell International Law Journal*, 45:1, pp. 227–55.

Samatas, M. 1993. 'The populist phase of an underdeveloped surveillance society: political surveillance in post-dictatorial Greece', *Journal of the Hellenic Diaspora*, 19:1, pp. 31–70.

Sampson, S.L. 1981–83. 'Muddling through in Rumania (or: why the mamaliga doesn't explode)', *International Journal of Rumanian Studies*, 3:1–2, pp. 165–85.

Saridakis, G. and H. Spengler. 2012. 'Crime, deterrence and unemployment in Greece: a panel data approach', *The Social Science Journal*, 49:2, pp. 167–74.

Schwarz, A.G., T. Sagris and Void Network. 2010. *We Are an Image from the Future: the Greek Revolt of December 2008*, Oakland, Calif.: AK Press.

Seferiades, S. 1999. *Low Union Density Amidst a Conflictive Contentious Repertoire: Flexible Labour Markets, Unemployment, and Trade Union Decline in Contemporary Greece*, EUI Working Paper SPS, no. 99/6, Florence: European University Institute.

Siani-Davies, P. 2003. 'Introduction: international intervention (and non-intervention) in the Balkans', in P. Siani-Davies (ed.), *International Intervention in the Balkans since 1995*, London: Routledge, pp. 1–31.

———— 2005. *The Romanian Revolution of December 1989*, Ithaca, NY: Cornell University Press.

Siani-Davies, P. and S. Katsikas. 2009. 'National reconciliation after civil war: the case of Greece', *Journal of Peace Research*, 46:4, pp. 559–75.

Simou, E. and E. Koutsogeorgou. 2014. 'Effects of the economic crisis on health and healthcare in Greece in the literature from 2009 to 2013: a systematic review', *Health Policy*, 115:2–3, pp. 111–19.

Sinn, H-W. and T. Wollmershäuser. 2012. 'Target loans, current account balances and capital flows: the ECB's rescue facility', *International Tax and Public Finance*, 19:4, pp. 468–508.

Sotiropoulos, D. 2012. 'The paradox of non-reform in a reform-ripe environment: lessons from post-authoritarian Greece', in S. Kalyvas, G. Pagoulatos and H. Tsoukas (eds), *From Stagnation to Forced Adjustment: Reforms in Greece, 1974–2010*, London: Hurst, pp. 9–29.

Spanou, C. 2012. 'The quandary of administrative reform: institutional and performance modernization', in S. Kalyvas, G. Pagoulatos and H. Tsoukas (eds), *From Stagnation to Forced Adjustment: Reforms in Greece, 1974–2010*, London: Hurst, pp. 171–94.

Spourdalakis, M. 1988. *The Rise of the Greek Socialist Party*, London: Routledge.

—— 2008. '2007 Greek elections: signs of major political realignment, challenges and hopes for the left', *Studies in Political Economy*, 82, pp. 171–86.

—— 2013. 'Left strategy in the Greek cauldron: explaining Syriza's success', *Socialist Register*, 49, pp. 98–119.

Spraos, J. 1991. 'Government and the economy: the first term of PASOK', in S. Vryonis Jr. (ed.), *Greece on the Road to Democracy: from the Junta to PASOK 1974–1986*, New York: Caratzas, pp. 169–92.

Springler, E. 2005–2006. 'Financial liberalization, stock markets and growth in economies with underdeveloped financial markets', *European Political Economy Review*, 3:2, pp. 53–86.

Stamatis, G.A. 2012. *Homeless in Greece in the Current Financial Crisis: What Perspectives?*, Athens: University of Athens Medical School.

Stavrianakos, K., A. Pachi, K. Paplos, D. Nikoviotis, E. Fanouraki, A. Tselebis, D. Lekka, E. Karakasidou, V.Kontaxakis and G. Moussas. 2013. 'Suicide attempts before and during the financial crisis in Greece', *European Psychiatry*, 28, Supplement 1, 1.

Stavrou, N.A. 1988. 'Ideological foundations of the Panhellenic Socialist Movement', in N.A. Stavrou (ed.), *Greece Under Socialism: a NATO Ally Adrift*, New Rochelle, NY: Caratzas, pp. 11–40.

Stefanakis, Z., A. Vgontzas, M. Basta, M. Tsougkou, A. Kastanaki, J. Fernandez-Mendoza and M. Sfakiotaki. 2013. 'Suicidality in psychiatric inpatients and economic crisis in Greece', *European Psychiatry*, 28, Supplement 1, 1.

Strogylis, A. 1995. *Παναγής Παπαληγούρας: ο Ευρωπαίος Πολιτικός*, Athens: Odysseas.

Tagkalakis, A. 2013. 'The unemployment effects of fiscal policy: recent evidence from Greece', *IZA Journal of European Labor Studies*, 2:11, pp. 1–32.

Telloglou, T. 2009. *Το Δίχτυο. Φάκελος Siemens*, Athens: Skai.

Teperoglou, E. and E. Tsatsanis. 2014. 'Dealignment, de-legitimation and the implosion of the two-party system in Greece: the earthquake election of 6 May 2012', *Journal of Elections, Public Opinion and Parties*, 24:2, pp. 222–42.

The Albanian Centre for Competitiveness and International Trade (ACIT). 2012. *Study on the Economic Impact of the Greek Crisis in Albania*, Tirana: ACIT.

Theodorikakou, O., A. Alamanou and K. Katsadoros. 2013. '"Neo-homelessness" and the Greek crisis', *European Journal of Homelessness*, 7:2, pp. 203–11.

Theodossopoulos, D. 2013. 'Infuriated with the infuriated? Blaming tactics and discontent about the Greek financial crisis', *Current Anthropology*, 54:2, pp. 200–21.

Thomadakis, S.B. 1995. 'The Greek economy and European integration: prospects for development and threats of underdevelopment', in D. Constas and T.G. Stavrou (eds), *Greece Prepares for the Twenty-First Century*, Washington DC: Woodrow Wilson Center Press, pp. 101–23.

Tinios, P. 2012. 'The pensions merry-go-round: the end of a cycle?', in S. Kalyvas, G. Pagoulatos and H. Tsoukas (eds), *From Stagnation to Forced Adjustment: Reforms in Greece, 1974–2010*, London: Hurst, pp. 117–31.

BIBLIOGRAPHY

Transparency International. 2012. *National Integrity System Assessment: Greece*, Athens: Transparency International—Greece.

Trantidis, A. 2014. 'Reforms and collective action in a clientelist system: Greece during the Mitsotakis administration (1990–93)', *South European Society and Politics*, 19:2, pp. 215–34.

Triandafyllidou, A., R. Gropas and H. Kouki. 2013. 'Introduction: is Greece a modern European country?' in A. Triandafyllidou, R. Gropas and H. Kouki (eds), *The Greek Crisis and European Modernity*, Basingstoke, England: Palgrave Macmillan, pp. 1–24.

Trichet, J-C. 2010. 'State of the union: the financial crisis and the ECB's response between 2007 and 2009', *Journal of Common Market Studies*, 48:1, Annual Review, pp. 7–19.

Tsakalotos, E. 1991. 'Structural change and macroeconomic policy: the case of Greece (1981–85)', *International Review of Applied Economics*, 5:3, pp. 253–76.

Tsakatika, M. and C. Eleftheriou. 2013. 'The radical left's turn towards civil society in Greece: one strategy, two paths', *South European Society and Politics*, 18:1, pp. 81–99.

Tsimas, P. 2011. *Τὸ Ἡμερολόγιο τῆς Κρίσης. Νέα Υόρκη, Σεπτέμβριος 2008/Ἀθήνα, Ὀκτώβριος 2011*, Athens: Metaichmio.

Tsoucalas, C. 1969. *The Greek Tragedy*, London: Penguin.

——— 1995. 'Free riders in wonderland; or, of Greeks in Greece', in D. Constas and T.G. Stavrou, (eds), *Greece Prepares for the Twenty-First Century*, Washington DC: Woodrow Wilson Center Press, pp. 191–219.

Tsoukalis, L. 1991. 'The austerity program: causes, reactions and prospects', in S. Vryonis Jr. (ed.), *Greece on the Road to Democracy: from the Junta to PASOK 1974–1986*, New York: Caratzas, pp. 193–212.

——— 2013. 'International bubbles, currency union and national failures: the case of Greece and the euro', in A. Triandafyllidou, R. Gropas and H. Kouki (eds), *The Greek Crisis and European Modernity*, Basingstoke, England: Palgrave Macmillan, pp. 125–43.

Tsoukas, H. 2012. 'Enacting reforms: towards an enactive theory', in S. Kalyvas, G. Pagoulatos and H. Tsoukas (eds), *From Stagnation to Forced Adjustment: Reforms in Greece, 1974–2010*, London: Hurst, pp. 67–89.

Tzanelli, R. 2008. *Nation-Building and Identity in Europe: the Dialogics of Reciprocity*, Basingstoke, England: Palgrave Macmillan.

Tziovas, D. 2001. 'Beyond the Acropolis: rethinking Neohellenism', *Journal of Modern Greek Studies*, 19:2, pp. 189–220.

Tzogopoulos, G. 2013. *The Greek Crisis in the Media: Stereotyping in the International Press*, Aldershot: Ashgate.

Vamvakas, V. and P. Panagiotopoulos (eds). 2010. *Η Ελλάδα στη Δεκαετία του '80: Κοινωνικό, Πολιτικό και Πολιτισμικό Λεξικό*, Athens: To Perasma.

Varoufakis, Y. 2011. *The Global Minotaur: America, the True Origins of the Financial Crisis and the Future of the World Economy*, London: Zed.

——— 2013. 'We are all Greeks now! The crisis in Greece in its European and global context', in A. Triandafyllidou, R. Gropas and H. Kouki (eds), *The Greek Crisis and European Modernity*, Basingstoke, England: Palgrave Macmillan, pp. 44–58.

425

BIBLIOGRAPHY

———— 2014. 'Being Greek and an economist while Greece is burning! An intimate account of a peculiar tragedy', *Journal of Modern Greek Studies*, 32:1, pp. 1–23.

Vasardani, M. 2011. 'Tax evasion in Greece: an overview', *Bank of Greece, Economic Bulletin*, 35, pp. 15–25.

Vasilopoulou, S. and D. Halikiopoulou. 2013. 'In the shadow of Grexit: the Greek election of 17 June 2012', *South European Society and Politics*, 18:4, pp. 523–42.

Vasilopoulou, S., D. Halikiopoulou and T. Exadaktylos. 2014. 'Greece in crisis: austerity, populism and the politics of blame', *Journal of Common Market Studies*, 52:2, pp. 388–402.

———— Veremis, T. 2008. 'Andreas Papandreou, radical without a cause', in M. Mazower (ed.), *Networks of Power in Modern Greece: Essays in Honour of John Campbell*, Hurst: London, pp. 137–46.

Veremis, T., S. Kalyvas, T. Kouloumbis, G. Pagoulatos, L. Tsoukalis and H. Tsoukas. 2011. *H Ανατομία της Κρίσης. Η Παθογένεια της Ελληνικής Κοινωνίας μέσα από Άρθρα Δημοσιευμένα στην Εφημερίδα Καθημερινή*. Athens: Skai.

Vergopoulos, K. 1988. 'Economic crisis and modernization in Greece', *International Journal of Political Economy*, 17:4, pp. 106–40.

Verney, S. 2004. *The End of Socialist Hegemony: Europe and the Greek Parliamentary Election of 7th March 2004*, SEI Working Paper no. 80/EPERN Working Paper no. 15, Brighton, England: University of Sussex.

———— 2011. 'An exceptional case? Party and popular euroscepticism in Greece, 1959–2009', *South European Society and Politics*, 16:1, pp. 51–79.

———— 2012. 'The eurozone's first post-bailout election: the 2010 local government contest in Greece', *South European Society and Politics*, 17:2, pp. 195–216.

Vgontzas, A.N., A. Kastanaki, E. Michalodimitrakis, M. Basta, E. Koutentaki and N. Michalas. 2013. 'Suicides in the Greek island of Crete during the economic crisis: reality vs myth', *European Psychiatry*, 28, Supplement 1, 1.

Visvizi, A. 2012. 'The crisis in Greece and the EU-IMF rescue package: determinants and pitfalls', *Acta Oeconomica*, 62:1, pp. 15–39.

———— 2014. 'From *Grexit* to *Grecovery*: the paradox of the troika's engagement with Greece', *Perspectives on European Politics and Society*, 15:3, pp. 335–45.

Vlachadis, N. and Kornarou, E. 2013. 'Increase in stillbirths in Greece is linked to the economic crisis', *British Medical Journal*, 346:f1061.

Vlachadis, N., M. Vlachadi, Z. Iliodromiti, E. Kornarou and N. Vrachnis. 2014. 'Greece's economic crisis and suicide rates: overview and outlook', *Journal of Epidemiology and Community Health*, 68:12, pp. 1204–05.

Vlamis, P. 2013. *Greek Fiscal Crisis and the Repercussions for the Property Market*, Hellenic Observatory Papers on Greece and Southeast Europe, no. 76, London: The Hellenic Observatory, LSE.

Vlontzos, G. and M.N. Duquenne. 2013. 'Identification of decision making for food under economic crisis: the case of Greece', *Procedia Technology*, 8, pp. 306–14.

Volbert, A. and G.D. Demopoulos. 1989. *Stabilization Policies in Greece in the Context of Modern Macroeconomic Theory*, Berlin: Duncker and Humblot.

BIBLIOGRAPHY

Vrachnis, N., N. Vlachadis, Z. Iliodromiti, M. Vlachadi and G. Creatsas. 2014. 'Greece's birth rates and the economic crisis', *The Lancet*, 383: 9918, pp. 692–93.

Wallace, W. 1979. 'Grand Gestures and second thoughts: the response of member countries to Greece's application', in L. Tsoukalis (ed.), *Greece and the European Community*, Farnborough, England: Saxon House, pp. 21–38.

Xenakis, S. 2010. 'Resisting submission? The obstinacy of "Balkanist" characteristics in Greece as dissidence against "the West"', in L.K. Cheliotis (ed.), *Roots, Rites and Sites of Resistance: the Banality of Good*, Basingstoke, England: Palgrave Macmillan, pp. 178–96.

———— 2013. 'Normative hybridity in contemporary Greece: beyond "modernizers" and "underdogs" in socio-political discourse and practice', *Journal of Modern Greek Studies*, 31:2, 171–92.

Xenakis, S. and L.K. Cheliotis. 2013a. 'Spaces of contestation: challenges, actors and expertise in the management of urban security in Greece', *European Journal of Criminology*, 10:3, pp. 297–313.

———— 2013b. 'Crime and economic downturn: the complexity of crime and crime politics in Greece since 2009', *British Journal of Criminology*, 53:5, pp. 719–45.

Zahariadis, N. 2013a. 'Leading reform amidst transboundary crises: lessons from Greece', *Public Administration*, 91:3, pp. 648–62.

———— 2013b. 'The politics of risk-sharing: fiscal federalism and the Greek debt crisis', *Journal of European Integration*, 35:3, pp. 271–85.

———— 2016. 'Powering over puzzling? Downsizing the public sector during the Greek sovereign debt crisis', *Journal of Comparative Policy Analysis: Research and Practice*, 18:5, pp. 464–78.

Zarafonitou, C. 2009. 'Criminal victimisation in Greece and the fear of crime: a "paradox" for interpretation', *International Review of Victimology*, 16:3, pp. 277–300.

———— 2011. 'Fear of crime in contemporary Greece: research evidence', *Criminology* (Special Issue), October 2011, pp. 50–63.

Zettelmyer, J., C. Trebesch and M. Gulati. 2013. *The Greek Debt Restructuring: an Autopsy*, Peterson Institute Working Paper, WP 13–8, Washington DC: Peterson Institute for International Economics.

Ziomas, D., N. Bouzas and N. Spyropoulou. 2009. *Greece: Minimum Income Schemes: a Study of National Policies*, Brussels: European Commission DG Employment, Social Affairs and Equal Opportunities.

Zohios, G. 2011. 'Liberalization of closed professions: opening Pandora's box', *Competition Policy International Antitrust Chronicle*, 3:2.

Zombanakis, G.A., C. Stylianou, and A.S. Andreou. 2009. *The Greek Current Account Deficit: is it Sustainable After All?*, Bank of Greece Working Paper 98, Athens: Bank of Greece.

INDEX

About, Edmond, 335
Ackermann, Josef, 124, 195
AGET Heracles, 30, 44
Alavanos, Alekos, 231
Albanians, 286
Almunia, Joaquín, 105, 112, 116; on
    euro area, 97, 98; memo on Greece,
    102
Alogoskoufis, Giorgos, 60, 61, 62, 63,
    69, 73–74, 75, 76, 88, 94, 103; and
    2004 audit, 65; on austerity, 68; and
    banks, 82, 85
Alpha Bank, 198, 257–58
anarchists, 18, 90, 233, 234
Andreadis, Stratis, 21
Androutsopoulos, Adamantios, 15
Apoyevmatini (newspaper), 92
Argentina, economic crisis in, 8, 58,
    347n.24, 347n.25
Aristophanes; *The Birds*, 299
ATEbank, 86, 257, 258
Athens Indymedia, 292
Athens Paper Mills, 30, 48
Athens, Acropolis of, 128, 142, 198,
    239; Ermou street, 245; Exarcheia,
    89; impact of crisis on, 93, 237, 241,
    273, 276–77, 280, 285, 287–88; im-

pact of Olympic Games on, 53–54;
    mayor of, 325; Omonia Square, 233,
    287; Patission street, 287; Philopap-
    pos hill, 276; as site of protest, 18,
    142, 237–38, (*see also* Syntagma
    Square); Stadiou Street, 128, 199,
    244; Vasilissis Sofias Avenue, 169.
    See also graffiti; street art
Athens Stock Exchange (ASE), 13, 14,
    309, 311; boom, (1990s), 47; index
    of, 35, 56, 80, 81, 101, 106–107,
    110, 112, 114, 115, 181, 313, 322
audit of state finances, (2004), 54,
    62–68
austerity, (1970s), 14–15, 16, (1980s),
    32–35, (1990s), 40–43; Alogoskou-
    fis on, 68; anger at, 293–94; Karat-
    zaferis on, 196; measures during
    crisis, 99, 102, 119, 121, 168, 176,
    196–97; opinion polls on, 25, 153.
    See also fiscal consolidation; taxation
Austria, 63, 85, 161, 320; banks of,
    204; finance minister of, 176

Bakoyanni, Dora, 111, 128, 207, 209
Bank of Greece, 9, 26, 32, 34, 39, 53,
    74, 76, 208, 310, 315–16, 331; and

Greece, 133–34; extension of second programme, 310, 313, 314, 316–17, 321, 324; negotiating second programme, 161–63, 172–73, 178–80; second programme, 200–201, 206; third programme, 328–32. *See also* memorandum; support mechanism
Economic and Monetary Affairs Council (Ecofin council), 32, 33, 40, 49, 65, 68, 69, 84, 125; meetings, (2004–2005), 61, 62, 63, (2008), 83, (2009), 102, 105, 108, 109, 110, 112, (2010), 119, 130–31, 151, (2013), 306. *See also* Eurogroup
Economic and Monetary Union (EMU), 37–38, 45–47, 48–52, 53, 217; convergence criteria, 38; convergence programmes, 41, 44, 47
Economist (news magazine), 191
economy, culture of regulation, 19–20, 25–26, 251–52, 260–62; 'economic miracle', 13, 14; European during financial crisis, 86–88; fall in GDP during crisis, 8, 243, 248–49, 271; Greek model, 59–60; growth forecasts, 88, 113, 125, 135, 137, 140, 335; growth rate, (before crisis), 34, 42, 48, 58, 69, (during crisis), 102, 113, 153, 174, 309, 335; performance during crisis, 243–71; pessimism about, 58, 88, 93; under Andreas Papandreou governments, 29–36; under dictatorship, 13–15; under Giorgos Papandreou government, 113, 140, 153–54; under Konstantine Karamanlis governments, 19–22, 23–26; under Kostas Karamanlis governments, 5, 68–69, 76–77, 88, 101–102, 103; under Mitsotakis government, 41–42; under Simitis governments, 45, 48, 49,

58; under Tsipras governments, 335; use of 'recession' and 'depression', 8–9, 346–47n.22, 347n.25
Ecuador, 157, 167
EFG Eurobank Ergasis, 154, 257, 258
elections, European parliament, 47, (2009), 103, (2014), 229–30, 310; general, 17, 26, 32, 38–39, 44, 45, (2000), 50, 55, (2004), 58–59, (2007), 75, (2009), 105–106, (2012), 206–207, 209–210, (2015), 311–313, 332–33; local, 35, (2010), 144, 147–48; fiscal-electoral cycle, 18, 225
Electric Railway Athens-Piraeus (ISAP), 92, 146, 240
Eleftherotypia (newspaper), 143, 154, 282
elite, 337; narrative about, 20, 27–28, 36–37, 93–94, 223, 226, 262–63, 270, 298. *See also* Polytechnic Generation
Elliniki Halyvourgia, 239
Emboriki (Commercial) Bank, 21, 257, 260
emigration, 23, 285–86
Estonia, 320; economy of, 87
euro area summit, (2010), 129–30, (2011), 160, 172–73, 179–81, (2015), 328–30
euro area, central banks, 74, 130, 195, 200, 201, 307, 331; creation of, 53; crisis in, 6, 96–98, 127, 129–31, 167, 172, 174, 175–76, 178, 190–94; current account balance, 74; economic and fiscal governance, 149–50, 180, 191–92, 193, 306; end of crisis in, 193–94, 205–206, 305–306; potential flaws in, 51, 337–39; recycling of fiscal surplus, 73. *See also* euro; European Central Bank

and banking crisis, 84–85; budget
deficits, 54–55, 68; concept of debt,
279; and debt restructuring, 149,
163, 164; economy, 73, 86; emigration to, 23, 286; and euro, 121, 153,
192; exposure of banks to Greece,
124, 151, 164, 359n.27; and moral
hazard, 123, 136, 159; and possible
Greek exit from euro, 162, 174–75,
204, 211, 327; relations with Greece,
27, 63, 141–42, 161–62, 180, 200,
293, 299, 316, 320; and Second
World War, 157, 283, 313, 314; and
spring 2009 debt crisis, 97–98; and
third adjustment programme, 320,
328, 329, 331
Glezos, Manolis, 316
Goin' Through, 300
Golden Dawn, 92, 227–30, 280, 293,
299, 300, 324, 325; and elections,
207, 210, 227–28, 230, 312; ideology, 228; profile of voters, 229
Goldman Sachs, 48, 110, 115, 201,
236; 2001 currency swaps, 56–57
Gonzi, Lawrence, 83
graffiti, 273, 284, 293. See also street art
Grexit, 316, 320, 327; origins of term,
196. See also under euro; drachma
Grigoropoulos, Alexis, 89, 90, 301
Gurría, José Ángel, 127
Gysi, Gregor, 203

Hague, William, 191
Hamsun, Knut, 294
Handelsblatt (newspaper), 125
Hellenic Banking Association, 85
Hellenic Broadcasting Corporation
(ERT), 128, 308, 311, 318
Hellenic Financial Stability Fund
(HFSF), 257, 258, 315
Hellenic Postbank (TT), 168,
376–77n.29

Hellenic Railways Organisation (OSE),
82, 146, 155, 173, 201; TrainOSE,
168
Hellenic Statistical Authority (EL.
STAT), 109. See also National Statis-
tical Service
Hellenic Telecommunications Organ-
isation (OTE), 14, 42, 154, 260
Hessel, Stéphane, 235
Hollande, François, 232, 319, 327, 328
homelessness, 276
Hungary, 87, 101, 138
Hypo Real Estate Holdings, 85,
359n.27

Iceland, 26, 81, 87, 115, 125
Ieronymos II, Archbishop, 213
imports, 14, 309; controls, 20, 25, 26,
32–33. See also current account balance; exports
Independent Greeks (ANEL), 206,
207, 210; coalition with SYRIZA,
313, 324, 327, 332
Indignant movement, 167–68, 169,
189, 231–32, 235–36
inflation, 13–15, 16, 24, 25, 33; during
crisis, 5, 76, 80; efforts to control,
20, 31, 40, 49; after euro entry,
69–70, 254. See also deflation; prices
informal economy, 34, 103, 240–41,
254, 262–64, 278
Institute of International finance (IIF),
124, 172, 179, 194, 200, 203
institutions, the. See troika
Institution for Growth in Greece, 329
internal devaluation, 87, 137–138, 154,
249, 250–254. See also competitiveness
International Monetary Fund (IMF),
on adjustment programme, 143, 152,
249, 250, 260, 262, 271; agreement